Foundations of
Sport and
Exercise
Psychology

Robert S. Weinberg, PhD
Miami University

Daniel Gould, PhD
University of North Carolina at Greensboro

Human Kinetics

Library of Congress Cataloging-in-Publication Data

Weinberg, Robert S. (Robert Stephen)
    Foundations of sport and exercise psychology / Robert S. Weinberg,
Daniel Gould.
       p.   cm.
    Includes bibliographical references and index.
    ISBN 0-87322-812-X
    1. Sports--Psychological aspects. 2. Exercise--Psychological
aspects.   I. Gould, Daniel, 1952-   . II. Title.
GV706.4.W38   1995
796'.01--dc20
                                              94-47973
                                             CIP

ISBN: 0-87322-812-X

Developmental Editor: Anne Mischakoff Heiles
Assistant Editors: Jacqueline Blakley, Kirby Mittelmeier, John Wentworth
Copyeditor: John Wentworth
Proofreader: Pamela S. Johnson
Typesetters: Sandra Meier, Yvonne Winsor
Text Designer: Judy Henderson
Layout Artists: Denise Lowry, Tara Welsch
Photo Editor: Karen Maier
Cover Designer: Jack Davis
Photographer (cover): David Stoecklein/F-Stock
Illustrators: Paul To, John Walters, Craig Ronto
Info Art: Thomas•Bradley Illustration & Design
Printer: Braun-Brumfield

Printed in the United States of America

10 9 8 7 6 5 4 3 2 1

Human Kinetics
P.O. Box 5076, Champaign, IL 61825-5076
1-800-747-4457

Canada: Human Kinetics, Box 24040, Windsor, ON N8Y 4Y9
1-800-465-7301 (in Canada only)

Europe: Human Kinetics, P.O. Box IW14, Leeds LS16 6TR, England
(44) 532 781708

Australia: Human Kinetics, 2 Ingrid Street, Clapham 5062, South Australia
(08) 371 3755

New Zealand: Human Kinetics, P.O. Box 105-231, Auckland 1
(09) 309 2259

To Mom—who raised me, guided me, and believed in me no matter what.
I could not have asked for a better teacher and mentor!

Dan

To my family—the most important part of my life.

Bob

Contents

Preface

Behavior intrigues novelists and playwrights; husbands and wives; friends, lovers, and enemies; sons and daughters; and pet owners and politicians. In this book you will focus on how people behave in sport and exercise settings—what motivates them, what angers them, what scares them, how their emotions affect their performances, how their emotions can be moderated, and how their behaviors can be made more effective.

Perhaps you want to be a physical educator, coach, fitness instructor, athletic trainer, or even a sport psychologist. Or maybe you are just curious about the field. In any case, this book is for you. It is designed to give you an overview of sport and exercise psychology, to bridge the gap between research and practice, convey fundamental principles of professional practice, and capture some of the excitement of the world of sport and exercise.

Sport psychology has changed our lives and the lives of many athletes and coaches we have worked with and trained over the years. We feel enriched by our studies in this field, and we would like to give something back to it through this comprehensive, introductory text on sport and exercise psychology. Many books focus on research literature, addressing the needs of graduate students and professionals. Others relate practical experience but ignore the wealth of research from the past 25 years. Our goal has been to create a book for undergraduates that bridges up-to-date research and practice, capturing the best of what we have learned from coaches and scholars, exercisers and athletes. And we have hoped to write a book that you will find both illuminating and interesting.

When you finish the course, please write us with your comments. We wrote this textbook for you, and you are in the best position to give feedback to help us better meet your needs in the future. We hope you will enjoy learning about sport and exercise psychology as much as we do.

Acknowledgments

This book would not have been possible if not for the tireless work of countless dedicated sport and exercise psychologists throughout the world. It is because of their research, writing, and consulting that the field has advanced so far in recent years. And it is for this reason we acknowledge all their efforts.

We would also like to recognize the teachers, coaches, and athletes with whom we have had the opportunity to consult. Indeed, they have taught us a great deal about sport and exercise psychology.

We acknowledge reviewers Rainer Martens, Damon Burton, and Penny McCullagh for their thoughtful and helpful suggestions on an earlier version of the manuscript. Laura Finch and Eileen Udry also provided valuable assistance in field-testing the book's content in undergraduate sport and exercise psychology classes at the University of North Carolina at Greensboro. Kristen Davidson's assistance in indexing the text is also noteworthy.

We would like to thank the staff at Human Kinetics for helping make this book possible. In particular, Rainer Martens, publisher, for asking us to take on the project and for his support throughout all phases of it. And special kudos go to Developmental Editor Anne Mischakoff Heiles for the countless hours she spent editing things down to a manageable size and keeping the two of us in line. We also acknowledge the careful editorial assistance of Kirby Mittelmeier.

Finally, our families—Kathleen, Kira, and Josh; Deb, Kevin, and Brian—deserve a great deal of thanks for their patience in allowing us the time and space needed to write a book of this magnitude. Their unconditional social support was always there just when we needed it. So thanks, everybody.

Introduction:
Your Roadmap
to Understanding Sport
and Exercise Psychology

Most of you do not get into a car to begin a long trip without a destination in mind and a plan to get there. You pick a specific place and use a roadmap to find the best, most enjoyable route.

Ironically, though, some students read textbooks with no plan and no educational destination (as long as you get the next day's assignment completed on time). Failing to set a goal and plan of study with your textbooks is much like driving without a destination and roadmap: You spend a lot of time driving aimlessly.

Your understanding of sport and exercise psychology will come easier if you set a plan and keep a goal in mind while reading this text. You can use this introduction as a roadmap toward achieving two goals: (1) a better understanding of sport and exercise psychology and (2) knowledge of how to apply sport psychology in sport and exercise settings.

This book has seven major parts:

1. Getting Started—Introduction to Sport and Exercise Psychology
2. Understanding Participants
3. Understanding Sport and Exercise Environments
4. Understanding Group Processes
5. Enhancing Performance
6. Enhancing Health and Well-Being
7. Facilitating Psychological Growth and Development

Although these parts and their chapters work well when read in order, your instructor may elect to change the order to fit your particular class. That's okay, as we have designed each chapter to stand alone, without depending on knowledge from the previous chapters.

The practical roadmap we have included will help you move through the text in whatever order your professor assigns. The model (see Figure 1) will help you tie together the specifics into a coherent whole. In it you'll see seven stops—points of interest—on your journey to understanding sport and exercise psychology. Part I, Getting Started (chapters 1 and 2), is where you prepare for the journey. Here you will be introduced to the field of sport and exercise psychology, its history, and contemporary directions. You will also learn how

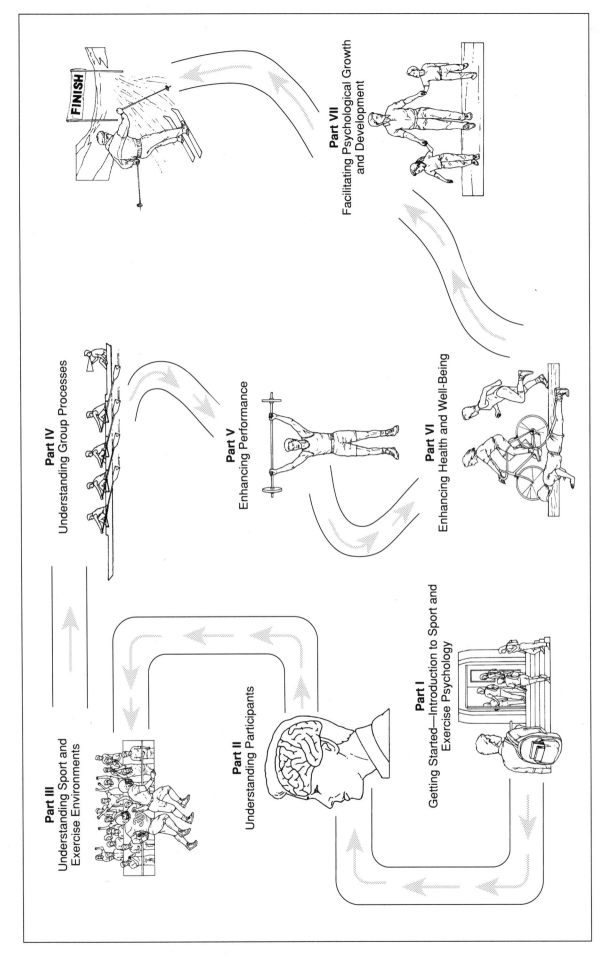

Figure 1. Roadmap to understanding sport and exercise psychology.

Part III
Understanding Sport and
Exercise Environments

Part II
Understanding Participants

Part I
Getting Started—Introduction to Sport and
Exercise Psychology

Part IV
Understanding Group Processes

Part V
Enhancing Performance

Part VI
Enhancing Health and Well-Being

Part VII
Facilitating Psychological Growth
and Development

FINISH

closely research and practice are linked and how you can make that connection even stronger.

The next stop on your journey is Part II—Understanding Participants. Effective teaching, coaching, and training rests on understanding the psychological make-up of the people you work with—what makes them tick! Hence, the four chapters in this part focus on individuals, whether they are exercisers, athletes, rehabilitation clients, or physical education students. It is important to understand people in terms of their personalities, motivational orientations, achievement motivation, competitiveness, and anxiety levels.

You must also consider the situations or environments in which people function. For this reason Part III, Understanding Sport and Exercise Environments, examines major environmental influences affecting sport and exercise participants. You will learn about competition and cooperation and how feedback and reinforcement influence people.

The fourth stop on your journey is Part IV, Understanding Group Processes, which focuses on the workings of groups. Most teachers, coaches, and exercise leaders work with groups, so it is critical to understand team dynamics, group cohesion, leadership, and communication.

Enhancing individual performance is a mainstay of sport and exercise psychology. For this reason, Part V, Enhancing Performance, is one of the longest stops on our journey, consisting of six chapters. Here you will learn how to develop a psychological skills training program to regulate arousal, use imagery to improve performance, enhance self-confidence, set effective goals, and strengthen concentration.

Part VI, Enhancing Health and Well-Being, introduces you to the joint roles of psychological and physical development in motivating people to exercise, enjoying the benefits of exercise, treating athletic injuries, and aiding rehabilitation. You will find critical information about combatting substance abuse, eating disorders, and overtraining.

One of the most important functions that sport and exercise professionals have is helping people with their psychological growth and character development. Part VII, Facilitating Psychological Growth and Development, concludes the text with discussions of four special issues: aggression, sportsmanship and character development, children in sport, and gender and sport.

Finally, we come to the finish. After covering the previous seven parts of the book you will have not only an excellent idea of what sport and exercise psychology involves, but specific knowledge of how to use the information effectively.

A roadmap does little good sitting in the car's glove compartment. This is also true of our Model to Understanding Sport and Exercise Psychology. So, before you read a chapter, see where it fits into the model. And as you read each chapter, ask yourself these questions:

1. What can I do as a professional to use this information effectively?
2. What personal and situational considerations will influence how I will use and modify this information?
3. Will my primary goal in using this information be to help participants enhance performance, develop and grow personally, or a combination of these objectives?
4. How can I integrate this information and derive efficient, effective strategies for practice?

We have tried to make this book user-friendly in several ways. Specifically, key point elements in each chapter summarize information that is crucial to remember. Case studies appear throughout the book to demonstrate how material presented applies to practical settings. You'll find exercises to complete to aid your understanding of material. Finally, review the summary and questions at the end of each chapter to know that you have a thorough grasp of the chapter's content.

PART

1

Getting Started—Introduction to Sport and Exercise Psychology

---

In this part we'll focus on getting you, the future sport and exercise science practitioner, started on your journey to understanding sport and exercise psychology. First, to inform you of the nature of sport and exercise psychology, we'll describe what this ever-growing field involves. Chapter 1, Welcome to Sport and Exercise Psychology, introduces you to the field, details some of its history, and defines its current status. Here we'll describe what sport and exercise psychologists do, discuss orientations to studying the field, and present the field's future directions and opportunities.

Chapter 2, Bridging Science and Practice, introduces the main ways sport psychology knowledge is gained and emphasizes the importance of teaming scientific and practical knowledge to allow you to be better able to psychologically assist students, athletes, and exercisers.

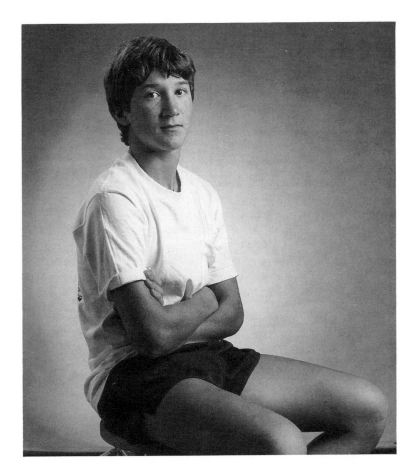

Welcome to Sport
and Exercise Psychology

Jeff, the point guard on the high school basketball team, becomes very nervous in competition—the more critical the situation, the more nervous he becomes and the worse he plays. Your biggest coaching challenge this season will be helping Jeff learn to manage stress.

Beth, fitness director for the St. Peters Hospital Cardiac Rehabilitation Center, runs an aerobic fitness program for recovering patients. She is concerned, however, that clients don't stick with their exercise programs after they start feeling better.

Mario wanted to be a physical educator ever since he can remember. He feels frustrated now by his high school students who have so little interest in learning life-long fitness skills. Mario's goal is to get the sedentary students motivated to engage in fitness activities.

Mary Jo is the head athletic trainer at Campbell State College. The school's star running back, Tyler Peete, has achieved a 99% physical recovery from knee surgery. The coaches notice, however, that he still favors his formerly injured knee in practice and is very hesitant when making cutbacks. Mary Jo knows that Tyler is physically recovered but needs to regain his confidence.

Tom, a sport psychologist and long-time baseball fan, just heard about a dream consulting position. The New York Mets owners, fed up with the lack of team cohesion, have asked him to design a psychological skills training program. If Tom can construct a strong program in the next week, he will be hired as the team's sport psychology consultant.

If you become a coach, an exercise leader, a physical educator, an athletic trainer, or even a sport psychologist, you also will encounter the kinds of situations Jeff, Beth, Mario, Mary Jo, and Tom faced. Sport and exercise psychology is a resource for solving such problems and many other practical concerns.

In this chapter you will learn about

■ what sport and exercise psychology is,
■ the field's history,
■ what sport and exercise psychology specialists do and their training, and
■ career opportunities in the field.

What Is Sport and Exercise Psychology?

Sport and exercise psychology is the scientific study of people and their behavior in sport and exercise activities.

Simply stated, sport and exercise psychology is the scientific study of people and their behavior in sport and exercise contexts. Sport and exercise psychologists identify principles and guidelines that professionals can use to help adults and children participate in and benefit from sport and exercise activities.

Most study in sport and exercise psychology aims at two objectives: (a) learning how psychological factors affect an individual's physical performance and (b) understanding how participation in sport and exercise affects a person's psychological development, health, and well-being. This study is pursued by asking the kinds of questions you see in Table 1.1.

Sport and exercise psychologists seek to understand and help elite athletes, children, the physically and mentally disabled, seniors, and average participants achieve peak performance, personal satisfaction, and development through participation.

Sport psychology applies to a broad population base. Although some professionals use it to help elite athletes achieve peak performance, many others are concerned more with children, the physically and mentally disabled, seniors, and average participants. Recently, some sport psychologists have focused on the psychological factors involved in exercise, developing strategies to encourage sedentary people to exercise or assessing the effectiveness of exercise as a treatment for depression. To reflect this broadening of interests, the field is now called sport *and exercise* psychology.

What Sport and Exercise Psychology Specialists Do

Contemporary sport psychologists pursue varied careers. They serve three primary roles in their professional activities: conducting research, teaching, and consulting (see Figure 1.1). We'll discuss each of these briefly.

Table 1.1 Typical Questions Studied in Sport and Exercise Psychology

Objective 1: Understand the effect of psychological factors on motor performance

- How does anxiety affect a basketball player's free-throw shooting accuracy?
- Does self-confidence influence a child's ability to learn to swim?
- How does coach reinforcement and punishment influence team cohesion?
- Does imagery training facilitate the recovery process in injured athletes and exercisers?

Objective 2: Understand the effect of physical activity on psychological development

- Does running reduce anxiety and depression?
- Do young athletes learn to be overly aggressive from participating in youth sports?
- Does participation in daily physical education classes facilitate a child's self-esteem?
- Does participation in college athletics enhance personality development?

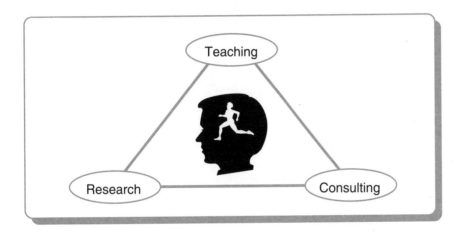

Figure 1.1 The roles of sport and exercise psychologists.

The Research Role

A primary function of any scholarly field is to advance the knowledge within the field. We do this by conducting research. Most sport and exercise psychologists in a university conduct research. They might, for example, study the motives children have for youth sport involvement, how imagery influences putting proficiency in golf, how running 20 minutes 4 days a week affects an exerciser's anxiety levels, and the relationship between movement education and self-concept in elementary physical education students. These psychologists then share their findings with colleagues and participants in the field. This sharing produces advances, discussion, and healthy debate at professional meetings and in journals (see Table 1.2).

The Teaching Role

Many sport and exercise psychology specialists teach university courses such as exercise psychology, applied sport psychology, and the social psychology

The History of Sport and Exercise Psychology

Sport psychology dates back to the turn of the 20th century (Wiggins, 1984). Its history falls into five periods which are highlighted here with some specific individuals and events from each period. These various periods have distinct characteristics and yet are interrelated. Together they contributed to the field's development and growing stature.

The Early Years (1895-1920)

In North America, sport psychology began in the 1890s. **Norman Triplett**, a psychologist from Indiana University and a bicycle-racing enthusiast, wanted to understand why cyclists sometimes rode faster when they raced in groups or pairs than when they rode alone (Triplett, 1898). First, he verified that his initial observations were correct by studying cycling racing records. To test his hunch further, he also conducted an experiment where young children were to reel in fishing line as fast as they could. Triplett found that children reeled in more line when they worked in the presence of another child. This experiment allowed him to predict more reliably when bicycle racers would have better performances.

In Triplett's day psychologists and physical educators were only beginning to explore psychological aspects of sport and motor skill learning. They measured athletes' reaction times, studied how people learn sport skills, and discussed the role of sport in personality and character development, but they did little to apply these studies.

Norman Triplett conducted the first experiment in sport psychology.

Period 1 — The Early Years   (1895-1920)

Highlights

- 1897   Norman Triplett conducts first social psychology and sport psychology experiment studying the effects of others on cycling performance.
- 1899   E.W. Scripture of Yale describes personality traits that he felt could be fostered via sport participation.
- 1903   G.T.W. Patrick discusses the psychology of play.
- 1914   R. Cummins assesses motor reactions, attention, and abilities as they pertain to sport.
- 1918   As a student, Coleman Griffith conducts informal studies of football and basketball players at the University of Illinois.

Period 2 — The Griffith Era
(1921-1938)

Highlights

- 1919-1931   Griffith publishes 25 sport psychology research articles.
- 1925   University of Illinois research in athletics laboratory established. Griffith appointed director.
- 1926   Griffith writes *Psychology of Coaching*.
- 1928   Griffith writes *Psychology of Athletics*.
- 1932   Research in athletics laboratory closes as a result of the Depression.
- 1938   Phillip Wrigley hires Griffith to be Chicago Cubs sports psychologist.
- 1938   Griffith takes a new position outside of sport psychology, signaling the end of an era.

The Griffith Era (1921-1938)

Coleman Griffith is credited with being the father of American sport psychology (Kroll & Lewis, 1970). A University of Illinois psychologist who also worked in the Department of Physical Welfare (Education and Athletics), Griffith developed the first laboratory in sport psychology, helped initiate one of the first coaching schools in America, and wrote two classic books, *Psychology of Athletics* and *Psychology of Coaching*. He also conducted a series of studies on the Chicago Cubs baseball team and developed psychological profiles of such legendary players as Dizzy Dean. He corresponded with Notre Dame football coach Knute Rockne about how best to psych teams up and questioned hall-of-famer Red Grange about his thoughts while running the football. Ahead of his time, Griffith worked in relative isolation, but his high-quality research and deep commitment to improving practice remain an excellent model for sport and exercise psychologists.

Coleman Griffith, the father of American sport psychology.

(continued)

The History of Sport and Exercise Psychology   (continued)

Preparation for the Future (1939-1965)

Franklin Henry at the University of California, Berkeley, was largely responsible for the field's scientific development.

He devoted his career to the scholarly study of the psychological aspects of sport and motor skill acquisition. Most important, Henry trained many other energetic physical educators who later became university professors and initiated systematic research programs. Some of his students became administrators who reshaped curriculums and developed sport and exercise science as we know it today.

Other investigators in the 1939-1965 period, such as Warren Johnson and Arthur Slatter-Hammel, helped lay the groundwork for future study of sport psychology. They helped create the academic discipline of exercise and sport science; however, applied work in sport psychology was still limited.

Franklin Henry, the main force responsible for the field's scientific development.

Bruce Ogilvie, father of North American applied sport psychology.

The Establishment of Academic Sport Psychology (1966-1977)

By the mid-1960s physical education had become an academic discipline, and sport psychology had become a separate component within this discipline, distinct from motor learning. Motor learning specialists focused on how people acquire motor skills (not necessarily sport skills) and on conditions of practice, feedback, and timing. In contrast, sport psychologists studied how psychological factors—anxiety, self-esteem, and personality—influence sport and motor skill performance and how participation in sport and physical education influence psychological development (e.g., personality, aggression).

Applied sport psychology consultants began working with athletes and teams. **Bruce Ogilvie** of San Jose State University was one of the first to do so and is often called the father of North American applied sport psychology. Concurrently with the increased interest in the field, the first sport psychology societies were established in North America.

Period 3 — Preparation for the Future (1939-1965)

Highlights

- 1938   Franklin Henry assumes position in Department of Physical Education at Univ. of California Berkeley, and establishes psychology of physical activity graduate program.
- 1949   Warren Johnson assesses precompetitive emotions of athletes.
- 1951   John Lawther writes *Psychology of Coaching*.
- 1965   First World Congress of sport psychology held in Rome.

Period 4 — The Establishment of Academic Sport Psychology (1966-1977)

Highlights

- 1966   Clinical psychologists Bruce Ogilvie and Thomas Tutko write *Problem Athletes and How to Handle Them* and begin to consult with athletes and teams.
- 1967   B. Cratty of UCLA writes *Psychology of Physical Activity*.
- 1967   First annual North American Society for the Psychology of Sport and Physical Activity (NASPSPA) held.
- 1974   Proceedings of NASPSPA conference published for the first time.

Period 5 — Contemporary Sport and Exercise Psychology (1978-Present)

Highlights

- 1979   *Journal of Sport Psychology* (now called *Sport and Exercise Psychology*) is established.
- 1980   U. S. Olympic Committee develops Sport Psychology Advisory Board.
- 1984   American television coverage of Olympic Games emphasizes sport psychology.
- 1985   U. S. Olympic Committee hires first full-time sport psychologist.
- 1986   The first applied scholarly journal, *The Sport Psychologist*, is established.
- 1986   The Association for the Advancement of Applied Sport Psychology is established.
- 1987   American Psychological Association Division 47 (Sport Psychology) is developed.
- 1988   U. S. Olympic team accompanied by officially recognized sport psychologist for the first time.
- 1989   *Journal of Applied Sport Psychology* begins.
- 1991   AAASP establishes "certified consultant" designation.
- 1992   *Contemporary Thought on Performance Enhancement* begins.

Contemporary Sport and Exercise Psychology (1978-Present)

Since the mid-1970s we have witnessed tremendous growth in sport and exercise psychology, especially in the applied area. Later in this chapter you will learn about contemporary sport and exercise psychology in detail.

Sport and Exercise Psychology Around the World

Sport and exercise psychology thrives worldwide. Salmela (1992), for instance, has estimated that 2700 individuals work in the field today in over 61 different countries. Most sport and exercise psychology specialists live in North America and Europe, and major increases in activity have occurred in Latin America, Asia, and Africa in the last decade.

Sport psychologists in Russia and Germany began working at about the time that Coleman Griffith began his work at the University of Illinois. The International Society of Sport Psychology (ISSP) was established in 1965 to promote and disseminate information about sport psychology throughout the world. ISSP has sponsored eight World Congresses of Sport Psychology—focusing on such topics as human performance, personality, motor learning, wellness and exercise, and coaching psychology—that have been instrumental in promoting awareness and interest in the field. Since 1970, ISSP has also sponsored the *International Journal of Sport Psychology*.

Credit for much of the development of sport psychology internationally goes to Italian sport psychologist Ferruccio Antonelli, who was both the first president of the ISSP and the first editor of *IJSP*. Sport and exercise psychology is now well-recognized throughout the world as both an academic area of concentration and a profession. The prospect of continued growth remains bright.

Ferruccio Antonelli.

of sport to undergraduate and graduate students. They may also teach such courses as personality psychology or developmental psychology if they work in a psychology department and courses such as motor learning and control or sport sociology if they work in a sport science program.

Table 1.2   American Sport and Exercise Psychology Journals and Organizations

Organizations

- *Association for the Advancement of Applied Sport Psychology*
  Overview: This organization is solely designed to promote research and practice in applied sport and exercise psychology. Three subareas focused on include: health psychology; intervention-performance enhancement; and social psychology.

- *American Psychological Association (APA) Division 47—Sport and Exercise Psychology*
  Overview: This is one of the newest of almost 50 divisions in the APA, the largest professional psychology organization in the United States. Both research and practice in sport psychology are emphasized in this organization.

- *North American Society for the Psychology of Sport and Physical Activity (NASPSPA)*
  Overview: This is the oldest organization focusing on the psychological aspects of sport and physical activity. The organization's main focus is on research in the subareas of motor development, motor learning and control, and social psychology and physical activity.

Journals

- *Journal of Applied Sport Psychology*
  Overview: Begun in 1989 this is the official journal of AAASP and publishes applied sport psychology research and professional practice articles.

- *Journal of Sport and Exercise Psychology*
  Overview: This journal publishes basic and applied sport and exercise psychology research studies. Begun in 1979 it is the oldest and most-respected research journal in the field.

- *The Sport Psychologist*
  Overview: This journal began in 1987 and publishes both applied research and professional practice articles designed to facilitate the delivery of psychological services to coaches and athletes.

The Consulting Role

A third important role is consulting with individual athletes or athletic teams to develop psychological skills for enhancing competitive performance and training. In fact, the U.S. Olympic Committee and some major universities employ full-time sport psychology consultants, and hundreds of other teams and athletes use consultants on a part-time basis for psychological skills training. Many sport psychology consultants work with coaches through clinics and workshops.

Some sport and exercise psychologists now work in the fitness industry, designing exercise programs that maximize participation and promote psychological and physical well-being. Sometimes consultants become adjuncts to support a sports medicine or physical therapy clinic, providing psychological services to injured athletes.

Coming Off the Bench: A Sport Psychology Consulting Case Study

Jerry Reynolds was referred to Ron Hoffman, Southeastern University sport psychology consultant, at the end of his freshman year of varsity basketball. Jerry had had a successful high school career, lettering in three sports and starting every basketball game. At Southeastern on a full scholarship, Jerry worked harder than anyone else on the team and improved his skills. Still he did not make the starting five. In the second half of the season's first contest, Coach Johnson put Jerry into the game. As he moved to the scorer's table and awaited the substitution whistle, Jerry found that he was much more nervous than ever before. His heart was pounding and he could not shut off his mind. He entered the game and had a disastrous performance. He threw the ball away several times, picked up two silly fouls, and failed to take an open shot. Coach Johnson took Jerry out. After the game, Jerry's coaches and teammates told him it was just nerves and to relax. But Jerry could not relax, and a pattern of high anxiety and deteriorating performance ensued. After a few more disasters Jerry rode the pine for the remainder of the season.

Jerry was hesitant about going to see a sport psychologist. He did not think he was mentally ill, and he was kind of embarrassed about the idea of going to see a "shrink." Much to Jerry's surprise, Dr. Hoffman was a regular guy and talked a lot like a coach. So Jerry agreed to meet with him every couple of weeks.

Working with Dr. Hoffman, Jerry learned it was common to experience anxiety when making the transition from high school to college ball. After all, 90% of the players he had defeated in high school were no longer competing. Hoffman also pointed out to Jerry that, after starting for 3 years in high school, it was no surprise if he had a hard time adjusting to coming off the bench and entering a game cold. He was experiencing a new kind of pressure, and his response to the pressure—his nervousness—was to be expected.

Dr. Hoffman taught Jerry how to relax by using a breathing technique called centering. He taught him to control negative thoughts and worries by stopping them with an image and replacing them with more positive affirmations. Jerry developed a mental preparation routine for coming off the bench, including stretches to keep loose and a procedure to help him focus as he waited at the scorer's table.

Jerry practiced these psychological techniques extensively in the off-season and refined them during early season practices and scrimmages. After he was able to come off the bench without falling apart, he worked on taking open shots and playing to his full potential quickly.

That season, Jerry accomplished his goal of coming off the bench and helping the team with a solid performance. He did not quite break in to the starting line-up, but Coach Johnson expressed his confidence in him by using him in tight situations. Jerry felt happy to be contributing to the team.

Clinical and Educational Sport Psychologists

Clinical sport and exercise psychologists treat those athletes and exercisers who have severe emotional disorders.

Clinical sport psychologists have extensive training in psychology to learn to detect and treat individuals with emotional disorders (e.g., severe depression, suicidal tendencies). They are licensed by State Boards to treat individuals with emotional disorders. They receive additional training in sport and exercise psychology and the sport sciences. Clinical sport psychologists are needed because, just as in the normal population, some athletes and exercisers develop severe emotional disorders and need special treatment (Heyman, 1987). Two prevalent areas in sport and exercise where the specialized skills of the clinical sport psychologist are needed are eating disorders and substance abuse.

Educational sport psychologists, however, are not trained to treat individuals with emotional disorders, nor are they licensed psychologists. Instead, they have extensive training in sport and exercise science, physical education, and

Sean McCann, Head of
the U.S. Olympic
Committee Sport
Psychology Program.

kinesiology and understand the psychology of human movement, particularly
as it is related to sport and exercise contexts. These specialists often have taken
advanced graduate training in psychology and counseling.

A good way to think of an educational sport psychologist is as a "mental
coach" who, through group and individual sessions, educates athletes and
exercisers about psychological skills and their development. Anxiety management, confidence development, and improved communication are some of the
areas that educational sport psychologists address. When educational sport
psychology consultants encounter an athlete with an emotional disorder, they
refer the athlete to either a licensed clinical psychologist or, preferably, a clinical
sport psychologist for treatment.

Clinical and educational sport and exercise psychologists must have a thorough knowledge both of psychology and exercise and sport science (see Table
1.3). In 1991 the Association for the Advancement of Applied Sport Psychology
(AAASP) began a certified consultant program, which requires advanced training in both psychology and the sport sciences to ensure that people have the

> Educational sport
> psychology special-
> ists are "mental
> coaches" who edu-
> cate athletes and
> exercisers about psy-
> chological skills and
> their development.
> They are not trained
> to work with individ-
> uals who have
> severe emotional
> disorders.

Table 1.3 The Relationship of Sport Science and Psychology Knowledge to Sport and Exercise Psychology	
Sport science knowledge domain	**Psychology knowledge domain**
Biomechanics	Abnormal psychology
Exercise physiology	Clinical psychology
Motor development	Counseling psychology
Motor learning and control	Developmental psychology
Sports medicine	Experimental psychology
Sport pedagogy	Personality psychology
Sport sociology	Physiological psychology

Sport and Exercise Psychology

necessary sport science and psychological training to call themselves sport and exercise consultants. This is designed to protect the public from unqualified individuals professing to be sport and exercise psychologists.

Sport and Exercise Psychology Orientations

Some coaches believe teams win games through outstanding defense, other coaches believe teams win through a wide-open offensive system, and still others believe wins come through a structured and controlled game plan. Like coaches, sport psychologists differ in how they view successful interventions. Contemporary sport and exercise psychologists may take, for instance, a behavioral, psychophysiological, or cognitive-behavioral approach to studying the field.

Behavioral Orientation

Those with a behavioral orientation view the primary determinants of an athlete's or exerciser's behavior as coming from the environment. Relatively little emphasis is placed on thoughts, personality, and perceptions. Instead the focus is on how environmental factors, particularly reinforcement and punishment, influence behavior. Heward (1978), for instance, found that professional minor league baseball players who received $10 per hit increased their batting averages over the course of a season. Allen and Iwata (1980) found that they could increase the amount of time that retarded children engaged in exercise by rewarding the children with the opportunity to play games they liked. These two examples demonstrate changing behavior through a systematic manipulation of the environment.

People with a behavioral orientation focus on how environmental factors influence behavior.

Psychophysiological Orientation

Psychophysiological sport and exercise psychologists believe the best way to study behavior during sport and exercise is to examine the physiological pro-

Dan Landers, leading proponent of psychophysiological sport and exercise psychology.

cesses of the brain and their influences on the physical activity. They typically assess heart rate, brain wave activity, and muscle action potentials, drawing relationships between these psychophysiological measures and sport and exercise behavior. An example is using biofeedback techniques to train elite marksmen to fire between heart beats, to improve accuracy (Landers, 1985).

Cognitive-Behavioral Orientation

Cognitive-behavioral psychologists assume that behavior is determined both by the environment and cognitions (thoughts)—how a person interprets the

Psychophysiological sport and exercise psychologists study behavior through its underlying psycho-physiological processes occurring in the brain.

Tara Scanlan of UCLA, leading cognitive-behavioral sport psychology researcher who has extensively studied stress, competition, and sport enjoyment.

Maureen Weiss, leading developmental sport psychology researcher studying children's self-esteem/ competence and motivation in sport from a cognitive-behavioral perspective.

A cognitive-behavioral orientation to sport and exercise psychology assumes that behavior is determined by both the environment and cognition, or thoughts and interpretation.

environment. They emphasize the athlete's or exerciser's cognitions, believing thought to be central in determining behavior. Cognitive-behavioral psychologists, might, for instance, develop self-report measures to assess self-confidence, anxiety, goal orientations, imagery, and intrinsic motivation. Then they would see how these assessments are linked to changes in an athlete's or exerciser's behavior. For example, elite collegiate wrestlers were asked to rate the sources of stress in competition (e.g., worry about not wrestling well, what my coach will think or say). Losing wrestlers turned out to worry more often about coach evaluation, losing, and making mistakes (Gould & Weinberg, 1985). Thus, links between the athletes' thoughts and behaviors (winning and losing) were examined.

The Present and Future of Sport and Exercise Psychology

Many universities now offer sport and exercise psychology courses, and some graduate programs include up to five or six different courses. Research and professional resources are increasingly available to students. Consulting and service opportunities are more plentiful, and more sport psychologists are helping athletes and coaches achieve their goals. Exercise psychology has opened new service and research opportunities for helping people enjoy the benefits of exercise.

Rod Dishman, University of Georgia, leading exercise psychology researcher.

Growth brings some accompanying problems. For example, sometimes unqualified people call themselves sport psychologists, or unethical individuals promise more to coaches, athletes, and exercise professionals than they can deliver. This is why the AAASP organization has begun to certify sport and exercise psychology consultants. Physical education, sport, and exercise leaders need to become informed consumers who can discriminate between legitimate, useful information and fads or gimmicks.

Many consultants now work part-time with elite amateur athletes through various National Sport Governing Bodies (NGBs) such as the U.S. Tennis Association and U.S. Skiing Association. Some NGBs and the U.S. Olympic Committee sponsor research on such issues as mental preparation and athlete stress. Several universities have full-time sport psychology consultants to serve their varsity athletes, and many professional teams employ a sport psychologist. There are full-time consulting sport psychologists and specialists who conduct research and service in the exercise-wellness area.

Despite today's opportunities to consult part-time with high-level, elite athletes, few full-time positions exist, and advanced graduate training is needed to become a qualified sport psychology specialist.

We believe the greatest gains in helping those in sport and exercise will come from supplying sport and exercise psychology information to physical education teachers, coaches, fitness instructors, and athletic trainers. With up-to-date sport and exercise psychology information these professionals make great strides toward achieving their various goals. In short, the field of sport and exercise psychology has much to offer you, the future physical education teachers, coaches, fitness specialists, and athletic trainers.

Summary

Sport and exercise psychology is the scientific study of the behavior of people engaged in sport and exercise activities. Researchers in the field have two major objectives: (a) to understand how psychological factors affect a person's motor performance and (b) to understand how participating in physical activity affects a person's psychological development. Despite enormous growth in recent years, sport psychology dates back to the early 1900s and is best understood within the framework of its five distinct periods.

Contemporary sport and exercise psychologists play a number of different roles, including conducting research, teaching, and consulting with athletes and exercisers. Not all of them are trained in the same way. Clinical sport and exercise psychologists are trained specifically in psychology to treat athletes and exercisers with severe emotional disorders, such as substance abuse or anorexia. Educational sport psychologists receive training in exercise and sport science and related fields and serve as mental coaches, educating athletes and exercisers about psychological skills and their development. They are not trained to assist people with severe emotional disorders. Approaches that can be taken to sport and exercise psychology include behavioral, psychophysiological, and cognitive-behavioral orientations.

Contemporary sport and exercise psychology concerns include fitness and exercise, the need for certifying sport psychology specialists, and the need to better inform and educate consumers (e.g., teachers, coaches, athletes, and exercisers) about the utility of sport psychology information.

Review Questions

1. What is sport and exercise psychology?

2. Identify two general objectives of sport and exercise psychology.

3. Describe the major accomplishments of the five periods in the history of sport and exercise psychology.

4. What contributions did Coleman Griffith and Franklin Henry make to sport and exercise psychology?

5. Describe three roles of sport and exercise psychology specialists.

6. Distinguish between clinical and educational sport psychology. Why is this distinction important?

7. Briefly describe the behavioral, psychophysiological, and cognitive-behavioral orientations to the study of sport and exercise psychology.

8. Why is there a need for certification in contemporary sport and exercise psychology?

9. What career opportunities are there in sport and exercise psychology?

References

Allen, L.D., & Iwata, B.A. (1980). Reinforcing exercise maintenance: Using existing high-note activities. *Behavior Modification, 4,* 337-354.

Gould, D., & Weinberg, R.S. (1985). Sources of worry in successful and less successful intercollegiate wrestlers. *Journal of Sport Behavior, 8,* 115-127.

Griffith, C.R. (1926). *Psychology of coaching.* New York: Scribners.

Griffith, C.R. (1928). *Psychology of athletics.* New York: Scribners.

Heward, W.L. (1978). Operant conditioning of a .300 hitter? The effects of reinforcement on the offensive efficiency of a barnstorming baseball team. *Behavior Modification, 2,* 25-39.

Heyman, S. (1987). Counseling and psychotherapy with athletes: Special considerations. In J.R. May & M.J. Ashen (Eds.), *Sport psychology: The psychological health of the athlete* (pp. 135-156). New York: PMA Publishing.

Kroll, W., & Lewis, G. (1970). America's first sport psychologist. *Quest, 13,* 1-4.

Landers, D.M. (1985). Psychophysiological assessment and biofeedback: Applications for athletes in closed-skilled sports. In J.H. Sandweiss & S.L. Wolf (Eds.), *Biofeedback and sports science* (pp. 63-105). New York: Plenum Press.

Salmela, J.H. (1992). *The world sport psychology source book* (2nd ed.). Champaign, IL: Human Kinetics.

Triplett, N. (1898). The dynamogenic factors in pacemaking and competition. *American Journal of Psychology, 9,* 507-553.

Wiggins, D.K. (1984). The history of sport psychology in North America. In J.M. Silva & R.S. Weinberg (Eds.), *Psychological foundations of sport* (pp. 9-22). Champaign, IL: Human Kinetics.

Bridging Science and Practice

Reading a sport and exercise psychology textbook and working professionally with exercisers and athletes are very different activities. To understand the relationship between the two, you must be able to integrate scientific textbook knowledge with practical experience.

In this chapter you will learn about

▌ sport and exercise psychology as a science,

▌ experiential knowledge from professional practice, and

▌ ways to integrate experiential and scientific knowledge to guide practice.

Understanding Sport and Exercise Psychology as a Science

Sport and exercise psychology is above all a science. It is important to understand that science is dynamic—something that scientists *do* (Kerlinger, 1973). Science is not a mere accumulation of facts discovered through detailed observations but a process, or method, of learning about the world through the systematic, controlled, empirical, and critical filtering of knowledge acquired through experience. In applying science to psychology, our goals are to describe, explain, predict, and allow control of behavior.

Let's take an example. Dr. Jennifer Jones, a sport psychology researcher, wants to study how movement education affects children's self-esteem. Dr. Jones first defines self-esteem and movement education and determines what age groups and particular children she wants to study. She then explains why she expects movement education and self-esteem to be related (e.g., the children would get recognition and praise for learning new skills). Dr. Jones is really after prediction and control: She wants to show that using movement education in similar conditions will consistently affect children's self-esteem in the same way. To test such things, science has evolved some general guidelines for research:

1. The scientific method dictates a *systematic approach* to studying a question. It involves standardizing the conditions, for example assessing the children's self-esteem under identical conditions with a carefully designed measure.

2. The scientific method involves *control* of conditions. Key variables, or elements in the research (e.g., movement education or changes in self-esteem), are the focus of study, with other variables controlled (e.g., the person doing the teaching) so as not to influence the primary relationship.

3. The scientific method is *empirical*, which means it is based on experience. Objective evidence must support beliefs, and this evidence must be open to outside evaluation and observation.

4. The scientific method is *critical*, meaning that it involves rigorous evaluation by the researcher and other scientists. Critical analysis of ideas and work helps ensure conclusions are reliable.

Theory

A theory is a set of interrelated facts presenting a systematic view of some phenomenon in order to describe, explain, and predict its future occurrences.

A scientist's ultimate goal is a *theory*, or a set of interrelated facts that presents a systematic view of some phenomenon in order to describe, explain, and predict its future occurrences. Theory allows scientists to organize and explain large numbers of facts in a pattern that helps others understand them. Theory then turns to practice.

One example is the *social facilitation theory* (Zajonc, 1965). Since Triplett's first reel-winding experiment on children (discussed in chapter 1), psychologists had studied how the presence of an audience affects performance, but their results were inconsistent. Sometimes people performed better in front of an audience, and other times they performed worse. Zajonc saw a pattern in the seemingly random results and formulated a theory. He noticed that when people performed simple tasks or tasks they knew well that having an audience influenced performance positively. However, when people performed unfamiliar or complex tasks, having an audience harmed performance. In his social facilitation theory, Zajonc contended that an audience creates arousal in the performer, which hurts performance on difficult tasks that were unlearned (or not well-learned) and helps performance on well-learned tasks.

Zajonc's theory increased our understanding of how audiences influence performance at many levels (students and professionals) and in many situations (sports, exercise, etc.). It consolidated many seemingly random instances into a theory basic enough for performers, coaches, and teachers to remember and to apply in a variety of circumstances. As the saying goes, nothing is more practical than a good theory!

Of course, not all theories are equally useful. Some are in early stages of development, and others have already passed the test of time. Some theories have a limited scope, and others a broad range of application. Some study few variables and others a complex matrix of variables and behaviors.

Studies and Experiments

Studies involve an investigator observing or assessing factors without changing the environment in any way. For example, a study comparing the effectiveness of goal setting, imagery, and self-talk in improving athletic performance might have a written questionnaire given to a sample of high school cross-country runners just before a race. The researchers could compare what techniques the fastest 20 runners used compared with the slowest 20 runners. They would not be changing or manipulating any factors, simply observing. But they would not know whether the goal setting, imagery, and self-talk caused some runners to go faster or whether running faster stirred the runners to set more goals, etc. Studies have limited ability to identify *causal* relations between factors.

Experiments differ from studies in that the investigator manipulates the variables along with observing them, then examines how changes in one variable affect changes in others. Runners might be divided into two equal groups. One, called the *experimental group*, would receive training in how to set goals and use imagery and positive self-talk. The other, called the *control group*, would not receive any psychological skills training. Then, if the experimental group outperformed the control group with other factors that could affect the relation controlled, the reason, or cause, for this would be known. A causal relation would be demonstrated!

Determining causal relationships is the main advantage of conducting experiments over conducting studies.

Strengths and Limitations of Scientifically Derived Knowledge

Each method of obtaining knowledge has strengths and limitations. The scientific method is no different in this regard (see Table 2.1). The major strength of scientifically derived knowledge is that it is reliable. Not only is the methodology systematic and controlled, but scientists are trained to be as objective as possible. One of their goals is to collect *unbiased* data, where the data or facts speak for themselves without being influenced by the scientist's personal interpretation.

Table 2.1 Strengths and Limitations of Scientifically Derived Knowledge	
Strengths	**Limitations**
Highly reliable	Reductionistic
Systematic & controlled	Lack of focus on external validity (practicality)
Objective & unbiased	Conservative—often slow to evolve

On the negative side, the scientific method is slow. It takes time to be systematic and controlled—more time than most practitioners have. For this reason, it's not always practical to insist that science guide all elements of practice.

Sometimes scientific knowledge is *reductionistic*. That is, because it is too complex to study all the variables of a situation at the same time, isolated variables may be selected that are of the most critical interest. By reducing a problem to smaller, manageable parts the whole picture may be compromised or diminished.

Another limitation of science is that in its emphasis on *internal validity*, or conforming to the rules of scientific methodology, it can overlook *external validity*, or whether the issue has true significance or utility in the real world. If a theory has no external validity, its internal validity doesn't count for much. Finally, scientific knowledge tends to be conservative. Because reliability must be judged by other scientists and the public, the dissemination of new ideas is slowed. A breakthrough in science usually comes after years of research.

Assessing Sport Psychology Research: The Case of Personality

Before applying research you need to assess it carefully. We will outline some common criteria you can use to evaluate research studies, using examples from the study of personality in sport and exercise settings (see chapter 3), which has suffered its share of flawed methodologies (see Martens, 1975; Vealey, 1992 for reviews of problems in sport personality research). We will highlight some problems to help you view research with a discerning skepticism.

1. *Clearly Defined Variables.* A first guideline is to look for clearly defined variables that ask the right questions; otherwise no firm conclusions can be drawn. For example, one thrust in early personality research was to distinguish the personality profiles of athletes from nonathletes. But a more fundamental question is what is an athlete? Does someone have to be a varsity team member or simply compete in sport to be considered an athlete? What makes someone an elite athlete? Without clear preliminary definitions researchers had difficulty determining whether athletes differ from nonathletes on personality characteristics.

2. *Inferring Cause and Effect.* If a study (as opposed to an experiment) found that football players are more aggressive than tennis players, it would not mean that playing football actually *causes* the players to be more aggressive. It might be that more aggressive individuals are attracted to aggressive contact games such as football. In essence, football did not cause the aggression; rather there is merely a relationship between playing football and exhibiting aggressive behavior. So care must be taken in inferring cause and effect relationships.

3. *Sampling Procedures and Generalizing.* Early personality research had a common error in its sampling procedures—that is, it used many athletes from one or two teams as subjects and then generalized across many teams. Let's say that 50 soccer players are chosen from three teams as subjects for a study on the effects of soccer on personality. It must be recognized that any conclusions the research draws are based on a sample of only three teams and the unique individuals on those teams. Thus, the findings may not be typical of (*generalizable to*) other teams and athletes. That is, the findings may not really apply to other athletes and teams.

4. *Appropriate Measures.* Most early sport personality researchers selected tests for their convenience rather than for the underlying conceptual structure of the particular test, or personality inventory. In fact, they often measured normal athletes by scales that had been developed for identifying clinical abnormality (mental illness): These scales were not appropriate for a normal

population. Sport and exercise psychologists now are developing personality tests that are specific to sport and exercise settings.

It takes time to verify scientific knowledge and many practitioners become impatient. Fortunately, they can supplement research studies with other sources of knowledge to guide their practice.

Understanding Professional Practice Knowledge

Professional practice knowledge refers to knowledge gained through experience. It might result, for example, from all the time you spent helping exercisers, athletes, and PE students enhance their performance and well-being. Professional practice knowledge comes from many sources or ways of knowing (see Table 2.2). Although exercise leaders, coaches, and athletic trainers ordinarily do not use the scientific method, they do use theoretically derived sport and exercise principles to guide their practice.

Table 2.2   Methods of Knowing
Scientific method
Systematic observation
Single case study
Shared public experience
Introspection (examining your thoughts or feelings)
Intuition (immediate apprehension of knowledge in the absence of a conscious rational process)

Based on Martens (1987).

Think of a volleyball coach, Theresa Hebert, working with the high school team. She develops her coaching skills in a variety of ways. Before the season she reflects (*uses introspection*) on how she wants to coach this year. During team tryouts she *systematically observes* the new players as they serve, hit, and play the back and front rows. Last season the team captain and star setter struggled, so Coach Hebert wants to learn as much about her as possible to help her more. To do this, she talks with other players, teachers, and the setter's parents. In essence, she *conducts a case study*. Shared public experience occurs. She and her assistant coaches *compare notes* scouting the next opponent. Coach Hebert often uses *intuition*. She decides to start Sarah over Rhonda today, the two players having similar ability, because it feels right to her. Of course, these methods are not equally reliable; however, in combination they lead to effective coaching. Like her players, Coach Hebert will sometimes make mistakes. But these errors or miscalculations also become sources of information to her.

Professional practice knowledge is guided trial-and-error learning. Whether you become a physical therapist, coach, teacher, exercise leader, or athletic trainer, you will use your knowledge to develop strategies and then to evaluate their effectiveness. With experience, the exercise and sport science professional becomes more proficient and more knowledgeable in practical ways.

Strengths and Limitations of Professional Practice Knowledge

Table 2.3 lists the major strengths and limitations of professional practice knowledge. This practical knowledge is usually more holistic than scientifically derived knowledge, reflecting the complex interplay of many factors—psychological, physical, technical, strategic, and social. And unlike science, professional practice knowledge tends to absorb novel or innovative practices. Coaches, teachers, exercise leaders, and trainers enjoy using new techniques. Another plus is that practical theories do not have to wait to be scientifically verified, so they can be used immediately.

Table 2.3 Strengths and Limitations of Professional Practice Knowledge	
Strengths	**Limitations**
Holistic	Less reliable
Innovative	Lack of explanations
Immediate	Greater susceptibility to bias

On the down side, professional practice can produce fewer and less precise explanations than science can. It is more affected by bias rather than being objective. Practical knowledge tends to be less reliable and definitive than scientifically based knowledge. Often a teacher knows a method works, but does not know why. This can be a problem if he wants to use the method in a new situation or revise it to help a particular student.

Integrating Scientific and Professional Practice Knowledge

The gap you may sense between reading a textbook and pursuing professional activities is part of a larger division between scientific and professional practice knowledge. Yet bridging this gap is paramount, for the combination of the two kinds of knowledge is what makes for effective applied practice.

There are several causes for this gap (Gowan, Botterill, & Blimkie, 1979). Until recently few opportunities existed to transfer results of research to professionals working in the field—physical educators, coaches, exercise leaders, athletes, exercisers, and trainers. Second, some sport and exercise psychologists were overly optimistic about using research to revolutionize the practice of teaching sport and physical activity skills. While basic laboratory research was being conducted in the 1960s and 1970s, there was little connection to actual field situations (external validity). The gap must close, with practitioners and researchers communicating to integrate their worlds.

An Active Approach to the Utilization of Sport and Exercise Psychology

To effectively use sport and exercise psychology in the field requires actively developing knowledge. The practitioner must blend sport and exercise psychology scientific knowledge with professional practice knowledge. Reading a book like this, taking a course in sport and exercise psychology, or working as a teacher, coach, or exercise leader is simply not enough. You must actively integrate scientific knowledge with your professional experiences and temper these with your own insights and intuition (see Table 2.4).

To take an active approach means applying the scientific principles identified in subsequent chapters of this book to your practice environments. Relate these principles to your own experiences as an athlete, exerciser, and/or physical education student. In essence, use the gym, the pool, or the athletic field as a mini-experimental situation where you test your sport and exercise psychology thoughts and principles. Evaluate how effective they are and in what situations they seem to work the best. Modify and update them when needed by keeping current regarding the latest sport and exercise psychology scientific findings.

In using this active approach, however, it is imperative that you have realistic expectations of sport and exercise psychology research findings. The majority of sport and exercise psychology research findings are judged significant based on probability. Hence, these findings probably won't hold true 100% of the time. They should work or accurately explain behavior the majority of the time. When they do not seem to adequately predict or explain behavior, analyze the situation relative to the explanation for why the principle works and see if you need to consider overriding personal or situation factors working in your practice environment.

Table 2.4 Actively Applying Sport and Exercise Psychology Knowledge
Apply scientific principles in your professional work settings
Evaluate the utility of scientific principles in the particular context in which you are involved
Keep current by updating and modifying your scientific knowledge base
Hold realistic expectations relative to the strengths and limitations of scientific principles

Sport and Exercise Psychology as an Art

It is especially important to recognize the individuality of students, exercisers, and athletes. Psychology is a social science. It is different from physics: Whereas inanimate objects do not change much over time, human beings do. Humans involved in sport and exercise also think and manipulate their environment, which makes behavior more difficult (but not impossible) to predict. Coach "Doc" Counsilman (Kimiecik & Gould, 1987), legendary Olympic swim coach and key proponent to a scientific approach to coaching, best summed up the need to consider individuality when he indicated that coaches coach by using general principles, the science of coaching. The art of coaching enters as they recognize when and in what situations to individualize these general principles. This same science-to-practice guiding principle holds true in sport and exercise psychology.

The science of coaching focuses on the use of general principles. The art of coaching is recognizing when and how to individualize these general principles.

Summary

The field of sport and exercise psychology is above all a science. For this reason it is imperative that you understand the basic scientific process and

James "Doc" Counsilman—the dean of coaching science of practical sport psychology.

how scientific knowledge is developed. Scientific knowledge alone, however, is not enough to guide professional practice. You must understand also how professional practice knowledge develops and, most importantly, how to integrate scientific knowledge with the knowledge gained from professional practice. This active process of integrating scientific and professional practice knowledge will greatly benefit you in using psychological skills as you work in applied sport and exercise settings.

Review Questions

1. Define science and explain four of its major goals.

2. What is a theory and why are theories important in sport and exercise psychology?

3. Distinguish between a research study and an experiment. Give an example of each.

4. Identify the strengths and limitations of scientifically derived knowledge.

5. What is professional practice knowledge and how does it develop?

6. Identify the strengths and limitations of professional practice knowledge.

7. Describe the gap between research and practice, why it exists, and how it can be bridged.

8. Describe the active approach to using sport and exercise psychology.

9. How is sport and exercise psychology like an art?

References

Gowan, G.R., Botterill, C.B., & Blimkie, C.J.R. (1979). Bridging the gap between sport science and sport practice. In P. Klavora & J.V. Daniel (Eds.), *Coach, athlete and the sport psychologist* (pp. 3-9). Ottawa, Canada: Coaching Association of Canada.

Kerlinger, F.N. (1973). Foundations of behavioral research (2nd ed.). New York: Holt, Rinehart & Winston.

Kimiecik, J., & Gould, D. (1987). Coaching psychology: The case of James "Doc" Counsilman. *The Sport Psychologist*, **1**, 350-358.

Martens, R. (1975). *Social psychology and physical activity*. New York: Harper & Row.

Martens, R. (1987). Science, knowledge and sport psychology. *Sport Psychologist*, **1**, 29-55.

Vealey, R.S. (1992). Personality in sport: A comprehensive view. In T.S. Horn (Ed.), *Advances in sport psychology* (pp. 25-59). Champaign, IL: Human Kinetics.

Zajonc, R.B. (1965). Social facilitation. *Science*, **149**, 269-274.

PART

Understanding Participants

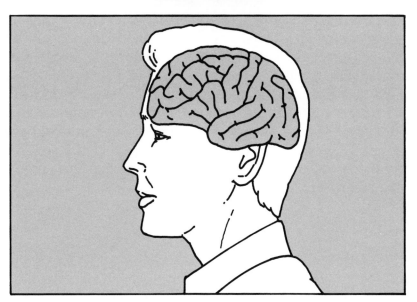

A re successful athletes distinguished by certain key personality characteristics? What motivates people to participate in physical activity? Why are some people so motivated to achieve competitive success, whereas others dread the mere thought of competition? And how does one psych up for optimal performance without psyching out?

These are just some of the important questions addressed during the first stop on our journey to understanding sport and exercise psychology. In particular, this part focuses on personal factors—personality characteristics, individual orientations, and emotions—that affect performance and psychological development in sport, physical education, and exercise settings. The part consists of four chapters.

Chapter 3, on personality, is an important chapter because to work effectively with students, athletes, and exercisers you need to understand what makes them tick as individuals. Thus, the information in this chapter will help you better understand the psychological make-up of those you will work with.

Motivation is one of the most studied issues in sport and exercise psychology. Chapters 4 and 5 focus on elements of motivation. In chapter 4, a person-by-situation interactional model of motivation is presented and used to help us understand motivation in a variety of physical activity contexts. Achievement motivation, competitiveness, and attributions (the explanations we use to account for our behavior) are discussed in chapter 5. The information in these two chapters will help you understand why some people are go-getters while others seem to lack motivation. You'll learn how situational factors (including your actions) influence participant motivation. Most importantly, you will be presented with effective strategies for enhancing a person's level of motivation.

The final chapter in the section, chapter 6, examines arousal and anxiety. Here you'll learn why students and athletes become uptight and how psyching up influences performance. Major sources of stress affecting participants in sport and exercise will also be identified.

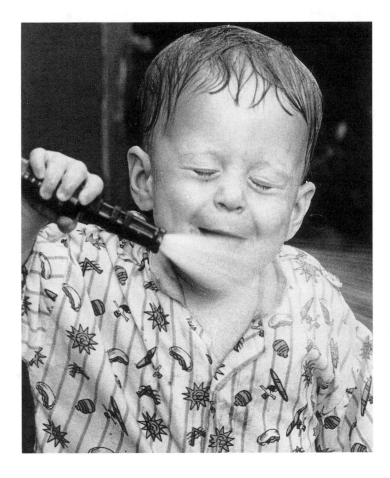

CHAPTER 2

Personality and Sport

By 1994 over 1,000 articles had been published on aspects of sport personality (Ruffer, 1976a, 1976b; Vealey, 1989), most of them written during the 1960s and 1970s. This voluminous research demonstrates how important researchers and practitioners consider the role of personality in sport and exercise settings. Researchers have asked, for example, what causes some students to be excited about physical education classes, whereas others don't even bother to "dress out"; why some exercisers stay with their fitness program, whereas others lose motivation and drop out; whether personality tests should be used to select athletes for teams; and whether athletic success can be predicted by an athlete's personality type.

In this chapter you will learn about

▌ what personality is,

▌ how personality can be measured,

▌ the relationship between personality and behavior in sport,

▌ how to assess personality tests and research for practicality and validity,

▌ how to use what you know of personality in sport and exercise settings, and

▌ how to better understand people's personalities.

What Makes Up Personality?

Have you ever tried to describe your own personality? If you have, you probably found yourself listing adjectives like funny, outgoing, happy, stable, and so on. Maybe you remembered how you reacted in various situations. Is there more to personality than these kinds of attributes? Many theorists have attempted to define personality and they agree on one description: *uniqueness*. In essence, personality refers to the characteristics—or blend of characteristics—that make a person unique.

One of the best ways to understand personality is through its structure. Think of personality as divided into three separate but related levels (see Figure 3.1; Hollander, 1967; Martens, 1975):

- A psychological core
- Typical responses
- Role-related behavior

> Personality is the sum of those characteristics that make a person unique.

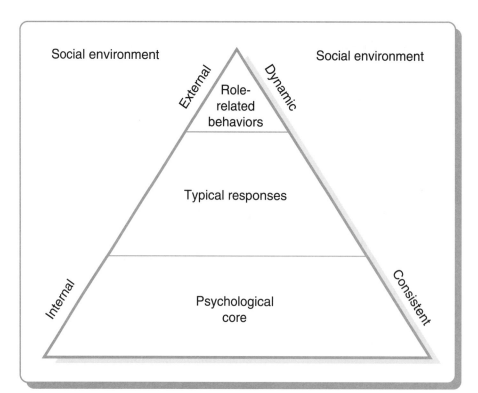

Figure 3.1 A schematic view of personality structure. Adapted from Martens (1975).

Psychological Core

The most basic level of your personality is called the *psychological core*. The deepest component, it includes your attitudes and values, interests and motives, and beliefs about yourself and your self-worth. In essence, the psychological core represents the centerpiece of your personality and is "the *real* you," not who you want others to think you are. For example, your basic values might revolve around the importance of family, friends, and religion in your life.

Typical Responses

Typical responses are the ways we each learn to adjust to the environment, or how we usually respond to the world around us. For example, you might be happy-go-lucky, shy, and even-tempered. Often your typical responses are good indicators of your psychological core. That is, if you consistently respond to social situations by being quiet and shy, you are likely introverted, not extroverted. However, if someone observed you being quiet at a party and from that evidence alone concluded you were introverted, that person could well be mistaken—it may have been this particular situation that caused you to be quiet. Your quietness may not have been a typical response.

Role-Related Behavior

How you act based on what you perceive your social situation to be is called *role-related behavior*. This behavior is the most changeable aspect of personality: Your behavior will change as your perceptions of the environment change. Different situations require playing different roles. On the same day you might play the roles of student at a university, coach of a Little League team, employee, and friend. Likely you'll behave differently in each of these situations; for example, you'll probably exert more leadership as a coach than as a student or employee. Roles can conflict with each other. For example, a parent who is

coaching her child's soccer team might feel a conflict between her coaching and parenting roles.

Why Study Personality Structure?

The three levels of personality encompass a continuum from internally driven to externally driven behaviors (see Figure 3.1). To simplify it, liken your levels of personality to a chocolate-covered cherry: The outside wrapper is seen by all (role-related behavior), the chocolate layer (typical responses) is seen by those who go to the trouble to take off the wrapper, and the cherry center is seen only by the people interested or motivated enough to bite into the candy to see what's there (psychological core).

The psychological core is not only the most internal of the three levels and the hardest to get to know, it is also the most stable part of your personality and remains fairly constant over time. On the other end of the continuum are the most external role-related behaviors, which are subject to the greatest influence from the external environment. For example, you may always tell the truth because being truthful is one of your core values. But your behavior may vary in some areas, such as being aloof in your role as a fitness director and affectionate in your role as a parent. Usually your responses lie somewhere in between because they result from the interaction of your psychological core and role-related behaviors.

Both stability and change are desirable in personality. The core, or stable, aspect of personality provides the structure we need to function effectively in society, whereas the dynamic, or changing, component allows for learning. As coaches, physical educators, trainers, and exercise leaders we can be more effective when we understand the different levels of personality structure beyond the role-related behaviors particular to a situation. Getting to know the real person (psychological core) and typical modes of response produces insight into motivation, actions, and behavior. In essence, we need to know what makes people tick to decide the best way to help them. Especially when working long-term with people, such as over a season or more, it's helpful to understand more about their individual core values (i.e., psychological core).

The study of personality helps us work better with students, athletes, and exercisers.

Approaches to Personality

Psychologists have looked at personality from several viewpoints. Three of their major ways of studying personality in sport and exercise have been called the trait, situation, and interactional approaches.

Trait Approach

The trait approach assumes that the fundamental units of personality—its traits—are relatively stable. That is, personality traits are enduring and consistent across a variety of situations. Taking the trait approach, psychologists consider that the causes of behavior generally reside within the person. They minimize the role of situational or environmental factors. Traits are considered to predispose a person to act a certain way, regardless of the situation or circumstances. If an athlete is competitive, for example, he or she will be predisposed to playing hard and giving all, regardless of the situation or score. A predisposition, however, does not mean that the athlete will always act this way; it simply means that the athlete is likely to be competitive in sport situations.

The most noted of the trait proponents in the 1960s and 1970s included Gordon Allport, Raymond Cattell, and Hans Eysenck. Cattell developed a personality inventory with 16 independent personality factors (16 PF) that he believed describe a person (1965). Eysenck and Eysenck (1968) viewed traits as relative, the two most significant traits ranging on continuums from introversion to extroversion and from stability to emotionality. They argued that personality can best be understood by considering traits that are relatively enduring and stable over time.

However, simply knowing an individual's personality traits will not always help us predict how he or she will behave in a particular situation. For example, some people anger easily during sport activity, whereas others seldom get angry. Yet the individuals who tend to get angry in sport probably will not anger in other situations. So simply knowing an individual's personality traits does not necessarily predict (or tell you) whether he or she will act on them. The predisposition toward anger does not tell us what specific situations will provoke that response. This observation led some researchers to study personality by focusing on the situation or environment, rather than personality traits, that might trigger behaviors.

The trait approach, which dominated the early study of personality, did not take into consideration the particular situations that might also influence an individual's behavior.

Situation Approach

The situation approach, on the other hand, argues that behavior is determined largely by the situation or environment. It draws from social learning theory (Bandura, 1977), which explains behavior in terms of observational learning (modeling) and social reinforcement (feedback). Simply stated, environmental influences and reinforcements shape the way you behave. You might act confident, for instance, in one situation but tentative in another, regardless of your particular personality traits. Furthermore, if the influence of the environment is strong enough, the effect of personality traits will be minimal. For example, if you are introverted and shy, you still might act assertively or even aggressively if you saw someone getting mugged. Many football players are gentle and shy off the field, but the game (situation) requires them to act aggressively. Thus, the situation would be a more important determinant of their behavior than their particular personality traits.

Although the situation approach is not as widely embraced by sport psychologists as the trait approach, Rushall and Siedentop (1972) contend that you can influence behavior in sport and physical education by changing the reinforcements in the environment. Still, the situation approach, like the trait approach, cannot truly predict behavior. A situation can certainly influence behavior, but some people will not be swayed by the situation.

Situations alone are insufficient to accurately predict behavior—an individual's personality traits need also to be considered.

Interactional Approach

The interactional approach considers situation and person as codeterminants of behavior—that is, as variables that together determine behavior. In other words, knowing both an individual's psychological traits and particular situation are helpful to understand behavior. Researchers using an interactional approach ask these kinds of questions:

- Will extroverts perform better in a team situation and introverts in an individual (i.e., nonteam) situation?
- Will highly motivated people stick with a formal exercise program longer than exercisers with low self-motivation?
- Will self-confident children prefer competitive sport and youngsters with low self-confidence prefer noncompetitive sport situations?

Using the Interactional Approach

Most sport and exercise psychologists favor the interactional approach to studying behavior. Bowers found that the interaction between persons and situations could explain twice as much behavior as traits or situations alone (1973). The interactional approach requires investigating how people in sport and physical activity react individually in particular settings.

For example, Fisher and Zwart (1982) studied the anxiety athletes showed in different basketball situations—before the game, during the game, and after the game. Here are a few of the game situations:

- With 2 seconds left and the score tied 70-70, you have just been fouled and your free throw might win the game.
- The crowd is very loud and directs most its comments toward you.
- You have just made a bad play and your coach is criticizing you.
- You are in the locker room after losing a game you really expected to win.

Given these situations, the athletes were asked to report to what degree they would react in these ways (worded as in the study):

a. Get an uneasy feeling
b. React overemotionally
c. Want to avoid the situation
d. Get a "choking" feeling
e. Enjoy the challenge

Both situations and psychological traits need to be considered to understand and predict behavior.

The athletes' reactions to each basketball situation are colored by their particular mental and emotional make-up. Pilar, who is usually anxious and uptight, may "choke" before shooting free throws with a tied score, whereas Pat, who is laid back and less anxious, might enjoy the challenge. How would you react?

The Interactional Approach: A Case Study

Madonna and Cher enroll in an exercise class. Madonna has high self-esteem, and Cher has low self-esteem. The class is structured so that each participant takes a turn leading the exercises. Because she is confident in social situations and about how she looks, Madonna really looks forward to leading the class. Cher, on the other hand, is not confident getting up in front of people and feels embarrassed by how she looks. Not surprisingly, Cher loses interest in the class and drops out after 2 months.

The Measurement of Personality

When research is conducted appropriately, it can shed considerable light on how personality impacts behavior in sport and exercise settings. Psychologists have developed ways to measure personality, which help our understanding of personality traits and states. Many psychologists distinguish between an individual's typical style of behaving *(traits)* and the situation's effects on behavior *(states)*. This distinction between psychological traits and states has been critical in the development of personality research in sport. However, even though a given psychological trait predisposes someone to behave in a certain way, the behavior doesn't necessarily occur in all situations. Therefore, you should consider *both traits and states* as you attempt to understand and predict behavior.

Trait and State Measures

Until recently, almost all of the trait and state measures of personality in sport psychology came from general psychological inventories, without specific reference to sport or physical activity. Examples of such inventories include

- the State-Trait Anxiety Inventory (Spielberger, Gorsuch, & Lushene, 1970),
- the Test of Attentional and Interpersonal Style (Nideffer, 1976),

Table 3.1 Trait Sport Confidence Inventory

Think about how self-confident you are when you compete in sport. Answer the questions below based on how confident you *generally* feel when you compete in your sport. Compare your self-confidence to the most self-confident athlete you know. Please answer as you really feel, not how you would like to feel (circle number).

1. Compare your confidence in your ability to execute the skills necessary to be successful to the most confident athlete you know.

   Low　　　　　Medium　　　　High
   1　2　3　4　5　6　7　8　9

2. Compare your confidence in your ability to perform under pressure to the most confident athlete you know.

   Low　　　　　Medium　　　　High
   1　2　3　4　5　6　7　8　9

3. Compare your confidence in your ability to concentrate well enough to be successful to the most confident athlete you know.

   Low　　　　　Medium　　　　High
   1　2　3　4　5　6　7　8　9

Adapted from Vealey, R.S. (1986).

- the Profile of Mood States (McNair, Lorr, & Droppleman, 1971), and
- the Eysenck Personality Inventory (Eysenck & Eysenck, 1968).

Look at these sample questions from trait (Trait Sport Confidence Inventory) and state (State Sport Confidence Inventory) measures of confidence in Tables 3.1 and 3.2. They highlight the differences between trait and state measures of confidence in a *sport* context.

Now look at some of the questions and response formats from the Test of Attentional and Interpersonal Style and the Profile of Mood States (POMS; see Tables 3.3 and 3.4). Notice that the questions do not directly relate to sport or

Table 3.2   State Sport Confidence Inventory

Answer the questions below based on how confident you feel *right now* about competing in the upcoming contest. Compare your self-confidence to the most self-confident athlete you know. Please answer as you really feel, not how you would like to feel (circle number).

1. Compare the confidence you feel right now in your ability to execute the skills necessary to be successful to the most confident athlete you know.

   Low 1 2 3   Medium 4 5 6   High 7 8 9

2. Compare the confidence you feel right now in your ability to perform under pressure to the most confident athlete you know.

   Low 1 2 3   Medium 4 5 6   High 7 8 9

3. Compare the confidence you feel right now in your ability to concentrate well enough to be successful to the most confident athlete you know.

   Low 1 2 3   Medium 4 5 6   High 7 8 9

Adapted from Vealey, R.S. (1986).

Table 3.3   Test of Attentional and Interpersonal Style

I get caught up in my thoughts and become oblivious to what is going on around me.

I have difficulty clearing my mind of a single thought or idea.

It is easy for me to direct my attention and focus narrowly on something.

At stores, I am faced with so many choices I can't make up my mind.

I am good at rapidly scanning crowds and picking out a particular person or face.

Scoring

0 = Never
1 = Rarely
2 = Sometimes
3 = Frequently
4 = Always

Adapted from Nideffer, R. (1976).

Table 3.4   Profile of Mood States
Energetic Tense Fatigued Confused Full of pep Annoyed **Scoring** 0 = Not at all 1 = A little 2 = Moderately 3 = Quite a bit 4 = Extremely

Adapted from McNair, Lorr, and Droppleman (1971).

physical activity. Rather, they are general and related to overall attentional styles and mood.

Situation-Specific Measures

Although general scales provide some useful information about personality traits and states, situation-specific measures will predict behavior more reliably for given situations because they consider both the personality of the participant and the specific situation (interactional approach). For example, a researcher named Sarason observed that some students did poorly on tests when they became overly anxious (1975). These students were not particularly anxious in other situations, but taking exams made them freeze up. Sarason devised a

We can predict behavior better when we have more knowledge of the specific situation and how individuals respond to particular types of situations.

situationally specific scale to measure how anxious a person usually feels before taking exams (test anxiety). This situation-specific test could predict anxiety right before exams (state anxiety) better than a general test of trait anxiety.

Sport-Specific Measures

Sport-specific mea-
sures of personality
predict behavior in
sport settings better
than general person-
ality tests do.

Sport-specific tests provide more reliable and valid measures of personality traits and states in sport and exercise contexts. For example, rather than test how anxious you are before giving a speech or going out on a date, a coach might test how anxious you are before competition (especially if excess anxiety proves detrimental to your performance). A sport-specific test of anxiety assesses precompetitive anxiety better than a general anxiety test. Psychological inventories developed specifically for use in sport and physical activity settings include

- the Sport Competition Anxiety Test to measure competitive trait anxiety (Martens, 1977),
- the Competitive State Anxiety Inventory-2 to measure precompetitive state anxiety (Martens et al., 1982), and
- the Trait-State Confidence Inventory to measure sport confidence (Vealey, 1986).

Some tests have even been developed for a particular sport: These inventories can help identify a person's areas of psychological strength and weakness in that sport or physical activity. After gathering the results a coach can advise players on how to build the strengths and reduce or eliminate the weaknesses. Sport-specific inventories include

- the Tennis Test of Attentional and Interpersonal Style (Van Schoyck & Grasha, 1981—see Table 3.5 for sample questions),
- the Anxiety Assessment for Wrestlers (Gould, Horn, & Spreeman, 1984), and
- the Group Cohesion Inventory for Basketball (Yukelson, Weinberg, & Jackson, 1984).

Table 3.5   Sample Items
From the Tennis Test of Attentional and Interpersonal Style

When playing tennis, I find myself distracted by the sights and sounds around me.

When playing doubles, I am aware of the movements and positions of all the players on the court.

I am good at quickly analyzing a tennis opponent and assessing strengths and weaknesses.

When playing tennis, I get anxious and block out everything.

Scoring

0 = Never
1 = Rarely
2 = Sometimes
3 = Frequently
4 = Always

Adapted from Van Schoyck and Grasha (1981).

Consider Traits and States to Understand Behavior

Terry is in general a confident person; he usually responds to situations with higher state confidence than Tim, who is low trait-confident. As a coach you are interested in how confidence relates to performance and want to know how Tim and Terry are feeling immediately before a swimming test you are giving. Although Tim is not confident in general, he swam on his high school swim team and is confident in his swimming abilities. Consequently, his *state* confidence right before the race is high. Conversely, although Terry is highly confident in general, he has had little swimming experience and is not even sure he can finish the race. Thus, his state confidence is low right before the race. If you measured only Tim's and Terry's trait confidence, you would be unable to predict how confident they feel before swimming. On the other hand, if you observed Tim's and Terry's state confidence in a different sport— baseball, for example—their results might be different.

This example demonstrates the need to consider both trait and state measures to investigate personality. State and trait levels alone are less significant than the difference between a person's current state level and trait level. This difference score represents the impact of situation factors on behavior. Terry's and Tim's state anxiety levels differed because of experience in swimming (a situation factor).

Fluctuations Before and Throughout Competition

Feelings change before and during a competition. Usually states are assessed shortly before (within 30 minutes) the onset of competition or physical activity. Although a measurement can indicate how someone is feeling at that moment, these feelings might change during the competition. For example, Matthew's competitive state anxiety 30 minutes before playing a championship football game might be very high. But once he "takes a few good hits" and gets into the flow of the game, his anxiety might drop to a moderate level. In the fourth quarter, Matt's anxiety might increase again when the score is tied. Such fluctuations should be considered in evaluating personality and reactions to competitive settings.

Using Psychological Measures

The knowledge of personality is critical to success as a coach, teacher, or exercise leader. You may be tempted to use psychological tests to gather information about the people you want to help professionally. Bear in mind, however, that psychological inventories cannot actually predict athletic success. And they have sometimes been used unethically—or at least inappropriately—and administered poorly. Indeed, it isn't always clear how psychological inventories should be used! Yet it is essential that professionals understand the limitations and the uses and abuses of testing to know what to do and what not to do.

You want to be able to make an informed decision on how (or if) to use personality tests—that is, to be an informed consumer of psychological testing. These are some important questions to consider about psychological testing:

- Should psychological tests be used to help select athletes for a team?
- What qualifies someone to administer psychological tests?
- Should coaches give psychological tests to their athletes?
- What types of psychological tests should be used with athletes?
- How should psychological tests be administered to athletes?

In 1985 the American Psychological Association (APA) provided the following seven helpful guidelines on the use of psychological tests.

Know the Principles of Testing and Measurement Error

Before you administer and interpret psychological inventories, you should understand testing principles, be able to recognize measurement errors, and have well-designed and validated measures. Not all psychological tests have been systematically developed and made reliable. Making predictions or inferences about an athlete's behavior and personality structure on the basis of these tests would be misleading and unethical. Test results are not absolute or irrefutable.

Even valid tests that have been reliably developed may have measurement errors. Suppose you wish to measure self-esteem in 13- to 15-year-old physical education students. You choose a good test developed for adults, inasmuch as there are no tests specifically for youngsters. If the students do not fully understand the questions, however, the results would not be reliable. Similarly, if you give a test developed on a predominantly white population to African-American and Hispanic athletes, the results might be less reliable due to cultural differences. In these situations, a researcher should conduct pilot testing with that specific population to establish the reliability and validity of the test instrument.

People usually want to present themselves in a favorable light. Sometimes they answer questions in what they think is a "socially desirable" way, a response style known as "faking good." For example, an athlete may fear letting her coach know how nervous she gets before competition, so she skews her answers in a precompetitive anxiety test, trying to appear calm, cool, and collected.

Know Your Own Limitations

The American Psychological Association recommends that people administering tests be aware of the limitations of their training and preparation. However, some people do not recognize their own limited knowledge, or they use and interpret test results unethically, which can be damaging to the athletes. For instance, it would be inappropriate to use personality inventories developed to measure psychopathology (abnormality) such as schizophrenia or manic-depression to measure a more normal increase in anxiety. Furthermore, it is inappropriate to give physical education students a clinical personality test.

Do Not Use Psychological Tests for Team Selection

Using psychological tests to select players to a team is an abuse. For example, determining if an athlete has the "right" psychological profile to be a middle linebacker in football or point guard in basketball on the basis of psychological tests is unfair. Psychological tests are not accurate enough yet to predict behavior consistently.

Include Explanation and Feedback

Athletes, students, and exercisers should be told the purpose of the tests, what they measure, and how the test is going to be used—before they actually complete the tests. They should receive specific feedback about the results that allows them to gain insight into themselves from the testing process.

Assure Confidentiality

It is essential to assure people that their answers will remain confidential in whatever tests they take (and to ensure that this confidentiality is maintained!). With this assurance test takers are more likely to answer truthfully. When they fear exposure, they may fake good, which can distort the true findings of the test and make its interpretation virtually useless. Students in a physical education class might wonder if a test will affect their grades, and in these circumstances they will be more likely to exaggerate their strengths and minimize their weaknesses. If you do not explain the reasons for testing, test takers typically become suspicious and wonder if the coach will use the test to help select starters or weed out players.

Take an Intraindividual Approach

It is a mistake to compare an athlete's psychological test results with the norms. Athletes or exercisers might seem to score high or low in anxiety, self-confidence, or motivation in relation to other people, but the more critical point is to determine how they are feeling relative to how they usually feel (intraindividual approach). Use this psychological information to help them perform better and enjoy the experience.

Take the example of assessing an exerciser's motivation. It isn't as important to know if the individual's motivation to exercise is high or low compared

---

All psychological tests contain a degree of measurement error; exercise caution in interpreting their results.

Individuals need special training (e.g., certification, coursework) in psychological assessment or a degree in clinical psychology or psychiatry to be qualified to interpret personality test results.

Using personality inventories to select athletes to a team or to cut them from a team is an abuse of testing that should not be tolerated.

with other exercisers so much as compared with competing motivations (e.g., being with family or job responsibilities).

Understand the Structure of Personality

A clear understanding of personality structure provides you with some perspective for interpreting psychological tests. For example, to measure someone's personality, you would certainly be interested in her psychological core. You would select specific types of tests to gain an accurate understanding of the various aspects of her personality. Here are two examples.

Projective Tests. It is hard to measure personality directly. So *projective* tests usually include pictures or written situations, and the test takers are asked to project their feelings and thoughts about these materials. For example, someone might be shown a photo of an exhausted runner crossing a finish line at the end of a highly contested track race and be asked to write about what is happening. A high-achieving, confident person might emphasize how the runner made an all-out effort to achieve his goal, whereas a low-achiever might project feelings of sorrow for losing the race in a close finish.

Typical Responses. Projective tests are interesting but they are often difficult to score and interpret. Consequently, sport psychologists usually assess personality in sport by looking at typical responses. For instance, a coach wants

---

Dos and Don'ts in Personality Testing

Dos:

- Inform participants about the purpose of the personality test and exactly how it will be used.
- Allow only qualified individuals who have an understanding of testing principles and measurement error to give personality tests.
- Integrate personality test results with other information obtained about the participant.
- Use sport- and exercise-specific tests whenever possible, giving them in consultation with a sport psychologist.
- Use both state and trait measures of personality.
- Provide participants with specific feedback concerning the results of the test.
- Compare individuals against their own baseline levels rather than against normative information.

Don'ts:

- Do not use clinical personality tests that focus on abnormality to study an average population of sport and exercise participants.
- Do not use personality tests to decide who makes a team or program and who doesn't.
- Do not give or interpret personality tests unless you are qualified to do so by the APA or another certifying organization.
- Do not use personality tests to predict behavior in sport and exercise settings without considering other sources of information such as observational data and performance assessments.

to know more than that an athlete is generally anxious—he or she wants to know how the athlete deals with competitive anxiety. So a test that measures anxiety in sport would be more useful to a coach or sport psychologist than a test that measures anxiety in general. Likewise, a test that measures motivation for exercise would be more useful to an exercise leader than a general motivation test.

Personality Research in Sport and Exercise

The research from the 1960s and 1970s yielded few useful conclusions about the relationship of personality to sport performance. In part these meager results stemmed from methodological, statistical, and interpretive problems, which we will discuss later. Researchers were divided into two camps. Morgan (1980) described one group as taking a *credulous* viewpoint; that is, these researchers believed that personality is closely related to athletic success. The other group, he said, had a *skeptical* viewpoint, arguing that personality is not related to athletic success.

Relationship Between Personality and Behavior

Neither the credulous nor the skeptical viewpoint appears to have been correct. Rather, some relationship exists between personality and sport performance, but it is far from perfect. That is, although personality traits and states can help predict sport behavior and success, they are not precise. For example, the fact that some Olympic long-distance runners exhibit introverted personalities does not mean that a long-distance runner needs to be introverted to be successful. Similarly, although many successful middle linebackers in football have aggressive personalities, other successful middle linebackers do not.

We'll now turn our focus to the research on personality, sport performance, and sport preference. But remember that personality alone doesn't account for behavior in sport and exercise. Some caution is needed in interpreting the findings of personality research because, as discussed in chapter 2, an attribution, or assumption, of cause-and-effect relationships between personality and performance was a problem in many of the early studies.

Personality traits and states should be considered along with cognitive, physiological, sociological, and psychological variables to understand and predict behavior in sport and exercise.

Athletes and Nonathletes

Try to define an athlete. It isn't easy. Is an athlete someone who plays on a varsity or interscholastic team? Who demonstrates a certain level of skill? Who jogs daily to lose weight? Who plays professional sports? Who plays intramural sports? Keep this ambiguity in mind as you read about studies that have compared personality traits of athletes and nonathletes. As discussed in chapter 2, such studies have weakened this research and clouded its interpretation.

One large comparative study of athletes and nonathletes tested almost 2,000 college males using Cattell's 16 PF, which measures 16 traits (Schurr, Ashley, & Joy, 1977). No single personality profile was found that distinguished athletes (defined for the study's purposes as a member of a university intercollegiate team) from nonathletes. However, when the athletes were categorized by sport, several differences did emerge. For example, compared to nonathletes, athletes who played team sports exhibited

- less abstract reasoning,
- more extroversion,
- more dependency, and
- less ego strength.

Compared with nonathletes, athletes who played individual sports displayed

- higher levels of objectivity,
- more dependency,
- less anxiety, and
- less abstract thinking.

Hence, some personality differences appear to distinguish athletes and nonathletes, but these specific differences cannot yet be considered definitive. Schurr et al. (1977) found that team-sport athletes were more dependent, extroverted, and anxious but less imaginative than individual-sport athletes. Of course, it's possible that certain personality types are drawn to a particular sport rather than that participation in a sport somehow changes one's personality. The reasons for these differences remain unclear.

Female Athletes

As more women compete in sport, it is important to understand the personality profile of female athletes. In 1980 Williams found that successful female athletes differed markedly from the "normative" female in terms of personality profile. Compared with nonathletes, female athletes were found to be more

- achievement-oriented,
- independent,
- aggressive,
- emotionally stable, and
- assertive.

Most of these traits are desirable for sports. Apparently, outstanding athletes have similar personality characteristics, regardless of being male or female.

Positive Mental Health—The Iceberg Profile

After comparing personality traits of more successful with less successful athletes, Morgan developed a *mental health model* that he has found effective in predicting athletic success (Morgan, 1979, 1980; Morgan et al., 1987). Basically, the model suggests that positive mental health is directly related to athletic success and high levels of performance.

Morgan's model predicts that an athlete who scores above the norm on neuroticism, depression, fatigue, confusion, and anger and below the norm on vigor will tend to pale in comparison with an athlete who scores below the norm on all of these traits except vigor, on which he scores above the norm. Elite athletes in a variety of sports (e.g., swimmers, wrestlers, oarsmen, runners) are characterized by what Morgan called the *iceberg profile*. The iceberg profile of a successful elite athlete is formed by vigor being above the mean of the population and tension, depression, anger, fatigue, and confusion being below the mean of the population (see Figure 3.2). Notice that the profile looks like an iceberg, with all negative traits below the surface (population norms) and the one positive trait (vigor) above the surface. In contrast, less successful elite athletes have a flat profile, scoring at or below the 50th percentile on all psychological factors (see Figure 3.3).

The Mental Health Model—Predicting Performance

Morgan (1979) psychologically evaluated 16 candidates for the 1974 United States Heavyweight Rowing Team, correctly predicting 10 of the 16 finalists. You might think that these impressive statistics mean you should use psycho-

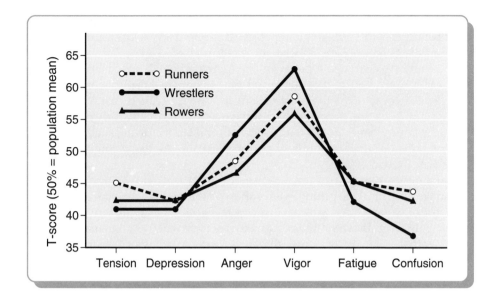

Figure 3.2 Iceberg profiles for elite wrestlers, distance runners, and rowers. Adapted from Morgan (1979).

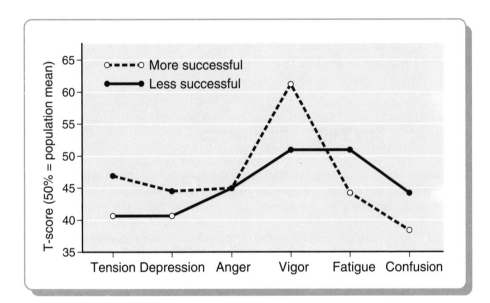

Figure 3.3 Psychological profiles of more successful and less successful elite athletes. Adapted from Morgan (1979).

logical tests for selecting athletes to a team. However, as you will later read, most sport psychologists vehemently oppose using psychological tests for team selection. Personality testing is far from perfect (only 10 of 16 were correctly predicted), and athletes might be unfairly and erroneously selected or cut from a team.

This type of personality data, however, is useful for discovering the kinds of psychological traits and states associated with successful athletes—and once these psychological factors are understood, athletes can work with sport psychologists and coaches to develop psychological skills for improving performance. For example, psychological skills training (see chapters 13 to 18) can help exercisers and athletes more effectively cope with anger and anxiety.

Exercise and Personality

Sport psychologists have more recently been investigating the relationships between exercise and personality. We will briefly review the relation between exercise and two personality dispositions: Type A behavior and self-concept.

Tests can help identify an athlete's psychological strengths and weaknesses, and this information can be used to develop appropriate psychological skills training.

Type A Behavior. The Type A behavior pattern is characterized by a strong sense of urgency, an excess of competitive drive, and an easily aroused hostility. The antithesis of the Type A behavior pattern is called Type B. Initially, a link was found between Type A behavior and increased incidence of cardiovascular disease. More recently, it is suspected that the anger-hostility component of the Type A construct is the most significant disease-related characteristic. Although the causes of Type A behavior have not been conclusively determined, considerable evidence points to the sociocultural environment, such as parental expectations of high standards of performance, as the likely origin (Girdano, Everly, & Dusek, 1990).

Early efforts to modify Type A behavior through exercise interventions have had mixed results. One positive study showed that a 12-week aerobics program was not only associated with reductions in Type A behavior but also helped participants significantly reduce cardiovascular reactivity to mental stress (Blumenthal et al., 1988). Thus, changing Type A behavior patterns through exercise could result in positive health benefits.

Self-Concept. Exercise appears to have a positive relationship also with self-concept (Sonstroem, 1984). Sonstroem suggested that these changes in self-concept might be associated with the *perception* of improved fitness rather than with actual changes in physical fitness. Although studies so far have not proved that changes in self-concept were produced by changes in physical fitness, exercise programs seem to lead to significant increases in self-esteem, especially with subjects initially low in self-esteem.

Cognitive Strategies and Success

The kinds of mental strategies athletes use for competition reflect their personalities. Recently some psychologists studied the cognitive (mental) strategies that distinguish successful athletes from less successful ones. For example, when Mahoney and Avener investigated gymnasts competing for berths on the United States Men's Gymnastics Team, they found that those who made the team coped better with anxiety, used more internal imagery, and had more positive self-talk than the gymnasts who didn't make the team (1977). Similarly, successful wrestlers maintained a high level of confidence, focused their thoughts on the match, and recovered better from mistakes than did other wrestlers (Gould, Weiss, & Weinberg, 1981).

In-Depth Interview Technique

Researchers recently have attempted to investigate the differences between successful and less successful athletes by taking a *qualitative* approach. In-depth interviews are conducted to probe the coping strategies that athletes employ before and during competition. The interview approach provides coaches, athletes, and sport psychologists with much more in-depth personality profiles of an athlete. For example, all 20 members of the 1988 U.S. Olympic freestyle and Greco Roman wrestling teams were interviewed. Compared with nonmedalist wrestlers, Olympic medal winners

- used more positive self-talk,
- had a more narrow and immediate focus of attention,
- were better prepared mentally for unforeseen negative circumstances, and
- had more extensive mental practice (Gould, Eklund, & Jackson, 1992).

Type A behavior patterns apparently can be altered through exercise, which could lead to reducing the risk of cardiovascular disease.

Exercise and increased levels of fitness appear to be associated with increases in self-esteem, especially for individuals initially low in self-esteem.

One wrestler described his ability to react automatically to adversity:

> Something I've always practiced is to never let anything interfere with what I'm trying to accomplish at a particular tournament. So, what I try to do is if something is trying to bother me . . . completely empty my mind and concentrate on the event coming up. . . . My coping strategy is just to completely eliminate it from my mind, and I guess I'm blessed to be able to do that. (Gould et al., 1992)

Medalists seemed able to maintain a relatively stable and positive emotional level because their coping strategies became automatic, whereas nonmedalists experienced more fluctuating emotions as a consequence of not coping well mentally. Take the following example of a nonmedalist Olympic wrestler:

> I had a relaxation tape that seemed to give me moments of relief. . . . It got to the point where what you would try to do was *not* think about wrestling and get your mind on other things. But inevitably . . . you would bind up and get tight, [your] pulse would pick-up, and your palms and legs and hands or feet [would be] sweating. You go through that trying to sleep, and I would resort to my relaxation tape. I don't think I coped very well with it really. (Gould et al., 1992)

Mental Plans

Some quotes from Olympic athletes will help in demonstrating the above mental strategies (Orlick & Partington, 1988).

> The plan or program was already in my head. For the race I was on automatic, like turning the program on cruise control and letting it run. I was aware of the effort I was putting in and also of my opponent's position in relation to me but I always focus on what I had to do next.

> Before I start I focus on relaxing, on breathing calmly. I feel activated but in control since I'd been thinking about what I was going to do in the race all through the warm-up. I used the period just before the start to clear my mind, so when I did actually start the race all my thoughts about what I would be doing in the race could be uncluttered.

> I usually try to work with my visualization on what is likely I'm going to use. Different wrestlers have different moves, you know. They always like to throw a right arm spin or something and I'll visualize myself blocking that and things like that.

Olympic medalists, unlike nonmedalists, internalize their mental strategies to the extent that they react automatically to adversity.

Canadian Olympic athletes learn a systematic series of mental strategies for before the competition and during it, including refocusing plans. Thus, athletes come not only prepared mentally to perform but also to handle distractions and unforeseen events both before and during the competition (Orlick & Partington, 1988). These mental plans especially help athletes whose sense of control (personality trait) is low by allowing them to feel more in control, regardless of situational influences. Table 3.6 provides an example of a detailed refocusing plan for a Canadian Olympic Alpine skier.

Table 3.6   Refocusing Plan for an Olympic Alpine Skier

Action	Strategy
Prevent hassle	Use adrenaline and anger as a positive instead of bringing me down. Let coaches or other personnel rectify the problem.
Delay in start	Relax, think of anything and everything that makes me happy.
Loss of ideal focus in race run	Think of course in "sections" and deal with mistakes as a mistake in previous "section"; entering the "new section," a refocusing occurs. Think and deal with the remainder of the course as previously rehearsed.
Mistake in race run	Deal with mistake as I would a loss of focus. Go for the future, not the past.
Poor performance—first run	Think of second run with a "nothing to lose" attitude.
Poor performance—final run	Determine what went wrong and why. Learn from the mistake, train, and see the mistake dissolve mentally and physically. Make the poor performance a challenge to defeat.

Adapted from Orlick, T. (1986)

Mental Strategies Used by Successful Athletes

- Practice specific plans to deal with adversity during competition to enhance confidence.

- Practice routines to deal with unusual circumstances and distractions before and during a competition.

- Concentrate wholly on the upcoming performance and block out irrelevant events and thoughts.

- Use several mental rehearsals prior to competition.

- Don't worry about other competitors before a competition—instead focus on what you can control.

- Develop detailed competition plans.

- Learn to regulate arousal and anxiety.

This skier's refocusing plan to meet the demands of the situation shows how important it is to study not only an athlete's personality profile but also an in-depth description of his or her cognitive strategies and plans. In this way, coaches can continually structure practices and training environments to meet the situation and maximize performance and personal growth.

Your Role in Understanding Personality

Now that you have learned something about the study of personality in sport and exercise settings, how can you use the information to better understand the individuals in your classes and on your teams? Many later chapters will explore the practical aspects of changing behaviors and developing psychological skills. In the meantime, use these guidelines to help you better understand the people with whom you work now and to consolidate what you have learned about personality structure.

1. Consider Both Personality Traits and Situations. To understand someone's behavior, consider both the person and his or her situation. Along with understanding personality, always consider the particular situation in which you are teaching or coaching.

2. Be an Informed Consumer. To know how and when to use personality tests, understand the ethics and guidelines for personality testing. This chapter has provided some guidelines and, as a professional, it is your responsibility to understand the dos and don'ts of personality testing.

3. Be a Good Communicator. Although formal personality testing can disclose a great deal about people, so can sincere and open communication. Asking questions and being a good listener can go a long way toward establishing rapport and finding out about a person's personality and preferences. A more detailed discussion of communication is presented in chapter 12.

4. Be a Good Observer. Another good way to gain valuable information about people's personalities is to observe their behavior in different situations. If you combine your observation of an individual's behavior with open communication, you'll likely get a well-rounded view and understanding of his or her personality.

5. Be Knowledgeable About Mental Strategies. A constellation of mental strategies facilitates the learning and performance of physical skills. Be aware of and implement these strategies appropriately in your programs, selecting them to benefit an individual's personality.

Summary

Understanding personality is central to improving your teaching and coaching effectiveness. Sport personality was the most popular research area in the 1960s and 1970s, when the trait approach guided most research efforts. Most researchers now take an interactional approach to the study of sport personality, as this approach considers personal and situational factors as equal determinants of behavior.

Although some differences have been found in comparing athletes with nonathletes and comparing athletes from different sports, the most interesting and consistent findings come from comparing more successful with less successful athletes. Successful athletes (particularly elite athletes) exhibit the iceberg profile, which is characteristic of positive mental health. These athletes, compared with their less successful counterparts, also tend to possess a variety of psychological skills, such as the ability to stay focused, adapt to unusual circumstances, remain confident, cope effectively with anxiety, and form detailed plans for mental preparation. As a professional in sport and exercise, your role in understanding personality will include good communication and observation skills to help you gather information about the personalities of people with whom you work.

Review Questions

1. Discuss the three levels of personality, including the stability of the different levels.

2. Compare and contrast the situation, trait, and interactional approaches to personality. Which approach is most common among sport psychologists today? Why?

3. Discuss three problems in early personality research in sport and exercise settings.

4. Compare and contrast state and trait *measures* of personality. Why are both needed for a better understanding of personality in sport?

5. Why are sport-specific personality inventories more desirable than general psychological inventories for measuring personality in sport and exercise? Name examples of both sport-specific and general personality measures.

6. Should psychological tests be used for team selection? Explain your answer.

7. Discuss four important guidelines when administering psychological tests and providing feedback from the results of these tests.

8. Discuss the research comparing the personalities of athletes and nonathletes. Do athletes have a unique personality profile?

9. Do male and female athletes have different personality profiles than male and female nonathletes? Do individual and team sport athletes have different personality profiles?

10. Discuss Morgan's mental health model and the "iceberg profile" as they relate to predicting athletic success. Can athletic success be predicted from psychological tests? Explain.

11. Compare and contrast the cognitive strategies of successful versus less successful athletes.

12. What is your role in understanding personality? When might you consider using personality tests? Discuss other ways to assess participants' personalities.

References

American Psychological Association. (1985). *Standards for educational and psychological testing.* Washington, DC: American Psychological Association.

Bandura, A. (1977). Self-efficacy: Toward a unifying theory of behavioral change. *Psychological Review*, **84**, 191-215.

Blumenthal, J.A., Emery, C.F., Walsh, M.A., Cox, D.K., Kuh, C.M., Williams, R.B., & Williams, R.S. (1988). Exercise training in healthy type A middle aged men: Effects on behavioral and cardiovascular responses. *Psychosomatic Medicine*, **50**, 418-433.

Bowers, K.S. (1973). Situationism in psychology: An analysis and a critique. *Psychological Review*, **80**, 307-336.

Cattell, R.B. (1965). The scientific analysis of personality. Baltimore: Penguin.

Eysenck, H.J., & Eysenck, S.B.G. (1968). *Eysenck Personality Inventory Manual*. London: University of London Press.

Fisher, A.C., & Zwart, E.F. (1982). Psychological analysis of athletes' anxiety responses. *Journal of Sport Psychology*, **4**, 139-158.

Girdano, D.A., Everly, G.S, & Dusek, D.E. (1990). *Controlling stress and tension: A holistic approach*. (3rd ed.). Englewood Cliffs, NJ: Prentice Hall.

Gould, D., Eklund, R., & Jackson, S. (1992). Coping strategies used by more versus less successful Olympic wrestlers. *Anxiety Research*.

Gould, D., Horn, T., & Spreeman, J. (1984). Competitive anxiety in junior elite wrestlers. *Journal of Sport Psychology*, **5**, 58-71.

Gould, D., Weiss, M., & Weinberg, R. (1981). The effects of model similarity and model task on self-efficacy and muscular endurance. *Journal of Sport Psychology*, **3**, 17-29.

Hollander, E.P. (1967). *Principles and methods of social psychology*. New York: Holt.

Mahoney, M.J., & Avener, M. (1977). Psychology of the elite athlete: An exploratory study. *Cognitive Therapy and Research*, **1**, 135-141.

Martens, R. (1975). The paradigmatic crisis in American sport personology. *Sportwissenschaft*, **5**, 9-24.

Martens, R. (1977). *Sport competition anxiety test*. Champaign, IL: Human Kinetics.

Martens, R., Burton, D., Vealey, R.S., Bump, L.A., & Smith, D. (1982, June). *Cognitive and somatic dimensions of competitive anxiety* (CSAI-2). Paper presented at NASPSPA Conference, University of Maryland, College Park.

McNair, D.M., Lorr, M., & Droppleman, L.F. (1971). *EDITS manual for POMS*. San Diego, CA: Educational and Industrial Testing Service.

Morgan, W.P. (1979). Prediction of performance in athletics. In P. Klavora & J.V. Daniel (Eds.), *Coach, athlete, and the sport psychologist* (pp. 173-186). Champaign, IL: Human Kinetics.

Morgan, W.P. (1980). The trait psychology controversy. *Research Quarterly for Exercise and Sport*, **51**, 50-76.

Morgan, W.P., Brown, D.R., Raglin, J.S., O'Conner, P.J., & Ellickson, K.A. (1987). Psychological monitoring of overtraining and staleness. *British Journal of Sports Medicine*, **21**, 319-328.

Nideffer, R.M. (1976). Test of attentional and interpersonal style. *Journal of Personality and Social Psychology*, **34**, 394-404.

Orlick, T., & Partington, J. (1988). Mental links to excellence. *The Sport Psychologist*, **2**, 105-130.

Ruffer, W.A. (1976a). Personality traits of athletes. *The Physical Educator*, **33**(1), 50-55.

Ruffer, W.A. (1976b). Personality traits of athletes. *The Physical Educator*, **33**(4), 211-214.

Rushall, B., & Siedentop, D. (1972). *The development and control of behavior in sport and physical education*. Philadelphia: Lea and Febiger.

Sarason, I.G. (1975). Test anxiety and the self-disclosing coping model. *Journal of Consulting and Clinical Psychology*, **43**, 148-153.

Schurr, K.T., Ashley, M.A., & Joy, K.L. (1977). A multivariate analysis of male athlete characteristics: Sport type and success. *Multivariate Experimental Clinical Research*, **3**, 53-68.

Sonstroem, R.J. (1984). Exercise and self-esteem. In R.L. Terjung (Ed.), *Exercise and sport science reviews* (pp. 123-155). Toronto: Collare.

Spielberger, C.D., Gorsuch, R.L., & Lushene, R.F. (1970). *Manual for the state-trait anxiety inventory*. Palo Alto, CA: Consulting Psychologists Press.

Van Schoyck, S.R., & Grasha, A.F. (1981). Attentional style variations and athletic ability: The advantages of a sports-specific test. *Journal of Sport Psychology*, **3**, 149-165.

Vealey, R.S. (1986). Sport-confidence and competitive orientations: Preliminary investigation and instrument development. *Journal of Sport Psychology*, **8**, 221-246.

Vealey, R. (1989). Sport personality: A paradigmatic and methodological analysis. *Journal of Sport and Exercise Psychology*, **11**, 216-235.

Vealey, R. (1992). Personality in sport: A comprehensive view. In T. Horn (Ed.), *Advances in sport psychology* (pp. 23-59). Champaign, IL: Human Kinetics.

Williams, J.M. (1980). Personality characteristics of the successful female athlete. In W.F. Straub (Ed.), *Sport psychology: An analysis of athlete behavior*. Ithaca, NY: Mouvement.

Yukelson, D., Weinberg, R., & Jackson, A. (1984). A multidimensional group cohesion instrument for intercollegiate basketball teams. *Journal of Sport Psychology*, **6**, 103-117.

Understanding Motivation

"Win one for the gipper!" "Go hard or go home!" "Give 110 percent!" Coaches frequently try to motivate athletes with inspirational slogans. Physical educators also want to motivate inactive children—who often seem more interested in playing video games than volleyball. And exercise leaders and physical therapists routinely face the challenge of motivating clients to stay with an exercise or rehabilitation program.

Although motivation is critical to the success of all these professionals, many do not understand the subject well. Success as a teacher, coach, or exercise leader requires a thorough understanding of motivation, including the factors affecting it and the methods of enhancing motivation in individuals and groups. In fact, often it is not technical knowledge of the sport or physical activity but the ability to motivate people that separates the very good instructors from the average ones.

Here, we will introduce you to the topic of motivation.

In this chapter you will learn about

▌ what motivation is and its components,

▌ typical views of motivation and whether they are useful,

■ a process view of motivation,

■ using the fundamentals of motivation to guide practice, and

■ developing a realistic view of motivation.

What Is Motivation?

Motivation is the direction and intensity of effort.

Motivation can be defined simply as the direction and intensity of one's effort (Sage, 1977).

Direction of Effort

The *direction of effort* refers to whether an individual seeks out, approaches, or is attracted to certain situations. For example, a high school student may be motivated to go out for the tennis team, a coach to attend a coaching clinic, a business woman to join an aerobics class, or an injured athlete to seek medical treatment.

Intensity of Effort

Intensity of effort refers to how much effort a person puts forth in a particular situation. For instance, a student may attend physical education class (approach a situation) but not put forth much effort during class. On the other hand, a golfer may want to make a winning putt so badly that he becomes overly motivated, tightens up, and performs poorly. Finally, a weightlifter may work out 4 days a week like her friends but differ from them in terms of the tremendous effort or intensity she puts into each workout.

Relationship of Direction and Intensity

While for discussion purposes it is convenient to separate the direction from the intensity of effort, for most people direction and intensity of effort are

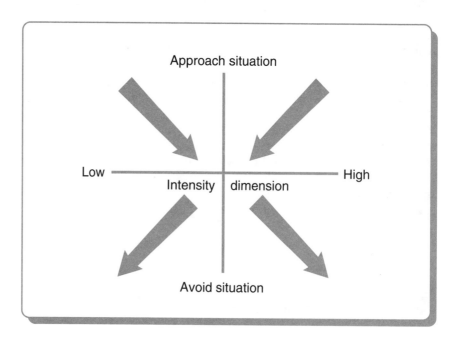

Figure 4.1 Direction and intensity aspects of motivation.

closely related (see Figure 4.1). For instance, students or athletes who seldom miss class or practice and always arrive early typically expend great effort during participation. Conversely, those who are consistently tardy and miss many classes or practices often exhibit low effort when in attendance.

Problems With Vaguely Defining Motivation

Although we have defined motivation using Sage's terms of intensity and direction, the term "motivation" is used in many ways in daily life. It is often vaguely defined or not defined at all. Motivation is discussed loosely in any of the following ways:

- As an internal personality characteristic (e.g., she is a highly motivated individual—a real go-getter)
- As an external influence (e.g., I need something to motivate me—to get me going on my running program)
- As a consequence or explanation for our behavior (e.g., I just wanted it too much and was overmotivated)

Vaguely defining motivation and using the term in so many different ways has two disadvantages. First, if coaches and teachers tell students or athletes that they need to be more motivated without telling them what they specifically mean by the term, the student or athlete will have to infer the meaning. This can easily lead to misunderstandings and conflict. An exercise leader, for example, may tell her students that they need to be "more motivated" if they want to achieve their desired levels of fitness, meaning that the students need to set goals and work hard toward achieving those goals. A student with low self-esteem, however, might mistakenly interpret the instructor's remarks as a description of his personality (e.g., I am lazy and do not care), which can negatively affect the student's involvement.

Second, as practitioners we develop specific strategies or techniques for motivating individuals, but we may not recognize how these various strategies interact. In chapter 8, you'll learn how extrinsic rewards, such as trophies and money, can sometimes have powerful positive effects in motivating individuals, but these strategies can often backfire and actually produce negative effects on motivation, depending on how the external rewards are used.

Multiple Uses of Motivation

In essence, motivation is the global term for the complex process governing the direction and intensity of effort. We understand the specifics of motivation through this broader, holistic context, much like a football coach views specific plays from the perspective of a larger game plan or offensive or defensive philosophy.

Sport and exercise psychologists view motivation from several specific vantages, including intrinsic and extrinsic motivation (see chapter 8), achievement motivation (see chapter 5), and motivation in the form of competitive stress (see chapter 6). These varied forms of motivation are the parts of the more general definition of motivation. By establishing this general orientation, specific motivational areas can be defined, better understood, and fit into a framework.

Views of Motivation

Each of us develops a personal view of how motivation works, a theory on what motivates people. Likely we do this from learning what motivates ourselves and seeing how other people are motivated. For instance, if someone has a physical education teacher she likes and feels is successful, she will probably try to use, or emulate, many of the same motivational strategies that the teacher uses.

Moreover, people often act out their personal views of motivation, both consciously and subconsciously. A coach, for example, might make a conscious effort to motivate students by giving them positive feedback and encouragement. Another coach may believe people are primarily responsible for their own behaviors and spend little time creating situations to enhance motivation.

Although there are thousands of individual views, most people fit motivation into one of three general orientations that parallel the approaches to personality discussed in chapter 3. These include

a. the trait-centered orientation,
b. the situation-centered orientation, and
c. the interactional orientation.

Participant-Centered or Trait-Centered View

The trait-centered view (also called the participant-centered view) contends that motivated behavior is primarily a function of individual characteristics. That is, the personality, needs, and goals of a student, athlete, or exerciser are the primary determinants of motivated behavior. Thus, coaches often describe an athlete as a "real winner," implying that this individual has a personal make-up that allows him to excel in sport. Similarly, another athlete may be described as a "loser" who has no get-up-and-go.

Some people have personal attributes that seem to predispose them to success and high levels of motivation, whereas others seem to lack motivation, personal goals, and desire. However, most of us would agree that we are in part affected by the situations in which we are placed. For example, if a teacher does not create a motivating learning environment, student motivation will consequently decline. Conversely, an excellent leader who creates a positive environment will greatly increase motivation. Thus, ignoring environmental influences on motivation is unrealistic and is one reason sport and exercise psychologists have *not* endorsed the trait-centered view for guiding professional practice.

Situation-Centered View

In direct contrast to the trait-centered view is the situation-centered orientation, which contends that motivation level is determined primarily by situation. For example, Brittany might be really motivated in her aerobic exercise class but unmotivated in a competitive sport situation.

Probably you would agree that situation influences motivation, but can you also recall situations in which you remained motivated despite a negative environment? For example, maybe you have played for a coach you didn't like who constantly yelled at you and criticized you, but still you did not quit the team or lose any of your motivation. In such a case the situation was clearly not the primary factor influencing your motivation level. For this reason, sport and exercise psychology specialists do not recommend the situation-centered view of motivation as the most effective for guiding practice.

Interactional View

The view of motivation most widely endorsed by sport and exercise psychologists today is the participant-by-situation interactional view. Interactionalists contend that motivation does not result solely from participant factors like personality, needs, interests, and goals nor from only situational factors like a coach's or teacher's style or the win-loss record of a team. Rather, the best way to understand motivation is to examine how these two sets of factors interact (see Figure 4.2).

The best way to understand motivation is to consider both the person and situation and how these two factors interact.

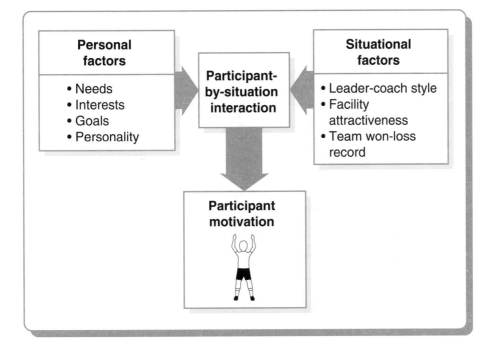

Figure 4.2 Participant-by-situation interactional model of motivation.

Interactional View of Motivation: A Research Example

Sorrentino and Sheppard (1978) studied 44 male and 33 female swimmers in three Canadian universities, testing them twice as they swam a 200-yard freestyle time trial swimming individually or as part of a relay team. The situational factor assessed was whether each swimmer had a faster split time when swimming alone or when swimming as part of a relay team. The researchers also assessed a personality characteristic in the swimmers, namely, their affiliation motivation. The objective of the study was to see whether each swimmer was oriented more toward social approval, viewing competing with others as a positive state, or more toward rejection, feeling threatened when facing an affiliation-oriented activity (like a relay), where he or she might let others down.

As the investigators predicted, the approval-oriented swimmers demonstrated faster times swimming in the relay than when swimming alone (see Figure 4.3). After all, they had a positive orientation toward seeking approval from others—their teammates. In contrast, the rejection-threatened swimmers who were overconcerned with letting their teammates down swam faster alone than they swam in the relay.

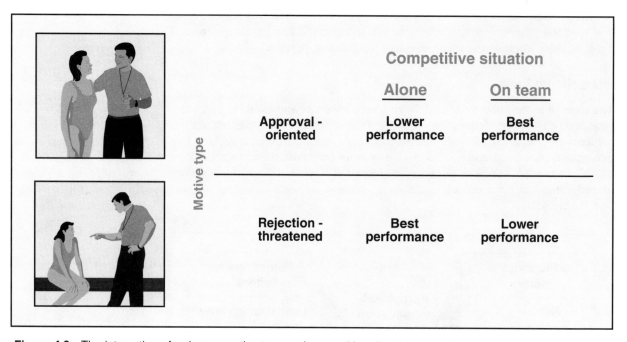

Figure 4.3 The interaction of swimmer motive type and competitive situation on performance.

From a coaching perspective, these findings show that the four fastest individual swimmers would not necessarily make the best relay team. Depending on the athletes' personalities, some would perform best in a relay and others would perform best individually. Many experienced team sport coaches agree that starting the most highly skilled athletes does not guarantee having the best *team* in the game.

The swimming study's results clearly demonstrate the importance of the interactional model of motivation. Knowing a swimmer's personal characteristics (motivational orientation) only was not the best way to predict behavior (individual split time) because degree of speed depended on the situation (performing individually or in a relay). Similarly, it would be a mistake to look only at the situation as the primary source of motivation, because best speed depended on whether a swimmer was more approval-oriented or rejection-threatened. The key, then, was understanding the *interaction* between the athlete's personal make-up and the situation. Rejection-threatened swimmers performed best in the individual event and approval-oriented swimmers performed best as part of a relay squad.

Five Guidelines to Build Motivation

The interactional model of motivation has important implications for teachers, coaches, trainers, exercise leaders, and program administrators. In fact, some

fundamental guidelines can be derived from this model for professional practice.

Guideline 1: Both Situations and Traits Motivate People

When attempting to enhance motivation, consider both situational and personal factors. Often when teachers, trainers, coaches, or exercise leaders work with students, athletes, or clients who seem to lack motivation, they immediately attribute this lack to the participant's personal characteristics. "These students don't care about learning," "This team doesn't want it enough," or "Exercise is just not a priority in these folks' lives"—such phrases ascribe personal attributes to people and serve, in effect, to dismiss the poor motivation and avoid the responsibility for helping the participants develop motivation. At other times, instructors fail to consider the personal attributes of their students or clients and instead put all the blame on the situation (e.g., "This material must be boring." Or, "What is it about my instructional style that inhibits the participant's level of motivation?").

In reality, low participant motivation usually results from a combination of personal and situational factors. Personal factors do cause people to lack motivation, but so do the environments in which people participate. And often it may be easier for an instructor to change the situation than to change the needs and personalities of the participants. The key, however, is not to focus attention *only* on the personal attributes of the participants or *only* on the situation at hand but to consider the interaction of these factors.

To enhance motivation you must analyze and respond not only to a player's personality, but also to the interaction of personal and situational characteristics.

Guideline 2: People Have Multiple Motives for Involvement

Consistent effort is necessary to identify and understand participant motives for involvement in sport, exercise, or educational environments. There are several ways to accomplish this.

Understand Why People Participate in Physical Activity.   Researchers know why most people participate in sport and exercise. The results of their

Table 4.1   Major Motives Cited for Youth Sport Participation
Improving skills Having fun Being with friends Experiencing thrills and excitement Achieving success Developing fitness

Based on Gould and Petlichkoff (1988).

Table 4.2 Major Motives Cited for Exercise Participation	
For initially joining	**For continuing involvement**
Health factors Weight loss Fitness Self-challenge Feel better	Program enjoyment Organization-leadership Activity type Social factors

Based on Wankel (1980).

studies are summarized in Tables 4.1 and 4.2. What motivates you to participate in sport and physical activity?

People Participate for More Than One Reason.   Most people have multiple motives for participation. For example, you may lift weights because you want to tone your body. Yet, lifting weights also makes you feel good, plus you enjoy the camaraderie of your lifting partners. Thus, you do not lift for only one reason.

Competing Motives for Involvement.   At times people have competing motives. For instance, a person may want to exercise at the club after work and also to be with her family. As a coach, teacher, or exercise leader, you'll want to be aware of such conflicting interests—they can have an important influence on participation.

People Have Shared and Unique Motives.   Although it is possible to identify why people usually participate in sport and exercise, we need to remember that motives for participation vary greatly and can be unique to each individual. Table 4.3 lists many different categories and motives people have for sport participation. Although you'll notice many familiar motives, you'll also see some that seem idiosyncratic.

Because people have such a diverse range of motives for sport and exercise participation, you need to be aware of your students', athletes', or exercisers' motives for involvement. Following these guidelines should improve your awareness:

1. Observe the participants and see what they like and do not like about the activity.
2. Informally talk to others (e.g., teachers, friends, and family members) who know the student, athlete, or exerciser and solicit information about the person's motives for participation.
3. Periodically ask the participants to write out or list their reasons for participation.

Table 4.3 Motivational Categories for Sport Participation

Category 1: Social approval
Parental approval
Peer approval
Coach approval

Category 2: Competition
Against time
Against fellow team members
Against rival teams

Category 3: Self-mastery
Achieving control of mind over body
Feeling more in control of body
    movements
Learning new skills

Category 4: Lifestyle
Habit
Lack of something better to do
Introduced to activity at an early age
Parents decided this for you

Category 5: Fear of failure
Critical comments from others
Self-criticism
How others might view your
    performance

**Category 6: Physical fitness and
    health**
Feeling healthy
Increased muscle tone
Keeping in good shape
Gaining greater physical strength

**Category 7: Friendship and personal
    associations**
Fellow team members
Athletes from other sports
Famous and well-known athletes

**Category 8: Success and
    achievement**
Participating in important contests
Achieving in training
Achieving personal goals

Category 9: Tangible pay-offs
Athletic scholarship
Travel
Extra attention

Category 10: Recognition
Peers
Public
Younger people
Older people
Special people

Category 11: Intimidation/control
Coach being angry at you
Coach directing and running your
    training

Category 12: Heterosexuality
Being more attractive to the opposite
    sex
Being dated because you are an
    athlete

**Category 13: Competing
    conditions—crowds**
Competing before a large enthusiastic
    audience
Being viewed as "favorite"
Competing with lots of noise and
    fanfare

**Category 14:
    Independence—individuality**
Deciding your own training schedule
Practicing alone
Helping the coach decide the training
    program
Being viewed as an individual

Category 15: "Family"
Team members becoming a substitute
    family
Confiding in coaches and teammates
Developing close relationships with
    coaches, teammates, and opponents

Category 16: Emotional release
Competing brings a sense of calmness
Letting your feelings come out
Feeling exhilarated

Category 17: Status
Being viewed as important
Having others look up to you
Having others treat you with respect
Feeling important

Category 18: Self-direction/awareness
Gaining a focus in life
Attaining a greater sense of
    confidence
Feeling better about yourself as a
    person
Feeling special

Category 19: Understanding reasons
Knowing the reasons for changing
    particular techniques
Understanding reasons for training
    regulations
Having the coach explain the reasons
    for directions

Adapted from Gauron (1984).

Because motives may change over time, you need to continue to monitor people's motives for participation even months after they've begun.

Motives Change Over Time.   Continue to monitor motives for participation: Research has shown that motives change over time. For instance, the reasons individuals cited for beginning an exercise program (e.g., health and fitness benefits) were not necessarily the same motives they cited for staying involved (e.g., social atmosphere of the program; Wankel, 1980). Consequently, continuing to emphasize fitness benefits and ignore the social aspect after people have begun the exercise program is probably not the most effective motivational strategy.

Guideline 3: Change the Environment to Enhance Motivation

Knowing why people become involved in sport and exercise is important, but this information alone is insufficient to enhance motivation. You need to use what you learn about your participants to structure the sport and exercise environment to meet their needs.

Competition or Recreation.   For example, many park district directors have learned that although some adult athletes prefer competition, others do not. Thus, the directors divide the traditional competitive softball leagues into "competitive" and "recreational" divisions. This choice enhances participation rates by giving people what they want.

Provide Multiple Opportunities.   Meeting participant needs isn't always simple. Structuring a situation to enhance motivation may mean constructing an environment to meet multiple needs. For example, elite performers demand rigorous training and work at a very intense level. Some coaches mistakenly think that world-class athletes need *only* rigorous physical training—the truth is these elite athletes often also want to have fun and enjoy the companionship of their fellow athletes. When coaches pay more attention to the motives of fun and fellowship along with optimal physical training, they enhance motivation and improve their athletes' performance.

To enhance motivation, teaching and coaching environments must be structured to meet the needs of all participants.

Adjust to Individuals Within Groups.   The most difficult but important component of structuring sport and exercise is individualizing coaching and teaching. That is, each exerciser, athlete, and student has his or her unique motives for participation, and effective instructors must provide an environment to meet these diverse needs. Experienced coaches have known this for years. Legendary football coach Vince Lombardi, for example, structured his coaching environment to meet individual athlete needs (Kramer & Schaap, 1968). Specifically, Lombardi had a reputation as a fiery, no-nonsense coach who was constantly on his players' backs. All-pro guard Jerry Kramer, for instance, has said that Lombardi *always* yelled at him. (But Coach Lombardi was also clever: Just when Kramer was discouraged enough to quit because of the criticism, Lombardi would provide some much-needed positive reinforcement.) In contrast to the more thick-skinned Kramer, his teammate—all-pro quarterback Bart Starr—was extremely self-critical. Lombardi recognized this and treated Starr in a much more positive way than he treated Kramer. Lombardi understood that these two players' different personalities and needs required a coaching environment flexible enough for both.

Of course, individualizing is not always easy to accomplish. Physical educators may teach six different classes of 35 students each, and aerobics instructors can have classes with as many as 100 students in them. Without assistants it is impossible to structure the instructional environment in the way Lombardi did. This means today's physical educators must be both imaginative and realistic in individualizing their environments.

Of course, a junior high school physical educator cannot get to know her students nearly as well as a personal trainer with one client or a basketball

Pro Football Hall of Fame Coach Vince Lombardi.

coach with 15 players on his team. However, the physical educator could have students identify on index cards their motives for involvement ("What do you like about physical education class?"), assess the frequency that various motives are mentioned, and structure the class environment to meet the most frequently mentioned motives. If more students indicated they preferred noncompetitive activities over traditional competitive class activities, the instructor could choose to structure class accordingly.

You might offer options within the same class and have half the students play competitive volleyball on one court and the other half play noncompetitive volleyball on a second court.

Guideline 4: Leaders Influence Motivation

As an exercise leader, physical educator, or coach you have a critical role to influence participant motivation. At times your influence may be indirect and you won't even recognize the importance of your actions. For example, a physical educator who is energetic and bubbly will on personality alone give considerable positive reinforcement in class. Over the school year her students come to expect her upbeat behavior. However, she may have a bad day and, although she does not act negatively in class, she might not be up to her usual cheeriness. Because they know nothing about her circumstances, her students perceive that they did something wrong and consequently become discouraged. Unbeknownst to the teacher, her students are influenced by her inaction (see Figure 4.4).

You too will have bad days as a professional and will need to struggle through them, doing the best job you can. The key thing to remember is to be aware that your actions (and inaction) on such days can influence the motivational environment. Sometimes you may need to act more upbeat than you feel. If that's not possible, inform your students that you're not quite yourself so they don't misinterpret your behavior.

As a leader, recognize that you are critical to the motivational environment and that you influence motivation both directly and indirectly.

Figure 4.4 "She was pretty upset with us tonight. I wonder what we did wrong."

Guideline 5: Use Behavior Modification to Change Undesirable Participant Motives

We have emphasized the need for structuring the environment to facilitate participant motivation because the exercise leader, trainer, coach, or teacher usually has more direct control over the environment than over the motives of individuals. This does not imply, however, that it is inappropriate to attempt to change a participant's motives for involvement.

A young football player, for example, may be involved in his sport primarily to inflict injury on others. This player's coach will certainly want to use behavior modification techniques (see chapter 8) to change this undesirable motive. That is, the coach will reinforce good clean play, punish aggressive play designed to inflict injury, and simultaneously discuss appropriate behavior with the player. Similarly, a cardiac rehabilitation patient beginning exercise at doctor's orders may need behavior modification from her exercise leader to gain intrinsic motivation to exercise. Behavior modification techniques to modify undesirable participant motives are certainly appropriate in some settings.

Use behavior modification techniques to change undesirable motives and strengthen weak motives.

Developing a Realistic View of Motivation

Motivation is a key variable in both learning and performance in sport and exercise contexts. People sometimes forget, however, that motivation is not the *only* variable influencing behavior. Sportswriters, for instance, typically ascribe a team's performance to motivational attributes—the extraordinary efforts of the players; laziness; the lack of incentives that follow from million-dollar, no-cut professional contracts; or a player's ability (or inability) to play in clutch situations. A team's performance, however, often hinges on nonmotivational factors, such as injury, playing a better team, being overtrained, or failing to learn new skills. Besides the motivational factors of primary concern to us here, biomechanical, physiological, sociological, medical, and technical-tactical factors are also significant to sport and exercise and warrant consideration in any analysis of performance.

Some motivational factors are more easily influenced than others. It is easier for an exercise leader to change her reinforcement pattern, for instance, than it is for her to change the attractiveness of the building. (This is not to imply that cleaning up a facility is too time-consuming to be worth the trouble! Consider, for example, how important facility attractiveness is in the health club business.) Professionals need to consider what motivational factors they can influence and how much time (and money) it will take to change them. As you read the case study, think about how to realistically develop effective strategies for enhancing participant motivation.

Breathing Life Into the Gym: A Case Analysis of a Physical Educator's Plan for Enhancing Student Motivation

Kim is a 2nd-year physical education teacher at Kennedy Junior High School, the oldest building in the district. The school is pretty run down and is scheduled to be closed in the next 5 years, so the district doesn't want to invest any money in fixing it up. During the first several weeks of class, Kim notices that her students are not very motivated to participate.

Kim realizes that student motivation would likely improve if the facility were revamped, but she also knows that renovation is unlikely. So, she decides to take it into her own hands to improve things. First, she cleans up the gym and gets permission to take the old curtains down. Next, she brightens the gym by backing all the bulletin boards with color and hanging physical fitness posters on the walls. She also talks to the custodian, thanking him for helping get rid of those old curtains and asking about changing his cleaning schedule so the gym gets swept up right after lunch.

Of course Kim realizes that improving the physical environment is not enough to motivate her students to participate in class. She herself must also play an important role. She reminds herself to make positive, encouraging remarks during class and to be upbeat and optimistic. Perhaps the most important thing Kim does to enhance her students' motivation is to ask them what they like and dislike about gym class. Students tell her that fitness testing and exercising at the start of class are not much fun. However, these are mandated in the district curriculum and must be done. (Besides, many of her students are couch potatoes and badly need the exercise!)

Kim works to make the fitness testing a fun part of a goal-setting program, where each class earns points for improvement. She tallies the results on a bulletin board for students to see. The "student of the week" award also focuses on the one youngster who makes the greatest effort and shows the most progress toward her or his fitness goal. Exercising to rap music is also popular with students.

Through talking to her students, Kim is surprised to learn of their interest in sports other than the "old standards," volleyball and basketball. They say they'd like to play tennis, swim, and golf. Unfortunately, swimming and golfing are not possible because of a lack of facilities, but Kim is able to introduce tennis into the curriculum by obtaining racquets and balls through a United States Tennis Association program in which recreational players donate their used equipment to the public schools.

At the end of the year, looking back, Kim is generally pleased with the changes in her students' motivation. Sure, some kids are still not interested, but most seem genuinely excited about what they are learning. In addition, the students' fitness scores have improved over those of previous years. Finally, her student of the week program is a big hit—especially for those hard-working students with average skills who are singled out for their personal improvement and effort.

Summary

Motivation has been defined as the direction and intensity of effort. Among models of motivation, the participant-by-situation interactional view is the most useful for guiding professional practice. Five fundamental observations derived from this model are good guidelines:

1. Participants are motivated both by situations and their internal traits.
2. It is important to understand participant motives for involvement.
3. Structure situations to meet participant needs.
4. Recognize that as a teacher, coach, or exercise leader you play a critical role in the motivational environment.
5. Use behavior modification to change undesirable participant motives.

To develop a realistic view of motivation, recognize nonmotivational influences on sport performance and behavior and learn to assess whether motivational factors may be readily changed.

Review Questions

1. Explain the direction and intensity aspects of motivation.

2. Identify three general views or orientations to motivation. Which should be used to guide practice?

3. How does Sorrentino and Sheppard's swimming relay study support the interactional model of motivation?

4. Describe five fundamental guidelines of motivation for professional practice.

5. What are the primary motives people have for participating in sport? What are their primary motives for participating in exercise activities?

6. List at least three ways to improve understanding of someone's motives for sport and physical activity involvement.

7. How can you directly and indirectly influence motivation in your program?

8. When is it appropriate to use behavior modification techniques to alter motivation for sport and exercise involvement?

9. What major factors besides motivation should you consider to understand performance and behavior in exercise and sport settings?

10. Give examples of motivational factors that are readily influenced.

References

Kramer, J. & Shaap, D. (1968). *Instant replay: The Green Bay diary of Jerry Kramer.* New York: Signet.

Sage, G.H. (1977). *Introduction to motor behavior: A neuropsychological approach* (2nd ed.). Reading, MA: Addison-Wesley.

Sorrentino, R.M., & Sheppard, B.H. (1978). Effects of affiliation-related motives on swimmers in individual versus group competition: A field experiment. *Journal of Personality and Social Psychology*, **36**(7), 704-714.

Wankel, L.M. (1980). Involvement in vigorous physical activity: Considerations for enhancing self-motivation. In R.R. Danielson & K.F. Danielson (Eds.), *Fitness motivation: Proceedings of the Geneva Park workshop* (pp. 18-32). Toronto: Ontario Research Council on Leisure.

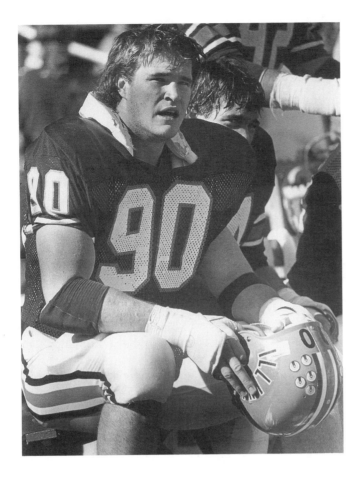

Achievement Motivation and Competitiveness

Dan is a co-captain and center on his high school football team. His team does not have outstanding talent, but if everyone gives maximum effort and plays together, the team should have a successful season. When the team's record slips below .500, however, Dan becomes frustrated with some of his teammates who don't seem to try as hard as he does. Despite being more talented, these players don't seek out challenges, are not as motivated, and in the presence of adversity often give up. Dan wonders what he can do to motivate some of his teammates.

Teachers, coaches, and exercise leaders often wonder why some individuals are highly motivated and constantly strive for success, while others seem to lack motivation and avoid evaluation and competition. Fortunately, sport psychology offers information to help you understand the motivational differences in people and create climates that enhance motivation.

In this chapter you will learn about

▮ achievement motivation—what it is and how it influences learning and performance,

▮ theories that explain why some people are so strongly achievement oriented and others are not,

▮ ways that people develop achievement motivation, and

▮ ways to facilitate achievement motivation.

What Is Achievement Motivation?

Achievement motivation is the tendency to strive for success, persist in the face of failure, and experience pride in accomplishments.

To understand how achievement motivation influences performance you should first know what the term means and how it relates to competitiveness. The term was coined over 50 years ago to refer to a person's efforts to master a task, achieve excellence, overcome obstacles, perform better than others, and take pride in exercising talent (Murray, 1938). Achievement motivation is a person's orientation to strive for task success, persist in the face of failure, and experience pride in accomplishments (Gill, 1986).

Not surprisingly, coaches, exercise leaders, and teachers have an interest in achievement motivation: These are the precise characteristics that allow athletes to achieve excellence, exercisers to gain high levels of fitness, and students to maximize learning.

Because achievement motivation has been considered a personality factor, sport psychologists have viewed it like personality, progressing from a trait-oriented view of a person's "need for achievement" to an interactional view that emphasizes more changeable achievement goals and how these affect and are affected by the situation. Achievement motivation in sport is popularly called *competitiveness*.

Competitiveness

In sport and exercise settings achievement motivation focuses on self-competition, whereas competitiveness influences behavior in socially evaluative situations.

Competitiveness is defined by Rainer Martens as "a disposition to strive for satisfaction when making comparisons with some standard of excellence in the presence of evaluative others" (Martens, 1976, p. 3). Basically, he views competitiveness as achievement behavior in a competitive context, with social evaluation as a key component. It is important to look at a situation-specific achievement orientation: Some people who are highly achievement oriented in one setting (e.g., competitive sports) are not in other settings (e.g., math class).

Martens' definition of competitiveness is limited to those situations where one is evaluated by or has the potential to be evaluated by knowledgeable others. Yet, many people compete with themselves (e.g., trying to exceed your own running time from the previous day), even when no one else evaluates the performance. The level of achievement motivation would bring out this self-competition whereas the level of *competitiveness* would influence behavior in socially evaluated situations. For this reason, we discuss achievement motivation and competitiveness together in this chapter.

Motivation Effects

Achievement motivation and competitiveness deal not just with the final outcome or the pursuit of excellence—they deal also with the psychological journey of getting there. If we understand why motivation differences occur in people, we can intervene positively. Thus, we are interested in how a person's competitiveness and achievement motivation influence a wide variety of behaviors, thoughts, and feelings, including the following:

- **Choice of activity** (e.g., seeking out opponents of equal ability to *compete* against or looking for players of greater or lesser ability to *play with*)
- **Effort to pursue goals** (e.g., how often you practice)
- **Intensity** of effort in the pursuit of goals (e.g., how consistently hard you try during a workout)
- **Persistence** in the face of failure and adversity (e.g., when the going gets tough do you work harder or take it easier?)

Theories of Achievement Motivation

Three theories have evolved over the years to explain what motivates people to act:

- Need achievement theory
- Attribution theory
- Achievement goal theory

Need Achievement Theory

Need achievement theory (Atkinson, 1974; McClelland, 1961) is an interactional view that considers both personal and situational factors as important predictors of behavior. Five components make up this theory (see Figure 5.1), including

- personality factors or motives,
- situational factors,
- resultant tendencies,
- emotional reactions, and
- achievement-related behaviors.

Personality Factors.   According to the need achievement view, each of us has two underlying achievement motives: to achieve success and to avoid failure (see Box 1 of Figure 5.1). The motive to achieve success is defined as "the capacity to experience pride or satisfaction in accomplishments," whereas motive to avoid failure is "the capacity to experience shame or humiliation as a consequence of failure" (Gill, 1986, p. 60). The theory contends that our behavior will be influenced by our balance of these motives. In particular, high achievers demonstrate high motivation to achieve success and low motivation to avoid failure. They enjoy evaluating their abilities and are not preoccupied with thoughts of failure. In contrast, low achievers demonstrate low motivation to achieve success and high motivation to avoid failure. They worry and are preoccupied with thoughts of failure. The theory makes no clear predictions for those with moderate or other levels of each motive (Gill, 1986).

Situational Influences.   As you learned in chapter 3, information about traits alone is not enough to accurately predict behavior. Situations must also be considered. In need achievement theory two primary considerations are the *probability for success* in the situation or task and the *incentive value of success*. Basically, the probability for success depends on whom you compete against and the difficulty of the task. That is, your chance of winning a tennis match

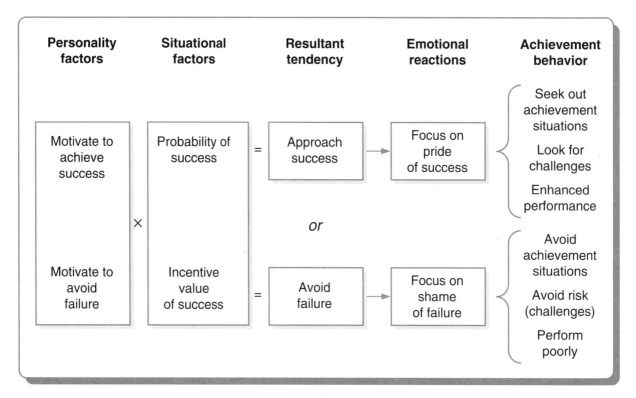

Figure 5.1 Need achievement theory.

would be lower against Steffi Graf than against a novice. The value you place on success, however, would be greater, as it is more satisfying to beat a skilled opponent than it is to beat a beginner. Settings that offer a 50-50 chance of succeeding (e.g., a difficult but attainable challenge) provide high achievers the most incentive for engaging in achievement behavior. However, low achievers do not see it this way.

Resultant Tendencies.   The third component of Figure 5.1 is the *resultant* or *behavioral tendency* derived by considering an individual's achievement motive levels in relation to situational considerations (e.g., probability of success or incentive value of success). The theory is best at predicting situations where there is a 50-50 chance of success. That is, high achievers seek out challenges in this situation because they enjoy competing against others of equal ability or performing tasks that are not too easy or too difficult.

Low achievers, on the other hand, avoid such challenges, instead opting either for easy tasks where success is guaranteed or for unrealistically hard tasks where failure is almost certain. Low achievers sometimes prefer very difficult tasks because no one expects them to win. For example, losing to Michael Jordan one-on-one in basketball certainly would not cause shame or embarrassment. Low achievers do not fear failure—they fear the negative evaluation associated with failure. A 50-50 chance of success causes maximum uncertainty and worry and thus increases the possibility of demonstrating low ability or competence. If low achievers cannot avoid such a situation, they become preoccupied and distraught because of their high need to avoid failure.

Pride and Shame.   Both high and low achievers want to experience pride and minimize shame, but their personality characteristics interact differently with the situation to cause them to focus more on pride or shame. High achievers focus more on pride, whereas low achievers focus more on shame and subsequent worry.

Achievement Behavior.   The fifth component of the need achievement theory indicates how the four previous components interact to influence behavior. High achievers select more challenging tasks, prefer intermediate risks, and perform better in evaluative situations. Low achievers avoid intermediate risk, perform worse in evaluative situations, and avoid challenging tasks—by selecting either tasks so difficult they are certain to fail or tasks so easy they are guaranteed success.

Significance of Theory.   These performance predictions of the need achievement theory serve as the framework for all contemporary achievement

High achievers select challenging tasks, prefer intermediate risks, and perform better when evaluated. Low achievers avoid challenging tasks, avoid intermediate risks, and perform worse when evaluated.

motivation explanations. That is, even though more recent theories offer different explanations for the thought processes underlying achievement differences, the behavioral predictions between high and low achievers are basically the same. The most important contribution of need achievement theory is its task preference and performance predictions.

Attribution Theory

Attribution theory focuses on how individuals explain their successes and failures.

Attribution theory focuses on how people explain their successes and failures. This view, originated by Heider (1958) and extended and popularized by Weiner (1985, 1986), holds that literally thousands of possible explanations for success and failure can be classified into a few categories (see Figure 5.2). These most basic attribution categories are *stability* (being either fairly permanent or unstable), *causality* (an internal or external factor), and *control* (a factor that is or is not under our control).

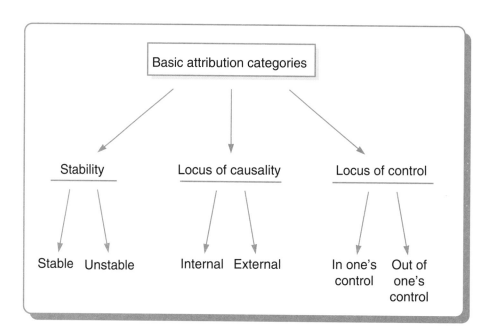

Figure 5.2 Weiner's basic attribution categories.

Attributions as Causes of Success and Failure.   A performance's success or failure can be attributed to a variety of possible explanations (attributions). For example, you may win a swimming race and attribute your success to

- a stable factor (e.g., your talent or good ability) or an unstable factor (e.g., good luck),
- an internal cause (e.g., your tremendous effort in the last 50 meters) or an external cause (e.g., an easy field of competitors), and
- a factor you can control (e.g., your race plan) or a factor out of your control (e.g., your opponents' physical conditioning).

Or you may drop out of an exercise program and attribute your failure to

- a stable factor (e.g., your terrible talent) or an unstable factor (e.g., the terrible instructor),
- an internal cause (e.g., your bad back) or an external cause (e.g., exercise facility too far from your home), and
- a factor you can control (e.g., your lack of effort) or a factor out of your control (e.g., the cost of the program).

Why Attributions Are Important.   Attributions affect expectations of future success or failure and emotional reactions (Biddle, 1993; McAuley, 1993). Attributing performance to certain types of stable factors has been linked to expectations of future success. For example, if Susie, an elementary physical education student, ascribes her performance success to a stable cause (e.g., her high ability), she will expect the outcome to occur again in the future and will be more motivated and confident. She may even ask her parents if she can sign up for after-school gymnastics. In contrast, if Zachary attributes his performance success in tumbling to an unstable cause (e.g., luck), he won't expect it to occur regularly and his motivation and confidence will not be enhanced. He probably wouldn't pursue after-school gymnastics. Of course, a failure also can be ascribed to a stable cause, such as low ability, which would lessen confidence and motivation, or to an unstable cause (e.g., luck), which would not.

Attributions to internal factors and to factors in our control (e.g., ability, effort) rather than to external factors or factors out of our control (e.g., luck, task difficulty) often result in emotional reactions like pride and shame. For example, a lacrosse player will experience more pride (if successful) or shame (if unsuccessful) if she attributes performance to internal factors rather than to luck or an opponent's skill (see Table 5.1).

How performers explain or attribute their performance affects their expectations and emotional reactions, which in turn influence future achievement motivation.

Table 5.1 **Attributions and Achievement Motivation**	
Attributions	**Psychological result**
Stability factors	*Expectancy of future success*
Stable	Increase expectation of success
Unstable	Decrease expectation of success
Causality factors	*Emotional influences*
Internal cause	Increased pride or shame
External cause	Decreased pride or shame
Control factors	*Emotional influences*
In one's control	Increased motivation
Out of one's control	Decreased motivation

Achievement Goal Theory

Recently both psychologists and sport exercise psychologists have focused on *achievement goals* as a way of understanding differences in achievement (Duda, 1993; Dweck, 1986; Maehr & Nicholls, 1980; Nicholls, 1984; Roberts, 1993). According to the achievement goal theory, three factors (see Figure 5.3) interact to determine a person's motivation: achievement goals, perceived ability, and achievement behavior. To understand someone's motivation, we must understand what success and failure mean to that person. And the best way to do that is to examine a person's achievement goals and how they interact with his or her perceptions, or perceived ability, of competence (self-worth).

Outcome and Task Orientations.   Holly may compete in bodybuilding because she wants to win trophies and have the best physique of anybody in the area. She has adopted an *outcome goal orientation* (also called a competitive goal orientation), where the focus is on comparing herself to and defeating others. Holly feels good about herself when she wins (has high perceived ability), but not so good about herself (has low perceived ability) when she loses.

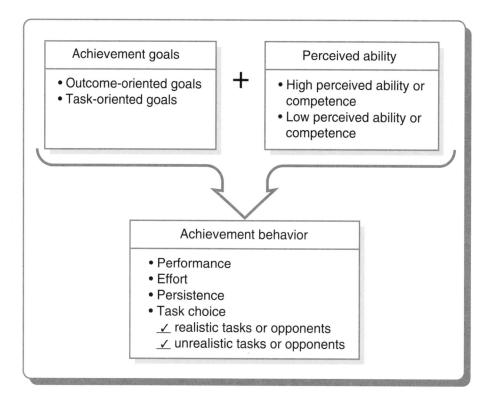

Figure 5.3 Three key factors in the achievement goal approach.

An outcome goal orientation focuses on comparing performance with and defeating others, whereas a task goal orientation focuses on comparing performance with personal standards and personal improvement.

It is best to adopt a task orientation, which emphasizes comparisons with your own performance standards rather than with the performance of others.

Sarah also likes to win contests, but she primarily takes part in bodybuilding to see how much she can improve her strength and physique. She has adopted a *task goal orientation* (also called a mastery goal orientation), where the focus is on improving relative to her own past performances. Her perceived ability is not based on a comparison with others.

For a particular situation, some people can be both task and outcome oriented. For example, a person might want to win the local Turkey trot but also to set a personal best time for the race. However, according to achievement goal researchers, most people tend to be either task or outcome oriented.

The Value of a Task Orientation. Sport psychologists argue that a task orientation more often than an outcome orientation will lead to a strong work ethic, persistence in the face of failure, and optimal performance. This orientation can protect a person from disappointment, frustration, and a lack of motivation when a performance is exceeded by others (which we often cannot control). Because focusing on personal performance provides greater control, we are more motivated and persist longer in the face of failure.

Task-oriented people also select moderately difficult or realistic tasks and opponents. They do not fear failure, and because their perception of ability is based on their own standards of reference, it is easier for them to feel good about themselves and demonstrate high perceived competence than it is for an outcome-oriented person.

Problems With Outcome Orientations. In contrast to task-oriented individuals, outcome-oriented people will have more difficulty maintaining high perceived competence. They judge success by how they compare to others, but they cannot necessarily control how others perform. After all, at least half of the competitors must lose, which can lower a fragile perceived competence. People who are outcome oriented and have low perceived competence demonstrate a low or maladaptive achievement behavioral pattern (Duda, 1993). That is, they are likely to reduce their efforts, cease trying, or make excuses. To

protect their self-worth they are more likely to select tasks where they are guaranteed success or where they are so outmatched no one would expect them to do well. They tend to perform less well in evaluative situations (see the case study of Dave).

What Theories of Achievement Motivation Tell Us

To compare how these three theories explain achievement motivation, Table 5.2 summarizes major predictions from each of them, showing how high and low achievers differ in terms of their motivational attributions, goals, task choices, and performance. We next discuss how a person's achievement motivation and competitiveness develop.

Negative results of an outcome orientation:

- Losing lowers perceived competence
- Losing results in reduced effort
- Avoidance of challenges
- Choking in evaluative situations

Problems Associated With an Outcome Goal Orientation

After years of hard work, Dave became a member of the U.S. Ski Team. He had always set outcome goals for himself: becoming the fastest skier in his local club, winning regional races, beating arch rivals, and placing at nationals. Unfortunately, he got off to a rocky start on the World Cup circuit. He wanted to be the fastest American downhiller and to place in the top three at each World Cup race, but with so many good racers it became impossible to beat them consistently. To make matters worse, because of his lower world ranking, Dave skis well back in the pack, after the course has been chopped up by the previous competitors, which makes it virtually impossible to place in the top three.

As Dave becomes more frustrated by his failures, his motivation declines. He no longer looks forward to competitions; he either skis out of control, totally focused on finishing first, or skis such a safe line through the course that he finishes well back in the field. Dave blames his poor finishes on the wrong ski wax and equipment. He does not realize that his outcome goal orientation, which served him well at the lower levels of competition where he could more easily win, is now leading to lowered confidence, self-doubts, and less motivation.

Table 5.2	What Theories of Achievement Motivation Tell Us	
	High achiever	**Low achiever**
Motivational orientation	High motivation to achieve success	Low motivation to achieve success
	Low motivation to achieve failure	High motivation to achieve failure
	Focuses on the pride of success	Focuses on shame and worry that may result from failure
Attributions	Ascribes success to stable factors and internal factors in one's control	Ascribes success to unstable factors and external factors out of one's control
	Ascribes failure to unstable factors and external factors out of one's control	Ascribes failure to stable factors and internal factors in one's control
Goals adopted	Usually adopts task goals	Usually adopts outcome goals
Task choice	Seeks out challenges and able competitors/tasks	Avoids challenges; seeks out very difficult or very easy tasks/competitors
Performance	Performs well in evaluative conditions	Performs poorly in evaluative conditions

Developing Achievement Motivation and Competitiveness

Is achievement motivation learned? At what age do children develop achievement tendencies? Can they be influenced by sport and exercise professionals?

Achievement motivation and competitiveness are believed to develop in three stages (Scanlan, 1988; Veroff, 1969). These stages are sequential—you must move through one stage before progressing to the next (see Figure 5.4). Not everyone makes it to the final stage, and the age at which each stage is reached varies considerably.

1. **Autonomous competence stage**. In this stage, which is thought to occur before the age of 4 years, a child focuses on mastering his or her environment and on self-testing. For example, Brandon is a preschooler who is highly motivated to learn to ride his tricycle, and he couldn't care less that his sister Eileen can ride better than he can. He rarely compares himself to others.

2. **Social comparison stage**. In the social comparison stage, which begins at about the age of 5 years, a child focuses on directly comparing his or her performance to others, unlike the autonomous stage with its self-referenced standards. This stage is the "who is faster, bigger, smarter, and stronger stage," as children seem preoccupied with comparing themselves to others.

3. **Integrated stage**. The integrated stage involves both social comparison and autonomous achievement strategies. The person who fully masters this integration knows when it is appropriate to compete and compare himself or herself to others and when it is appropriate to adopt self-referenced standards.

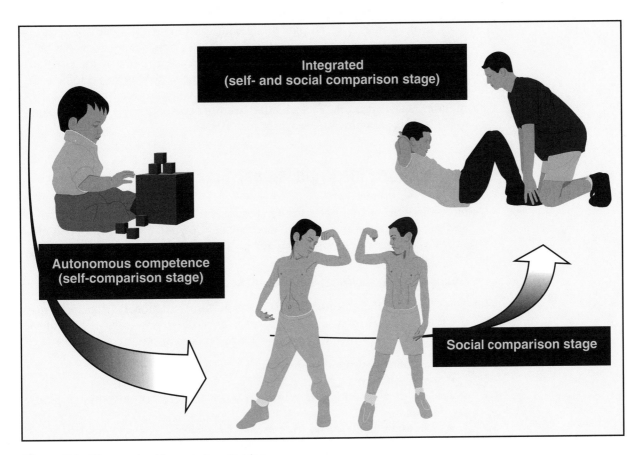

Figure 5.4 Stages of achievement motivation.

This stage, which integrates components from the previous two stages, is the most desirable. There is no typical age for entering this stage.

Why Distinguish Between Stages?

Recognizing the developmental stages of achievement motivation and competitiveness helps us to understand better the behavior of people we work with, especially children. Thus, we will not be surprised when a preschooler is disinterested in competition or when fourth and fifth graders seem preoccupied with it. An integrated achievement orientation, however, must ultimately be developed, and it is an important responsibility to teach children when it is appropriate or inappropriate to compete and compare themselves socially.

Influencing Stages of Achievement Motivation

The social environment in which a person functions has important implications for achievement motivation and competitiveness. Significant others can play an important role in creating a positive or negative climate.

Parents, teachers, and coaches play an especially important role. Teachers and coaches directly and indirectly create motivational climates. They define tasks and games as competitive or cooperative, group children in certain ways (e.g., picking teams through a public draft where social comparison openly occurs), and differentially emphasize task or outcome goals (Ames, 1987; Roberts, 1993).

As professionals, we can play significant roles in creating climates that enhance participant achievement motivation. For example, young gymnasts (ages 9 to 14 years) with strong mastery (task) goals perceived that their coaches encouraged mastery goals. A pressuring coaching style was found to be negatively related to these goals. When the gymnasts perceived coaches as demanding a task focus, they then tended to emphasize both mastery and outcome goals (Piparo, Lewthwaite, & Hasbrook, 1990).

Implications for Professional Practice

Now that you have a better understanding of what achievement motivation and competitiveness involve and how they develop and influence psychological states, you can draw implications for professional practice.

Recognize Interactional Factors in Achievement Motivation

You know now that the interaction of personal and situational factors influences the motivation particular students, athletes, and exercisers have to achieve. What should you watch for to guide your practice? In essence you assess their

- stage of achievement motivation,
- goal orientations,
- what they attribute their performance to (attributions they typically make), and
- the situations they tend to approach or avoid.

Let's take two examples. Jose performs well in competition, seeks out challenges, sets mastery goals, and attributes success to stable internal factors like ability. These are desirable behaviors and he is most likely a high achiever. You see, however, that Felix avoids competitors of equal ability, gravitates toward extreme competitive situations—where either success or failure is almost certain—focuses on outcome goals, becomes tense in competitions, and attributes failure to his low ability (or success to external, unstable factors such as luck. He demonstrates maladaptive achievement behavior and will need your help and guidance.

Felix may even suffer from *learned helplessness*, an acquired condition in which a person perceives that his or her actions have no effect on the desired outcome of a task or skill (Dweck, 1980). In other words, the person feels doomed to failure and that nothing can be done about it. He or she probably makes unhelpful attributions for failure and feels generally incompetent (see Helpless and Hopeless Johnny).

Guiding Achievement Orientation and Competitiveness

- Consider the interaction of personal and situational factors in influencing achievement behavior.
- Emphasize task or mastery goals and downplay outcome goals.
- Monitor and alter your attributional feedback.
- Assess and correct inappropriate participant attributions.
- Help participants determine when to compete and when to focus on individual improvement.

Emphasize Mastery Goals

There are several ways to help prevent maladaptive achievement tendencies or rectify learned helpless states. One of the most important strategies is to help people set task goals and downplay outcome goals. Society emphasizes athletic outcomes and student grades, so downplaying outcome goals is not always easy to do. Luckily, however, sport and exercise psychologists have learned a great deal about goal setting (see chapter 17).

Monitor and Alter Attributional Feedback

In addition to downplaying outcome goals and emphasizing task or individual-specific mastery goals, it is critical that you be conscious of the attributions you make while giving feedback. It is not unusual for teachers, coaches, or exercise leaders to unknowingly convey subtle but powerful messages via attributions that accompany their feedback. Adults influence a child's interpretations of performance success—and future motivation—by how they give feedback (Horn, 1987). For example, notice how this physical educator provides feedback to a child in a volleyball instructional setting:

> You did not bump the ball correctly. Bend your knees more and contact the ball with your forearms. Try harder—you'll get it with practice.

The coach not only conveys instructional information to the young athlete but also informs the child that he can accomplish the task. The instructor also includes the message that persistence and effort pay off.

Helpless and Hopeless Johnny

Johnny is a fifth grader in Ms. Roalston's second period physical education class. He is not a very gifted student, but he can improve with consistent effort. However, after observing and getting to know Johnny, Ms. Roalston has become increasingly concerned. He demonstrates many of the characteristics of learned helplessness that she learned about in her university sport psychology and sport pedagogy classes.

- Johnny seldom tries new skills, usually opting instead to go to the back of the line.

- When Johnny does try a new skill and fails in his first attempt he says he is no good at sports, so why even try.

- His reaction to initial failure is embarrassment and decreased effort.

- He feels so bad about his physical competence that he just wants to get out of the gym as quickly as possible.

Johnny has all the characteristics of learned helplessness. Ms. Roalston remembers that learned helplessness is not a personality flaw nor the fault of Johnny. Rather, it results from an outcome goal orientation, maladaptive achievement tendencies, previous negative experiences with physical activity, and corresponding attributions to uncontrollable, stable factors, especially low ability. Equally important, learned helplessness can vary from being specific to a particular activity (e.g., learning to catch a baseball) to more general to a domain (e.g., learning any sport skill). Ms. Roalston knows that learned helplessness can be overcome by giving Johnny some individual attention, repeatedly emphasizing mastery goals, and downplaying outcome goals. Attributional retraining or getting Johnny to change his low ability attributions for failure will also help. It will take some time and hard work, but she will make helping get Johnny out of his helpless hole a major goal for the year.

In contrast, consider the effects of telling that same child the following:

You did not bump the ball correctly! Your knees were not bent and you did not use your forearms. Don't worry, though—I know baseball is your game, not volleyball.

Although well-meaning, this message informs the young athlete that he will not be good at volleyball, so don't bother trying.

Of course you should not make unrealistic attributions (e.g., telling an exerciser that with continued work and effort she will look like a model when in fact her body type makes this unlikely). Rather, the key is to emphasize mastery goals by focusing on individual improvement and then to link attributions to those individual goals (e.g., "I'll be honest. You'll never have a body like Cindy Crawford, but with hard work you can look and feel a lot better than you do now").

When you work with children, attributing performance failure to their low effort may be effective only if they believe they have the skills they need to ultimately achieve the task (Horn, 1987). If Jimmy feels that he is totally inept

Table 5.3	**Attributional Guidelines for Providing Instructor Feedback**	
	Dos	**Don'ts**
Student/client failure	Emphasize the need to try harder and exert effort. However, link such attributions to individual goals and capabilities.	Make low ability attributions that signify a lack of personal improvement is not possible.
Student/client success	Attribute success to ability. Attribute success to high effort.	Attribute success to luck. Attribute success to task ease.
General		Make insincere or false attributions of any kind.

at basketball, telling him that he didn't learn to dribble because he did not try will not increase his achievement motivation—it may only reinforce his low perception of ability. Do not make low effort attributions with children under the age of 9 unless you also reassure them that they have the skills to accomplish the task. Most importantly, the child must believe he has the skills to perform the task.

Assess and Correct Inappropriate Attributions

It is important to monitor and correct inappropriate or maladaptive attributions that participants make themselves. Many performers who fail (especially those with learned helplessness) attribute their failure to low ability, saying things like "I stink" or "why even try, I just don't have it." Teaching children in classroom situations to replace lack-of-ability attributions with lack-of-effort attributions helped alleviate performance decrements after failure—it was more effective even than actual success (Dweck, 1975)! If you hear students or clients make incorrect attributions for successful performances, like "that was a lucky shot," correct them and indicate that it was hard work and practice that made the shot successful, not luck. You have an important responsibility to ensure that participants use attributions that will facilitate achievement motivation and efforts.

Teaching children in classroom situations to replace lack-of-ability attributions with lack-of-effort attributions helped alleviate performance decrements following failure.

Determine When Competitive Goals Are Appropriate

You also are responsible for helping participants determine when it is appropriate to compete and when it is appropriate to focus on individual improvement. Competing is sometimes a necessity in society (for example, to make an athletic team or to gain admission to a highly selective college). At times, however, competing against others is counterproductive. You wouldn't encourage a basketball player to not pass off to teammates who have better shots or a cardiac rehabilitation patient to exceed the safe training zone to be the fastest jogger in the group.

Teach exercisers and athletes to develop judgment about the appropriateness of their goals.

The key, then, is developing judgment, and through discussion you can help students, athletes, and exercisers make good decisions in this area. Society emphasizes social evaluation and competitive outcomes so much that you will need to counterbalance by stressing a mastery (as compared to an outcome) orientation (see chapter 7 for additional guidelines). Talking to someone once or twice about this issue is not enough: Consistent, repeated efforts are necessary to promote good judgment about appropriate competition.

Make consistent and repeated use of achievement motivation strategies.

Summary

High and low achievers can be distinguished by the tasks they select to be evaluated on, the effort they exert during competition, their persistence, and their performance. High achievers usually adopt mastery (task) goals. They attribute success to stable and internal factors like ability and failure to unstable, controllable factors like effort. Low achievers, on the other hand, judge themselves more on outcome goals and attribute successes to luck or task ease (external, uncontrollable factors) and failure to low ability (an internal, stable attribute).

Achievement motivation and its sport-specific counterpart, competitiveness, develop through stages that include (a) an autonomous stage where the individual focuses on mastery of her environment, (b) a social comparison stage where comparing oneself to others is emphasized, and (c) an integrated stage that focuses on both self-improvement and social comparison. The goal is for the individual to reach an autonomous, integrated stage and to know when it is appropriate to compete and compare socially and when to adopt a self-referenced focus of comparison.

Parents, teachers, and coaches significantly influence the achievement motivation of children. They can create climates that enhance achievement and counteract learned helplessness. They can best do this by (a) recognizing interactional influences on achievement motivation, (b) emphasizing individual mastery goals and downplaying outcome goals, (c) monitoring and providing appropriate attributional feedback, (d) teaching participants to make appropriate attributions, and (e) discussing with participants when it is appropriate to compete and compare themselves socially and when it is appropriate to adopt a self-referenced focus.

Review Questions

1. What is the difference between achievement motivation and competitiveness?

2. In what ways does achievement motivation influence participant behavior?

3. Explain and distinguish three theories to explain achievement motivation.

4. How do high and low achievers differ in the types of challenges and tasks they select?

5. What are attributions? Why are they important in helping understand achievement motivation in sport and exercise settings?

6. Distinguish between an outcome (competitive) versus a task (mastery) goal orientation. Which should be most emphasized in sport, physical education, and exercise settings? Why?

7. Identify the three stages of achievement motivation and competitiveness. Why are these important?

8. How does a teacher's or coach's attributional feedback influence participant achievement?

9. What is learned helplessness? Why is it important?

References

Ames, C. (1987). The enhancement of student motivation. In D.A. Klieber & M. Maehr (Eds.), *Advances in motivation and achievement* (pp. 123-148). Greenwich, CT: JAI Press.

Atkinson, J.W. (1974). The mainstream of achievement-oriented activity. In J.W. Atkinson & J.O. Raynor (Eds.), *Motivation and achievement* (pp. 13-41). New York: Halstead.

Biddle, S. (1993). Attribution research and sport psychology. In R.N. Singer, M. Murphey, & L.K. Tennant (Eds.), *Handbook of research on sport psychology* (pp. 437-464). New York: Macmillan.

Duda, J.L. (1993). Goals: A social-cognitive approach to the study of achievement motivation in sport. In R.N. Singer, M. Murphey, & L.K. Tennant (Eds.), *Handbook of research on sport psychology* (pp. 421-436). New York: Macmillan.

Dweck, C.S. (1975). The role of expectations and attributions in the alleviation of learned helplessness. *Journal of Personality and Social Psychology*, **31**, 674-685.

Dweck, C.S. (1986). Motivational processes affecting learning. *American Psychologist*, **41**, 1040-1048.

Dweck, C.S. (1980). Learned helplessness in sport. In C.M. Nadeau, W.R. Halliwell, K.M. Newell, & G.C. Roberts (Eds.), *Psychology of motor behavior and sport—1979* (pp. 1-11). Champaign, IL: Human Kinetics.

Gill, D.L. (1986). *Psychological dynamics of sport*. Champaign, IL: Human Kinetics.

Heider, F. (1958). *The psychology of interpersonal relations*. New York: Wiley & Sons.

Horn, T.S. (1987). The influence of teacher-coach behavior on the psychological development of children. In D. Gould & M.R. Weiss (Eds.), *Advances in pediatric sport sciences: Vol. 2. Behavioral issues* (pp. 121-142). Champaign, IL: Human Kinetics.

Maehr, M., & Nicholls, J. (1980). Culture and achievement motivation: A second look. In N. Warren (Ed.), *Studies in cross-cultural psychology, Vol. 2* (pp. 53-75). New York: Academic Press.

Martens, R. (1976). *Competitiveness in sport*. Paper presented at the International Congress of Physical Activity Sciences. Quebec City.

McAuley, E. (1993). Self-referent thought in sport and physical activity. In T.S. Horn (Ed.), *Advances in sport psychology* (pp. 101-118). Champaign, IL: Human Kinetics.

McClelland, D. (1961). *The achieving society*. New York: Free Press.

Murray, H.A. (1938). *Explorations in personality*. New York: Oxford University Press.

Nicholls, J. (1984). Concepts of ability and achievement motivation. In R. Ames & C. Ames (Eds.), *Research on motivation in education: Student motivation, Vol. 1* (pp. 39-73). New York: Academic Press.

Piparo, A.J., Lewthwaite, R., & Hasbrook, C.A. (1990, October). *Social correlates of children's sport goal orientations: Coach behaviors and societal influences*. Paper presented at the annual meeting of the Association for the Advancement of Applied Sport Psychology, San Antonio, TX.

Roberts, G. (1993). Motivation in sport: Understanding and enhancing the motivation and achievement of children. In R.N. Singer, M. Murphey, & K.L. Tennant (Eds.), *Handbook of research on sport psychology* (pp. 405-420). New York: Macmillan.

Scanlan, T.K. (1988). Social evaluation and the competition process: A developmental perspective. In F.L. Smoll, R.A. Magill, & M.J. Ash (Eds.), *Children in sport* (3rd ed.) (pp. 135-148). Champaign, IL: Human Kinetics.

Veroff, J. (1969). Social comparison and the development of achievement motivation. In C.P. Smith (Ed.), *Achievement-related motives in children* (pp. 46-101). New York: Russell Sage Foundation.

Weiner, B. (1985). An attribution theory of achievement motivation and emotion. *Psychological Review*, **92**, 548-573.

Weiner, B. (1986). *An attribution theory of motivation and emotion*. New York: Springer-Verlag.

Arousal, Stress, and Anxiety

Jason comes to bat in the bottom of the final inning with two outs and two men on base. With a hit his team will win the district championship; with an out his team will lose the biggest game of the season. Jason steps into the batter's box, his heart pounding and butterflies in his stomach, and has trouble maintaining concentration. He thinks of what a win will mean for his team and of what people might think of him if he does not deliver. Planting his cleats in the dirt, Jason squeezes the bat, says a little prayer, and awaits the first pitch.

If you're involved in athletics, you have probably faced the elevated arousal and anxiety of situations such as Jason's. Sport and exercise psychologists have long studied the causes and effects of arousal, stress, and anxiety in the competitive athletic environment and other areas of physical activity. Many health care professionals are interested in both the physiological and psychological benefits of regular exercise. Does regular exercise lower stress levels? Will patients with severe anxiety disorders benefit from intensive aerobic training and need less medication? Students too experience stress and anxiety over exams and learning. Consider how stress-provoking learning to swim can be for people who have had a bad experience in water. How can teachers reduce this anxiety?

In this chapter you will learn about

▮ the nature of stress and anxiety (what it is and how it is measured),

▮ the sources of anxiety and stress,

▮ how and why arousal and anxiety-related emotions affect performance, and

▮ ways to regulate arousal, stress, and anxiety.

Defining Arousal, Stress, and Anxiety

Although people use the terms *arousal*, *stress*, and *anxiety* interchangeably, sport and exercise psychologists find it important to distinguish among them. They use precise definitions for the phenomena they study to have a common language, reduce confusion, and diminish the need for long explanations.

Arousal

Arousal is a general physiological and psychological activation varying on a continuum from deep sleep to intense excitement.

Arousal is "a general physiological and psychological activation of the organism [person] that varies on a continuum from deep sleep to intense excitement" (Gould & Krane, 1992, pp. 120-121). The term refers to the intensity dimensions of motivation at a particular moment, falling along a continuum (see Figure 6.1) ranging from not at all aroused (i.e., coma) to completely aroused (i.e., frenzy). Highly aroused individuals are mentally activated and experience increased heart rate, respiration, and sweating. Arousal is not automatically associated with either pleasant or unpleasant events. You might be highly aroused by learning you have won 10 million dollars. Yet you might be equally aroused by learning of the death of a loved one.

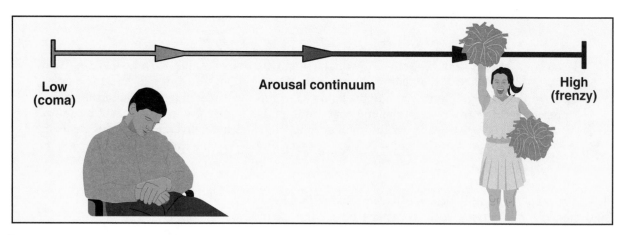

Figure 6.1 The arousal continuum.

Anxiety

Anxiety is a negative emotional state with feelings of nervousness, worry, and apprehension associated with activation or arousal of the body. Thus, anxiety has a thought component (e.g., worry and apprehension) called *cognitive* anxiety. It also has a *somatic* anxiety component, which is the degree of physical activation perceived.

State Anxiety.   We sometimes refer to anxiety to discuss a stable personality component; other times, we use the term to describe a changing mood state. *State anxiety* refers to the ever changing mood component and is defined as an emotional state "characterized by subjective, consciously perceived feelings of apprehension and tension, accompanied by or associated with activation or arousal of the autonomic nervous system" (Spielberger, 1966, p. 17). For example, a player's level of state anxiety would change from moment to moment during a basketball game. She may have a slightly elevated level of state anxiety (feeling somewhat nervous and noticing her heart pumping) prior to tip-off, a lower level once she settles into the pace of the game, and an extremely high level (feeling very nervous and her heart racing) in the closing minutes of a tight contest.

Anxiety is a negative emotional state with feelings of nervousness, worry, and apprehension associated with activation or arousal of the body.

State anxiety is a temporary, ever changing emotional state of subjective, consciously perceived feelings of apprehension and tension, associated with activation of the autonomic nervous system.

Cognitive state anxiety concerns the degree to which one worries or has negative thoughts, whereas *somatic* state anxiety concerns the moment-to-moment changes in perceived physiological activation (which come not from a change in activity but from the stress).

Trait Anxiety.   Unlike state anxiety, *trait anxiety* is part of the personality—an acquired behavioral tendency or disposition that influences behavior. In particular, trait anxiety is

> a motive or acquired behavioral disposition that predisposes an individual to perceive a wide range of objectively nondangerous (physically or psychologically nondangerous) circumstances as threatening and to respond

to these with state anxiety reactions disproportionate in intensity and magnitude of the objective danger (Spielberger, 1966, p. 17)

Trait anxiety is a behavioral disposition to perceive objectively nondangerous circumstances as threatening and to respond with disproportionate state anxiety.

For instance, two field goal kickers with equal physical skills may be placed under identical pressure (e.g., to kick the winning field goal at the end of the game) and yet have entirely different state anxiety reactions because of their personalities—that is, their levels of trait anxiety. Rick is more laid back (low trait-anxious) and does not perceive kicking the game-winning field goal as overly threatening. Thus, he does not experience more state anxiety than would be expected in such a situation. Ted, however, is high trait-anxious and consequently perceives the chance to kick (or, in his view, to miss) the winning field goal as very threatening. He experiences tremendous state anxiety—much more than we would expect in such a situation. (For an efficient summary of the interrelationships among arousal, trait anxiety, and state anxiety see Figure 6.2.)

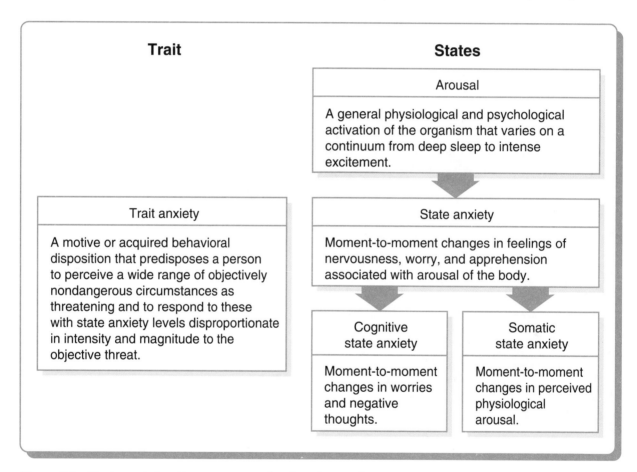

Figure 6.2   The interrelationship among arousal, trait anxiety, and state anxiety.

Measuring Arousal and Anxiety

Sport and exercise psychologists measure arousal, state anxiety, and trait anxiety in various physiological ways and by using psychological self-reporting measures. To measure *arousal* they look at changes in these physiological signs: heart rate, respiration, skin conductance (recorded on a voltage meter), and biochemistry (changes in substances such as catecholamines are assessed). They look also at how people rate their arousal level with a series of statements (such as "my heart is pumping," "I feel peppy"), using numerical scales ranging from low to high.

To measure state anxiety psychologists use both global and multidimensional self-report measures. On the global ones, people rate how nervous they feel on self-report scales from low to high. A total score is calculated by summing the scores of individual items. Using the multidimensional self-report measures is similar, but people rate how worried (cognitive state anxiety) and how physiologically activated they feel on self-report scales ranging from low to high. Subscale scores for cognitive and somatic anxiety are obtained by summing scores for items representing each type of state anxiety.

Psychologists also use global and multidimensional self-reports to measure trait anxiety. The formats for these measures are similar to state anxiety assessments, but instead of people rating how anxious they feel right at that moment, they are asked how they *typically* feel.

Self-report measures (that is, rating yourself on questions from these scales) may help you better understand the differences among cognitive state anxiety, somatic state anxiety, and trait anxiety (see Tables 6.1 and 6.2 for sample questions).

Table 6.1   Competitive State Anxiety Inventory–2 (CSAI-2)

Directions: Below are several statements that athletes have used to describe their feelings before competition. Read each statement and then circle the appropriate number to the right of the statement to indicate how you *feel at this moment*. There are no right or wrong answers. Don't spend too much time on any one statement, but choose the answer that best describes your feelings.

	Not at all	Some-what	Moderately so	Very much so
1. I am concerned about this competition.	1	2	3	4
2. I feel nervous.	1	2	3	4
3. I feel at ease.	1	2	3	4
4. I have self-doubts.	1	2	3	4
5. I feel jittery.	1	2	3	4
6. I feel comfortable.	1	2	3	4
7. I am concerned that I may not do as well in this competition as I could.	1	2	3	4
8. My body feels tense.	1	2	3	4
9. I feel self-confident.	1	2	3	4

Adapted from Martens, Vealey, and Burton (1990).

Relationship Between Trait and State Anxiety

A direct relationship exists between a person's levels of trait anxiety and state anxiety. Research has consistently shown that those who score high on trait anxiety measures experience more state anxiety in highly competitive, evaluative situations. This relationship is not perfect, however. A high trait-anxious athlete may have a tremendous amount of experience in a particular situation and for that reason may not perceive a threat and the corresponding high state anxiety. Similarly, some high trait-anxious people learn coping skills to help them reduce the state anxiety they experience in evaluative situations. Still, generally speaking, knowing a person's level of trait anxiety is usually helpful in predicting how he or she will react to competition, evaluation, and threatening conditions.

High trait-anxious people usually have more state anxiety in highly competitive, evaluative situations than low trait-anxious people do.

Table 6.2 **Sport Competition Trait Anxiety Test (SCAT)**			

Directions: Below are some statements about how persons feel when they compete in sports and games. Read each statement and decide if you *hardly ever*, *sometimes*, or *often* feel this way when you compete in sports and games. If your choice is hardly ever, blacken the square labeled A; if your choice is sometimes, blacken the square labeled B; and if your choice is often, blacken the square labeled C. There are no right or wrong answers. Do not spend too much time on any one question. Remember to choose the word that describes how you *usually* feel when competing in sports and games.

	Hardly ever	Sometimes	Often
1. Before I compete I feel uneasy.	A ☐	B ☐	C ☐
2. Before I compete I worry about not performing well.	A ☐	B ☐	C ☐
3. When I compete I worry about making mistakes.	A ☐	B ☐	C ☐
4. Before I compete I am calm.	A ☐	B ☐	C ☐
5. Before I compete I get a queasy feeling in my stomach.	A ☐	B ☐	C ☐
6. Just before competing I notice my heart beats faster than usual.	A ☐	B ☐	C ☐

Adapted from Martens, Vealey, and Burton (1990).

Stress and the Stress Process

Stress is a process, a sequence of events that will lead to a particular end. It is defined as "a substantial imbalance between demand [physical and/or psychological demands] and response capability, under conditions where failure to meet that demand has important consequences" (McGrath, 1970, p. 20). According to a simple model that McGrath proposed, stress consists of four interrelated stages, which are depicted in Figure 6.3: environmental demand, perception of demands, stress response, and behavioral consequences. We will briefly describe the individual stages here.

Stage 1: Environmental demand. In the first stage of the stress process some type of demand is placed on an individual. The demand might be physical or psychological, such as a physical education student having to execute a newly learned volleyball skill in front of her class or parents pressuring a young athlete to win the race.

Stage 2: Perception of demands. People do not perceive demands in exactly the same way. This is reflected in Stage 2 of the stress process, the individual's perception of the physical or psychological demand. For instance, two eighth graders may perceive having to demonstrate a newly learned volleyball skill in front of class quite differently. Maya may enjoy the attention of being in front of the class, whereas Issaha may feel threatened. That is, Issaha perceives an imbalance between the demands placed on him (having to demonstrate in front of the class) and his ability to meet those demands. Maya perceives no such imbalance, or perceives it only to a nonthreatening degree.

A person's level of trait anxiety greatly influences how he or she perceives the world. High trait-anxious people tend to perceive more situations (especially evaluative and competitive ones) as threatening than low trait-anxious people

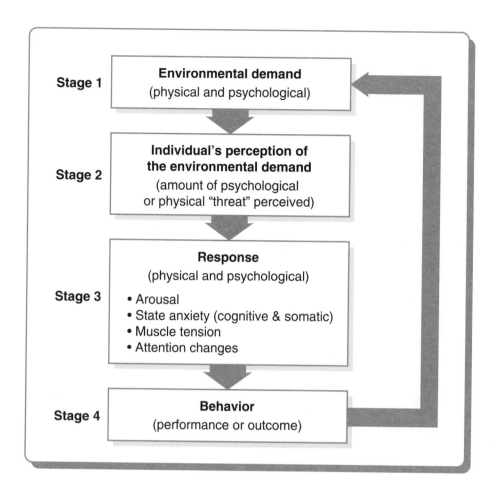

Figure 6.3 The stress process.

do. For this reason trait anxiety is an important influence in Stage 2 of the stress process.

Stage 3: Stress response. The third stage of the stress process is the individual's physical and psychological response to a perception of the situation. If someone's perception of an imbalance between demands and response capability causes her to feel threatened, increased state anxiety results, bringing with it increased worries (cognitive state anxiety), heightened physiological activation (somatic state anxiety), or both. Other reactions, such as changes in concentration and increased muscle tension, accompany increased state anxiety.

Stage 4: Behavioral consequences. The fourth stage is the actual behavior of the individual under stress. If the volleyball student we met earlier perceives an imbalance between capability and demands and feels increased state anxiety, does his performance deteriorate? Or does the increased state anxiety increase intensity, thereby improving performance?

The final stage of the stress process feeds back into the first. If a student becomes overly threatened and performs poorly in front of the class, the other children may laugh, and this negative social evaluation would become an additional demand on the child (Stage 1). The stress process, then, is a continuing cycle (see Figure 6.3).

Implications for Practice

The stress process has a number of implications for practice. If a corporate fitness specialist is asked by her company's personnel director to help develop a stress-management program for the company's employees, for example, Stage

Stress occurs when there is a substantial imbalance between physical and psychological demands placed on an individual and his or her response capability, under conditions where failure to meet the demand has important consequences.

1 of the model suggests that she determine what demands are placed on the employees (e.g., increased workloads, unrealistic scheduling demands, hectic travel schedules). An analysis of Stage 2 might lead her to question who is experiencing or perceiving the most stress (e.g., individuals in certain divisions or with certain jobs or those with certain personality dispositions). Stage 3 would call for studying the reactions the employees are having to the increased stress—somatic state anxiety, cognitive state anxiety, attention-concentration problems, and so on. Stage 4 analysis would focus on the behavior of employees feeling increased stress, such as greater absenteeism, reduced productivity, or decreased job satisfaction. By understanding this stress cycle the fitness director can target her efforts to reduce stress. She might suggest physical activity (most likely in Stage 3) or other means of stress management (e.g., time-management seminars, restructured work schedules). She has a better grasp of the specific causes and consequences of stress, which allows her to design more effective stress-management activities.

Sources of Anxiety and Stress

There are literally thousands of specific sources of stress. Exercise psychologists have shown that major life events—a job change or a death in the family—as well as daily hassles—an auto breakdown or a problem with a co-worker—cause stress and affect physical and mental health (Willis & Campbell, 1992). In athletes, stressors include worry about performing up to capabilities, financial costs and time needed for training, self-doubts about talent, and relationships or traumatic experiences outside of sport, such as the death of a family member (Scanlan, Stein, & Ravizza, 1991). These thousands of specific stress sources fall into some general categories determined by both situation and personality.

Situational Sources of Stress

There are two general sources of situational stress: (a) the importance placed on an event or contest and (b) the uncertainty that surrounds the outcome of that event (Martens, 1987).

Event Importance.   In general, the more important the event, the more stress-provoking it is. Thus, a championship contest is more stressful than a regular season game, just as a job interview is more stressful than watching television at home. Little League baseball players, for example, were observed each time they came to bat over an entire baseball season (Lowe, 1971). The batters' heart rates were recorded while at bat, as were their nervous mannerisms on deck. How critical the situation at bat was in the game (e.g., bases loaded, two outs, last inning, close score, etc.) and how important the game was in the season standings were both rated. The more critical the situation, the more stress and nervousness the young athletes exhibited.

The importance placed on an event is not always obvious, however. An event that may seem insignificant to most people may be very important for one particular person. For instance, a regular-season soccer game may not seem particularly important to most players on a team that has locked up a championship. Yet, it may be of major importance to a particular player who is being observed by a college scout. You must continually assess the importance participants attach to activities.

The more important an event, the more stress-provoking it will be.

Uncertainty.   Uncertainty is a second major situational source of stress—and the greater the uncertainty, the greater the stress.

Often we cannot do anything about uncertainty. For example, when two evenly matched teams are scheduled to compete, there is maximum uncertainty, but little can or should be done about it. After all, the essence of sport is to match up evenly matched athletes and teams. However, at times teachers, coaches, and sports medicine professionals create unnecessary uncertainty by not informing participants of such things as the starting line-ups, how to avoid injury in learning high-risk physical skills (e.g., vaulting in gymnastics), or what to expect while recovering from a serious athletic injury. Trainers, teachers, and coaches should be aware of how they might unknowingly create uncertainty in participants.

> The greater the degree of uncertainty an individual feels about an outcome or others' feelings and evaluations, the greater the state anxiety and stress.

Personal Sources of Stress

Some people will characterize situations as important and uncertain, viewing them with greater anxiety than other people will. Two personality dispositions that consistently relate to heightened state anxiety reactions are high trait anxiety and low self-esteem (Scanlan, 1986).

> High trait anxiety and low self-esteem are related to heightened state anxiety reactions in athletes.

Trait Anxiety.   As previously discussed, trait anxiety is a personality factor that predisposes a person to view competition and social evaluation as more or less threatening. A high trait-anxious person perceives competition as more threatening and anxiety provoking than a low trait-anxious person does.

Self-Esteem.   Self-esteem is also related to perceptions of threat and corresponding changes in state anxiety. Low self-esteem athletes, for example, have less confidence and experience and more state anxiety than do athletes with high self-esteem. Strategies for enhancing self-confidence are important means of reducing the amount of state anxiety individuals experience.

How Arousal and Anxiety Affect Performance

One of the most compelling relationships that sport and exercise psychologists study is how arousal and anxiety affect performance positively and negatively. Most of us recognize readily enough when our nerves make us feel vulnerable and out of control. But how exactly do physiological and psychological arousal function to the advantage of one person and the detriment of another? How does it happen that even in our own performance on a single afternoon, we can notice fluctuations in anxiety levels and their effects?

Sport and exercise psychologists have studied the relation of anxiety and performance for decades. They haven't reached definitive conclusions, but they have illuminated aspects of the process that have several implications for helping people psych up and perform better rather than psyching out and performing poorly. Some 50 years ago study concentrated on drive theory, which was used in the 1960s and 1970s to explain social facilitation. In the past quarter century psychologists have found the inverted-U theory more convincing, and more recently they have proposed some variations and newer hypotheses, including the concepts of zones of optimal functioning, the catastrophe phenomenon, and the reversal theory. We will discuss these briefly.

Drive Theory

Psychologists first saw the relationship between arousal and performance as a direct, linear one (Spence & Spence, 1966). In their view, called *drive theory*, as an individual's arousal or state anxiety increases, so too does his or her performance: The more psyched up an athlete becomes, for example, the better she or he performs. Most athletes, of course, can remember that they also sometimes became overly aroused or overly anxious and then performed more poorly. So little scholarly support now exists for the drive theory (Martens, Vealey, & Burton, 1990).

You may recall the *social facilitation theory* (the example of a theory we used in chapter 2). Zajonc had observed a pattern in the seemingly random way in which people sometimes performed better in front of an audience, and at other times performed worse. His observation was that when people performed tasks they knew well or that were simple, having an audience was a positive effect, whereas when they performed less familiar or more complex tasks, their performance suffered. So Zajonc's social facilitation theory contended that an audience creates arousal in the performer, which hurts performance on difficult tasks that are not yet learned but helps performance on well-learned tasks.

An audience need not be present for social facilitation to occur. The theory refers more broadly to the effects of the presence of others on performance, including coaction, or performing a task simultaneously with others. Zajonc (1965) used drive theory to show that the presence of others increases arousal in the performer and that this increased arousal (drive) increases or brings out the performer's dominant response (the most likely way to perform the skill). When people perform well-learned or simple skills (e.g., sit-ups), the dominant response is correct (positive performance) and the increased arousal facilitates performance. When they perform complex or unlearned skills (e.g., a novice golfer learning to drive a golf ball), others being present increases arousal and causes the dominant response more often to be incorrect (poorer performance). Thus, social facilitation theory predicts that coactors or an audience (that is, others being present) inhibits performance on tasks that are complex or have not been learned thoroughly and enhances performance on tasks that are simple or have been learned well.

The implications are that you would want to eliminate audiences and evaluation as much as possible in learning situations. For example, if you were teaching a gymnastic routine, you would not want to expose youngsters to an audience too soon. It is critical that instructors eliminate or lessen audience and coaction effects in learning environments to make them as arousal-free as possible. However, when participants are performing well-learned or simple tasks, you might want to encourage people to come watch.

While the drive/social facilitation theory explains how an audience hurts performance when one is learning new skills, it does not explain so well how an audience affects a person performing well-learned skills. It predicts that as arousal increases, performance increases proportionately in a straight line. If this were true, we would expect highly skilled athletes to consistently excel in all high-pressure situations. Yet nervousness and choking in the clutch occur even at the elite level. For this reason, we can only conclude that on well-learned skills an audience may sometimes enhance performance and at other times inhibit it. The views presented next will give you a better understanding of how increased arousal/anxiety influences performance on well-learned tasks.

> Social facilitation theory predicts that the presence of others helps performance on well-learned or simple skills and inhibits or lessens performance on unlearned or complex tasks.

Inverted-U Hypothesis

Dissatisfied with the drive theory, most sport psychologists turned to the *inverted-U hypothesis* to explain the relationship between arousal states and performance (Landers & Boutcher, 1986). This view holds that at low arousal levels performance will be below par (see Figure 6.4); the exerciser or athlete is not psyched up. As arousal increases, so too does performance—up to an optimal point where best performance results. Further increases in arousal, however, cause performance to decline. So this view is represented by an inverted-U that reflects high performance with the optimal level of arousal and lesser performance with either low or very high arousal.

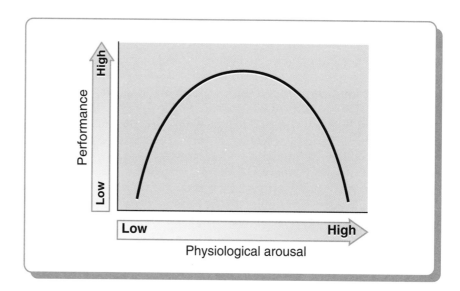

Figure 6.4 The inverted-U arousal-performance relationship.

Most athletes, coaches, and sport psychologists accept the inverted-U theory. After all, most people have experienced being underaroused, optimally aroused, and overaroused. But despite its wide acceptance, the hypothesis has had criticism recently (Hardy, 1990). Critics question the shape of the arousal curve, whether optimal arousal always occurs at the midpoint of the arousal continuum, and the nature of the arousal itself. Their questions have led to the development of other views.

Hanin's Zones of Optimal Functioning (ZOF)

Yuri Hanin, a noted Russian sport psychologist, presented an alternative view that he calls *zones of optimal functioning*. He found that top athletes each have a zone of optimal state anxiety in which best performance occurs (1980, 1986). Outside this zone, poor performance occurs. His view differs from the inverted-U hypothesis in two important ways. First, the optimal level of state anxiety does not always occur at the midpoint of the continuum but varies from individual to individual. That is, some athletes have a zone of optimal functioning at the lower end of the continuum, some in the midrange, and others at the upper end (see Figure 6.5). Second, the optimal level of state

A person's zone of optimal functioning may be at the lower, the middle, or the upper end of the state anxiety continuum.

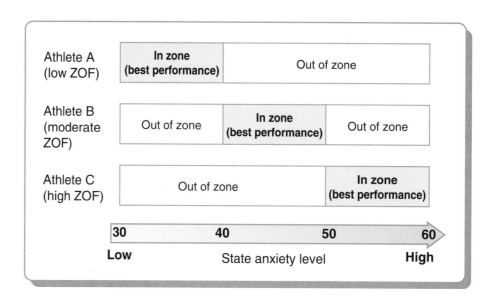

Figure 6.5 Zones of optimal functioning (ZOF).

anxiety is not a single point but a bandwidth. Thus, coaches and teachers should help participants identify and reach their own, specific optimal zone of state anxiety.

Multidimensional Anxiety Theory

Hanin's ZOF hypothesis did not examine whether the components of state anxiety—cognitive and somatic anxiety—affect performance differently. These state anxiety components are generally thought to differentially influence performance. That is, physiological (somatic) arousal and worry (cognitive arousal)

Home Court Advantage: Myth or Reality?

One way spectators influence performance is by providing support and encouragement for the home team. In fact, in many of our team sports, teams battle throughout the season for the best record so that they can have the home court advantage during the playoffs. But, do teams really win more at home than on the road?

Research has found that teams do win more at home, with the advantage being fairly small in football and baseball but quite large in basketball and hockey. Since the latter are played in intimate indoor sites, compared to the more open air stadiums of baseball and football, it may be that the proximity of the fans to the action and the noise level they are able to generate in enclosed facilities enhance player performance. The continual flow of activity in hockey and basketball might also make it easier for a crowd to get emotionally involved and thus play a part in motivating and arousing the players. The increased level of involvement is reflected in elevated noise levels and emotional outbursts, such as sustained booing of referees or opposing coaches.

Despite the evidence supporting the home court advantage during the regular season, recent findings have indicated that this advantage might be lost in the playoffs and championship games; in fact, the home court might even become a disadvantage. For example, Baumeister and Steinhilber (1984) found in baseball World Series played from 1924 to 1982 that in series that went at least five games the home team won 60% of the first two games but only 40% of the last two games. And in the 26 series that have gone to a final and deciding seventh game, the home team won only 38% of the time. To test the generalizability of these results, a similar analysis was conducted on professional basketball. Home teams won 70% of the first four games. However, during the fifth and sixth games, the home team's winning percentage was 46%, dropping to a dismal 38% for the deciding seventh game.

Thus, the home court "advantage" turned to a disadvantage as games became more critical and the pressure mounted. To determine how and why this occurred, game statistics were gathered. In both baseball and basketball, the visiting team's performance remained fairly constant throughout the series. However, the home teams had a significant decrease in performance as games became more critical, producing more errors in baseball and lower foul shooting in basketball. In essence, home teams were choking under pressure instead of getting a lift from fans. Researchers argue that supportive spectators can create expectations for success, which in turn can increase self-consciousness in athletes, causing them to think too much instead of simply playing and performing automatically, which is characteristic of highly skilled athletes.

However, there appears to be a shift in the success of home teams in basketball over the past 10 years. Specifically, from 1984 to 1994, the home team won 18 consecutive seventh and deciding games during the National Basketball Association playoffs. It's possible that coaches and athletes have become more knowledgeable about putting too much pressure on themselves in critical games, thus reducing self-consciousness and letting the emotion of home town fans carry them to victory.

affect performers differently. Your heart racing or pounding and your mind reiterating negative predictions can affect you differentially.

The *multidimensional anxiety theory* predicts that cognitive state anxiety (worry) is negatively related to performance. That is, increases in cognitive state anxiety lead to decreases in performance. But it predicts that somatic state anxiety (physiologically manifested) is related to performance in an inverted-U, with increases in the anxiety facilitating performance up to an optimal level, after which performance declines with additional anxiety. Thus, state anxiety is multidimensional and its two components have different influences on performance. Although studies have shown that these two anxiety components differentially predict performance, the precise predictions of multidimensional anxiety theory have not been consistently supported (Gould & Krane, 1992).

The catastrophe model predicts that with low worry, increases in arousal or somatic anxiety are related to performance in an inverted-U manner. With great worry the increases in arousal improve performance to an optimal threshold beyond which additional arousal causes a rapid and dramatic decline in performance.

Hardy's Catastrophe Model

Hardy's more recent *catastrophe view* addresses another piece of the puzzle. According to his model, performance depends on the complex interaction of arousal and cognitive anxiety (1990). The catastrophe model predicts that physiological arousal is related to performance in an inverted-U fashion, but only when an athlete is not worried or has low cognitive state anxiety (see Figure 6.6a). If cognitive anxiety is high (the athlete is worrying), however, the increases in arousal at some point reach a kind of threshold just past the point of optimal arousal level, and afterward a rapid decline in performance—a "catastrophe"—occurs (see Figure 6.6b). So arousal (somatic anxiety) can have markedly different effects, depending on the amount of cognitive anxiety. Moreover, in conditions of high worry, once overarousal and the catastrophe occur, performance deteriorates *dramatically*. This is different than the steady decline predicted by the inverted-U hypothesis because recovery takes longer. The performer must completely relax to again reach the optimal level of functioning.

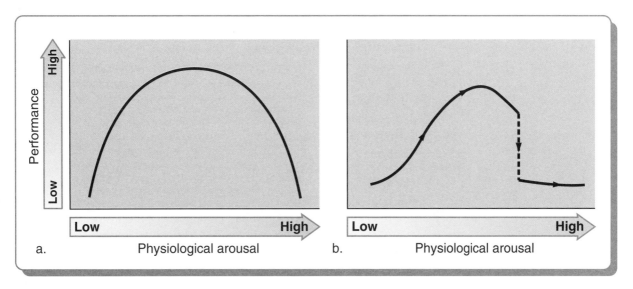

Figure 6.6   Catastrophe theory predictions. (a) Arousal-performance relation under low cognitive state anxiety; (b) Arousal-performance relation under high cognitive state anxiety.

Catastrophe theory has received good initial scientific support. The message for practice is that for optimal performance an ideal arousal level isn't enough: It is also necessary to manage or control cognitive state anxiety (worrying).

Reversal Theory

Kerr's application of *reversal theory* (1985) contends that how arousal affects performance depends basically on an individual's *interpretation* of his or her arousal level. Joe might interpret high arousal as a pleasant excitement, whereas Jan might interpret it as an unpleasant anxiety. She might see low arousal as relaxation, whereas Joe sees it as boring. Athletes are thought to make quick shifts—*reversals*—in their interpretations of arousal. So an athlete may perceive arousal as positive one minute and then reverse the interpretation to negative the next minute.

Martens suggests that looking at arousal as a pleasant or unpleasant state is fundamental to understanding its relationship to athletic performance (1987). If a person interprets arousal positively (called *positive psychic energy*), that will affect performance positively. If, on the other hand, someone interprets it negatively (*negative psychic energy*), that will affect performance negatively. So having high positive psychic energy and low negative psychic energy should result in an athlete performing at his or her best. Martens' observations are based on practical experience working with athletes, and not on research, but his view has strong intuitive appeal.

How a performer interprets arousal may influence performance.

Significance of the Arousal-Performance Views

Let's summarize what these recent views tell us for practice. The zones of optimal functioning, multidimensional anxiety, catastrophe, and reversal theories offer several guidelines (Gould & Udry, 1994):

1. Arousal is a multifaceted phenomenon consisting of both physiological activation and an athlete's interpretation of that activation (e.g., state anxiety, confidence). We must help performers find the optimal mixture of these emotions needed for best performance.

2. Arousal and state anxiety do not necessarily have a negative effect on performance. The effects can be positive and facilitating or negative and debili-

tating, depending largely on how the performer interprets changes. In addition, self-confidence is critical to facilitating heightened arousal as positive (psyching up) as opposed to negative (psyching out).

3. Some optimal level of arousal leads to peak performance, but the optimal levels of physiological activation and arousal-related thoughts (worry) are not necessarily the same!

4. Both the catastrophe and reversal theories suggest that interaction between levels of physiological activation and arousal-related thoughts appear more important than absolute levels of each. Some people perform best with relatively low optimal arousal and state anxiety, whereas others perform best with higher levels.

5. An optimal level of arousal is thought to be related to peak performance, but it is doubtful that this level occurs at the midpoint of the arousal continuum. Excessive arousal likely does not cause slow, gradual declines in performance but "catastrophes" that are difficult to reverse.

Why Arousal Influences Performance

Understanding why arousal affects performance can help you to regulate arousal, both in yourself and others. For instance, if heightened arousal and state anxiety lead to increased muscle tension in Nicole, a golfer, then progressive muscle relaxation techniques may reduce her state anxiety and improve performance. Thought control strategies, however, may work better for Shane, another golfer, who needs to control excessive cognitive state anxiety.

There are at least two explanations for how increased arousal influences athletic performance: (a) increased muscle tension and coordination difficulties and (b) changes in attention or concentration levels.

Muscle Tension and Coordination Difficulties.   Many people who experience great stress report muscle soreness, aches, and pains. Athletes who experience high levels of state anxiety might say, "I don't feel right"; "My body doesn't seem to follow directions"; or "I tensed up" in critical situations. Comments like these are not surprising: Increased arousal and state anxiety cause increased muscle tension and can interfere with coordination.

For example, some high trait-anxious and low trait-anxious college students were watched closely as they threw tennis balls at a target. As you might expect, the high trait-anxious students experienced considerably more state anxiety than the low trait-anxious subjects (Weinberg and Hunt, 1976). Moreover, electroencephalograms (EEGs) monitoring electrical activity in the students' muscles showed that increased state anxiety caused the highly anxious individuals to use more muscular energy before, during, and after their throws. Thus, increased muscle tension and coordination difficulties contributed to the students' inferior performance.

Attention-Concentration Changes.   Nideffer (1976) proposed that increased arousal and state anxiety influence athletic performance through changes in attention and concentration. First, increased arousal causes a narrowing of a performer's attentional field (Landers, Wang, & Courtet, 1985). For example, Joe is a goalie in ice hockey and needs to maintain a broad but optimal focus of attention as three opponents break into his end of the ice. If he becomes preoccupied with Tim, who has the puck, and does not attend to the other players on the periphery, Tim will simply pass off to a teammate on the wing for an easy score. Under normal conditions, Joe can maintain his optimal attentional focus (see Figure 6.7a), but if he is underaroused (see Figure 6.7b),

Increased arousal and state anxiety cause increased muscle tension and can interfere with coordination.

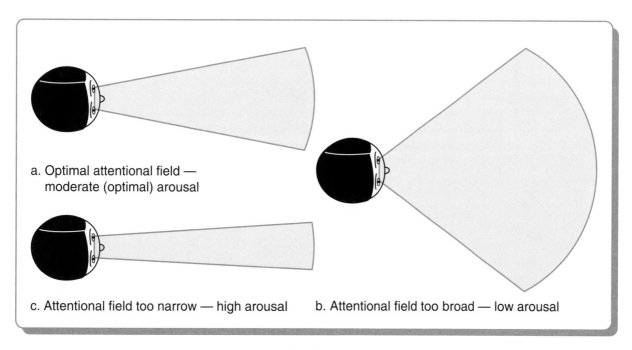

a. Optimal attentional field —
   moderate (optimal) arousal

c. Attentional field too narrow — high arousal   b. Attentional field too broad — low arousal

Figure 6.7   Attentional narrowing under conditions of high arousal.

his attention focus may be too broad, focusing on both task-relevant (e.g., the opposing players) and irrelevant cues (e.g., the crowd). When he experiences excessive levels of arousal and state anxiety, however, his attention focus narrows too much, and he is unable to survey the entire playing surface (see Figure 6.7c). One athlete who experienced severe anxiety problems put it this way: "When the pressure is on, it is like I am looking through the tube in a roll of toilet paper." In psychological terms, increased arousal causes a narrowing of the attentional field, which negatively influences performance on tasks requiring a broad external focus.

When arousal is increased, performers also tend to scan the playing environment less often. For example, Tony is a wrestler who experiences high levels of arousal and state anxiety. He becomes preoccupied with executing one move on an opponent so does not visually or kinetically scan the opponent's total body position for other potential opportunities. Thus, Tony's performance deteriorates as he scans less often and, consequently, potential scoring opportunities go undetected.

Arousal and state anxiety also cause changes in attention and concentration levels by affecting attention style (Nideffer, 1976). Athletes must learn to shift their attention to appropriate task cues (see chapter 18). For example, a quarterback in football needs to shift from a broad external span when surveying the field for open receivers to a narrow external focus when delivering a pass. Also, each individual has a dominant attention style. Increased arousal can cause performers to shift to a dominant attention style that may be inappropriate for the skill at hand.

Finally, increased arousal and state anxiety causes athletes to attend to inappropriate cues. For instance, most athletes perform well-learned skills best when they fully concentrate on the task. Unaware of their levels of concentration, they perform on automatic pilot or in a "flow zone" (see chapter 18). Unfortunately, excessive cognitive state anxiety causes some performers to

Arousal and state anxiety narrow the attention field, decrease environmental scanning, and cause a shift to dominant attention style and inappropriate cues.

focus on inappropriate task cues by "worrying about worrying" and becoming overly self-evaluative. This, in turn, affects optimal concentration.

Implications for Practice

You can integrate your knowledge of arousal, stress, and anxiety by considering implications for professional practice. Five of the most important guidelines are to

1. identify the optimal combination of arousal-related emotions needed for best performance;
2. recognize how personal and situational factors interact to influence arousal, anxiety, and performance;
3. recognize the signs of increased arousal and anxiety in sport and exercise participants;
4. tailor coaching and instructional practices to individuals; and
5. develop confidence in performers to help them cope with increased stress and anxiety.

Identify Optimal Arousal-Related Emotions

One of the most effective ways to help people achieve peak performance is to increase their awareness of how arousal-related emotions can lead to peak performances (see chapter 14 for specific techniques). Once this is accomplished, various psychological strategies (e.g., imagery and developing preperformance routines) can help the performer learn to regulate arousal.

Think of arousal as an emotional temperature, and arousal-regulation skills as a thermostat. The athlete's goals are to identify the optimal emotional temperature for his best performance and then to learn how to "set" his thermostat to this temperature—either by raising (psyching up) or lowering (chilling out) his emotional temperature.

Recognize the Interaction of Personal and Situational Factors

As with other behaviors, you can best understand and predict stress and anxiety by considering the interaction of personal and situational factors (see Figure 6.8). For instance, many people mistakenly assume that the low trait-anxious athlete will always be the best performer because she will achieve an optimal level of state anxiety and arousal needed for competition. In contrast, the high trait-anxious athlete is assumed to consistently choke. But this is not the case.

Where the importance placed on performance is not excessive and there is a good deal of certainty, you might expect a high trait-anxious swimmer to experience some elevated arousal and state anxiety because she is predisposed to perceive most competitive situations as somewhat threatening. It seems likely that she would move close to her optimal level of arousal and state anxiety. In contrast, a low trait-anxious competitor may not perceive the situation as very important because he does not feel threatened. Hence, his level of arousal and state anxiety remain low and he has trouble achieving an optimal performance.

In a high-pressure situation, where the meet has considerable importance and the outcome is highly uncertain, these same swimmers react quite differently. The high trait-anxious swimmer perceives this situation as even more important than it is and responds with very high levels of arousal and state anxiety: She overshoots her optimal level of state anxiety and arousal. The low

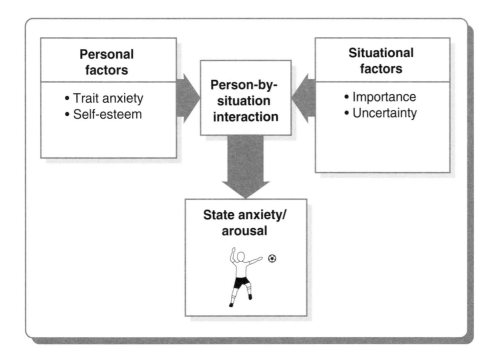

Figure 6.8 Interactional model of anxiety.

trait-anxious swimmer also experiences increased state anxiety, but because he tends to perceive competition and social evaluation as less threatening, his state anxiety and arousal will likely be in an optimal range.

Looking at the interaction of personal factors (such as self-esteem and trait anxiety) and situational factors (such as event importance and uncertainty) is a better predictor of arousal, state anxiety, and performance than looking at either set of these factors alone.

Recognize Arousal and State Anxiety Signs

The interactional approach has several implications for helping exercise and sport participants manage stress. Chief among them is the need to identify people who are experiencing heightened stress and anxiety. This is not easy to do. Coaches, for example, have been found to be inaccurate predictors of their athletes' anxiety levels. Hanson and Gould found that only one of four college cross-country coaches accurately read their athletes' state and trait anxiety levels (1988). Coaches who could accurately read the anxiety levels did not think it was an easy task—rather, they worked hard to learn about their athletes.

You can more accurately detect a person's anxiety levels if you are familiar with the signs and symptoms of increased stress and anxiety (see Table 6.3). Although no specific number or pattern of symptoms characterize a high level of stress, those people who experience high levels of state anxiety often exhibit a number of these signs. The key is to notice changes in these variables between stressful and unstressful environments (e.g., when a normally positive athlete becomes negative).

One of the best but often overlooked ways to understand what people are feeling is to ask them. Encourage your participants to freely talk about their feelings with you, and be empathetic by trying to see things from their perspectives (i.e., how you would feel in their situation at their level of experience). This allows you to associate specific behavioral patterns with varying levels of stress and anxiety and to better read their anxiety levels.

To accurately detect an individual's anxiety level you need to know the various signs and symptoms of increased stress and anxiety.

Table 6.3 Symptoms of Heightened State Anxiety and Arousal	
* Cold, clammy hands	* Feel ill
* Constant need to urinate	* Headache
* Profuse sweating	* Cotton mouth
* Negative self-talk	* Constantly sick
* Dazed look in eyes	* Sleeping difficulties
* Increased muscle tension	* Consistently perform better in non-evaluative situations
* Inability to concentrate	
* Butterflies in stomach	

Tailor Coaching Strategies to Individuals

Sometimes arousal and state anxiety will need to be reduced, other times maintained, and other times facilitated.

It is important to individualize teaching, exercise, and coaching practices. At times, arousal and state anxiety levels will need to be reduced, at other times maintained, and at still other times facilitated (see chapter 14 for specific strategies). The teacher or coach should recognize when and with whom arousal and state anxiety need to be enhanced, reduced, or maintained.

For example, if a student or athlete with high trait anxiety and low self-esteem must perform in a highly evaluative environment, the teacher or coach would best de-emphasize the importance of the situation and emphasize the performer's preparation to execute. A pep talk stressing the importance of the situation and performing well would only add stress and increase arousal and state anxiety beyond an optimal level. Someone with moderate levels of trait anxiety and self-esteem may be best left alone in the same highly evaluative situation. This individual's arousal and state anxiety would be elevated, but in all likelihood not excessive. However, an athlete with very low trait anxiety and high self-esteem, performing in a nonthreatening environment, may need a pep talk to increase arousal. The keys, then, are to know a person's personal characteristics, read the current level of state anxiety, and treat the individual appropriately.

Develop Confidence in Performers

One of the most effective methods of helping people control their stress and anxiety is to assist them in developing their confidence. Highly confident people who believe in their abilities experience less state anxiety. Two important strategies are fostering a positive environment and instilling a positive orientation to mistakes and losing (see chapter 16 for other excellent strategies).

One major source of stress is uncertainty, which often results when athletes or students participate in negative practice environments. For instance, some coaches harp on mistakes that players make, yelling and screaming all through practice. Then on game day, these same coaches say how confident they are in their athletes' abilities. But after hearing so much negative feedback in practice, the athletes may not believe what the coach says on game day.

A productive approach for facilitating confidence is to create a positive practice environment. Give frequent and sincere encouragement. That way, when athletes encounter stressful environments, they will have confidence in their abilities to meet the demands of their situations.

Foster a positive, productive orientation to mistakes—and even to losing. Typically, when individuals make mistakes, they become frustrated and often overly aroused and anxious. This leads to unproductive attention changes and increased muscle tension, which further deteriorate performance.

It is useful to teach people to view mistakes in a more productive light. Just as legendary UCLA basketball coach John Wooden did with his players, good sport psychologists teach performers not to view mistakes as bad or evil, but as building blocks to success (Smoll & Smith, 1979). No performer is happy to make mistakes, but getting upset only makes a mistake a *complete* mistake. Instead, try to gain at least a partial success by staying cool and learning from the mistake: Use it as a building block to success. Mastering this strategy reduces anxiety, making for a more productive learning and performance environment.

Summary

Stress, arousal, and anxiety each have distinct meanings. Stress is a process. It occurs when people perceive an imbalance between the physical and psychological demands on them and their ability to respond. Some situations produce more state anxiety and arousal than others (e.g., events that are important and where event outcome is uncertain). Stress is also influenced by personality dispositions (e.g., trait anxiety and self-esteem). Performers with high trait anxiety and low self-esteem experience more state anxiety.

Arousal-related emotions, such as cognitive and somatic state anxiety, are related to performance. Hanin's optimal zones of functioning, Hardy's catastrophe model, and Martens' interpretation of reversal theory should be used to guide practice. An optimal recipe of emotions is related to peak performance, and when performers are outside this optimal range, poor performance results. This optimal combination of emotions needed for peak performance does not necessarily occur at the midpoint of the arousal/state anxiety continuum, and the relationship between arousal and performance depends on the level of cognitive state anxiety (worry) a performer exhibits.

An interactional model of motivation should guide teachers and coaches in their efforts to help students and athletes manage arousal and state anxiety. Creating a positive environment and a productive orientation to mistakes and losing is an effective way to manage stress.

Review Questions

1. Distinguish between the terms arousal, state anxiety, trait anxiety, cognitive state anxiety, and somatic state anxiety.

2. How can arousal and anxiety be measured?

3. Define stress and identify the four stages of the stress process. Why are these stages important? How can they guide practice?

4. What are the major sources of situation stress?

5. Identify two personal sources of stress.

6. What is social facilitation theory? What implications does this theory have for practice?

7. Discuss the major differences in how arousal relates to performance according to the following theories:

   - Drive theory
   - Inverted-U hypothesis
   - Multidimensional anxiety theory
   - Zone of optimal functioning
   - Catastrophe model
   - Reversal theory

8. Describe the major signs of increased state anxiety in athletes.

9. Give an example of how you should tailor coaching strategies to individuals trying to deal with stress and anxiety.

References

Baumeister, R.F., & Steinhilber, A. (1984). Paradoxical effects of supportive audiences on performance under pressure: The home field disadvantage in sports championships. *Journal of Personality and Social Psychology*, **43**, 85-93.

Gould, D., & Krane, V. (1992). The arousal-athletic performance relationship: Current status and future directions. In T. Horn (Ed.), *Advances in sport psychology* (pp. 119-141). Champaign, IL: Human Kinetics.

Gould, D., & Udry, E. (1994). Psychological skills for enhancing performance: Arousal regulation strategies. *Medicine and Science in Sports & Exercise*, **26**(4), 478-485.

Hanin, Y.L. (1980). A study of anxiety in sports. In W.F. Straub (Ed.), *Sport psychology: An analysis of athlete behavior* (pp. 236-249). Ithaca, NY: Mouvement.

Hanin, Y.L. (1986). State trait anxiety research on sports in the USSR. In C.D. Spielberger & R. Diaz-Guerreo (Eds.), *Cross-cultural anxiety* (Vol. 3, pp. 45-64). Washington, DC: Hemisphere.

Hanson, T.W., & Gould, D. (1988). Factors affecting the ability of coaches to estimate their athletes' trait and state anxiety levels. *The Sport Psychologist*, **2**, 298-313.

Hardy, L. (1990). A catastrophe model of performance in sport. In J.G. Jones & L. Hardy (Eds.), *Stress and performance in sport* (pp. 81-106). Chichester, England: Wiley.

Jones, J.G., & Hardy, L. (1989). Stress and cognitive functioning in sport. *Journal of Sport Sciences*, **7**, 41-63.

Kerr, J.H. (1985). The experience of arousal: A new basis for studying arousal effects in sport. *Journal of Sport Sciences*, **3**, 169-179.

Landers, D.M., & Boutcher, S.H. (1986). Arousal-performance relationships. In J.M. Williams (Ed.), *Applied sport psychology: Personal growth to peak performance* (pp. 163-184). Palo Alto, CA: Mayfield.

Landers, D.M., Wang, M.Q., & Courtet, P. (1985). Peripheral narrowing among experienced and inexperienced rifle shooters under low- and high-stress conditions. *Research Quarterly*, **56**, 122-130.

Lowe, R. (1971). *Stress, arousal, and task performance of Little League baseball players.* Unpublished doctoral dissertation. University of Illinois, Urbana.

Martens, R. (1987). *Coaches guide to sport psychology.* Champaign, IL: Human Kinetics.

Martens, R., Vealey, R.S., & Burton, D. (Eds.) (1990). *Competitive anxiety in sport.* Champaign, IL: Human Kinetics.

McGrath, J.E. (1970). Major methodological issues. In J.E. McGrath (Ed.), *Social and psychological factors in stress* (pp. 19-49). New York: Holt, Rinehart, & Winston.

Nideffer, R.M. (1976). *The inner athlete.* New York: Crowell.

Scanlan, T.K. (1986). Competitive stress in children. In M.R. Weiss & D. Gould (Eds.), *Sport for children and youths* (pp. 118-129). Champaign, IL: Human Kinetics.

Scanlan, T.K., Stein, G.L., & Ravizza, K. (1991). An in-depth study of former elite figure skaters—Part 3. Sources of stress. *Journal of Sport Exercise Psychology*, **13**(2), 103-120.

Smoll, F.L., & Smith, R.E. (1979). *Improving relationship skills in youth sport coaches.* East Lansing, MI: Michigan Institute for the Study of Youth Sports.

Spence, J.T., & Spence, K.W. (1966). The motivational components of manifest anxiety: Drive and drive stimuli. In C.D. Spielberger (Ed.), *Anxiety and behavior.* New York: Academic Press.

Spielberger, C.D. (1966). Theory and research on anxiety. In C.D. Spielberger (Ed.), *Anxiety and behavior* (pp. 3-22). New York: Academic.

Weinberg, R.S., & Hunt, V.V. (1976). The interrelationships between anxiety, motor performance, and electromyography. *Journal of Motor Behavior*, **8**(3), 219-224.

Willis, J.D., & Campbell, L.F. (1992). *Exercise psychology.* Champaign, IL: Human Kinetics.

Zajonc, R.B. (1965). Social facilitation. *Science*, **149**, 269-274.

PART

III

Understanding Sport and Exercise Environments

I n Part II we learned how a person's psychological make-up influences her or his behavior in physical education, sport, and exercise contexts. People do not exist in vacuums, however, and as we learned, a person-by-situation interactional model is the best way to psychologically understand behavior.

In Part III, we'll focus on two major classes of situational factors that influence behavior. Chapter 7 examines the important environmental impact that competition and cooperation have on a person's behavior. Virtually everything we do as professionals in sport, teaching, and exercise settings involves competition or cooperation to some degree. In this chapter we'll learn that competition and cooperation are learned behaviors, how they influence performance, positive and negative effects of competitive and cooperative settings, and ways to balance competition and cooperation so that healthy development is maximized.

Chapter 8 focuses on feedback and reinforcement. You will learn how these factors affect learning and performance. We offer guidelines for giving feedback and reinforcement to people in sport and exercise settings. The chapter closes with an examination of how rewards can both enhance and undermine the natural, intrinsic motivation of participants.

Understanding Competition and Cooperation

Basketball is a sport in which success, as symbolized by the championship, requires that the community goal prevail over selfish impulses. . . . The less conflict there is off-court, the more the inevitable friction of competition can be minimized . . . teams develop when talents and personalities mesh.

Bill Bradley

Tennis players are continually taking out of the sport and never putting anything back. . . . They are strictly individualists today, self-centered, with no recognition of authority and no feeling for the roots and traditions to which countless people have contributed over the years. They seem to feel the game belongs to them. . . . The problem is that when the goal of sport is only to win and preserve status, with no broader appreciation of the significance of sport, serious consequences often result.

Fred Perry

Former all-star basketball player, Senator Bill Bradley, and tennis great Fred Perry sound like the blind men exploring the elephant (or, in this case, sport). According to Bradley, whose experience is the more cooperative world of basketball, competitive sport brings out cooperative efforts among teammates seeking a common goal. According to Perry, whose experience is in the more individual game of tennis, it can produce self-centered athletes. But virtually all sport and physical activity involve environments of both competition and co-operation.

In this chapter you will learn about

▌ what competition and cooperation are and what factors influence them,

▌ psychological studies of competition and cooperation,

▌ social processes and developmental factors influencing competition and coop-eration, and

▌ guidelines for balancing competitive and cooperative effort.

Defining Competition and Cooperation

Morton Deutsch defined *competition* as a situation in which rewards are distrib-uted unequally among participants (1949a). In essence, the goals of the partici-pants are interdependent in a negative way: If one person achieves the goal, the other person cannot. In sport, one athlete wins and the other athlete loses. Or the first-place winner receives $10,000, second place $5,000, and last place nothing but a handshake. Conversely, Deutsch defined *cooperation* as a situation in which the goals of the participants are mutually interdependent: Each person depends on the other to reach his or her goals. A tennis doubles team, for example, can't win a match (its goal) unless the players work together to make this happen. They win or lose together.

Although research concerning competition dates back to the turn of the century (Triplett, 1898), the first concerted effort to study competition was initiated by Deutsch who noted that few everyday situations are purely coopera-tive or competitive. He argued that most social interactions involve some kind of goal-directed behavior that rewards the person (or persons) for achieving the goal while requiring some type of cooperative effort from everyone involved. Basketball is a good example—each player on a team should be cooperating in an attempt to win the game, but players might also be competing against each other for playing time and a starting position in the line-up.

Although the reward definition of competition guided early psychological research on competition/cooperation, Rainer Martens proposed another defini-tion and approach to competition that focuses on social evaluation (1975). His model was developed specifically as a framework to study competition in sport and exercise environments, taking into account the many social influences that impact competitive behaviors in sport. Understanding these influences helps in structuring the activity environment to maximize the participants' personal development. Thus, Martens' *social evaluation approach* is more useful than the reward approach for understanding the competitive process in sport.

Competition as a Process

According to Martens, competition is more than a single event; rather it involves a process that encompasses several events or stages. This process of competition, which involves four distinct stages, is illustrated in Figure 7.1. Though distinct, these stages are linked to each other, as shown in the figure. The competitive process will be experienced differently by different individuals. Therefore, the person is at the focal point of the process and can influence the relationship among the different stages. Personal attributes such as previous experience, ability, motivation, and attitudes are just some of the factors that might influence a person's responses in competition. As with any social process, each stage is influenced by the other stages as well as by external factors in the environment such as feedback and external rewards.

The four stages of competition are (a) the objective competitive situation, (b) the subjective competitive situation, (c) the response, and (d) the consequences of the response.

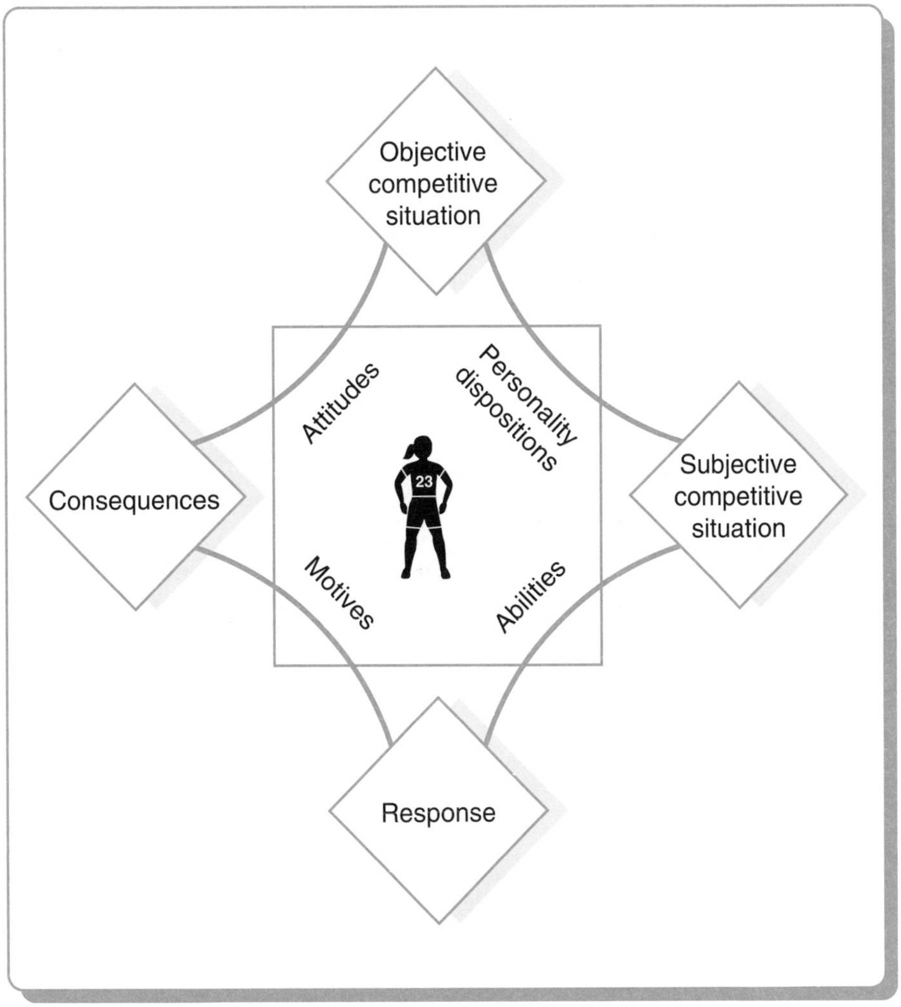

Figure 7.1 The competitive process. Adapted from Martens (1975).

Stage 1—Objective Competitive Situation

Martens proposes an alternative definition of the objective competitive situation, stemming from social evaluation theory (Festinger, 1954), that includes a standard for comparison and at least one other person. The comparison standard can be an individual's past performance level (e.g., 4:10 in the mile run), an idealized performance level (e.g., a 4-minute mile), or another individual's performance (e.g., your main rival has run a 4:05 mile). The primary thing that distinguishes a competitive situation from other comparison situations is that the criteria for comparison are known by the person in position to evaluate the performance.

Consider these examples with Martens' definition in mind. You go out alone for a 3-mile jog, setting a goal for yourself to run this distance in 21 minutes

In an objective competitive situation "an individual's performance is compared with some standard of excellence, in the presence of at least one other person who is aware of the criterion for comparison." (Martens, 1975, p. 70).

(your previous best was 22 minutes). This would not be considered competition because *only you* are aware of the standard of excellence you are striving to beat. However, if you ran with a friend and told her about your goal to run 3 miles in 21 minutes, it would be competition because your friend is aware of the criteria for evaluation and can evaluate your performance.

Some people argue that the first example is also competition inasmuch as you are competing against yourself. Martens would not necessarily disagree with this point of view, but he argues that to study competition scientifically, we must delimit its scope. Without another person involved to evaluate the comparison process, almost anything might be called competition. How would one know if you were trying to run 3 miles in 21, 20, or 19 minutes? By having another person there, the exact parameters of competition can be well-defined. Martens states that most activities commonly thought to be competitive are indeed covered by his definition so we really don't lose much by limiting the definition to include another person. His definition is useful because it begins by seeking out the objective competitive situation.

Stage 2—Subjective Competitive Situation

Regardless of whether people are in an objective competitive situation because they seek it or because circumstances place them in it, they must evaluate the situation in some way. This brings into play the next stage, the *subjective competitive situation*, which involves how the person perceives, accepts, and appraises the objective competitive situation. Here the individual's unique background and attributes become important. Such factors as perceived ability, motivation, importance of the competitive situation, and the opponent may well influence the subjective appraisal of the competitive setting.

For example, one gymnast may look forward to competing in a championship meet as a means of gaining experience, whereas another facing the same objective situation may dread the upcoming meet. Similarly, one runner in an adult fitness class may want to turn every jog into a race, whereas another avoids comparisons to other runners in his class.

People with a high level of competitiveness tend to seek out competitive situations and be more motivated to achieve in them than people with lower levels of competitiveness. Trait competitiveness alone, however, will not adequately predict how a person will respond to a particular competitive situa-

Objective Versus Subjective Outcomes of Competition

Deutsch defined competition as a situation in which rewards are distributed unequally among participants based on their performances. Martens views this definition as inadequate to study competition in sport because it does not take into consideration the subjective as well as objective rewards inherent in sport competition. For example, say you have a chance to play Michael Jordan in a one-on-one basketball game, the first player to score 21 points winning the game. You obviously do not expect to beat the best player in the world, so you set a goal for yourself to score 5 points. If you lose the competition 21-6 (objective outcome) but are happy to have scored more than 5 points (subjective outcome), then you would consider yourself successful, even though you lost on the scoreboard. On the other hand, Michael Jordan might be disappointed that you scored even 1 point off him. As you can see, it is quite possible for the goals strived for and the rewards sought to be entirely different for each competitor. Deutsch's reward definition is not sensitive to these differential outcomes and goals in sport competition; thus, the competition model proposed by Martens is more useful for studying competitive behavior in sport and physical activity.

Table 7.1 Sport Orientation Questionnaire				
The following statements describe reactions to sport situations. We want to know how you usually feel about sports and competition. Read each statement and circle the letter that indicates how much you agree or disagree with each statement on the scale: A, B, C, D, or E. There are no right or wrong answers; simply answer as you honestly feel. Do not spend too much time on any one statement. Remember—choose the letter that describes how you *usually* feel.				
	Strongly agree	**Slightly agree**	**Neither agree nor disagree**	**Slightly disagree**	**Strongly disagree**
1. I am a determined competitor.	A	B	C	D	E
2. Winning is important.	A	B	C	D	E
3. I am a competitive person.	A	B	C	D	E
4. I set goals for myself when I compete.	A	B	C	D	E

Adapted from Gill and Deeter (1988).

tion—other situational variables (e.g., type of sport, coach, parents, teammates) also exert strong influences on behavior.

But since competitiveness is such an important personal factor in the competitive process, let's take a closer look at how Gill and Deeter tried to more clearly define this term. They first developed the Sport Orientation Questionnaire (SOQ) to provide a reliable and valid measure of competitiveness (1988) (see Table 7.1). Using the SOQ, they found three types of competitive orientations, all of which represent different subjective outcomes of a competitive situation.

- *Competitiveness* is an enjoyment of competition and desire to strive for success in competitive sport settings. A competitive person simply loves to compete and actively seeks competitive situations.
- *Win orientation* is a focus on interpersonal comparison and winning in competition. It is more important to beat other competitors than to improve on personal standards.
- *Goal orientation* is a focus on personal performance standards. The goal is to improve one's own performance, not to win the competition.

A person's competitive orientation affects how he or she perceives the competitive situation. For example, Gill found that males scored higher on the competitive and win orientations and females higher on goal orientation (1988). Athletes vary greatly in their competitive orientations, but Gill's study suggests that more are oriented toward improving their own performances (goal orientation) than on winning. The various orientations athletes have to the competitive situation impact how they subjectively perceive the objective competitive situation. These different orientations of course need to be considered by anyone structuring a sport program.

The personality characteristic that best predicts how people appraise the objective competitive situation is competitiveness.

Stage 3—Response

According to Martens' competitive process model, after a person appraises a situation, she decides to either approach or avoid it. The chosen response initiates the third stage of the model. If the decision is not to compete, then the response stops there. However, a response to compete can occur at the behavioral, physiological, and/or psychological levels. For example, at the behavioral level, you might decide what type of opponent you prefer to play— someone better than you, so you might improve; someone worse than you, so you can make sure you win; or someone equal to you, so you have a challenging competition. On a physiological level, your response might be that your heart starts to beat fast and your hands become cold and clammy. Several psychological factors, both internal and external, can also affect a person's response. Motivation, confidence, and perceived ability level are just a few of the internal factors affecting the response. Facilities, weather, time, and opponent ability are some external influences.

Stage 4—Consequences

The final stage of the competitive process results from comparing the athlete's response to the standard of comparison. Consequences are usually seen as being either positive or negative, and many people equate positive consequences to success and negative consequences to failure. However, as we discussed earlier, the athlete's *perception* of the consequences are more important than the objective outcome. For example, although you might have lost the game, you might still perceive the outcome as positive if you played well and met your own standard of excellence.

These feelings of success and failure do not occur in isolation: They feed back into the process and affect subsequent competitive events. A Little League baseball player who strikes out three times with runners in scoring position but who is encouraged and instructed in proper batting technique may yet improve his batting average. This should contribute to a more positive outlook in future games and change the way the player approaches the next objective competitive situation. Another player who is criticized for striking out three times might develop a more apprehensive and negative approach to future games. Modifying the rules (e.g., not keeping score) or the facilities and equipment (e.g., lowering the rim in basketball) can also influence perceptions of

success and failure. Here are some useful and appropriate modifications for young participants:

- Lower the basket in basketball
- Use smaller balls for basketball, volleyball, or football
- Do not keep score officially
- Allow a player to stay at bat until he or she hits the ball into fair territory
- Rotate positions on the team

The following case study shows how Martens' model might be applied by a junior high school physical education teacher.

Using Martens' Model

Martens' model is useful to demonstrate how competition can be enhanced or decreased during its different stages. In the objective competitive situation, for example, a person competes against some standard of excellence. Competition could be accentuated by making the standard of comparison simply beating an opponent, or it could be reduced by making the standard one's past performance. Thus, a runner's goal might be to improve her 10K time by 5 seconds instead of to finish in a certain position.

In a subjective competitive situation, a coach might manipulate the situation by emphasizing to the gymnast the importance of the competition and settling

A Case Study Demonstrating the Model of Competition

Bill is a physical education teacher at a junior high school. He has been teaching volleyball skills the past few weeks and recently the class has started to play some competitive games. Mark, who is outgoing and athletic, looks forward to the competition—he enjoys the challenge and the chance to show his classmates his skills. John, on the other hand, is shy and not very athletic. He is nervous and apprehensive about the competition because he is unsure of his skills and afraid of embarrassing himself.

Bill is aware that Mark views competition positively, whereas John would like to avoid competition at all costs (subjective competitive situation). Mark likes to compete against people as good or better than him because he sees this as a challenge, whereas if John has to compete, he likes to play against a weaker opponent so that he doesn't look too bad (response).

In a competition, Mark handles winning and losing very well because his self-esteem is not threatened if he should play poorly or his team should lose. He has succeeded often in sport, receiving supportive feedback from coaches and parents in the past. In contrast, John has experienced a lot of failure, often receiving criticism and even ridicule for his athletic endeavors. Naturally he feels threatened and apprehensive about losing or performing poorly (consequences).

Because Bill understands this process of competition and how students are different, he structures his physical education class to meet the needs of both John and Mark. Of course he tries always to be positive and encouraging to his students. He also sets up different types of learning situations and lets students choose among them. For example, on one court he sets up teams and a competition for those who seek out a challenge and enjoy the excitement of competition. On another court, the emphasis is on learning and improvement of skills, not on competing. On this court students still unsure of themselves can learn without the pressure of competition. Bill attempts to structure his physical education class so that students enjoy themselves, acquire skill, and develop a positive feeling toward sport and physical activity.

for nothing less than first place. Having parents and friends at the meet might also accentuate the importance of performing well, which would probably increase the pressure and anxiety the athlete feels. Conversely, the coach could focus on team cooperation and encourage players to give each other emotional support. The coach could tell the gymnasts to "go out and do your best—enjoy yourselves." This orientation would of course influence the gymnasts' subjective perception of the competitive situation.

It is important that administrators, coaches, and parents know how to help performers feel more successful about sport experiences. Taking a participant-centered approach by modifying rules, facilities, and equipment to provide more action, more scoring, closer games, and more personal involvement can create positive experiences for all participants.

In essence, competition is a "learned" social process (rather than being innate) influenced by the social environment (including coaches, parents, sport psychologists, etc.). Competition is inherently neither good nor bad. It is simply a process, and the quality of leadership largely determines whether it is a positive or negative experience for the participant. Thus, you should consider the many factors that can influence the relationship between the objective competitive situation, subjective competitive situation, response, and consequences of the competitive process.

Psychological Studies

People have been competing in sports for hundreds of years, but only recently have sport psychologists begun to systematically study competitive and cooperative behaviors in sport. It might be useful to review some of the classic and pioneer psychological investigations into the processes of competition and cooperation.

Triplett's Cyclists

The first experiment that investigated the effects of competition on performance was documented in 1898 by Norman Triplett (whose influence we discussed briefly in chapter 1). Triplett noted that racers showed varying performances (as measured in time) when they raced alone, with a pacer, or in competition with another racer. By consulting the records of the Racing Board of the League of American Wheelmen, he found that cyclists were faster when racing against or with another cyclist than when racing alone against the clock.

Deutsch's Puzzles

In Deutsch's classic study (1949b) college students were required to solve puzzle problems over 5 weeks under both competitive and cooperative instructions. Students in the competitive condition were told that a reward (grade in the class) would be given to the person within the group with the best average of number of puzzles solved. Students in the cooperative condition were told that they would be evaluated by their group's ranking in relation to four other groups who were also solving puzzles. In essence, the students' appraisal of the objective competitive situation was manipulated to change their subjective appraisal and evaluation of the competitive situation (to be either more competitive or cooperative). Results revealed that students in the competitive group were self-centered, directed their efforts at beating others, had closed communication, and exhibited group conflict and mistrust. Students in the cooperative group, however, communicated openly, shared information, developed friendships, and actually solved more puzzles than their competitive counterparts.

One implication from Deutsch's study is that teams work together better when they have a common goal and when reaching that goal produces similar rewards for all participants. For example, if one basketball team member is most interested in the scoring title and the others are interested in winning their division, a potentially counterproductive conflict of interests exists. Consequently, it is important for coaches to make sure that all players understand their roles and strive toward common goals. This can be accomplished by emphasizing the unique role and contribution of each team member.

In 1982, Deutsch called for a planned reduction of competitive situations in society. He had concluded from decades of research that the resolution of conflict can be accomplished by communication, coordination, shared goals, and control of threat.

Competition or Cooperation and Aggression

It's not news that a primary focus on winning and beating an opponent can produce hostility and aggression among teams. Fighting has erupted in professional and college sports that encourage contact and collision between players, such as football, hockey, and basketball. It is not the competition per se that produces the aggressive behavior and hostility. Rather, the feelings and behavior stem from the focus on doing whatever it takes to win, even when this means unfair play or injuring an opponent. In his book *They Call Me Assassin* (1980), former pro footballer Jack Tatum describes the premeditated, deliberate attempts at injuring opposing players to take them out of commission.

Helping athletes work together to strive for mutual goals and reducing the overemphasis and pressure on winning not only creates a positive social environment—it also improves performance. For example, two teammates

Reducing Competition Through Cooperation

Sherif and Sherif conducted three field experiments with 11- and 12-year-old boys in isolated camps (1969). First, two groups were formed and each was provided the opportunity to develop a strong group identity. Sport and games were a large part of the groups' activities, and teamwork and group identity were emphasized. In the next phase of the study, intergroup conflict was deliberately induced, much of it through sport competitions that emphasized a winner and a loser. In addition, refreshments were put on a camp table for a party, and one group was invited up first. The first group ate almost all the food, leaving little for the second group, which naturally felt resentful.

The third phase attempted to reduce or eliminate the hostility that the experimenters had helped to build, but the boys maintained their dislike and ill will toward each other. Finally, situations were contrived, such as repairing a leak in the camp's waterpipe and fixing a damaged food supply truck, that forced the two groups to cooperate for what the experimenters termed "superordinate goals." These situations were set up so that neither group could achieve a highly desired outcome without the help of the other group. The results of these cooperative efforts was the reduction of hostility and intergroup conflict and the development of friendships and communication between the groups. These studies underscore the critical roles that the social context and the emphasis placed on competition play in determining whether competition is beneficial and productive. Inherently, competition is neither good nor bad.

competing for a starting position might develop hostility and try to undermine each other's play (or, as suggested by figure skater Tonya Harding's involvement in the attack on Nancy Kerrigan, competition for the same spot might lead to one competitor deliberately injuring another). Or, these teammates could cooperate by trying to help each other be the best player possible because in the long run this will help the team as a whole. Two rivals might focus solely on beating each other, with no concern about how they play, as long as they win. Or, they could view each other as allies, in the sense that each plays better because of the high performance level of the other. A great performance by one spurs the other to even greater heights (this is how basketball great Magic Johnson viewed Larry Bird). Thus, the way competition is viewed by performers determines whether its impact is positive or negative.

How Do Competition and Cooperation Score?

We can see the potential negative effects of competition when we look at the relation between competition and performance. Johnson & Johnson (1985) thoroughly analyzed 122 studies conducted from 1924 to 1981 for the effects of competitive and cooperative attitudes on performance. Sixty-five studies showed that cooperation produced higher achievement and performance than competition, with only 8 studies showing the opposite. Furthermore, in 108 studies cooperation promoted higher achievement than independent or individualistic work, whereas the opposite occurred in only 6 studies. The superiority of cooperation held across a variety of tasks involving memory and the quality, accuracy, and speed of performance. It certainly appears that we should promote cooperation over competition in physical education and sport.

However, the nature of the experimental tasks in many of these studies called for a cooperative strategy over a competitive strategy. That is, because of the nature of the task, if subjects had chosen to compete, their performances would be poorer than when they cooperated. As noted earlier, it's not that competition itself produces negative consequences—it is the overemphasis on winning that is counterproductive. In fact, competitive orientations often lead to high levels of achievement in individual as well as team sports. For example, although Michael Jordan needed to cooperate with his teammates to form a unit that won three straight titles, it is generally recognized that his extremely competitive nature was what really drove him to reach the highest level of success and excellence. In essence, many situations in the world of sport and physical activity call for a blend of cooperative and competitive strategies and orientations. Finding the right mix for the specific situation is the real challenge.

Experimental Games: Prisoner's Dilemma

Psychologists have also studied competition and cooperation through the use of experimental games. The "prisoner's dilemma," based on the not-uncommon strategy of questioning more than one prisoner suspected of the same crime, is the most popular of these games. The prisoners are usually separated, and each is told that the co-conspirator has confessed to obtain an advantage in the final proceedings. Each prisoner is then urged separately to "make a deal," confess, and obtain a lighter sentence by testifying against the other.

The most advantageous thing for both prisoners to do is to maintain their innocence. However, each prisoner has to guess the behavior of the other to decide whether to cooperate with the police or to cooperate with each other. For example, if both prisoners choose not to confess, they will both spend only a short time in jail on minor charges. However, if one prisoner chooses to confess, and implicate the partner, he will get off scot-free while the partner gets the jail term.

In a sport setting, for example, two highly sought college athletes might have been recruited by means that violated NCAA regulations. One athlete has second thoughts and is told by an NCAA investigator that if he goes public with these irregularities, his penalty will be significantly reduced, but others involved will be severely punished. If he doesn't go public now, the NCAA can still pursue and prove some minor violations. Therefore, the athlete must decide whether to cooperate with his teammate in keeping their secret or with the investigator by "ratting" on his teammate.

Competitors Drawing in Cooperators.   An example of a prisoner's dilemma game using money as incentive is illustrated in Figure 7.2. In another interesting study, Kelley and Stahelski used the prisoner's dilemma to investigate how effective competitive responses were compared with cooperative ones (1970). The game was repeated several times to allow each subject the opportunity to choose competitive or cooperative responses. Subjects chose few cooperative choices (Aa), even when a competitive style of play (Bb) resulted in losses for both players. Over a period of time, the number of cooperative choices rarely reached more than 50%.

In the second part of the study, competitive players were paired with cooperative players. Over a series of games, the competitive players were able to draw their cooperative partners into competition. In essence, cooperators began by cooperating but were forced into competitive responses by their opponents. The cooperators knew they were being forced to change their style of play and compete, whereas the competitors perceived only the conflict of the game and were oblivious to the cooperative overtures being offered. It appears, then, that competitive-oriented individuals can control the nature of a competition and draw cooperative-oriented performers into competition. Kelley and Stahelski (1970) conclude that "it is simply that the competitor's experience has been severely biased or limited by his or her tendencies to be aggressive, egotistic, exploitive, and rivalistic in interpersonal relationships" (p. 86).

The Prisoner's Dilemma Experimental Game. The first player may choose *A* (the cooperative choice) or *B* (the competitive choice). His or her payoff depends on the second player's choice, which may be *a* (cooperative) or *b* (competitive). If the choices are *Aa* then both players receive $4. If they are *Ba*, then the first player receives $7 and the second player $1. Conversely, if they are *Ab*, the first player receives $1 and the second player $7. If they are *Bb*, both players receive $1. The choices with the greatest payoff for both players over repeated trials of the game are *Aa* (the cooperative choices). In fact, a feature of experimental game behavior is a large percentage of *Bb* (competitive) responses, with a competitively oriented player usually imposing his or her style upon a cooperatively oriented player to the detriment of both.

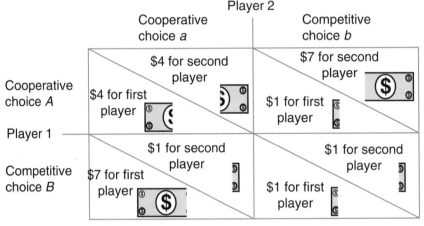

Figure 7.2 Prisoner's dilemma game.

Overcoming the Dilemma.   Usually a physical education teacher has both competitive- and cooperative-oriented students in class, and one solution is to group students according to their degree of competitiveness. In this way both competitive- and cooperative-oriented students have a chance to explore and derive satisfaction from their class experience. Another solution is to structure some activities that are best performed competitively and others that are oriented toward cooperation.

Cross-Cultural Studies of Competition and Cooperation

One way to understand how competitive and cooperative orientations are learned is to study their development in different cultures. For example, in one study (Madsen & Shapira, 1970) Anglo-American children, particularly those in urban areas, showed higher degrees of competition than Mexican children. Children raised in cooperative and sometimes communal environments, such as the kibbutz in Israel, exhibit the highest level of cooperation (Madsen & Shapira, 1977). Some studies demonstrate that the way parents reward or punish success and failure affects the development of competitive or cooperative orientations. For instance, American mothers typically were found to reward their children after success, whereas Mexican mothers typically rewarded their children after both success and failure.

The findings indicate that cultures differ in fostering competitive or cooperative attitudes. It is not enough to say that we are competitive by nature; rather the kinds of reinforcements we receive and our environment appear to be critical determinants of our attitudes. This idea is consistent with Sherif and Sherif's (1969) studies of summer camps, where the social environment and evaluations the boys received were critical in shaping their competitive or cooperative behaviors.

Is Competition Good or Bad?

As things now stand, the competitive ethic is a driving force in today's sports. You hear people say, "Competition brings out the best in us," "Without competition, even minimal productivity would disappear," and "To compete is to strive for goals and reach for success." Many Americans equate success with victory and doing well with beating somebody: They subscribe to an attitude attributed to former Green Bay Packer coach Vince Lombardi—winning isn't everything, it's the only thing. Thus, whether they call it the competitive urge, competitive spirit, or competitive ethic, many people consider this type of thinking synonymous with the American way of life.

For example, although a regular-season game in the National Football League can end in a tie (after one quarter of overtime), the Super Bowl is played out until some team finally wins. The assumption is that nobody would be satisfied with a Super Bowl that ended in a tie. We want a clear winner. Similarly, a coach's win-loss record is often the overriding criterion for his or her success. College presidents may claim that education is more important than athletics, but a coach who graduates all his players but doesn't achieve a winning record is seldom retained, much less rewarded. At the home level, some parents hold their children back a grade in school so with that extra year they can be bigger and stronger and thus more likely to achieve success in football.

The preoccupation with winning sometimes leads to cheating. One winner of the All-American Soap Box Derby was disqualified for cheating and forfeited his $7500 scholarship when officials discovered that an electromagnet gave his car an unfair starting advantage. The abuse of steroids to improve performance is also a form of cheating, highlighted by Ben Johnson's disqualification from winning the 1988 Olympic gold medal in the 100-meter dash.

Many elementary school physical education teachers complain about their overly competitive students. Some adult exercisers have trouble working at their own pace because they want to keep up with or be compared to their fitness-crazy friend. Some exercisers get caught up trying to do more than the "other guy." A growing number of experts, noting the overemphasis on winning, are proponents of cooperative sport and working together. In fact, new games have been developed that emphasize cooperation over competition (Orlick, 1978). The late tennis great Arthur Ashe says this about cultivating a cooperative mindframe:

> I associate the killer instinct with a heightened emotional state, and I would not want to be known as somebody who had it. . . . I like harmony in everything. To me, there should be harmony among the crowd, court officials, and even the ball boys. (1981, p. 176)

The potential negative effects of competition do not mean, however, that competition or competitive sport is necessarily bad or that it *causes* these negative consequences. There are also many instances where competition has produced positive, healthy outcomes. For example, author James Michener states,

> I am on the side of healthy competition. I love it. I seek it out. I prosper under its lash. I have always lived in a fiercely competitive world and

Competition is inherently neither good nor bad. It is neither a productive nor a destructive strategy—it is simply a process.

have never shied away. I live in such a world now and I would find life quite dull without the challenge. (1976)

Similarly, in his retirement speech, Magic Johnson told how much his rivalry with Larry Bird had meant to him. Magic felt he had to raise the level of his game to stay competitive with Bird. Their competition served these superstars as positive motivation to continually improve and refine their skills.

Especially in youth sport, the quality of adult leadership (e.g., parents, coaches) becomes crucial in determining whether competition positively or negatively affects young athletes. Any of you who have competed in sport know that competition can be fun, exciting, challenging, and positive. Coaches and teachers should teach youngsters when it is appropriate to compete and when it is appropriate to cooperate: An integrated approach offers the greatest opportunities for personal development and satisfaction.

Enhancing Cooperation

The positive outcomes produced by cooperative efforts are familiar to those in business, educational, and organizational settings. Yet most sports and games retain a competitive focus and most sport psychology texts emphasize the various psychological factors that enhance performance in competitive settings. Certainly, competitive sports offer positive benefits, including character development, discipline, and teamwork. With so much evidence from diverse fields of the positive effects of cooperation, however, let's look at how cooperative games might complement traditional competitive sport and physical education.

Component Structure of Games

Canadian sport psychologist Terry Orlick (1978) argues that the design of a game will largely influence the predominant behavioral response, be it competitive, individualistic, cooperative, or some combination of these. Competition

A Blend of Cooperation and Competition

We in the physical education field play a crucial role in the development of the attitudes of young athletes and sport participants. Coaches, for example, can convey a win-at-all-costs attitude that promotes unsportsmanlike and overaggressive behavior, or they can emphasize and reward fair play and skill development. One junior high school basketball coach who wanted to emphasize sportsmanship over winning gave rewards for sportsmanlike behaviors, including the biggest trophy at the end-of-year awards dinner for the player who displayed the best sportsmanship. The sportsmanship award became the most coveted award, and players worked hard during the season to win it. Cooperation enhances enjoyment of the activity, communication, and sharing of information. Often it produces superior performance to what competition yields. Consequently, focusing on cooperation as well as encouraging healthy competition in sport and physical activity appears to have many possible positive outcomes.

However, cooperation need not replace competition. We are advocating a blend of competition and cooperation in our sport and physical activity. Research has shown that competition has been emphasized to the exclusion of cooperation. The focus on winning at all costs is an imbalance that reflects the values of a large segment of our society. Sport experiences should emphasize a blending of competition and cooperation.

and cooperation are complementary relationships giving people scope to realize their unique potential in sport and physical activity. They have different potential interactions—ranging from purely cooperative to purely competitive—that are necessary to understand for a coach or exercise leader to structure a good mix of physical activities and games. Most activities can be classified into these categories, as defined by Orlick:

1. *Competitive means–competitive ends*. The goal is to beat someone else or everyone else from the outset to the end (e.g., a 100-yard race or the game King of the Mountain).

2. *Cooperative means–competitive ends*. Participants cooperate within their group but compete outside their group (e.g., soccer, basketball, football, and hockey, when team members work together and try to coordinate their movements to defeat an opponent). However, cooperation within teams (*cooperative independent means*) is not always ensured for all team members: A basketball player, for example, can hog the ball and not pass to teammates. To ensure cooperative independent means with younger athletes, a rule can be introduced, such as requiring everyone to receive a pass before a shot could be taken at the basket.

3. *Individual means–individual ends*. One or more players pursue an individual goal without cooperative or competitive interaction. Some examples might include cross-country skiing, calisthenics, and swimming.

4. *Cooperative means–individual ends*. Individuals cooperate and help each other achieve their own goals. For example, athletes can watch one another and provide feedback and cues so that both of them can improve their skills.

5. *Cooperative means–cooperative ends*. Players cooperate with each other from the outset to the end. Everybody works toward a common goal, sharing the

means as well as the ends (e.g., volleyball where the objective is to keep the ball from hitting the floor for as long as possible; each team is allowed only three hits before hitting the ball over the net, but the goal is not to make your opponents miss but to hit it over in such a way to ensure that they do *not* miss).

Philosophy of Cooperative Games

Although games that emphasize both cooperative means and cooperative ends are rare, some significant steps have been taken since the mid-1980s to develop alternatives to competitive games and sports (Orlick, 1978; Orlick, McNally, & O'Hara, 1978). Orlick argues that our competitive sport and games have become rigid, judgmental, highly organized, and excessively goal-oriented. There is little freedom from the pressure of evaluation and the psychological distress of disapproval. Many competitive sports for young athletes are designed by principles of elimination. In many sports there is only one winner and everyone else loses. This perceived failure is one reason for the large percentage of drop-outs from competitive youth sports (see chapter 24). Even worse, many young athletes are taught to delight in others' failures that enhance their own chances of victory. Children become conditioned to the importance of winning, making it more difficult to simply play for the fun of it, which is why most kids play sports in the first place. They don't learn how to help one another, be sensitive to another's feelings, or compete in a friendly, fun-filled way. The beauty of cooperative games lies in part in their versatility and adaptability (some of the benefits of unorganized sport are discussed in chapter 24). Most cooperative games require little or no equipment or money. Anyone can play, and the rules of the game can be altered to fit the specific constraints of the situation. Furthermore, through cooperation, children learn to share, empathize, and to work to get along better. The players in the game must help one another by working together as a unit, leaving no one out of the action, waiting for a chance to play. They have freedom to learn from mistakes rather than trying to hide them. This is not to say that cooperative games are inherently better than competitive ones, but that because some of the structure, goals, and outcomes differ in them, participants should have the option of choosing from a variety of physical activities.

Cooperative Games: An Example

In one study, 4-year-olds were exposed to 14 weeks of cooperative games, 2 days a week, using 12 different types of games. The children were asked to play together toward a common end rather than compete against other teams or individuals. The games were designed to tie all participants into continuous action. The responses of children playing these cooperative games were compared with children participating in regular physical education classes. Among the interesting results, children exposed to cooperative games engaged in three times as much cooperative behavior during "free play" in the gymnasium as did the control group of children who had not experienced cooperative games. Games played by children in the cooperative games group were characterized by sharing, concern for others, helping, and cooperation. Control group children tended to be centered on their own desires and making sure that they got what they needed or wanted. These differences were highlighted by comments from the teachers: "Now my kids think of everyone involved" (cooperation group); "Mine don't do that at all" (control group). "There's a definite difference in my classes. If there are not enough chairs, the children will share" (cooperation group); "If there are not enough chairs, they'll fight" (control group). "The most cooperation is visible at clean-up time. It constantly amazes me how the

majority team up and help each other. There is now no discrimination as to whether the mess is theirs or made by someone else'' (cooperation group). It is important to note that it was only during the last 6 weeks that these positive changes occurred—there were no differences during the program's first 8 weeks. This underscores the importance that such programs be systematic and carried out over time (Orlick, McNally, & O'Hara, 1978).

Cooperative Games in the Gymnasium/Playing Field

Professional educators and coaches need to foster cooperative learning in physical education classes and on sport teams, especially among young participants. Next, we suggest ways to implement cooperative games and activities into your program (see Orlick, 1978). First, it is important for coaches and physical educators to determine what they want to accomplish in their classes or on the athletic field. If having fun, learning skills, reducing stress, providing maximum participation, and enhancing social relationships are deemed important outcomes from coaches and physical educators, then integrating some cooperative games into our programs and curricula appears appropriate. This is not to say that cooperative games should be the main or only type of games taught, but they should be included to complement other activities and competitive events. Often, cooperative games require only a modification of the rules in our existing sports and games. To implement a cooperative approach to learning follow these general principles:

- maximize participation
- maximize opportunities to learn sport/movement skills
- do not keep score of games
- maximize opportunities for success
- give positive feedback

Some specific examples of rule modifications that encourage cooperation include the following:

- volleyball—the goal is to keep the ball from hitting the ground; each team still gets only three hits
- soccer—there should be at least five passes to different players before a shot on goal can be attempted
- baseball—no strikeouts or walks allowed; every batter must hit the ball into fair territory to complete an at-bat

Summary

In this chapter we have looked at the concepts of competition and cooperation and how they relate to sport and physical activity. Overwhelming evidence from psychological studies suggests that cooperative activities produce more open communication, sharing, trust, friendship, and even enhanced performance than competitive activities do. These differences were found in laboratory and field settings, as well as in a variety of experimental games. People will compete even when it is irrational to do so, and once competition breaks out it's hard to stop.

Competitors tend to dictate things and draw cooperators into competition. One good way to break the competitive cycle is through activities that require the joint pooling of resources (i.e., superordinate goals). Some cross-cultural work has indicated that the environment and reinforcement patterns of adults help shape the competitive mindset. This means that coaches and parents can influence the development of young athletes by emphasizing either the competitive or cooperative aspects of sport.

Martens developed a model of sport competition as a framework for studying the competitive process. Competition is a four-stage process relying heavily on social comparison and evaluation. By understanding the framework, you can gain a better appreciation of the determinants and consequences of competitiveness and competitive behavior. How and why people choose to compete, athletes' evaluation of competition, the different potential responses to competition, and how competition affects athletes psychologically are just some of the questions that need to be explored.

Recent research has investigated the role of cooperation in sport and physical activity. Cooperative games are a viable alternative and complement to the traditional competitive games that dominate our culture. Table 7.2 presents a summary of some of the major guidelines gleaned from the research on competition and cooperation. We can all learn a great deal through participation in competitive sports. But we must be aware that an overemphasis on competition can undermine some of the values of competitive sport. Simply put, physical educators, coaches, and parents must work together to provide athletes the most enjoyable, meaningful, and educational sport experience.

Review Questions

1. *Winning isn't everything—it's the only thing.* Do you agree? Provide examples to support your point of view.

2. Discuss some of the common themes emerging from the psychological studies on competition and cooperation and their implications for sport and physical education.

Table 7.2   Guidelines for Competition and Cooperation
Blend competition and cooperation when teaching and coaching physical skills.
Remember that competition is a process.
Individualize instruction to meet each person's needs.
Stress cooperation to produce trust and open communication.
Structure games for children to include both competitive and cooperative elements.
When competition leads to a fierce rivalry, use superordinate goals to get the groups together.
When teaching and coaching, always be aware that aggressive competition will eventually cause others to compete, even if it's irrational.
Provide positive feedback and encouragement to students and athletes regardless of the outcome of the competition.
Provide opportunities for both the learning of sport skills and the practice of these skills in competition.

3. Describe the classic field experiments by Sherif and Sherif conducted at summer camps for boys. How was competition and hostility created and finally eliminated? What implications does this have for sport competition?

4. Describe how the prisoner's dilemma game helps us understand competition and cooperation.

5. Discuss some of the findings from the cross-cultural studies on competition and cooperation and their relevance to physical education teachers and coaches.

6. Discuss Martens' definition of the objective competitive situation. Do you agree or disagree with this definition? Why? Why did Martens define competition in this way?

7. Why is the reward definition of competition inadequate for use in competitive sport environments?

8. Describe the four stages of Martens' model of competition, including examples of each stage.

9. Discuss the three different competitive orientations from the work of Gill and Deeter.

10. Compare and contrast the five different component structures of games.

11. Discuss Orlick's basic philosophy of cooperative games. Make up three games that have cooperative means and cooperative ends and explain how they are cooperative.

References

Ashe, A. (1981). *Off the court*. New York: New American Library.

Bradley, B. (1986). *Life on the run*. New York: Bantam.

Deutsch, M. (1949a). A theory of cooperation and competition. *Human Relations*, **2**, 129-152.

Deutsch, M. (1949b). An experimental study of the effects of cooperation and competition upon group process. *Human Relations*, **2**, 199-231.

Deutsch, M. (1982). Interdependence and psychological orientation. In V.J. Derlega and J. Grzelak (Eds.), *Cooperation and helping behavior*. New York: Academic.

Festinger, L.A. (1954). A theory of social comparison processes. *Human Relations*, **7**, 117-140.

Gill, D.L. (1988). Gender differences in competitive orientation and sport participation. *International Journal of Sport Psychology*, **19**, 145-159.

Gill, D.L., & Deeter, T.E. (1988). Development of the Sport Orientation Questionnaire. *Research Quarterly for Exercise and Sport*, **59**, 191-202.

Grimsley, W. (1982, June 28). "Lack of respect": Biggest problem facing pro tennis. *Vancouver Sun*, p. C3.

Johnson, D.W., & Johnson, R.T. (1985). Motivational processes in cooperative, competitive, and individualistic learning situations. In C. Ames & R. Ames (Eds.), *Research on motivation in education* (vol. 2, pp. 249-286). Orlando, FL: Academic Press.

Kelley, H.H., & Stahelski, A.J. (1970). Social interaction basis of cooperators' and competitors' beliefs about others. *Journal of Personality and Social Psychology*, **36**, 385-418.

Madsen, M.C., & Shapira, A. (1970). Cooperative and competitive behavior of urban Afro-American, Anglo-American, Mexican-American and Mexican village children. *Developmental Psychology*, **3**, 16-20.

Madsen, M.C., & Shapira, A. (1977, August). Cooperation and challenge in four cultures. *Journal of Social Psychology*, **102**(2), 189-195.

Martens, R. (1975). Social psychology and physical activity. New York: Harper & Row.

Michener, J. (1976). *Sports in America*. New York: Random House.

Orlick, T. (1978). The cooperative sports and games book. New York: Pantheon.

Orlick, T., McNally, J., & O'Hara, T. (1978). Cooperative games: Systematic analysis and cooperative impact. In F. Smoll & R.E. Smith (Eds.), *Psychological perspectives in youth sports*. New York: Hemisphere.

Sherif, M., & Sherif, C.W. (1969). *Social psychology*. New York: Harper & Row.

Tatum, J., & Kushner, B. (1980). *They call me assassin*. New York: Avon.

Triplett, N. (1898). The dynamogenic factors in pacemaking and competition. *American Journal of Psychology*, **9**, 507-533.

Feedback, Reinforcement, and Intrinsic Motivation

People thirst for feedback. An exerciser feels like a klutz and hopes for a pat on the back, some telling instruction, and a camera to capture the moment she finally gets things right. You are probably taking this course because you think you might want to help people like that exerciser make sport and physical activity a lifetime habit. To create an environment that fosters pleasure in growth and mastery, professionals use motivational techniques based on the principles of reinforcement. *Reinforcement* is the use of rewards and punishments that increase or decrease the likelihood of a similar response occurring in the future. The principles of reinforcement are among the most widely researched and accepted in psychology. Their roots are firmly grounded in the theories of behavior modification and operant conditioning. B.F. Skinner, the most widely known and outspoken behavior theorist, has argued that teaching rests entirely on the principles of reinforcement:

> Teaching is the arrangement of reinforcers under which students learn. They learn without teaching in their natural environment, but teachers

arrange special reinforcements which expedite learning, hastening the appearance of behavior which would otherwise be acquired slowly or making sure of the appearance of behavior which might otherwise never occur. (1968, pp. 64-65)

In this chapter you will learn about

▮ what reinforcement is,

▮ positive and negative ways to influence behavior,

▮ ways to use behavior modification programs in sport,

▮ intrinsic motivation and external rewards,

▮ ways to increase intrinsic motivation, and

▮ flow—a special kind of intrinsic motivation.

Principles of Reinforcement

Two basic premises underlie reinforcing behavior.

- If doing something results in a good consequence (*positive reinforcement*), people tend to try to repeat the behavior to receive additional positive consequences.
- If doing something results in an unpleasant consequence (*negative reinforcement*), people tend to try not to repeat the behavior to avoid more negative consequences.

Imagine a physical education class on soccer skills where a player makes a pass to a teammate that leads to a goal. The teacher says, "Way to pass the ball to the open man, keep up the good work!" The player would probably try to repeat that type of pass in the future to receive more praise from the coach. Now imagine a volleyball player going for a risky jump serve and hitting the ball into the net. The coach yells, "Use your head—stop trying low percentage serves!" Most likely, this player would not try this type of serve again, wanting to avoid the criticism from the coach.

Reinforcement principles are more complex than you might think, however, in the real world. Often the same reinforcer will affect two people differently. For example, reprimanding one participant in an exercise class might make her feel that she is being punished, whereas it might provide attention and recognition for another person.

A second difficulty is people cannot always repeat the reinforced behavior. For instance, a point guard in basketball scores 30 points, although his normal scoring average is 10 points a game. He receives praise and recognition from the fans and media for his high scoring output and naturally wants to repeat this behavior. However, he is a much better passer than a shooter: When he tries hard to score more points he actually hurts his team and lowers his shooting percentage because he attempts more low-percentage shots.

You must also consider all the reinforcements available to the individual, as well as how he or she values them. For example, someone in an exercise program receives great positive reinforcement from staying in shape and looking good. But because of his participation in the program he spends less time with his spouse and children, which is a negative reinforcer that outweighs the positive reinforcer, so he drops out of the program. Often, coaches, teachers, and exercise leaders are unaware of these competing motives and reinforcers.

The principles of reinforcement are complex because people

- react differently to the same reinforcement,
- are unable to repeat desired behavior, and
- receive different reinforcers in different situations.

Positive and Negative Approaches to Influencing Behavior

There are positive and negative ways to teach and coach. The positive approach, by rewarding appropriate behavior, increases the likelihood of desirable responses occurring in the future. Conversely, the negative approach focuses on punishing undesirable behaviors, which should lead to a future reduction of these inappropriate behaviors. The positive approach is designed to strengthen desired behaviors by motivating participants to perform them and by rewarding them when they occur. The negative approach, however, attempts to eliminate unwanted behaviors through punishment and criticism. Thus, the primary motivation in this approach is fear.

Most coaches combine the positive and negative approaches in attempting to motivate and teach skills to their athletes (Smith, Zane, Smoll, & Coppel, 1983). However, sport psychologists agree that the predominant approach with sport and physical activity participants should be positive. Despite this consensus, some coaches support using a negative approach that emphasizes punishment as the primary motivator (Rushall, 1983). In our society aversive measures, through punishment, are perhaps the most widespread means of controlling behavior. For example, the judicial system often uses threats of punishment to deter breaking laws. Similarly, school achievement is often prompted by a fear of failure (i.e., repeating a grade).

Punishment certainly can control and change negative behavior, and it has advocates among coaches and teachers who take a negative approach to learning and performance. Some coaches assume that by punishing athletes for making mistakes, they can eliminate these errors: If players fear making mistakes, they will try harder not to make them. Novice coaches tend to emulate their fear-oriented counterparts (especially if the coach was perceived as successful). However, successful coaches who used a negative approach usually were also masters of strategy, teaching, or technical analysis. Often these were the attributes—not their negative approach—that made them successful.

Although some coaches still use threats of punishment as their primary motivational tool, a positive approach is recommended in working with athletes.

Drawbacks of Punishment

Clear evidence suggests that punishment and criticism can help eliminate undesirable behaviors. The evidence is equally compelling, however, that these modes of teaching have serious drawbacks that can undermine the effectiveness of punishment in eliminating negative behaviors.

Punishment usually works by arousing a fear of failure. An athlete who fears failure is not motivated by and does not enjoy the fruits of victory; rather he or she is just trying to avoid the agony of defeat.

This fear of failure usually causes a decrease in performance: An athlete becomes prone to choke under pressure. This occurs because the athlete focuses more on the consequences of losing and making mistakes than on what needs

Two Sides to Motivation

Indiana basketball coach Bobby Knight has a reputation for yelling, screaming, and using physical intimidation to get his players to perform up to their potential. Knight also is known as a brilliant defensive coach and tactician. He uses his strong sense of discipline to teach fundamental basketball skills. Many of his former players have spoken about the "other side" of Coach Knight, which includes caring for his players. In fact, Knight has an excellent record for players graduating on time and is known to help them in their personal lives even after they graduate. It is probably not the fear and intimidation that makes Bobby Knight a successful coach—it is his ability to combine this discipline with other aspects of coaching.

to be done to be successful. For example, a basketball player who worries that the coach will pull her from the game if she misses a shot or turns the ball over will likely become tentative and hesitant in her play. This is counter-productive—basketball requires confidence, assertiveness, and some risk taking. Playing it safe (because you're afraid of making a mistake) ultimately leads to poor performance. In fact, research has indicated that athletes having a high fear of failure not only perform more poorly in competition but are also more likely to get injured, enjoy the sport experience less, and drop out (Orlick & Botterill, 1975; Smith & Smoll, 1983).

Using punishment can unwittingly reinforce the undesirable behavior by drawing attention to it. In some cases, criticism may be the only way a student gets attention from the teacher. Singling out a student who disrupts the class provides the student with the attention he craves. The punishment reinforces and strengthens the very behavior it was intended to eliminate.

A third problem with emphasizing punishment is that it can create an unpleasant, aversive learning environment. Negative reinforcement can produce hostility and resentment between the coach and the athletes. Over time, students and athletes may lose motivation as they become discouraged by frequent criticism. Furthermore, the undesirable behaviors may not even be eliminated; rather, they may just be suppressed when the threat of punishment is present. In many cases, individuals are not taught the correct alternative behavior but learn only how to avoid punishment. For example, an exerciser may work hard in an aerobics class when the leader is watching her but slacken off when she is not being watched. People don't reach their potential because the internal motivation to work hard all the time has not really been developed.

Drawbacks to punishment and criticism are that

- *punishment can arouse fear of failure,*
- *punishment can act as a reinforcer, and*
- *punishment can hinder the learning of skills.*

Positive Reinforcement

Sport psychologists highly recommend a positive approach to motivation to avoid the potential negative side-effects of using punishment as the primary approach. Research demonstrates that athletes who play for positive-oriented coaches like their teammates better, enjoy their athletic experience more, like their coaches more, and have greater team cohesion (Martin & Hyrcaiko, 1983). So let's examine some of the principles underlying the effective use of positive reinforcement.

Choose Effective Reinforcers

Rewards should meet the needs of those receiving them. The best way to choose rewards is to know the likes and dislikes of the people you work with. For example, a physical education teacher might have students complete a questionnaire (see Table 8.1). This feedback might help a teacher pinpoint the type of reinforcer to use for each student. Sometimes you might want to reward the entire team or class rather than a particular individual or to vary the types of rewards (it can become monotonous to receive the same reinforcement repeatedly). These rewards are classified as *extrinsic* because they come from external sources (outside the individual), such as the coach or the teacher. Another classification of rewards are considered *intrinsic* because they reside within the participant. Examples are taking pride in accomplishment and feeling competent. Although coaches, teachers, and exercise leaders cannot directly offer intrinsic rewards, they can structure the environment to promote intrinsic motivation. We will further discuss the relationship between extrinsic rewards and intrinsic motivation later in the chapter.

Table 8.1 Reward Preferences

Please answer these questions and return the questionnaire to the coach.

Social rewards

Place a check beside the kinds of approval that you like others to show.

_____ Facial signs (e.g., smiles, nods, winks)

_____ Hand and body signs (e.g., clapping hands, holding thumbs up, clasping hands overhead)

_____ Physical contact (e.g., a pat on the back, a handshake, a hug)

_____ Praise about yourself (e.g., you're smart, very helpful, a nice person)

_____ Praise about your athletic skills (e.g., you have a great throwing arm, backhand, jumpshot)

_____ Other (be specific) _____

Activity rewards

What activities would you like to do more often during practice? Explain why you would like to do them.

1. _____   3. _____

2. _____   4. _____

(Examples: Have a free swim time; shoot baskets for fun; help the coach set up equipment; help the coach score time trials; lead the group; demonstrate skills; change playing positions for fun)

Outings as rewards

Place a check beside the things you would like to do with the whole team.

_____ See a film about sports.

_____ Tour a sports museum.

_____ Have a local professional athlete visit.

_____ Go to a competition or sports event of professionals or high-ranking amateurs.

_____ Visit a practice session for professional athletes.

_____ Have a team party or dance.

_____ Other events or activities (be specific) _____

_____

Material rewards

Place a check beside the things you would like to have or own.

_____ Team sweater

_____ Trophies

_____ Team uniform

_____ Personal chart that shows your progress from week to week

_____ Team jacket

_____ Other _____

Adapted from Martin and Lumsden (1987).

Schedule and Timing of Reinforcements

Appropriate timing and frequency (that is, choosing the best time to reinforce desired behaviors and deciding how often to give rewards) can ensure that

Different Types of Reinforcers

- Social reinforcers—praise, smile, pat on the back, publicity

- Material reinforcers—trophies, medals, ribbons, T-shirts

- Activity reinforcers—playing a game rather than drilling, playing a different position, taking a trip to play another team, getting a rest

- Special outings—going to a professional game, throwing a team party, hearing a presentation from a professional athlete

rewards are effective. During the initial stages of training or skill development, desirable responses should be reinforced often, perhaps on an almost continuous schedule. A continuous schedule requires rewarding after every correct response, whereas on a partial schedule behavior is rewarded intermittently. Research has indicated that continuous feedback not only acts as a motivator but also provides the learner with information about how she is doing. However, once a particular skill or behavior has been mastered or is occurring at the desired frequency, the schedule can be gradually reduced to intermittent (Martin & Pear, 1983).

Behavior reinforced intermittently rather than continuously will persist longer in the absence of further reinforcements. Thus, although continuous reinforcement is desirable for early learning, an intermittent reinforcement schedule is better once the behavior has been mastered. Intermittent reinforcement is less time consuming and makes the behavior persist.

All things being equal, the sooner after a response that a reinforcement is provided, the more powerful the effects on behavior. This is especially true when people are learning new skills, when it is easy to lose confidence if the skill isn't performed correctly. Once someone masters a skill, it is less critical to reinforce immediately, although it is still essential that the correct behaviors be reinforced at some point.

In the early stages of learning, continuous and immediate reinforcement is desirable; in the later stages of learning, intermittent, immediate reinforcement is effective.

Select Behaviors to Reward

Choosing the proper behaviors to reward is also critical. Obviously you cannot reward someone every time he does something right. You have to decide on the most appropriate and important behaviors and concentrate on rewarding them. Many coaches and teachers tend to focus their rewards purely on the outcome of performance (e.g., winning), but there are other behaviors that could and should be reinforced, which we will now discuss.

Reward Successful Approximations.   When individuals are acquiring a new skill, especially a complex one, they inevitably make mistakes. It may take days or weeks to master the skill, which can be disappointing and frustrating for the learner. It is helpful then to reward small improvements as the skill is learned. This technique, called *shaping*, allows people to continue to improve as they get closer and closer to the desired response. Specifically, individuals are rewarded for performances that approximate the desired performance. This spurs their motivation and provides direction for what they need to do next. For example, if players are learning the overhand volleyball serve, you might first reward the proper toss, then the proper motion, then good contact, and finally the execution that puts all the parts together successfully.

With difficult skills, shape the behavior of the learner by reinforcing close approximations of the desired behavior.

Reward Performance (Not Only Outcome).   With an emphasis on winning, most coaches tend to reward based on outcome. A baseball player hits a hard line drive down the third base line, but the third baseman makes a spectacular diving catch. In his next at-bat the same batter tries to check his swing and hits the ball off the end of the bat and just over the outstretched arm of the second baseman for a base hit. Rewarding the base hit but not the out would be sending the wrong message to the player. If an individual performs the skill correctly, that's all he or she can do. The outcome is sometimes out of the player's control, so the coach should focus on the athlete's performance instead of the performance's outcome.

Reward Effort.   It is imperative that coaches and teachers recognize effort as part of performance. Not everyone can be successful in sports. When sport and exercise participants (especially youngsters) know that they will be recognized for trying new and difficult skills—and not just criticized for performing incorrectly—they do not fear trying. All they can do is try as hard as they can, and if this is recognized, then they have nothing to fear. UCLA basketball coach John Wooden encapsulates this concept of focusing on effort instead of winning:

> You cannot find a player who ever played for me at UCLA that can tell you he ever heard me mention winning a basketball game. He might say I inferred a little here and there, but I never mentioned winning. Yet the last thing that I told my players, just prior to tip-off, before we would go out on the floor was, when the game is over, I want your head up—and I know of only one way for your head to be up—and that's for you to know you did your best. . . . This means to do the best you can do. That's the best; no one can do more. . . . You made that effort.

Reward Emotional and Social Skills. With the pressure to win, it is easy to forget the importance of fair play and being a good sport. Athletes who demonstrate good sportsmanship, responsibility, judgment, and other signs of self-control and cooperation should be recognized and reinforced.

Provide Knowledge of Results

Help participants by giving them information and feedback about the accuracy and success of their movements. This type of information, called *knowledge of results*, is typically provided by a teacher or coach after the completion of a response. For example, an athletic trainer working with an injured athlete on increasing her flexibility while rehabilitating from a knee injury asks the athlete to bend her knee back as far as possible. The trainer then tells the athlete that she has improved her flexibility from 50 degrees to 55 degrees since the week before. This feedback is a form of knowledge of results.

Benefits of Knowledge of Results. Knowledge of results can benefit athletes in several ways. First, athletes can learn specifically what they have been doing incorrectly and have a benchmark for performance. Using this information they can make adjustments on subsequent attempts.

Second, the information can be a valuable reinforcement, especially when someone has done something correctly or shown improvement. As a result, the person will try to duplicate or improve that performance on the next attempt.

Finally, the knowledge of results can be motivating. Often participants are unable to detect improvement by watching their own performance, so the instructor becomes a vital source of motivation toward continued practicing.

Knowledge of results helps people improve performance by providing specific feedback regarding the correctness (or incorrectness) of their response and by enhancing their motivation.

Types of Knowledge of Results. Verbal praise, facial expressions, and pats on the back are easy, effective ways to reinforce desirable behaviors. Statements such as "Well done!," "Way to go!," "Keep up the good work!," and "That's a lot better!" can be powerful reinforcers. However, this reward becomes more effective when you identify the specific behaviors you are pleased with. For instance, a track coach might say to a sprinter, "Way to get out of the blocks—you really pushed off strongly with your legs." Or an aerobics instructor might say to a participant who is working hard, "I like the way you're pumping your arms while stepping in place." This coach and instructor have identified exactly what the participants were doing well.

Provide Contingent, Sincere Feedback

When you give feedback to athletes, students, and exercisers, it is important that the feedback be sincere and contingent on some behavior. Whether it is praise or criticism, the feedback needs to be tied to (*contingent on*) a specific behavior or set of behaviors. It would be inappropriate, for example, to tell a student in a physical education class who is having difficulty learning a new gymnastic skill, "Way to go, keep up the good work!" Rather, the feedback should be specific and tied to performance. Inform the athlete how to perform the skill correctly, such as, "Make sure you keep your chest tucked close to your body during the tumbling maneuver." Such feedback, when sincere, demonstrates that you care and are concerned with helping the learner.

Negative Reinforcement

Positive reinforcement should be the predominant way to change behavior; in fact, most researchers suggest that 80% to 90% of reinforcement should be

Guidelines for Using Punishment

- Be consistent by giving everyone the same type of punishment for breaking similar rules.

- Punish the behavior, not the person—convey to the individual that it's his or her behavior that needs to change.

- Allow athletes input in making up punishments for breaking rules.

- Do not use physical activity as a punishment.

- Make sure the punishment is not perceived as a reward, or simply as attention.

- Impose punishment impersonally—do not berate the person or yell. Simply inform him of his punishment.

- Do not punish athletes for making errors while they are playing.

- Do not embarrass individuals in front of teammates or classmates.

- Use punishment sparingly but enforce it when you use it.

positive. Although punishment has potential negative side-effects, especially if it's used too often, there are times when punishment might be necessary to eliminate unwanted behaviors.

Modifying Behavior in Sport

The systematic application of the basic principles of positive and negative reinforcement to help produce desirable behaviors and eliminate undesirable behaviors has been given various names in the sport psychology literature: contingency management (Siedentop, 1980), behavioral coaching (Martin & Lumsden, 1987), and behavior modification (Donahue, Gillis, & King, 1980).

All of these terms refer to attempts to structure the environment through the systematic use of reinforcement, especially during practice. In general, behavioral techniques are used in sport and physical activity settings to help individuals stay task oriented and motivated throughout a training period. In what follows we'll highlight a few studies that have used behavioral techniques in sport settings and then offer some guidelines for designing behavior programs.

Evaluating Behavioral Programs

The evidence to date suggests that systematic reinforcement techniques can effectively modify various behaviors including specific performance skills, coaching and teaching behaviors, and error reduction. Behavioral techniques have also successfully changed attendance at practice, sportsmanship, and team support. Some programs have effectively used behavioral techniques to increase output by swimmers in practice (McKenzie & Rushall, 1974), improve physical fitness activities (Keefe & Blumenthal, 1980), improve picking up and stacking weights (Darden & Madsen, 1972), decrease off-task behaviors of figure skaters (Hume, Martin, Gonzalez, Cracklen, & Genthon, 1985), reduce errors in tennis, football, and gymnastics (Allison & Ayllon, 1980), and help golfers keep their head still while putting (Simek & O'Brien, 1981). Let's look closely at a few examples of successful behavioral programs.

Feedback and Reinforcement in Football. The study by Komaki & Barnett is a good example of using feedback and praise to improve specific performance skills (1977). Barnett coached a Pop Warner football team and wanted to know if his players were improving in the basic offensive plays. He and Komaki targeted three specific plays run out of the wishbone offense (a formation that requires specific positioning of the running backs and quarterback) and the five players (center, quarterback, and running backs) responsible for their proper execution. They broke each play into five stages. For example, one play included (a) quarterback-center exchange, (b) quarterback–right halfback fake, (c) fullback blocking end, (d) quarterback decision to pitch or keep, and (e) quarterback action.

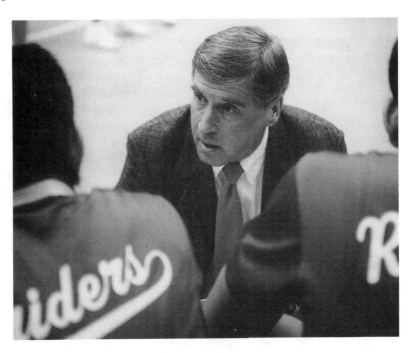

After collecting data during an initial baseline period (10 practices or games), the coach systematically reinforced and provided feedback for Play A, Play B, and Play C. This feedback included

- demonstrating the correct behaviors at each stage,
- a checklist of parts that were successfully executed, and
- praise and recognition for performing each stage correctly.

To test the effectiveness of the behavioral program, the authors compared the percentage of stages performed correctly for each play during baseline and reinforcement (about 2 weeks) periods. Correct performances increased on Play A from 62% at baseline to 82%, on Play B from 54% to 82%, and on Play C from 66% to 80%.

Recording and Shaping in Basketball.   Another behavioral program targeted both performance and nonperformance behaviors (Siedentop, 1980). A junior high school basketball coach was distressed that his players criticized each other so often in practice while failing to concentrate on shooting skills. The coach decided to award points for daily practice in layups, jump shooting, free throw drills, and for being a team player (which meant that you encouraged your teammates during play and practice). In this system, points were deducted if the coach saw an instance of a "bad attitude." An "Eagle effort board" was posted in a conspicuous place in the main hall leading to the gymnasium, and outstanding students received an "Eagle effort" award at the postseason banquet.

The program produced some dramatic changes: After just a few weeks, jump shooting improved from 37% to 51%, layups increased from 68% to 80%, and foul shooting improved from 59% to 67%. But the most dramatic improvement was in the team player category. Before implementation of the behavioral program, 4 to 6 instances of criticism were detected during each practice session, along with 10 to 12 instances of encouragement among teammates. After only a few sessions, over 80 encouraging statements were recorded during a practice

Improving Attendance—A Behavioral Approach

A swimming team was showing poor attendance and punctuality at practices. To solve the problem, the swim coach made an attendance board with each swimmer's name. She placed the board prominently on a wall by the swimming pool where everyone could see it (see Table 8.2). In the first phase of the program, swimmers who came to practice received a check on the board next to their names. In the second phase, swimmers had to show up on time to receive a check. In the final phase, swimmers had to show up on time and swim for the entire session to receive a check. Results indicated a dramatic increase in attendance at each phase of the study with increases of 45%, 63%, and 100% for the three phases, respectively (McKenzie & Rushall, 1974).

Then a public program board was developed on which swimmers could check off each lap of a programmed workout. The group increased its performance output by 27%, equivalent to an additional 619 yards for each swimmer during the practice session! The public nature of the attendance and program boards clearly served a motivational function: Every swimmer could see who was attending, who was late, who swam the entire period, and how many laps each swimmer completed. Coaches and swimmers commented that peer pressure and public recognition helped make the program successful, along with the attention, praise, and approval of coaches after swimmers' checks were posted on the board.

Table 8.2 Attendance Board

Swimmer	Show up					Show up on time					Show up on time and swim entire practice				
	M	T	W	Th	F	M	T	W	Th	F	M	T	W	Th	F
Antonio															
Marcus															
Maria															
Ken															
Othello															
Karen															
Josh															
Kira															
Kathleen															
Bob															

session. (Recorders noted there were probably more but they couldn't record all of them quickly enough!) At the end of the season the coach commented, "We were more together than I ever could have imagined."

Implementing Behavioral Programs

Clearly, behavioral techniques can produce positive changes in a variety of behaviors. As behavioral techniques are applied, the following guidelines can increase the effectiveness of intervention programs.

Target the Behaviors

When initiating a program, identify only a couple of behaviors to work with. If participants focus on changing just a couple of behaviors, they avoid being overwhelmed and confused by trying to do too much too fast. Also, it is difficult to observe simultaneously what all the participants are doing, and by tracking only one or two behaviors you can more accurately record the targeted behaviors and reinforce fairly.

Define Targeted Behaviors

Try to define behaviors in a way that makes them readily observable and easy to record. For example, number of laps, attendance, foul shooting percentage, and correct execution of a skill are relatively objective, concrete behaviors. But such behaviors as hustle and effort are more difficult to pinpoint, quantify, and measure. Individuals need to be told specifically what types of behaviors are expected of them so they can modify their behavior accordingly.

Record the Behaviors

Record observable behaviors on a checklist to give participants feedback. Coaches and teachers are usually too busy to record the behaviors in question, but often assistant coaches, managers, trainers, or teacher aides can be enlisted to help. If so, they will need to be taught how to record the behaviors.

Provide Meaningful Feedback

Detailed feedback will enhance motivation (Rushall, 1979). If someone can see a simple set of checkmarks on an easy-to-read graph that clearly displays her progress, it encourages self-praise, attention, teacher/coach praise, and knowledge of improvement that help in motivation. Public display of this feedback can stimulate peer interaction that might reinforce increased output. However, some people find this type of display embarrassing and aversive. The focus should always be on self-improvement; avoid creating unhealthy competition among teammates. A team meeting might be appropriate to help determine the exact location and nature of the public display.

State the Outcomes Clearly

Athletes and students want to be clear on what behaviors are required and what will be the result of their performing or not performing these behaviors. If being eligible to start in the next game is the reward for certain practice behaviors, the coach should clarify this along with which specific behaviors need to be demonstrated.

Tailor the Reward System

Many athletes and students are fairly well motivated already, but they need a systematic program to direct their motivation. The less motivated athletes and students are, the more they might need to initially rely on external rewards. But the strongest kind of motivation over the long haul is internal motivation, and that should always be encouraged.

Intrinsic Motivation and Extrinsic Rewards

The world of sport uses extrinsic rewards extensively. Most leagues have post-season banquets in which such awards as medals, trophies, ribbons, money, and jackets are given to participants. Elementary school teachers frequently give stickers and toys to reward good behavior in their students. Advocates of extrinsic rewards argue that rewards will increase motivation, enhance learning, and increase desire to continue participation. The systematic use of rewards can certainly produce some desired changes in behavior in sport, physical education, and exercise settings.

The Additive Approach

We know that motivation has two sources: extrinsic and intrinsic. With *extrinsic* rewards motivation comes from other people through positive and negative reinforcements. But individuals also participate in sport and physical activity for *intrinsic* reasons. Those who are intrinsically motivated strive inwardly to be competent and self-determining in their quest to master the task at hand. These people enjoy competition, like the action and excitement, focus on having fun, and want to learn skills to the best of their ability. People who participate for the love of sport and exercise would be considered intrinsically motivated, as would those who play for pride. The practical question concerns what happens when we *combine* extrinsic rewards and intrinsic motivation.

Do Extrinsic Rewards Undermine Intrinsic Motivation?

Intuitively, it seems that combining extrinsic and intrinsic motivation would produce more motivation. For instance, adding extrinsic rewards (e.g., trophies) to an activity that is intrinsically motivating (e.g., intramural volleyball) should increase motivation accordingly. Certainly you would not foresee these extrinsic rewards as *decreasing* intrinsic motivation. But let's take a further look at the effect of extrinsic rewards on intrinsic motivation.

Most early researchers and practitioners viewed intrinsic and extrinsic motivation as additive (i.e., the more the better). Some people, however, noted the undermining effect of extrinsic rewards on intrinsic motivation. For example, Albert Einstein commented about exams, "This coercion had such a deterring effect that, after I passed the final examination, I found the consideration of any scientific problems distasteful to me for an entire year" (Bernstein, 1973, p. 88). When people see themselves as the cause of their behavior, they consider themselves intrinsically motivated. Conversely, when people perceive the cause of their behavior external to themselves (i.e., I did it for the money), they consider themselves extrinsically motivated. And, often, the more an individual is extrinsically motivated, the less he or she will be intrinsically motivated (deCharms, 1968).

What Does Research Say?

Researchers as well as theorists began in the late 1960s to systematically test the relationship between extrinsic rewards and intrinsic motivation. Edward Deci used a Parker Brothers game called SOMA, which is composed of many different shaped blocks that can be arranged to form various patterns (1971, 1972). Half the subjects (college students) were offered one dollar for each of the three puzzles they were able to solve in the allotted time, whereas the other half worked on the same puzzles with no mention of reward. After the subjects completed the three puzzles, the experimenter left the room and observed

Undermining Intrinsic Motivation

An old man lived in the country on a farm. He wanted to live in peace and quiet but some youngsters kept coming to play baseball on his beautiful lot and made a lot of noise to boot. After continually chasing them from his property, the old man decided on a different tactic. The next day, when the kids came around, instead of chasing them off, he asked to talk to them. He said that he was kind of lonely and actually enjoyed the kids coming around to play baseball, making noise and having lots of fun. So he offered to pay each child 25 cents every time they played baseball on his property. The kids thought this was too good to be true—to actually be paid for playing baseball! After a couple of days of this, the old man came out and apologized to the kids, explaining that he didn't have enough money to pay them each a quarter (he was living only on social security), but he would gladly pay them 15 cents. The kids still thought this was great, but the old man had to reduce it a few days later to 10 cents. Finally, after a few more days, he told the kids that he could pay them only 5 cents. The indignant kids responded, "Who do you think we are? We're not going to play in your yard for only a nickel!" And they went off in a huff, never to return.

Being paid for working on an intrinsically interesting activity can decrease a person's intrinsic motivation for the activity.

through a one-way mirror the subjects' willingness to work on the puzzle during an 8-minute break. Interesting magazines were on the table in front of them along with the puzzles. Thus, the amount of time spent working on the puzzle during the free session was Deci's measure of intrinsic interest in the task. The subjects receiving a reward spent significantly less free time (106 seconds) working on the puzzles than did subjects receiving no reward (206 seconds).

In a later study called "Turning Play Into Work," Lepper and Greene (1975) used nursery school children as subjects and selected an activity that was intrinsically motivating for these children—drawing with felt pens. Each child was asked to draw in one of three reward conditions. In the "expected reward" condition, the children agreed to draw a picture in order to receive a Good Player certificate. In the "unexpected reward" condition, the award was given to unsuspecting children after they completed the task. In the "no-reward" condition, the children neither anticipated nor received an award. One week later, the children were unobtrusively observed for their interest in the same activity in a free-choice situation. The children who drew with the felt pen for expected rewards showed a drop in intrinsic motivation, whereas the other two groups continued to use the felt pens just as much as they had before the experiment. When the expected reward was removed, the prime reason for the first group's using the felt pen was also removed, although they were initially intrinsically motivated to use the felt pen (Lepper, Greene, & Nisbett, 1973). This study demonstrates potential long-term effects of extrinsic rewards and the importance of studying how the reward is administered.

How rewards are perceived by the recipient is critical in determining whether they will increase or decrease intrinsic motivation.

Cognitive Evaluation Theory

To help explain the potential differential effects of rewards on intrinsic motivation, Deci and his colleagues developed a useful conceptual approach called *cognitive evaluation theory* (Deci, 1975; Deci & Ryan, 1985). The theory asserts that there are two processes by which extrinsic rewards can affect intrinsic motivation. One process is termed *controlling* and produces a decrease in intrinsic motivation. The other process is termed *informational* and can cause either an increase or a decrease in intrinsic motivation, depending on the type of information.

Controlling Aspect

People feel a direct conflict between being controlled by someone's use of rewards and their needs for self-determination. That is, people who are intrinsically motivated feel they do things because they *want* to rather than for external reward. When people feel controlled by a reward (e.g., I'm only playing because of the money), the reason for their behavior resides outside of themselves. In the story about the kids playing baseball on the farmer's property, they were originally intrinsically motivated to play baseball just for the fun of it. But their intrinsic motivation turned to extrinsic motivation when money was introduced. In a sense, they were controlled by the money as it became the major reason for playing instead of just for enjoyment.

Informational Aspect

The informational aspect affects intrinsic motivation by altering how competent someone feels. When a person receives a reward for achievement, such as the most valuable player award, this provides positive information of competence and should lead to increased intrinsic motivation. In essence, for rewards to enhance intrinsic motivation, they should be contingent on specific levels of performance or behavior. However, negative information (striving for an award but not receiving it) will decrease feelings of competence and lower intrinsic motivation.

Controlling Versus Informational Aspects of Reward

In the cognitive evaluation theory, every reward potentially has both controlling and informational aspects. How the reward will affect intrinsic motivation depends on whether the recipient perceives it to be more controlling or more informational. For example, on the surface, recognizing individuals or teams with trophies seems to be positive. However, although the reward's message seems to be about the athletes' competence, the players may perceive that the coach is giving them these rewards to control their behavior (i.e., make sure they don't join another team next year). It is the message behind the reward that is crucial: It must be made clear to the athlete that the reward provides positive information about her competence and is not meant to control her behavior.

Consider how young athletes sometimes feel that they must excel to satisfy their parents. Parents who derive vicarious satisfaction from their children's athletic accomplishments frequently pressure their children to win at all costs. The controlling aspect of athletic awards becomes more obvious than the informational aspect as the young athletes perceive the need to win trophies to satisfy their parents' vicarious needs.

- Rewards that are perceived to control a person's behavior or that provide information suggesting that he or she is not competent *decrease* intrinsic motivation.
- Rewards that emphasize the informational aspect and provide positive feedback about competence *increase* intrinsic motivation.

How Extrinsic Rewards Affect Intrinsic Motivation in Sport

External rewards have potential drawbacks. Richard Todd, NFL quarterback, described the enthusiasm of his former University of Alabama team: "It was fun for those fellows. They were not getting paid for it." Magic Johnson was once asked if he received any outrageous offers while being recruited by various college basketball teams. He responded, "I received my share of offers for cars and money. It immediately turned me off. It was like they were trying to buy me, and I don't like anyone trying to buy me." Notice that what Magic Johnson was really referring to was the controlling aspect of rewards. He did not like anyone trying to control him through bribes and other extrinsic incentives. Although what these athletes have to say implies that rewards may undermine intrinsic motivation in sport, let's take a look at what some of the research has found.

Scholarships

One of the first assessments of how extrinsic rewards affect intrinsic motivation in a sport setting was Dean Ryan's study of scholarship and nonscholarship collegiate football players (1977, 1980). Players on scholarship reported that they were enjoying football less than their nonscholarship counterparts. Moreover, scholarship football players exhibited less intrinsic motivation every year they held their scholarship, so their lowest level of enjoyment occurred during their senior year. Ryan later surveyed male and female athletes from different schools in a variety of sports (1980). Again, scholarship players reported less intrinsic motivation than nonscholarship players. However, male wrestlers on scholarship and female athletes on scholarship from six different sports reported higher levels of intrinsic motivation than those who were not on scholarship.

These results can be explained by the distinction between the controlling and informational aspects in rewards. Scholarships can have an informational function—they tell athletes that they are good. This would be especially informative to wrestlers and women, who receive far fewer scholarships than other athletes. Remember that in 1980, few athletic scholarships were available to women and wrestlers. Compare this with some 80 scholarships awarded to Division I football teams, which would make the informational aspect of receiving a football scholarship less positive confirmation of outstanding competence.

Football is the prime revenue-producing sport for most universities. Look at how football scholarships are sometimes used. Some coaches use the scholarship as leverage to control the player's behavior. Players often feel they have to perform well or lose their scholarships. Sometimes players who are not performing up to the coaches' expectations are made to participate in distasteful drills. Some athletes say that coaches holding scholarships over their heads turn what used to be play into work. Under these conditions, the scholarship's controlling aspect is more important than its informational aspect, which evidently decreases intrinsic motivation among these scholarship players.

> Athletic scholarships can either decrease or increase athletes' level of intrinsic motivation, depending on which is more emphasized—the controlling or the informational aspect.

Success and Failure

Competitive success and failure can also affect intrinsic motivation. By manipulating subjects' perceived success and failure on a motor task, Weinberg and his colleagues revealed that people had higher levels of intrinsic motivation after success than after failure (Weinberg, 1979; Weinberg & Jackson, 1979; Weinberg & Ragan, 1979). Success and failure have high informational value in competition, and males exhibited significantly higher levels of intrinsic motivation after success than after failure. In contrast, females did not vary much across success and failure conditions, which suggests that competitive success is more important for males than for females (Deaux, 1977). When males succeed, they feel good and exhibit high intrinsic interest in the task, but when they lose, they quickly lose interest and intrinsic motivation decreases. Females do not appear to be as threatened as males by the information contained in competitive failure, likely because their egos are not typically as invested in display success as are their male counterparts. A study on young hockey players performing a balance task also showed that positive feedback increased feelings of competence, which in turn increased intrinsic motivation, whereas the reverse proved true for negative feedback (Vallerand, 1983; Vallerand & Reid, 1984).

> Competitive success tends to increase intrinsic motivation, whereas competitive failure tends to decrease intrinsic motivation.

We tend generally to focus on who won or lost a competition, which represents the *objective* outcome. However, sometimes you play well but still lose to a superior opponent, whereas other times you play poorly but still win because of a weak opponent. These *subjective* outcomes also appear to determine an athlete's intrinsic motivation. People who perceive that they performed well show higher levels of intrinsic motivation than those with lower perceptions of success (McAuley and Tammen, 1989). Winning and losing are less important in determining intrinsic motivation than is how well people perceive (subjectively) they performed. The old adage, "it's not whether you win or lose, but how you play the game" applies in determining a performance's effect on intrinsic motivation. In fact, coaches and parents can enhance the intrinsic motivation of young athletes by providing subjective feedback focusing on what they did well, despite an objective loss.

Increasing Intrinsic Motivation

Rewards do not inherently undermine intrinsic motivation. It is the job of coaches, physical educators, and exercise leaders to structure and use rewards (as well as other strategies) in ways that increase perceptions of success and, by extension, the intrinsic motivation of the participants. Here are some suggestions for increasing intrinsic motivation. For each one, analyze how the process leads from the structuring or use of rewards to a participant's getting information that leads to a perception of competence, which in turn leads to greater intrinsic motivation.

• *Provide for Successful Experiences*. Perceived success strengthens feelings of personal competence. For example, lowering the basket for young basketball players and structuring practice to provide successful experiences will enhance feelings of competence. Similarly, give positive feedback about what young athletes are doing right.

• *Give Rewards Contingent on Performance*. Tie rewards to the performance of specific behaviors to increase their informational value. Rewarding based on proper execution of plays, good sportsmanship, helping other teammates, or mastering a new skill provides information about the individual's competence. You should make clear to the participants that the rewards are specifically for doing things well and that you are not trying to control them in any way. Emphasize the informational aspect of the rewards.

• *Use Verbal and Nonverbal Praise*. Many people forget how powerful praise can be. Praise provides positive feedback and helps athletes continue to strive to improve. This is especially important for athletes who are second string and get little recognition and for students who are not particularly skilled in sport and physical activity. For example, overweight participants in an exercise class need plenty of positive feedback to stay motivated and feel good about themselves. A simple pat on the back or "good job" can acknowledge each athlete's contribution to the team or achievement of a personal goal.

• *Vary Content and Sequence of Practice Drills*. As you likely know, practices in sport and exercise can get tedious and boring. One way to break the monotony and maintain motivation levels is to vary the kinds of drills and how they are sequenced. Such variety can also give young athletes an opportunity to try new positions or assignments. They not only have more fun but gain an awareness and appreciation of the demands of different positions and of their abilities to handle them. Similarly, exercise leaders should strive to vary the content

and format of their classes to keep motivation high (dropout rates in exercise programs all too frequently reach over 50%).

- *Involve Participants in Decision Making.* Allow participants more responsibility for making decisions and rules. Doing so will increase their perception of control and lead to feelings of personal accomplishment. For example, they might suggest how to organize a practice session, make up team or class rules, establish a dress code, or, if they are ready, proceed with game strategy. They might plan a new or innovative drill for practice. People perceive they have greater competency when they are active in the learning process.

- *Set Realistic Performance Goals.* Not all participants are highly skilled or will be winners in competition. However, people can learn to set realistic goals based on their own abilities. These goals need not be based on objective performance outcomes; rather, they might be in terms of minutes played, keeping emotional control, or simply improving over a previous performance. Performance goals based on a personal level of performance (e.g., to improve your time in the mile run from 4:33 to 4:25) leave participants in control of their performance (i.e., they don't depend on how well an opponent plays) and make success more likely. In turn, reaching performance goals is a sign of competence that affects motivation positively. A more detailed discussion of how to set goals is presented in chapter 17.

Flow—A Special Case of Intrinsic Motivation

Some of the most innovative studies of enhancing intrinsic motivation come from the work of Mihalyi Csikszentmihalyi (1975). Whereas many researchers have tried to determine which factors undermine intrinsic motivation, Csikszentmihalyi investigated exactly what makes a task intrinsically motivating. He examined rock climbing, dancing, chess, music, and amateur athletics—all activities that people do with great intensity but usually for little or no external reward. He determined common elements that make these activities intrinsically interesting.

Csikszentmihalyi calls the holistic sensation people feel when they are totally involved, or on automatic pilot, *flow*. He argues that the flow experience occurs when your skills are equal to your challenge. Intrinsic motivation is at its highest and maximum performance is achieved. However, if the task demands are greater than your capabilities, you become anxious and perform poorly. Conversely, if your skills are greater than the challenges of the task, you become bored and perform less well.

Note in Figure 8.1 that flow is obtained when both capabilities (skills) and challenge are high. For example, if an athlete has a high skill level and the opponent is also highly skilled (e.g., high challenge), then the athlete may achieve flow. But if an athlete with less ability is matched against a strong opponent (high challenge), it will produce anxiety. Combining low skills and low challenge results in apathy, whereas high skills and low challenge results in boredom. By structuring exercise classes, PE, and competitive sports to be challenging and creative, you foster better performance, rich experiences, and longer involvement in physical activity.

How Do People Achieve Flow?

Coaches and teachers, if they knew how, would likely want to help students and athletes achieve this narrow framework of flow. If so, the logical question

Essential Elements of Flow

- *Complete absorption in the activity*
  "The court—that's all that matters. . . . Sometimes I think of a problem, like fighting with my girlfriend, and I think that's nothing compared to the game. You can think about a problem all day but as soon as you get in the game, the hell with it. . . . When you're playing basketball, that's all that's on your mind."

- *Merging of action and awareness*
  You are aware of your actions but not of the awareness itself. "The only thing that goes through my mind is performing well. I really don't have to think, though. When I'm playing [volleyball], it just comes to me. It's a good feeling. And when you're on a roll, you don't think about it at all. If you step back and think why you are so hot, all of a sudden you get creamed."

- *Loss of self-consciousness*
  "[In rock climbing] one tends to get immersed in what is going on around him, in the rock, in the moves that are involved . . . search for handholds . . . proper position of the body—so involved he might lose the consciousness of his own identity and melt into the rock."

- *A sense of control*
  You are not actively aware of control; rather, you are simply not worried by the possibility of lack of control. "At times when I have super concentration in a [racquetball] game, nothing else exists—nothing except the act of participating and swinging at the ball. The other player must be there to play the game, but I'm not concerned with him. I'm not competing with him at that point. I'm attempting to place the ball in the perfect spot, and it has no bearing on winning and losing."

- *No goals or rewards external to the activity*
  You participate purely because of the activity itself, without seeking any other reward. "The most rewarding part [of chess] is the competition, the satisfaction of pitting your mental prowess against someone else. . . . I've won trophies and money, but considering expenses of entry fees, chess association, et cetera, I'm usually on the losing side financially."

- *Effortless movement*
  "It was just one of those programs that clicked. It's just such a rush, like you feel it could go on and on and on, like you don't want it to stop because it's going so well. It's almost as though you don't have to think, it's like everything goes automatically without thinking. It's like you're in automatic pilot, so you don't have any thoughts."

is, how does one get into a flow state? Research with figure skaters (Jackson, 1992) found that the following factors were most important for getting into flow:

- *Positive mental attitude.* Confidence, positive thinking, and high motivation helped the skaters achieve flow. The fact that you've self-talked being positive with yourself to actually be able to say to yourself, "This is what I want to do, this is what I have to do to do it" . . . it has to do with this feeling internally like nothing is going to stop you from getting what you want (Jackson, 1992, p. 171).

- *Positive precompetitive and competitive affect.* Being relaxed, controlling anxiety, and enjoying the activity contribute to flow. Several athletes reported finding a balance between calmness and arousal. As one skater said, "Relaxation and confidence, but you have to be on edge, you can't be too relaxed. You have to be concerned about something" (Jackson, 1992, p. 171).

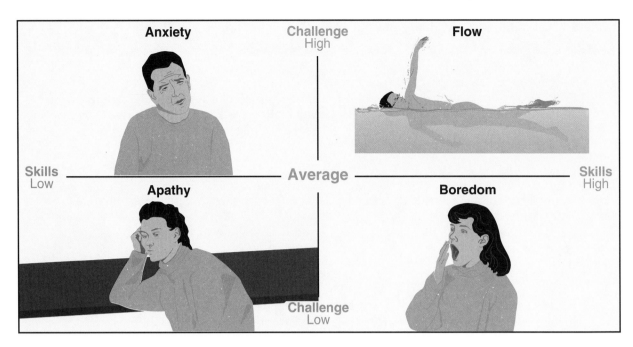

Figure 8.1   A flow model. Adapted from Kimiecik and Stein (1992).

• *Maintaining appropriate focus.* Keeping a narrow focus, staying in the present, focusing before the performance, and focusing on key points in one's program. One skater described the positive result of focusing fully on the upcoming performance. "The fact that you're so focused, you're able to concentrate easily" (Jackson, 1992, p. 172).

• *Physical readiness.* Having done the necessary training/preparation beforehand, working hard, and feeling that you are physically ready and able to have good practice sessions before competing.

Can individuals control these thoughts and feelings? The figure skaters Jackson interviewed expressed varied beliefs, ranging from flow being controllable to the opposite:

> Yeah, I think you can increase it. It's not a conscious effort. If you try to do it, it's not going to work. I don't think it's something you can turn on and off like a light switch. (Jackson, 1992, p. 174)

How to Increase the Chances of Flow Occurring

• Be well trained

• Maintain appropriate focus

• Enjoy the activity at hand

• Keep confident and think positive

• Channel energies and stay relaxed

Factors Preventing or Disrupting Flow

Although it's important to understand how to enhance the likelihood of flow occurring, it is equally important to understand what factors may prevent or disrupt it (Jackson, 1992). These factors include the following:

- *Physical problems/mistakes*—Injuries, mistakes, and fatigue
- *Inability to maintain focus*—Losing concentration, distractions, surprises, or interruptions before or during performance
- *Negative mental attitude*—Negative self-talk, self-critical attitude, and not believing in yourself

Flow doesn't just happen. Rather, your mental and physical state and your environmental influences seem to interact to make it more or less likely that flow will actually occur. Professionals can try to structure the environment and provide feedback to maximize the possibility of athletes reaching and maintaining a flow state. However, participants themselves also need to be aware of the factors that influence the occurrence of the flow state (see Table 8.3) and mentally and physically prepare for competition and physical activity accordingly.

Table 8.3 Factors That Facilitate and Disrupt Flow States

Factors facilitating flow	Factors disrupting flow

Positive mental attitude
  Confidence
  Positive thinking
  High motivation
	Physical problems/mistakes
	  Physical problems
	  Mistakes by self
	  Mistakes by partner

Positive competitive affect
  Being relaxed
  Controlling anxiety
  Enjoying what you are doing
	Inability to maintain focus
	  Losing concentration
	  Distractions
	  Interruptions

Maintaining appropriate focus
  Staying in the present
  Very narrow focus
  Focusing on key points
	Negative mental attitude
	  Negative self-talk
	  Doubting self
	  Self-critical attitude

Physical readiness
  Being well trained
  Working hard
  Being well prepared	

Summary

We have learned that both extrinsic and intrinsic motivation have great importance to skill performance and behavior change. We discussed two basic approaches to reinforcement: positive control and negative control. A positive approach is recommended, although punishment is sometimes necessary to change behavior. Rewards and punishments in the form of behavioral intervention programs can be systematically used in sport and exercise contexts to enhance motivation.

We discussed the potential undermining effects extrinsic rewards have on intrinsic motivation. Cognitive evaluation theory has demonstrated that extrinsic rewards can either increase or decrease intrinsic motivation, depending on whether the reward is more informational or controlling. Examples of the effect of extrinsic incentives on intrinsic motivation in sport such as scholarships and winning and losing were explored. We learned that different strategies can enhance intrinsic motivation and that the special state of *flow* is the epitome of intrinsic motivation.

Review Questions

1. Discuss the two principles of reinforcement and why they are more complex than they first appear.

2. Discuss the differences between the positive and negative approaches to teaching and coaching. Based on the research, which one is more beneficial and why?

3. Discuss three of the potential negative side-effects of using punishment.

4. Discuss the different types of reinforcers along with the effectiveness of continuous and intermittent reinforcement schedules.

5. Discuss three things other than success that a coach or physical educator can reinforce.

6. Discuss what you believe to be the three most important guidelines for implementing behavioral programs in sport and exercise settings.

7. For an individual who is intrinsically motivated, the introduction of extrinsic rewards will increase motivation. Discuss the accuracy of this statement and why you agree or disagree.

8. Discuss cognitive evaluation theory as a way to help explain the relation between extrinsic rewards and intrinsic motivation. Compare the informational versus the controlling aspect of rewards.

9. Discuss the results of Ryan's studies on scholarships and intrinsic motivation. What are the implications of the findings?

10. Explain the effects of success and failure on intrinsic motivation, including findings from research studies. What implications do these findings have for the practitioner?

11. Discuss three ways to increase intrinsic motivation.

12. Discuss the concept of flow. What are its major characteristics? In what sort of activity is flow most likely to occur?

13. Discuss three factors that help people get into flow and three barriers that inhibit it.

References

Allison, M.G., & Ayllon, T. (1980). Behavioral coaching in the development of skills in football, gymnastics, and tennis. *Journal of Applied Behavior Analysis*, **13**, 297-314.

Bernstein, F. (1973, March 16). *The New Yorker*, pp. 87-88.

Csikszentmihalyi, M. (1975). *Beyond boredom and anxiety.* San Francisco: Jossey-Bass.

Darden, E., & Madsen, C.H. (1972). Behavior modification for weightlifting room problems. *College Student Journal,* **6,** 95-99.

Deaux, K. (1977). Sex differences in social behavior. In T. Blass (Ed.), *Personality variables in social behavior.* Hillsdale, NJ: Erlbaum.

deCharms, R. (1968). *Personal causation.* New York: Academic Press.

Deci, E.L. (1971). Effects of externally mediated rewards on intrinsic motivation. *Journal of Personality and Social Psychology,* **18,** 105-115.

Deci, E.L. (1972). The effects of contingent and noncontingent rewards and controls on intrinsic motivation. *Organizational Behavior and Human Performance,* **8,** 217-229.

Deci, E.L. (1975). *Intrinsic motivation.* New York: Plenum.

Deci, E.L., & Ryan, R.M. (1985). *Intrinsic motivation and self-determination in human behavior.* New York: Plenum.

Donahue, J.A., Gillis, J.H., & King, H. (1980). Behavior modification in sport and physical education: A review. *Journal of Sport Psychology,* **2,** 311-328.

Hume, K.M., Martin, G.L., Gonzalez, P., Cracklen, C., & Genthon, S. (1985). A self-monitoring feedback package for improving freestyle figure skating practice behaviors. *Journal of Sport Psychology,* **7,** 333-345.

Jackson, S. (1992). Athletes in flow: A qualitative investigation of flow states in elite figure skaters. *Journal of Applied Sport Psychology,* **4,** 161-180.

Keefe, F.J., & Blumenthal, A.J. (1980). The life fitness program: A behavioral approach to making exercise a habit. *Journal of Behavior Therapy and Experimental Psychiatry,* **11,** 31-34.

Komaki, J., & Barnett, F. (1977). A behavioral approach to coaching football: Improving the play execution of the offensive backfield on a youth football team. *Journal of Applied Behavioral Analysis,* **10,** 657-664.

Lepper, M.R., & Greene, D. (1975). Turning play into work: Effects of adult surveillance and extrinsic rewards on children's intrinsic motivation. *Journal of Personality and Social Psychology,* **31,** 479-486.

Lepper, M.R., Greene, D., & Nisbett, R.E. (1973). Undermining children's intrinsic interest with extrinsic rewards: A test of the overjustification hypothesis. *Journal of Personality and Social Psychology,* **28,** 129-137.

Martin, F., & Lumsden, J. (1987). *Coaching: An effective behavioral approach.* St. Louis: Times Mirror Mosby.

Martin, G.L., & Hrycaiko, D. (1983). *Behavior modification and coaching: Principles, procedures, and research.* Springfield, IL: Charles C. Thomas.

Martin, G.L., & Pear, J.J. (1983). *Behavior modification: What it is and how to do it* (2nd ed.) Englewood Cliffs, NJ: Prentice-Hall.

McAuley, E., & Tammen, V.V. (1989). The effects of subjective and objective competitive outcomes on intrinsic motivation. *Journal of Sport & Exercise Psychology,* **11,** 84-93.

McKenzie, T.L., & Rushall, B.S. (1974). Effects of self-recording on attendance and performance in a competitive swimming training environment. *Journal of Applied Behavior Analysis,* **7,** 199-206.

Orlick, T.D., & Botterill, C. (1975). *Every kid can win.* Chicago: Nelson-Hall.

Rushall, B.S. (1979). *Psyching in sports.* London: Pelham.

Rushall, B.S. (1983). Coaching styles: A preliminary investigation. In G.L. Martin and D. Hrycaiko (Eds.), *Behavior modification and coaching: Principles, procedures, and research* (pp. 299-320). Springfield, IL: Charles C. Thomas.

Ryan, E.D. (1977). Attribution, intrinsic motivation, and athletics. In L.I. Gedvilas & M.E. Kneer (Eds.), *Proceedings of the NAPECW/NCPEAM National Conference* (pp. 346-353). Chicago: Office of Publications Services, University of Illinois at Chicago Circle.

Ryan, E.D. (1980). Attribution, intrinsic motivation, and athletics: A replication and extension. In C.H. Nadeau, W.R. Halliwell, K.M. Newell, & G.C. Roberts (Eds.), *Psychology of motor behavior and sport—1979* (pp. 19-26). Champaign, IL: Human Kinetics.

Siedentop, D. (1980). The management of practice behavior. In W.F. Straub (Ed.), *Sport psychology: An analysis of athletic behavior*. Ithaca, NY: Mouvement Publications.

Simek, T.C., & O'Brien, R.M. (1981). *Total golf: A behavioral approach to lowering your score and getting more out of your game*. Huntington, NY: B-Mod Associates.

Skinner, B.F. (1968). *The technology of teaching*. New York: Appleton-Century-Crofts.

Smith, R.E., & Smoll, F.L. (1983). Psychological stress in youth sports: Sources, effects, and intervention strategies. In N.J. Smith (Ed.), *Sports medicine: Health care for young athletes*. Evanston, IL: American Academy of Pediatrics.

Smith, R.E., Zane, N.W.S., Smoll, F.L., & Coppel, D.B. (1983). Behavioral assessment in youth sports: Coaching behaviors and children's attitudes. *Medicine and Science in Sports and Exercise*, **15**, 208-214.

Vallerand, R.J. (1983). Effect of differential amounts of positive verbal feedback on the intrinsic motivation of male hockey players. *Journal of Sport Psychology*, **5**, 100-107.

Vallerand, R.J., & Reid, G. (1984). On the causal effects of perceived competence on intrinsic motivation: A test of cognitive evaluation theory. *Journal of Sport Psychology*, **6**, 94-102.

Weinberg, R.S. (1979). Intrinsic motivation in a competitive setting. *Medicine and Science in Sport*, **11**, 146-149.

Weinberg, R.S., & Jackson, A. (1979). Competition of extrinsic rewards: Effect on intrinsic motivation and attribution. *Research Quarterly*, **50**, 494-502.

Weinberg, R.S., & Ragan, J. (1979). Effects of competition, success/failure, and sex on intrinsic motivation. *Research Quarterly*, **50**, 503-510.

PART

IV

Understanding Group Processes

This part consists of four chapters, all focusing on group interaction. Group issues are especially important to professionals in our field because of the amount of time we spend working in or with groups. In chapter 9, Group and Team Dynamics, you'll learn how groups are formed and how they function. Chapter 10, Group Cohesion, examines whether a tight-knit (cohesive) group is necessary for optimal performance and discusses ways to develop cohesion.

This part's final two chapters focus on leadership (chapter 11) and communication (chapter 12). Groups do not thrive unless someone exerts leadership, and effective leadership requires effective communication. You'll learn the essentials of good communication and leadership and ways to build these skills in others.

CHAPTER 60

Group and Team Dynamics

Inside or outside of sport, people tend to act among others differently from how they act alone. The study of group dynamics can be fascinating and of course has its applications to sport and exercise. Most sport activities, even so-called individual sports, require groups or teams. Competition almost always involves more than one person. Other forums for group physical activities include exercise groups, fitness clubs, and physical education classes. Almost any position in the sport and exercise field requires the understanding of the processes and dynamics of groups.

In this chapter you will learn about

▌ what makes up a group,

▌ how a group becomes a team,

▌ how groups are structured,

▌ how to develop an effective team climate, and

▌ maximizing individual performance in team sports.

The importance of understanding and studying group behavior is underscored by a quote from Cartwright and Zander's classic text on group dynamics, *Group Dynamics: Research and Theory* (1968):

> Whether one wishes to understand or improve human behavior, it is necessary to know a great deal about the nature of groups. Neither a coherent view of people nor an advanced social technology is possible without dependable answers to a host of questions concerning the operation of groups, how individuals relate to groups, and how groups relate to larger society.

We can readily apply this statement to sport and physical activity. To understand behavior in sport and physical activity, we have to understand the nature of sport and exercise groups. We'll begin by defining what we mean by the term "group."

What Is a Group?

Distinguishing characteristics of sport/exercise groups:

- A collective identity
- A sense of shared purpose or objectives
- Structured modes of communication
- Personal and/or task interdependence
- Interpersonal attraction

You may think it's easy to define what a group is, but it can be quite complex. For example, a football team, badminton class, karate club, and exercise class might all be considered groups. But what about several people meeting at noon to play basketball or getting together to go to the volleyball game on Thursday nights? A collection of individuals is not necessarily a group.

The key defining characteristic of a group is the *interaction* among members. Group members have to depend on each other and share common goals. There need to be feelings of interpersonal attraction among group members and open lines of communication. Groups also exhibit task interdependence—they must interact to get the job done. For example, players on a football team must interact on offense and defense, depending on each other to do specific tasks. Most importantly, a group needs a feeling of collective identity where members view the group as a unit unto itself, distinguishable from other groups. When we think about sport teams, what usually comes to mind is a group of athletes working together to achieve their individual and collective goals.

How a Group Becomes a Team

A group of athletes does not necessarily form a team. Becoming a team is really an evolutionary process. In fact, groups go through a four-stage developmental sequence to move from a mere collection of individuals to a team (Tuckman, 1965). Although the duration of each stage might vary for different groups, the sequence they follow is invariable in the process of team development. These four stages include:

- Forming
- Storming
- Norming
- Performing

Forming

In this first stage of team development, team members familiarize themselves with other team members. Individuals try to determine if they belong in the group and, if so, in what role. After each athlete has found her place within the structure of the team, interpersonal relationships are formed and tested, including relationships between leaders (i.e., coaches) and team members. Athletes lacking a strong team identification will have difficulty forming positive relationships with other team members. Coaches can help by developing strategies to ease team interaction.

Storming

The second stage of team formation, storming, is characterized by rebellion against the leader, resistance to control by the group, and interpersonal conflict. Infighting occurs as individuals and the leader establish their roles and status within the group. This conflict can extend to the physical; fights and other altercations may even break out as teammates vie for a spot on the team. Most of this infighting is social and interpersonal in nature. In this stage, coaches need to communicate with athletes objectively and openly. Their evaluations of each athlete's strengths and weaknesses, as well as his role on the team, will help relieve uncertainty, a chief source of stress for athletes. Relieving stress should reduce the hostilities.

Norming

During norming, the third stage, hostility is replaced by solidarity and cooperation. Instead of watching out for their individual well-being, the athletes work together to reach common goals. Group cohesion (see chapter 10) occurs during this stage, as members pull together and build team unity. This pulling together can be a catalyst for improved satisfaction among team members; it can also set the grounds for future success. Team roles stabilize, and a respect develops for each player's unique contribution to the team. Instead of competing for status or recognition, players strive for economy of effort and task effectiveness.

Performing

In this final stage, team members band together to channel their energies for team success. Structural issues are resolved, and interpersonal relationships have stabilized. Roles are well defined, and the players help one another to succeed—the primary goal is team success. The coach gives each player feedback about his special contributions and makes sure no one feels left out.

Team Building: A College Swim Team

A college swim coach noticed that his team was not meshing. New members didn't know their teammates and there was little camaraderie. To develop a team concept, the coach scheduled get-togethers such as picnics, soccer games, and other social events. He asked team members to interview each other and report to the rest of the team what they had learned. The idea was to develop team awareness, communication, and interdependence, so that when a swimmer felt competitive stress, he could obtain some psychological security by knowing that team members would understand his responses to the situation.

Structure of the Group

Every group develops its own structure, which begins to emerge upon the group's first meeting. A group's structure depends largely on the interactions of its members—how they perceive one another and what they expect out of themselves and each other. For a group of athletes to become an effective team, certain structural characteristics must develop. Two of the most important are group roles and group norms.

Group Roles

A role consists of the set of behaviors required or expected of the person occupying a certain position in a group. Teachers, parents, corporate executives, and health professionals, for example, all have specific roles within their professions and within society. Coaches are expected to perform such behaviors as teaching, organizing practices, interacting with other school officials, and being a good role model.

A team, like any other group, plays formal and informal roles. Formal roles are dictated by the nature and structure of the organization. Athletic director, coach, team captain, and the like are examples of specific formal roles within a sport organization. A point guard in basketball, setter in volleyball, goalie in hockey, and other formal roles all have specific performance roles within a team. Each of these roles has specific associated expectations. Usually, individuals are either trained or recruited to fill specific roles, such as when a football coach recruits a place kicker, or a high school baseball coach converts an outfielder to a catcher.

Informal roles evolve from interactions among group members. For example, the power and social structure of gangs evolve through informal means (see William Whyte's 1943 classic work on the social structure of street gangs). In sport organizations, informal roles *evolve*. For instance, because of her strong personality and athletic ability, Jill is looked to for leadership even though she is not her team's official captain. In contact and collision sports a common informal role is the enforcer—someone who makes sure that no teammate gets bullied, roughed up, or physically intimidated. Another informal team role is the mediator, a diplomatic player who mediates disputes among teammates, or even between a coach and players.

> Two different types of roles exist within any group or team. Formal roles (e.g., coach or team captain) are dictated by the structure of the organization; informal roles evolve out of the dynamics of the group.

You can improve a team's effectiveness by making sure players understand (*role clarity*) and accept their roles (*role acceptance*). People in a specific role usually have a different perspective of the role's requirements than do other members of the group. For example, if a basketball coach wants a player to concentrate on defense and rebounding instead of scoring, then this needs to be clearly communicated to the player. Unclear roles hurt team performance. For example, if two players on the same basketball team each think his role is to direct the team's offense, conflict will likely result over who brings the ball up court. Similarly, an athletic trainer and team doctor must agree on their roles so that athletes and coaches know whom to see for injury evaluation and whom to see for decisions on playing availability.

An effective goal-setting program (see chapter 17) can clarify roles. Helping players set goals in specific areas gives them direction and focus. If a football coach wanted a defensive lineman to focus on stopping the run instead of on sacking the quarterback, setting a specific goal would clarify the lineman's role. In fact, open communication can clarify everyone's role for everyone else. If a coach groups her players and tells each one exactly what she expects of her individually and describes how her role fits in to the team concept, then everyone should know not only her own role but the roles of all her teammates.

Role acceptance is also important to enhance a group's structure. Players who don't start or get significant playing time can easily feel left out and confused about their contribution to the team. Coaches can help players accept their roles by minimizing the status differences among roles and emphasizing that the success of the team depends on each individual's contribution. When their responsibilities are perceived as important contributions to team success, players are more willing to accept and carry out their roles.

Norms

A *norm* is a level of performance, pattern of behavior, or belief. Norms can be either formally established or informally developed by a group. Each norm carries specific expectations and behaviors that group members are expected to follow. Individuals usually receive pressure to adhere to group norms. Sometimes a group uses positive or negative sanctions to enforce conformity. On a sport team, the norm might involve dress and hairstyle, the interactions between rookies and veterans, or who takes control in critical situations. Deviation from the expected behaviors might result in informal or formal sanctions. For example, when Michael Jordan played at the end of a close basketball game, he was expected to receive the ball and make something positive happen (which he usually did). If a rookie decided to take the last shot himself, he would be violating the norm and would most assuredly receive some kind of censure.

In industrial settings, a level or rate of performance called the *norm for productivity* is established by the group as acceptable. Anything falling below or above this level is not supported by the group. A norm for productivity can also apply to sport. The captain or top performer on a team is often a role model who sets the norm of productivity. For example, when Dan Gable, Olympic gold medalist, was wrestling at the University of Iowa, he put in unbelievable hours of practice time. And because Gable was considered the best wrestler in his weight classification in the country, his teammates adopted his standards.

Because norms can have powerful effects on behavior, it is imperative for a coach or teacher to establish positive group norms or standards. One good method is to enlist the formal and informal leaders of a team to set positive examples. Dan Gable took the initiative and set the norm himself. But often the coach or teacher will need to encourage leaders to set high standards of achievement. Whenever possible, include all team members in decision making about norms adopted by the team. Some additional methods for sport leaders to establish and enforce group norms were developed by Zander (1982):

- Show individual team members how the group's standards (norms) can contribute to more effective team performance and team unity.
- Assess adherence to team standards and reward those who adhere and sanction those who do not.
- Point out to each team member how his or her contribution toward developing and maintaining the standards contribute to the team's success.

Developing an Effective Team Climate

Team climate develops from how players perceive the interrelationships among the group members. Although the coach will certainly have his or her own perception of the team, it is the players' perceptions and evaluations that set the team's climate. Still, the coach has the strongest influence on establishing

The Pressure of Social Norms

Norms can have an enormous influence on individual members of a group, as demonstrated by the classic experiment conducted by Solomon Asch (1956). Seven students were asked to judge which of three lines was like the standard line (see Figure 9.1). The standard line was 5 inches in length, while the comparison lines were 5 inches, 4 inches, and 6-1/4 inches. All but one of the subjects (the naive subject) was told beforehand by the experimenter to give incorrect responses. Subjects answered out loud, one at a time, with the naive subject going next to last. Although it was clear that comparison line "a" was the correct answer, one-third of the naive subjects conformed to the group norm, even with as few as three other subjects. Thus, even when someone knows the correct response, she feels pressure to conform to the norms of the group by choosing a response she knows to be incorrect.

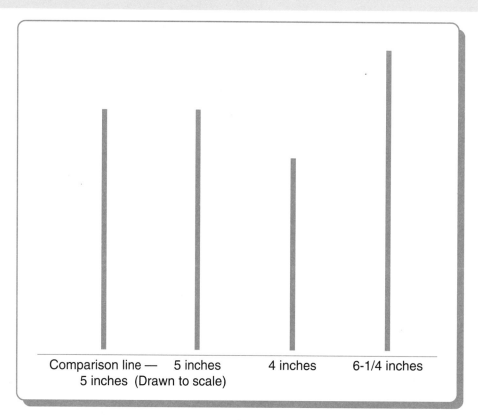

Comparison line — 5 inches 4 inches 6-1/4 inches
5 inches (Drawn to scale)

Figure 9.1 Typical comparison lines used in Asch's study of group effects on individual judgments.

team climate (Fisher et al., 1982). Some of the factors of team climate are more easily changed than others, but they all can affect the effective functioning of a group (Zander, 1982).

Social Support

Social support refers to "an exchange of resources between at least two individuals perceived by the provider or the recipient to be intended to enhance the well-being of the recipient" (Shumaker & Brownell, 1984, p. 13). Expressing emotional support (e.g., affection) or appraisal support (e.g., performance feedback), giving information (e.g., advice and role clarification), offering emotionally sustaining behaviors (e.g., empathy), and listening to the concerns and feelings of the other person are all examples of supportive social behaviors (Albrecht & Adelman, 1984).

Athletes need the emotional support of teammates, coaches, parents, and friends. Positive support is especially important when an athlete feels she is not performing well or realizing her potential. Conversely, negative responses from team members or coaches—such as harsh criticism, sarcasm, and lack of attention—can simply devastate some athletes. Mike Krzyzewski, men's basketball coach at Duke University, says the first thing he does at the beginning of the season is make sure all his players fit into the team concept and support each other. Creating an effective team climate that involves mutual support and respect is number one on his list in preparing his teams for the rigors of competition.

> Functions of social support include
>
> - providing appraisal, information, reassurance, and companionship,
> - reducing uncertainty during times of stress,
> - aiding in mental and physical recovery, and
> - improving communication skills.

Proximity

People are more likely to bond when they are near each other. Although physical proximity alone will usually not develop a team concept, close contact with teammates promotes interaction. Locker rooms and road trips ensure close proximity. Some college coaches promote team unity by having athletes live together in a residence hall. This interaction combined with a similarity of attitudes can help establish team identity.

Distinctiveness

When a group feels distinct, its feelings of unity and oneness increase. Street gangs use distinctive dress and special initiation rites to set themselves apart from other gangs. In sport, distinctiveness is traditionally achieved through team uniforms and mottos, special initiation rites, or special privileges. Athletes differ from other people in their intensive physical training programs, reduced time for social activities, and close relationships with team members. Some teams such as the Boston Celtics, New York Yankees, Notre Dame football team, UCLA basketball team, and Iowa wrestling team foster distinctiveness (e.g., the Celtics are known for their kelly green uniforms, which are distinct from all other teams'). By making team members feel unique and distinct from other teams, a coach helps develop and mold a team concept.

Fairness

How fairly athletes think they are being treated by the coach will influence their level of commitment, motivation, and satisfaction. Athletes interpret fairness on three central issues (Anshel, 1990):

- The degree of compatibility between the coach's and the player's assessments of the player's skills and contributions to the team.
- How the coach communicates his or her views to the athletes.
- The athlete's perception that the coach is trying to help him or her improve and be happy.

Fairness, or lack of it, can bring a team close together or tear it apart. Coaches need to deal with athletes honestly, openly, and fairly. Athletes need to feel they are treated fairly, even if they are not entirely happy with certain decisions.

Similarity

Similarity among team members in commitments, attitudes, aspirations, and goals are important to positive team climate. As Zander (1982) notes,

> Birds of a feather flock together and create a more distinct entity when they do. People too form a better unit if they are alike, and an effective leader develops oneness within a set by encouraging likeness among members. To do this, they recruit persons who will interact well because of similar purpose, background, training, experience, or temperament. . . . Persons whose beliefs do not fit together will have a hard time forming a strong group. (p. 3)

Team members usually differ in ethnicity, race, socioeconomic background, personality, and ability. It is up to the coach to get a diverse bunch of athletes working together so that they become more similar than dissimilar. Some ways to develop commonality among team members include shared group performance goals, expectations for proper behavior and dress, codes of conduct for games and practices, and clarity of team roles. The more this group of individuals feels similar to one another, the greater the probability of their developing a strong team concept.

Team Climate Questionnaire

It is useful for a coach to assess how athletes are feeling. Table 9.1 presents sample questions from a checklist to measure athletes' feelings about being members of the team and their perceptions of the coach's behavior and attitudes. Athletes' responses give the coach valuable information about team climate and possible ways to enhance team cohesion. Because coaches want to look at

Table 9.1   Team Climate Questionnaire

Using the following code, please write in the appropriate number for each statement.

1 = never occurs, 2 = sometimes occurs, 3 = usually occurs, 4 = always occurs

_____ 1. I make many of the decisions that affect the way I play.

_____ 2. I can count on the coach to keep the things I say confidential.

_____ 3. People on the coaching staff pitch in to help each other out.

_____ 4. I have enough time to do the things the coach asks me to learn and perform.

_____ 5. I can count on my coach to help me when I need it.

This checklist was developed by Francis and Young (1979). Adapted from M. Anshel, *Sport Psychology: From Theory to Practice*, 2nd edition. © 1994 by Gorsuch Scarisbrick, Publishers (Scottsdale, AZ). Used with permission.

changes occurring over the course of a season, athletes should respond to the checklist at preseason and then periodically throughout the season to monitor changes. Players should be told that this is not a test and that there are no right or wrong answers. Keep the responses anonymous so athletes are more likely to respond honestly.

Individual and Team Performance in Sport

Because it's their job to get individual players to play together as a team, coaches need to know how interactions among team members affect performance on the athletic field (or court). Most coaches and sport psychologists agree that a group of the best individuals usually does not make the best team. Take the 1991 men's NCAA basketball semifinals, where Duke beat previously undefeated UNLV. The consensus was that UNLV had the superior talent—including two All-Americans, Larry Johnson and Stacey Augmon—but Duke played better team basketball. Similarly, in the NBA it is rare for a player to win the scoring title on a championship team. Simply stated, a good team is more than the sum of its parts. How well a team works together is a key factor in the equation.

Individual abilities of team members are often not good predictors of how a team will perform.

Steiner's Model

Ivan Steiner developed a model to show the relation between individual abilities or resources on a team and how team members interact (1972). Steiner's model is shown by this equation:

$$\text{actual productivity} = \text{potential productivity} - \text{losses due to faulty group processes}$$

Potential productivity refers to a team's possible best performance, given each player's ability, knowledge, and skill (both mental and physical) as well as the demands of the task. Thus, a hockey team with six outstanding players who can shoot, play defense, pass, and skate would be considered to possess excellent group resources. According to Steiner's model, individual ability is probably the most important resource for sport teams—thus, the team made up of the best individuals will usually achieve the most success.

However, Steiner's model implies that a team's actual productivity will not usually match its potential productivity. Only when a team effectively uses its available resources to match the demands of the task will its actual productivity or performance approach its potential performance. Specifically, a group's actual performance usually falls short of its potential productivity because of faulty group processes. In a team situation, group process refers to the complex interactions that help the team transform its individual resources into a collective performance. A volleyball team, for example, would have to have precise teamwork between setters, spikers, and blockers to achieve their potential.

There are two kinds of losses due to faulty group processes: *motivation losses* and *coordination losses*. Motivation losses occur when team members do not give 100% effort. Perhaps players feel that one or two stars can "carry the load" and thus they slacken off. Coordination losses occur when the timing between teammates is off or when ineffective strategies are used. For example, in a doubles match in tennis, if the ball is hit right down the middle of the court and neither player goes for it because they think the other is going to take it, that is a loss of coordination. Similarly, a soccer team that does not keep proper spacing and stay in position is not working well together.

Sports that require complex interaction or cooperation such as basketball, soccer, football, and volleyball are more susceptible to coordination losses than sports requiring fewer interactions and less coordination (e.g., swimming and track and field). Basketball, soccer, and volleyball coaches typically spend much time and effort to fine tune coordination, timing, and team movement patterns. Swimming coaches spend most of their time developing individual swimming technique, giving less time to integrative skills such as transitions among relay team members.

How Individual Skills Relate to Group (Team) Performance

In 1954 Comrey and Deskin investigated the relation between individual and group performance to see how faulty group processes reduce productivity. Using a pegboard assembly task and with subjects performing alone and in groups, they found that no matter what level of motor skills individuals brought to the task, when two or more people tried to interact in precise ways, their ability to anticipate one another's movements and time their own actions accordingly was at least as important as their individual performance qualities. In 1974 Jones studied professional teams, focusing on statistics of individual players, such as their runs batted in and batting average in baseball; points, assists, rebounds, and steals in basketball; and singles rankings in tennis to see how these statistics related to team success. He found a positive relation between team effectiveness and individual performance success, but this relation was weakest in basketball, which has the most complex interactions. Thus, it appears that where more cooperation and interaction are necessary, the importance of individual ability decreases and the importance of group process increases.

When teams of *two* people play, they apparently work best together if they are close in ability. One investigation revealed that the best predictor of success was the averaged ability of the two players (i.e., summing the abilities of the two-person team), but a large difference in ability between partners had a negative effect on performance (Gill, 1979). The closer teammates are in ability, the more likely they are to put to full use their combined abilities. When a superior player is paired with an inferior player, the better player will often try to do too much (i.e., play above her ability level) and wind up making mistakes. In tennis, for example, the top singles players rarely win at doubles (John McEnroe and Martina Navratilova are exceptions). Usually, the top doubles teams are made up of two very good players who complement each other—not one star and another good player who have trouble putting their skills together.

Ringelmann Effect

So we know from these studies that individual abilities do not neatly sum up to group or team performance. This is consistent with Steiner's model, which noted that potential productivity could be reduced by faulty group processes (1972). But what causes these losses, and how much potential productivity is lost? The answers to these questions began to emerge from an obscure, unpublished study on individual and group performance on a rope-pulling task that Ringelmann conducted nearly 100 years ago (cited by Ingham, Levinger, Graves, & Peckman, 1974). He observed individuals and groups of two, three, and eight people pulling on a rope. If there were no losses due to faulty group processes, then it could be assumed that if each individual pulled 100 pounds, then groups of two, three, and eight would be able to pull 200, 300, and 800 pounds, respectively. However, the relative performance of each individual showed a progressive decline as the number of people in the group increased. That is, two-person groups pulled only 93% of their individual potential, three-person groups 85%, and eight-person groups only 49%.

Since some of the early methodology and descriptions had been incomplete in Ringelmann's study, Ingham et al. (1974) attempted to replicate Ringelmann's findings while extending the work. They first had individuals and groups of two, three, four, five, and six persons perform the rope-pulling task. Results were similar to Ringelmann's study: Groups of two performed at 91% of their potential and groups of three at 82% of their potential. However, contrary to what Ringelmann found, increases in group size did not lead to corresponding decreases in efficiency. Rather, there was a general leveling off, where groups of six pulled at an average of 78% of their potential (see a comparison of the Ringelmann and Ingham studies in Table 9.2).

Ingham and his colleagues then wanted to determine whether the losses resulting from increased group size were due to poor coordination or reduced motivation. To separate these two, coordination was eliminated as a factor by testing only one subject at a time, blindfolding the subject, and having trained helpers pretend to pull on the rope (subjects thought the other members of the group were pulling on the rope, but they were not). Any decrease in performance was then attributed to a loss in motivation rather than a loss in coordination (because only the real subject was actually pulling the rope). The results were almost identical to their first study—average performance dropped to 85% in the three-person groups, with no further decrease in individual perfor-

The phenomenon by which individual performance decreases as the number of people in the group increases is known as the Ringelmann Effect.

Table 9.2 Relationship Between Group Size and Rope-Pulling Performance								
	Percentage of potential productivity for groups differing in size							
	1	2	3	4	5	6	7	8
Ringelmann study	100	93	85					49
Ingham (study 1)	100	91	82	78	78	78		
Ingham (study 2)	100	90	85	86	84	85		

mance as group size increased. They concluded that the differences between actual and potential performance were not due to a decrease in coordination but to a decrease in motivation.

Social Loafing

Psychologists call the phenomenon of individuals within a group or team putting forth less than 100% effort (due to losses in motivation) *social loafing*. Two experiments using shouting and clapping as group tasks found that the average sound each person produced decreased from the solo performance to 71% in two-person groups, 51% in four-person groups, and 40% in six-person groups. When the scientists controlled for coordination, they found that two-person groups performed at 82% of their potential and six-person groups at 74% of their potential (Latane, Williams, & Harkins, 1979).

Why does social loafing occur on sport teams, and what can coaches do about it?

Emphasize the Importance of Individual Pride.   When you stress the team concept, some players might not recognize the importance of their own contribution to the team. All players should be challenged to examine their responsibility to the team and how they can improve for the team's benefit.

Increase Identifiability.   When team members believe that their individual performances are identifiable (i.e., known to others), social loafing may be eliminated because players no longer feel anonymous (Williams, Harkins, & Latane, 1981). Studies of swimmers found that they swam faster in relays than in individual events only when individual times in relays were announced (i.e., high identifiability). However, swimmers swam slower in relays than individual events when individual times were not announced in relays (i.e., low identifiability). Coaches and exercise leaders should monitor individual efforts consistently and give feedback to athletes in practice as well as competition. By evaluating individual efforts, coaches make athletes aware of their concern and that they are not lost in the crowd.

Videotaping or observational checklists from team sport practices and games can also provide increased identifiability. For example, at Ohio State University, the late Woody Hayes increased the identifiability of football linemen by filming and specifically grading each player on each play, providing "lineman of the week" honors, and awarding helmet decals to players who showed individual effort and performance. It's important to include practices as well as games in your evaluation because many players don't get a lot of actual game time.

What Causes Social Loafing?

- Athletes might believe that teammates are less motivated than themselves, and not wanting to play the role of a sucker, they put forth less effort.

- Athletes may feel that working hard doesn't bring much recognition since they get "lost in the crowd" anyway.

- Athletes may feel that they don't really have to try hard since their teammates will take up the slack.

- Athletes may feel that they can hide in the crowd and avoid the negative consequences of not trying hard.

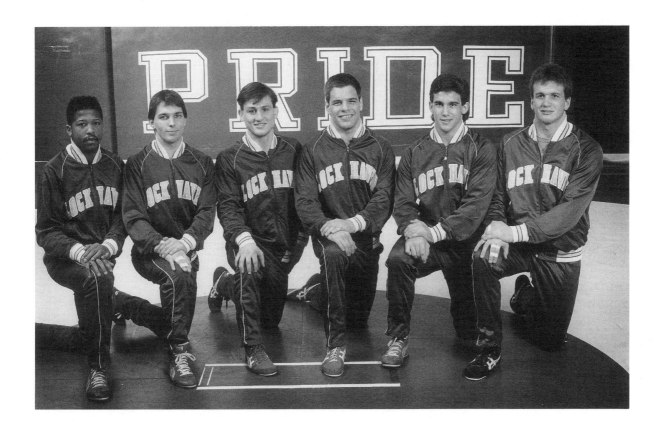

Determine Specific Situations Where Loafing May Occur.   Through videotape or other observations, coaches should determine what situations seem to elicit loafing. Social loafing can sometimes be appropriate. For example, a basketball center gets a rebound and throws an outlet pass to the guard but does not follow the ball down the floor. She is in effect taking a rest on the offensive end to make sure she is ready on the defensive end, which may be appropriate if she is tired.

If changes need to be made, coaches should structure the practice sessions and competitions so that each player can economize efforts without interfering with team performance. For example, during a particularly tough part of the season, coaches might incorporate low-intensity practices into the schedule or complement high-intensity practices with fun activities. This will help keep players sharp and minimize loafing.

Conduct Individual Meetings to Discuss Loafing.   It is important to discuss loafing with each player individually. A player may have reasons for motivational loss that are more complex than feeling lost in the crowd or assuming someone else will get the job done. Good communication is essential to learn why an athlete is not giving full effort. For example, athletes may have other commitments that place them under stress and require energy and time expenditure. Thus, the athlete may be economizing effort just to get through the day both physically and mentally.

Summary

To understand behavior in sport and physical activity we need to understand sport groups. Much of sport competition is conducted in a team context; thus, the dynamics of groups weigh heavily in understanding how sport teams function. Groups form in a process that involves four stages (forming, storming, norming, and performing), structures, roles, and norms as they relate to group structure. Developing a team concept is usually one of a coach's central missions. Coaches also are concerned with group performance, particularly the relationship of individual abilities to group performance. Although research suggests a positive relationship between individual abilities and group performance (i.e., the best individuals make the best team), this relationship is far from perfect. As suggested by Steiner's model, losses due to faulty group processes can undermine team performance. Coordination losses and motivational problems can also detract from team performance. Research indicates that these losses tend to be motivational in nature, however, suggesting social loafing. Coaches can reduce social loafing by increasing identifiability and personal responsibility.

Review Questions

1. Discuss why most definitions of a *group* agree that a *collection of individuals* is not necessarily a group.

2. Describe the four stages of team development and the key events that characterize each stage.

3. List some formal and informal roles in a sport you're familiar with. Who decides on these roles? What are the defining characteristics that identify each role?

4. What might happen to a team when the roles are clearly defined yet only partially accepted (i.e., only some of the players are willing to accept their roles)?

5. Provide examples of some norms you have experienced while participating in sport or exercise programs. Was there a norm for productivity? If so, how was this norm developed?

6. Explain at least three techniques you might use to improve a team's climate.

7. Discuss an experience you have had where Steiner's model of productivity was applicable and actual productivity was less than potential productivity. Was the loss due to a lack of coordination or motivation?

8. Describe several tasks that might replicate the Ringelmann effect.

9. How would you identify social loafing? How could your team captains help you to alleviate or overcome social loafing? What would you say to players to get them to realize they are loafing and that the team needs them to stop?

10. As an exercise leader, describe three principles from this chapter that would help build unity within your class or group.

References

Albrecht, T.L., & Adelman, M.B. (1984). Social support and life stress: New directions for communication research. *Human Communication Research*, **1**, 3-22.

Anshel, M. (1990). *Sport psychology: From theory to practice.* Scottsdale, AZ: Gorsuch Scarisbrick.

Asch, S. (1956). Studies of independence and conformity: A minority of one against a unanimous majority. *Psychological Monographs, 70*, (9, Whole No. 416).

Cartwright, D., & Zander, A. (1968). *Group dynamics: Research and theory* (3rd ed.) New York: Harper & Row.

Comrey, A., & Deskin, G. (1954). Group manual dexterity in women. *Journal of Applied Psychology, 38*, 178.

Fisher, A.C., Mancini, U.H., Hirsch, R.L., Proulx, T.J., & Staurowsky, E.J. (1982). Coach-athlete interactions and team climate. *Journal of Sport Psychology, 4*, 388-404.

Francis, D., & Young, D. (1979). *Improving work groups: A practical manual for team building.* San Diego, CA: University Associates.

Gill, D.L. (1979). The prediction of group motor performance from individual member abilities. *Journal of Motor Behavior, 11*, 113-122.

Ingham, A.G., Levinger, G., Graves, J., & Peckham, V. (1974). The Ringelmann effect: Studies of group size and group performance. *Journal of Experimental Social Psychology*, 371-384.

Jones, M.B. (1974). Regressing group on individual effectiveness. *Organizational Behavior and Human Performance, 11*, 426-451.

Latane, B., Williams, K.D., & Harkins, S.G. (1979). Many hands make light the work: The causes and consequences of social loafing. *Journal of Personality and Social Psychology, 37*, 823-832.

Shumaker, S.A., & Brownell, A. (1984). Toward a theory of social support: Closing conceptual gaps. *Journal of Social Issues, 40*, 11-36.

Steiner, I.D. (1972). Group process and productivity. New York: Academic Press.

Tuckman, B.W. (1965). Developmental sequence in small groups. *Psychological Bulletin, 63*, 384-399.

Whyte, W.F. (1943). Street corner society: The social structure of an Italian slum. Chicago: University of Chicago Press.

Williams, K., Harkins, S., & Latane, B. (1981). Identifiability and social loafing: Two cheering experiments. *Journal of Personality and Social Psychology, 40*, 303-311.

Zander, A. (1982). *Making groups effective.* San Francisco: Jossey-Bass.

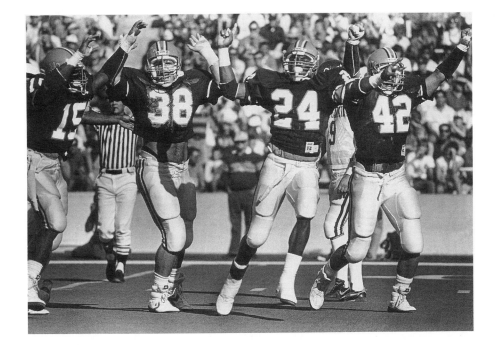

CHAPTER 10

Group Cohesion

> This club grew up together. Nobody here thinks of himself. There are no media-seekers, and that's important because everyone shares in the appreciation. I've enjoyed a lot of teams. We've been close, but I'm enjoying the game more now, with this club, than any time in my career.
>
> *Darrell Evans*

Detroit Tiger player Darrell Evans reflected on the importance of team cohesion in the early success of the Tiger team, which started the season with a record of 32 and 7. Manager Sparky Anderson downplayed individual heroes, considering the team just 25 players working together to play good, solid baseball. After his retirement, football great Joe Namath told a reporter that what he would miss most was the tremendous feeling of comradeship he shared with his teammates. Not only athletes but also participants in exercise classes often remark that they feel a greater commitment to the exercise program when they develop friendships with other class members.

Players and coaches often attribute team success or failure to how well the team works together as a cohesive unit. When a highly favored team is upset by a less talented team, the coach may say, "We just didn't play well as a team. Everyone seemed concerned about his own individual statistics instead of doing what it took to win the game."

Yet we cannot always credit success to team cohesion. Some teams win despite an apparent lack of cohesion. The Oakland Athletics in the early 1970s and the New York Yankees in the late 1970s won the World Series amidst publicity about the lack of harmony of their ball clubs, which had frequent battles among players and between players and coaches (Billy Martin and Reggie Jackson, for example). The most successful German Olympic and world championship rowing teams reportedly were the teams with the most internal conflict (Lenk, 1969). So, a key question is whether cohesive teams are more successful than teams that lack cohesion.

In this chapter you will learn about

▌ what cohesion is,

▌ how cohesion is measured,

▌ a model for the cohesion-performance relationship,

▌ correlates of cohesion such as conformity, satisfaction, and team stability, and

▌ guidelines for building team cohesion.

Definitions of Cohesion

In 1950, Festinger, Schacter, and Back defined cohesion as "the total field of forces which act on members to remain in the group" (p. 164), a definition that subsequently influenced thinking in sport. They felt that two distinct forces act on members to remain in a group. The first class of forces, *attractiveness of the group*, refers to the individual's desire for interpersonal interactions with other group members and a desire to be involved in group activities. Just being with the group and interacting with each other gives group members a sense of satisfaction. The second class of forces, *means control*, refers to the benefits that a member can derive by being associated with the group. For example, playing for a highly ranked college football team might increase an athlete's recognition and value in the draft.

Task cohesion refers to the degree that group members work together to achieve common goals and objectives, whereas *social cohesion* reflects the interpersonal attraction among group members.

Between 1950 and 1970, several other definitions of group cohesion were proposed. Their common thread was that cohesion consisted of two basic dimensions: task cohesion and social cohesion. *Task cohesion* reflects the degree to which members of a group work together to achieve common goals. In sport, a common goal would be winning a championship, which in part depends on the team's coordinated effort or teamwork. *Social cohesion*, on the other hand, reflects the degree to which members of a team like each other and enjoy each other's company. Social cohesion is often equated with interpersonal attraction. In an exercise class, for example, a common goal would be enhanced fitness. And it has been shown that adherence to the exercise program increases as the social cohesion of the group increases (Spink & Carron, 1992).

The distinction between task and social cohesion is important conceptually and helps explain how teams can overcome conflict to succeed. Take the examples of the New York Yankees and Oakland Athletics, teams that certainly appeared low in social cohesion (team members fought, formed cliques, and exchanged angry words). However, these teams obviously had a high degree of task cohesion—they wanted to win the World Series. It didn't matter if Reggie Jackson didn't get along with manager Billy Martin—they shared the goal of winning. In terms of working together effectively, the teams had excellent field work and could turn double plays, hit cut-off men, and advance runners as good or better than any other teams.

Task Versus Social Cohesion

The New York Yankees in the late 1970s were a classic case of a team that apparently did not get along well together (low social cohesion) yet were able to win pennants and World Series (high task cohesion). The major personalities in conflict in the "Bronx Zoo" (as some people called it) were owner George Steinbrenner, manager Billy Martin, and star outfielder Reggie Jackson. Steinbrenner and Martin had strong personalities that often clashed (in fact Steinbrenner fired Martin three times). Steinbrenner wanted to make managerial decisions instead of focusing on front office decisions. But Martin wanted to be in total control of what happened on the field and felt that Steinbrenner was usurping his authority. To add to the stew, Reggie Jackson was an outspoken, strong-willed player who frequently and openly disagreed with both Martin's and Steinbrenner's decisions. As this circus unfolded throughout the season, other players were inevitably drawn into the melee.

It seemed unlikely that such a team could "hang together" for even a single season, yet for several years the Yankees were probably the most successful team in professional baseball. The key to understanding its success is to understand the difference between social and task cohesion. That is, despite the team's infighting and bickering (i.e., low social cohesion), it had a strong desire to win and be the best (i.e., high task cohesion). When Reggie Jackson came to bat, he would try his hardest, both for Reggie Jackson and for the success of the team. Similarly, in making managerial decisions, winning was always foremost in Billy Martin's mind, regardless of what he thought about Reggie Jackson or George Steinbrenner. Thus, the shared common goal of winning the World Series overcame the lack of interpersonal attraction among players and management.

To reflect the task and social components of cohesion, in 1982 Carron refined the definition of cohesion, proposing "a dynamic process which is reflected in the tendency for a group to stick together and remain united in the pursuit of its goals and objectives" (1982, p. 124).

Conceptual Model of Cohesion

Carron's definition is more useful for sport and exercise settings than Festinger et al.'s earlier one. Carron later developed a conceptual system as a framework for systematically studying cohesion in sport and exercise. His approach to the study of cohesion can be seen in Figure 10.1.

Carron's model outlines four major antecedents affecting the development of cohesion in sport and exercise settings:

- Environmental factors
- Personal factors
- Team factors
- Leadership factors

The *environmental factors*, which are the most general and remote, refer to the normative forces holding a group together. Some examples are players being under contract to the management, athletes holding scholarships, regulations specifying the minimum playing time in a youth sport program, and exercisers paying an extra fee for their class. These influences can hold a group together, although other factors such as age, geography, or eligibility requirements can also play an important role. Carron also notes an unwritten value—namely, if

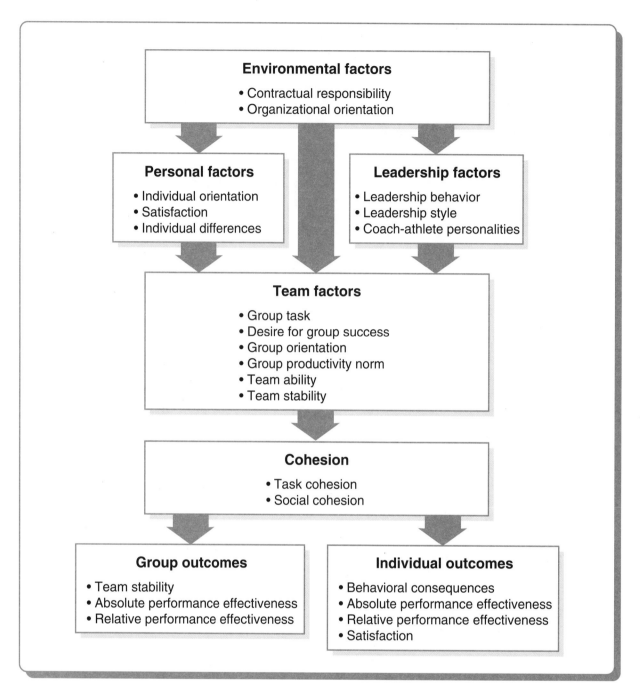

Figure 10.1 Carron's conceptual model for cohesiveness in sport teams. Adapted from Carron (1982).

an athlete leaves a team he or she may be labeled a quitter. This deters some players from leaving a team.

Environmental factors are fairly constant and usually apply to all teams within a given league. But a great deal of variation occurs within the *personal factors*, which refer to the individual characteristics of group members, such as participation motives. Bass, for example, identified three primary motives: task motivation, affiliation motivation, and self-motivation (1962). Task motivation and affiliation motivation are closely associated with task and social cohesion, respectively. If you have high task motivation, you would contribute to a group's task cohesion. Similarly, athletes high in affiliation motivation would contribute to social cohesion. Self-motivation refers to the attempt to obtain personal satisfaction by performing up to one's level of ability and it seems to contribute to both social and task cohesion.

Leadership factors include the leadership style and behaviors that professionals exhibit and the relationships they establish with their groups. These factors will be discussed more thoroughly in chapter 11.

Team factors refer to group task characteristics (individual versus team sports), group productivity norms, desire for group success, and team stability. Carron (1982) argues that teams that stay together a long time and have a strong desire for group success also exhibit high levels of group cohesion.

Measuring Cohesion

To determine the relationship between cohesion and performance we need to be able to measure cohesion. Two kinds of measures have been developed: questionnaires and sociograms.

Questionnaires

Most early research on cohesion utilized the Sport Cohesiveness Questionnaire developed by Martens, Landers, and Loy (1972). This questionnaire has 7 items that measure either interpersonal attraction or direct ratings of closeness or attraction to the group. Unfortunately, no reliability or validity measures were established on the Sport Cohesiveness Questionnaire, and most items address only social cohesion. To account for the multidimensional nature of cohesion, Yukelson, Weinberg, and Jackson developed a 22-item tool called the Multidimensional Sport Cohesion Instrument (1984). It includes four broad dimensions of team cohesion:

- Attraction to the group
- Unity of purpose
- Quality of teamwork
- Valued roles

The first factor, attraction to the group, reflects social cohesion. The final three factors can be collectively considered as relating to task cohesion since they all have to do with working together as a team in pursuit of common goals. While the Multidimensional Sport Cohesion Instrument was designed for basketball teams, it's versatility allows it to be used with other team sports.

More recently, the Group Environment Questionnaire (GEQ) was developed, distinguishing between the individual and the group and between task and social concerns (see Table 10.1; Widmeyer, Brawley, & Carron, 1985). It is conceptually based and systematically developed, in terms of establishing reliability and validity (Brawley, Carron, & Widmeyer, 1987; Carron, Widmeyer, & Brawley, 1985). The model has two major categories: a member's perception of the group as a totality (*group integration*) and a member's personal attraction to the group (*individual attraction to the group*). The members' perceptions of the group as a unit and their perceptions of the group's attraction for them can be focused on task or social aspects. Thus, four constructs can be identified (see Figure 10.2):

- Group integration—task
- Group integration—social
- Individual attractions to group—task
- Individual attractions to group—social

The Group Environment Questionnaire focuses on how attractive the group is to individual members and on how the members perceive the group. The GEQ is accepted for assessing team cohesion.

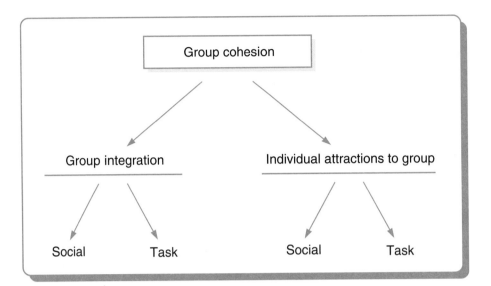

Figure 10.2 Conceptual model of group cohesion for the GEQ. Adapted from Carron, Widmeyer, and Brawley (1985).

Table 10.1 Group Environment Questionnaire (GEQ): Sample Items		
	Strongly disagree	Strongly agree
Attraction to group–task subscale I do like the style of play of this team.	1 2 3 4 5 6 7 8 9	
Attraction to group–social subscale Some of my best friends are on this team.	1 2 3 4 5 6 7 8 9	
Group integration–task subscale We all take responsibility for any loss or poor performance by our team.	1 2 3 4 5 6 7 8 9	
Group integration–social subscale Our team would like to spend time together in the off season.	1 2 3 4 5 6 7 8 9	

Note. The GEQ is scored by adding up all questions for each subscale. The higher the score, the higher the individual feels about that particular aspect of group cohesion (scoring reverses for negatively worded items). For example, an attraction to the group–task scores can range from 4 to 36. Comparisons can be made among individuals or among groups.

Adapted from Carron, Brawley, and Widmeyer (1985).

Sociograms

Questionnaires have been the most popular way to measure group cohesion, but they do not show how particular individuals relate to each other, whether cliques are developing, and if some group members are socially isolated. A sociogram is a tool to measure social cohesion. It discloses affiliation and attraction among group members, including

- the presence or absence of cliques,
- members' perceptions of group closeness,
- friendship choices within the group,
- the degree to which athletes perceive interpersonal feelings similarly,
- social isolation of individual group members, and
- extent of group attraction.

To generate information for the sociogram you ask individual group members specific questions, such as, "Name the three people in the group you would most like to invite to a party and the three people you would least like to invite," "Name the three people you would most like to room with on road trips and the three you would least like to room with," and "Name three people you would most like to practice with during the off-season and the three you would least like to practice with." Confidentiality must be assured and honesty of responses needs to be encouraged.

Based on the responses to the questions, a sociogram is created (see Figure 10.3), which should reveal the pattern of interpersonal relationships in a group. In creating a sociogram, the most frequently chosen individuals are placed toward the center of the sociogram and less frequently chosen individuals placed outside. Notice that the arrows in Figure 10.3 indicate the direction of choice. Reciprocal choice is represented by arrows going in both directions between two individuals. In the baseball team represented in the figure, you can see that Tom is the person everyone seems to like. Larry is isolated from the team and is disliked by several members, so there is a problem that a coach would need to address. Jay and Bob form a closed unit and are not really involved with the rest of the team. Knowing about these relationships might help the coach deal with interpersonal problems before they become disruptive.

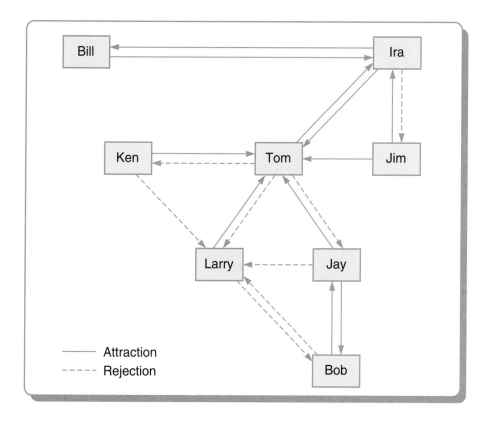

Figure 10.3 Sociogram for measuring team cohesion.

Cohesion and Performance Success

Fans, coaches, and sport psychologists seem to have an enduring fascination with how team cohesion relates to performance success. On an intuitive level, you might assume that the higher the level of team cohesion, the greater the team's success. Why else spend so much time trying to develop team cohesion? However, the cohesion-performance relation is not obvious. In fact, several reviews of the research literature have cited the contradictory nature of the results (e.g., Carron, 1982). We will now review the literature, considering measurement of cohesion, task characteristics, and direction of causality.

Type of Measurement

Think back to the breakdown of task and social cohesion. Almost all the studies reporting a negative relation between cohesion and performance used only an *interpersonal attraction* measure, such as a sociogram or the interpersonal attraction items from the Sport Cohesiveness Questionnaire (e.g., Landers & Lueschen, 1974; Lenk, 1969). In essence, teams high in interpersonal attraction were more likely to be unsuccessful.

When both task cohesion and social cohesion were assessed, however, mixed results were found. That is, positive relationships between cohesion and performance were found for task measures of cohesion but not for social measures such as friendship and interpersonal attraction (e.g., Widmeyer & Martens, 1978). Much of the research before 1985 used some measure of social cohesion but often had no measure of task cohesion, which probably accounts for the inconsistent findings.

Task Demands

A second explanation for the confusing cohesion-performance results involves the diversity of task demands that sport teams face. We can characterize the nature of interactions among team members along a continuum, from being interactive to coactive (see Figure 10.4). *Interactive* sports require team members to work together and coordinate their actions. Players on a soccer team, for example, have to constantly pass the ball to each other, maintain certain positions, coordinate offensive attacks, and devise defensive strategies to stop opponents from scoring. *Coactive* sports require little, if any, team interaction and coordination to achieve their goals. For instance, members of a golf or bowling team have little to do with each other in terms of coordinated activity. Baseball is a good example of a sport that is both interactive and coactive: Batting or catching a fly ball is coactive, whereas making a double play or hitting the cut-off man is interactive.

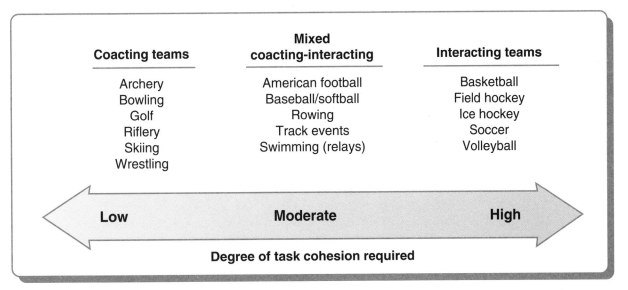

Figure 10.4   Relation of task cohesion and the sport.
From Bryant J. Cratty, *Psychology in Contemporary Sport: Guidelines for Coaches and Athletes.* Copyright © 1983 by Prentice-Hall. Adapted by permission.

The distinction between interactive and coactive tasks further helps us understand the varied cohesion-performance results. Positive cohesion-performance relations are reported most often for team sports that require extensive interaction, coordination, and cooperation among team members, such as basketball (Gruber & Gray, 1982), hockey (Ball & Carron, 1976), and volleyball (Bird, 1977). On the other hand, sports such as bowling (Landers & Lueschen, 1974), riflery (McGrath, 1962), and rowing (Lenk, 1969) are predominantly coactive, requiring independent performance with little interaction and integration. Typically they show no relation between cohesion and performance or even a negative relation.

From an intuitive perspective these findings make sense, especially when we consider task cohesion. For instance, in basketball, a team's success depends on all members working closely together. Good team defense requires switching assignments, calling out screens, and blocking out for rebounding. A smooth offense requires distribution of passes, movement without the ball, screens away from the ball, and proper spacing among teammates. These maneuvers require close teamwork, with members understanding their roles and having common goals.

Now think of a track and field team. Although each athlete's score on a particular event will be part of the team score, the athletes do not really have to work with each other to achieve their goals (except for runners in a relay team). Pole vaulters, long jumpers, hurdlers, sprinters, and middle distance runners compete at their own specialty. As long as the athletes on the track

Cohesion increases performance for interacting sports (e.g., basketball) but decreases or shows no effect on performance for coacting sports (e.g., bowling).

and field team do their best, how well they get along matters little to the team's performance.

Direction of Causality

The direction of causality refers to whether cohesion leads to performance success or performance success leads to cohesion. In other words, will a team that works together on and off the field be more successful, or do players like each other more and work together well because they are successful? Researchers have investigated these questions from two perspectives:

- Cohesion to performance—cohesion measures preceding performance
- Performance to cohesion—performance measures preceding cohesion

At first they relied heavily on correlational data in trying to predict performance from cohesion. Researchers assessed early season cohesion and tried to determine if it would predict later season success (e.g., Widmeyer & Martens, 1978). Or, attempting to study the causal effects of performance on cohesion, they measured performance early in the season and tried determining if this would predict later season cohesion (e.g., Ruder & Gill, 1982).

The relation between cohesion and performance appears to be circular, with performance success leading to increased cohesion, which in turn leads to increased performance.

Direction of causality proves difficult to establish due to many uncontrolled factors such as previous team success, coaching, or talent. To more directly assess the performance and cohesion relation, a couple of researchers employed a *cross-lagged panel design*, which incorporates time factors into the measurement. Using this design, Carron and Ball tested cohesion in 12 intercollegiate hockey teams at early season, midseason, and end of season (1977). They also assessed team performance in terms of win-loss percentage at midseason and at the end of the season (see Figure 10.5). None of the correlations were significant as far as cohesion predicting later performance. However, significant correlations were found between early performance and later cohesion. That is, the relation between early season performance and later season cohesion is stronger than vice versa. The same stronger effects of performance on cohesion were

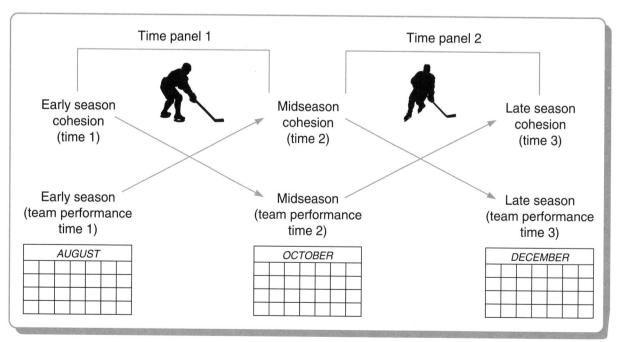

Figure 10.5 Cross-lagged correlations for cohesion and performance in Carron and Ball's study of hockey players. Adapted from Carron and Ball (1977).

Cohesion-Performance Findings—A Summary

- In general, positive relations are found between cohesion and performance for interactive tasks.

- No relation or negative relations are found in general between cohesion and performance for coactive tasks.

- Positive relations are found in general between task cohesion and performance, rather than between social cohesion and performance.

- Performance appears to have a stronger effect on cohesion than cohesion has on performance.

- The relation between cohesion and performance appears to be circular, with performance success leading to increased cohesion, which in turn leads to increased performance.

---

found in a study of intercollegiate female field hockey players (Williams and Hacker, 1982). However, additional research suggests that the relation between cohesion and performance is circular. Performance seems to affect later cohesion and then the changes in cohesion affect subsequent performance (Landers, Wilkinson, Hatfield, & Barber, 1982; Nixon, 1977).

Other Correlates of Cohesion

Although researchers have focused predominantly on the relation between cohesion and performance, other potentially important factors are also associated with cohesion. We will review these factors here.

Team Satisfaction

Satisfaction and cohesion are highly similar except that cohesion is about groups, whereas satisfaction is an individual construct. Although consistently strong relations have been found to exist between cohesion and satisfaction (e.g., Carron & Chelladurai, 1982), two different models are used to explain the relation between cohesion, satisfaction, and performance.

One model (A) hypothesizes a circular relation, with team cohesion leading to success, which leads to feelings of satisfaction, which tend to strengthen and reinforce team cohesion. The other model (B) hypothesizes that performance success leads to higher cohesion, which in turn leads to greater satisfaction. Thus, both the models suggest that there is indeed a relation between satisfaction, cohesion, and performance. However, model A suggests that cohesion directly enhances performance whereas model B argues that performance success leads to cohesion. But in either case, leaders do well in building group cohesion because being in a cohesive group is satisfying and also indirectly and directly enhances performance.

Conformity

Psychological research has found that the more cohesive the group, the more influence the group has on its individual members. This means there will be greater pressure on individual members to conform to the attitudes and behavior of the group. Group members might feel pressure about clothing style, hairstyle, practice habits, or game behavior. For example, when the Detroit

Pistons won consecutive NBA titles in 1989 and 1990 they were known as the "bad boys," and the norm was to play rough, tough, aggressive, intimidating basketball. Rookies and new players had to adapt to this norm and style of basketball to fit in with the team.

Highly cohesive groups demonstrate a greater conformity to the group's norm for productivity. A norm for productivity can be either high or low, and thus conformity to this norm may result in a member having higher or lower productivity. In either case, conformity and compliance of individual members is enhanced by the group's cohesion.

The more cohesive a group is, the greater influence it will have on individual group members to conform to group norms.

Stability

Stability refers to the turnover rate for group membership as well as to how long group members have been together. It would seem logical that teams that remain relatively constant across a certain period of time would be more stable, cohesive, and ultimately successful. In fact, Carron (1984) suggests that team cohesion and stability are related in a circular fashion. That is, the longer the team has been together, the more likely it is that cohesiveness will develop, and the more cohesive the team becomes, the less likely it is that members will choose to leave. Let's look at some research that has investigated this issue.

A study of 18 German Federation Soccer teams across a single season showed that teams with few line-up changes were more successful than those that changed constantly (Essing, 1970). A study of major league baseball teams supported this finding (Loy, 1970). A third study tried to determine if there is an optimal time to keep a group of players together to maximize cohesion and subsequent success. It found that in major league baseball, teams with a half life of 5 years were the most successful (a team's half-life was defined as the time it took for the starting roster to reduce to half of its original size) (Donnelly, Carron, & Chelladurai, 1978).

More recently, Brawley, Carron, and Widmeyer (1988) studied sport groups (including elite sport athletes, recreation sport athletes, and fitness classes) for relation between cohesion and the group's resistance to disruption (e.g., personnel changes or internal conflict). They then compared the groups that exhibited either high or low cohesion on their perceived resistance to disruption.

- Teams higher in cohesion can better resist disruption than teams lower in cohesion.
- Teams that stay together longer tend to be more cohesive, which leads to improvements in performance.

There was a reliable positive relation between group cohesion and group resistance to disruption: Teams higher in cohesion exhibited a higher perceived resistance to disruption than teams lower in cohesion.

Group Goals

Most people think individuals set their own goals. But in group situations, such as sport teams or exercise groups, goals are often set for the group. A group's goals are not merely the sum of the personal goals of group members; they are shared perceptions that refer to a desirable state for the group as a unit. The question is, What relation is there between group goals and cohesion? One study of volleyball, hockey, basketball, and swimming teams revealed the following:

- Members who perceived that their team engaged in group goal setting for competition had higher levels of cohesion.
- The higher the level of satisfaction with team goals, the higher the level of team cohesion.
- Although individual group members' perceptions of cohesion changed across a season, cohesion was still related to team satisfaction and group goals throughout the season (Brawley, Carron, & Widmeyer, 1993).

Athletes who perceive that a team goal encourages them to increase effort and practice drills designed to achieve that goal (e.g., in basketball, shifting successfully from a field goal or rebound to a full court press) will likely feel satisfied with team practice goals. This probably would happen as team members received feedback that the drills were correctly completed (i.e., the goal was reached) and perceived that team effort was high and attention was focused. In this way the group's goals can enhance its feelings of unity and cohesion.

Adherence to Exercise

With dropout rates from formal exercise programs at about 50%, researchers have been investigating ways to reduce this discouraging statistic. One innovative approach has focused on team building and how group cohesion might enhance adherence to exercise programs. It has been found that dropouts from exercise programs hold lower perceptions of their exercise class's task and social cohesion than participants who stay with the program (Carron & Spink, 1993; Spink & Carron, 1992, 1993). Exercisers with higher feelings of cohesion are absent from class or late to class less often than exercisers with lower cohesion.

In 1993 some sport psychologists attempted to build cohesiveness in exercise classes through a team approach (Spink & Carron, 1993). Instructors were trained in team building strategies to enhance adherence by improving group cohesion. They learned that distinctiveness contributes to a sense of group identity, unity, and cohesiveness. Some emphasized distinctiveness by having a group name, making up a group T-shirt, or handing out neon headbands (see Table 10.2 for strategies to enhance cohesiveness). Their classes showed higher levels of cohesion and significantly fewer dropouts and late arrivals than the classes not exposed to team building. This suggests that cohesion is an important ingredient in exercise settings as well as in traditional sport settings.

Exercise classes with high feelings of group cohesion have fewer dropouts and late arrivals than classes low in cohesiveness. Cohesiveness can be increased by exercise leaders.

Building Team Cohesion

Cohesion doesn't always enhance group performance, but it can certainly create a positive environment that elicits positive interactions among group members.

Table 10.2   Specific Strategies Suggested by Fitness Class Instructors to Enhance Group Cohesiveness

Factor	Example of intervention strategies used
Distinctiveness	Have a group name. Make up a group T-shirt. Hand out neon headbands and/or shoelaces. Make up posters/slogans for the class.
Individual positions	Divide pool into areas by fitness level. Have signs to label parts of the group. Use specific positions for low-, medium-, and high-impact exercisers. Let participants pick their own spot and encourage them to keep it throughout the year.
Group norms	Have members introduce each other. Encourage members to become fitness friends. Establish a goal to lose weight together. Promote a smart work ethic as a group characteristic.
Individual sacrifices	Ask two or three people for a goal for the day. Ask regulars to help new people. Ask people who aren't concerned with weight loss to make a sacrifice for the group on some days (more aerobics) and people who are to also make a sacrifice on other days (more mat work).
Interaction and communication	Use partner work and have them introduce themselves. Introduce the person on the right and left. Work in groups of five and take turns showing a move.

Adapted from Carron and Spink (1993).

Sport psychologists (e.g., Anshel, 1990; Carron, 1984; Yukelson, 1984) have suggested guidelines for developing team cohesion. Their ideas, though specific to sport teams, apply to teaching and exercise settings.

Communicate Effectively

An effective group consists of members who communicate easily and efficiently with one another (see chapter 12 for a detailed discussion on effective communi-

Barriers to Group Cohesion

- A clash of personalities in the group

- A conflict of task or social roles among group members

- A breakdown in communication among group members or between the group leader and members

- One or more members struggling for power

- Frequent turnover of group members

- Disagreement on group goals and objectives

cation). Communication's role in group cohesion is described here by Terry Orlick:

> Harmony grows when you really listen to others and they listen to you, when you are considerate of their feelings and they are considerate of yours, when you accept their differences and they accept yours, and when you help them and they help you. (1990, p. 143)

Team building requires a climate of openness where airing problems and matters of concern is not just appropriate but encouraged. Increases in communication have a circular relation with increased group cohesiveness (Carron, 1993). As communication about task and social issues increases, cohesiveness develops. As a result, group members are more open with each other, volunteer more, talk more, and listen better. The group leader plays a major role in integrating the group into a unit that communicates openly and performs with a sense of pride, excellence, and collective identity (Yukelson, 1993).

What Coaches Can Do

As long as communication is effective and open, coaches can foster team cohesion in several other ways as well. We'll discuss here what coaches can do to help build cohesion and then turn to what the players themselves can do.

Explain Individual Roles in Team Success.   Coaches should clearly outline individual roles to team members, stressing the importance of each player's role to team success. The more team members who perceive their roles as unimportant, the more apathetic the team. It's not easy to keep everyone on a football team happy and involved when some players never get to play in real games. Coaches need to carefully explain to these athletes what their roles are on the team and give them opportunities to contribute.

When players understand what is required of their teammates, they can begin to develop support and empathy among themselves. The coach can help

this process by having players observe and record the efforts of their teammates in different positions. Also, during practice, you might assign a player to play a position other than her usual position. For example, a spiker in volleyball who is upset at the setter's poor passes could be asked to set during practice. This way she can see how hard it is to set the ball in just the right spot for the spiker.

Develop Pride Within Subunits.   In sports where subunits naturally exist, such as football, hockey, and track and field, coaches should foster pride within these groups. Players need the support of their teammates, especially those playing the same position. The offensive linemen for the Washington Redskins in the 1980s called themselves "the hogs" because they did all the dirty work. The linemen took pride in this name and in what they contributed to overall team success. And the running backs and quarterback really appreciated the linemen's contributions—after all, their success depended on how well those hogs blocked.

Set Challenging Team Goals.   Setting specific, challenging goals has a positive impact on individual and group performance (see chapter 17). Goals set a high norm for productivity and keep the team focused on what they need to accomplish. As they reach goals, players should collectively feel encouraged to take pride in their accomplishments and strive toward new goals. These goals need to be clearly defined for them to foster group cohesiveness in their pursuit. The goals should be performance based (relating to players' abilities) rather than outcome based (winning).

Encourage Team Identity.   A coach can encourage team identity (by ordering team jackets and scheduling social functions, for example), but these should not interfere with the development of subunit identity. The two should work hand-in-hand. Teams should be made to feel special and in some sense different from other groups.

Avoid Formation of Social Cliques.   As compared to subunits, which are groups of athletes working at a similar position or task, social cliques usually

Figure 10.6 T-shirts can help build unity in a group and make members feel special.

benefit only a few athletes—at the expense of alienating most team members. Players often form cliques when the team is losing, their needs are not being met, or when coaches treat athletes differently, setting them apart from each other (e.g., starters vs. substitutes). Cliques tend to be disruptive to a team, and coaches should quickly determine why they are forming and take the steps to break them up. Changing roommate assignments on trips and encouraging team functions are ways to battle clique development.

Avoid Excessive Turnover.   Excessive turnover decreases cohesion and makes it difficult for members to establish close rapport. They feel unfamiliar with each other and uncertain about the group's longevity. Of course, high school and college teams will lose players each year to graduation. In this case, the veteran players should be asked to help integrate the new players into the team. Team expectations can be shared in a warm, sincere, open manner, making the new player feel at ease with his or her new team and teammates.

Conduct Periodic Team Meetings to Resolve Conflict.   Throughout the season coaches should conduct team meetings to allow for positive and negative feelings to be honestly, openly, and constructively expressed. A team can resolve its internal conflicts, mobilize its resources, and take intelligent action only if it has a means for consensually validating its own experience. Teams can talk about learning from mistakes, redefining goals, and maintaining good sportsmanship. Or they can simply express positive or negative feelings. The group leader or coach needs to steer the group to deal constructively with problems.

Stay in Touch with Team Climate.   Within any formal organization lies an informal, interpersonal network that can greatly affect the organization's functioning. A coach should identify the team members who have high interpersonal prestige and status on the team. They can be communication links between the coaching staff and players, helping coaches to stay in touch with the team's attitudes and feelings. This link gives coaches and athletes a vehicle for expressing ideas, opinions, and feelings regarding what's happening on the team.

Know Something Personal About Each Group Member.   Athletes appreciate it when the coach makes a special effort to know about their lives outside the context of the team. Even simple things, such as knowing and remembering a birthday or an exceptional grade in class, shows an athlete that you care. Being aware of potentially negative personal events, such as a divorce in the family or break-up with a boyfriend or girlfriend, and making yourself available to listen also demonstrates that you care.

What Group Members Can Do

So far our guidelines have been targeted at coaches. But team unity is not just the coach's responsibility—group members can also promote team cohesion. Here are some ways team members can improve communication and build a strong, cohesive unit.

Get to Know Teammates.   The better team members know each other, the easier it is to accept individual differences. Players should take time to get to know their teammates, especially the new members on the team.

Help Teammates Whenever Possible.   Being a team means that players are mutually interdependent. Helping each other out creates team spirit and brings teammates closer.

Give Teammates Positive Reinforcement. Supporting teammates instead of being negative and critical goes a long way toward building trust and support. Team members should be especially sensitive, positive, and constructive when a teammate is going through adversity. The help and support given to this player also helps the team.

Be Responsible. Team members should not get into the habit of blaming others for their poor performances. Blaming serves no useful purpose. When things are not going well, players need to try to make positive, constructive changes and get themselves back on track.

Communicate Honestly and Openly With the Coach. Team members should communicate with the coach openly and honestly. The better everyone understands each other, the better the chances for team success and harmony.

Resolve Conflicts Immediately. If a team member has a complaint or a conflict with the coach or a teammate, she should take the initiative to resolve the situation and clear the air. Players should not just gripe, complain, and vent their feelings. It is important to respond to the problem quickly so that negative feelings don't build up and explode later.

Give 100% Effort at All Times. Working hard, especially in practice, helps bring the team together. Dedication and commitment are contagious. Setting a good example usually has a positive impact on a team's unity.

Summary

We began by defining team cohesion as a dynamic process reflected in the group's tendency to stick together while pursuing its goals and objectives. By measuring cohesion, researchers have found that it is multidimensional and comprises both task and social cohesion. Task cohesion refers to working together as a team to achieve goals, whereas social cohesion refers to the interpersonal attraction among team members.

Carron's model of cohesion indicates that four factors affect the development of cohesion: environmental factors, personal factors, team factors, and leadership factors. Most recent research has examined the relation of cohesion and performance. Unfortunately, this relation is complex and studying it must involve three important factors: (a) measurement of cohesion, (b) type of task, and (c) direction of causality. Generally speaking, task cohesion is more closely related to performance than is social cohesion, and cohesion is more important for interacting sports than for coacting sports. In addition, the cohesion-performance relation appears to be circular, with team success enhancing cohesion, which leads in turn to success. Cohesion is positively related to other important constructs such as satisfaction, conformity, and stability. Both coaches and team members have responsibility for developing team cohesion, and sport psychologists can suggest many helpful guidelines.

Review Questions

1. Discuss the different definitions of cohesion, including the difference between task and social cohesion.

2. Discuss Carron's conceptual model of cohesion, focusing on the four antecedents of cohesion.

3. Discuss how measuring cohesion has developed via questionnaires.

4. Explain how a sociogram can help a coach understand the interpersonal attraction and cohesion of a team. Draw a hypothetical sociogram of a team and explain what information this gives the coach regarding the development of cohesion.

5. The cohesion-performance relation has resulted in inconsistent findings in the research literature. Explain how the types of measures employed and the demands of the task have impacted on this relation.

6. Does cohesion lead to winning or does winning lead to cohesion? Discuss this question and its implications for coaches in light of the research literature.

7. Although researchers have focused on the cohesion-performance relation, cohesion appears to be related to several other potentially important variables. Discuss the relation of cohesion and conformity and of cohesion and satisfaction.

8. You are a new coach who has inherited a team that had a great deal of dissension and in-fighting last season. Using the guidelines provided, discuss what you would do before and during the season to build cohesion in your team.

9. Although it is often considered the job of a coach to build team cohesion, athletes can also help in the process. If you were an athlete on a team lacking in cohesion, what might you do to build team unity?

10. How could you enhance group cohesion in exercise classes? What would you do to enhance attendance and adherence in an exercise class?

References

Anshel, M. (1990). *Sport psychology: From theory to practice.* Scottsdale, AZ: Gorsuch Scarisbrick.

Ball, J.R., & Carron, A.V. (1976). The influence of team cohesion and participation motivation upon performance success in intercollegiate ice hockey. *Canadian Journal of Applied Sport Sciences*, **1**, 241-275.

Bass, B.M. (1962). *The orientation inventory.* Palo Alto, CA: Consulting Psychologists Press.

Bird, A.M. (1977). Development of a model for predicting team performance. *Research Quarterly*, **48**, 24-32.

Brawley, L., Carron, A., & Widmeyer, W. (1987). Assessing the cohesion of teams: Validity of the Group Environment Questionnaire. *Journal of Sport Psychology*, **9**, 275-294.

Brawley, L., Carron, A., & Widmeyer, W. (1988). Exploring the relationship between cohesion and group resistance to disruption. *Journal of Sport and Exercise Psychology*, **10**, 199-213.

Brawley, L., Carron, A., & Widmeyer, W. (1993). The influence of the group and its cohesiveness on perception of group goal-related variables. *Journal of Sport and Exercise Psychology*, **15**, 245-266.

Carron, A.V. (1982). Cohesiveness in sport groups: Interpretations and considerations. *Journal of Sport Psychology*, **4**, 123-138.

Carron, A.V. (1984). Cohesion in sport teams. In J.M. Silva and R.S. Weinberg (Eds.), *Psychological foundations of sport* (pp. 340-351). Champaign, IL: Human Kinetics.

Carron, A.V. (1993). The sport team as an effective group. In J. Williams (Ed.), *Applied sport psychology: Personal growth to peak performance* (pp. 110-121). Mountain View, CA: Mayfield.

Carron, A.V., & Ball, J.R. (1977). Cause effect characteristics of cohesiveness and participation motivation in intercollegiate ice hockey. *International Review of Sport Sociology*, **12**, 49-60.

Carron, A., & Chelladurai, P. (1982). *Cohesiveness, coach-athlete compatibility, participation orientation and their relationship to relative performance and satisfaction.* Paper presented at the North American Society for Sport Psychology and Physical Activity, College Park, MD.

Carron, A.V., & Spink, H.S. (1993). Team building in an exercise setting. *The Sport Psychologist*, **7**, 8-18.

Carron, A., Widmeyer, W., & Brawley, L. (1985). The development of an instrument to assess cohesion in sport teams: The Group Environment Questionnaire. *Journal of Sport Psychology*, **7**, 244-267.

Donnelly, P., Carron, A.V., & Chelladurai, P. (1978). *Group cohesion and sport* (Sociology of Sport Monograph Series). Ottawa, Ontario: Canadian Association for Health, Physical Education and Recreation.

Essing, W. (1970). Team line-up and team achievement in European football. In G.S. Kenyon (Ed.), *Contemporary psychology of sport* (pp. 349-354). Chicago: Athletic Institute.

Festinger, L., Schacter, S., & Back, K. (1950). *Social pressures in informed groups: A study of a housing project.* New York: Harper.

Gruber, J.J., & Gray, G.R. (1982). Responses to forces influencing cohesion as a function of player status and level of male varsity basketball competition. *Research Quarterly for Exercise and Sport*, **53**, 27-36.

Landers, D.M., & Lueschen, G. (1974). Team performance outcome and cohesiveness of competitive coaching groups. *International Review of Sport Sociology*, **2**, 57-69.

Landers, D.M., Wilkinson, M.O., Hatfield, B.D., & Barber, H. (1982). Causality and the cohesion-performance relationship. *Journal of Sport Psychology*, **4**, 170-183.

Lenk, H. (1969). Top performance despite internal conflict: An antithesis to a functional proposition. In J.W. Loy & G.S. Kenyon (Eds.), *Sport, culture and society: A reader on the sociology of sport* (pp. 224-235). New York: Macmillan.

Loy, J.W. (1970). *Where the action is: A consideration of centrality in sport situations.* Paper presented at the meeting of the Second Canadian Psychomotor Learning and Sport Psychology Symposium, Windsor, Ontario.

Martens, R., Landers, D., & Loy, J. (1972). *Sports cohesiveness questionnaire.* Washington, DC: AAHPERD.

McGrath, J.E. (1962). The influence of positive interpersonal relations on adjustment and effectiveness in rifle teams. *Journal of Abnormal and Social Psychology*, **65**, 365-375.

Nixon, H.L. (1977). "Cohesiveness" and team success: A theoretical reformulation. *Review of Sport and Leisure*, **2**, 36-57.

Orlick, T. (1990). *In pursuit of excellence* (2nd ed.). Champaign, IL: Human Kinetics.

Ruder, M.K., & Gill, D.L. (1982). Immediate effects of win-loss on perceptions of cohesion in intramural and intercollegiate volleyball teams. *Journal of Sport Psychology*, **4**, 227-234.

Spink, K.S., & Carron, A.V. (1992). Group cohesion and adhesion in exercise classes. *Journal of Sport and Exercise Psychology*, **14**, 78-86.

Spink, K.S., & Carron, A.V. (1993). The effects of team building on the adherence patterns of female exercise participants. *Journal of Sport and Exercise Psychology*, **15**, 50-62.

Widmeyer, W.N., Brawley, L.R., & Carron, A.V. (1985). *The measurement of cohesion in sport teams: The group environment questionnaire.* London, Ontario, Canada: Sports Dynamics.

Widmeyer, W.N., & Martens, R. (1978). When cohesion predicts performance outcome in sport. *Research Quarterly*, **49**, 372-380.

Williams, J.M., & Hacker, C.M. (1982). Causal relationships among cohesion, satisfaction, and performance in women's intercollegiate field hockey teams. *Journal of Sport Psychology*, **4**, 324-337.

Yukelson, D. (1984). Group motivation in sport teams. In J. Silva and R. Weinberg (Eds.), *Psychological foundations of sport.* Champaign, IL: Human Kinetics.

Yukelson, D. (1993). Communicating effectively. In J. Williams (Ed.), *Applied sport psychology: Personal growth to peak performance* (pp. 122-136). Mountain View, CA: Mayfield.

Yukelson, D., Weinberg, R., & Jackson, A. (1984). A multidimensional group cohesion instrument for intercollegiate basketball teams. *Journal of Sport Psychology*, **6**, 103-117.

CHAPTER 11

Leadership

Who can forget the fourth-quarter comeback under the leadership of San Francisco 49er quarterback Joe Montana that beat the Dallas Cowboys in the 1981 NFC championship game? Or the final game of the 1980 NBA play-offs where, in his first season, Magic Johnson assumed the center position when Kareem Abdul-Jabbar was injured, provided offensive leadership, and scored over 30 points to defeat the Philadelphia 76ers for the championship?

In the world of sport, coaches like Knute Rockne, John Wooden, Pat Head Summitt, Vince Lombardi, and Casey Stengal or players like Nancy Lieberman Cline, Magic Johnson, Joe Montana, and Wayne Gretsky have shown great leadership capacity. It is easy to think of people who are great leaders, but it is much more difficult to determine what makes them leaders. For decades psychologists have studied leadership. In fact, more than 3,500 studies on leadership have been published (Stogdill, 1974), and researchers are still investigating leadership concepts.

In this chapter you will learn about

▌ what leadership is,
▌ how psychologists study leadership,
▌ research into sport leadership,
▌ the Multidimensional Model of Sport Leadership,
▌ factors affecting sport leadership, and
▌ what makes successful leadership in sport and exercise settings.

What Is Leadership?

Leadership might broadly be considered "the behavioral process of influencing individuals and groups toward set goals" (Barrow, 1977, p. 232). This definition is useful because it encompasses many dimensions of leadership. In sport and exercise these dimensions include decision-making processes, motivational techniques, giving feedback, establishing interpersonal relationships, and directing the group or team confidently.

A leader knows where the group or team is going (i.e., its goals and objectives) and provides the direction and resources to help it get there. Coaches who are good leaders provide not only a vision of what to strive for but also the day-to-day structure, motivation, and support to translate vision into reality. Coaches, teachers, and exercise specialists are leaders who seek to assure each participant maximum opportunities to achieve success. And coaches also try to ensure that individual success helps achieve team success.

Leader or Manager?

A manager takes care of such things as scheduling, budgeting, and organizing, whereas a leader is more concerned with the direction of an organization, including its goals and objectives.

A manager is generally concerned with planning, organizing, scheduling, budgeting, staffing, and recruiting. Although leaders often perform these same functions (or delegate them to others), they act in some other critical ways. For example, leaders help determine the direction the organization or team pursues, including its goals and objectives. They try to provide the resources and support to get the job done. Many coaches become excellent managers as they tackle operations that keep things running smoothly. But this is different from provid-

---

Leadership in Sports: An Example

It's the final play-off game between the Cleveland Browns and Denver Broncos, and the winner will go on to the Super Bowl. Cleveland is ahead with 2 minutes left when the Broncos receive the ball on their own 2-yard line. It will take a miracle to drive down the field 98 yards to win the game. Quarterback John Elway has often led the Broncos from the edge of defeat to victory with breathtaking fourth-quarter finishes. Besides having great physical talent, Elway is a leader. In the huddle at the 2-yard line, he tells his teammates that they will win this game. He tells them to remain poised and to concentrate on carrying out their assignments. His teammates believe in him and work hard because they know John Elway can do the impossible. They respect not only his athletic skills but also his mental toughness, drive, and dedication. Under Elway's leadership the Broncos methodically drive down the field against all odds and score a touchdown.

ing the leadership needed for players and teams to grow and mature. "Too many teams are overmanaged and underled" (Martens, 1987, p. 33).

How Are Leaders Chosen?

Usually leaders and coaches are appointed by someone in authority. For example, in health clubs, owners choose the managers, and in schools the principal chooses the teachers. Similarly, in college sports, the athletic director (with some feedback from a search committee) commonly selects coaches.

Sometimes, however, leaders simply emerge from the group and take charge, such as with captains and coaches of intramural or club teams. Many leaders who emerge are more effective than appointed leaders because they have the respect and support of team or group members. They probably have special leadership skills or high ability in the particular sport or exercise.

Researchers have tried to identify these special leadership skills, hoping to be able to predict and select those likely to become leaders. They have also researched if situation factors produce effective leadership and if environment might be structured to better develop leadership abilities. We will review the earlier research into industrial and organizational leadership and the studies it stimulated in sport settings. Then we will discuss how sport psychologists have studied leadership effectiveness.

Trait Approach

In the 1920s researchers tried to determine what characteristics or personality traits were common to great leaders in business and industry. They considered leadership traits to be relatively stable personality dispositions, such as intelligence, assertiveness, independence, and self-confidence. These researchers were proponents of the trait theory and argued that successful leaders have certain personality characteristics that make it likely for them to be leaders no matter what situation they are in. This would mean, for example, that Joe Montana would be a great leader not only on the football field but also in other sports and aspects of life such as business and community affairs.

The trait approach lost favor around the end of World War II, when Stogdill (1948) reviewed over 100 trait theory studies of leadership and found only a couple of consistent personality traits. Although certain traits might be helpful for a leader to have, they are certainly not essential. Nor do they guarantee successful leadership.

Attempts were also made in sport to identify successful coaches according to the trait view. For example, one study profiled typical coaches as tough-minded, authoritarian, willing to bear the pressure of fans and the media, emotionally mature, independent in their thinking, and realistic in their perspective (Ogilvie & Tutko, 1966, 1970). The study, however, did not provide documented evidence to support this coaching profile.

In fact, no particular set of traits seems to characterize effective sport leadership. For example, Charles Barkley is a leader on the basketball floor although he would not fit any typical psychological profile of effective leadership. Because an ideal leadership style among coaches and athletes has not been found, little sport research today uses the trait approach to leadership theory.

Leaders have a variety of personality traits. There are no specific traits that make a leader successful.

Behavioral Approach

Research next focused on discovering universal *behaviors* of effective leaders. Behaviorists argued that anyone could be taught to become a leader by simply learning the behaviors of other effective leaders. Thus, unlike trait theory, the behavioral approach argues that leaders are made, not born.

Leaders in Business, Military, Government, and Education

To describe how leaders in business, military, educational, and government organizations behave or go about doing their jobs, researchers at the Ohio State University developed the *Leader Behavior Description Questionnaire* (LBDQ). Using it, they found that most of what leaders do falls into two categories: *consideration* and *initiating structure*. Consideration refers to friendship, mutual trust, respect, and warmth between the leader and subordinates. Leaders who scored high on consideration had good rapport and communication with others. Initiating structure refers to such behavior as setting up rules and regulations, channels of communications, procedural methods, and well-defined patterns of organization to achieve goals and objectives. Leaders who scored high on initiating structure were active in directing group activities, communicating, scheduling, and experimenting with new ideas. These two categories are distinct but also compatible. For instance, successful leaders tend to score high on both consideration and initiating structure.

Leaders in Sport

Successful leaders tend to score high on both initiating structure and consideration.

Leaders in sport and exercise settings work both through interpersonal relationships and providing direction, goals, and structure to their team or class. For example, when a coach takes over a new team, she must establish open lines of communication, good interpersonal relations, and clear goals and objectives. To study leadership behaviors in sport, psychologists devised several sport-specific questionnaires. We will describe three useful methodologies and some of their findings.

Communication.   Effective communication is a key ingredient to successful coaching and teaching, especially with younger players (6 to 16 years). For example, effective coaches communicate well to instruct and correct an error (e.g., "get down on one knee on a ground ball and block it with your body"), rather than simply yelling nonspecific feedback (e.g., "you did that incorrectly!") (see chapter 12 on effective communication).

Most hockey coach behaviors apparently are communicative. Danielson, Zelhart, and Drake revised the *Leadership Behavior Description Questionnaire* and administered it to 160 young hockey players, ages 12 to 18, wanting to determine which behaviors these athletes believed their coaches exhibited (1975; see Table 11.1, which shows the eight coaching behaviors identified in this study and descriptions of each).

Instruction and Demonstration.   Former UCLA basketball coach John Wooden is a coaching legend in basketball, winning an unprecedented 10 of 12 NCAA basketball championships and coaching, among other greats, Kareem Abdul-Jabbar and Bill Walton. What was John Wooden's secret? Using the *event recording* technique for 30 hours of observation, Tharp and Gallimore (1976) identified 10 categories of behavior Wooden exhibited. Most of his behaviors involved giving instructions (what to do and how to do it); often he also encouraged intensity and effort.

For example, in communicating he spent about 50% of his time in verbal instruction, 12.7% in hustling players to intensify instruction, 8% in scolding and reinstructing with a combination statement, 6.9% in praising and encouraging, and 6.6% in simple statements of displeasure (i.e., scolding; Tharp & Gallimore, 1976).

Table 11.1 Coaching Behavior as Perceived by High School Hockey Players	
Behavior	**Examples**
Competitive training	Training, performance, and motivation
Initiation	An open approach to solving problems using new methods
Interpersonal team operation	Getting team members to work together for efficiency
Social	Social interaction outside athletics
Representation	Representing the team favorably in contacts with outsiders
Organization communication	Concern for organization or communication with little concern for interpersonal support
Recognition	Feedback and reinforcement as rewards for performance and participation
General excitement	Arousal and activation; involves a disorganized approach to team operation

Adapted from Danielson, Zelhart, and Drake (1975).

In event recording an investigator lists several typical coaching behaviors and then records when and how often these behaviors occur. Usually more than one rater records the behaviors. Having two or more raters verifies that people can consistently observe the same behavior, improving the study's reliability. For example, if three raters watch a coach during a game and agree that she used punishment five times, the conclusion would be considered more reliable than if only one rater observed the coach.

Studying Wooden, the researchers noted that his demonstrations rarely lasted longer than 5 seconds, but they were so clear that they left an image in memory, much like a textbook sketch. Wooden models with his body most often during patterned offensive drills, half-court scrimmage when he will whistle down play. He promptly demonstrates the correct way to perform the act (modeling positive) and then imitates the incorrect way the player has just performed (modeling negative) (Tharp & Gallimore, 1976, p. 77).

Reactive and Spontaneous Behaviors.   Researchers have wanted to look at coaching behaviors in general to develop guidelines for training coaches (Smith, Smoll, & Hunt, 1977; Smoll, Smith, Curtis, & Hunt, 1978). The *Coaching Behavior Assessment System* (CBAS) was developed for coding and analyzing the behavior of coaches in natural field settings. Coaching behaviors turn out to be either reactive or spontaneous (see Table 11.2). *Reactive* behaviors are responses to a specific player behavior, for example, when a coach instructs after an error. *Spontaneous* behaviors, on the other hand, are initiated by the coach. For example, a coach might yell encouragement to his players as they go onto the field.

Other studies have used the CBAS to assess specific coaching behaviors and how they affect young athletes. These behaviors relate in general to a leadership style that emphasizes the positive. About two thirds of all observed coaching behaviors were found to be positive, falling into the categories of

- positive reinforcement ("You really got down on that ground ball. Keep up the good work.");

Coach Wooden focused his coaching on telling players what to do and how to do it. He accomplished this through short demonstrations modeling the correct behavior.

Table 11.2 Categories of Coaching Behavior From the Coaching Behavior Assessment System

Class I. Reactive behaviors

Responses to desirable performance

Reinforcement	A positive, rewarding reaction (verbal or nonverbal) to a good play or good effort
Nonreinforcement	Failure to respond to a good performance

Responses to mistakes

Mistake-contingent encouragement	Encouragement given to a player following a mistake
Mistake-contingent technical instruction	Instructing or demonstrating to a player how to correct a mistake he or she has made
Punishment	A negative reaction, verbal or nonverbal, following a mistake
Punitive technical instruction	Technical instruction following a mistake given in a punitive or hostile manner
Ignoring mistakes	Failure to respond to a player mistake

Responses to misbehavior

Keeping control	Reactions intended to restore or maintain order among team members

Class II. Spontaneous behaviors

Game-related

General technical instruction	Spontaneous instruction in the techniques and strategies of the sport (not following a mistake)
General encouragement	Spontaneous encouragement that does not follow a mistake
Organization	Administrative behavior that sets the stage for play by assigning duties or responsibilities

Game-irrelevant

General communication	Interactions with players unrelated to the game

Adapted from Smoll and Smith (1980).

- general technical instruction ("Keep your head down when you complete your golf swing."); and
- general encouragement ("Keep up the good work!").

Players demonstrate greater self-esteem at the end of a season when they have played for coaches who frequently use mistake-contingent encouragement and reinforcement. They rate their teammates and their sport more positively when they have played for coaches who use high amounts of general technical instruction.

Many coaches learned by attending a workshop to communicate positively with young athletes. The youngsters reported that they liked their teammates more, felt these coaches were knowledgeable, rated their coaches better as teachers, had a greater desire to play again the next year, and had higher levels of enjoyment than other young players whose coaches did not attend the workshop.

Interactional Approach

Trait and behavioral approaches emphasize personal factors at the expense of considering the interaction between people and their situational constraints (see chapter 3). Many researchers in industry and general psychology have proposed interactional models of leadership (see Horn, 1992, for a review of the literature). These interactional theories have important implications for effective leadership in sport and exercise settings.

1. No one set of characteristics ensures successful leadership. Investigators believed that great leaders had in common personality traits that suited them for leadership roles and distinguished them from nonleaders. However, leaders have not been predicted solely by their personality traits.

2. Effective leadership fits the specific situation. Some leaders function better in certain situations than in others. Coaches have been fired from team positions, for example, when administrators thought they weren't providing effective leadership, only to be hired by another team where they were immediately successful. These coaches probably did not suddenly change their leadership styles or the way they coached—rather, their leadership styles and behavior fit better in their new settings.

3. Leadership styles can be changed. If you hear someone say, "Some people have what it takes and others don't," don't believe him. In fact, coaches and other leaders can alter their styles and behaviors to match a situation's demands. Here are two examples of leadership styles and how they might change to fit a situation. *Relationship-oriented leaders* develop interpersonal relationships, keep open lines of communication, maintain positive social interactions, and assure that everyone is involved and feeling good (like the consideration function described earlier; Fiedler, 1967). On the other hand, *task-oriented leaders* primarily work to get the task done and meet their objectives (like the initiating structure function described earlier). Their focus is performance and productivity rather than creating good interpersonal relations.

> A relationship-oriented leader focuses on developing and maintaining good interpersonal relationships; a task-oriented leader focuses on setting goals and getting the job done.

Leadership in Sport: An Interactional Coaching Example

Forest Gregg was NFL coach of the year as head football coach of the Cleveland Browns during the 1976 season, yet he was fired from his position the very next year. Apparently Gregg by nature was extremely task oriented. During the 1976 season leader-member relations were good because of a winning record; the situation was very structured and the leader's position was strong because of the support of owner Art Modell. Gregg's task-oriented style of leadership predictably would be effective. However, during the next season the team had a losing record and leader-member relations deteriorated. Gregg's position and power weakened. Football, of course, was still a structured sport, and thus task structure was still favorable. According to Fiedler's classification scheme, a structured situation with poor leader-member relations and weak position power would represent a moderately favorable situation. Gregg remained task oriented and autocratic, but the situation (moderately favorable) called for a relationship-oriented approach. Gregg's leadership did not fit the new situation. (Straub, 1978)

Relationship-Oriented Versus Task-Oriented Leadership

People can change from a relationship-oriented style to a task-oriented style (or vice versa) depending on the situation. Fiedler's research demonstrates that in either very favorable or unfavorable situations a task-oriented leader is more effective. However, in moderately favorable situations, a relationship-oriented leader is more effective. A physical education teacher in an inner city school that lacks facilities, leadership, and community support might have to be very task oriented. Getting things done and setting goals would override developing positive interpersonal relations. Conversely, a physical education teacher in a lower middle class school where the facilities are poor but the community support is good (moderately favorable situation) might be more effective as a relationship-oriented leader. Thus, sport and exercise professionals need to be flexible in their leadership styles, tailoring them to meet the demands of the situation. If a coach feels more comfortable with one type of leadership style than another, he should seek out situations where this style would be most effective.

Highly skilled players are typically task oriented, and coaches who have a more relationship-oriented style appear to be more effective with these players. Conversely, lower skilled players need more continuous instruction and feedback: A task-oriented coach would be more appropriate for them. This does not mean that lower skilled individuals do not need or want a caring, empathetic coach or that higher skilled participants do not need specific feedback and instruction. It is a matter of what should be emphasized. Getting the task done and providing a supportive environment are both necessary for effective leadership.

Jerry Faust was one of the most successful high school football coaches in the country when he became head coach at the University of Notre Dame. Faust could not maintain Notre Dame's standard of winning and was fired after several seasons. He may not have altered his coaching behavior to fit the maturity level of college, versus high school, players. The maturity level of participants needs to be considered to determine the most effective leadership style, and this too is a matter of an interactional approach to leadership.

Consider these specific relationships between leadership styles and maturity level:

- Most elementary and junior high school athletes require a low task orientation and high relationship orientation.
- Most high school athletes require high levels of both task-oriented and relationship-oriented behaviors.
- Most college athletes require low relationship-oriented and high task-oriented behaviors (Chelladurai & Carron, 1977).

Younger athletes especially need relationship-oriented leadership for their best performance, personal growth, and development. Traditional sport practices, which emphasize autocratic behaviors, may actually hinder the development of athletic maturity:

> People on the high school level talk about sport programs and how they develop a kid's self-discipline and responsibility. I think the giveaway that most of this stuff preached on the lower level is a lie, is that when you go to college and professional levels, the coaches still treat you as an adolescent. They know damn well that you were never given a chance to become responsible or self-disciplined. Even in the pros you are told when to go to bed, when to turn your lights off, when to wake up, when to eat, and what to eat. (All-pro football player George Sauer as cited in Sage, 1978, p. 225)

The effectiveness of an individual's leadership style stems from matching the situation.

The Multidimensional Model of Sport Leadership

The leadership models we have discussed so far were derived from nonsport settings, such as industry and the military, and they are excellent frameworks for understanding leadership. Yet, they are not specific to sport or physical activity. P. (Chella) Chelladurai (1978, 1990) developed the *Multidimensional Model of Leadership* specifically for athletic situations. Chelladurai's leadership model conceptualizes leadership as an interactional process. That is, he argues that leader effectiveness in sport is contingent on situational characteristics of both the leader and the group members. Thus, effective leadership can and will vary depending on the characteristics of the athletes and constraints of the situation (see Figure 11.1).

According to Chelladurai, athlete satisfaction and performance (box 7 in the figure) depend on three types of leader behavior: required (box 4), preferred (box 6), and actual (box 5). The situation (box 1), leader (box 2), and members (box 3) lead to these three kinds of behavior, so they are called antecedents.

If we put this model in interactional terms, leader characteristics are the personal factor, whereas characteristics of the situation and members are the situation factors. Chelladurai hypothesizes that a positive outcome—that is, optimal performance and group satisfaction—occurs if the three aspects of leader behavior agree. If the leader behaves appropriately for the particular situation and these behaviors match the preferences of the group members, they will achieve their best performance and feel satisfied. For example, a supervisor tells an exercise leader to concentrate on good communication and relations with the participants in her class (i.e., to be relationship-oriented), and the participants want this behavior in a leader: They perform optimally and find satisfaction. We'll now take a closer look at the three types of leader behavior and how the antecedent conditions affect them.

> Optimal performance and satisfaction are achieved when a leader's required, preferred, and actual behaviors are consistent.

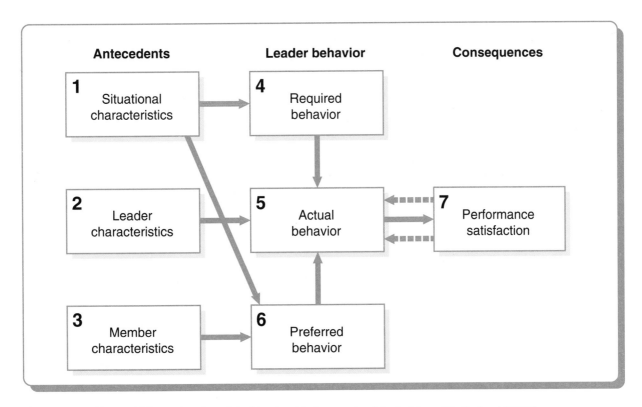

Figure 11.1 The multidimensional model of leadership for sports. Adapted from Chelladurai (1980).

Required Leader Behavior

The situation demands that a leader behave in certain ways. In other words, the organizational system itself dictates behaviors, and people are expected to conform to the established norms. For example, physical education teachers are expected to behave in certain ways in front of their students, fellow teachers, and parents (e.g., high school PE teachers shouldn't attend the same parties as their students). Similarly, coaches are expected to behave in specific ways with reporters, other coaches, and spectators. Management goals, program structure, and the social, cultural, and economic environment all may prescribe an exercise leader's behavior.

Preferred Leader Behavior

Group members also have preferences for specific leader behaviors. Some members want to stress achievement, others affiliation. Age, gender, skill, and experience influence what kind of guidance, social support, and feedback they prefer. An adult in rehabilitation after anterior cruciate ligament (knee reconstruction) surgery, for example, probably expects to have more input into program planning than a young athlete does.

Sometimes group members become used to certain behaviors and grow to prefer them. For instance, the owner of the Los Angeles Raiders football team, Al Davis, has traditionally advocated a loose leadership style, allowing players individualism off the field as long as they perform well on the field. Players on his team have grown to prefer this style of leadership.

Actual Leader Behavior

Actual leader behaviors are simply the behaviors the leader exhibits, such as initiating structure or being considerate. According to Chelladurai, the leader's characteristics, such as personality, ability, and experience (box 2 in Figure 11.1) affect these behaviors directly. Actual behavior is believed to be indirectly affected by group preferences and what the situation dictates. For example, a professional sports team usually has winning as a goal, and its coach would likely adopt task-oriented behaviors. Although winning is among a high school team's goals, the experience itself is also valued, and a coach would likely adopt consideration-oriented behaviors. Characteristics of both the situation and group members would influence the coaches.

Performance and Satisfaction

Performance and satisfaction are jointly affected by the congruence, or match, of required, preferred, and actual leader behaviors. They are not independent of each other. For example, if the athletes are task oriented, satisfaction and performance are *both* enhanced.

Research on the Multidimensional Model of Leadership

Researchers have tested both the accuracy and the usefulness of Chelladurai's multidimensional model, applying the model in interesting ways. We'll discuss briefly a couple of these applications. (For a more detailed analysis of the Multidimensional Model of Leadership, see Chelladurai, 1990, and Horn, 1992.)

Leadership Scale for Sports

The *Leadership Scale for Sports* (LSS) was developed to measure leadership behaviors, including the athletes' preferences for specific behaviors, athletes' perceptions of their coaches' behaviors, and coaches' perceptions of their own behavior (e.g., Chelladurai & Saleh, 1978; Chelladurai, Malloy, Imamura, & Yamaguchi, 1987; Chelladurai et al., 1988). The LSS has five dimensions:

• Training (instructional behaviors)—A coach oriented toward training and instruction scores high in trying to improve the athletes' performances by giving technical instruction on skills, techniques, and strategies; by emphasizing and facilitating rigorous training; and by coordinating the activities of team members.

• Democratic behavior (decision-making style)—A coach with a democratic style allows athletes to participate in decisions about the group's goals, practice methods, and game tactics and strategies.

• Autocratic behavior (decision-making style)—An autocratic coach is typically aloof from the players and stresses personal authority in working with them. Input from athletes is generally not invited.

• Social support (motivational tendencies)—A coach who scores high in social support shows concern for the welfare of individual athletes and attempts to establish warm relationships with them. Unlike a coach who stresses positive feedback during performance, a social support–oriented coach's behaviors are independent of (not contingent on) the athlete's performance and typically extend beyond the athletic arena.

- Positive feedback (motivational tendencies)—A coach who scores high in positive feedback consistently praises or rewards athletes for good performance. Positive feedback is contingent on the performance and limited to the athletic context.

Antecedents of Leadership

Some studies have concentrated on the conditions, or *antecedents*, that affect leader behavior, whereas others have focused on the *consequences* of leader behavior—that is, how it affects member performance and satisfaction.

Studies of the conditions that affect leader behavior have produced many insights, including the following:

- As people get older and mature athletically, they increasingly prefer an autocratic coaching style. Thus, coaches of college athletes should adopt a more autocratic style than high school coaches.
- Males prefer training and instruction behaviors and an autocratic coaching style more than females do. Hence, coaches should be more directive with males and provide plenty of instructional feedback.
- Females prefer a democratic and participatory coaching style allowing them to help make the decisions. Coaches and other group leaders should allow females opportunities for input.
- Athletes who have high task motivation prefer more training and instruction, whereas those with high affiliation motivation prefer more social support.
- Athlete preference for training and instruction progressively decreases through high school but increases again in college.
- Athlete preference for social support progressively increases throughout high school and into college. Empathy and understanding are critical for working with high school–age and college-age populations.
- Compared to their low-skilled counterparts, highly skilled athletes perceive their coaches as trainers and instructors, democratic in style, and as providing more positive feedback. Thus, leadership style should be adjusted to fit the level of the athletes.
- Athletes from the United States, Great Britain, and Canada do not differ notably in the coaching styles they prefer. Japanese university athletes prefer more social support and autocratic behaviors than Canadian athletes, and they perceive their coaches to be more autocratic. Thus, cultural background may influence leadership preferences.
- Athletes who play highly interactive team sports, such as basketball, prefer an autocratic coaching style more than do athletes in coacting sports, such as bowling. Thus, the volleyball team should be coached differently from the track team.

Consequences of Leadership

According to Chelladurai (1990), when a coach leads in a style that matches group member preferences, optimal performance and satisfaction result. Using Chelladurai's model to investigate the consequences of how a sport leader behaves, researchers have found the following:

- Athletes' not getting the coaching style they prefer clearly affects their satisfaction. Especially with training and instruction and positive behaviors, the greater the discrepancy, the less the satisfaction.

• The relationship between athlete satisfaction and leadership discrepancy varies by sport. Leadership that could produce satisfaction among basketball players, for example, would not predict satisfaction among wrestlers and track-and-field athletes. Clearly, if you value athlete satisfaction, you need to identify the players' preferences for leadership style for the specific activity.

• High frequencies of rewarding behavior, social support, and democratic decision-making are generally associated with high satisfaction among athletes.

• High frequencies of social support are related to poorer team performance (i.e., win-loss record). The increased social support did not *cause* the team to lose more. More likely, losing teams need more social support from leaders to sustain motivation.

• When a coach reports developing the same decision style that his or her athletes prefer and perceive, coaching effectiveness is rated highly.

Four Components of Effective Leadership

We have emphasized that personal traits alone do not account for leadership. Yet research has identified some common and consistent components of effective leaders, including qualities of great leaders and leadership styles. Research has also identified general strategies to produce more effective leadership in physical education, sport, and exercise settings, including manipulating situational factors and promoting certain group member characteristics.

The four components of effective leadership are really a composite of many different approaches to the study of leadership. No one approach is best—they all make some contribution to understanding what makes effective leadership. Consistent with the interactional model, the four components together show that behavior is best understood as an interaction between personal and situational factors.

Qualities of Effective Leaders

Effective leadership has four separate components (Martens, 1987; see Figure 11.2). Although there isn't one distinct set of essential core personality traits that assure a person will become a leader, successful leaders appear to have these qualities in common:

- Intelligence
- Assertion
- Empathy
- Intrinsic motivation
- Flexibility
- Ambition
- Self-confidence
- Optimism

These are necessary, but not sufficient, qualities to become a leader—that is, presence of all these qualities doesn't guarantee a leader. And these qualities will be needed to a greater or lesser degree depending on the preferences of group members and the specific situation.

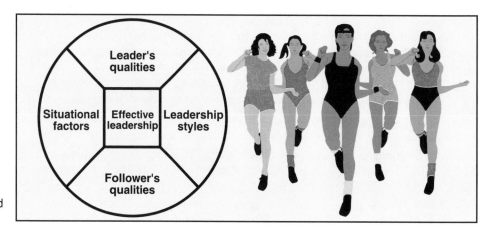

Figure 11.2 The four components of effective leadership. Adapted from Martens (1987).

Leadership Style

We have talked about democratic or autocratic coaching styles. As you might expect, the democratic style coach is typically athlete-centered, cooperative, and relationship oriented. Conversely, the autocratic style coach is usually win oriented, very structured, and task oriented. A coach need not be all one or the other. We can effectively integrate and blend both democratic and autocratic leadership styles (Blake & Moulton, 1969). The challenge is determining what style best suits the circumstances. The appropriate coaching style depends most on situation factors and member characteristics.

Situational Factors

A leader should be sensitive to the specific situation and environment. Several situation factors come into play when planning for effective leadership in sport (Martens, 1987), including

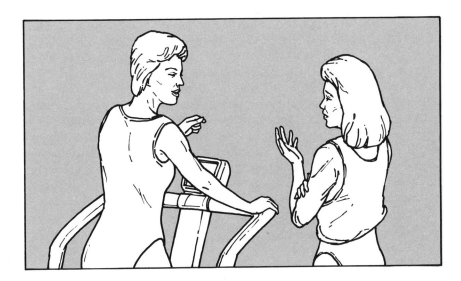

Figure 11.3 "I really feel comfortable with Anne's low-key style of leading our exercise class."

- team versus individual sports,
- interactive (e.g., basketball) versus coactive (bowling) sports,
- size of the team,
- time available,
- number of assistants, and
- tradition.

Member Characteristics

The characteristics of the followers (athletes in sport settings) are also important in determining how effective leadership is. The need for a mesh between the characteristics and style of leaders and participants shows how important the interactional process is. For example, higher skill athletes prefer a more relationship-oriented coach, and female athletes prefer a democratic coach. Specific participant characteristics that determine whether leadership will be effective in sport and exercise include

- gender,
- ability level,
- personality,
- nationality,
- age, and
- experience.

Summary

Leadership refers to the process of influencing people toward set goals. Its study has a rich history in the industrial, military, and psychological literatures. Most of this study has been from three major approaches. The trait approach assumes great leaders possess a set of universal personality traits that are essential for effective leadership. The behavioral approach assumes that a relatively universal set of behaviors are characteristic of successful leaders. The interactional approach posits that it is the interaction of the situation and a leader's behaviors that determine effective leadership. This approach assumes that there is not one best type of leader but that leadership style and effectiveness depend on fitting the situation and qualities of the group's members.

Chelladurai, who developed the Multidimensional Model of Sport Leadership, considers group performance and member satisfaction to depend on how well three types of leader behavior—required, preferred, and actual—mesh, the antecedents being the characteristics of the situation, the leader, and the members. Positive outcomes, performance, and group satisfaction occur if the three types of leader behavior are congruent. That is, if a coach or other leader uses behaviors prescribed for the particular situation that are consistent with the preferences of the members, optimal performance and member satisfaction will result. The Leadership Scale for Sport was established to help test the model, and its use has supported the model. Effective leadership in sport apparently depends on the qualities of the leader, leadership style, situational factors, and characteristics of the followers.

Review Questions

1. Compare and contrast the trait, behavioral, and interactional approaches to leadership.

2. Discuss three practical implications and principles that can be drawn from the psychological literature on leadership.

3. Describe three major results of the Coaching Behavior Assessment System and how it applies to coaching and teaching.

4. Discuss event recording as a technique for studying leadership behaviors in sport.

5. Describe the major tenets of Chelladurai's Multidimensional Model of Leadership, including the three antecedents and three types of leader behaviors.

6. List three findings each from studies about the antecedent conditions and the consequences of leadership behaviors in sport.

7. Discuss the four components of effective leadership. What implications do these have for leaders in coaching, teaching, or exercise settings?

8. Describe how you might apply some of the principles and findings derived from Chelladurai's model to coaching, teaching, or exercise training.

References

Barrow, J. (1977). The variables of leadership: A review and conceptual framework. *Academy of Management Review*, **2**, 231-251.

Blake, R., & Moulton, J. (1969). *Building a dynamic corporation through grid organization development*. Reading, MA: Addison Wesley.

Chelladurai, P. (1978). *A contingency model of leadership in athletics*. Unpublished doctoral dissertation, Department of Management Sciences, University of Waterloo, Canada.

Chelladurai, P. (1990). Leadership in sports: A review. *International Journal of Sport Psychology*, **21**, 328-354.

Chelladurai, P., & Carron, A.V. (1977). A reanalysis of formal structure in sport. *Canadian Journal of Applied Sport Sciences*, **2**, 9-14.

Chelladurai, P., Imamura, H., Yamaguchi, Y., Oinuma, Y., & Miyauchi, T. (1988). Sport leadership in a crossnational setting: The case of Japanese and

Canadian university athletes. *Journal of Sport & Exercise Psychology*, **10**, 374-389.

Chelladurai, P., Malloy, D., Imamura, H., & Yamaguchi, Y. (1987). A cross-cultural study of preferred leadership in sports. *Canadian Journal of Sport Sciences*, **12**, 106-110.

Chelladurai, P., & Saleh, S.D. (1978). Preferred leadership in sports. *Canadian Journal of Applied Sport Sciences*, **3**, 85-92.

Danielson, R.R., Zelhart, P.F., & Drake, C.J. (1975). Multidimensional scaling and factor analysis of coaching behavior as perceived by high school hockey players. *Research Quarterly*, **46**, 323-334.

Fiedler, F. (1967). *A theory of leadership effectiveness*. New York: McGraw-Hill.

Horn, T. (1992). Leadership effectiveness in the sport domain. In T. Horn (Ed.), *Advances in sport psychology* (pp. 151-200). Champaign, IL: Human Kinetics.

Martens, R. (1987). *Coaches guide to sport psychology*. Champaign, IL: Human Kinetics.

Ogilvie, B.C., & Tutko, T.A. (1966). Problem athletes and how to handle them. London: Palham Books.

Ogilvie, B.C., & Tutko, T.A. (1970). Self-perceptions as compared with measured personality of selected male physical educators. In G.S. Kenyon (Ed.), *Contemporary psychology of sport* (pp. 73-78). Chicago, IL: The Athletic Institute.

Sage, G. (1978). Humanistic psychology and coaching. In W.F. Straub (Ed.), *Sport psychology: An analysis of athlete behavior* (pp. 215-228). Ithaca, NY: Mouvement.

Smith, R.E., Smoll, F.L., & Hunt, E. (1977). A system for the behavioral assessment of athletic coaches. *Research Quarterly*, **48**, 401-407.

Smoll, F.L., Smith, R.E., Curtis, B., & Hunt, E. (1978). Toward a mediational model of coach-player relationships. *Research Quarterly*, **49**, 528-541.

Stogdill, R.M. (1948). Personal factors associated with leadership: Survey of literature. *Journal of Psychology*, **25**, 35-71.

Stogdill, R.M. (1974). *The handbook of leadership*. New York: Free Press.

Straub, W.F. (1978). *Sport psychology: An analysis of athlete behavior*. Ithaca, NY: Mouvement.

Tharp, R.G., & Gallimore, R. (1976, January). What a coach can teach a teacher. *Psychology Today*, **9**, 74-78.

CHAPTER 12

Communication

Communication is integral to our daily lives. Do you remember Jason, our Little League baseball player from chapter 6 who came to bat in the last inning with two men on and two outs? Now it's the championship game, Jason's team is losing 3-2 and, again, there's a lot of pressure. The count goes to 2 and 2 and then Jason is fooled, swings at a bad pitch, and misses. The head coach says:

> Jason, I can't believe you actually swung at that pitch. How many times have I told you to lay off bad pitches? That was just stupid. You let us all down and we may never get another chance to win the championship.

Right after that, the assistant coach comes up to Jason and says:

> Don't worry about it, Jason. It's just a game. The pitcher made a really good pitch and you had to protect the plate with two strikes on you. Maybe next time you could choke up on the bat a little more and shorten your swing. But I know you tried your best out there.

Jason received very different messages from his coaches about his performance, and of course the two messages would have far different effects. Thanks to the assistant coach, Jason will not hang his head because he knows he has done his best. Next time he'll choke up on the bat a bit more and come through. If Jason had received only the head coach's message, who knows if there would even be a next time?

This scene underscores how important communication is in sport and exercise settings. No matter how brilliant a coach is in planning strategy and knowing the technical aspects of the game, success depends on being able to communicate effectively with the athletes. This is true also for physical education teachers and exercise leaders. In essence, it's not what you know, but how well you can communicate that information to others.

Breakdowns in communication often are at the root of problems when coaches talk to athletes or teachers to students. These remarks probably sound familiar: "I just can't talk to him," "If I've told her once I've told her a thousand times," and "When I talk to her it goes in one ear and out the other." On the other side, athletes and students often have these things to say about coaches and teachers: "He never explains why he does things," "She's so hard to approach," and "He's always shouting and yelling." Clearly, there are problems on both sides of communication. Repairing these communication gaps is essential in the learning and coaching environment.

In this chapter you will learn about

▌ what process all communication follows,

▌ three types of communication,

▌ sending messages effectively,

▌ listening effectively,

▌ what causes breakdowns in communication, and

▌ how to communicate effectively.

The Communication Process

All communication follows the same basic process (see Figure 12.1):

1. One person decides to send a message to another.
2. The sender then translates (*encoded*) thoughts into a message.
3. The message is channelled (usually through spoken words but sometimes through nonverbal means, such as sign language) to the receiver.
4. The message is received and interpreted (*decoded*).
5. The receiver then thinks about the message and responds internally, such as being interested, getting mad, feeling relieved, and so on.

Purposes of Communication

Although the same process occurs in all communications, the purposes of the communication can vary. You might communicate to

- *persuade* a person in an aerobics class that she can lose weight by exercising regularly,
- *evaluate* how well a gymnast performs her routine on the balance beam,
- *inform* students on how to perform a new volleyball skill,
- *motivate* your team to psych up for a tough opponent, or
- *solve* problems dealing with a conflict between two of the players on your team.

Communication may incorporate several purposes at once. For example, let's say an aerobic dance instructor wants to include harder and more vigorous movements in the class's exercise regimen. She would use motivation and persuasion to convince the class of the benefits of this added exercise and then inform them how to perform the new skill.

Types of Communication

Communication occurs in three basic ways: intrapersonally, interpersonally, and nonverbally. Usually when we talk about communicating, we mean *interpersonal communication*, which involves at least two people and a meaningful exchange. The sender intends to affect the response of a particular person or persons. The message or content may be received by the person for whom it was intended, by persons for whom it was not intended, or both. Sometimes that message gets distorted so that the sender's intended response does not transmit.

Intrapersonal communication is the communication we have with ourselves. We talk a lot to ourselves, and this inner dialogue is important. What we say to ourselves usually helps shape and predict how we act and perform. For instance, perhaps a youngster in a physical education class is afraid of performing a new skill, the tennis serve, and tells himself that he can't do it and will look foolish if he tries—this intrapersonal communication increases the chances that he will not execute the skill properly. Self-talk can also affect motivation. If someone is trying to lose weight and tells herself that she's looking slimmer and feeling good, she is improving her motivation with her self-talk. (See chapter 18 for more on self-talk.)

Inner dialogue, or *intrapersonal communication*, affects motivation and behavior.

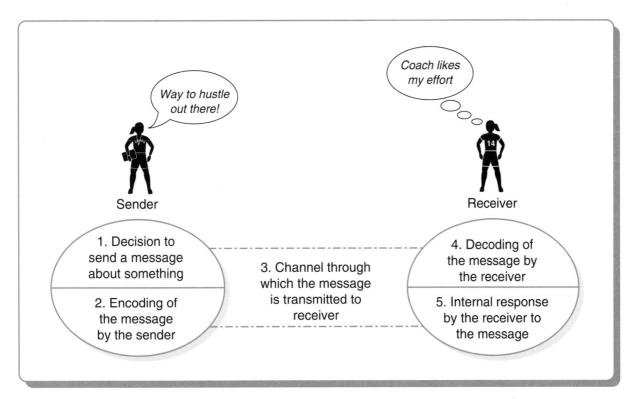

Figure 12.1 The process of communication. Adapted from Martens (1987).

As much as 50% to 70% of human communication is nonverbal.

Nonverbal communication, or nonverbal cues, are also critical to imparting and receiving information. In one study, subjects watching a tennis match were shown only the players between points—they never saw a player actually hit a ball or play a point. Still, about 75% of the time they could pick out who was winning the match. The players exhibited nonverbal cues between points strong enough to communicate who was ahead or behind.

Sending Messages Effectively

Effective communication is often the difference between success and failure for teachers, coaches, and exercise leaders. Thus, it is important to understand how to send effective messages, both verbally and nonverbally. We will briefly discuss interpersonal and intrapersonal communication, but our focus will be on nonverbal communication, which is more subtle but critical to the imparting and receiving of information.

Verbal Messages

Verbal messages should be sent clearly and received and interpreted correctly. Breakdowns occur because communications are sent ineffectively, not received, or are misinterpreted. Often the problem is with the transmission of the message. Some people talk too much, rambling on about things that bore or distract others, while others talk too little and thus don't communicate enough information. Table 12.1 provides guidelines for sending effective verbal messages.

Nonverbal Messages

People are often unaware of the many nonverbal cues they use in communicating. They also often ignore the nonverbal cues coming their way, which are a rich source of information. Understanding various kinds of nonverbal communication improves both sending and receiving messages (see Yukelson, 1992, for an in-depth discussion).

Nonverbal messages are less likely to be under conscious control and therefore are harder to hide. They can give away our unconscious feelings and attitudes. People tend to believe nonverbal messages. For example, an exercise leader asks a young woman how she is feeling just before starting an aerobics class. The young woman shrugs, looks down, frowns, and mutters, "Oh, fine." Although her words say everything is okay, the leader knows otherwise from the nonverbal messages being conveyed.

Although nonverbal messages can be powerful, they are often difficult to interpret accurately. Thus, we have to be cautious in interpreting them and try to correctly judge the context.

Physical Appearance.   Often our first impression of a person comes from physical appearance. We might think someone fat, skinny, handsome, sloppy, attractive, or homely. A very small thing might convey a large message. For example, 20 years ago a male athlete who walked into a coach's office wearing an earring would likely have been quickly escorted out. Now it is more accepted for males to wear earrings, and a different message is conveyed. Dress and hairstyles convey powerful information. And sometimes what we wish to convey is misinterpreted by others.

Posture.   How we carry ourselves also sends a message. Slumped posture conveys low self-image or depression, whereas erect posture conveys control and energy. Our gait and the way we walk carry messages. Someone who

Table 12.1 Guidelines for Sending Effective Verbal Messages

1. **Be direct.**
   People weak in this area assume others know what they want or feel. Rather than expressing their message directly, they hint at what they have in mind—or they tell someone else, hoping the message will get to the right person indirectly.

2. **Own your messages.**
   Use "I" and "my," not "we" or "the team," when referencing your messages. You disown your messages when you say, "The team feels . . . ," or "Most people think you are . . . ," when what you're saying is really what *you* believe. Using others to bolster what you have to say implies cowardice in expressing your own messages.

3. **Be complete and specific.**
   Provide the person to whom you are speaking with all the information he or she needs to fully understand your message. Watch for leaps in logic, unknown assumptions, and unstated intentions.

4. **Be clear and consistent. Avoid double messages.**
   "I really want to play you, Mary, but I don't think this is a good game for you. I think you're a fine athlete, but you'll just have to be patient." This example of a double message—acceptance and rejection—leaves Mary confused and probably hurt. Double messages send contradictory meanings and are usually sent when a person is afraid to be direct.

5. **State your needs and feelings clearly.**
   Because our society frowns on those who wear their emotions on their sleeves, we tend not to reveal our feelings and needs to others. Yet if you want to develop close relationships, you need to share your feelings.

6. **Separate fact from opinion.**
   State what you see, hear, and know, and then clearly identify any opinions or conclusions you have about these facts. You say to your son when he returns home late one night, "I see you've been out with the Williamson kid again." In the context in which it is spoken, the message is received by your son, but he is not certain exactly what your concern is about the Williamson boy. A better way to send this message would be to say "That was the Williamson kid, wasn't it?" (verifying a fact), and then, "I'm concerned that you spend time with him. I'm afraid he'll get you into trouble" (stating your opinion). Although your son may not be pleased with your opinion, at least he'll understand it.

7. **Focus on one thing at a time.**
   Have you ever begun discussing how to execute a particular skill and abruptly switched to complaining about how the team hasn't been practicing well? Organize your thoughts before speaking. Disjointed messages do not transmit well.

8. **Deliver messages immediately.**
   When you observe something that upsets you or that needs to be changed, don't delay sending a message. Sometimes holding back can result in your exploding later about a little thing. Responding immediately also makes for more effective feedback than a delayed response.

9. **Make sure your message does not contain hidden agendas.**
   This means that the stated purpose of the message is not the same as the real purpose. Hidden agendas and disguised intentions destroy relationships. To determine if your message contains hidden agendas, ask yourself these two questions:
   - Why am I saying this to this person?
   - Do I want him or her to hear this, or is there something else involved?

(continued)

Table 12.1   (continued)

10. **Be supportive.**
    If you want another person to listen to your messages, don't deliver them with threats, sarcasm, negative comparisons, or judgments. Eventually the person will avoid communicating with you or simply tune you out whenever you speak. Your cumulative messages need to demonstrate support.

11. **Be consistent with your nonverbal messages.**
    You may tell your player it is okay to make an error, but your body gestures and facial expressions contradict your words. Conflicting messages confuse your athlete and hinder future communication.

12. **Reinforce with repetition.**
    That is, you should repeat your message. Get the point? That's correct. Repeat key points to reinforce what you are saying. However, don't overrepeat, as this results in the other person not listening. You can also reinforce messages by using additional channels of communication—show a picture or video along with explaining the skill, for example.

13. **Make your message appropriate to the receiver's frame of reference.**
    Messages can be much better understood if you tailor them to the experiences of the person with whom you are communicating. It is inappropriate, for example, to use complex language when speaking to young athletes. They do not have the vocabulary to understand what you're saying.

14. **Look for feedback that your message was accurately interpreted.**
    Watch for verbal and nonverbal signals that the person to whom you are speaking is receiving the message you intended. If no signal is given, ask questions to solicit the feedback: "Do you understand what I am telling you, Susan?" or "Are you clear about what you should do?"

Adapted from Martens (1987).

During competition, an athlete's spirit is telegraphed to her opponent by how she moves.

shuffles along with his head down and his hands in his pockets conveys sadness, whereas a bouncy step suggests a sense of control and confidence.

Athletes often recognize frustrated or discouraged opponents by how they move. When they see an opposing player hanging his head, they know it's time to "go in for the kill." Great tennis players like Bjorn Borg and Chris Evert knew the importance of posture and never let their opponents know how they were feeling: Whether they made a great shot or blew an easy one, they looked and acted the same. This made Evert and Borg tougher to beat because opponents could not tell when they were down.

Gestures.   People's gestures often convey messages, whether they want them to or not. For instance, folding your arms across your chest usually expresses that you're not open to others, whereas locking your hands behind your head connotes superiority. Coaches often express themselves through gestures—sometimes if they verbalize their thoughts to officials they risk getting thrown out of the game!

Body Position.   This refers to the personal space between you and others and the position of your body with respect to others. Body position is really an aspect of *proxemics*, which is the study of how people communicate by the way they use space.

An example of body position language is the coach's surrounding himself or herself with starting players, rather than with reserves. Many coaches stand next to starting players, connoting favoritism. John Thompson, basketball coach for Georgetown University, makes it a habit to sit instead among the reserves to make them feel like valued members of the team.

Touching.   Touching is a powerful form of nonverbal communication that can be used to calm or to express affection or other feelings, depending on the situation. We have become freer in recent years with the use of touching in sport, including more embracing between males than was socially acceptable years ago. A gentle pat on the back or an arm around the shoulder can often effectively communicate caring and empathy.

Facial Expression.   Your face is the most expressive part of your body. When listening to others, people often study facial expressions and eye movements to try to find deeper meaning in their messages. Eye contact is particularly important in communicating feelings. Getting eye contact usually means your listener is interested in your message. When people feel uncomfortable or embarrassed, they tend to avoid direct eye contact and look away. The smile is the universal bridge across language barriers and one of the most efficient ways of communicating. Smiles and other facial expressions can both invite verbal communication and give feedback about how effective communication was.

Voice Characteristics.   Verbal communication is often powerfully reinforced or undercut by the sound of a voice. As the adage goes, "it's not what you say but how you say it." The voice's quality often betrays true feelings, moods, and attitudes, revealing what we might never state verbally. Voice characteristics include pitch (high or low), tempo (speed), volume (loudness or softness), rhythm (cadence), and articulation (enunciation).

Nonverbal messages are harder to hide and consciously control than verbal messages are, so they are often more accurate indicators of how a person feels.

Receiving Messages Effectively

So far we've focused on one side of communication: the sender. However, people spend 40% of their communication time listening (Sathre, Olson, & Whitney, 1973). Yet although they learn writing and speaking skills, they seldom receive any formal training in listening. Before you read about how to improve listening skills, complete the short listening skills test in Table 12.2 to learn what specific skills you need to improve.

Active Listening

"Sure, my athletes can come to see me anytime they want. I have an open door policy."

"Aw, the coach doesn't really listen to us. All he's interested in is telling us what to do."

As this example illustrates, some people think they are available to others in ways they really are not. People feel more comfortable expressing their true ideas and feelings to someone who wants to listen. Good listening shows sensitivity and encourages an open exchange of ideas and feelings. If you really want people to come by and confide in you, you need to make a concerted effort to listen.

The most useful way to improve listening is to listen actively. *Active listening* involves attending to main and supporting ideas, acknowledging and responding, giving appropriate feedback, and paying attention to the speaker's total communication. Active listening also involves nonverbal communication such as direct eye contact and nodding to confirm that you understand the speaker. In essence, the listener shows concern for the content, the intent, and the feelings of the message.

Table 12.2 Listening Skills Test

Rating scale	Never 1	Seldom 2	Sometimes 3	Often 4
1. You find listening to others uninteresting.	1	2	3	4
2. You tend to focus attention on the speaker's delivery or appearance instead of the message.	1	2	3	4
3. You listen more for facts and details, often missing the main points that give the facts meaning.	1	2	3	4
4. You are easily distracted by other people talking, chewing gum, rattling paper, and so on.	1	2	3	4
5. You fake attention, looking at the speaker but thinking of other things.	1	2	3	4
6. You listen only to what is easy to understand.	1	2	3	4
7. Certain emotion-laden words interfere with your listening.	1	2	3	4
8. You hear a few sentences of another person's problems and immediately start thinking about all the advice you can give.	1	2	3	4
9. Your attention span is very short, so it is hard for you to listen for more than a few minutes.	1	2	3	4
10. You are quick to find things to disagree with, so you stop listening as you prepare your argument.	1	2	3	4
11. You try to placate the speaker by being supportive through head-nodding and uttering agreement, but you're really not involved.	1	2	3	4
12. You will change the subject when you get bored or uncomfortable with it.	1	2	3	4
13. As soon as someone says anything that you think reflects negatively on you, you jump in to defend yourself.	1	2	3	4
14. You second-guess the speaker, trying to figure out what he or she *really* means.	1	2	3	4

Now add up your score. The following subjective scale will give you some help in determining how well you listen.

14–24	Excellent
25–34	Good
35–44	Fair
45–56	Weak

Adapted from Martens (1987).

An active listener often paraphrases what the speaker has said. Some typical lead-ins for a paraphrase follow:

- What I hear you saying is . . .
- Let me see if I've got this right. You said . . .
- What you're telling me is . . .

Asking specific questions to allow the person to express his or her feelings is also part of active listening. These are examples of questioning and paraphrasing.

Statement: "I am thinking about increasing my exercise times from 3 days a week to 5 days a week, but I'm not sure this is the best thing to do right now."

Question: "What do you gain or lose by increasing your exercise times?"

Paraphrase: "It sounds as though you're struggling with trying to balance getting fit and other demands in your life."

By paraphrasing a person's thoughts and feelings, you let her know that you're listening and you care. Often this leads to more open communication and exchange, as the speaker senses that you're interested. When you ask questions, avoid using the interrogative "why" because this word can seem judgmental. Rosenfeld and Wilder (1990) offer additional suggestions for improving active listening skills:

- *Don't mistake hearing for listening*. Hearing and listening are distinct activities. Hearing is simply receiving sounds, whereas listening is an active process. Hearing someone does not mean you're listening to the meaning of their message. It is frustrating to the speaker when a receiver hears but doesn't listen. If you find yourself not listening, practice focusing your concentration on the speaker.

- *Mentally prepare to listen*. Listening sometimes requires mental preparation. For example, before having an important discussion with someone, develop a mental game plan for the exchange. That is, rehearse in your mind attending very carefully to the meaning of the speaker's message. You should try to save difficult discussions for when your energy level is high so you can sustain intensity and listen actively.

Active listening enhances communication because the speaker feels that he or she is being heard, acknowledged, and provided with appropriate feedback.

Supportive Listening

Being a supportive listener communicates that you are "with" the speaker and value his message. Here are some tips for supportive listening:

1. *Use supportive behaviors as you listen*. These communicate the message that the other person is acknowledged, understood, and accepted. Supportive listening behaviors

- describe the other's behavior instead of trying to evaluate or attack it,
- focus on immediate thoughts and feelings,
- are not calculated or manipulative,
- are empathic, not indifferent, and
- remain open to new ideas, perspectives, and the possibility of change.

Along with these behaviors use active *attending behaviors*, such as nodding your head and making clear, direct eye contact.

2. *Use conforming behaviors as you listen*. Part of effective communication is letting people know you are with them in the conversation and understand their message, even if you do not agree with it. Interrupting or failing to either

verbally or nonverbally acknowledge what someone is saying is disconcerting to the speaker. Use conforming behaviors along with supportive behaviors to show you are paying attention, accepting, and understanding.

3. *Use both verbal and nonverbal listening behaviors.* Nonverbal behaviors that communicate interest and attention include

- standing no more than a few feet from the person,
- maintaining eye contact,
- making appropriate facial gestures,
- facing each other, and
- maintaining an open posture.

Verbal behaviors should communicate an understanding and acknowledgment of what the speaker is saying and feeling.

Aware Listening

Be *aware* that people react differently to the way you communicate. Here are tips for being an aware listener:

1. *Be flexible.* There is no one best listening strategy. Different situations require different strategies (think of the interactional model). People prefer or feel more comfortable with one style of listening than another. Some people simply like to talk and appear unconcerned about your understanding. Others will give you time to think about what they've said and provide opportunities for feedback.

2. *Be alert for barriers and breakdowns in communication.* Barriers involve "noise," such as people talking while you are trying to communicate with others. For example, coaches and athletes often have to speak above the roar

of a crowd. It is useful to develop strategies to deal with noise such as using nonverbal signals. *Breakdowns* occur when messages are misinterpreted or misdirected. Often, we do not know a breakdown has occurred until something bad happens that can be traced back to the breakdown. We'll discuss breakdowns at greater length in what follows.

Breakdowns in Communication

Communicating effectively requires skill and effort from both parties. The process can be complicated and often breaks down. Breakdowns can result from either sender or receiver failures.

Sender Failures

Senders may transmit a message poorly. Ambiguous messages, for example, are ineffective communications. Say a coach tells an athlete that if she continues to do well in practice, she will be in the starting lineup when the season opens. Over the next few weeks, the coach says nothing about her not starting, so 2 days before the start of the season the athlete is taken aback when she is listed as a reserve. In this case, the coach should have been more specific about the criteria for starting and given the athlete ongoing feedback.

Inconsistent messages also cause communication breakdowns. Nothing is more frustrating than hearing one thing today and the opposite tomorrow. Consistency is critical to building trust and rapport. For example, if a coach is always supportive during practice but is harsh and critical during games, athletes get confused and may even fall apart during competitions.

Often inconsistency results when verbal and nonverbal channels conflict. A physical education teacher might offer encouraging words to a student attempting a new skill while her body language and facial expression convey disappointment and impatience. Inconsistent communication produces insecurity and anxiety in those receiving it. Physical educators want to establish credibility in their communications, and consistency is a good route toward this goal. And it's necessary to be consistent not only with each participant but also among participants. For example, say a coach tells her team that anyone late to practice will not play in the next game. If the coach then enforces this policy when a couple of reserves are late for practice, she must also enforce it if the star player is late.

Use active and supportive listening techniques to avoid most of the breakdowns that prevent effective communication.

Communicating With Consistency

- Never miss an opportunity to praise an athlete for doing something right.

- Always recognize the greetings of others—a hello and a smile are easy ways to communicate positive feelings.

- If you have an open door policy for your athletes, show that you are sincere about it.

- Try to show the same compassion on the field as you do in the locker room or office.

- Be consistent in administering discipline. (Anshel, 1990)

Receiver Failures

Ineffective communication is a double-edged sword. Receivers as well as senders can contribute to miscommunication. As an illustration, let's look at Mary, an exercise leader. She is talking to Cindy, a member of her aerobics class who has missed several classes. "Cindy, I've missed you the past several weeks," says Mary. "If you don't keep up your regular exercise, you'll get fat again. In fact, I already see those love handles." Mary's intent was to motivate Cindy to stop missing exercise classes, but Cindy heard only the "getting fat" and "love handles" part. Overweight for many years, she is too sensitive to comments about her weight. What she heard Mary saying was that she was getting fat, and she started feeling depressed because she had worked so hard to lose the weight. Had Mary been more sensitive, however, she could have simply told Cindy that she missed her in class and was glad to see her back and exercising. Thus, in this case there was a problem in both the sending and the receiving.

Along with misinterpreting the message, failing to listen is another way receivers can cause problems. For example, a teacher might convey information very well, but if her students are looking out the window or thinking about an upcoming party, communication will break down. The receiver shares responsibility with the sender and should make every effort to listen to the message being sent.

Confrontation

Communication breakdowns often lead to confrontations. A *confrontation* is usually a face-to-face discussion among people in conflict. Despite its negative connotations, when properly used confrontation can help both parties understand the issues more clearly without feeling undue stress, guilt, or inadequacy. Confrontations are useful not only for major conflicts, but also for minor conflicts to help "clear the air."

When to Use Confrontation

Avoid confrontations when you are angry. It has been said that someone who speaks when he is angry will make the best speech he will forever regret. Many people feel uncomfortable with confrontations because they anticipate a negative, stressful encounter. They avoid the meeting and let things fester. Other people jump to arguments and escalate feelings of hostility. Neither approach produces a productive resolution of the problem.

So, in what situations should you use confrontation? Decide by considering the purposes a confrontation might serve. It should not be to put other people "in their place" but should lead to carefully examining the behavior and its consequences.

How to Use Confrontation

Once you decide that confrontation can be useful and appropriate, you need to know how to confront. Following are some general guidelines to make confrontations more productive and less stressful (Anshel, 1990; Martens, 1987).

Express Feelings Constructively.   People often use anger to release strong emotional feelings and tension—and this venting of feelings might make us feel better for the moment. But, usually, our response to anger is guilt, an upset

stomach, or a headache. Also, when we are angry we tend to make irrational and cruel statements without thinking about the consequences of what we say.

We cannot eliminate anger from our emotional make-up, but we can learn how to deal with it. A first step is realizing that getting angry isn't necessarily bad. It's what we *do* with this anger that makes it constructive or destructive.

• Do not attack a person's character or personality in anger. Communication should aim to improve future situations. Providing specific information and instruction—instead of attacking character—can produce more desirable behavior change and still maintains a positive working relationship.

• When you feel angry or upset, try to identify the exact feelings by name. For example, "I am annoyed with you," or "Your behavior disappoints me." Sometimes just recognizing feelings can ease them before you fly off the handle.

• Take time to gather yourself. If you let your anger speak, your message will probably not be constructive to anyone. Try turning away or taking a very brief walk. Sometimes getting away from the situation for a moment gives you time to cool down and evaluate.

Think!   Before you start screaming commands or blurting out insults, think of the consequences. Will what you are about to say produce a successful confrontation? That is, will it get across your message without embarrassing and shaming the other person? Take a deep breath and back off for even a few seconds. This can be the difference between a positive interchange and a disaster.

Understand.   Ask yourself if you are accurately understanding the person and situation. To help, ask directed questions to get information, establish facts, and clarify perceptions—not to instill guilt and cause embarrassment. Let the person know that you are trying to understand his or her position. Understanding is not always easy in the midst of a confrontation, but allowing the person to express feelings without your being judgmental will often lead to a resolution.

Communication: Individual Differences

After teaching volleyball skills for several weeks, Curt is observing students in an actual game. Two of the players, Carlos and Matthew, are not following through on their service motions, and their serves are landing in the net. Observing this, Curt calls out, "How many times have I told you to follow through on your serves? Didn't you listen to anything I've said the past 3 weeks?" Matthew does not react well to criticism, and he feels hurt and embarrassed in front of his classmates. He labors to stay focused on the game, but he makes more errors and incurs more criticism. Carlos, on the other hand, is less sensitive than Matt, experienced in sport, and understands how to react to mistakes. Criticism makes him more determined to show everyone that he can serve the ball properly. He uses the teacher's criticism to motivate himself and focus on improving the skill.

Be Empathetic.   Being aloof, antagonistic, or sarcastic does not convey that you care—it only produces distrust and resentment. Your goal in a confrontation should be to resolve the problem mutually without dominating or intimidating someone. Putting yourself in the other person's shoes is the essence of empathy. It is asking yourself how you would feel under similar circumstances. If you were receiving a message, how would you feel if you were criticized and yelled at? Unfortunately, many adults in leadership positions don't know how it feels to be on the receiving end of destructive comments. Professionals must think about how their comments and critiques will feel to recipients. This doesn't mean to never criticize but to be sincere and sensitive to how others are feeling.

Be Tentative.   In most sport situations, tentativeness can lead to indecision and harm performance, but this is not what happens in confronting a person. Being a little tentative helps the person to consider what you are saying. If you come on too strong, the person might feel under attack. Tentative does not mean being "wishy washy." It simply means that you are inviting the person to examine the problem as you see it.

Proceed Gradually.   Beginning the confrontation with accusations and critical remarks does not get things off to a good start. Give the other person time to absorb what you say and understand the nature of the problem. Throwing too much information at someone too rapidly causes overload and confusion.

Criticism

Although we generally want to be positive, there are times when criticism is necessary. Unfortunately, many people take criticism as a threat to self-esteem. When they feel threatened, their immediate response is to become defensive. They concentrate on defending themselves instead of on listening to the message. Some exemplary research indicates that the "sandwich approach" is the most effective way to give criticism (Smith, Smoll, & Curtis, 1979; Smith, Smoll, & Hunt, 1977). The *sandwich approach* is a technique to offer constructive feedback in a sensitive yet effective manner. It consists of three sequential elements:

1. A positive statement
2. Future-oriented instructions
3. A compliment

Dos and Don'ts When Initiating Confrontation

Dos

- Do convey that you value your relationship with the person.

- Do go slowly and think about what you want to communicate.

- Do try to understand the other person's position.

- Do listen carefully to what the other person is trying to communicate.

Don'ts

- Don't communicate the solution. Rather, focus on the problem. We are often overly anxious to tell others what they must do instead of letting them figure it out.

- Don't stop communicating. Even if the confrontation isn't going as you planned, keep communicating about the problem in a constructive manner.

- Don't use "put-downs." Sarcasm and attacks usually alienate people. A confrontation is not a competition, and the idea is not to win it. The idea is to solve a problem together.

- Don't rely on nonverbal hints to communicate your thoughts. You need to be direct and forthright in communicating. Now is not the time for subtle nonverbal cues.

- Don't discuss the problem with others before confronting the person. This can make the person defensive and uptight.

Let's take a closer look. After a participant makes a mistake, he or she typically anticipates a negative remark from the coach or teacher. Often the person will tune out the anticipated unpleasant message and never hear it. To assure the individual attends to the first comment, it should be positive. Appropriate positive statements might be "Nice try, Janet," "Good effort, Marty," or "That was a tough pitch to hit." Once the person is receptive to the opening positive statement, he or she will also pay attention to the second part, the instructional feedback.

The key aspect of the sandwich approach is the future-oriented instruction. After gaining the person's attention, provide the critical instructional feedback—behaviors or strategies to use the next time the person performs the skill. The reason for keeping the instruction future oriented is to keep the person from thinking about the error immediately (thinking about an error will often result in repeating it). The feedback should be positive to keep the individual focused on it. The message should be what to do next time—not one that ridicules, embarrasses, or criticizes. For instance,

- after a ground ball goes through a player's legs, say, "Next time you get a hard grounder, just get down on one knee and block the ball with your body," or

- after a student trying a new skill on the balance beam falls off, say, "You really need to concentrate on keeping your eyes looking forward to help maintain your balance."

The final part of the sandwich is a compliment. After the instructional feedback, make sure the individual still feels good about the performance. Ending the interaction on a positive note makes it more likely that the instruction will be remembered. It also helps build trust and rapport; the individual realizes that making a mistake isn't the end of the world and that people can learn from their errors.

Let's look at two examples of the complete sandwich.

1. Max drops a pass from the quarterback that would have been a sure touchdown. "All right, Max, that was a good pass pattern. Next time make sure you watch the ball into your hands. Hang in there, you'll get it next time."

2. Sally keeps getting out of step during her aerobics dance class. "Sally, you're really working hard out there. Next time try to slow down and not get ahead of the music. You're looking good. Keep up the good work."

Summary

Effective communication takes work and effort. Basically we communicate in three ways: intrapersonally, interpersonally, and nonverbally. Nonverbal communication is an important source of information, and much of what we convey to others is through nonverbal cues.

Some 40% of the time we communicate through listening. Active listening, involving paraphrasing, questioning, and supportive behaviors, is useful for promoting open, honest communication. However, effective communication is complex, and breakdowns often occur either in sending or receiving the message. Confrontation is a way of communicating, and although most people view confrontation negatively, it can lead to a mutual solution. Part of successfully resolving a problem is recognizing when and why a confrontation may be appropriate. The chapter concluded with suggestions for communicating criticism effectively, including using the sandwich approach. Success as a teacher, coach, or exercise leader requires good communication skills above and beyond the technical aspects of the skills to be imparted.

Review Questions

1. Discuss the five steps comprising the communication process.

2. Compare and contrast the three types of communication.

3. Describe three types of nonverbal communication, giving examples from applied settings.

4. Define active listening. How can practitioners enhance their listening skills?

5. Discuss three breakdowns in communication, including practice examples of each type.

6. Describe the 5-step process you would use when confronting someone.

7. Discuss the sandwich approach to constructive critiques after a mistake.

8. Give three guidelines for consistency in communication.

9. What guidelines would you follow to express anger constructively?

10. Suggest guidelines for communicating with empathy.

References

Anshel, M. (1990). *Sport psychology: From theory to practice.* Scottsdale, AZ: Gorsuch Scarisbrick.

Martens, R. (1987). *Coaches guide to sport psychology.* Champaign, IL: Human Kinetics.

Rosenfeld, L., & Wilder, L. (1990). Communication fundamentals: Active listening. *Sport Psychology Training Bulletin,* **1**(5), 1-8.

Sathre, S., Olson, R.W., & Whitney, C.I. (1973). *Let's talk.* Glenview, IL: Scott, Foresman.

Smith, R.E., Smoll, F.E., & Curtis, D. (1979). Coach effectiveness training: A cognitive-behavioral approach to enhancing relationship skills in youth sport coaches. *Journal of Sport Psychology,* **1**, 59-75.

Smith, R.E., Smoll, F.L., & Hunt, E. (1977). A system for the behavioral assessment of athletic coaches. *Research Quarterly,* **48**, 401-407.

Yukelson, D. (1992). Communicating effectively. In J. Williams (Ed.), *Sport psychology: Peak performance to personal growth.* Palo Alto, CA: Mayfield.

P A R T

V

Enhancing Performance

One of the main questions asked by sport and exercise psychologists is, How can we use psychological techniques to help people perform more effectively? In fact, this question has been a major focus of sport psychology since the field's early days. In this part we'll try to convey what progress has been made toward answering this question.

Chapter 13 introduces you to psychological skills training. Here you'll discover that psychological skills are like physical skills and can be taught, learned, and practiced. You'll learn how to enhance performance in your students, athletes, and exercisers by teaching mental skills.

Chapters 14 through 18 then focus on specific topics within psychological skills training for performance enhancement. In chapter 14 we'll examine arousal regulation and reduction, which will equip you to help athletes psych up rather than psych out. You'll become familiar with a variety of health-related stress-management techniques as well. Chapter 15 discusses the much publicized topic of imagery (or visualization). You will learn how to augment physical practice with mental practice techniques and strategies. Self-confidence is the focus of chapter 16. Here the relationship between confidence and performance is emphasized, as well as confidence-building methods. One of the best ways to build confidence is by effectively setting goals. Thus, in chapter 17 you'll learn about effective goals and goal-setting skills for enhancing confidence, other psychological skills, and performance. Finally, the section ends with chapter 18 and a discussion of the all-important topics of attention and concentration. Here we'll focus on how you can improve performance via enhanced concentration and attentional skills.

Introduction to Psychological Skills Training

Jim's high school basketball team is behind 67-66 with 1 second left on the clock when Jim is fouled in the act of shooting and awarded two shots. The opposing coach calls a time-out to try to ice Jim and let the pressure build. Jim's coach tells him to just relax and shoot the foul shots like he does in practice. But Jim knows how important the game is to his teammates, his coach, the school, his friends, and his family in the audience. He starts to think about how awful he would feel if he let everybody down, and this worry starts to affect him physically. As he approaches the free-throw line, the muscles in his shoulders and arms tighten up. As a result, he rushes his shots, lacks rhythm in his release, misses both free throws, and his team loses the game.

The next day in practice, Jim's coach tells him to work more on his free-throw shooting, recommending that he stay after every practice to shoot 100 free throws. The coach feels that the extra practice will help Jim perfect his free-throw technique so that he won't choke at the next big game.

Many coaches attempt to correct poor performance by having an athlete simply put in more practice time. Often, however, the real problem is not a lack of physical skills but mental skills. Jim's problem was that he had not developed (or been taught) the psychological skill of relaxation. Having Jim rehearse free throws will not help him overcome the pressures of shooting when the game is on the line. Jim needs to develop skills to relax physically and mentally under great pressure. Other athletes need to improve or enhance concentration, confidence, motivation, or mental preparation. These skills can be developed through psychological skills training (PST).

In this chapter you will learn about

▮ why PST is important,

▮ why coaches and leaders neglect PST,

▮ three phases in PST,

▮ who should conduct PST programs,

▮ when and how to implement PST, and

▮ ethical considerations and common problems in designing PST programs.

Why PST Is Important

Which of the following sport and exercise experiences have you had?

- You walked off a playing field in disgust after losing a game you felt you should have won.
- You choked at a critical point in a competition.
- You felt depressed because you weren't recovering from an injury quickly enough.
- You lacked the desire or motivation to exercise.
- Your mind wandered during a competition.
- You became angry and frustrated with your performance and put yourself down.

All sport and exercise participants fall victim to mental letdowns and mistakes. Conversely, most sport performers also know what it feels like to be "in the zone," where everything seems to come together effortlessly and performance is exceptional. Mental and emotional components often overshadow and transcend the purely physical and technical aspects of performance. In any sport, a player's success (or failure) results from a combination of physical (e.g., strength, speed, balance, coordination) and mental (e.g., concentration, confidence, anxiety management) abilities. Most coaches consider that sport is at least 50% mental (see Figure 13.1), with certain sports such as golf, tennis, and figure skating consistently receiving percentages in the 80% to 90% range. Jimmy Connors, known for his mental tenacity and toughness, has often stated

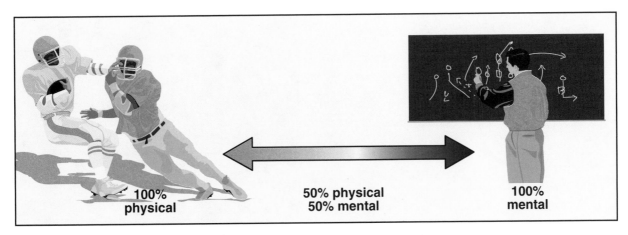

Figure 13.1 Continuum of importance of mental and physical skills for performance success.

that professional tennis is 95% mental. Still, serious athletes typically allot 10 to 20 hours a week to physical practice and little, if any, time to mental practice. This doesn't make sense.

A "B" tennis player usually plays against other "B" players, similar in ability. Likewise, a nationally ranked swimmer will probably compete against other high caliber swimmers. Of course athletes sometimes are clearly overmatched in physical skills or, conversely, are clearly superior to their opponents. In these cases, the outcome probably results from differences in physical skills and abilities. In most competitions, however, players win or lose depending on how they (and their opponents) perform that particular day. Physical ability being fairly equal, the winner is usually the athlete who has better mental skills. Observe fluctuations in your own day-to-day performance. How come on some days you can't do anything wrong, whereas on other days you can't do anything right? You know you haven't lost your physical skills—it's your mental skills that fluctuate.

> Psychological factors account primarily for day-to-day performance fluctuations— abilities are relatively stable.

Why Sport and Exercise Participants Neglect PST

If psychological skills are so important for success, the logical question is, Why do people spend so little time working on developing psychological skills to enhance performance? There are three basic reasons why PST is neglected by many coaches and participants.

Lack of Knowledge

Many people don't really understand how to teach or practice PST skills. For example, some coaches teach concentration by shouting, "Will you concentrate out there?" or "Will you get your mind on what you're supposed to be doing?" The implicit assumption is that the player knows how to concentrate but is just not doing it. Another common practice (remember Jim's errant free throws?) is telling a player to "just relax" as he goes into an important performance. But this is not easily done without training in relaxation skills. A track-and-field coach would not expect a 100-meter runner to perform well in the 440 if she hadn't been running that distance in practice. Similarly, relaxation and concentration need to be practiced to become effective tools for competition. We do not mean to criticize coaches and athletes. Unfortunately, many of them have not had access to techniques for teaching and learning psychological skills.

Psychological skills training programs establish a scientific basis for the effective development of psychological skills. Applied sport psychology has been rapidly evolving since the 1980s. The days of telling players, "Don't choke," "Get psyched up," "Be confident," "Stay loose," "Be mentally tough," and "Concentrate" are on their way out. We are learning that such advice needs action-oriented approaches that provide a plan for improving the mental skills to heed them and enhance performance.

Psychological Skills Are Viewed As Unchangeable

It is a misconception that some people enter the world equipped with mental skills—that champions are born rather than made. It is commonly assumed that athletes like Steffi Graf, Ken Griffey, Jr., and Wayne Gretsky were blessed with a mental toughness and competitive drive as part of their personality. It doesn't quite work that way. Yes, we are all born with certain physical and psychological predispositions, but skills can be learned and developed, depending on the experiences we encounter in our lives. No great athlete ever achieved stardom without endless hours of practice, honing and refining physical skills and techniques. Although some athletes do possess exceptional physical skills, they had to work hard to develop their talents to become champions. Staying calm under pressure, maintaining concentration despite distractions, and keeping confident in the face of failure are simply not innate. Rather, they are skills that need systematic practice and integration with physical skills.

Lack of Time

A third reason coaches and athletes cite for not practicing psychological skills is too little time. They say they barely have adequate time to practice physical skills, much less mental skills. Yet these same people reason that they lost a particular game or competition because "I wasn't up for the game today," "I just couldn't seem to concentrate," "I got too tight and choked," or "I lost confidence in my game." You would think that if coaches thought their teams lost because of poor concentration, they would make time to practice concentration skills. Instead they typically add time to physical practice. The issue is one of priorities. If you believe that mental skills are important and you know how to practice them, you will find time for them.

Psychological skills training is often neglected due to lack of knowledge, perceived lack of time, and the belief that psychological skills are innate and can't be taught.

Myths About PST

Several myths still flourish about the use of psychological techniques in optimizing performance (Gould & Eklund, 1991). These myths (i.e., not grounded on fact or empirical data), only confuse what sport psychology consultants can (and cannot) do to help athletes maximize their performance.

Myth #1—PST Is Only for "Problem" Athletes.   Many people wrongly think that all sport psychologists work with athletes who are messed up or have psychological problems. This is not the case (see chapter 1). *Clinical* sport psychologists are typically licensed to practice clinical psychology in a particular state and are trained to treat various mental disorders, including some sport-related problems such as substance abuse, eating disorders, and severe depression. However, only about 10% of athletes exhibit behaviors and mental disorders that require the expertise of a clinical sport psychologist. Rather, most athletes' psychological needs can be addressed by *educational* sport psychologists who focus on helping develop mental skills in athletes who have a normal range of functioning. (It's important to note that neither type of sport psychologist is better or more essential than the other. Both clinical and educational sport psychologists have unique roles to help people improve performance and psychological well-being.) Table 13.1 gives examples of the different PST needs addressed by educational and clinical sport psychologists.

Table 13.1 Topics Addressed by Sport Psychologists	
Educational sport psychologists	**Clinical sport psychologists**
Goal setting	Eating disorders
Imagery	Substance abuse
Arousal regulation	Personality disorders
Concentration	Severe depression/anxiety
Mental preparation	Psychopathology

Myth #2—PST Is Only for Elite Training.   PST is *not* only for the elite. PST is suitable for all athletes, including young, developing athletes (Gould, 1988; Hellstedt, 1987; Weiss, 1991), special populations such as the mentally retarded (Travis & Sachs, 1991), the physically challenged (Asken, 1991), and the deaf (Clark & Sachs, 1991). Dedicated professionals work to help improve performance and personal growth. Popular magazines and news media tend to focus on Olympic and professional athletes who work with sport psychology consultants, but many other groups receive sport psychology consultation as well.

Myth #3—PST Provides "Quick Fix" Solutions.   Many people mistakenly think that sport psychology offers a quick fix to psychological problems. Sometimes athletes and coaches expect learning how to concentrate or to stay calm under pressure to be accomplished in one or two lessons. Actually, psychological skills take time and practice to develop. And PST is not magical—it won't turn an average player into a superstar. However, it will help athletes reach their potential and maximize their abilities.

Myth #4—PST Is Not Useful.   Some people still think that sport psychology is "hocus pocus" without anything positive to offer. However, substantial research published in scholarly journals—and anecdotal reports from athletes and coaches in the popular press—indicate that psychological skills do in fact enhance performance (e.g., Greenspan & Feltz, 1989; Gould, Tammen, Murphy, & May, 1989; Orlick & Partington, 1988, 1989). Advances and new methods are sometimes scary, and sometimes people have extreme reactions or expectations. Sport psychology is neither a magic elixir nor useless bunk. People in the physical activity professions should have realistic expectations of what psychological skills training can and cannot do to enhance performance and well-being.

Psychological skills can be learned but they must be practiced over time and integrated into a person's daily training regimen.

PST Knowledge Base

The knowledge from which PST developed has been derived from basically two sources. One source is original research studies conducted with elite athletes, and the other is the experience of coaches and athletes. Let's take a look at each of these sources.

Elite Athlete Research

More successful players differ from the less successful in the development of their psychological skills.

Several studies that have compared successful and less successful athletes in terms of psychological skills consistently showed that more successful athletes had better concentration, higher levels of self-confidence, more task-oriented thoughts (rather than outcome oriented; see chapter 5), and lower levels of anxiety (Williams, 1986). Successful athletes also had more positive thoughts and used more positive imagery to visualize success. They tended to be more determined and show more commitment than their less successful counterparts.

Athlete and Coach Experiences

Increasingly, sport psychology researchers are asking coaches and athletes about the content and core sport psychology topics to be included in PST programs. For example, Gould, Tammen, Murphy, and May (1989) surveyed elite coaches and athletes with the United States Olympic Committee National Governing Body sport programs. The coaches and athletes rated relaxation training, concentration, imagery, concentration and attention training, stress management, and self-talk strategies as very important topics.

In another study, Canadian Olympic athletes who performed up to their potential had developed plans for competition, performance evaluation, and dealing with disruptions. They could overcome adversity and performance blocks by sticking to their plans. They could channel performance anxiety and arousal positively (Orlick & Partington, 1989).

Olympians who achieved peak performance demonstrated a total commitment to pursuing excellence, which was not evidenced by their less successful counterparts. They set daily training goals, used simulations in practice to replicate competitive environments, and used imagery to help focus attention and visualize successful outcomes (see Table 13.2).

With both Olympic and professional athletes, the issues and problems that consistently arise are coping with anxiety, coping with training stress and fatigue, developing mental plans, maintaining motivation, staying focused, and enhancing confidence. Other issues they report include interactions with friends and family, communication problems with coaches and fellow athletes, dealing with the media, and dealing with injuries.

In summary, the topics coaches and athletes would find useful in PST programs include the following:

- Arousal regulation
- Imagery (mental preparation)
- Confidence building
- Increasing motivation and commitment (goal setting)
- Attention/concentration skills (self-talk, mental plans)

The specific topics you choose for a PST program will depend on the particular athletes, their orientations and experience, and other personal factors that they bring to the competitive situation.

Table 13.2 **Psychological Skills of Successful Performers**
Developing competitive plans
Daily training goals
Simulations in practice
High confidence
Task-oriented thoughts
Positive imagery
Overcoming obstacles by planning

Data from Orlick and Partington (1989).

PST Effectiveness

To learn how effective PST programs are in improving sport performance requires the accumulation of well-controlled, outcome-based intervention studies conducted in competitive environments. These kinds of studies are costly and time consuming, and they depend on the willingness of coaches and athletes to participate and the ability to adequately control the environment.

Greenspan and Feltz (1989) reviewed 23 published studies of the effectiveness of various psychological interventions (e.g., stress inoculation, imagery, relaxation, reinforcement, systematic desensitization) in competitive settings including skiing, boxing, golf, karate, tennis, figure skating, volleyball, gymnastics, and basketball. They concluded that, in general, educationally based psychological interventions effectively improve competitive performance in collegiate and adult athletes. Vealey (1994) found that 9 of 12 studies testing psychological interventions in sport showed improved performance, with most interventions being cognitive or cognitive-behavioral in nature. Although these initial reports appear encouraging, we still need more controlled studies on elite athletes, youth sport, and recreational athletes before drawing conclusions.

Educationally based psychological skills training enhances sport performance.

Three Phases of PST Programs

Although PST programs take many forms to suit participant needs, they generally follow a set structure with three distinct phases: education, acquisition, and practice. We'll now discuss what each of these phases involves.

Education Phase

Because many sport participants are unfamiliar with how mental skills can enhance performance, the first phase of any PST program is educational. In the education phase participants soon recognize the importance of learning PST and how the skills affect performance. This is usually easy to accomplish: Just ask participants how important they think the mental side of sport performance is. Most will say that it is very important. Then you ask, "How often do you practice developing mental skills compared with practicing physical skills?" Usually the answer is "hardly ever." This then leads into explaining that psychological skills can be learned, just like physical skills.

The education phase may last as little as an hour or as long as several hours over the course of a few days. The gist of what you will explain is the importance of developing psychological skills. For example, in teaching the skill of regulating arousal states, you would explain the causes of anxiety and the relation of arousal and performance. You would tell athletes to learn to find their own optimal level of arousal. Some arousal is desirable, but skilled athletes have learned how to turn this tension or anxiety into positive energy, rather than debilitating tension that can deter performance. Learning to control arousal states is critical; give examples of well-known athletes in the particular sport to reinforce the importance of developing mental skills.

> Psychological skills need to be learned and practiced. Expect improvement as you develop these skills and refine them over time.

Acquisition Phase

The second phase, acquisition, focuses on strategies and techniques to learn the different psychological skills. Both formal and informal meetings are devoted to the learning of these skills. For example, when developing arousal regulation skills, formal meetings might focus on positive coping statements to replace negative self-statements that surface under stressful competitive conditions. You would follow these formal sessions with individual sessions to teach athletes how to use positive coping in actual competitive settings. Here you tailor specific strategies to an athlete's unique needs and abilities (Seabourne, Weinberg, Jackson, & Suinn, 1985). One athlete might worry too much about failure (cognitive anxiety): For her, a cognitively based strategy to change thought patterns might be most appropriate (Meichenbaum, 1977). Another athlete may suffer from increased muscle tension (somatic anxiety): For him, a physically based relaxation technique, such as progressive relaxation (Jacobson, 1938), might be the best choice.

> Tailor training programs to meet individual needs. You can provide general information to the group or team, but be specific when developing an individual's PST program.

Practice Phase

The practice phase has three primary objectives:

- To automate skills through overlearning
- To teach people to systematically integrate psychological skills into their performance situations
- To simulate skills you will want to apply in actual competition

When developing arousal regulation, for example, the athlete would begin the practice phase after becoming proficient in relaxation and cognitive coping skills. You might guide athletes through an imagined competitive situation requiring relaxation and coping skills. During the practice phase, a performer might progress from guided imagery practice to self-directed imagery to using imagery in a practice session as if it were a real competition. Finally, the athlete incorporates arousal control strategies into preparing for and participating in actual competitions.

During the practice phase it is helpful to keep a logbook in which the athlete records the frequency and perceived effectiveness of the arousal control strategies used in practice and competition. A log helps to systematically chart progress and provide feedback for areas of improvement. For example, after every practice athletes record how tense they felt, if their relaxation techniques helped, and the actual relaxation procedure used.

Learning psychological skills should progress from practices and simulations to actual competition.

Who Should Conduct PST?

Ideally, a PST program should be planned, implemented, and supervised by a qualified sport psychology consultant. However, unless you are at the highest level of competition, it is often not feasible to have a consultant administer the program. Usually a sport psychology consultant sets up the program and then either monitors it periodically or trains the coaching staff to implement it.

The selection of a qualified sport psychology consultant is critical. In 1991 the Association for the Advancement of Applied Sport Psychology (AAASP) adopted certification criteria for people in applied sport psychology. Basically, certification requires a person to have extensive backgrounds in both the sport and psychological sciences and some practical, supervised experience in implementing PST with athletes and teams. AAASP certification ensures a certain experience, background, and competence in applied sport psychology. However, the specific fit between the skills, abilities, and orientations of the sport psychology consultant and the needs and goals of the sport coaches and athletes always needs to be considered.

Coaches, of course, see athletes on a daily basis, whereas a sport psychologist does not. Thus coaches are in a position to administer psychological interventions over the course of a season. In working with the Houston Astros minor league player development program, Smith and Johnson (1990) developed an innovative consultation model that we present in the following case study.

When to Implement a PST Program

It is best to initiate a PST program during the off-season or preseason when there is more time to learn new skills and athletes are not so pressured with winning. Some athletes report that it can take several months to a year to fully understand new psychological skills and integrate them into actual competitions. Mental training is an ongoing process that needs to be integrated with physical practice over time.

Often coaches and athletes want to start a PST program in the middle of the season, usually because of some precipitating situation, such as a batter in a hitting slump. They become desperate to find a solution, but mental training in such a situation is rarely effective. A high jumper wouldn't change jumping technique right before a big meet; she would want extensive practice over several weeks or months. Similarly, athletes cannot expect to learn new psychological skills overnight.

Implement psychological skills training in the off-season for best results.

The time needed for practicing mental skills will vary according to what is being practiced and how well it is learned. If a new psychological skill is being learned, special 10- to 15-minute training sessions 3 to 5 days a week may be

Smith and Johnson's Model of Service Delivery

A sport psychology consultant can train one or more qualified individuals within a sport organization to provide psychological services to athletes and coaches. The consultant then oversees the program and provides ongoing supervision of the actual trainers.

Smith (a sport psychology consultant) trained Johnson (a manager in the Houston Astros organization with a master's degree in psychology). In an intensive 6-week training program before spring training, Johnson received extensive sport psychology reading materials and met with Smith for several days about using psychological interventions in sport. Smith also accompanied Johnson to spring training for 10 days of hands-on training plus a series of orientation workshops for staff and players. Weekly and sometimes daily telephone supervision continued throughout the remainder of spring training and the regular season along with two additional 4-day blocks of personal contact. Smith helped oversee the program but Johnson implemented the day-to-day development of psychological skills.

necessary. The first or last 10 to 15 minutes of practice is often a good time for training. (Session content will determine whether it is better held at the beginning or end of practice.) As athletes become more proficient, they may be able to integrate the mental training more with physical training and may need fewer special training sessions. Once a skill has been effectively integrated into physical practice, it should be tried during simulated competition before being used during actual competition. Homework assignments can also be given; but unless the athletes are self-directed, it is better to supervise most mental training practice.

If a sport psychology consultant (who is not typically present on a daily basis) implements the training, some scheduling adjustments may be necessary. Under such circumstances, fewer and longer mental training sessions are usually held. Sport psychology consultants typically start with some group sessions to explain general principles and their philosophy. They then follow up by meeting athletes individually (e.g., Botterill, 1990; Halliwell, 1990). It is critical that athletes be assigned training exercises to practice between meetings with the sport psychology consultant. And the coach can help assure compliance and feedback by conducting the training exercises—or at least providing time for athletes to practice.

Ideally, PST continues as long as athletes participate in their sport. Larry Bird, Jackie Joyner-Kersee, Wayne Gretsky, Monica Seles, Greg Louganis, Kristi Yamaguchi—all highly skilled and physically talented athletes—have all been known for continually integrating the mental aspects of their sports into physical practice.

Mental training should continue throughout an athlete's sport participation.

Although PST is an ongoing process, an athlete's *first exposure* to a formal PST program should last 3 to 6 months. Learning, practicing, and integrating new mental skills requires this much time. The specific sport, time available, existing mental skills, and commitment of the participants also play parts in determining how much time to allot to the formal program.

Designing and Implementing a PST Program

You have learned why PST is important, who should conduct the program, when to implement it during the season, and how much time to spend on it. We'll now outline some key aspects of developing and implementing PST programs.

Discussing Your Approach to Developing Psychological Skills

It is important to spell out to participants exactly what kind of PST services can be provided. You should explain the distinction between educational and clinical sport psychology consultants. Psychological skills training is an *educational* approach to mental training. If more serious mental problems are encountered (e.g., substance abuse, eating disorders), explain that the sport psychology consultant will make a referral to a qualified therapist or counseling center.

Emphasizing the educational approach also helps dispel the idea that seeing a sport psychology consultant means something must be "wrong" with a person. Younger athletes especially can be sensitive to the idea that they "have to see a psychologist." You can explain that most people applaud the extra effort of an athlete who stays after practice to work with the coach on a particular move or to improve technique. Similarly, an athlete recognizing the need to work on concentration skills should also be applauded.

If you asked participants to name the mental skills they would like to develop, they might list such diverse topics as positive mental attitude, mental toughness, aggressiveness, self-motivation, character, leadership, self-confidence, anxiety management, concentration, competitiveness, and communication skills. It isn't possible to develop all these skills, nor does each athlete need to. What is important is to assess each person's specific strengths and weaknesses in psychological skills so that programs can be individualized.

Assessing Athletes' Mental Skills

In first evaluating athletes' psychological strengths and weaknesses, bear in mind that not only psychological factors influence performance. A baseball player, for example, may attribute his slump to overanxiousness when in reality his problem is biomechanical, concerning a "hitch in his swing." Thus, combined input from coaches, biomechanists, physiologists, and teachers is often useful. Two clues that athletes might benefit from mental training are that they perform better in practice than in competition or poorer in important competitions than in unimportant ones.

An oral interview and written psychological inventories can provide useful subjective and objective information. We recommend the semistructured interview, which includes general questions with opportunities to use the athlete's responses to form follow-up questions (Orlick, 1980). The interview is a good time to determine where the athlete needs help and to start building the trust critical to any therapeutic relationship. Table 13.3 shows examples of key interview items.

Table 13.3   Sample Interview Items

Tell me about your involvement in your sport, summarizing what you consider important events, both positive and negative. (This is a good starting point because it lets athletes talk about themselves and become comfortable.)

Describe in detail the thoughts and feelings surrounding your best and worst performances.

What do you believe is your greatest psychological strength? Your biggest weakness?

Try to describe any psychological problems you are having now.

What is your relationship with your coach?

You should also try some psychological inventories to assess various skills. Here are some of the ones most popular with sport psychology consultants:

- Test of Attentional and Interpersonal Style (Nideffer, 1976)
- Sport Competition Anxiety Test (Martens, 1977)
- Psychological Skills Inventory for Sport (Mahoney, Gabriel, & Perkins, 1987)
- Trait-State Sport Confidence Inventory (Vealey, 1986)

Some sport-specific inventories have also been developed, such as the Tennis Test of Attentional and Interpersonal Style (Van Schoyck & Grasha, 1981) and the Anxiety Assessment for Wrestlers (Gould, Horn, & Spreemann, 1983).

Once the interview and psychological inventories have been completed, the evaluator should give written feedback to each athlete to highlight his or her specific psychological strengths and weaknesses in sport performance. This assessment should conclude with a section identifying the type of psychological skills appropriate for each athlete. It is important to provide people with the opportunity to react to the consultants' evaluations and to agree on how to proceed. If a sport psychology consultant works with an entire team, it is essential that the coach, who is more likely to know the team's mental strengths and weaknesses, is also involved in the assessment. A sample needs assessment is provided in the following case study.

Beware of anyone who presents a "canned" mental training program that does not provide individual assessment and ignores the specific needs of athletes. It takes more time and effort to individualize the programs, but the more attention paid to individual needs, the more likely the program will succeed.

Needs Assessment for a Soccer Player

Motivation:

Your motivation and drive to do well are extremely high. You are a self-starter and are motivated to improve yourself. You hang in there even when the going gets tough, and you can be counted on to give 100% effort. This area is definitely one of your key strengths.

- You are concerned with developing and maintaining self-discipline.
- You stick to tasks (even difficult ones) until they're completed.
- Whenever you reach a goal, you set a higher one.
- You persist even in the face of failure.
- You have a strong desire to achieve.
- You like to take on challenging tasks.
- You exhibit commitment to the tasks you undertake.

The only potential problem I see is that your motivation and drive for success might make you push yourself harder than you should. This could result in increased anxiety and actually undermine your performance.

Anxiety:

You show some strengths and some potential areas for improvement in this area. Unlike many athletes, you seem more relaxed during games than during practice. It is possible that you feel you must play well in practice to increase the possibility of playing time during the game. Perhaps you get so involved in the game that you don't have time to think and, therefore, you just react. Given your present position as a runner, which emphasizes speed and quickness, you can probably function well on instinct since ball handling is at a minimum. Here are specific situations that cause you some anxiety:

- You worry about performing up to your level of ability.
- You worry about making mistakes.
- You worry about not performing well.
- You worry about what your coach might think or say.

These worries may be tied to the pressure you put on yourself because you tend to be a perfectionist. Being a perfectionist is a double-edged sword—it can push you toward higher achievement but at the same time cause stress because it is impossible to be perfect. Over time, this could take the fun out of the game for you.

Concentration:

You appear able to focus well while you're playing and to block out distractions, such as crowd noises. Your concentration sometimes is compromised from distractions that you create. That is, the inability to forget mistakes and other negative thoughts interferes with your concentration. This, in turn, takes away from the fluid, automatic, and relaxed fashion in which you would like to be performing. Sometimes, too much thinking can be counterproductive. This would particularly be true of fast-moving sports such as soccer (especially indoor soccer).

Confidence:

This is probably the area that you will want to work on the most. Although anxiety, concentration, and confidence are all interrelated, I believe that in your case, confidence controls the other two. One overriding concern is the adjustment from outdoor to indoor soccer. It's likely that some of the things you previously did by instinct, you now have to think about, and this can decrease confidence. Second, with minimum playing time, it's hard to develop your

(continued)

Needs Assessment for a Soccer Player   *(continued)*

confidence and get into the flow of the game. These probably converge in causing you not to be confident on the ball, which used to be one of your strengths. Your confidence should improve as you feel more secure and familiar with the indoor game, but there are ways to speed up the process. Some specific areas where your confidence is lacking include the following:

- Your ability to make critical decisions during competition
- Your ability to perform under pressure
- Your ability to execute successful strategy
- Your ability to execute the skills necessary to be successful

And here are some of the areas in which your confidence is high:

- Your ability to relate successfully to teammates and coaches
- Your physical conditioning
- Your ability to improve your skills
- Your ability to control your emotions
- Your ability to put forth the effort to succeed

There are a couple of areas in which overconfidence might be a problem, including concentration and persistence to achieve your goal. I would like to explore these with you.

Summary

Strengths:

- Strong desire to succeed
- Confidence in your ability to succeed
- Ability to relax during competitions
- Confidence in your ability to relate well to teammates and coaches
- Your physical conditioning

Areas of Improvement:

- Forgetting about mistakes
- Maintaining confidence despite early errors
- Remaining relaxed during practice
- Worrying about performing up to your ability
- Perfectionistic attitude

Recommendations

- Learn thought stopping
- Change negative to positive self-talk
- Focus on having fun while competing hard
- Develop cue words to help concentration
- Learn relaxation techniques
- Think confidently

Determining Which Psychological Skills to Include

After the assessment comes the decision about which psychological skills to emphasize during the program. This decision should be based on the coaches' and athletes' answers to these questions:

- How many weeks of practice or preseason are available?
- How much practice time will be devoted weekly to PST?

- How interested are the athletes in receiving PST?
- Will there still be time to practice mental skills after the competitive season begins?

When there isn't sufficient time and commitment for a comprehensive training program, rather than superficially working on all the needed skills, it is better to prioritize objectives and emphasize a few skills initially.

The first thing to do is differentiate between psychological skills and methods (Vealey, 1988): *skills* are qualities to be obtained; *methods* are procedures or techniques employed to develop these skills. Table 13.4 is an overview of methods for developing and enhancing psychological skills. The basic PST methods include four traditional techniques for developing skills, including arousal regulation (chapter 14), imagery (chapter 15), goal setting (chapter 17), and attention/thought control (chapter 18). Vealey emphasizes that productive physical practice and the understanding of the physical and mental processes that influence performance will foster psychological skills.

Using these methods, Vealey proposes several skills that a well-rounded PST program can develop (see Table 13.5). These skills reflect areas of personal growth and performance enhancement. A human development model focuses on growth and change to help people gain control of their lives, both inside and outside sport (Vealey, 1988).

Whatever methods and skills are included in the PST program, they will be more effective if psychological objectives appropriate to the individual accompany them (Seabourne et al., 1985; Silva, 1982). The objectives should be easily understood and defined in measurable terms (see Table 13.6 for an example). Such definitions clarify the objective and expected outcomes. They give a clear foundation for planning how to accomplish the objectives and assessing how effective the strategies were in achieving objectives.

Table 13.4 Methods for Developing Psychological Skills

Foundation methods	Psychological skills methods
Physical practice	Goal setting
Education	Imagery
	Physical relaxation
	Thought/attention control

Adapted from Vealey (1988).

Table 13.5 Psychological Skills Developed in PST Programs

Foundation skills	Performance skills	Facilitative skills
Volition	Optimal physical arousal	Interpersonal skills
Self-awareness	Optimal mental arousal	Lifestyle management
Self-esteem	Optimal attention	
Self-confidence		

Adapted from Vealey (1988).

Table 13.6   A Sample of Psychological Skills, Objectives, and Outcomes

Objective 1: positive mental attitude	Objective 2: coping with mistakes and failures	Objective 3: handling the high-stress situation
Don't make negative statements at games or practices.	Accept that mistakes and failures are necessary to the learning process.	Learn to interpret the situation as a challenge, not a threat.
Change "I can't" statements to "I can" statements.	Don't make excuses. Accepting responsibility will help turn failures into successes.	Recognize too much tension. Achieve appropriate differential relaxation.
Always give 100%.	Stay positive even after a mistake.	Keep thoughts positive and focused on the task.
Don't talk while coaches talk.	Support teammates—even when they are making mistakes.	Imagine goal of performing well under high-stress situations.
Hustle during all plays and drills.	Keep focused on the task rather than dwelling on mistakes.	Focus on appropriate cues.

Adapted from Gould (1983).

Designing a PST Schedule

Needs have been assessed, psychological skill objectives identified, and specific strategies delineated to achieve the objectives. Now comes the training schedule. Maybe 1 or 2 days a week before or after practice could serve as a formal meeting time for educating participants on imagery, anxiety management, attentional control, goal setting, and other psychological skills. In general, it is better to hold frequent short meetings rather than less frequent long meetings.

Informal meetings allow the sport psychology consultant to impart information and build rapport. Many athletes who hesitate to sign up for a formal meeting are willing to talk informally. Informal meetings can occur during social events, on bus or plane rides to competitions, at the hotel, at meals, or any other time and place. These informal meetings complement the structured meetings and individualize content to each athlete.

A critical point in setting up a training schedule is determining when to start and how long the training should last. As we noted earlier, it is best to develop psychological skills just before the season begins or during the off-season when coaches and athletes can focus on developing skills, instead of on practice, games, travel, and winning. But the key is to systematically schedule PST into the daily practice regimen.

Formal and informal meetings with coaches and athletes are opportunities for the PST consultant to enhance communication and build rapport.

Evaluating the Program

Evaluating psychological skills development and change is an important but often overlooked element of PST programs. There are ethical obligations to show the effectiveness of the program (Smith, 1989), but practical considerations as well:

- An evaluation provides feedback for gauging the program's effectiveness and for modifying the program as necessary.
- An evaluation allows participants to suggest changes in how the program is conducted.

- An evaluation is the only way to objectively judge if the program has achieved its goals.

Ideally, the evaluation should include interviews and written rating scales to supply both qualitative and quantitative feedback. Also useful to coaches and athletes is objective performance data. For example, if one of the program goals was to help a basketball player relax while shooting free throws under pressure, then free-throw percentage in critical situations (e.g., last 5 minutes of a game when there is less than a 5-point difference in the score) would be a good statistic for evaluation. The following questions are useful for evaluating the effectiveness of a PST program:

- What techniques appeared to work best?
- Was enough time allotted to practice the psychological skills?
- How useful were the team sessions?
- How useful were the individual sessions?
- Was the consultant available?
- Was the consultant knowledgeable, informative, and easy to talk with?
- Should anything be added to or deleted from the program?
- What were the major strengths and weaknesses of the program?

Partington and Orlick (1987a, 1987b) developed a sample sport psychology evaluation form and data on what makes a consultant effective from both the coaches' and athletes' points of view (see Table 13.7). Sport psychologists are continually learning, and their programs will continue to change and evolve in the future.

Ethical Considerations

Sport psychology is a young profession, and only recently has its organizations—such as the Association for the Advancement of Applied Sport Psychology and the Canadian Society for Psychomotor Learning and Sport Psychology—developed ethical guidelines (see Nideffer, 1981, and Heyman, 1984, for a thorough presentation of the complex ethical issues and interrelationships involved in applied sport psychology). These guidelines are modifications of the American Psychological Association's Ethical Standards (1981), and at their core is the general philosophy that sport psychology consultants should respect the dignity and worth of the individual and honor the preservation and protection of fundamental human rights. Consultants are committed to increasing the knowledge of human behavior and of people's understanding of themselves and others in the sport environment. The essence of this philosophy is that the athlete's welfare must be foremost in mind.

There are nine areas (and principles) outlined in the American Psychological Association's ethical guidelines:

1. Responsibility
2. Competence
3. Moral and legal standards
4. Public statements
5. Confidentiality
6. Welfare of the client
7. Professional relationships
8. Assessment techniques
9. Research with human participants

These concerns should be considered in implementing PST programs.

Table 13.7 The Sport Psychology Consultant Evaluation Form

Name _____ Consultant's name _____

Sport _____

Please rate your sport psychology consultant on each of the following characteristics by using a number from 0 to 10 as shown on the scale below.

Not at all										Yes, definitely
0	1	2	3	4	5	6	7	8	9	10

Ratings

1. Consultant characteristics

   Had useful knowledge about mental training that seemed to apply directly to my sport. _____

   Seemed willing to provide an individual mental training program based on my input and needs. _____

   Seemed open, flexible, and ready to cooperate with me. _____

   Had a positive, constructive attitude. _____

   Proved to be trustworthy. _____

   Was easy for me to relate to (i.e., I felt comfortable and that he or she understood me). _____

   Provided clear, practical, concrete strategies. _____

2. How effective was this consultant?

	Hindered										Helped
Effect on you:	−5	−4	−3	−2	−1	0	+1	+2	+3	+4	+5
Effect on team:	−5	−4	−3	−2	−1	0	+1	+2	+3	+4	+5

3. Do you have any recommendations to improve the sport psychology consultation service? Please write suggestions on the back of this sheet.

Adapted from Partington and Orlick (1987b).

Common Problems in Implementing PST Programs

By attending to some common problems athletes, coaches, and consultants have encountered in implementing PST programs, you can avoid hampering your program's effectiveness. We've already touched on some of these problems in various contexts. We'll now provide some specific examples.

Lack of Conviction

Many people involved in sport resist change, no matter what the change happens to be. Thus, consultants often have to convince coaches and athletes that developing psychological skills will facilitate individual and team success. One good "selling point" is the example of highly visible athletes known for their psychological skills. Diver Greg Louganis, for instance, has exemplified exceptional psychological skills. People who watched the 1988 Olympics remember seeing Louganis hit his head on the board during a dive, resulting in an injury that required sutures. Yet Louganis was able to regain his composure, successfully execute his next dive, and win a gold medal. He had acquired psychological skills of concentration and anxiety management.

Lack of Time

Coaches frequently claim that there just isn't enough time to practice mental skills. However, time can usually be found if mental skills training is made a priority. This is another reason to convince coaches and athletes of the benefits of PST. It is important to get a commitment to set specific times during or after practice to devote to PST. If you value acquiring mental skills, it makes sense to set time aside to practice them.

Lack of Sport Knowledge

Coaches sometimes point out that a consultant lacks sport-specific knowledge. Having some playing or coaching experience indeed helps the consultant understand the specific problems athletes experience and talk about them in the sport's jargon. This helps build the trust and rapport essential for an effective consultant-athlete relationship. However, although it is good to have sport-specific experience, it is not absolutely essential as long as consultants acquaint themselves with the nature of the sport and its competitive environment. They can view videotapes, watch practices, and attend competitions to learn about the sport.

Lack of Follow-Up

Some coaches and consultants implement a PST program enthusiastically but provide little follow-up once the program is under way. Psychological skills, like any skills, need to be practiced to be learned well enough to use in tight spots. Following up throughout the season—by making time for PST and meeting with athletes to discuss their progress—is important.

A sport psychology consultant needs to be aware of these potential problems and be ready to deal with them if necessary. Many consultants make mistakes in their first years of consulting because they weren't aware of the nuances of setting up and implementing PST programs. Homework and planning should be prerequisites for any sport psychology consultant to work with athletes and teams. However, good preparation, careful thought, and a sense of commitment can lead to a rewarding experience. After all, helping individuals reach their potential both inside and outside the world of sport is what it's all about.

Summary

We have addressed many general issues relating to the integration and implementation of a psychological skills training program. Athletes and coaches generally acknowledge the importance of mental skills but fail to practice them in any systematic fashion. Often they don't allot adequate time for mental training because they lack the knowledge to implement such a program or erroneously believe that mental skills cannot be taught. Athletes of virtually all ages and skill levels can benefit from PST, and mental skills training should continue for as long as an athlete participates in competitive sport. Real benefits from PST will occur only with long-term systematic practice. A first step is psychological needs assessment to determine the specific components of a PST program. The program should be tailored to individual differences and needs. The initial PST program should probably last 3 to 6 months and start during the preseason or off-season. There are advantages to having a sport psychology consultant implement a PST program, but it's also possible for a coach or other

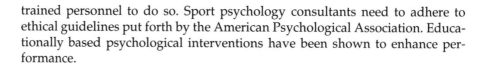

trained personnel to do so. Sport psychology consultants need to adhere to ethical guidelines put forth by the American Psychological Association. Educationally based psychological interventions have been shown to enhance performance.

Review Questions

1. Discuss three reasons why PST training is important.

2. Discuss three reasons why coaches and athletes often neglect PST and why the myths concerning PST training are false.

3. Provide specific examples of how PST derives its knowledge base from elite athlete research and athlete/coach experiences.

4. Describe the three phases of PST training—education, acquisition, and practice.

5. What empirical evidence is there that PST enhances sport performance?

6. Who should conduct PST programs? Include AAASP criteria for certification as part of your answer.

7. When is the best time to implement PST programs and why?

8. How much time should individuals spend practicing PST and why?

9. How would you assess an individual's psychological strengths and weaknesses via an interview and written psychological inventories?

10. Describe how Vealey breaks down PST programs into psychological methods and psychological skills. Give examples of each.

11. Why is it important to evaluate PST effectiveness? What specific questions would you use to evaluate effectiveness?

12. Discuss the importance of ethical standards in implementing PST programs. What are five APA ethical principles that PST programs need to adhere to?

13. Discuss three common problems in implementing PST programs and how you might solve them.

References

American Psychological Association (1981). Ethical principles of psychologists. *American Psychologist*, **36**, 633-638.

Asken, M.J. (1991). The challenge of the physically challenged: Delivering sport psychology services to physically disabled athletes. *The Sport Psychologist*, **5**, 370.

Botterill, C. (1990). Sport psychology and professional hockey. *The Sport Psychologist*, **4**, 369-377.

Clark, R.A., & Sachs, M.L. (1991). Challenges and opportunities in psychological skills training in deaf athletes. *The Sport Psychologist*, **5**, 392.

Gould, D. (1988). Sport psychology: Future directions in youth sport research. In F.L. Smoll, R.A. Magill, & M.J. Ash (Eds.), *Children in sport* (3rd ed., pp. 317-344). Champaign, IL: Human Kinetics.

Gould, D., & Eklund, R.C. (1991). The application of sport psychology for performance optimizations. *The Journal of Sport Science*, **1**, 10-21.

Gould, D., Horn, T., & Spreemann, J. (1983). Competitive anxiety in junior elite wrestlers. *Journal of Sport Psychology*, **5**, 58-71.

Gould, D., Tammen, V., Murphy, S., & May, J. (1989). An examination of the U.S. Olympic sport psychology consultants and the services they provide. *The Sport Psychologist*, **3**, 300-312.

Greenspan, M.J., & Feltz, D.F. (1989). Psychological interventions with athletes in competitive situations: A review. *The Sport Psychologist*, **3**, 219-236.

Halliwell, W. (1990). Providing sport psychology consulting services to a professional sport organization. *The Sport Psychologist*, **4**, 369-377.

Hellstedt, J.C. (1987). Sport psychology at a ski academy: Teaching mental skills to young athletes. *The Sport Psychologist*, **1**, 56-68.

Heyman, S.R. (1984). Cognitive interventions: Theories, applications, and cautions. In W.F. Straub & J.M. Williams (Eds.), *Cognitive sport psychology* (pp. 289-303). Lansing, NY: Sport Science Associates.

Jacobson, E. (1938). *Progressive relaxation.* Chicago: University of Chicago Press.

Mahoney, M.J., Gabriel, T.J., & Perkins, T.S. (1987). Psychological skills and exceptional athletic performance. *The Sport Psychologist*, **1**, 181-199.

Martens, R. (1977). *Sport competition anxiety test.* Champaign, IL: Human Kinetics.

Meichenbaum, D. (1977). *Cognitive-behavior modification: An integrative approach.* New York: Plenum.

Nideffer, R.M. (1976). Test of attentional and interpersonal style. *Journal of Personality and Social Psychology*, **34**, 394-404.

Nideffer, R.M. (1981). *The ethics and practice of applied sport psychology.* Ithaca, NY: Mouvement Publications.

Orlick, T. (1980). *In pursuit of excellence.* Champaign, IL: Human Kinetics.

Orlick, T., & Partington, J. (1988). Mental links to excellence. *The Sport Psychologist*, **2**, 105-130.

Orlick, T., & Partington, J. (1989). *Psyched: Inner views of winning.* Ottawa, Canada: Coaching Association of Canada.

Partington, J., & Orlick, T. (1987a). The sport psychology consultant: Olympic coaches' views. *The Sport Psychologist*, **1**, 95-102.

Partington, J., & Orlick, T. (1987b). The sport psychology consultant evaluation form. *The Sport Psychologist*, **1**, 309-317.

Seabourne, T., Weinberg, R.S., Jackson, A., & Suinn, R.M. (1985). Effect of individualized, nonindividualized and package intervention strategies on karate performance. *Journal of Sport Psychology*, **7**, 40-50.

Silva, J.M. (1982). Performance enhancement in competitive sport environments through cognitive intervention. *Behavior Modification*, **6**, 443-446.

Smith, R.E. (1989). Applied sport psychology in the age of accountability. *Journal of Applied Sport Psychology*, **1**, 166-180.

Smith, R.E., & Johnson, J. (1990). An organizational empowerment approach to consultation in professional baseball. *The Sport Psychologist*, **4**, 347-357.

Travis, C.A., & Sachs, M.L. (1991). Applied sport psychology and persons with mental retardation. *The Sport Psychologist*, **5**, 382.

Van Schoyck, S.R., & Grasha, A.F. (1981). Attentional style variations and athletic ability. The advantages of a sports-specific test. *Journal of Sport Psychology*, **3**, 149-165.

Vealey, R.S. (1986). Conceptualization of sport-confidence and competitive orientation: Preliminary investigation and instrument development. *Journal of Sport Psychology*, **8**, 221-246.

Vealey, R.S. (1988). Future directions in psychological skills training. *The Sport Psychologist*, **2**, 318-336.

Vealey, R. (1994). Current status and prominent issues in sport psychology intervention. *Medicine and Science in Sport and Exercise*, **26**, 495-502.

Weiss, M.R. (1991). Psychological skill development in children and adolescents. *The Sport Psychologist*, **5**, 335.

Williams, J.M. (1986). Psychological characteristics of peak performance. In J.M. Williams (Ed.), *Applied sport psychology: Personal growth to peak performance* (pp. 123-132). Palo Alto, CA: Mayfield.

CHAPTER 14

Arousal Regulation

The thing that always worked best for me whenever I felt I was getting too tense to play good tennis was to simply remind myself that the worst thing—the very worst thing that could happen to me—was that I'd lose a bloody tennis match. That's all!

Rod Laver, former tennis player

You can bring your whistle and you can bring your flag, but if you don't bring your guts you might as well stay home.

Football official

I love the pressure. I just look forward to it.

Daly Thompson, Olympic decathlon gold medalist

Depending on the person and the situation, there are different ways of coping with the pressures of competitive sports. A golfer preparing to knock in a 20-foot putt would control arousal differently than a wrestler climbing into the ring. The relation between arousal and performance can be complicated (see chapter 6), but athletes in competitive sport need to learn to control their arousal. They should be able to increase it—to psych up—when they're feeling lethargic and decrease it when the pressure to win causes anxiety and nervousness.

Many coaches used to mistakenly think that all athletes need to psych up to play their best. But in fact, more often athletes need to tone *down* anxiety and pressure in competitive sport. The key is for individuals to find their optimal levels of arousal—to psych up without psyching out. Although psyching up may be helpful at times, the problem often becomes psyching out. In fact, one of the frequent reasons athletes give for failing to reach their potential is that they couldn't cope effectively with competitive anxiety.

Our society values winning and pressures coaches and athletes to be successful. The inability to effectively cope with the pressures in competitive sport can lead not only to decreases in performance but also to physical illness and mental distress. Continued pressure sometimes causes burnout in sport and exercise (see chapter 23) and can lead to ulcers, migraine headaches, and hypertension.

In this chapter you will learn about

▮ increasing self-awareness of anxiety and arousal regulation states,

▮ techniques and on-site relaxation tips to reduce anxiety, and

▮ techniques to raise arousal and help get psyched up for competition.

Self-Awareness of Anxiety

The first step toward controlling arousal levels is to be more aware of them during practices and competitions. This typically involves self-monitoring and recognizing how emotional state affects performance. If you are an athlete you can probably identify certain feelings associated with top performances and other feelings associated with poor performances. To increase awareness of your arousal states, we recommend the following process.

First, think back to your best performance—some athletes refer to this special state as "playing in the zone." Try to visualize the actual competition as clearly as possible, focusing on what you felt and thought at that time. Don't rush: Take at least 5 minutes to relive the experience. Now complete the items in Table 14.1. Because you are reconstructing your best performance, for *played*

Table 14.1						**Checklist of Performance States**		
Played extremely well	1	2	3	4	5	6	Played extremely poorly
Felt extremely relaxed	1	2	3	4	5	6	Felt extremely anxious
Felt extremely confident	1	2	3	4	5	6	Felt extremely unconfident
Felt in complete control	1	2	3	4	5	6	Had no control at all
Muscles were relaxed	1	2	3	4	5	6	Muscles were tense
Felt extremely energetic	1	2	3	4	5	6	Felt extremely fatigued
Self-talk was positive	1	2	3	4	5	6	Self-talk was negative
Felt extremely focused	1	2	3	4	5	6	Felt extremely unfocused
Felt effortless	1	2	3	4	5	6	Felt great effort
Had high energy	1	2	3	4	5	6	Had low energy

extremely well, you would circle the number 1. For the second item, if you felt moderately anxious, you might circle number 4. There are no right or wrong answers; the goal is to see better the relation between your psychological states and performances. After completing Table 14.1 for your best performance, repeat the process for your worst performance.

After completing this exercise, compare how you responded to the two performances. Most people find that their thoughts and feelings are distinctly different when comparing playing well and playing poorly.

This is the beginning of awareness training. If you want to better understand the relation between your thoughts, feelings, and performance, monitor yourself by completing the checklist immediately after each practice or competitive session over the next few weeks. Of course, your psychological state will vary during a given session. If you feel one way during the first half of a basketball game, for example, and another way during the second half, simply complete two checklists. You are only estimating your feeling states—absolute precision is virtually impossible. If you are diligent with this procedure, however, you will quickly enhance your awareness, which is a giant step toward reaching your optimal level of arousal consistently. Remember that the most important thing is to understand the relation between how you feel on the inside and how you perform on the outside.

> You must increase your awareness of your psychological states before you can control your thoughts and feelings.

Anxiety Reduction Techniques

Excess anxiety can produce inappropriate muscle tension, which can in turn diminish performance. When your muscles become too tense, your movements appear awkward, jerky, rigid, and uncoordinated. And it is all too easy to develop excess muscle tension. The common thinking is "the harder you try, the better you will perform." This reasoning is incorrect.

As a quick, practical exercise, rest your dominant forearm and hand palm down on a desktop or table. Now, tense all the muscles in your hand and wrist and then try to tap your index and middle fingers quickly back and forth. Do

---

Trying Harder Isn't Always Better

In a study conducted with 400-meter runners, the runners were first asked to run all out (i.e., give 110%). A few days later, the same runners were asked to run at 95% of their capacity. Interestingly enough, the runners ran faster at 95% than at 110%. Why this happened involves the effect that muscle tension can have on skilled performance. Specifically, when running at 110% runners were using all their energies and muscular capacities. However, running—like most other sport activities—is performed most effectively when some muscles are contracting while others are relaxing. Thus, by using *all* of their muscles, agonists and antagonists, the runners were using muscles that prevented them from running as fast as they could. Running at 95%, they expended a great deal of muscular effort but relaxed the antagonist muscles that hinder maximum performance.

Consider a baseball pitcher who is overthrowing her fast ball—that is, trying too hard to throw the ball fast. Not only does the pitch not go as fast, it is also less accurate. Trying to throw the ball as fast as she can, the pitcher uses all the muscles in her arm. However, for accuracy, as well as speed, some of the muscles in the arm (particularly the flexor muscles like the biceps) need to relax as the extensor muscles (such as the triceps) do most of the work.

this for about 30 seconds. Now try to relax the muscles in your hands and fingers and repeat the exercise. You will probably discover that muscular tension slows your movements and makes them less coordinated, as compared with muscles that are relaxed.

We'll now present some relaxation procedures often used in sport and physical activity settings. Virtually all these techniques were designed to help people cope with stressful events they encounter in everyday life—only recently have they been applied to sport and exercise situations.

Progressive Relaxation (Muscle Relaxation)

Edmund Jacobson's *progressive relaxation* technique (1938) forms the cornerstone for many modern relaxation procedures. He named the technique progressive because the procedure progresses from one muscle group to the next, until all major muscle groups are completely relaxed. The technique has been modified considerably over the years, but its purpose remains to help people learn to feel tension in their muscles and then be able to let go of this tension.

General Progressive Relaxation Instructions. Progressive relaxation involves tensing and relaxing specific muscles. These tension-relaxation cycles develop your awareness of the difference between tension and lack of tension. Each cycle involves maximally contracting one specific muscle group and then attempting to fully relax that same muscle group while focusing on the different sensations of tension and relaxation. With skill, you can detect tension in a specific muscle or area of the body, like the neck, and then relax that muscle. Some people even learn to use the technique during breaks in an activity, such as a time-out.

You can create conditions that are conducive to relaxing.

- Find a quiet place.
- Dim the lights.
- Loosen tight-fitting clothing.
- Lie down in a comfortable position.

Using Progressive Relaxation. The first few sessions of progressive relaxation will probably take up to 30 minutes. With practice, less time is necessary: After three or four practice sessions, you might be able to relax within 5 to 10 minutes. When you can achieve relaxation regularly within 10 minutes, you can omit the muscle tension component. The goal of progressive relaxation is to learn to completely relax in a short time, which can be extremely valuable in many activities, such as a dive or a high jump. After learning the technique well, you can use a cue word, such as "relax," to trigger relaxation within a few seconds.

Basic Tenets of Progressive Relaxation

- It is possible to learn the difference between tension and relaxation.

- Tension and relaxation are mutually exclusive. It's not possible to be relaxed and tense at the same time.

- Progressive relaxation involves systematically contracting and relaxing each major muscle group in the body.

- Relaxation of the body through decreased muscle tension will, in turn, decrease mental tension.

Specific Instructions for Progressive Relaxation

In each step you'll first tense a muscle group and then relax it. Pay close attention to how it feels to be relaxed as opposed to tense. Each phase should take about 5 to 7 seconds. For each muscle group, perform each exercise twice before progressing to the next group. As you gain skill, you can omit the tension phase and focus just on relaxation. It is usually a good idea to record the following instructions on tape, or you might even invest a few dollars in a progressive relaxation recording.

1. Get comfortable. Loosen tight clothing and uncross your legs. Take a deep breath, let it out slowly, and relax.

2. Raise your arms, extend them in front of you, and make a tight fist with each hand. Notice the uncomfortable tension in your hands and fingers. Hold that tension for 5 seconds, then let go halfway and hold for an additional 5 seconds. Let your hands relax completely. Notice how the tension and discomfort drain from your hands, replaced by comfort and relaxation. Focus on the contrast between the tension you felt and the relaxation you now feel. Concentrate on relaxing your hands completely for 10 to 15 seconds.

3. Tense your upper arms tight for 5 seconds and focus on the tension. Let the tension out halfway and hold for an additional 5 seconds, again focusing on the tension. Now relax your upper arms completely for 10 to 15 seconds and focus on the developing relaxation. Let your arms rest limply at your sides.

4. Curl your toes as tight as you can. After 5 seconds relax the toes halfway and hold for an additional 5 seconds. Now relax your toes completely and focus on the spreading relaxation. Continue relaxing your toes for 10 to 15 seconds.

5. Point your toes away from you and tense your feet and calves. Hold the tension hard for 5 seconds, then let it out halfway for another 5 seconds. Relax your feet and calves completely for 10 to 15 seconds.

6. Extend your legs and raise them about 6 inches off the floor and tense your thigh muscles. Hold the tension for 5 seconds, let it out halfway and hold for another 5 seconds before relaxing your thighs completely. Concentrate on your feet, calves, and thighs for 30 seconds.

7. Tense your stomach muscles as tight as you can for 5 seconds, concentrating on the tension. Let the tension out halfway and hold for an additional 5 seconds before relaxing your stomach muscles completely. Focus on the spreading relaxation until your stomach muscles are completely relaxed.

8. To tighten your chest and shoulder muscles, press the palms of your hands together and push. Hold for 5 seconds, then let go halfway and hold for another 5 seconds. Now relax the muscles and concentrate on the relaxation until your muscles are completely loose and relaxed. Concentrate also on the muscle groups that have been previously relaxed.

9. Push your back to the floor as hard as you can and tense your back muscles. Let the tension out halfway after 5 seconds, hold the reduced tension and focus on it for another 5 seconds. Relax your back and shoulder muscles completely, focusing on the relaxation spreading over the area.

10. Keeping your torso, arms, and legs relaxed, tense your neck muscles by bringing your head forward until your chin digs into your chest. Hold for 5 seconds, release the tension halfway and hold for another 5 seconds, and then relax your neck completely. Allow your head to hang comfortably while you focus on the relaxation developing in your neck muscles.

(continued)

Specific Instructions for Progressive Relaxation   *(continued)*

11. Clench your teeth and feel the tension in the muscles of your jaw. After 5 seconds, let the tension out halfway and hold for 5 seconds before relaxing. Let your mouth and facial muscles relax completely with your lips slightly parted. Concentrate on totally relaxing these muscles for 10 to 15 seconds.

12. Wrinkle your forehead and scalp as tight as you can, hold for 5 seconds, and then release halfway and hold for another 5 seconds. Relax your scalp and forehead completely, focusing on the feeling of relaxation and contrasting it with the earlier tension. Concentrate for about a minute on relaxing all of the muscles of your body.

13. Cue-controlled relaxation is the final goal of progressive relaxation. Breathing can serve as the impetus and cue for effecting relaxation. Take a series of short inhalations, about one per second, until your chest is filled. Hold for 5 seconds, then exhale slowly for 10 seconds while thinking to yourself the word *relax* or *calm*. Repeat the process at least five times, each time striving to deepen the state of relaxation that you're experiencing.

Breath Control

Breathing is key to achieving relaxation. In fact, proper breathing is one of the easiest, most effective ways to control anxiety and muscle tension. When you are calm, confident, and in control, your breathing is likely smooth, deep, and rhythmical. When you're under pressure and tense, your breathing is likely short, shallow, and irregular.

Many athletes performing under pressure fail to coordinate their breathing with the performance of the skill. Research has demonstrated that breathing in and holding your breath increases muscle tension, whereas breathing out decreases muscle tension. For example, most discus throwers, shot-putters, and baseball pitchers learn to breathe out during release. Some athletes are even known as "grunters" because they exhale audibly each time they perform. Unfortunately, as pressure builds in a competition, the natural tendency is to hold your breath, which increases muscle tension and interferes with the coordinated movement necessary for maximum performance.

Similarly, in athletic rehabilitation settings, rhythmic breathing is important to maximize the effectiveness of stretching and lifting movements.

Practicing Breath Control.   As with any skill, breath control takes practice to develop. One technique focuses on breathing from the diaphragm instead of the chest. By focusing on the lowering (inhalation) and raising (exhalation) of the diaphragm, you'll experience a greater sense of stability, centeredness, and relaxation (Nideffer, 1985).

Applying Breath Control.   The best time to use breath control during competition is when there is a break in the action, such as a time-out, before serving in tennis, just prior to putting a golf ball, or preparing for a free throw in basketball. The slow and deliberate inhalation-exhalation sequence will help maintain your composure and control over anxiety during particularly stressful times. By focusing on your breathing, you'll be less likely to focus on irrelevant cues or distractions, such as spectator or opponent antics. Deep breathing also helps relax shoulder and neck muscles; it allows you to feel strong, centered, and ready for action. Finally, deep breathing provides a short mental break from the pressure of competition and can renew your energy.

Breath Control Procedure

Inhalation

Inhale deeply and slowly through your nose and notice how your diaphragm presses downward. Breathe from your stomach and diaphragm in a relaxed, easy manner, and then let the air fill and expand your central and upper chest. Push your stomach fully outward as you breathe in. This inhalation phase should last about 5 seconds.

Exhalation

Exhale slowly through your mouth. You should feel the muscles in your arms and shoulders relax. As you breathe out and relax, you should begin to feel centered and well anchored to the ground. Your legs should feel relaxed, yet solid and firm. The entire exhalation phase should last about 7 seconds. It's important to exhale slowly and steadily.

Some relaxation procedures focus more directly on relaxing the mind than progressive relaxation and deep breathing do. It is argued that relaxing the mind will in turn relax the body. Both physical and mental techniques will produce a relaxed state, but through different paths. We'll now discuss some of the techniques for relaxing the mind.

Relaxation Response (Mental Relaxation)

Herbert Benson (1975), a physician at the Harvard Medical School, popularized a scientifically sound way of relaxing that he called the *relaxation response*. Benson's method applies the basic elements of meditation but eliminates any spiritual or religious significance. Many athletes have used meditation to mentally prepare for competition, asserting that it improves their ability to relax, concentrate, and become energized. The state of mind produced by meditation is characterized by keen awareness, effortlessness, relaxation, spontaneity, and focused attention—many of the same elements that describe peak performance.

Four Elements Underlying the Relaxation Response

- *A quiet place.* This will assure that distractions and external stimulation are minimized.

- *Comfortable position.* Sit in a comfortable chair in a position you can maintain for a while. (Do not lie down in bed—you do not want to fall asleep.)

- *Mental device.* This is the critical element in the relaxation response and involves focusing your attention on a single thought or word and repeating it over and over. Select a word that does not stimulate your thoughts, such as *relax*, *calm*, or *easy*, repeating the word while breathing out. Every time you exhale, repeat your word.

- *A passive attitude.* A passive attitude is important but can be difficult to achieve. You have to learn to let it happen, allowing the thoughts and images that enter your mind to move through as they will, making no attempt to attend to them. If something comes to mind, let it go and refocus on your word. Don't worry about how many times your mind wanders; continue to refocus your attention on your word.

The relaxation response teaches you to quiet the mind, concentrate, and reduce muscle tension.

Learning the relaxation response takes time. You should practice it about 20 minutes a day. You will discover how difficult it is to control your mind and focus on one thought or object. But staying focused on the task at hand is important to many sports. The relaxation response teaches you to quiet the mind, which will help you to concentrate and reduce muscle tension. However, it is not a technique to use right before an event or competition.

Autogenic Training

Autogenic training has been used extensively in Europe but less in North America. The training, developed in Germany in the early 1930s by Johannes Schultz and later refined by Schultz and Luthe (1969), consists of a series of exercises designed to produce two physical sensations: warmth and heaviness. Basically, it is a technique of self-hypnosis. Attention is focused on the sensations you are trying to produce. As in the relaxation response, it is important to let the feeling happen without interference. The autogenic training program is based on six hierarchical stages, which should be learned in order:

1. Heaviness in the extremities
2. Warmth in the extremities
3. Regulation of cardiac activity
4. Regulation of breathing
5. Abdominal warmth
6. Cooling of the forehead

Phrases such as "My right arm is heavy," "My right arm is warm and relaxed," "My heartbeat is regular and calm," "My breathing rate is slow, calm, and relaxed," and "My forehead is cool" are all examples of commonly used verbal stimuli in an autogenic training program. One reason that autogenic technique has not caught on in North America is that it takes a long time. It usually takes several months of regular practice, 10 to 40 minutes a day, to become proficient, to experience heaviness and warmth in the limbs, and to produce the sensation of a relaxed, calm heartbeat and respiratory rate accompanied by warmth in the abdomen and coolness in the forehead.

Systematic Desensitization

Systematic desensitization has been demonstrated to be highly successful in sport (Smith, 1984). Originally developed by Joseph Wolpe (1958), systematic desensitization is really a form of counterconditioning. Wolpe argues that people learn to become anxious in the presence of certain stimuli, such as snakes or heights. Systematic desensitization is a gradual counterconditioning using relaxation as the incompatible response. For example, whenever someone with a snake phobia gets too close to a snake and becomes anxious, he is asked to relax. In time, the relaxation response helps to desensitize the anxiety felt when being close to a snake.

If an athlete has developed a strong fear (as opposed to some mild anxiety) that is undermining his or her performance, systematic desensitization is helpful. For example, a diver might develop a strong fear of injury after hitting her head on the diving board during a dive. Or a football running back might be afraid to make that first hard cut after returning from knee surgery. Other athletes might simply fall apart in front of a hostile crowd or when performing in front of their family and friends. In these cases, the athletes have developed intense fears that prevent them from performing up to their abilities.

Such athletes would first learn progressive relaxation. Next, an anxiety hierarchy would be established, consisting of about 10 scenes arranged by the inten-

sity of anxiety they elicit—from the least anxiety producing to the most anxiety producing (see the example in Table 14.2 of an individualized anxiety hierarchy for a volleyball player with a history of choking during service and return of serves). The third step is to imagine the first scene of the hierarchy for about 10 to 15 seconds. Athletes are instructed to signal any sign of tension by raising their hands. They then try to relax by using the progressive relaxation procedures. Once the first scene can be imagined without any anxiety reaction, the second scene is presented. The pairing of the potentially anxiety-producing situations with relaxation (if necessary) is continued until the most anxiety-producing situation can be dealt with effectively. In essence, athletes slowly become desensitized to the situation that was causing the most anxiety. Thus, the volleyball player in Table 14.2 would eventually be able to cope effectively with the pressure of serving or returning serve at the end of a close game.

Biofeedback

In most relaxation procedures, one of the goals is to become aware of muscular tension, as well as other autonomic nervous system reactions such as heart rate or respiration rate. Biofeedback is a technique specifically designed to

Table 14.2   **Individualized Anxiety Hierarchy for a Volleyball Player**
1. Participating in a regular practice session.
2. Participating in pregame warm-up drill.
3. Listening to the announcer introduce the team.
4. Preparing for the first play of the game.
5. Serving the ball when winning 10-2.
6. Preparing to serve the ball after I have made a good play.
7. Preparing to return serve when we are winning 10-2.
8. Preparing to return serve after I have just made an error.
9. Preparing to serve the ball for game point. The score is 14-13.
10. Preparing to receive the ball for game point. The score is 13-14.

teach people to control physiological or autonomic responses. It ordinarily involves an electronic monitoring device that can detect and amplify internal responses not ordinarily known to us. These electronic instruments provide visual or auditory feedback of physiological responses such as muscle activity, skin temperature, or heart rate (see Figure 14.1).

For example, a tennis player might feel muscle tension in her neck and shoulder before serving on important points in a match. Electrodes could be attached to specific muscles in the player's neck and shoulder region, and she would be asked to relax these specific muscles. Excess tension in the muscles would then cause the biofeedback instrument to make a loud, constant clicking noise. The tennis player's goal would be to quiet the machine by attempting to relax her shoulder and neck muscles. Relaxation could be accomplished through any of the relaxation techniques such as visualizing a positive scene or using positive self-talk. The key point is that the lower the noise level, the more relaxed the muscles are. Such feedback atunes the player to her tension levels and whether they are decreasing or increasing.

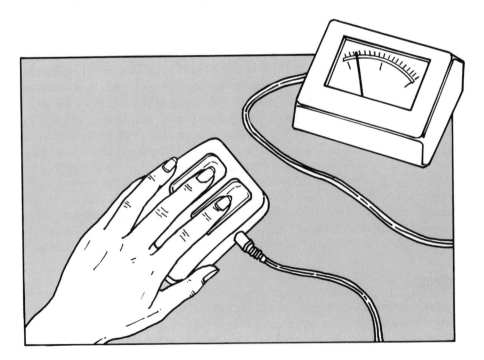

Figure 14.1 A form of biofeedback—measuring skin temperature.

Once the tennis player learns to recognize and reduce muscle tension in her shoulders and neck, she then needs to be able to transfer this knowledge to the tennis court. Daniels and Landers (1981) suggest doing this by interspersing sessions of nonfeedback within the training regimen. Gradually, the duration of these nonfeedback sessions (time away from the biofeedback device) is increased, and the tennis player depends less on the biofeedback signal while maintaining an awareness of physiological changes. With sufficient practice and experience, the tennis player can learn to identify the onset of muscle tension and control it so that her serve remains effective in clutch situations.

The most comprehensive approach to the study of biofeedback and sport performance has been carried out by Landers and colleagues (e.g., Daniels & Landers, 1981; Wilkinson, Landers, & Daniels, 1981). They worked with rifle shooters who through biofeedback trained themselves to fire between heartbeats, which improved performance. Although it should be noted that not all studies of biofeedback demonstrate enhanced performance (e.g., French, 1978), it has been shown to consistently reduce anxiety and muscle tension. Biofeedback appears to be effective in increasing awareness of tension levels and providing a mechanism for coping with precompetitive anxiety.

Biofeedback training can help people to become more aware of their autonomic nervous system reactions and subsequently to control these reactions.

Cognitive-Affective Stress-Management Training

Cognitive-affective stress-management training (SMT), developed by Ron Smith (1980), is one of the most comprehensive stress-management approaches. SMT is a skills program designed to teach a person a specific integrated coping response using relaxation and cognitive components to control emotional arousal. Such diverse professionals as bankers, business executives, social workers, and college administrators have applied it, and recently athletes have joined them (Crocker, Alderman, Murray, & Smith, 1988). Athletes have proven to be an ideal target population: They acquire the coping skills (e.g., muscular relaxation) somewhat more quickly than other groups, face stressful athletic situations frequently enough to permit careful monitoring of their progress, and perform in ways that can be readily assessed.

A theoretical model of stress underlies SMT (see Figure 14.2) that includes both cognitively based and physiologically based intervention strategies (derived from the work of Ellis, 1962; Lazarus, 1966; and Schachter, 1966). This model accounts for the situation, the person's mental appraisal of the situation, the physiological response, and the actual behavior. The program offers specific intervention strategies, such as relaxation skills, cognitive restructuring, and self-instructional training to help deal with the physical and mental reactions to stress. Combining mental and physical coping strategies will eventually lead to an integrated coping response.

Smith's cognitive-affective SMT program has four separate phases:

1. *Pretreatment assessment.* During this phase the consultant conducts personal interviews to assess what kinds of circumstances produce stress, the player's responses to stress, and how stress affects performance and other behaviors. She or he also assesses the player's cognitive and behavioral skills and deficits and administers written questionnaires to supplement the interview. This information is used to tailor a program to suit the player.

2. *Treatment rationale.* During the treatment rationale, or educational phase, the focus is on helping the player understand his or her stress response by analyzing personal stress reactions and experiences. It is important to emphasize that the program is *educational*, not psychotherapeutic, in design. Participants should understand that the program is designed to increase their self-control and that the level of coping ability they achieve depends on their efforts.

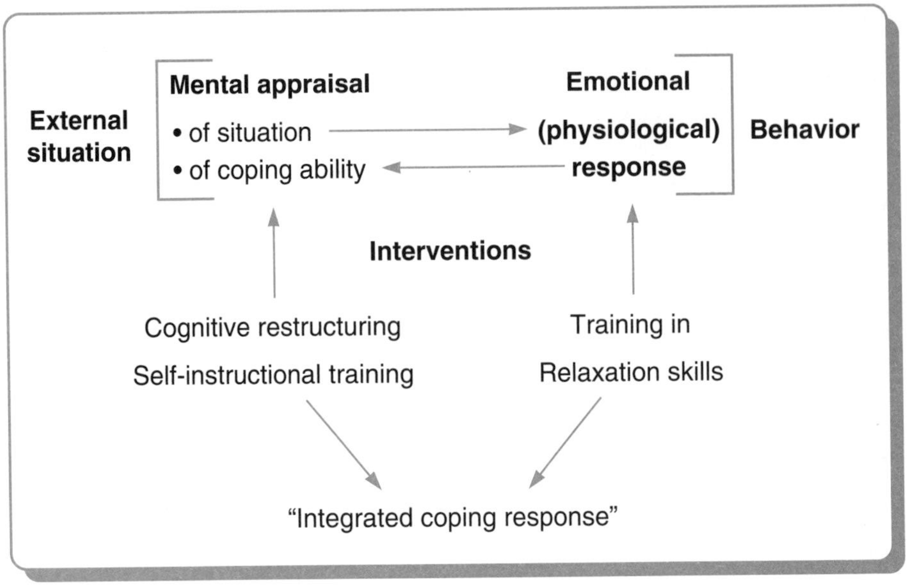

External situation → Mental appraisal • of situation • of coping ability → Emotional (physiological) response → Behavior

Interventions

Cognitive restructuring
Self-instructional training

Training in
Relaxation skills

"Integrated coping response"

Figure 14.2 Mediational model of stress underlying the cognitive-affective stress-management program together with the major intervention strategies used in the development of the integrated coping response. Adapted from Smith (1980).

3. *Skill acquisition.* The major objective of the SMT program is to develop an *integrated coping response* (see Figure 14.2) by acquiring both relaxation and cognitive intervention skills. In the skill acquisition phase participants receive training in muscular relaxation, cognitive restructuring, and self-instruction. The muscular relaxation comes from progressive relaxation. Cognitive restructuring is the attempt to identify irrational or stress-inducing self-statements, which are typically related to the fear of failure and disapproval (e.g., "I know I'll mess up," "I couldn't stand to let my teammates and coaches down," or "If I'm not successful, I won't be worth anything"). Then, these statements are restructured into more positive thoughts (e.g., "I'm still a good person whether I win or lose," and "Don't worry about losing—just play one point at a time"). (Changing negative self-statements into positive self-statements is discussed in more detail in chapter 18.) Self-instructional training teaches people to provide themselves with specific instructions to improve concentration and problem solving. This training teaches specific, useful self-commands, especially in stressful situations. Examples of such commands include, "Don't think about fear, just think about what you have to do," "Take a deep breath and relax," and "Take things one step at a time, just like in practice."

4. *Skill rehearsal.* To facilitate the rehearsal process, the consultant intentionally induces different levels of stress (typically by using films, imaginary rehearsals of stressful events, and other physical and psychological stressors), even high levels of emotional arousal that exceed actual competitions (Smith, 1980). These arousal responses are then reduced through the use of coping skills the participants have acquired. Warning: The procedure of induced affect can produce high levels of arousal, so only trained clinicians should employ this procedure.

On-Site Relaxation Tips

In addition to the well-developed and carefully structured techniques we've discussed so far, other on-site procedures can also help you cope with competitive stress. These techniques are not backed with scientific, empirical research but come from applied work with athletes (Weinberg, 1988). You should choose the strategies that best work for your situation.

1. Smile when you feel tension coming on. A simple and effective cue is to smile in the face of tension. It is difficult if not impossible to be mad or upset when you are smiling. By smiling, you take the edge off an anxiety-producing situation. It keeps things in perspective so you can forget about the pressure and enjoy the competition.

2. Have fun—enjoy the situation. Athletes highly skilled in their sport convey a sense of enjoyment and fun. Most of them look forward to and even relish pressure situations. For example, Al Oerter, four-time Olympic gold medalist in the decathlon, says, "I love competing in the Olympics. That's what training is all about." Similarly, former tennis great Billie Jean King says, "I like the pressure, the challenge—it's exciting; I choose to be here!" Enjoying the game also helps keep young players from burning out. Try to keep winning and losing in perspective and focus on enjoying the experience without undue concern for the outcome.

3. Set up stressful situations in practice. Practicing under simulated pressure can be good preparation for actual pressure situations. As you become more accustomed to playing under pressure, you will not be as negatively affected by it. You can create pressure in practice in many ways. Some college basketball coaches invite students to practices, asking them to scream and boo so that the players feel how it is on an opponent's home floor with the crowd against them. Football coaches will set the stage for a 2-minute drill by telling the team there are 2 minutes left in the game and they are down by 2 points on their own 20-yard line with 2 time-outs left—the offense must then move the ball into field goal range.

4. Slow down, take your time. Many athletes report that when they are feeling frustrated and mad, they start to perform too quickly. It is as if the easiest way to cope with all the anger and pressure is to hurry up and finish. For example, tennis players and golfers tend to rush their shots when they get anxious. Conversely, some athletes take too much time between shots, and their thinking disrupts performance. You can find the middle ground if you develop highly consistent preshot routines and perform them regularly before

each golf shot or tennis serve, regardless of the situation and pressure (see chapter 18).

5. Stay focused on the present. Thinking about what just happened or what might happen usually only increases anxiety. You can be sure that worrying about a fly ball you just dropped will not help you catch the next one that comes your way. In fact, worry makes you more anxious and increases your chances of missing. Similarly, thinking about what might happen on the next point or shot only increases pressure and anxiety (see chapter 18 for methods of focusing on the present).

6. Come prepared with a good game plan. Indecisiveness produces anxiety. Making decisions can be stressful, and in sport competition athletes and coaches have to make literally hundreds of decisions during the course of a game or match. Think of the decisions a point guard in basketball, quarterback in football, golfers, baseball pitchers, tennis players, or soccer players have to make. But if you come prepared with a specific game plan or strategy, decision making will be easier. For example, deciding what pitch to throw from behind in the count often causes baseball pitchers stress. Some pregame scouting can give pitchers a good idea of the best pitches to use if they fall behind to certain batters.

Arousal-Inducing Techniques

So far we have focused on anxiety-management techniques to reduce excess anxiety levels. There are times, however, when you need to pump yourself up because you are feeling lethargic and underenergized. Perhaps you have taken an opponent too lightly and she has surprised you. Or you're feeling tired in the 4th quarter. Or you're lethargic about your rehabilitation exercises. That is, you are below your optimal zone of functioning (see chapter 6) and need to generate some arousal or activate yourself to reach your optimal arousal level. Certain behaviors, feelings, and attitudes signal that you are underactivated:

- Moving slowly; not getting set
- Mind wandering; easily distracted
- Lack of concern about how well you perform
- Lack of anticipation or enthusiasm
- Heavy feeling in the legs; no bounce

You need to be aware of how activated you feel so you can take the steps to increase or decrease your arousal level.

You don't have to experience all of these signs to be underactivated. The more you notice, however, the more likely you need to increase arousal. Although these feelings can appear at any time, they usually indicate you are not physically or mentally ready to play. Maybe you didn't get enough rest, played too much (i.e., overtrained), or are playing against a significantly weaker opponent. The quicker you can detect these feelings, the quicker you can start to get yourself back on track. Here are suggestions for generating more energy and activating your system:

1. Increase breathing rate. Breathing control and focus produce energy and reduce tension. Short deep breaths tend to activate and speed up the nervous system. Along with the accelerated breathing rate, you may want to say "energy in" with each inhalation and "fatigue out" with each exhalation.

2. Act energized. At times when you feel lethargic and slow, acting energetically can help recapture your energy level. For example, football players often bang against each other's shoulder pads in the locker room before games to get themselves pumped up. Many athletes like to jump rope or take a little jog just before starting a competition to "get the butterflies out."

3. Use mood words/positive statements. The mind can certainly affect the body. For example, saying or thinking mood words (e.g., strong, forward, tough, aggressive, move, quick, fast, hard) can be energizing and activating. Positive self-statements can also energize you. Some examples include "hang in there," "I can do it," "get going," and "get tough."

4. Listen to music. Music can be a source of energy prior to competition. Many athletes use cassettes with headphones just before competitions. And listening to upbeat music while exercising can generate enthusiasm and emotion.

5. Use energizing imagery. Imagery is another way to generate positive feelings and energy (see chapter 15). Imagery involves visualizing something that is energizing to you. A sprinter, for example, might imagine a cheetah running swiftly over the plains. A swimmer might imagine moving through the water like a shark.

Summary

The ability to control arousal is a critical psychological skill for success in competitive sport. Anxiety-management techniques can help you cope with stressors in nonsport situations, as well. The first step is to become aware of the situations in competitive sport that cause you anxiety and how you respond to these events. A variety of anxiety-management methods can then be used, including both physical relaxation (progressive relaxation, breath control) and mental relaxation (relaxation response, autogenic training, cognitive-affective stress-management training) techniques. Different people feel more comfortable with different techniques; each person should choose the technique that works best in a particular situation. Several on-site techniques also help people cope with competitive anxiety. These techniques need to be practiced before being applied in actual competitions.

Sometimes energy levels need to be raised. Increased breathing, imagery, music, positive self-statements, and simply acting energized can all help increase arousal. The ability to regulate your arousal level is indeed a skill. To perfect that skill, you need to practice arousal regulation techniques in a systematic fashion, integrating them into your regular physical practice sessions whenever possible.

Review Questions

1. Discuss two ways to help athletes increase awareness of their psychological states.

2. Give two practical examples where giving 110% effort may deter performance.

3. Discuss the four basic tenets of progressive relaxation and give some general instructions for using this technique.

4. Describe the exhalation and inhalation phases of breath control. When might you use breath control?

5. Describe the four elements of the relaxation response and how to use it.

6. Describe systematic desensitization as a relaxation procedure and give an example of using it in a sport setting.

7. How does biofeedback work? Provide an example of its use in working with athletes.

8. Describe the mediational model of stress underlying the development of the cognitive-affective stress-management technique.

9. Discuss the four phases of cognitive-affective stress-management, comparing and contrasting cognitive structuring and self-instructional training.

10. Discuss three strategies for on-site reductions in anxiety and tension.

11. An athlete is having trouble getting psyched up for competition: How would you help her get energized?

References

Benson, H. (1975). The relaxation response. New York: Morrow.

Crocker, P., Alderman, R., Murray, F., & Smith, R. (1988). Cognitive-affective stress-management training with high performance youth volleyball players: Effects on affect, cognition, and performance. *Journal of Sport and Exercise Psychology*, **10**, 448-460.

Daniels, F.S., & Landers, D.M. (1981). Biofeedback and shooting performance: A test of disregulation and systems theory. *Journal of Sport Psychology*, **4**, 271-282.

Ellis, A. (1962). *Reason and emotion in psychotherapy*. New York: Lyle Stuart.

French, S.N. (1978). Electromyographic biofeedback for tension control during gross motor skill acquisition. *Perceptual and Motor Skills*, **47**, 883-889.

Jacobson, E. (1938). Progressive relaxation. Chicago: University of Chicago Press.

Lazarus, R.S. (1966). *Psychological stress and the coping process*. New York: McGraw-Hill.

Nideffer, R.M. (1985). *Athletes' guide to mental training*. Champaign, IL: Human Kinetics.

Schachter, S. (1966). The interaction of cognitive and physiological determinants of emotional state. In C. Spielberger (Ed.), *Anxiety and behavior*. New York: Academic Press.

Schultz, J., & Luthe, W. (1969). *Autogenic methods* (vol. 1). New York: Grune and Stratton.

Smith, R.E. (1980). A cognitive-affective approach to stress management training for athletes. In C.H. Nadeau, W.R. Halliwell, K.M. Newell, & G.C. Roberts (Eds.), *Psychology of motor behavior and sport* (pp. 54-72). Champaign, IL: Human Kinetics.

Smith, R.E. (1984). Theoretical and treatment approaches to anxiety reduction. In J. Silva and R. Weinberg (Eds.), *Psychological foundations in sport and exercise* (pp. 157-170). Champaign, IL: Human Kinetics.

Weinberg, R.S. (1988). *The mental advantage: Developing your psychological skills in tennis*. Champaign, IL: Human Kinetics.

Wilkinson, M.O., Landers, D.M., & Daniels, F.S. (1981). Breathing patterns and their influence on rifle shooting. *American Marksman*, **6**, 8-9.

Wolpe, J. (1958). *Psychotherapy by reciprocal inhibition*. Stanford, CA: Stanford University Press.

Imagery

Before every shot I go to the movies inside my head. Here is what I see. First, I see the ball where I want it to finish, nice and white and sitting up high on the bright green grass. Then, I see the ball going there; its path and trajectory and even its behavior on landing. The next scene shows me making the kind of swing that will turn the previous image into reality. These home movies are a key to my concentration and to my positive approach to every shot.

Jack Nicklaus (1976)

Jack Nicklaus believes that rehearsing shots in his mind before actually swinging is critical to his success. In fact, Nicklaus has said that hitting a good golf shot is 10% swing, 40% stance and setup, and 50% the mental picture of how the swing should occur. Another example is former Olympic athlete Dwight Stones, who visioned his high jumps in his imagination before performing them. Sometimes in his mind's eye he missed the jump—so he kept practicing in his head until he cleared the bar. Then, and only then, did he attempt the jump. Gold medalist Jean Claude Killy mentally rehearsed his slalom races before actually skiing down the mountain. He would run through the course in his head, seeing each turn, feeling his body respond to each mogul and shift in direction. Nicklaus, Stones, and Killy are only three of the many athletes who use imagery to enhance performance.

Only recently have coaches and researchers begun to understand the potential of imagery for improving sport performance. In using imagery in sport you "think with your muscles." As scientific evidence accumulates supporting the effectiveness of imagery in improving sport performance, more and more athletes and coaches are including mental rehearsal in training. Imagery has also helped athletes with rehabilitation after injury.

In this chapter you will learn about

▮ what imagery is,

▮ how and when imagery works,

▮ the effectiveness of imagery,

▮ different uses of imagery in training, rehabilitation, and competition,

▮ different types of imagery,

▮ training exercises for vividness and controllability, and

▮ how to set up an imagery training program.

What Is Imagery?

You probably have heard several of the different terms that describe an athlete's mental preparation for competition, including *visualization*, *mental rehearsal*, *imagery*, and *mental practice*. These terms all refer to creating or recreating an experience in the mind. The process involves recalling from memory pieces of information stored from experience and shaping these pieces into meaningful images. These experiences are essentially a product of your memory, experienced internally by recalling and reconstructing previous events. Imagery is actually a form of simulation. It is similar to a real sensory experience (e.g., seeing, feeling, or hearing), but the entire experience occurs in the mind.

All of us use imagery to recreate experiences. Have you ever watched the batting technique of a great baseball player and tried to copy the swing? Have you ever mentally reviewed the steps and the music of an aerobic dance workout before going to the class? We are able to accomplish these things because our minds can remember events and recreate pictures and feelings of them.

Our minds can also imagine or picture events that have not yet occurred. Although imagery relies heavily on memory, we can build an image from several parts of memory. For example, an athlete rehabilitating from a shoulder separation could see herself lifting her arm over her head, even though she has not been able to do this before. Many football quarterbacks view films of the defense they will be facing and then, through imagery, see themselves using certain offensive sets and strategies to offset the specific defensive alignments. Tennis great Chris Evert carefully rehearsed every detail of a match, including her opponent's style, strategy, and shot selection. Here is how she described using imagery to prepare for a tennis match:

> Before I play a match, I try to carefully rehearse what is likely to happen and how I will react in certain situations. I visualize myself playing typical points based on my opponent's style of play. I see myself hitting crisp

Through imagery you can recreate previous positive experiences or picture new events to prepare yourself mentally for performance.

deep shots from the baseline and coming to the net if I get a weak return. This helps me mentally prepare for a match and I feel like I've already played the match before I even walk on the court.

Involving All Senses

Imagery can, and should, involve as many senses as possible. Even when imagery is referred to as "visualization," the kinesthetic, auditory, tactile, and olfactory senses are all potentially important. The kinesthetic sense is particularly important to athletes because it involves the sensation of bodily position or movement that arises from the stimulation of sensory nerve endings in muscles, joints, and tendons. In essence, the kinesthetic sense is the feeling of our body as it moves in different positions. Using more than one sense helps to create more vivid images, thus making the experience more real.

Let's look at how you might use a variety of senses as a baseball batter. First, you obviously use *visual* sense to watch the ball as the pitcher releases it and it comes toward the plate. You employ *kinesthetic* sense to know where your bat is and to transfer your weight at the proper time to maximize power. You use *auditory* sense to hear the sound of the bat hit the ball. You can also use your *tactile* sense to feel how the bat feels in your hands. Finally, you might use your *olfactory* sense to smell the freshly mowed grass.

Besides using your senses, learning to attach various emotional states or moods to your imagined experiences is also important. Recreating emotions (e.g., anxiety, anger, joy, or pain) through imagery can help control these states. For instance, an aerobic dance instructor might get angry after making a mistake during her routine. Later, using imagery, she might imagine getting angry but then controlling that anger by redirecting her thoughts back to her routine. In one case study, a hockey player had difficulty dealing with officiating calls that went against him. He would get angry, lose his cool, and then not concentrate on his assignment. The player was instructed to visualize himself getting what he perceived to be a bad call, but then to use the cue words "stick to ice" to remain focused on the puck. Another example is a soccer player who tore an Achilles tendon. He felt angry when he thought he wasn't recovering quickly enough and would get down and not work hard at his exercises. But through imagery, he turned his anger into a positive emotion that stimulated him to work even harder toward rehabilitation.

> When using imagery, involve as many senses as possible and recreate or create the emotional feeling associated with the task or skill you're trying to execute.

Does Imagery Work?

To determine if imagery indeed does enhance performance, sport psychologists look at three different kinds of evidence: anecdotal reports, case studies, and scientific experiments.

Anecdotal reports, people's reports of isolated occurrences, are numerous (Jack Nicklaus's and Chris Evert's remarks are examples). Many of our best athletes and national coaches include imagery in their daily training regimen, and ever more athletes report using imagery to help recover from injury. A study conducted at the United States Olympic Training Center (Murphy, Jowdy, & Durtschi, 1990) found that 90% of Olympic athletes used some form of imagery and 97% of these athletes felt it helped their performance. In addition, 94% of the coaches of Olympic athletes used imagery during their training sessions, with 20% using it at every practice session. In fact, Peter Karns, the 1976 Olympic Biathlon coach, credits an imagery training program for a vast improvement in his team's performance.

Although anecdotal reports might be the most interesting pieces of evidence supporting imagery effectiveness, they are also the least scientific. A more scientific approach is the use of *case studies*, which closely monitor the use of imagery over time to determine if it helped to improve performance. The first case study concerns a field goal kicker from Colorado State University, Clark Kemble (Titley, 1976). During the 1973 season, Kemble missed a few relatively easy field goals at crucial times in the game, sometimes causing his team to lose in the final seconds. Afterward, during the off-season, Kemble diligently used imagery to visualize himself making field goals in important games under all types of game conditions and to see himself bounce back from a missed field goal attempt. During the next two seasons, he went on to kick many field goals near the ends of games to help Colorado State win, and he was also perfect on extra points. To top that off, he kicked a 63-yard field goal to break the NCAA record!

Another case study followed three college basketball players who all had some problems with their free throws, especially down the stretch of a game when the opposing team's fans were loud and waving their arms to distract them (Lane, 1980). The players used imagery to practice controlling their anxiety and focusing their attention during pressure situations. Two of the three players improved their free throw percentage by 11% and the other by 15%. These improvements were especially evident at away games where the pressure and distractions were greatest and where they had had particular difficulty the season before. Interestingly, the free throw percentage of their teammates who didn't use imagery actually decreased from the previous season.

In a third case study Dr. Richard Suinn, a sport psychologist, was given the opportunity to work with the 1976 United States Olympic ski team (it followed a disappointing Winter Games showing in 1972). First, he divided the team into two groups equally matched for ski-racing ability. One group received imagery training and the other acted as a control group. It became evident to the coach that the skiers practicing imagery were improving more rapidly than those in the control group (Suinn, 1976). The coach then called off the experiment and insisted that all his skiers be given the opportunity to train using imagery!

The scientific *experimental evidence* in support of imagery also is impressive and clearly demonstrates the value of imagery in learning and performing motor skills (Feltz & Landers, 1983; Richardson, 1967a, 1967b; Weinberg, 1981). Among experimental evidence, several studies have demonstrated the effectiveness of imagery in basketball, football, swimming, karate, skiing, volleyball, tennis, and golf.

Two factors seem to determine to what extent imagery can improve performance: the nature of the task and the skill level of the performer. Symbolic learning theory (discussed in detail later in this chapter) has shown that tasks involving mostly cognitive components (nature of the task), such as decision making and perception, show the greatest positive benefits from imagery rehearsal (Feltz & Landers, 1983). The performer practicing mentally "can think about what kinds of things might be tried, the consequences of each action can be predicted to some extent based on previous experiences with similar skills, and the performer can perhaps rule out inappropriate courses of action" (Schmidt, 1982, p. 520). In addition, the performer can rehearse the temporal and spatial regularities of a skill. For instance, to make the right decision to finish off a fast break, a basketball point guard might visualize running a break and note the changing positions of the offensive and defensive players.

Another important potential factor to consider in the effectiveness of imagery is the performer's skill level. Experimental evidence shows that imagery significantly helps performance for both novice and experienced performers, although there are somewhat stronger effects for experienced players (Feltz & Landers, 1983). Imagery may help novice performers learn cognitive elements relevant to successful performance of the skill. A physical education teacher, for example, might have the students picture themselves serving a volleyball after she demonstrates the skill. For experienced performers, imagery appears to help refine skills and prepare for making decisions and perceptual adjustments rapidly. For example, Olympic gold medalist Greg Louganis used imagery to help prepare himself to make minute changes in his dive based on his body positioning during different phases. He pictured himself making a perfect dive and feeling different points of the dive.

The nature of the task and the skill level of the performer affect how imagery will enhance performance. Novice and highly skilled performers who use imagery on cognitive tasks show the most positive effects.

How Imagery Works

How can just thinking about jumping over the high bar, hitting a perfect tennis serve, healing an injured arm, or sinking a golf putt actually help athletes accomplish these things? In essence, we can generate information from our own memory that is essentially the same as an actual experience, and, consequently, imagining events can have a similar effect on our nervous system as would the real, actual experience. "Imagined stimuli and perceptual or 'real' stimuli have a qualitatively similar status in our conscious mental life" (Marks, 1977, p. 285). Just think about your dreams. Perhaps you dreamed a big slobbering dog chased you and you woke up in a cold sweat, only to find that the dog was only in your imagination. Sport psychologists have proposed three theoretical explanations of this phenomenon.

Psychoneuromuscular Theory (Programming Muscles for Action)

The psychoneuromuscular theory originated with Carpenter (1894), who proposed the *ideo-motor principle* of imagery. According to his principle, imagery facilitates the learning of motor skills because of the nature of the neuromuscular activity patterns activated during the imaginal process. That is, vivid imagined events innervate the muscles somewhat like physically practicing the movement. These slight neuromuscular impulses are identical (but reduced in magnitude) to those produced during actual performance (although these impulses may be so minor that they do not actually produce movement). Thus, although the magnitude of the muscle activity is reduced during imagery, the activity is a mirror image of the actual performance pattern.

The first scientific support of this phenomenon came from the work of Edmund Jacobson (1931), who reported that the imagined movement of bending the arm created small muscular contractions in the flexor muscles of the arm. In research with downhill skiers, Suinn (1972, 1976) monitored the electrical activity in the skiers' leg muscles as they imagined skiing the course and found that the muscular activity changed during their imaginings. Muscle activity was highest when the skiers were imagining themselves skiing rough sections in the course, which would actually require greater muscle activity (also see studies by Hale, 1982, and Harris & Robinson, 1986).

When you vividly imagine yourself performing a movement, you use similar neural pathways to those you use in actual performance of the movement. Let's take the example of trying to perfect your golf swing. Your goal is to make your swing as fluid and natural as possible to achieve a consistent and accurate drive off the tee. To accomplish this, you take a bucket of balls to the driving range and practice your swing continually, trying to automate it (i.e., groove your swing). In effect, you are strengthening the neural pathways that

You can program muscles for a golf swing by practice on a driving range and by *imagining* yourself executing a perfect swing.

control the muscles related to your golf swing. You also can strengthen these neural pathways by *imagining* that you are executing a perfect swing. Through the imagery, your body believes that you are actually practicing the serve, so in effect you are programming your muscles and preparing your body to perform.

Symbolic Learning Theory (Understanding Movement Patterns)

Sackett (1934) argued that imagery can help athletes *understand* their movements. His symbolic learning theory suggests that imagery may function as a coding system to help people understand and acquire movement patterns. That is, one way individuals learn skills is by becoming familiar with what needs to be done to successfully perform them. By creating a motor program in the central nervous system, a mental blueprint is formed for successfully completing the movement. For example, in a doubles match in tennis, if a player knows how her partner will move on a certain shot, she will be able to better plan her own course. Similarly, a volleyball player needs to be familiar with the defensive team's position to decide where best to place his shots.

In a thorough review of over 60 studies in the literature, Feltz and Landers (1983) found that subjects using imagery, or some other form of mental practice, performed consistently better on tasks that were primarily *cognitive* (mental) in nature than on those that were more purely motoric. For example, lifting weights or kicking a soccer ball are predominantly motoric, whereas playing chess or a quarterback deciding which receiver to throw the ball to are mostly cognitive. This research supports the symbolic learning theory. Of course, most sport skills have both motor and cognitive components, so imagery can be effective in helping a variety of skills.

Psychological Skills Hypothesis

Sport psychologists have recently argued that imagery also works through the development and refinement of psychological skills. For example, imagery can improve concentration, reduce anxiety, and enhance confidence—all important psychological skills for maximizing performance. And imagery is a convenient, effective tool to practice and learn a variety of psychological skills. For instance, several intervention techniques, such as stress inoculation training and stress-management training, that have as their primary focus reducing and coping with anxiety, employ imagery as a key component in the process. People visualize themselves successfully coping with stress in tough situations. A golfer, for example, might visualize herself standing over a 10-foot putt that would win a tournament. In the past, she has tightened up and missed. Now, in her mind, she sees herself taking a deep breath and relaxing her muscles as she goes through her preshot routine. With a relaxed body and mind, she visualizes sinking the putt and winning the tournament.

In summary, all three explanations—psychoneuromuscular, symbolic learning, and psychological skills—assert that imagery can help program an athlete both physically and mentally, and all three have support from research, although the psychoneuromuscular theory has been questioned as of late. Thus, imagery might be regarded as a strong mental blueprint of how to perform a skill, which should result in quick and accurate decision making, increased confidence, and improved concentration. In addition, the increased neuromuscular activity in the muscles help make the skill's movements more fluid, smooth, and automatic.

Different theories maintain that imagery works by producing muscle activity, providing a mental blueprint, or improving other psychological skills. All three theories have received some support in the literature—thus, imagery likely works in a variety of ways.

Uses of Imagery

Athletes can employ imagery in many ways to improve both physical and psychological skills:

1. Improve concentration. By visualizing what you want to do and how you want to react in certain situations, you can prevent your mind from wandering. You can imagine yourself in situations where you generally lose your concentration (e.g., after missing an easy shot in basketball, forgetting a step in an aerobic dance class, or dropping a pass in football) and then imagine yourself remaining composed and focused on the next play or step.

2. Build confidence. For example, if you have had trouble with serving in recent matches, you might imagine hitting hard, accurate volleyball serves to build up your self-confidence. An official who has her confidence shaken when the crowd starts booing her calls against the home team could visualize herself taking control and maintaining confidence and impartiality on subsequent calls. Seeing yourself perform well in your mind makes you feel you can perform under adverse circumstances.

3. Control emotional responses. You can visualize situations that have caused problems in the past, such as choking under pressure or getting angry because of your own errors or officials' calls. You can then picture yourself dealing with these events in a positive way, such as taking a deep breath and focusing on your breathing as you concentrate on the task at hand.

4. Practice sport skills. Probably the best-known use of imagery is practicing a particular sport skill. Some examples include putting a golf ball, executing

a takedown in wrestling, throwing the javelin, doing a routine on the balance beam, or swimming the backstroke—all performed in the mind. You can practice skills to fine tune them or pinpoint weaknesses and visualize correcting them. A physical education teacher might have his students imagine the proper execution of a backward roll as they wait in line for their turn (imagery can be particularly useful during waiting periods). An aerobics instructor might have her students imagine a sequence of movements as they listen to the music before physically attempting the steps (Figure 15.1).

Figure 15.1 Imaging is a way to practice movement skills.

5. Practice strategy. Imagery can be used to practice either team or individual strategies. A quarterback, for example, might visualize different defenses and what plays he would call to counteract them. A hockey goalie might imagine what he would do on a breakaway as three players converge on the goal. A softball pitcher might visualize how to pitch to different batters on the opposing team, based on their strengths and weaknesses. Hank Aaron, the all-time leading home run hitter, visualized the different types of pitches a particular pitcher might throw him to prepare himself mentally to bat.

6. Cope with pain and injury. Imagery is useful for coping with pain and injury. It can help speed up recovery of the injured area and keep skills from deteriorating. It is hard for athletes to go through an extended layoff. But instead of feeling sorry for themselves, they can imagine doing practice drills and thereby facilitate recovery. (We'll further discuss using imagery during injury rehabilitation later in this chapter.)

Imagery can enhance a variety of skills to improve performance and can facilitate the learning of new techniques and strategies.

Types of Imagery

Athletes usually use imagery from an internal or external perspective (Mahoney & Avener, 1977). Which perspective is used depends on the athlete and the situation. Gymnasts who qualified for the 1976 U.S. Olympic team, for example, reported using internal imagery more frequently than external imagery. We'll look briefly at each perspective.

Internal Imagery

Internal imagery refers to imagining the execution of a skill from your own vantage point. As if you had a camera on your head, you see only what you would see if you actually executed the particular skill. As a softball pitcher, for instance, you would see the batter at the plate, the umpire, the ball in your glove, and the catcher's target, but not the shortstop, second baseman, or anything else out of your normal range of vision. Because internal imagery is done from a first person perspective, the images would emphasize the feel of the movement. As a softball pitcher, you would feel your fingers gripping the ball, the stretch of your arm during the backswing, the shift of weight, and finally the extension of your arm upon release.

External Imagery

In *external imagery*, you view yourself from the perspective of an external observer. It is as if you are watching yourself in the movies or on videotape. For example, if a baseball pitcher imagined pitching from an external perspective, he would see not only the batter, catcher, and umpire, but also all the other fielders. However, there would be little emphasis on the kinesthetic feel of the movement because the pitcher is simply watching himself perform it.

Regarding performance results, few differences have been established between external and internal imagery (e.g., Meyers, Cooke, Cullen, & Liles, 1979). According to one study, "It was virtually impossible to characterize subjects as strictly internal or external imagers because individual's images varied considerably both within and between images. In essence, the notion of stable and extreme imaginal styles was not supported by the data" (Epstein, 1980, p. 218). In fact, most Olympic athletes surveyed by Murphy et al. (1990) indicated that they use both internal and external imagery.

However, although the research is inconclusive, some evidence suggests that internal imagery might indeed yield better results than external imagery. For instance, one study found that internal imagery produced more electrical activity in the biceps muscle than external imagery when subjects imagined flexing their arm (Hale, 1982). Internal imagery makes it easier to bring in the kinesthetic sense, feel the movement, and approximate actual performance skills. For example, using an internal perspective, a golfer might become more aware of how her body feels and looks during her swing.

Many people switch back and forth between internal and external imagery. The important thing appears to be getting a good, clear, controllable image, regardless of whether it is from an internal or external perspective.

Whether a person uses an internal or external image appears to be less important than choosing a comfortable style that produces clear, controllable images.

Basics of Imagery Training

The first step in setting up an imagery training program is to evaluate the athlete's or student's current imagery skill level. Like all psychological techniques, imagery is a skill acquired through practice. Some athletes are pretty good at it, whereas others may not even be able to get an image in their minds.

Vividness

Good imagers use all of their senses to make their images as vivid and detailed as possible. It is important to recreate or create as closely as possible the actual experience in your mind. The closer images are to the real thing, the better the transfer to actual performance. Pay particular attention to environmental detail, such as the layout of the facilities, type of surface, and closeness of spectators. Experience the emotions and thoughts of the actual competition. Try to feel the anxiety, concentration, frustration, exhilaration, or anger associated with your performance. All of this will make the imagined performance more real.

If you have trouble getting clear, vivid images, first try to imagine things that are familiar to you, such as the furniture in your room. Then use the arena or playing field where you normally play and practice. Here, you will be familiar with the playing surface, grandstands, background, colors, and other environmental details. You can practice getting vivid images with the three vividness exercises that follow. (We also recommend trying the exercises in *Put Your Mother on the Ceiling* by Richard DeMille, 1973.)

Controllability

Another key to successful imagery is learning to manipulate your images so they do what you want them to. Many athletes have difficulty controlling their images and often repeat their mistakes. A baseball batter might visualize his strike outs; a tennis player, her double faults; a hockey goalie, a puck going

Vividness Exercises

1. **Imagining home.** Imagine that you are home in your living room. Look around and take in all the details. What do you see? Notice the shape and texture of the furniture. What sounds do you hear? What is the temperature like? Is there any movement in the air? What do you smell? Use all your senses and take it all in.

2. **Imagining a positive performance of a skill.** Select a particular skill in your sport and visualize yourself performing it perfectly. Perform the skill over and over in your mind and imagine every feeling and movement in your muscles. For example, in serving a tennis ball, start by seeing yourself in the ready position, looking at your opponent and the service court, and then pick the spot where you want the serve to go. See and feel how you start the service motion and release the ball at the perfect height, the toss going just where you want. Feel your back arch and your shoulder stretch as you take the racquet back behind your head. Feel your weight start to transfer forward and your arm and racquet reach high to contact the ball at just the right height and angle. Feel your wrist snap as you explode into the ball. Now see and feel the follow-through with your weight coming completely forward. The ball goes exactly where you wanted it to, forcing a high floating return from your opponent. You close in on the net and put the ball away with a firm crosscourt volley.

3. **Imagining a positive performance.** Recall as vividly as possible a time when you performed very well. If you can recall a finest hour in recent memory, use that. Your visualization will cover three specific areas of recall—visual, auditory, and kinesthetic.

   First, visually recall a picture of how you looked when you were performing well. Notice that you look different when you're playing well compared to when you're playing poorly. You walk differently; you carry your head and shoulders differently. When an athlete is confident on the inside, it shows on the outside. Try to get as clear a picture as possible of what you look like when you are playing well. Review films of successful performances to help crystallize the image.

   Now reproduce in your mind the sounds you hear when you are playing well, particularly the internal dialogue you have with yourself. There is often an internal silence that accompanies your best performances. Listen to it. What is your internal dialogue like? What are you saying to yourself, and how are you saying it? What is your internal response when faced with adversity during play? Recreate all the sounds as vividly as you can.

   Finally, recreate in your mind all the kinesthetic sensations you have when playing well. How do your feet and hands feel? Do you have a feeling of quickness, speed, or intensity? Do your muscles feel tight or relaxed? Stay focused on the sensations associated with playing well.

past him for a goal; or a gymnast, falling off the uneven parallel bars. Controlling your image helps you to picture what you want to accomplish instead of seeing yourself make errors. You can practice by doing the controllability exercises we've provided.

Developing an Imagery Training Program

Now that you know the fundamentals and principles underlying the effectiveness of imagery and how to improve vividness and controllability, the final step is to set up an imagery training program. To be effective, imagery should become part of the daily routine. It is important to tailor imagery programs to the needs, abilities, and interest of each athlete.

Tailor imagery programs to the athlete's individual needs, abilities, and interests.

Imagery Evaluation

Because imagery is a skill, athletes differ in how well they can do it. To evaluate an athlete's imagery skill level we recommend using the Sport Imagery Questionnaire (Martens, 1982) to measure how well athletes can use all their senses while imaging. After compiling feedback from the questionnaire, athletes and coaches can determine which areas to incorporate into the athlete's daily training regimen. If you want to see how good your own imagery skills are, just follow the instructions in Table 15.1. There are no right or wrong answers; the evaluation should take 10 to 15 minutes.

Controllability Exercises

1. **Controlling performance.** Imagine working on a specific skill that has given you trouble in the past. Take careful notice of what you were doing wrong. Now imagine yourself performing that skill perfectly while seeing and feeling your movements. For example, a basketball player might see and feel herself shooting a free throw perfectly, getting nothing but net.

   Now, think about a competitive situation in which you have had trouble in the past. Taking the basketball example, you might see yourself shooting two free throws at the end of a game with your team down by one point. See yourself remaining calm as you sink both shots.

2. **Controlling performance against a tough opponent.** Picture yourself playing a tough opponent who has given you trouble in the past. Try to execute a planned strategy against this person just as you would for a competition. Imagine situations in which you are getting the best of your opponent. For example, a quarterback might imagine different defenses and see himself calling the correct audible at the line of scrimmage to beat each defense. Then, he would actually see himself carrying out the successful play. Whatever your sport, make sure you control all aspects of your movements as well as the decisions you make.

3. **Controlling emotions.** Picture yourself in a situation where you tense up, become angry, lose concentration, or lose confidence (e.g., missing a field goal, blowing a breakaway layup, missing an empty net in soccer, or missing a jump and falling on the ice). Recreate the situation, especially the feelings that accompany it. For example, feel the anxiety of playing in a championship game. Then use anxiety-management strategies (see chapter 14) to feel the tension drain out of your body and to focus on what you need to do to execute your skills. Try to control what you see, hear, and feel in your imagery.

Table 15.1   Sport Imagery Questionnaire

Read the following descriptions of four general sport situations. For each one, imagine the situation and provide as much detail from your imagination as possible (using all the senses—seeing, hearing, feeling, tasting, and smelling) to make the image as real as you can. Think of a specific example of the situation (e.g., the skill, the people involved, the place, the time). Now close your eyes and take a few deep breaths to become as relaxed as you can. Put aside all thoughts. Keep your eyes closed for about 1 minute as you try to imagine the situation as vividly as you can. Your accurate appraisal of your images will help you determine which exercises you will want to emphasize in the basic training exercises.

After you have completed imagining the situation described, rate the four dimensions of imagery by circling the number that best describes the image you had.

1 = No image present
2 = Not clear or vivid, but a recognizable image
3 = Moderately clear and vivid image
4 = Clear and vivid image
5 = Extremely clear and vivid image

For each situation, pick the number that answers each of these four questions:

a. How vividly did you see yourself doing this activity?   1   2   3   4   5

b. How clearly did you hear the sounds of doing the activity?   1   2   3   4   5

c. How well did you feel yourself making the movements?   1   2   3   4   5

d. How clearly were you aware of your mood?   1   2   3   4   5

Practicing alone

Select a specific skill in your sport such as hitting a backhand, vaulting over the bar, swimming the breaststroke, or kicking a goal. Now imagine yourself performing this skill at the place where you normally practice (gymnasium, pool, field, rink, court) without anyone else present. Close your eyes for about 1 minute and try to see yourself at this place, hear the sounds, feel your body perform the movement, and be aware of your state of mind or mood.

a.   c.
b.   d.

Practicing with others

You are doing the same activity but now you are practicing the skill with your coach and your teammates present. This time, however, you make a mistake that everyone notices.

a.   c.
b.   d.

Watching a teammate

Think of a teammate or acquaintance performing a specific skill unsuccessfully in competition such as dropping a pass, falling off the balance beam, or missing an empty net.

a.   c.
b.   d.

Playing in a contest

Imagine yourself performing in a competition. You are performing very skill-fully and the spectators and teammates are showing their appreciation.

a.		c.	
b.		d.	

Scoring

Now determine your imagery scores and see what they mean. First, add the ratings for your four answers to part *a* in each section, your four answers to part *b* in each section, and so on, recording them below.

Total dimension score

a. Visual	_____	+	_____	+	_____	+	_____	= _____
b. Auditory	_____	+	_____	+	_____	+	_____	= _____
c. Kinesthetic	_____	+	_____	+	_____	+	_____	= _____
d. Mood	_____	+	_____	+	_____	+	_____	= _____

For each dimension, your top possible score is 20 and your lowest possible score is 4. The closer you came to 20 on each dimension, the more skilled you are in that particular area. Lower scores mean you need to work on those aspects of your imagery.

Adapted from Martens (1982, September).

The imagery program need not be complex or cumbersome and should fit well into the athlete's daily training regimen. What follows are tips and guidelines for implementing a successful imagery training program.

Proper Setting.   People highly skilled in the use of imagery can perform the technique almost anywhere. But these people are rare. For the beginner, it's best to practice in a setting with no distractions. Some people like to practice imagery in their rooms before going to sleep, others in the locker room before competition, and others during a break at school or work. As skills develop, people learn to use imagery amid distractions and even in actual competition.

Relaxed Concentration.   Imagery preceded by relaxation is more effective than imagery alone (Weinberg, Seabourne, & Jackson, 1981). So before each imagery session, relax by using deep breathing, progressive relaxation, or some other relaxation procedure that works for you. Relaxation is important for two reasons: (a) it lets you forget everyday worries and concerns and concentrate on the task at hand and (b) it results in more powerful imagery because it won't have to compete with other events.

Realistic Expectations and Sufficient Motivation.   Some athletes are quick to reject such nontraditional training as imagery, believing that the only way to improve is through hard physical practice, drills, and blood and sweat. They are skeptical that thinking about and visualizing a skill can help improve its performance. Such negative thinking and doubt undermine imagery effectiveness. Other athletes believe that imagery can help them become the next Barry Sanders or Steffi Graf, as if imagery is the magic that can transform them into the players of their dreams. The truth is, imagery can improve athletic skills if you work at it systematically. Excellent athletes are usually intrinsically

For imagery to be effective, it should be built into an athlete's daily routine.

motivated to practice their skills for months and even years. Such dedication and motivation is needed to develop psychological skills, also. Yet many athletes do not commit to practice imagery systematically. Remember that efforts in a systematic imagery program are rewarded in the near future.

Vivid and Controllable Images.   Try to use all your senses and to feel the movements as if they were occurring. Many Olympic teams visit the actual competition sites months in advance so they can visualize themselves performing in that exact setting, with its color, layout, construction, and grandstands. Moving and positioning your body as if you were actually performing the skill can make the imagery and feeling of movement more vivid. For example, instead of lying down in bed to image kicking a soccer goal, stand up and kick your leg as if you were actually performing the skill. Also, since imagery can be used during quick breaks in the action, it is important to learn to image with your eyes open as well as closed. Work on controlling images to follow your instructions and produce the desired outcome.

Positive Focus.   In general, focus on positive outcomes such as kicking a field goal, getting a base hit, completing a successful physical therapy session, scoring a goal, or doing a perfect routine. Sometimes using imagery to recognize and analyze errors is beneficial (Mahoney & Avener, 1977) because nobody is perfect and we all make mistakes every time we play. It is also important, however, to be able to leave the mistake behind and focus on the present. Try using imagery to prepare for the eventuality of making a mistake and effectively coping with the error.

For trouble with a particular mistake or error, we suggest the following: First try to imagine the mistake and determine the correct response. Then immediately imagine performing the skill correctly. The image of the correct response (along with the feeling of that response) should then be repeated several times, and this should be followed immediately with actual physical practice. This will help an athlete absorb what it looks and feels like to perform the skill well.

Imagining successful outcomes helps program the body to execute skills. The better athletes can visualize successful performances, the stronger their motor program will become. But errors and mistakes are part of competition, so you should be prepared to deal with them effectively.

Videotapes.   Many athletes can get good, clear images of their teammates or frequent opponents but have trouble imaging themselves. This is because it is difficult to visualize something you have never seen. The challenge is to capture that perfect shot, pass, jump, kick, or routine and lock it in for use with mental practice. A videotape can provide just this feedback—a picture of how you look performing at your best. Seeing yourself on videotape for the first time is quite eye-opening, and the typical comment is, "Is that me?"

A good procedure is to film athletes practicing, carefully edit the tape (usually in consultation with the coach or athlete) to identify the perfect, or near perfect, skills, and then duplicate the sequence repeatedly on the tape. The athlete observes her skills in the same relaxed state prescribed for imagery training. After watching the film for several minutes, she closes her eyes and images the skill.

A program called *Sybervision* (DeVore & DeVore, 1981) shows professional athletes in different sports hitting the basic shots perfectly. Along with repeated footage of these perfect movements, the tape also brings in auditory cues, such as the thwack of the bat as Rod Carew hits the ball. This approach still awaits scientific scrutiny, but it appears to offer promise.

Image Execution and Outcome.   Imagery should include both the execution and end result of the skills. Many athletes image the execution of the skill and not the outcome, or vice versa. Athletes need to be able to feel the movement and control the image so they see the desired outcome. For instance, divers must first be able to feel their body in different positions throughout the dive. Then they see themselves making a perfectly straight entry into the water.

Image in Real Time.   A final principle is to image in real time (Nideffer, 1985). In other words, the time spent imaging a particular skill should be equal to the time the skill actually takes to occur. If a golfer normally takes 20 seconds as part of a preshot routine before putting, then his image of this routine should also take 20 seconds. Because athletes tend to image faster than the actual time it takes to perform the skill, it is a good idea to time the skill. Imaging in real time makes the transfer from imagery to real life easier.

When to Use Imagery

Although imagery can be used virtually any time, there are some specific times when it appears to be most useful:

- Before and after practice
- Before and after competition
- During breaks in the action (in practice and competition)
- During personal time
- When recovering from injury

Examples of When Different Professionals Use Imagery

- Physical education teacher—After finishing a period of vigorous physical activity, ask students to sit down and try to imagine themselves feeling relaxed and calm. Have them practice while they wait in line to participate in an activity.

- Volleyball coach—Before matches, reserve a quiet, dark room for players to visualize themselves performing against a specific opponent.

- Exercise leader—During a cool down period, ask participants to visualize how they want their bodies to look and feel.

- Basketball coach—Before practice, have players imagine their specific assignments for different defenses and offensive sets.

- Tennis coach—During changeovers, instruct players to visualize what type of strategy and shots they want to use in the upcoming game.

- Swimming coach—After every practice, give swimmers 5 minutes to pick a certain stroke and imagine doing it perfectly.

- Gymnastics coach—Just prior to their performing any skill, instruct gymnasts to image themselves completing the skill or routine successfully.

- Football coach—Before each game, have assistant coaches call out different plays to their respective units and ask players to imagine what they would do in each situation.

- Track-and-field coach—Ask athletes to visualize their events the night before competition and see themselves carrying out the movements and strategy to perfection.

Before and After Practice.   One way to schedule imagery systematically is to include it before and after each practice session. Limit these sessions to about 10 minutes (most athletes have trouble concentrating any longer than this on imagery; Murphy et al., 1990). To focus concentration and get ready, before practice athletes should visualize the skills, routines, and plays they expect to perform. After each practice, athletes should review the skills and strategies they worked on. Because they have just finished working out, the feel of the movement should be fresh in their minds, which will help create clearer, more detailed imagery than usual.

Before and After Competition.   Imagery focuses an athlete on the upcoming competition by reviewing in their minds exactly what they want to do, including different strategies for different situations. Imagery before a contest helps fine-tune actions and reactions. The best time to use precompetition imagery depends on the person. Some athletes like to visualize right before the start of a competition, whereas others like to image an hour or two beforehand. Some athletes image at two or three different times before the competition. What's important is that imagery fit comfortably into the pre-event routine. It should not be forced or rushed.

Imagery before a competition can help an athlete concentrate and fine-tune actions for the event.

After competition, athletes can replay the things they did successfully and get a vivid, controllable image. Similarly, students in physical education classes can imagine themselves correcting an error in the execution of a skill they just learned and were practicing. You can also replay unsuccessful events, imagining performing successfully or choosing a different strategy.

Imagery can also be used to strengthen the blueprint and muscle memory of those skills already performed well. Larry Bird was a great shooter, but he still practiced his shooting every day. Similarly, good performance of a skill does not mean you need not image.

During Breaks in the Action.   Most sporting events have some extended breaks in the action during which an athlete can use imagery to prepare for what's ahead. In many sports, there is a certain amount of "dead time" after each shot, and this is an ideal opportunity to use imagery.

During Personal Time.   Athletes can also use imagery at home (or any other appropriate quiet place). It may be difficult to find a quiet spot before practicing, and there may be days when the athlete does not practice at all. In such cases, athletes should try to set aside 10 minutes at home so that they do not break their imagery routine. Some athletes like to image before they go to sleep; others prefer doing it when they wake up in the morning.

> Set a time every day to practice imagery without interruption.

When Recovering From Injury.   Athletes have been trained to use imagery with relaxation exercises to reduce anxiety about an injury. They have used imagery to rehearse emotions they anticipate experiencing upon return to competition. Through imagery, athletes can mentally rehearse physical and performance skills, thereby staying sharp and ready for return.

Positive images of healing or full recovery have been shown to enhance recovery. Ieleva and Orlick (1991) found that positive healing and/or performance imagery was related to faster recovery times. (Similarly, terminally ill cancer patients have used imagery to see themselves destroying and obliterating the bad cancer cells. Reportedly in a number of cases, the cancer has gone into remission; see Simonton, Matthews-Simonton, & Creighton, 1978). Imagery can also help athletes, such as long-distance runners, fight through a pain threshold and focus on the race and technique instead of on their pain.

Summary

Imagery refers to creating or recreating an experience in the mind. It is a form of simulation that involves recalling from memory pieces of information stored there from all types of experiences and shaping them into meaningful images. Imagery appears to work either through minute neural firings in the muscles or symbolic coding patterns in the central nervous system. Anecdotal, case study, and experimental evidence demonstrate that imagery can be a powerful technique to enhance performance. Imagery has many uses including reducing anxiety, building confidence, enhancing concentration, recovering from injury, and practicing specific skills and strategies.

There are basically two types of imagery—internal and external. People need not use one or the other exclusively. Whatever kind of imagery is comfortable to the individual should be practiced systematically, just like physical skills. Both types of imagery involve not only the visual sense but kinesthetic, auditory, tactile, and olfactory senses, as well.

Motivation and realistic expectations are critical to imagery training. Evaluation, using the Sport Imagery Questionnaire, should occur before the training program begins. Basic training in imagery includes exercises in vividness and controllability. Practicing imagery should become routine, a regular part of a training regimen.

Athletes should initially practice imagery in a quiet setting in a relaxed, attentive state. They should focus on developing positive images, although it is also useful to visualize failures occasionally to allow coping skills to develop. Both the execution and outcome of the skill should be imaged, and imaging should occur in real time. Imagery can be used before and after practice and competition, during breaks in the action, and during personal time. Imagery can also benefit the rehabilitation process.

Review Questions

1. What is imagery? Discuss recreating experiences and involving all the senses.

2. What are three uses of imagery? Provide practical examples for each.

3. Compare and contrast the psychoneuromuscular and symbolic learning theories as they pertain to imagery.

4. Describe some anecdotal and some experimental evidence supporting the effectiveness of imagery in improving performance, including the nature of the task and ability level.

5. Compare and contrast internal and external imagery and their comparative effectiveness.

6. Describe two exercises each to improve vividness and controllability of imagery.

7. What is the importance of vividness and controllability in enhancing the quality of imagery?

8. Discuss three of the basic elements of a successful imagery program including why they are important.

References

Carpenter, W.B. (1894). *Principles of mental physiology*. New York: Appleton.

DeMille, R. (1973). *Put your mother on the ceiling: Children's imagination games*. New York: Viking Press.

DeVore, S., & DeVore, G. (1981). *Sybervision: Muscle memory programming for every sport*. Chicago: Chicago Review Press.

Epstein, M.L. (1980). The relationship of mental imagery and mental rehearsal on performance of a motor task. *Journal of Sport Psychology*, **2**, 211-220.

Feltz, D.L., & Landers, D.M. (1983). The effects of mental practice on motor skill learning and performance: A meta-analysis. *Journal of Sport Psychology*, **5**, 25-57.

Hale, B.D. (1982). The effects of internal and external imagery on muscular and ocular concomitants. *Journal of Sport Psychology*, **4**, 379-387.

Harris, D.V., & Robinson, W.J. (1986). The effects of skill level on EMG activity during internal and external imagery. *Journal of Sport Psychology*, **8**, 105-111.

Ievleva, L., & Orlick, T. (1991). Mental links to enhance healing: An exploratory study. *The Sport Psychologist*, **5**, 25-40.

Jacobson, E. (1931). Electrical measurements of neuromuscular states during mental activities. *American Journal of Physiology*, **96**, 115-121.

Lane, J.F. (1980). Improving athletic performance through visuo-motor behavior rehearsal. In R.M. Suinn (Ed.), *Psychology in sports: Methods and applications* (pp. 316-320). Minneapolis: Burgess.

Mahoney, M.J., & Avener, M. (1977). Psychology of the elite athlete: An exploratory study. *Cognitive Therapy and Research*, **1**, 135-141.

Marks, D.F. (1977). Imagery and consciousness: A theoretical review from an individual differences perspective. *Journal of Mental Imagery*, **2**, 275-290.

Martens, R. (1982, September). *Imagery in sport*. Paper presented at the Medical and Scientific Aspects of Elitism in Sport Conference, Brisbane, Australia.

Meyers, A.W., Cooke, C.J., Cullen, J., & Liles, L. (1979). Psychological aspects of athletic competitors: A replication across sports. *Cognitive Therapy and Research*, **3**, 361-366.

Murphy, S., Jowdy, D., & Durtschi, S. (1990). *Imagery perspective survey*. Unpublished manuscript, U.S. Olympic Training Center, Colorado Springs.

Nicklaus, J. (1976). *Play better golf*. New York: King Features.

Nideffer, R.M. (1985). *Athlete's guide to mental training*. Champaign, IL: Human Kinetics.

Richardson, A. (1967a). Mental practice: A review and discussion (Part 1). *Research Quarterly*, **38**, 95-107.

Richardson, A. (1967b). Mental practice. A review and discussion (Part 2). *Research Quarterly*, **38**, 263-273.

Sackett, R.S. (1934). The influences of symbolic rehearsal upon the retention of a maze habit. *Journal of General Psychology*, **13**, 113-128.

Schmidt, R.A. (1982). *Motor control and learning: A behavioral emphasis*. Champaign, IL: Human Kinetics.

Simonton, O.C., Matthews-Simonton, S., & Creighton, J.L. (1978). *Getting well again*. New York: Bantam.

Suinn, R.M. (1972). Behavioral rehearsal training for ski racers. *Behavior Therapy*, **3**, 519.

Suinn, R.M. (1976, July). Body thinking: Psychology for Olympic champs. *Psychology Today*, pp. 38-43.

Titley, R.W. (1976, September). The loneliness of a long-distance kicker. *The Athletic Journal*, **57**, 74-80.

Weinberg, R.S. (1981). The relationship between mental preparation strategies and motor performance: A review and critique. *Quest*, 195-213.

Weinberg, R.S., Seabourne, T.G., & Jackson, A. (1981). Effects of visuo-motor behavior rehearsal, relaxation, and imagery on karate performance. *Journal of Sport Psychology*, **3**, 228-238.

CHAPTER 16

Self-Confidence

The key thing is that you always try and be positive. As an official, you are always wrong 50% of the time according to the players or coaches. Everyone is going to miss some calls but you can't let that get you down. I always try to make my calls in a confident, self-assured manner and convey to the players that I am in control. I always try to do my homework and prepare for the game, as that builds my own sense of confidence. If I feel confident in myself and my abilities, then everything else seems to fall into place.

High school basketball official

The whole thing is never to get negative about yourself. Sure, it's possible that the other guy you're playing is tough, and that he may have beaten you the last time you played, and okay, maybe you haven't been playing all that well yourself. But the minute you start thinking about these things you're dead. I go out to every match convinced that I'm going to win. That's all there is to it.

Jimmy Connors

Former tennis great Jimmy Connors and the high school basketball official capture the critical role that confidence plays in mental outlook and ultimate success. In fact, research has indicated that the most consistent factor distinguishing highly successful from less successful athletes is confidence (Gould, Weiss, & Weinberg, 1981). What this means is that top athletes, regardless of the sport, consistently display a strong belief in themselves and their abilities.

In this chapter you will learn about

▐ what confidence is,

▐ the benefits of confidence,

▐ how expectations affect performance,

▐ self-efficacy theory,

▐ confidence and performance,

▐ assessing self-confidence, and

▐ building self-confidence.

Defining Self-Confidence

No doubt you've heard athletes say things like "I felt confident even though I was behind," "I really felt confident in my shot," "I just never felt confident in my game today," and "The entire team felt confident that we would win." Although you hear the word *confidence* all the time, few people can define it precisely. Sport psychologists define confidence as *the belief that you can successfully perform a desired behavior*. In essence, self-confidence is to expect success. The desired behavior might be kicking a soccer goal, staying on an exercise regimen, recovering from a knee injury, serving an ace, hitting a home run, or getting a bulls-eye. You believe you will get the job done. A college basketball player talks about self-confidence:

> The whole thing is to have a positive mental approach. As a shooter, you know that you will probably miss about 50% of your shots. So you can't get down on yourself just because you miss a few in a row. In fact, when I do miss several shots in a row I feel that I am more likely to make the next one since I'm a 50% shooter. If I feel confident in myself and my abilities, then everything else seems to fall into place.

Confident athletes believe in themselves. Most importantly, they believe in their ability to acquire the necessary skills and competencies, both physical

A Case Study—Overcoming a Psychological Barrier

Before 1954 most people claimed there was no way to run a mile in less than 4 minutes. Many runners were timed at 4:03, 4:02, and 4:01, but most runners agreed that to get below 4 minutes was physiologically impossible. Roger Bannister, however, did not. Bannister felt certain that he could break the 4-minute barrier under the right conditions—and he did. Bannister's feat was impressive, but what's really interesting is that in *the next year more than a dozen runners broke the 4-minute mile*. Why? Did everyone suddenly get faster or start training harder? Of course not. What happened was that runners finally believed it could be done. Until Roger Bannister broke the barrier, runners had been placing psychological limits on themselves because they felt it just wasn't possible to break the 4-minute mile.

and mental, to reach their potential. Less confident players doubt whether they are good enough or have what it takes to be successful.

When you doubt your ability to succeed or expect something to go wrong, you are creating what is called a *self-fulfilling prophesy*—which means that expecting something to happen actually helps cause it to happen. Unfortunately, this is common in athletics. Negative self-fulfilling prophesies are psychological barriers that lead to a vicious cycle: The expectation of failure leads to actual failure, which lowers self-image and increases expectations of future failure.

Benefits of Confidence

Confidence is characterized by a high expectancy of success. It can help individuals in the following areas:

- Positive emotions
- Concentration
- Goals
- Effort
- Game strategies
- Momentum

We'll discuss each of these briefly.

- Confidence arouses positive emotions. When you feel confident, you are more likely to remain calm and relaxed under pressure. This state of mind and body allows you to be aggressive and assertive when the outcome of the competition lays in the balance.

- Confidence facilitates concentration. When you feel confident, your mind is free to focus on the task at hand. When you lack confidence, you tend to worry about how well you are doing or how well others think you are doing. A preoccupation with avoiding failure will impair concentration by making you more easily distracted.

- Confidence affects goals. Confident people tend to set challenging goals and pursue them actively. Confidence allows you to reach for the stars and realize your potential. People who are not confident tend to set easy goals and never push themselves to the limits (see goal setting in chapter 17).

- Confidence increases effort. How much effort someone expends and how long she will persist in pursuit of that goal depends largely on confidence (Weinberg, Yukelson, & Jackson, 1980). When ability is equal, the winners of competitions are usually the athletes who believe in themselves and their abilities. This is especially true where persistence is essential, such as running a marathon, playing a 3-hour tennis match, or enduring painful rehabilitation sessions.

- Confidence affects game strategies. People in sport commonly refer to "playing to win" or, conversely, "playing not to lose." These phrases sound similar but they produce very different styles of play. Confident athletes tend to play to win—they are usually not afraid to take chances and they take control of the competition to their advantage. When athletes are not confident, they play not to lose—they are tentative and try to avoid making mistakes. For example, a confident basketball player who comes off the bench will try to make things happen by scoring, stealing a pass, or getting an important rebound to ignite the team. A less confident player will try to avoid making a mistake, like turning over the ball or missing a shot. They are content just not to mess up and are less concerned with making something positive happen.

• Confidence affects psychological momentum. Athletes and coaches refer to momentum shifts as critical determinants of winning and losing. Being able to produce positive momentum or reverse negative momentum is an important asset. Highly skilled athletes are better able to rebound from adversity (i.e., being behind) than their less elite counterparts (Ransom & Weinberg, 1985). And confidence appears to be a critical ingredient in this process. People who are confident in themselves and their abilities have a "never give up" attitude. They view situations in which things are going against them as challenges and react with increased determination. For example, we associate Wayne Gretsky, Magic Johnson, Joe Montana, Steffi Graf, and Jackie Joyner-Kersee with the confidence to reverse momentum when the outlook looks bleak.

Optimal Confidence

Although confidence is a critical determinant of performance, it will not overcome incompetence. Confidence can take an athlete only so far. The relation between confidence and performance can be represented by the form of an inverted-U (see Figure 16.1). Performance improves as the level of confidence increases—up to an optimal point, whereupon further increases in confidence produce corresponding decrements in performance.

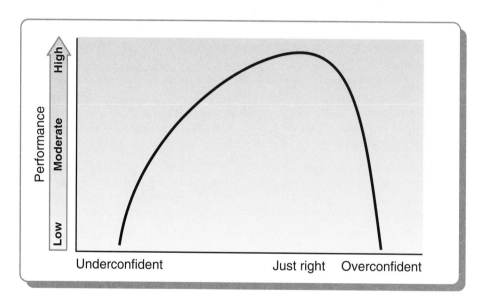

Figure 16.1 The inverted-U illustrating the confidence-performance relation.

Optimal self-confidence means being so convinced that you can achieve your goals that you will strive hard to do so. It does not necessarily mean you will always perform well, but it is essential to reaching your potential. You can expect to make some errors and bad decisions, and you might lose concentration occasionally. But a strong belief in yourself will help you deal with errors and mistakes effectively and keep you striving toward success. Each person has an optimal level of self-confidence, and performance problems can arise with either too little or too much confidence.

Lack of Confidence

Many people have the physical skills to be successful but lack confidence in their ability to perform these skills under pressure—when the game or match is on the line. For example, a volleyball player consistently hits strong and accurate spikes during practice. In the match, however, her first spike is blocked back in her face. She starts to doubt herself and becomes tentative and conservative in subsequent spikes and thus loses her effectiveness.

Self-doubts undermine performance: They create anxiety, break concentration, and cause indecisiveness. Individuals lacking confidence focus on their shortcomings rather than on their strengths, distracting themselves from concentrating on the task at hand. Sometimes athletes in the training room doubt their ability to fully recover from injury. Exercisers often have self-doubts about the way they look or their ability to stay with a regular exercise program. Lack of confidence is often tied to a specific skill, but it can overflow into performance of other skills.

Overconfidence

Overconfident people are actually falsely confident. That is, their confidence is greater than their abilities warrant. Their performance declines because they believe that they don't have to prepare themselves or exert the effort to get the job done. You cannot be overconfident if your confidence is based on skill and ability. As a general rule, overconfidence is much less a problem than underconfidence. When it does occur, however, the results can be just as disastrous.

In the mid-1970s Bobby Riggs lost a famous ''battle of the sexes'' tennis match against Billie Jean King.

It was mainly a case of overconfidence on my part. I overestimated myself. I underestimated Billie Jean's ability to meet the pressure. I let her pick the surface and the ball because I figured it wouldn't make a difference, that she would beat herself. Even when she won the first set, I wasn't worried. In fact, I tried to bet more money on myself. I miscalculated. I ran out of gas. She started playing better and better. I started playing worse. I tried to slow up the game to keep her back but she kept the pressure on. (Tarshis, 1977, p. 48)

A more common situation is when two players or teams of different abilities play each other. The better player or team often approaches the competition overconfident. They slight preparation and play haphazardly, which may well cause them to fall behind early in the competition. The opponent, meanwhile, starts to gain confidence, making it even harder for the overconfident player to come back and win the competition. This scenario happens even to the best athletes, but they will usually not let it happen often.

False overconfidence is seen sometimes when athletes attempt to cover self-doubts. Most coaches encourage athletes to be confident, so players usually aren't comfortable showing self-doubt. Thus, they fake overconfidence to hide actual feelings of self-doubt.

> People strive for an individual, optimal confidence level but sometimes become either overconfident or underconfident.

Expectations Influence Performance

Research has shown that giving people a sugar pill for extreme pain (telling them that it's morphine) can produce as much relief as a pain killer. The powerful effect of expectations on performance is evident in many aspects of daily life, including sport.

It's easy to get down on yourself after several poor performances or to develop self-doubt if you've lost to a particular opponent several times in a row. And these negative self-expectations can affect your future performance and how others perceive your effectiveness. Maintaining confidence under adversity is important not only for athletes but also for officials. Here is what a professional tennis umpire has said on the subject:

> The chair umpire in tennis is a job that requires individuals who have confidence in themselves and are not easily shaken. The players hit the ball so hard and fast and close to the lines that it is virtually impossible to be absolutely certain of all the calls. But . . . you can't start to doubt yourself, because once you do, you start to lose control of the match. In the end the players will respect you and your calls more if you show them that you are confident in your judgment and your abilities.

Self-Expectations and Performance

There have been some interesting studies to demonstrate the relation of expectations and performance. In one study, subjects were each paired with someone they thought clearly stronger in arm strength and then instructed to arm wrestle (Nelson & Furst, 1972). Remarkably, in 10 of the 12 contests, the objectively weaker subject (whom both subjects believed was stronger) won the competition. Clearly, the most important factor was not actual physical strength but who the competitors expected to win.

In another study two groups of subjects were told that they were lifting either more weight or less weight than they really were (Ness & Patton, 1979). (For example, someone who had already lifted 130 pounds was told he was given 130 pounds again, when in fact he was given 150 pounds, or vice versa.) A third group of subjects was told nothing about how much weight they were

> Positive expectations for success have been shown to produce positive effects in many fields of life, including sport.

lifting. Results indicated that subjects lifted the most weight when they thought they were lifting less—that is, when they believed and expected they could lift the weight.

In a study conducted on the 1976 U.S. Men's Olympic gymnastics team (Mahoney & Avener, 1977) researchers interviewed gymnasts to assess their level of confidence. Most were extremely confident and expected success. However, a few gymnasts reported experiencing occasional doubts about their abilities. The gymnasts with self-doubts tended to perform worse during the qualifying meet than those who expressed no self-doubts. Among the 12 finalists, the gymnasts who exhibited the strongest expectations of success in the meet tended to perform best.

In summary, these studies demonstrate the critical role of self-expectations on an athlete's performance.

> Expecting to beat a tough opponent or successfully perform a difficult skill can produce exceptional performance because psychological barriers are overcome.

Coach Expectations and Athlete Performance

The idea that a coach's expectations could affect athlete performance evolved from a classic study, where Rosenthal and Jacobson (1968) informed teachers that a standardized test of academic ability had identified certain children in each of their classes as "late bloomers" who could be expected to show big gains in academic achievement and IQ over the course of the school year. In fact, these children had been selected at random, so there was no reason to expect they would show greater academic progress than their classmates. But at the end of the school year, these "late bloomers" did in fact achieve greater gains in IQ scores than the other children. Rosenthal and Jacobson suggested that the false test information made the teachers expect higher performance from the targeted students, which led them to give these students more attention, reinforcement, and instruction. The students' performance and behavior thus conformed to the teachers' expectations that they were gifted students.

Studies in physical education classrooms (Martinek & Johnson, 1979) and competitive sport environments (Horn, 1984) also indicate that teacher and coach expectations can alter student and athlete performance. The process is a form of self-fulfilling prophesy that does not occur in all situations: Some teachers and coaches let their expectations affect their interaction with students and athletes, but others do not.

A sequence of events seems to occur in athletic settings that explains the expectation-performance relationship (Horn, 1986).

Step 1. Coaches form expectations. Coaches usually form expectations for their athletes and teams. Sometimes their expectations come from an individual's race, physical size, gender, or socioeconomic status. These expectations are called *person cues*. The exclusive use of person cues to form judgments about an athlete's competence could certainly lead to inaccurate expectations. Coaches also use *performance information*, such as past accomplishments, skill tests, practice behaviors, and other coaches' evaluations. When these sources of information lead to an accurate assessment of the athlete's ability and potential, there's no problem. However, inaccurate expectations (either too high or too low), especially when they are inflexible, will typically lead to inappropriate behaviors on the part of the coach. This brings us to the second step in the sequence of events—the self-fulfilling prophesy.

Step 2. Coaches' expectations influence their behavior. Among teachers and coaches who behave differently if they have high or low expectancies of a given student or athlete, behaviors usually fit into one of the following categories:

Frequency and quality of coach-athlete interaction

- Coach spends more time with high-expectancy athletes.

- Coach shows more warmth and positive affect toward high-expectancy athletes.

Quantity and quality of instruction

- Coach lowers his expectations of what skills some athletes will learn, thus establishing a lower standard of performance.
- Coach allows the low-expectancy athletes less time in practice drills.
- Coach is less persistent in teaching difficult skills to low-expectancy athletes.

Type and frequency of feedback

- Coach provides more reinforcement and praise for high-expectancy athlete after a successful performance.
- Coach provides less beneficial feedback to low-expectancy athletes such as praise after a mediocre performance.
- Coach gives high-expectancy athletes more instructional and informational feedback.

Step 3. Coaches' behaviors affect athletes' performances. In this step the coaches' expectancy-biased treatment of athletes affects performance both physically and psychologically. It is easy to understand that athletes who consistently receive more positive and instructional feedback from coaches will show more improvement in their performance and enjoy the competitive experience more. Look at these ways athletes are affected by the negative, biased expectations of their coaches:

- Low-expectancy athletes exhibit poorer performance due to less effective reinforcement and playing time.
- Low-expectancy athletes exhibit lower levels of self-confidence and perceived competence over the course of a season.
- Low-expectancy athletes attribute their failure to lack of ability, thus substantiating the notion that they aren't any good and have little chance to succeed in the future.

Step 4. The athletes' performances confirm the coaches' expectations. Step 3 of course communicates to coaches that they were correct in their initial assessment of the athletes' ability and potential. Few coaches observe that their

Examples of Coach Expectations Affecting Athlete Behavior

Example 1

During the course of a volleyball game, Kira (a high-expectancy player) attempts to spike the ball despite the fact that the set-up was poor, pulling her away from the net. The spike goes into the net, but the coach says, "Good try, Kira, just try to get more elevation on your jump so you can contact the ball above the level of the net." When Janet (a low-expectancy player) does the same thing, the coach says, "Don't try to spike the ball when you're not in position, Janet. You'll never make a point like that."

Example 2

During a basketball practice, Bill (a high-expectancy player) is having trouble running a new offensive pattern. The coach stops the practice and spends a couple of minutes explaining why and how certain formations are being used so that Bill can better understand what is expected of him. A little while later, Jim (a low-expectancy player) experiences the same difficulty. The coach pulls Jim from the scrimmage, saying, "No problem. We'll work on it more later." Of course this happens to Jim again and again, and "later" never comes.

behavior and attitudes help produce this result. And not *all* athletes will allow a coach's behavior or expectations to affect their performance or psychological reactions. Some athletes look to other sources, such as parents, peers, or other adults, to form perceptions of their competency and abilities. Their support and information can often help athletes resist the biases communicated by a coach.

Clearly, sport and exercise professionals, including trainers and rehabilitation specialists, need to be aware of how they form expectations and how their behavior is affected. Early in the season coaches should determine how they form expectations and whether their sources of information are reliable indicators of an individual's ability. Initial assessments can of course be wrong. Coaches should also monitor the quantity and quality of reinforcement and instructional feedback they give to make sure all participants get their fair share. Such actions help ensure that each participant has a fair chance to reach her potential and enjoy the athletic experience.

> Your expectations of others affects not only your own behavior but the feelings and behavior of others.

Self-Efficacy Theory

Psychologist Albert Bandura (1977, 1986) formulated a clear and useful conceptual model of self-efficacy that brought together the concepts of confidence and expectations. *Self-efficacy*, the perception of one's ability to perform a task successfully, is really a situation-specific form of self-confidence. For our purposes, we'll use the terms interchangeably. Bandura's theory of self-efficacy has been the most extensively used theory for investigating self-confidence in sport and motor performance settings. The theory places self-efficacy as a common cognitive mechanism for mediating motivation and behavior.

Sources of Efficacy

According to Bandura's theory, you might predict or expect self-efficacy to be derived from four principal sources of information: performance accomplishments, vicarious experiences (modeling), verbal persuasion, and emotional arousal. These four categories of efficacy information are not mutually exclusive in terms of the information they provide, although some are more influential than others. The relation between the major sources of efficacy information, efficacy expectations, and performance is diagrammed in Figure 16.2. We'll discuss each source in the sections that follow.

Bandura's Self-Efficacy Theory

- If someone has the requisite skills and sufficient motivation, then the major determinant of his or her performance is self-efficacy. Self-efficacy alone is not enough to be successful—an athlete must also want to succeed and have the ability to succeed.

- Self-efficacy affects an athlete's choice of activities, level of effort, and persistence. Athletes who believe in themselves will tend to persevere, especially under adverse conditions.

- Although self-efficacy is task-specific, it can generalize to other similar skills and situations.

- Self-efficacy is related to goal setting, with those exhibiting high self-efficacy being more likely to set challenging goals.

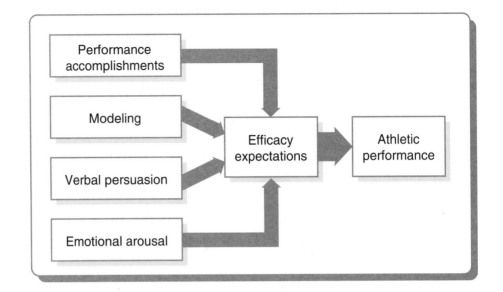

Figure 16.2 Relations among sources of efficacy information, efficacy expectations, and athletic performance. Adapted from Feltz (1984).

Performance Accomplishments.   Performance accomplishments provide the most dependable basis for self-efficacy judgments because they are based on one's mastery experiences. If experiences are generally successful, they will raise the level of self-efficacy. However, repeated failures will result in lower efficacy expectations. For example, if a field goal kicker has kicked the winning field goal in several games as time was running out, he will have a high degree of self-efficacy that he can do it again. Similarly, an athlete rehabilitating from a wrist injury will persist in exercise after seeing steady improvement in the range of motion and wrist strength. Research studies in diving and gymnastics show that performance accomplishments increase self-efficacy and subsequent performance (McAuley, 1985). Coaches can help athletes experience the feeling of successful performance by such tactics as guiding a gymnast through a complicated move, letting young baseball players play on a smaller field, or lowering the basket for young basketball players.

Modeling.   Physical educators and coaches often use demonstration, or *modeling*, to help students learn new skills. Students see how to do the skill technically and gain confidence that they too can do it. For example, seeing a team member complete a difficult move on the uneven parallel bars can reduce anxiety and help convince other gymnasts that they can also accomplish this move. Although vicarious experiences are generally not as potent as actual performance accomplishments in building self-efficacy, they have a demonstrated effectiveness (see studies of self-efficacy in muscular endurance tasks, Gould & Weiss, 1981; in gymnastics, McAuley, 1985; and in competitive persistence, Weinberg, Gould, & Jackson, 1979).

According to Bandura (1965, 1974; also see McCullagh, Weiss, & Ross, 1989), modeling can be best understood through a four-stage process: attention, retention, motor reproduction, and motivation.

In order to learn through watching, careful *attention* must be given to the model. Our ability to attend depends on respect for the person observed, interest in the activity, and how well we can see and hear. The best teachers and coaches do not overload you with information, expect you to focus your attention on all the specific elements of the skill, or show the skill only one quick time. Rather, they focus on a few key points, demonstrate several times, and let you know exactly what to look for.

For effective modeling to occur, the observed act must be committed to memory. This *retention* can be accomplished through mental practice tech-

Instructors must consider how they will get, focus, and keep observers' attention when modeling skills.

niques, analogies (e.g., tell the athlete to liken the tennis serve motion to throwing a racquet), or by having individuals verbally repeat the key points aloud (e.g., "put your right foot in, take your right foot out" in the elementary physical education hokey-pokey dance). The key is to help the observer remember the modeled act.

Even if people attend to the physical skills demonstrated and remember how to do them, they still may not be able to perform if they have not learned *motor reproduction*, that is, how to coordinate their muscle actions with their thoughts. For example, you could know exactly what a good approach and delivery in bowling looks like and even be able to mimic the optimal physical action, but without physical practice to learn the timing, you will not roll strikes. When modeling sport and exercise skills, you must make sure you have taught lead-up skills, provided optimal practice time, and considered the progression of how to best order related skills.

The final stage in the modeling process is *motivation*, and it affects all the other stages. Without being motivated, an observer will not attend to the model, make efforts to remember what was seen, and practice the act. The key, then, is to motivate the observer through praise, through the promise of earning rewards, by imparting the importance of learning the modeled act, or by utilizing models who will motivate them.

Tips for Giving Effective Demonstrations

Try to determine whether each tip fits the category of attention, retention, motor reproduction, or motivation.

- Inform learners of the importance of the skill for the game or activity.

- Point out a high-status model (e.g., professional athlete) who effectively uses the skill to be modeled.

- Make sure participants do not face any distractions and that they can all see and hear.

- Make eye contact with the learner as you convey instructions about the modeled act.

- Demonstrate complex skills from several angles (e.g., tennis serve for both left- and right-handed individuals).

- Focus learner attention on only three or four key points of the skill.

- Repeat demonstrations of complex skills.

- Make sure instructions always slightly precede the skill or segment of the skill being demonstrated.

- Have the learners mentally rehearse what was shown immediately after observing the demonstration.

- Practice the skill immediately after it has been demonstrated and mentally rehearsed.

- Have observers name the subunits or parts of the skill.

- Always follow slow-motion demonstrations with at least one demonstration performed at full speed.

- Reinforce correct performance of the modeled act.

- With children, focus on fewer key points and emphasize mental practice.

Verbal Persuasion.   Coaches, teachers, and peers often use persuasive techniques to influence behavior. An example would be a baseball coach telling a player, "I know you're a good hitter, so just hang in there and take your swings. The base hits will eventually come." These leaders are important to athletes and students and can be helpful in encouraging self-efficacy. When a psychological barrier is present, coaches and instructors sometimes even resort to deception to persuade performers that they can perform certain skills. Using deception is tricky, however, and can undermine credibility and trust.

Emotional Arousal.   Bandura (1977) suggests that perceptions of arousal affect behavior by altering efficacy expectations. For instance, some athletes may interpret increases in their physiological arousal or anxiety (such as heart beating fast or shallow breathing) as a fear that they cannot perform the skill successfully. If this perception of anxiety can be reduced through relaxation techniques (see chapter 14), then it is hypothesized that self-efficacy will be increased. Feltz (1984) suggests that if an athlete's interpretation of arousal changes from negative to positive, self-efficacy should be enhanced, but evidence so far is not conclusive.

Self-efficacy theory has provided a model to study the effects of self-confidence on sport performance, persistence, and behavior.

Assessing Self-Confidence

Now that you understand the relation of confidence and performance and that effectiveness can be hampered by overconfidence or underconfidence, the next step is to identify confidence levels in a variety of situations. Athletes might do this by answering the following questions:

- When am I overconfident?
- How do I recover from mistakes?
- When do I have self-doubt?
- Is my confidence consistent throughout the event?
- Am I tentative and indecisive in certain situations?
- Do I look forward to and enjoy tough, highly competitive games?
- How do I react to adversity?

Table 16.1 presents a more formal and detailed self-confidence inventory to assess confidence levels.

To score your overall confidence, add up the percentages in each of the three columns and then divide by 10. The higher your score on the "Confident" column, the more likely you are to be at your optimal level of confidence during competition. High scores in the "Underconfident" or "Overconfident" columns present some potential problem areas. To determine specific strengths and weaknesses, look at each item. The scale assesses confidence both in physical and mental terms. You can use this questionnaire to inform you of areas you need to work on.

Building Self-Confidence

Many people believe you either have confidence or you don't. Confidence can be built, however, through work, practice, and planning. Jimmy Connors is a good example. Throughout his junior playing days, his mother taught him to always hit out and go for winners. Because of this playing style he lost some matches he should have won. Yet Connors said he never could have made it without his mother and grandmother. "They were so sensational in their sup-

Table 16.1   Sport Confidence Inventory

Read each question carefully and think about your confidence with regard to each item as you competed over the last year or season. For each item indicate the percent of time you feel you have had too little, too much, or just the right degree of confidence. Below is an example to give you some confidence in filling out the inventory correctly.

You are a pole vaulter:	Underconfident (%)	Confident (%)	Overconfident (%)
How confident are you each time you attempt to clear 17 feet?	20	70	10

The three answers should always add up to 100%. You may distribute this 100% any way you think is appropriate. You may assign all 100% to one category, split it between two categories, or, as in the example, divide it among all three categories.

How confident are you with respect to . . .	Underconfident (%)	Confident (%)	Overconfident (%)
1. Your ability to execute the skills of your sport or exercise?	_____	_____	_____
2. Your ability to make critical decisions during the contest?	_____	_____	_____
3. Your ability to concentrate?	_____	_____	_____
4. Your ability to perform under pressure?	_____	_____	_____
5. Your ability to execute successful strategy?	_____	_____	_____
6. Your ability to put forth the effort needed to succeed?	_____	_____	_____
7. Your ability to control your emotions during competition?	_____	_____	_____
8. Your physical conditioning or training?	_____	_____	_____
9. Your ability to relate successfully with your coach(es)?	_____	_____	_____
10. Your ability to come back when behind?	_____	_____	_____

Adapted from ACEP (1989).

port, they never allowed me to lose confidence. They just kept telling me to play the same way, and they kept assuring me that it would eventually come together. And I believed them (Tarshis, 1977, p. 102).

Confidence can be improved through the following:

- Performance accomplishments
- Acting confidently
- Thinking confidently
- Imagery
- Physical conditioning
- Preparation

Performance Accomplishments

We have already discussed the influence of performance accomplishments on self-efficacy. The same points apply to confidence, but we'll elaborate on some of those points here. The concept is simple: Successful behavior increases confidence and leads to further successful behavior. The successful accomplishment might be beating a particular opponent, coming from behind to win, fully extending your knee during rehabilitation, or exercising continuously for 30 minutes.

Of course, when a team loses 8 games in a row, it will be hard-pressed to feel confident about winning the next game, especially against a good team. Confidence is crucial to success, but how can you be confident without previous success? It appears to be a "catch-22" dilemma: "We're losing now because we're not feeling confident, but I think the reason the players don't feel confident is that they have been losing."

You are certainly more likely to feel confident about performing a certain skill if you can consistently execute it during practice. That's why good practices and preparing physically, technically, and tactically to play your best enhances confidence. For the most part, performance accomplishments build confidence, and confidence then improves subsequent performance. Nothing elicits confidence like experiencing in practice what you want to accomplish in the competition.

Similarly, an athlete rehabilitating a shoulder separation needs to experience some success in improving range of motion to keep up her confidence that she will eventually regain full range of motion. Short-term goals can help her feel she has made progress and thus enhance her confidence (also see chapter 17).

A coach should structure practices to simulate actual performance conditions. For example, if foul shooting under pressure has been a problem in the past, each player could shoot an extra 100 free throws during practice. However, that would not simulate actual game action. It would be better for each player to sprint up and down the floor several times before shooting any free throw (since this is what happens during a game). Furthermore, to create pressure, a coach might require each player to make five free throws in a row or to continue this drill until they do. This can create a little pressure and fatigue (just like in the game). As the players start to consistently make their free throws under these conditions, it will build confidence that they can do the same thing in a game.

> Performance accomplishments represent the most powerful way to build confidence. Manipulate or create situations that allow participants to experience success and a sense of accomplishment.

Acting Confidently

Thoughts, feelings, and behaviors are interrelated: The more an athlete acts confidently, the more likely she is to feel confident. This is especially important when you begin to lose confidence and your opponent, sensing this, begins to gain confidence. Acting confidently is also important for sport and exercise professionals. An aerobics instructor should project confidence when leading her class if she wants to have a high-spirited workout. An athletic trainer should act confidently when treating athletes so they feel trust and confidence during the rehabilitation process.

Athletes should try to display a confident image during competition. They can demonstrate their confidence by keeping their head up high—even after a critical error. Many people give themselves away through body language and movements that indicate they are lacking confidence.

Acting confidently can also lift spirits during difficult times. If someone walks around with slumped shoulders, head down, and a pained facial expression, he communicates to all observers that he is down, which works to pull him even further down. It is best to keep your head up, shoulders back, and facial muscles loose to indicate that you are confident and will persevere. This will keep opponents guessing.

Thinking Confidently

Confidence consists of thinking you can and will achieve your goals. As a collegiate golfer noted, "If I think I can win, I'm awfully tough to beat." A positive attitude is essential to reaching potential. Athletic performers need to discard negative thoughts ("I'm so stupid," "I can't believe I'm playing so bad," "I just can't beat this person," or "I'll never make it") and replace them with positive thoughts ("I'll keep getting better if I just work at it," "Just keep calm and focused," "I can beat this guy," or "Just hang in there and things will get better").

Thoughts should be instructional and motivational rather than judgmental. Correcting technique, encouragement, and cues to perform the skill more successfully should be the focus of self-talk (see chapter 18). This is sometimes difficult to do, but the result will be a more enjoyable and successful athletic experience.

Fast Is What You Think It Is

Kenya's Gregg Parini won the 1980 NCAA Division III 50-yard freestyle in 21.49 seconds but worried the next winter about successfully defending his title. Gregg's coach thought a major barrier preventing Gregg from going faster was his conception of what is fast. So he told Gregg that a major difference between swimmers going 20 plus seconds and those going 19 plus was positive thinking. After all, what's the difference between a 20 plus and 19 plus? One second in a race that covers half the distance of a football field. That's almost nothing.

The coach suggested to Gregg that he was limiting himself by what he thought was fast for a Division III swimmer. Twenty-one plus was fast enough to win Division III, so that's what Gregg swam. Then, the coach asked him what he'd be shooting for if he were swimming in Division I. "Twenty-plus" was Gregg's reply. Gregg won the 1981 Division III Nationals in 20.83. (Bell, 1982, pp. 44-45)

Imagery

As you recall if you've read chapter 15, one use of imagery is to help build confidence. In imagery you can see yourself doing things that you either have never been able to do or have had difficulty doing. For example, a golfer who consistently has been slicing the ball off the tee can imagine himself hitting the ball straight down the fairway. A long-distance runner can see herself beating an arch rival after losing to her the last five races. A football quarterback can visualize different defensive alignments and then try to counteract these with specific plays and formations. Similarly, trainers can help injured athletes build confidence by having them imagine getting back on the playing field and performing well.

Physical Conditioning

Being in your best possible physical shape is another key to feeling confident. In most sports athletes now train year round to improve strength, endurance, and flexibility. Training and following good nutrition habits helps you know that you can stay out there as long as necessary to get the job done.

Preparation

Jack Nicklaus has said in interviews, "As long as I'm prepared, I always expect to win." The flip side of this is that you can't expect to win if you're unprepared. Being prepared gives you confidence that you have done everything possible to ensure success. A plan gives you confidence because you know what you're going to try to do. Many athletes enter a competition without a strategy. But there should always be a plan of attack, which requires that you have at least a general idea of what you want to accomplish and how you will do it.

Research with Olympic athletes indicates that the most successful have the most detailed plans and strategies of what they want to do. They also have alternative strategies (Gould, Eklund, & Jackson, 1992; Orlick, 1986). For example, a miler should go into every race with both a plan on how to run the race and an adjustment strategy if the pace of the race dictates such a move. A good plan considers not only your own abilities but your opponent's.

Good preparation also includes a set precompetition routine. Knowing exactly what will happen and when it will happen gives you confidence and puts your mind at rest. Being sure when you will eat, practice, stretch out, and arrive at the competition helps build confidence that extends to the competition itself. (See chapter 18 for more on precompetition routines.)

Summary

Confidence is crucial in determining performance and can be built systematically. A strong belief in your mental and physical abilities is essential to reaching your potential. Research has demonstrated how expectations can both harm and enhance performance. Bandura's theory of self-efficacy provides a sound theoretical foundation to study the relation between confidence and performance. Self-efficacy becomes an important predictor of performance only when one has the requisite skills and sufficient motivation to accomplish the task.

Confidence is all-consuming, involving the way we think, feel, and act. Because these factors are so closely tied, it is important that we maintain confidence in each of these areas. We should always strive for a strong sense of confidence without becoming either overconfident or underconfident. Confidence levels will almost certainly fluctuate, but we should always believe in ourselves and our capabilities.

Review Questions

1. What is self-confidence? How is it related to expectations?

2. How does confidence (or a lack of it) set up psychological barriers for performance? Provide examples to support your answer.

3. What are two studies that demonstrate the important role that expectations can have on performance?

4. Discuss the implications Rosenthal and Jacobson's study on expectancy effects has for coaches and physical education teachers.

5. Explain and recapitulate the 4-step process for how coaches' expectations might influence their own behavior and that of their athletes. What specific types of feedback or instruction would characterize coaches' behavior toward high-expectancy and low-expectancy athletes?

6. What is self-efficacy? How does it affect behavior?

7. Discuss the four sources of self-efficacy. What evidence supports that these different sources influence efficacy expectations?

8. Discuss Bandura's four-stage modeling process.

9. Discuss three characteristics of confidence and how these would be related to athletic performance.

10. Describe the relationship between self-confidence and athletic performance, including the ideas of overconfidence and underconfidence.

11. Discuss three strategies for building self-efficacy and describe how they affect sport performance.

References

Bandura, A. (1965). Vicarious processes: A special case of no-trial learning. In L. Berkowitz (Ed.), *Advances in experimental social psychology* (Vol. 2). New York: Academic Press.

Bandura, A. (1974) (Ed.). *Psychological modeling: Conflicting theories.* New York: Lieberton.

Bandura, A. (1977). Self-efficacy: Toward a unifying theory of behavioral change. *Psychological Review*, **84**, 191-215.

Bandura, A. (1986). *Social foundations of thought and actions: A social cognitive theory*. Englewood Cliffs, NJ: Prentice Hall.

Bell, K. (1982). *Winning isn't normal*. Austin, TX: Keel.

Feltz, D.L. (1984). Self-efficacy as a cognitive mediator of athletic performance. In W.F. Straub & J.M. Williams (Eds.), *Cognitive sport psychology* (pp. 191-198). Lansing, NY: Sport Science Associates.

Gould, D., Eklund, R.C., & Jackson, S.A. (1992). 1988 U.S. Olympic wrestling excellence: I. Mental preparation, precompetitive cognition, and affect. *The Sport Psychologist*, **6**, 358-382.

Gould, D., & Weiss, M. (1981). The effects of model similarity and model talk on self-efficacy and muscular endurance. *Journal of Sport Psychology*, **3**, 17-29.

Gould, D., Weiss, M., & Weinberg, R. (1981). Psychological characteristics of successful and nonsuccessful Big Ten wrestlers. *Journal of Sport Psychology*, **3**, 69-81.

Horn, T.S. (1984). Expectancy effects in the interscholastic athletic setting: Methodological considerations. *Journal of Sport Psychology*, **6**, 60-76.

Horn, T. (1986). The self-fulfilling prophesy theory: When coaches' expectations become reality. In J.M. Williams (Ed.), *Sport psychology: Peak performance to personal growth*. Palo Alto, CA: Mayfield.

Mahoney, M.J., & Avener, M. (1977). Psychology of the elite athlete: An exploratory study. *Cognitive Therapy and Research*, **1**, 135-141.

Martinek, T., & Johnson, S. (1979). Teacher expectations: Effects on dyadic interactions and self-concept in elementary age children. *Research Quarterly*, **50**, 60-70.

McAuley, E. (1985). Modeling and self-efficacy: A test of Bandura's model. *Journal of Sport Psychology*, **7**, 283-295.

McCullagh, P., Weiss, M.R., & Ross, D. (1989). Modeling considerations in motor skill acquisition and performance: An integrated approach. In K. Pandolf (Ed.), *Exercise and Sport Science Reviews* (Vol. 17, pp. 475-513). Baltimore, MD: Williams & Wilkins.

Nelson, L.R., & Furst, M.L. (1972). An objective study of the effects of expectation on competitive performance. *Journal of Psychology*, **81**, 69-72.

Ness, R.G., & Patton, R.W. (1979). The effects of beliefs on maximum weightlifting performance. *Cognitive Therapy and Research*, **3**, 205-211.

Orlick, T. (1986). *Psyching for sport: Mental training for athletes*. Champaign, IL: Human Kinetics.

Ransom, K., & Weinberg, R.S. (1985). Effect of situation criticality on performance of elite male and female tennis players. *Journal of Sport Behavior*, **8**, 144-148.

Rosenthal, R., & Jacobson, L. (1968). *Pygmalion in the classroom: Teacher expectations and pupils' intellectual development*. New York: Holt, Rinehart & Winston.

Tarshis, B. (1977). *Tennis and mind*. New York: Tennis Magazine.

Weinberg, R.S., Gould, D., & Jackson, A. (1979). Expectancies and performance: An empirical test of Bandura's self-efficacy theory. *Journal of Sport Psychology*, **1**, 320-331.

Weinberg, R.S., Yukelson, D., & Jackson, A. (1980). Effect of public versus private efficacy expectations on competitive performance. *Journal of Sport Psychology*, **2**, 340-349.

CHAPTER 17

Goal Setting

I want to lose 10 pounds.

I want to fully recover from my injury by August 15.

My goal is to make the starting line-up.

I want to be able to bench press my own weight.

I intend to improve my golf game and win the club tournament.

My objective is to become a high school varsity basketball coach.

People often set goals like those above in sport and exercise activities. You may be thinking, then, Why devote an entire chapter to goal setting if people already set goals on their own?

The problem is not getting people to identify goals. It is getting them to set the right kind of goals—ones that provide direction and enhance motivation—and helping them learn how to stick to and achieve their goals. As most of us have learned from the New Year's resolutions we've made, it is much easier to set a goal than follow through on it.

Seldom are goals to lose weight or to exercise set realistically in terms of commitment, difficulty, evaluating progress, and specific strategies to achieve them. Most people do not need to be convinced that goals are important; they need instruction on setting effective goals and designing a program to achieve them.

In this chapter you will learn about

▌ defining goals,

▌ the latest goal-setting research,

▌ basic goal-setting principles,

▌ the nuts and bolts of designing a goal-setting program, and

▌ common goal-setting problems and how to overcome them.

Types of Goals

Many people define a goal as an objective, a standard, an aim of some action, or a level of performance or proficiency. Some people talk about very *subjective* aims or objectives such as having fun, doing the best they can, or enjoying themselves. Other focus on more *objective* aims, such as lifting certain amounts of weight, running so many laps, or scoring a set number of points during a basketball game—that is, reaching a particular standard in an event or on a task (McClements, 1982).

Understanding Objective Goals

Sport and exercise psychologists usually distinguish between subjective and objective goals, spending most of their time helping their clients or students set and achieve objective goals. They might define these goals as "attaining a specific standard of proficiency on a task, usually within a specified time" (Locke, Shaw, Saari, & Latham, 1981, p. 145). Attempting to attain a specified level of weight loss within 3 months, a certain team win-loss record by the end of the season, and a lower performance time by the next competition are all examples of objective goals. Our definition of objective goals includes both performance goals and outcome goals (Burton, 1984; Martens, 1990).

A goal is attaining a specific standard of proficiency on a task, usually within a specified time.

Outcome Goals.   Outcome goals typically focus on a competitive result of an event such as winning a race, earning a medal, or scoring more points than an opponent. Thus, achieving these goals depends not only on your own efforts but on the ability and play of your opponent. You could play the best tennis match of your life and still lose—and thus fail to achieve your outcome goal of winning the match.

Performance Goals.   Performance, or process, goals focus on achieving standards or performance objectives that are compared with your own previous performances. For this reason performance goals tend to be more flexible and within your control. For example, if you play tennis, you might set a goal of improving the percentage of top spin first serves that enter the service zone from 70% to 80%. You can make much more precise adjustments to this goal (e.g., increase the goal from 80% to 82%) than you can to an outcome goal, which has only two levels (win or lose). Achieving a performance goal does not depend on your opponent's behavior, only on your own. Also, performance goals are generally associated with less anxiety and superior performance during competition compared to outcome goals. For these reasons, performance goals are commonly emphasized for use with athletes.

Outcome goals focus on achieving a victory in a competitive contest, whereas performance goals focus on achieving standards based on one's own previous performances, not the performances of others.

Goal-Setting Effectiveness

Psychologists (especially business psychologists) have studied goal setting as a motivational technique, focusing on whether setting specific, difficult goals improves performance more than setting no goals or setting the goal of simply doing your best.

Goal-Setting Research

Studies conclude that goal setting works and works well (Locke et al., 1981; Mento, Steel, & Karren, 1987). In fact over 90% of the studies show that goal setting has a consistent and powerful effect on behavior, whether with elementary school children or professional scientists, whether with brainstorming or with loading logs onto trucks. Goal setting is a behavioral technique that works!

Researchers have examined the relation between various types of goals (e.g., specific or general, long term or short term) and physical fitness tasks (e.g., the number of sit-ups performed within 3 minutes, performance times in a swimming event, free-throw shooting in basketball; see Weinberg, 1992, for a detailed review). In one study college students in an 8-week basketball course set either specific or general goals for fundamental basketball skill tasks (e.g., defensive footwork, free-throw shooting, dribbling). Setting specific rather than general goals enhanced performance, though not on all tasks. Specifically, goal setting appeared to enhance performance on low-complexity tasks better than on high-complexity tasks (Burton, 1989a).

Although both general psychology and sport psychology research show considerable early evidence that goal setting is a powerful technique for enhancing performance, it is not a fool-proof method. It must be implemented with thought, understanding of the process, and planning. Systematic goal-setting programs are needed along with monitoring the process to determine when and where goal setting is most effective in a program.

Goal setting is an extremely powerful technique for enhancing performance, but it must be implemented correctly.

Why Goal Setting Works

Researchers have two ways to explain how goals influence behavior: (a) as a direct mechanistic view and (b) as an indirect thought process view. The *direct mechanistic* explanation specifies that goals influence performance in one of four direct ways (Locke & Latham, 1985):

1. Goals direct attention to important elements of the skill being performed.
2. Goals mobilize performer efforts.
3. Goals prolong performer persistence.
4. Goals foster the development of new learning strategies.

First, goals direct performer attention to important elements of the skill, which may not normally be attended to. For example, when soccer players set specific goals to improve their games, they focus on the particular skills that need improving such as corner kicks, movement off the ball, and winning 50-50 balls.

Goals also mobilize effort and persistence by providing incentives. For instance, a swimmer may not want to practice on a given day and finds it difficult to muster her efforts to do so. However, by dividing the distance she needs to swim into 10 equal parts, or goals, she has incentives that seem reasonable.

Similarly, safely losing 50 pounds may seem like an insurmountable goal requiring considerable persistence. However, by setting a subgoal of losing 1 to 2 pounds weekly and charting subgoal accomplishment, you are much more likely to stay motivated and persist with the weight loss program.

Finally, a hidden advantage of goal setting is the development of new learning strategies. A goalie in ice hockey, for instance, may learn new strategies for clearing the puck after a save when he sets his goal of stopping more shots on goal.

The *indirect thought process* explanation proposes that goals influence performance indirectly by affecting a performer's psychological state, including such factors as confidence level, anxiety, and satisfaction (Burton, 1984; Garland, 1985). Burton (1989b) contends that athletes who set outcome goals experience more anxiety and lower self-confidence in competition because their goals are not in their complete control. In contrast, athletes who set performance goals experience less anxiety and enhanced self-confidence because their goals do not depend on their opponents' behavior, only on their own.

In Burton's (1989b) study, intercollegiate swimmers participated in a 5-month goal-setting program emphasizing performance (versus outcome) goals. All the swimmers learned to set performance goals. More importantly, swimmers who were high (as compared to low) in goal-setting ability demonstrated less anxiety, higher confidence, and improved performance. In other words, goals apparently influence performance indirectly through effects on psychological state. Thus, the effects of goal setting on psychological states should be monitored.

Basic Goal-Setting Principles

Several basic goal-setting principles can be identified from research and practice (Gould, 1993; see Figure 17.1 for the most important of these principles). The correct application of these principles provides a strong foundation for designing a goal-setting program.

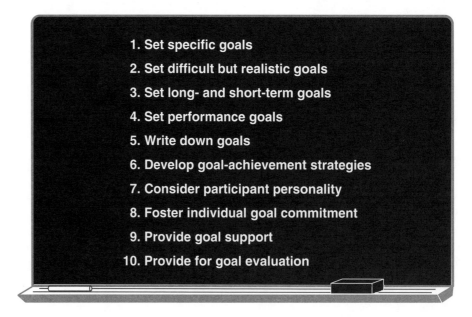

Figure 17.1 Ten basic principles of goal setting.

1. Set specific goals
2. Set difficult but realistic goals
3. Set long- and short-term goals
4. Set performance goals
5. Write down goals
6. Develop goal-achievement strategies
7. Consider participant personality
8. Foster individual goal commitment
9. Provide goal support
10. Provide for goal evaluation

1. Set Specific Goals

Specific goals effect behavior change better than general goals do. However, many teachers, coaches, and exercise leaders still tell their students or clients simply "to do their best." Goals should be stated in very specific, measurable, and behavioral terms. For example, a goal to improve your golf game is too vague. A better goal would be to lower your golf handicap from 14 over par to 11 by improving the accuracy of your short iron approach shots to the green. Similarly, a goal to lower your cholesterol level is broad and imprecise compared to lowering your cholesterol level from 290 to 200 by eliminating an evening snack of high-fat potato chips and beginning an exercise program of walking 4 days a week. To be effective, goals must be stated in specific terms.

Specific goals, as compared to general "do your best" goals, are most effective for producing behavioral change.

2. Set Difficult but Realistic Goals

Effective goals are difficult enough to challenge a participant yet realistic enough to achieve. Goals are of little value if no effort is needed to achieve them, and participants soon lose their interest in the goal-setting program. But goals that are too difficult to achieve lead to frustration, reduced confidence, and poor performance. The secret is to strike a balance between goal challenge and achieveability, which is no easy task. Professionals must know the capabilities and commitment of the individuals they are working with. As professional experience is gained, it's easier to judge capabilities and how long improvement will take to occur.

If someone does not have extensive experience with the activity or the individuals involved in her program, it is better to err on the side of setting goals that can be more easily achieved. That way, participants will not become frustrated. However, as soon as it becomes clear that the goals are being easily mastered, more challenging goals should be set.

3. Set Long- and Short-Term Goals

Unfortunately, major behavior change does not occur overnight. Thus, both long- and short-term goals should be set. One way to employ this principle is to think of a staircase with a long-term goal (or dream) at the top, the present level of ability at the lowest step, and a sequence of progressively linked short-term goals connecting the top and bottom of the stairs. Figure 17.2 depicts a goal-setting staircase used with a group of 8- to 11-year-old figure skaters. The skaters had a long-term goal of achieving the next test level (performing a prescribed set of skills) but were not ready to test at the time. Thus, the coach charted a progression of skills, or short-term goals, that would prepare the young skaters to achieve the next test level. The goal-setting staircase was posted, and each time a skater mastered a particular skill, a gold skate sticker was placed on the graph until all the subgoals were accomplished and the long-term test goal was achieved.

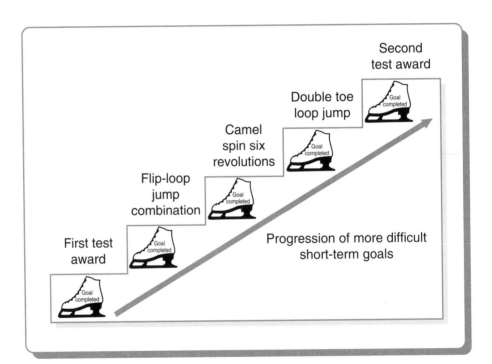

Figure 17.2 Beginning figure skater second test level goal-setting staircase.

This short- and long-term goal-setting staircase has been successfully adapted and used with elite athletes including several World and Olympic champions. It can be also easily adapted for exercise programs.

Short- and long-term goals can be linked. Terry Orlick (1986) developed a form (see Table 17.1) that links an athlete's long-term goals with a series of more immediate short-term physical and psychological goals. The form also creates a progression of goals, starting with some that can be achieved immediately and leading to more difficult and distant objectives. Orlick's approach can be successfully employed in a variety of sport and exercise settings.

4. Set Performance Goals

It is difficult not to think about winning or how your performance compares with others. After all, winning and losing receive much more attention from others than do an individual's personal goal achievements. Not surprisingly,

Table 17.1   Short- and Long-Term Goals Questionnaire

1. Dream Goal (long-term)—What is your long-term dream goal? What is potentially possible in the long term if you stretch all your limits?

2. Dream Goal (this year)—What is your dream goal for this year? What is potentially possible if all your limits are stretched this year?

3. Realistic Performance Goal (this year)—What do you feel is a realistic performance goal that you can achieve this year (based on your present skill level, your potential for improvement, and your current motivation)?

4a. Goal of Self-Acceptance—Can you make a commitment to accept yourself and to learn from the experience, regardless of whether you achieve your ultimate performance goal this year?

4b. If you do not meet your desired performance goal, to what extent will you still be able to accept yourself as a worthy human being?

    Complete self-   0 1 2 3 4 5 6 7 8 9 10   Complete and full
    rejection   self-acceptance

5. Can you set an on-site goal of best *effort* (giving everything you have that day) and be satisfied with achieving that single goal?

6. Focused Psychological Goal (this year)—What do you feel is an important goal for you to focus on this year in terms of your psychological preparation or mental control? Some examples are a *specific* goal related to psychological readiness for the event, focus control within the event, distraction control, confidence, coping with hassles or setbacks, and improving interpersonal harmony or relationships.

7. Daily Goal—(A) Set a personal goal for *tomorrow's* training session. Write down one thing you would like to do, accomplish, or approach with a special focus or intensity. (B) Can you set a personal goal before going to *each* training session this year?

8. What do you think you or others could do to increase the harmony among team members this year?

Adapted from Orlick (1986).

then, athletes often cite as their goals such outcomes as winning games, winning championships, or beating particular opponents.

Ironically, the best way to win a championship or beat a particular opponent is to focus on performance goals. Too much emphasis placed on outcome goals creates anxiety during competition, and the athlete spends undue time worrying instead of focusing on the task at hand.

The key, then, is to continually emphasize performance goals. For every outcome goal an athlete sets, there should be several performance goals that would lead to that outcome. For example, if you are working with the members of a junior high school softball team who want to win the city championship, you should emphasize the relevant performance goals of improving fielding percentage, team batting average, and stolen bases. Encourage efforts to achieve these goals and chart progress toward them throughout the season.

For every outcome goal an athlete sets, he should set several performance goals that will lead to that outcome.

5. Write Down Goals

The old adage "out of sight, out of mind" might be remembered for goal-setting procedures. Several sport psychologists (Botterill, 1983; Harris & Harris, 1984; McClements, 1982) have recommended that once goals are set they should be recorded and placed where they can be easily seen.

There are several ways to record goals. You can have students, athletes, or exercisers simply write down their goals on a 3-by-5 card, or you can formulate complex behavioral contracts. No one strategy is optimal. However, the more efficient the method of recording, the more useful it is. For example, writing down goals on a card and posting the card in a locker or on the bedroom mirror at home is more effective and time efficient than an in-depth, behavioral contract that is signed and placed in a drawer never to be looked at again. Athletes who use training logs often find it useful to include sections where they record goals and their progress toward them.

6. Develop Goal-Achievement Strategies

Setting goals without corresponding goal-achievement strategies is like driving a car to a strange city without consulting a map. Strategies must be developed to accompany the goals you set.

Chipping a bucket of golf balls onto a practice green 3 days a week is a strategy to achieve the goal of lowering your handicap by three shots. Participating in a walking program that burns 2500 calories a week is a strategy to achieve a weight-loss goal of 20 pounds in 5 months. Strategies should be specific and indicate how much and how often they are to be performed.

Athletes should build flexibility into their goal-achievement strategies. Instead of saying you will lift weights on Monday, Wednesday, and Friday, it is better to say you will lift 3 days a week. That way, if you cannot lift on one of the designated days, you can lift on another day and still achieve your goal.

7. Consider Participant Personality

When helping sport and exercise participants set and achieve goals it is important to consider their personalities. An individual's motivation and goal orientations influence the goals she adopts and how well the goal-setting process functions. High achievers (see chapter 5 on achievement motivation), whose personalities are characterized by high levels of motivation to achieve success and low levels of motivation to avoid failure, will readily seek out and adopt challenging but realistic goals. In contrast, low achievers with high levels of motivation to avoid failure and low levels of motivation to achieve success will avoid challenging goals and seek to adopt either very easy or very difficult goals.

Similarly, children in the social comparison stage of achievement tend to focus on competitive and outcome goals. Competitive people also focus on outcome goals, whereas task-oriented athletes will be much more open to performance goals.

Understanding and recognizing these personality differences will help you know what to expect from the people you help set goals for. High achievers and task-oriented athletes should respond well to your goal-setting efforts. For low achievers and outcome-oriented athletes, you will need to repeatedly emphasize the importance of setting realistic performance goals. You will then need to monitor them to ensure they do not gravitate back to more familiar outcome goals. Extra efforts to focus on performance goals will also be necessary with young children. Goal setting should be easier once youngsters reach the integrated stage and feel comfortable focusing on personal improvement.

8. Foster Individual Goal Commitment

A person will not achieve a goal without commitment to achieving it. Instructors should promote this commitment by encouraging progress and providing consistent feedback.

Teachers or coaches should not set their students' or athletes' goals for them, either directly or indirectly. Instead, make your participants part of the goal-setting process by soliciting their input and letting them set their *own goals*.

9. Provide Goal Support

Other people also can support athletes, students, and exercisers in their goal setting. Too often this does not occur. For example, a high school lacrosse coach whose team is competing for the district championship may have her athletes set a series of performance goals. Meanwhile, the athletes' parents, teachers, and friends frequently ask the players about winning the championship. Educating these significant others about the importance of performance (rather than outcome) goals can be accomplished through letters to parents, staff meeting announcements, and stories in the school newspaper.

Spousal support is a critical factor affecting exercise adherence (Dishman, 1988). Thus, many corporate fitness specialists have found it useful to involve spouses in weight loss and conditioning programs and invite them to support the achievement of the participant's goals.

Finally, fitness professionals need to show a genuine interest in the people with whom they work. They should review their participants' goals, ask about their progress, empathize with their struggles, and foster a caring, upbeat, and encouraging atmosphere.

Enlist support from significant others to make goal setting effective.

10. Provide for Goal Evaluation

Performance feedback about progress is absolutely essential if goals are going to effectively change performance and behavior. Yet the failure to provide goal evaluation and feedback is common.

Goal evaluation strategies should be initiated at the start of the goal-setting program and continually implemented as the program progresses. Evaluation

Goal evaluation and feedback are essential parts of facilitating behavior change.

can take many forms (see Table 17.2 for some examples). The key is to be consistent. Too often, people spend considerable time defining and setting goals only to have all their work wasted because they don't follow through with essential evaluation and feedback.

Table 17.2 Forms of Goal Evaluation	
Goal	**Goal evaluation strategy**
Lose 20 pounds in 6 months	Client informs fitness instructor of his or her weight weekly
Increase free-throw shooting percentage from 65% to 72% by the end of the season	Team manager charts free-throw percentage statistics after each game and calculates year-to-date free-throw average
To attend injury rehabilitation clinic 3 days a week until recovery	Attendance posted weekly at rehabilitation center and coach is notified of attendance
To improve concentration levels during practice	Coach gives player weekly report card rating practice concentration on a 0 (low) to 10 (high) scale
To improve class cooperation in elementary school physical education class	Teacher tallies cooperative acts on behavioral checklist during week and charts improvement of varying classes on gym bulletin board

Designing a Goal-Setting System

Just as a basketball coach develops a game plan from individual plays, the fitness professional should develop a goal-setting system or plan from the 10 basic goal-setting principles we have just discussed. Although there are many different goal-setting systems, most of them include three basic stages:

1. Instructor-leader preparation
2. Education and acquisition
3. Implementation and follow-up

We'll discuss each of these stages separately.

Instructor-Leader Preparation

An effective instructor, trainer, or coach does not want to enter a physical activity setting unprepared. Time is needed for the thought and preparation that must precede effective goal setting. The time spent on preparing the goal-setting process saves hours of work once the program is implemented.

Assess Abilities and Needs. The first thing required is an assessment of the participant's abilities and needs. Based on his knowledge of the athlete, the fitness professional should identify the areas he thinks most need improvement. When little is known about the athlete's background, it can also be useful to develop a list of all the skills needed in her activity. Then the athlete is asked to rate her ability relative to each of the skills identified.

Set Goals in Diverse Areas.   Too often people consider only performance-related goals. Goals can and should be set in a variety of areas including

- individual skills,
- team skills,
- fitness levels,
- playing time,
- enjoyment, and
- psychological skills.

Table 17.3 lists sample goals in each of these areas.

Table 17.3	Areas in Which Goals Can Be Set
Goal area	**Goal**
Individual skills	I will decrease my time by .4 seconds in the 400-meter dash by increasing my speed in the initial 100 meters through a more explosive start.
Team skills	Our high school wrestling team will increase the percentage of successful takedowns achieved from 54% to 62% by midseason.
Fitness	A homemaker will lower his or her resting heart rate from 71 beats per minute to 61 beats per minute by participating in a 50-minute aerobic dance class at least 3 days per week for the next 5 months.
Playing time	A junior in high school will earn a varsity football letter by participating in at least 16 different game quarters during the season.
Enjoyment	A veteran professional tennis player will enjoy touring more by identifying and visiting one new restaurant and historic site in each tour city.
Psychological skills	A diver will attempt to regain her confidence on an inward 2-1/2 dive by visualizing a successful dive before each practice attempt and repeating at least one positive self-statement.

Identify Influences on Goal-Setting Systems.   Goals can't be set in a vacuum. The athlete's potential, commitment, and opportunities for practice must be assessed before goals can be set. For instance, it does little good to establish after-hours practice goals for an athlete who is not committed or disciplined enough to do them. It would be more effective for this person to have goals that he can achieve during regular practice times—or, better yet, to set a goal of becoming more independent and disciplined enough to practice on his own.

Plan Goal-Achievement Strategies.   Strategies must be planned that participants can use to achieve their goals. Goals are not effective unless they are tied to specific and realistic strategies.

Education and Acquisition

Once the preparation and planning stage has been completed, the coach, teacher, or exercise leader can begin educating the athlete directly on the most effective ways to set goals. This involves imparting basic goal-setting information and principles.

Schedule Meetings.   A formal meeting or a series of brief, less formal meetings should be scheduled before practices or classes. In these meetings the coach and athlete can identify examples of effective and ineffective goals. Participants should not be expected to be able to list goals right on the spot. Instead, they can be introduced to goal setting and given time to think. The coach or instructor can schedule a follow-up meeting or subsequent practice to discuss specific goals.

Focus on One Goal.   Unless an athlete has considerable experience in setting goals, it is better to set just one goal at a time. The coach can help each individual select one goal from his or her list. The athlete will then focus on correctly defining the goal and outlining realistic strategies to achieve it. After participants have learned to set and achieve a single goal, they might be ready to try multiple goals.

Implementation and Follow-Up

Once participants have learned to set goals, the next step is to list the goals that have been identified as appropriate. The coach or instructor will need to assist in the goal evaluation and follow-up process.

Identify Appropriate Goal Evaluation Procedures.   You want to avoid designing a goal-setting system that is impossible for you as a coach, teacher, or fitness instructor to keep up with. For example, anticipate the busiest time of your year and estimate how much time you will have available for goal evaluation and follow-up.

Moreover, be sure to identify the most effective system for managing goal evaluation and follow-up. Many coaches streamline the evaluation process by having managers keep and post practice and game statistics related to player goals. Similarly, some physical educators schedule periodic skills tests during class when students receive feedback about their performance progress toward their goals. In these cases, the feedback process costs the instructor or coach little time.

Provide Support and Encouragement.   Throughout the season the coach needs to ask participants about their goals and publicly encourage their goal progress. Showing enthusiasm about the goal-setting process supports the athletes and keeps them motivated to fulfill their goals.

Plan for Goal Reevaluation.   Goal setting is not a perfect science, and sometimes the goals that have been set don't work out. For example, a tennis player may set a goal to hit 40% of her first serves in and find that, with practice, she has little trouble hitting 50% of her first serves in. In such a case, her goal must be modified to challenge her. Other athletes will set initial goals that are too difficult and need to be made easier. Injuries and illness might also require an athlete to modify his goals. It is necessary to reevaluate goals intermittently. Modifying and reestablishing goals is a normal part of the process.

Goal setting is not a perfect science. Plan for periodic goal reevaluation.

Common Problems in Goal Setting

Goal setting is not a difficult psychological technique to understand, but this doesn't mean that problems will not arise in implementing a goal-setting program (Gould, 1993). Some common problems include

- failing to set specific goals,
- setting too many goals too soon,
- failing to adjust goals when they are not being achieved,
- failing to set performance goals, and
- not initiating goal-setting evaluation and follow-up procedures.

By understanding and anticipating these problems you can reduce their effects and even circumvent some problems altogether.

Failing to Set Specific Goals

The most frequent problem people in sport and exercise settings have is failing to set specific goals. Even when activity participants are told how important it is to state goals in specific, behavioral terms, they often identify goals in a general, vague way. For example, "improving my tennis serve" might be the stated goal, instead of "improving the accuracy of good serves from 60% to 70% by developing a more consistent ball toss."

It is important for the physical fitness professional to monitor initial goals and give feedback about their specificity. Additionally, we need to teach people to form a numerical goal that includes an improved percentage or number of some behavior. Finally, when establishing sport skill goals, the performer should be asked to include specific characteristics of improved technique in the goal statement (e.g., "improve downhill running by shortening stride length," or "improve the percentage of strikes thrown by bending my back more").

Setting Too Many Goals Too Soon

Novices at setting goals tend to take on too many goals at once. Their desire to improve leads them to become overzealous and unrealistic. On the practical side, monitoring, tracking, and providing individualized feedback across time becomes virtually impossible for the fitness leader when participants have too many goals. Plus, when too many goals are set at once, they are all almost invariably abandoned.

Inexperienced goal setters should set only one or two goals at a time. Making the goals short term (e.g., achieved within 2 weeks rather than 5 months) keeps them in the foreground and maximizes the performer's enthusiasm. Tracking the goal and providing feedback is also easier over a shorter time period. Multiple, simultaneous goals can be set once the individual has gained experience.

Initially, only one or two goals should be set. Participants can set more goals at once after gaining experience.

Failing to Adjust Goals

Adjusting goals, especially lowering them, once they have been set can be difficult. For example, in one study swimmers had no difficulty adjusting goals upward, but after an injury or illness found adjusting goals downward to be extremely difficult from a psychological perspective (Burton, 1989b).

Two things can reduce this problem. First, right from the start of your goal-setting program discuss the need to adjust goals upward and downward. That way, participants will view adjustments as a normal part of the process rather than as indicating a problem on their part. Second, if goals must be lowered due to illness or injury, make the adjustment part of a staircase of goals (see Figure 17.3) that ultimately surpasses the original goal. In that way, the person can view the lowered goal as a temporary setback to be ultimately overcome.

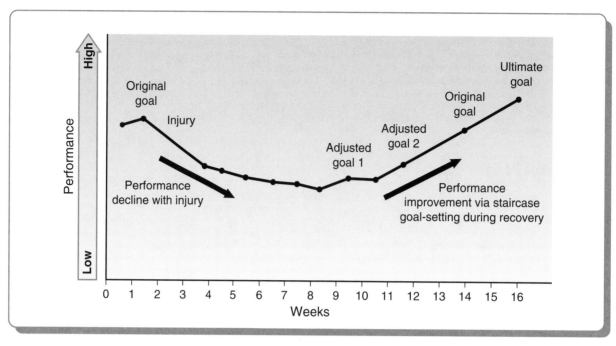

Figure 17.3   Adjusting goals downward: Maintaining a positive perspective through a staircase approach.

Failing to Set Performance Goals

Failure to set performance goals rather than outcome goals occurs frequently with athletes in competitive sports. Performance goals should be emphasized throughout the athletic season. Coaches and exercise leaders need to be alert to not unconsciously stress outcome goals. Instead, they should evaluate the players' performance goals as thoroughly after a win as after a loss.

Not Initiating Follow-Up and Evaluation

A lack of follow-up and evaluation is one of the major factors in the failure of goal-setting programs. It is imperative to develop a goal-setting follow-up and evaluation plan and to examine it critically for ease and efficiency. It must be simple to implement. Goal setting without follow-up and evaluation is simply a waste of time and effort.

Summary

Goals are objectives or aims of actions. They may be subjective or objective and directed toward performance or toward outcome. The research on goal setting demonstrates that goals are a powerful means for effecting behavior change, either directly or indirectly. Goals influence behavior directly by bringing a performer's attention to important elements of the skill or task, increasing motivation and persistence, and facilitating the development of new learning strategies. They influence behavior indirectly by causing changes in important psychological factors such as self-confidence, anxiety, and satisfaction. Basic goal-setting principles include setting specific goals, difficult but realistic goals, both short- and long-term goals, and performance goals. Other basic principles of effective goal setting are the need to write down goals, develop goal-achievement strategies, consider participant personality, foster individual goal commitment, provide goal support, and provide for goal evaluation. These 10 goal-setting principles form the foundation of a three-stage goal-setting system that involves instructor-leader preparation, education and acquisition, and follow-up.

Failing to set specific goals, setting too many goals too soon, failing to readjust goals, failing to set performance goals, and not initiating goal-setting follow-up and evaluation are common goal-setting problems that a good program needs to address.

Review Questions

1. What's the difference between subjective and objective goals? Between performance and outcome goals?

2. Compare and contrast the "direct mechanistic" and "indirect thought process" explanations of goal setting.

3. Identify a basic goal-setting principle or guideline that relates to each of the following areas: goal specificity; goal difficulty; short- versus long-term goals; performance versus outcome goals; writing down goals; strategies for achieving goals; participant personality; individual commitment; goal support; and goal evaluation.

4. Why do sport psychologists recommend that athletes focus on performance over outcome goals?

5. What is a goal-setting staircase and why is it important?

6. What are the three basic stages to consider in designing a goal-setting system? What should happen during each stage?

7. Identify five common problems with goal setting.

8. Why is it important to adjust goals periodically?

References

Botterill, C. (1983). Goal setting for athletes with examples from hockey. In G.L. Martin & D. Hrycaiko (Eds.), *Behavior modification and coaching: Principles, procedures, and research*. Springfield, IL: Charles C. Thomas.

Burton, D. (1984). Evaluation of goal setting training on selected cognitions and performance of collegiate swimmers. (Doctoral dissertation, University of Illinois, 1983.) *Dissertation Abstracts International*, **45**, 116A.

Burton, D. (1989a). The impact of goal specificity and task complexity on basketball skill development. *The Sport Psychologist*, **3**, 34-47.

Burton, D. (1989b). Winning isn't everything: Examining the impact of performance goals on collegiate swimmers' cognitions and performance. *The Sport Psychologist*, **3**, 105-132.

Dishman, R.K. (Ed.) (1988). *Exercise adherence: Its impact on public health*. Champaign, IL: Human Kinetics.

Garland, H. (1985). A cognitive mediation theory of task goals and human performance. *Motivation and Emotion*, **9**, 345-367.

Gould, D. (1993). Goal setting for peak performance. In J. Williams (Ed.), *Applied sport psychology: Personal growth to peak performance* (2nd ed., pp. 158-169). Palo Alto, CA: Mayfield.

Harris, D.V., & Harris, B.L. (1984). *The athlete's guide to sports psychology: Mental skills for physical people*. New York: Leisure Press.

Locke, E.A., & Latham, G.P. (1985). The application of goal setting to sports. *Journal of Sport Psychology*, **7**, 205-222.

Locke, E.A., Shaw, K.N., Saari, L.M., & Latham, G.P. (1981). Goal setting and task performance. *Psychological Bulletin*, **90**, 125-152.

Martens, R. (1990). *Coaches guide to sport psychology*. Champaign, IL: Human Kinetics.

McClements, J. (1982). Goal setting and planning for mental preparations. In L. Wankel & R.B. Wilberg (Eds.), *Psychology of sport and motor behavior: Research and practice*. Proceedings of the Annual Conference of the Canadian Society for Psychomotor Learning and Sport Psychology. Edmonton, Alberta, Canada: University of Alberta.

Mento, A.J., Steel, R.P., & Karren, R.J. (1987). A meta-analytic study of the effects of goal-setting on task performance: 1966-1984. *Organizational Behavior and Human Decision Processes*, **39**, 52-83.

Orlick, T. (1986). *Psyching for sport: Mental training for athletes*. Champaign, IL: Human Kinetics.

Weinberg, R.S. (1992). Goal setting and motor performance: A review and critique. In G.C. Roberts (Ed.), *Motivation in sport and exercise* (pp. 177-197). Champaign, IL: Human Kinetics.

CHAPTER 18

Concentration

If your mind is going to wander during practice, it's going to do the same thing in a match. When we were all growing up in Australia, we had to work as hard mentally as we did physically in practice. If you weren't alert, you could get a ball hit off the side of your head. What I used to do was force myself to concentrate more as soon as I'd find myself getting tired, because that's usually when your concentration starts to fail you. If I'd find myself getting tired in practice, I'd force myself to work much harder for an extra ten or fifteen minutes, and I always felt as though I got more out of those extra minutes than I did out of the entire practice.

Rod Laver

The key to running the 1500 meters is to just concentrate on what you're trying to do and not allow other things to start clouding your mind. Oftentimes, loss of concentration for a brief moment will be enough to make the difference in winning and losing.

Sebastian Coe

Many athletes mistakenly believe that it's important to concentrate only during actual competition. Yet the old adage "Practice makes perfect" applies aptly to concentration skills. Like other psychological skills, concentration develops through dedication and practice. Rod Laver describes how he worked on concentration during all of his practices. He understood that without developing concentration in practice, he wouldn't have it for a competitive match.

Sebastian Coe underscores a second important aspect of concentration—that is, winning or losing is often decided by a small attentional lapse. Even in competitions lasting hours or days, a brief loss of concentration can mar total performance and even affect outcome. Thus, it is critical to concentrate throughout a competition, despite potential distractions such as crowd noise, weather conditions, or irrelevant thoughts.

In this chapter you will learn about

- the meaning of concentration,
- different types of attentional focus,
- how to shift attentional focus,
- attentional problems, including choking,
- self-talk,
- how to measure attentional ability, and
- how to improve attentional focus.

What Is Concentration?

A useful definition of concentration contains two parts: focusing attention on the relevant cues in the environment and maintaining that attentional focus. And sport psychologists have demonstrated that having the proper attentional focus is conducive to good performance.

Focusing on Relevant Environmental Cues

Part of the definition refers to focusing on the *relevant* environmental cues. Irrelevant cues need to be either eliminated or disregarded. Let's return to the example we have used before of a basketball player shooting two free throws at the end of a game with only a couple of seconds left and her team down by one point. What cues in our basketball player's environment are relevant or irrelevant? A relevant cue might be making sure she goes through her normal preshot routine—bouncing the ball three times, taking a deep breath, looking up at the basket, and focusing on the front of the rim. Irrelevant cues include the players lined up for the rebound and the home town fans behind the backboard waving their hands and making a lot of noise. The attentional ability to focus on the preshot routine and the rim, while eliminating all extraneous noise and movements, is critical to the successful execution of the foul shot.

Maintaining Attentional Focus

Maintaining attentional focus for the duration of the competition is also part of concentration. Many athletes have moments of greatness, yet few can sustain

Goals will not be effective unless they are tied to specific and realistic strategies for achieving them.

Attentional Focus

A quarterback in football has to distinguish between what is relevant and irrelevant. When he stands behind the center and looks over the defense, he first must recognize the specific defensive formation to determine if the play that was called will work. If he believes the linebackers are all going to blitz, he might decide to change the long pass he originally called to a quick pass over the middle. Of course, the linebackers are probably trying to fool the quarterback into thinking they are going to blitz when they really aren't—a cat and mouse game occupying the quarterback's attentional focus.

Now the quarterback has the ball and has dropped back to throw a pass. He sees one of his men open and is about ready to release the ball when, out of the corner of his eye, he sees a 250-pound lineman getting ready to slam into him. Is this lineman a relevant or irrelevant cue for the quarterback? If he can release the ball before being tackled by the lineman, then the lineman is an irrelevant cue, even though the quarterback knows he will be hit hard right after he releases the ball. However, if the quarterback determines that the defensive lineman will tackle him before he can release the ball, then the lineman becomes a relevant cue that should signal the quarterback to "scramble out of the pocket" to get more time to find an open receiver.

a high level of play for an entire competition. Chris Evert was never the most physically talented player on the women's tour, but nobody could match her ability to stay focused throughout a match. She was virtually unaffected by irrelevant cues, such as bad line calls, missed easy shots, crowd noise, and opponent antics. Her concentration helped make her a champion.

Maintaining focus over long time periods is no easy task. Tournament golf, for example, is usually played over 72 holes. Say after playing great for 70 holes, you have 2 holes left in the tournament and lead by a stroke. On the 17th hole, just as you prepare to hit your drive off the tee, an image of the championship trophy flashes in front of your mind. This momentary distraction causes you to lose your focus on the ball and hook your drive badly into the trees. It takes you three more strokes just to get on the green, and you wind up with a double bogey. You lose your lead and wind up in second place. Thus, one lapse in concentration over 72 holes cost you the championship.

Now consider a runner competing in a marathon. You might think that in a race of 2 or 3 hours a few attention lapses wouldn't matter much. Nothing could be farther from the truth. Studies of the cognitive strategies of elite marathon runners found that the most successful marathoners used a combination of an *associative attentional strategy* (monitoring bodily functions and feelings, such as heart rate, muscle tension, and breathing rate) and a *dissociative attentional strategy* (distraction) during the race (Silva & Applebaum, 1989). Less successful marathoners used a dissociative strategy almost exclusively throughout the race. Dissociative attentional strategies "tune out" physiological feedback from the body to help deal with the boredom and fatigue of the marathon. However, this lack of attentional focus to what's happening in the body can often result in being unprepared for important changes, such as muscle cramps or "hitting the wall," where you suddenly feel you can go no farther.

Fatigue certainly affects concentration. When the body is fatigued, it can be difficult to keep the mind in tow for extended periods of time. As Rod Laver noted, the minute you feel yourself getting a little tired is when you have to force yourself to concentrate harder.

Concentration is the ability to maintain focus on relevant environmental cues.

Types of Attentional Focus

Most people think concentration is an all-or-none phenomenon—that either you're concentrating or you're not. However, research in sport psychology reveals that several types of attentional focus are appropriate for specific sports and activities.

To date, the most useful research on the role of attentional style in sport has developed from the theoretical framework of Nideffer (1976, 1981), who views attentional focus along two dimensions: *width* (broad versus narrow) and *direction* (internal versus external).

- A *broad* attentional focus allows a person to perceive several occurrences simultaneously. This is particularly important in sports where athletes have to be aware of and sensitive to a rapidly changing environment (i.e., they must respond to multiple cues). Two examples are a basketball point guard leading a fast break and a soccer player dribbling the ball up field.
- A *narrow* attentional focus occurs when you respond to only one or two cues, such as when a baseball batter prepares to swing at a pitch or a golfer lines up a putt.
- An *external* attentional focus directs attention outward on an object, such as a ball in baseball or a puck in hockey, or on an opponent's movements, such as in a doubles match in tennis.
- An *internal* attentional focus is directed inward on thoughts and feelings, such as when a coach analyzes plays without having to perform, or when a high jumper prepares to start his run-up or a bowler readies her approach.

By combining width and direction of attentional focus, four different categories emerge, appropriate to various situations and sports (see Table 18.1).

Shifting Attentional Focus

Often it is necessary to shift attentional focus during an event. Let's take a golf example. As a golfer gets ready to step up to the ball before teeing off, she

Table 18.1 Four Different Types of Attentional Focus	
Broad-External	**Broad-Internal**
Used to rapidly assess a situation (e.g., a football quarterback rapidly assesses the positioning of the defensive backs)	Used to analyze and plan (e.g., developing a game plan or strategy)
Narrow-External	**Narrow-Internal**
Used to focus exclusively on one or two external cues (e.g., the ball)	Used to mentally rehearse an upcoming performance or control an emotional state (e.g., mentally rehearse golf putting or taking a breath to relax)

needs to assess the external environment: the direction of the wind, length of the fairway, positioning of water hazards, trees, and sand traps. This requires a broad-external focus. After appraising this information, she might recall previous experience with similar shots, note current playing conditions, and analyze the information she's gathered to select a particular club and determine how to hit the ball. These considerations require a broad-internal focus.

Once she has formulated a plan, she might monitor her tension, image a perfect shot, or take a deep, relaxing breath as part of a preshot routine. She has moved into a narrow-internal focus. Finally, shifting to a narrow-external focus, she addresses the ball. At this time, her focus is directly on the ball. This is not the time for other internal cues and thoughts, which would probably interfere with the execution of the shot. Golfers have ample time to shift attentional focus because they themselves set the pace.

Attentional Problems

Many athletes recognize that they have problems concentrating for the duration of a competition. Usually, these concentration problems are caused by

Can You Identify the Proper Attentional Focus?

See if you can identify the proper attentional focus of a football quarterback under time duress. Blank spaces are provided to fill in the proper attentional focus (the answers, which correspond to the numbers in the blanks, are given afterward).

As the quarterback calls the play, he needs a ____(1)____ focus to analyze the game situation, including the score, what yard line the ball is on, the down, and time left in the game. He also considers the scouting reports and the game plan that the coach wants him to execute in calling the play. As the quarterback comes up to the line of scrimmage his focus of attention should be ____(2)____ while he looks over the entire defense and tries to determine if the play originally called will be effective. If he feels that another play might work better, he may change the play by calling an "audible" at the line of scrimmage. Next the quarterback's attention shifts to a ____(3)____ focus to receive the ball from the center. Mistakes sometimes occur in the center-quarterback exchange because the quarterback is still thinking about the defense or what he has to do next instead of making sure he receives the snap without fumbling.

If a pass play was called, the quarterback drops back into "the pocket" to look downfield for his receivers. This requires a ____(4)____ perspective so the quarterback can evaluate the defense and find the open receiver while at the same time avoiding onrushing linemen. Finally, after spotting a specific receiver, his focus becomes ____(5)____ as he concentrates on throwing a good pass.

Within a few seconds, the quarterback shifts attentional focus several times to effectively understand the defense and pick out the correct receiver. (See examples of different types of attentional focus in Figures 18.1, 18.2, 18.3, and 18.4.)

Answers to Proper Attentional Focus

1. Broad-internal
2. Broad-external
3. Narrow-external
4. Broad-external
5. Narrow-external

(continued)

Can You Identify the Proper Attentional Focus? *(continued)*

Figure 18.1   Broad-internal attentional focus. Adapted from Weinberg (1988).

Figure 18.2   Broad-external attentional focus. Adapted from Weinberg (1988).

Figure 18.3   Narrow-internal attentional focus. Adapted from Weinberg (1988).

Figure 18.4   Narrow-external attentional focus. Adapted from Weinberg (1988).

When the environment changes rapidly, attentional focus must also change rapidly.

inappropriate attentional focus. They are not focusing on the proper cues; rather, they become distracted by thoughts, other events, and emotions. We'll now discuss some of the typical problems athletes have in controlling and maintaining attentional focus.

Attending to Past Events

Some people cannot forget about what has just happened—especially if it was a bad mistake. Focusing on past events has been the downfall of many talented athletes, as doing so prevents them from focusing on the present. An example of how attending to past mistakes and actions can ruin concentration is described in the following case study.

Attending to Future Events

Concentration problems can also involve attending to future events. Younger athletes especially tend toward future-oriented thinking, usually focusing on the consequences of certain actions. Such thinking often takes the form of "what if" statements:

- What if we lose the game?
- What if I strike out again?
- What if I make another error?
- What if I get injured?
- What if I let my teammates down?
- What if I can't adhere to my new exercise program?

This kind of future-oriented thinking and worry negatively affects concentration, making mistakes and poor performance more likely. Worry is not only a distraction but can also cause excess muscle tension that further inhibits performance (see chapter 14).

Thinking of the past or the future are irrelevant cues that often lead to performance errors.

Some future-oriented thinking has nothing to do with the situation. Your mind wanders without much excuse. For example, athletes report thinking during the heat of competition about such things as what they need to do at school the next day, what they have planned for that evening, their girlfriend or boyfriend, and what they are going to wear on an upcoming date. These irrelevant thoughts are often involuntary—suddenly you just find yourself thinking about things that have nothing to do with the present exercise or competition. Such concentration lapses are very frustrating and certainly affect performance.

Attending to Past Mistakes: A Gymnastics Example

A gymnast performing on the balance beam has a virtually flawless first routine, putting her in first place. On her second routine she again performs flawlessly until the very end, where she loses balance on her dismount, falling on her hands and knees instead of landing on her feet. The judges penalize her for this mistake, and she falls from first to third place. With one more round to go there still is a chance to win. However, as she awaits her next turn, she continues to replay the missed dismount in her mind, becoming angry with herself for missing a move that she had perfected. If she had only hit her dismount, she would still be in first place. As she mounts the beam for her final round she isn't paying close enough attention to her routine—she has lost her concentration. She loses her balance on a difficult move and falls off the beam.

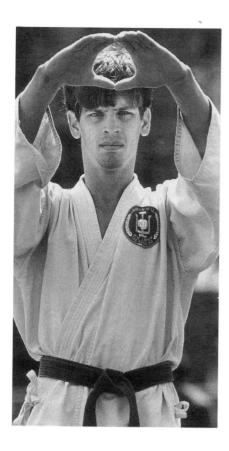

Attending to Too Many Cues

One of the difficult aspects of remaining focused throughout a long exercise bout or competition is that there are many distractions in the environment competing for your attention. For example, people with a broad-external focus seem to notice everything happening in their vicinity, even things that have nothing to do with the activity. Spectators, for example, can distract them. Perhaps they start thinking about the audience and want to impress friends and family. But in trying to impress others, they may attempt things beyond their capabilities. A basketball player might try long-range shots outside her normal shooting range. A baseball player might try for a home run instead of just making good contact with the ball.

Spectators affect some people's concentration and subsequent performance by making them try too hard. We all want to look good when playing in front of people we know and care for, so we often start to press, tighten up, and try too hard. This usually results in poorer play instead of better, which makes us feel embarrassed and causes us to tighten up even more. Of course, some people actually play better in front of audiences they know. For many others, knowing people in the audience is a powerful distraction.

It is important to focus on only the relevant cues in the athletic environment and eliminate distractions.

Overanalysis of Body Mechanics

Another type of inappropriate attention is focusing too much on body mechanics and movements. Of course we're not saying an internal-narrow focus is *always* bad. When you're learning a new skill, you need to focus internally to get the kinesthetic feel of the movement. If you're learning to ski downhill, for instance, you might focus on the transfer of weight, the positioning of the skis, positioning your poles, and simply keeping from falling down or running into other people. As you attempt to integrate this new movement pattern, your performance is likely to be uneven. This is what practice is all about—focusing on improving your technique by getting a better feel of the movement.

The problem arises when internal-narrow thinking continues after you have learned the skill. At this point, the skill should be virtually automatic, and your attention should be primarily on what you're doing and on one or two key cue words to keep you focused. If you are skiing in a competition for the fastest time, you should not be focusing on body mechanics. Rather, you should be externally focused on where you're going, skiing basically on automatic pilot.

Once a skill is well learned, an over-emphasis on body mechanics is detrimental to performance.

This doesn't mean that no thinking occurs once a skill is well learned. But an emphasis on technique and body mechanics during competition is usually detrimental to performance because the mind gets in the way of the body. The more you analyze, the more likely you are to break the natural smooth movements characteristic of high levels of performance, especially when rapid decisions and reactions are imperative.

Choking—An Attentional Problem

Although most players and coaches have difficulty defining choking, almost everyone agrees that it impairs performance. Read the three scenarios that follow and determine if the athlete choked or not.

When people think of choking, they tend to focus on the bad performance at a critical time of the game or competition, such as a missed shot, dropped pass, poor kick, or bad throw. However, choking is much more than the actual behavior—it is a process that leads to impaired performance. The fact that you missed a free throw to lose a game does not necessarily mean you choked. The more important questions to answer are why and how you missed the free throw. We'll now take a closer look at the process characteristic of what we have come to call choking.

How to Recognize Choking

Behaviorally, we infer that athletes are choking when their performance progressively deteriorates and they cannot regain control over performance with-

---

Did These Performers Choke?

A basketball game is tightly fought, the lead shifting after each basket. Finally with 2 seconds left and her team down by 2 points, steady guard Julie Lancaster gets fouled in the act of shooting and is awarded two foul shots. Julie is a 90% free-throw shooter. She steps up to the line, makes her first shot but misses her second, and her team loses. Did Julie choke?

Jane is involved in a close tennis match. After splitting the first 2 sets with her opponent, she is now serving for the match at 5-4, 30-30. On the next 2 points, Jane double faults to lose the game and even the set at 5-5. However, Jane then comes back to break serve and hold her own serve to close out the set and match. Did Jane choke?

Bill Moore is a baseball player with a batting average of .355. His team is playing a one-game play-off to decide who will win the league championship and advance to the district finals. Bill goes 0 for 4 in the game, striking out twice with runners in scoring position. In addition, in the bottom of the ninth, he comes up with the bases loaded and one out—all he needs to do is hit the ball out of the infield to tie the game. Instead he grounds into a game-ending—and game-losing—double play. Did Bill choke?

out outside assistance. In other words, we infer choking from a pattern of behavior. An example is the gymnast who allows an early mistake of falling off the balance beam to upset her and cause additional errors once she's back on the beam. Similarly, we can infer that a baseball player is choking when he drops an easy fly ball and then makes matters worse by overthrowing the cutoff man. Choking usually occurs in a situation of emotional importance to

Table 18.2   The Choking Process
Conditions leading to choking
1. Important competition 2. Critical plays in a competition 3. Evaluation by coaches, peers, and parents

Physical changes	**Attentional changes**
1. Increased muscle tension 2. Increased breathing rate 3. Racing heart rate	1. Internal focus 2. Narrow focus 3. Reduced flexibility

Performance impairment
1. Timing and coordination breakdown 2. Muscle tightness and fatigue 3. Rushing 4. Inability to attend to task-relevant cues

Adapted from Nideffer (1993).

the athlete. A golfer is more likely to choke on the 18th hole of a tournament than on the third hole in a friendly round with his pals. (This does not mean that only tournaments are important; playing with friends might be equally important and stressful to some people, depending on their level of competition.)

Sensing pressure causes your muscles to tighten. Your heart rate and breathing increase; your mouth gets dry while your palms get damp. The key breakdown occurs at the *attentional* level: Instead of focusing externally on the relevant cues in your environment (e.g., the ball, the opponent's movements), your attention becomes narrow and internal as you focus on your own worries and fears of losing and failing. At the same time, the increased pressure reduces your flexibility to shift your attentional focus—you have problems changing your focus as the situation dictates. Impaired timing and coordination, fatigue, muscle tension, and poor judgment and decision making soon follow (the choking process is shown in Table 18.2).

Now look at a practical example of the choking process by following the sequence of events Tom, a high school freshman, experiences in his first championship baseball game.

Self-Talk

Anytime you think about something, you are in a sense talking to yourself. This self-talk can take many forms, but for convenience it can be categorized into two types: positive and negative. Positive self-talk is an asset that enhances self-esteem, motivation, attentional focus, and performance. Self-talk that helps you focus on the present and keep your mind from wandering is considered positive. It usually has either a motivational component (e.g., "I can do it," or "Just hang in there a little longer") or an instructional component (e.g., "Keep your eye on the ball," or "Bend your knees").

A Classic Case of Choking

Tom's inexperience and the importance of this championship game already are combining to make him feel nervous when the school newspaper adds to the pressure by printing an article that calls Tom's hitting power the key to the team's success. In addition, Tom knows that his friends and family will be coming out to watch him play.

Under this pressure, during the game Tom feels muscle tension in his neck and shoulders, where stress usually hits him. His heart is racing and his breathing is labored and shallow. He feels rushed, as if things are happening too fast around him. This feeling might be why he feels overanxious at the plate and swings at bad pitches.

Tom's attention is also affected—his concentration becomes narrow and internally focused. He is distracted by his own thoughts and feelings and has trouble concentrating on the coach's instructions. His thoughts become focused on "not messing up" and disappointing his teammates, family, and friends.

Tom's state, both psychologically and physically, is conducive to making mistakes. Sure enough, he comes up with the bases loaded and one out in the 4th inning and needs to make good contact with the ball. Instead, Tom swings at bad pitches and strikes out. This makes him even more frustrated, and he starts thinking about his batting as he plays the field. When a line drive comes sailing out to centerfield, he lunges at it at the last second, only to have the ball go under his glove for a triple. This is a classic case of choking.

Negative self-talk is critical and self-demeaning and gets in the way of reaching goals; it is counterproductive and anxiety producing. Saying things like, "That was a stupid shot," "You stink," or "How can you play so bad?" does not enhance performance or create positive emotions. Rather, it creates anxiety and fosters self-doubt.

How Self-Talk Works

We are not disturbed by things, but rather the view we take of them.

Epictetus

Thoughts play a critical role in shaping emotional responses to events. Most people assume that events themselves determine their emotional and physical responses, but this is not the case. Events in and of themselves do not cause depression, anger, anxiety, hopelessness, or frustration—it is how the event is interpreted that determines the response. The relation among an event, self-talk, and response is displayed in Table 18.3. As the table demonstrates, self-talk plays a key role in reactions to situations, and these reactions affect future actions and feelings.

Table 18.3	Process of Self-Talk	
Event (environmental stimulation)	**Self-talk (perception/evaluation)**	**Response (emotional, physiological, behavioral)**
Missing an important shot in a tennis match	"What an idiot I am—I'll never win now."	Anger, hopelessness, increased muscle tension
Missing an important shot in a tennis match	"Keep your eye on the ball—this match isn't over."	Better concentration, optimism, calmness
A setback in rehabilitating a knee injury	"I'll never get back in the starting lineup."	Hopelessness, anger, frustration
A setback in rehabilitating a knee injury	"This type of injury just takes time to heal, so I need to continue to work hard."	Optimism, motivation, increased effort

Uses of Self-Talk

Although positive self-talk is crucial for concentration, the uses of self-talk extend into several other areas. Here are some ways to use cue words as self-talk to help your performance:

• *Skill acquisition*. When learning skills, use self-talk as cue words to focus attention. For example, an aerobics instructor might use simple cue words like *turn*, *stretch*, *pull*, or *reach* to focus attention on the next movement for learning a new routine.

• *Breaking bad habits*. When breaking a bad habit, you need to decide on the best self-instructional cue (or cues) to make the new response automatic. The greater the change, the more self-instruction necessary. A golfer who doesn't keep her head down throughout the execution of her shot should use a cue word such as *stay* or *ball* to remind herself to keep her head down.

- *Initiate action.* Self-talk can be motivating. Runners can increase their speed by using such cue words as *quick* or *fast*. A tennis serve might be cued by *smooth, reach,* or *forward,* whereas a swimmer getting out of the blocks might use such words as *explode, stretch,* or *push.*

- *Sustain effort.* Although getting started is sometimes difficult, staying motivated and continuing to work hard can be just as tough. Positive, motivational self-talk (*keep it up, stay with it,* and *hang in there*) can help sustain effort when the body is fatigued.

Techniques to Improve Self-Talk

Several techniques or strategies can improve self-talk. Two of the most successful involve thought stopping and changing negative self-talk to positive self-talk.

Thought Stopping.   One way to cope with negative thoughts is to stop them before they harm performance. Learning to thought stop involves concentrating on the undesired thought briefly, then using a cue or trigger to stop the thought and clear your mind. The trigger can be a simple word like *stop* or a trigger like snapping your fingers or hitting your hand against your thigh. The most effective cue depends on the person.

Initially, it's best to restrict thought stopping to practice situations. Whenever you start thinking a negative thought, just say *stop* (or whatever cue you choose) aloud and then focus on a task-related cue. Once you have mastered this, try saying *stop* quietly to yourself. If there is a particular situation that produces negative self-talk (like falling during a figure skating jump), you might want to focus on that one performance aspect to stay more focused and aware of the particular problem. Old habits die hard, so thought stopping needs to be continually practiced.

Changing Negative Self-Talk to Positive Self-Talk.   It would be nice to eliminate all negative self-talk, but in fact almost everyone has negative thoughts from time to time. When they come, one way to cope with them is to change the negative thoughts into positive self-talk, which redirects attentional focus to provide encouragement and motivation.

First, list all the types of self-talk that hurt your performance or produce other undesirable behaviors. The goal here is to recognize which situations produce negative thoughts and why. Then try to substitute a positive statement for the negative one. When this is accomplished, create a chart with negative self-talk in one column and corresponding positive self-talk in another (see Table 18.4).

Use the same guidelines to practice changing self-talk from negative to positive as you used for thought stopping. That is, use it in practice before trying it in competition. Also, because most negative thoughts occur under stress, you should first try to halt the negative thought and then take a deep breath. As you exhale, relax and repeat the positive statement.

We'll return soon to our discussion of concentration. Let's now look at attentional skills—specifically, how to assess attentional strengths and weaknesses.

Assessing Attentional Skills

Before you try to improve concentration, you should be able to pinpoint problem areas, such as undeveloped attentional skills. Nideffer's distinctions of

Table 18.4 Negative and Positive Self-Talk

Negative self-talk	change to	Positive self-talk
You idiot—how could you miss such an easy shot?		Everyone makes mistakes—just concentrate on the next point.
I'll never recover from this injury.		Healing takes time. Just continue to exercise every day.
He robbed me on the line call—that ball was definitely in.		There's nothing I can do about it. If I play well I'll win anyway.
I'll take it easy today and work out hard tomorrow.		If I work hard today then the next workout will be easier.
That was a terrible serve.		Just slow down and keep your rhythm and timing.
I'll never stay with this exercise program.		Just take one day at a time and make exercise fun.
I never play well in the wind.		It's windy on both sides of the court. This just requires extra concentration.

attentional focus as internal or external and broad or narrow is useful in this regard. Nideffer argues that people have different attentional styles that contribute to differences in the quality of performance.

Test of Attentional and Interpersonal Style

Nideffer (1976) devised the Test of Attentional and Interpersonal Style (TAIS) to measure a person's attentional style, or disposition. The TAIS has 17 subscales, six of them measuring attentional style (the others measure interpersonal style and cognitive control). Notice in Table 18.5 that three of the scales indicate aspects of effective focusing (broad-external, broad-internal, and narrow focus)

Table 18.5 Attentional Scales of the TAIS

Scale	Description
Broad-external	High scores indicate an ability to integrate many external stimuli simultaneously.
External overload	High scores indicate a tendency to become confused and overloaded with external stimuli.
Broad-internal	High scores indicate an ability to integrate several ideas at one time.
Narrow focus	High scores indicate an ability to narrow attention when appropriate.
Reduced focus	High scores indicate chronically narrowed attention.
Internal overload	High scores indicate a tendency to become overloaded with internal stimuli.

and three assess aspects of ineffective focusing (external overload, internal overload, reduced focus).

Effective Versus Ineffective Attentional Styles

People who concentrate well (effective attenders) deal well with simultaneous stimuli from external and internal sources (see Figure 18.5). They have high scores on broad-external and broad-internal focusing and can effectively switch their attention from broad to narrow focus when necessary. They are also low on the three measures of ineffective attention we just mentioned, which means they can attend to many stimuli (both internal and external) and not become overloaded with information. They also can narrow their attentional focus when necessary without omitting or missing any important information.

In contrast, people who don't concentrate well (ineffective attenders) tend to become confused and overloaded by multiple stimuli, both internal and external. When they assume either a broad-internal or broad-external focus, they have trouble narrowing their attentional width. For example, they may have trouble blocking out crowd noises or movement in the stands. Furthermore, the high score on the reduced-focus scale indicates that when they assume a narrow focus, it is so narrow that important information is left out. A soccer player, for example, might narrow his attentional focus to the ball and fail to see an opposing player alongside him who steals the ball. For ineffective attenders to perform better in sport competition, they must learn to switch direction of attention at will and to narrow or broaden attention as the situation demands.

TAIS as a Trait Measure

Nideffer's Test of Attentional and Interpersonal Style is a *trait* measure of a person's generalized way of attending to the environment. It does not consider situational factors. Recall the interactional paradigm from chapter 3, a model

> Effective attenders can attend to several stimuli without getting overloaded and can narrow attentional focus without leaving out important information. Ineffective attenders are easily confused by multiple stimuli.

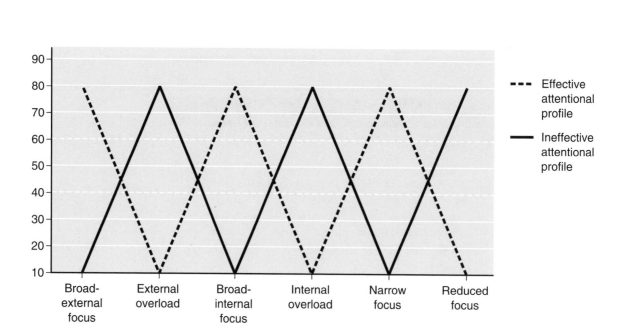

Figure 18.5 Effective and ineffective attentional profiles.

that more completely describes human behavior than the more traditional trait approach does. If a soccer coach used the TAIS to measure the attentional style of players without taking into consideration that different positions require different types of attentional focus, then she would gain little pertinent information for enhancing performance.

If it had sport-specific measures of attentional styles, the TAIS would be more useful because questions assessing attentional abilities would be directed at the specific skills employed in a particular sport. Sport-specific attentional style measures have been developed for tennis (Van Schoyck & Grasha, 1981) and pistol shooting (Etzel, 1979). Using sport-specific measures of attentional focus can help identify specific attentional weaknesses for athletes and coaches to work on.

Understanding a person's attentional style is a first step toward improving concentration skills. In the next section we suggest specific methods for improving attentional focus and shifting between types of attention.

Tips for Improving Concentration On Site

Being able to maintain a focus on relevant environmental cues is critical for effective performance. In describing ways to improve concentration, we'll focus first on things that can be done on the field of play. Then we'll suggest exercises that can be practiced at other times and places.

Tip #1—Practice With Distractions Present

It is amazing to observe how a small sound or movement by someone in the crowd can destroy a tennis player's or golfer's concentration. Yet many team

sport athletes (e.g., basketball, football, and soccer players) deal well with even hostile spectators who yell, wave their hands, and stomp their feet.

You can prepare yourself to cope with distractions by systematically practicing with typical distractions present. Some basketball coaches, for instance, have loud crowd noises piped in to get the players used to playing and shooting in that environment. Similarly, some tennis coaches have people stand around and talk or walk by the court from time to time to simulate match play.

Fans in individual sports such as tennis and golf tend to follow proper etiquette, keeping quiet and still during play and remaining passive. Conversely, team sport spectators often cheer loudly for the home team and even boo the visiting team. Thus, team sport athletes are exposed more to distractions and learn to play in spite of them. Individual sport athletes rarely face distractions in competition or practice and are thus less prepared to deal with them. Although practicing with distractions can help develop focus, many athletes avoid situations they find aversive. For example, if a baseball player does not like to bat when it's cold because it stings his hands, he will usually avoid practicing under such conditions. But then what happens when he has to bat in cold weather during an actual game? The more you practice under adverse conditions, the better prepared you will be to cope with these conditions during competition. Here's an example of how Jimmy Connors blocked out heat and humidity during a match to maintain his focus:

> It was hot out there—really hot—but I knew that if I started thinking too much about the sun, I wouldn't do my best. I didn't worry about it while I was on the court, but when I was sitting down, with the sun bearing down, it started to get to me a little. So I just blocked it out and pretended it wasn't there. That's what you have to do in tennis—not let yourself think about anything that can have a negative effect on your game (Tarshis, 1977, p. 45).

Tip #2—Use Cue Words

Put simply, cue words are used to trigger a particular response. They can be instructional (e.g., *follow-through, shoulders back, watch the ball, stretch*) or motivational or emotional (e.g., *strong, move, relax, hang in there, get tough*). The key is to keep the cue word simple and let it automatically trigger the desired response. For example, a gymnast performing a floor routine might use the cue word *forward* to make sure that she pushes ahead at a certain point during her performance. Similarly, a sprinter might say *explode* to make sure that he gets off the starting blocks well. Or, a figure skater might say *glide* to make sure she keeps her balance between jumps. It is important that these cue words be used in practice so that they become familiar and well learned before being used in competition.

Cue words are particularly useful when you are trying to vary or change a movement pattern—whether it be changing your golf swing, batting stance, aerobic dance routine, or service motion. In the training room, athletes could use cue words like *relax* or *easy* when stretching injured muscles and joints.

Attentional cues are also helpful for trying to break a bad habit. For instance, if a miler tends to tighten up in the last lap of a race and her stride becomes shorter, thus spoiling her rhythm, a cue such as *smooth, stretch,* or *relax* might help her keep focused on relaxing and lengthening her stride. Similarly, a hockey player might use the cue *stick to ice* to remind himself to keep his stick on the ice until he has control of the puck.

Cue words should be either instructional or motivational to help focus on the task at hand.

Tip #3—Employ Nonjudgmental Thinking

One of the biggest obstacles athletes face in maintaining concentration is the tendency to evaluate performance and classify it as good or bad. That is, they assign a positive or negative value to what they do. Such judgments tend to elicit personal, ego-involved reactions.

The process of evaluating and judging what you do on the athletic field or in exercise class usually results in performance declines. After you become judgmental about a portion of your performance or behavior, it is common to start generalizing. For example, a soccer player who misses a couple of opportunities to score a goal might think, "I always miss the easy ones," "I'm just a choke artist," or "I just can't kick one when I need to." Such thoughts and judgments make you lose your fluidness, timing, and rhythm. What happens is that your brain starts to override your body, causing excess muscle tension, excess effort, concentration lapses, and impaired decision making. Suppose someone in an exercise class misses a few workouts and thinks, "I just don't have what it takes to stay with the program." Such thinking undermines her motivation to adhere to an exercise program (see chapter 20).

Instead of judging the worth of a performance and categorizing it as either good or bad, you should learn to look at your actions nonjudgmentally. This doesn't mean you should ignore errors and mistakes but that you should see your performance as it is, without adding judgments. For instance, a baseball pitcher realizes he doesn't have good control today—he has walked four batters in the first 3 innings and thrown more balls than strikes. He knows that the manager is getting edgy and that if he continues this pattern he'll soon be taken out of the game. This observation could lead him to generalize that he's a bad pitcher and doesn't have control over his pitches. This thinking could lead to anger, frustration, and discouragement.

Instead, this pitcher could evaluate how he is pitching and notice that most of his pitches out of the strike zone have been high, rather than low. This might tell him that he is not following through properly and so the ball is getting away from him on delivery. In response, he focuses on getting a good wrist snap and following through to keep the ball from rising on him. In this way he has used his performance evaluation constructively, which translates into better performance and a more enjoyable experience.

Tip #4—Establish Routines

Routines can focus concentration and be extremely helpful to mental preparation for an upcoming performance. The effectiveness of routines has substantial support (see Cohn, Rotella, & Lloyd on golf, 1990; Feltz & Landers' mental rehearsal, 1983; Kirschenbaum, Ordman, Tomarken, & Holtzbauer on bowling, 1982; Lobmeyer & Wasserman on basketball, 1986; Moore on tennis, 1986; Nacson & Schmidt's set hypothesis, 1971; Orlick on skiing, 1986; and Schmidt's schema theory, 1975).

The mind often starts to wander during breaks in the action. Such times are ideal for routines. For example, a tennis player during changeovers might sit in a chair, take a deep breath, and image what she wants to do in the next game. Then she might repeat two or three cue words to help focus attention before taking the court. Routines can help structure the time before performance and between performances so that the athlete can be mentally focused when it's time to perform.

Routines can be used before or during an event to focus attention, reduce anxiety, eliminate distractions, and enhance confidence.

The routines of athletes vary from short and simple to complex and lengthy. Some border on superstition, such as wearing a lucky pair of socks, tying your shoelaces a certain way, or walking to the pitcher's mound without stepping on the foul lines. The routine needs to be comfortable and help sharpen focus as the time of performance nears. Preperformance routines structure the athlete's thought processes and emotional states, keeping the focus of attention in the present and on task-related cues. (See Table 18.6 for examples of preperformance routines for tennis and golf.)

Table 18.6   Sport-Specific Examples of Performance Routines
Golf shot
1. Take a deep breath.
2. Look at the fairway lie and assess the weather conditions and possible hazards.
3. Look at the target and decide on the shot required.
4. Picture your target and the shot you want to hit. Imagine not only your swing but also the trajectory of the ball and its final resting place.
5. Address the ball, adjusting and readjusting your position until you feel comfortable.
6. Feel the shot with your whole body.
7. Again picture the desired shot and, while feeling the shot, think *target*.
8. Think *target* and swing.
Tennis serve
1. Determine positioning and foot placement.
2. Decide on service type and placement.
3. Adjust racquet grip and ball.
4. Take a deep breath.
5. Bounce the ball for rhythm.
6. See and feel the perfect serve.
7. Focus on ball toss and serve to programmed spot.

"The Lucky Chair"

Tennis players Tom Okker and Ray Moore were preparing to face each other in the semifinals of the Paris Indoor Championships. As they emerged from the locker room they began briskly walking side by side. By the time they were halfway to the umpire's chair their brisk pace seemed like a race. "You bet it was a race," said Moore later. "It was a race to see who could reach the lucky chair first. Of course, neither of us wanted to admit it. I had played well in the tournament, beating Vilas and Tanner, and on both occasions I had sat to the left of the umpire. Okker had been using that side during matches as well. Neither of us wanted to risk breaking the routine, so here we were engaged in this farce of trying to reach a certain spot on the court before the other guy, when we were supposed to be walking side by side. At the last moment, that bloody Okker broke all the rules and sprinted the last couple of yards, so of course I had no chance. I mean the man's quick as a hare. I was livid." (Weinberg, 1988, p. 167)

Tip #5—Practice Eye Control

Eye control is another method to focus concentration. Our eyes tend to wander (just like our minds) and focus on such distractions (task-irrelevant cues) as crowd motions, opponents' antics, officials' signals, coaches' outbursts, and teammates' behavior instead of on the task at hand (task-relevant cues). Many a race has been lost near the end by looking at the opposition instead of focusing on the finish line. Watching the runners take off on a hit-and-run in baseball instead of staying focused on the pitch is an attentional error. Similarly, a gymnast's looking around at other competitors while preparing to start her own floor exercise is an inappropriate attentional focus.

The key to eye control is to make sure your eyes do not wander to irrelevant cues. How many times have you heard athletes in tennis, golf, baseball, soccer, or volleyball say "watch the ball." You hear it a lot because, as you know from experience, keeping your eyes on the ball is easier said than done.

Here are some techniques to use for eye control:

- Keep your eyes on the floor.
- Focus on the equipment.
- Focus on a spot on the wall.

For example, a basketball player on the free-throw line shooting in front of a hostile crowd may want to keep his head down and eyes on the floor until he is ready to look up at the basket and focus on the rim. A tennis player might focus on the strings of her racquet between points to keep from looking at the opponent or the crowd. Preparing to dive, a diver might focus on a spot on the wall. The key is to pick something that can maintain your focus of attention and prevent your eyes from wandering.

Tip #6—Stay Focused in the Present

The importance of keeping focused in the present cannot be overemphasized. Because the mind is so open to incoming messages, it is hard to keep a present focus. The mind wants to replay that missed shot and review that error in judgment or blown assignment. It also wants to look ahead to what might happen in the future. But past- and future-oriented thinking usually creates attentional problems.

Staying in the present requires a focused concentration throughout the event. It's okay to take an occasional brief mental break during stops in the action. But it is important then to have a cue word like *focus* to help bring you back into the present when it's time to start competing again.

Exercises to Improve Concentration

Besides the six tips to improve concentration on the field, several other techniques can increase concentration skills. They can be adapted to any sport.

Exercise #1—Learning to Shift Attention

This exercise can be practiced in its entirety or broken down into separate exercises (Gauron, 1984). Before starting the exercises, sit or lie down in a comfortable position and take a few deep breaths from the diaphragm. Begin the technique when you are comfortable and relaxed.

1. Pay attention to what you hear. Take each separate sound and label it, such as voices, footsteps, or the radio. Next, listen to all the sounds around you without attempting to label or classify them. Simply dismiss your thoughts and listen to the blend of sounds as if you were listening to music.

2. Now become aware of body sensations, such as the feeling of the chair, floor, or bed supporting you. Mentally label each sensation as you notice it. Before moving on to another sensation, let each sensation linger for a moment while you examine it closely, considering its quality and source. Finally, try to experience all of these sensations at once without labeling any of them. This will require a broad internal focus.

3. Turn your attention to your own thoughts and emotions. Let each emotion or thought just arise; do not try to specifically think about anything. Remain relaxed and at ease, no matter what you are thinking or feeling. Now try to experience each of your feelings and thoughts one at a time. Finally, see if you can just let go of all these thoughts and emotions and relax.

4. Open your eyes and pick an object across the room and directly in front of you. While looking straight ahead, see as much of the room and as many objects there as your peripheral vision allows. Now try to narrow your focus of attention to just the object centered in front of you. Continue to narrow your focus until that is the only object in view. Now expand your focus little by little, widening your perspective until you can see everything in the room. Think of your external focus as a zoom lens; practice zooming in and out, narrowing or broadening your attentional focus according to your preference.

By shifting your focus across internal-external and broad-narrow dimensions, this exercise helps you experience different attentional styles. The exercise also demonstrates why different perspectives are needed to perform the various skills required in different sports.

Exercise #2—Learning to Maintain Focus

Find a quiet place with no distractions. Choose an object to focus on (you might choose something related to the sport that you play, such as a hockey puck, soccer ball, baseball, or volleyball). Hold the object in your hands. Get a good sense of how it feels, its texture, color, and any other distinguishing characteristics. Now put the object down and focus your attention on it, examining it in great detail. If your thoughts wander, bring your attention back to the object.

Record how long you can maintain your focus on the object. It isn't easy to stay focused on one object. Once you are able to maintain focus for at least 5 minutes, start practicing with distractions present. Chart how long you can maintain your attention under these conditions. You will enhance your performance capabilities if you can become proficient at maintaining your concentration despite distractions and disruptions.

Exercise #3—Searching for Relevant Cues

The grid exercise has been used extensively in Eastern Europe as a precompetition screening device. It can give you a sense of what it means to be totally focused. The exercise requires a block grid containing two-digit numbers ranging from 00 to 99 (see Table 18.7). The object is to scan the grid and within a set period of time (usually 1 or 2 minutes) mark a slash through as many sequential numbers as possible (00, 01, 02, 03, etc.). The same grid can be used several times by just starting with a higher number (e.g., 33, 41, 51, etc.) than in your previous attempt. You can make new grids using any combination of numbers. People who intensely concentrate, scan, and store relevant cues reportedly score in the upper 20s and into the 30s in terms of how many numbers they find in sequence in 1 minute.

Table 18.7		Concentration Grid Exercise							
32	42	39	34	99	19	64	44	03	77
37	97	92	18	90	53	04	72	51	65
95	40	33	86	45	81	67	13	59	58
69	78	57	68	87	05	79	15	28	36
09	26	62	89	91	47	52	61	64	29
00	60	75	02	22	08	74	17	16	12
76	25	48	71	70	83	06	49	41	07
10	31	98	96	11	63	56	66	50	24
20	01	54	46	82	14	38	23	73	94
43	88	85	30	21	27	80	93	35	55

This exercise will help you learn to focus your attention and scan the environment for relevant cues (which is especially important in fast-moving sports such as basketball, hockey, and soccer), and you can modify it for different situations. For instance, you can scan the grid amidst different types of distractions, such as people talking or loud music. As your concentration improves, you will be better able to block out such distractions and focus exclusively on the task. And isn't this what most athletes want to accomplish in terms of concentration—complete absorption and the elimination of all distractions?

Exercise #4—Rehearsing Game Concentration

Using imagery or mental rehearsal is another good practice for concentration. For example, a football referee might picture making calls on different pass plays in which both offensive and defensive players make contact just as the ball is arriving. Sprinters might see themselves get a great start off the blocks, hit their strides, and then stay loose and relaxed during the last 20 yards in the race (where sprinters often tighten up). The use of imagery along with specific exercises is detailed in chapter 15.

Summary

Proper attentional focus is a key psychological skill in sport performance. The ability to maintain focus on relevant cues in the environment is critical for success in many sports. However, maintaining concentration and appropriate focus is difficult, and several problems may occur. These include future- and past-oriented thinking as well as attending to too many cues. Choking, which many athletes fear, is a process of improper attentional focus interacting with excess anxiety levels.

There are four types of attentional focus: broad-internal, broad-external, narrow-internal, and narrow-external. Different sports require different attentional focus for optimal performance. The ability to change attentional focus rapidly is an important skill in fast-moving sports. Attentional style can be measured by the Test of Attentional and Interpersonal Style (TAIS), and strengths and weaknesses can be assessed for developing programs to improve attentional focus. Practicing simple techniques and exercises will improve concentration skills.

Review Questions

1. Why is the ability to maintain focus on relevant cues essential to the definition of a proper attentional focus?

2. Explain the old saying, "fatigue makes cowards of us all." Include an athletic situation where fatigue is common and concentration requirements are high.

3. Why is concentration not an "all-or-none" phenomenon? Use athletic examples to explain the different types of concentration (according to Nideffer) and the situations for which they are appropriate.

4. Provide an example from a sport and discuss the kinds of shifts in attentional focus that Nideffer describes.

5. What are some attentional problems that affect focus and impair performance?

6. When is it appropriate to have an internal-narrow focus on body mechanics and movements? When is this focus inappropriate? What impact do physical and psychological skill development have on an appropriate attentional focus during competition?

7. Choking is a process, not solely a poor performance at a critical time. Describe this process, giving a specific sport example. What could the athlete have done to avoid choking?

8. Nideffer's Test of Attentional and Interpersonal Style (TAIS) is a trait measure of a person's generalized way of attending to the environment. What are the limitations inherent in a trait measure of an athlete's perceptions? What could be done to make the TAIS a better assessment tool?

9. What steps would you take in setting up an athletic practice using concentration-enhancing techniques? Explain why each technique is likely to get participants to focus on the relevant stimuli.

10. Discuss why routines work as preparation for performance and the best time to perform a routine.

11. How could you use mental imagery to learn to shift attention, maintain focus, and search for relevant cues?

12. Describe the different types and uses of self-talk. Give a practical example of thought stopping to enhance performance.

References

Cohn, P.J., Rotella, R.J., & Lloyd, J.W. (1990). Effects of a cognitive-behavioral intervention on the preshot routine and performance in golf. *The Sport Psychologist*, **4**, 33-47.

Etzel, E. (1979). Validation of a conceptual model characterizing attention among international rifle shooters. *Journal of Sport Psychology*, **1**, 281-290.

Feltz, D.L., & Landers, D.M. (1983). The effects of mental practice on motor skill learning and performance: A meta-analysis. *Journal of Sport Psychology*, **5**, 25-57.

Gauron, E. (1984). *Mental training for peak performance*. Lansing, NY: Sport Science Associates.

Kirschenbaum, D.S., Ordman, A.M., Tomarken, A.J., & Holtzbauer, R. (1982). Effects of differential self-monitoring and level of mastery on sports performance: Brain power bowling. *Cognitive Therapy and Research, 6*, 335-342.

Lobmeyer, D.L., & Wasserman, E.A. (1986). Preliminaries to free throw shooting: Superstitious behavior? *Journal of Sport Behavior, 9*, 70-78.

Moore, W.E. (1986). *Covert-overt service routines: The effects of a service routine training program on elite tennis players*. Unpublished doctoral dissertation, University of Virginia.

Nacson, J., & Schmidt, R.A. (1971). The activity-set hypothesis for warm-up decrement. *Journal of Motor Behavior, 3*, 1-15.

Nideffer, R. (1981). The ethics and practice of applied sport psychology. Ithaca, NY: Mouvement.

Nideffer, R. (1976). Test of attentional and interpersonal style. *Journal of Personality and Social Psychology, 34*, 394-404.

Orlick, T. (1986). *Psyching for sport: Mental training for athletes*. Champaign, IL: Leisure Press.

Schmidt, R.A. (1975). A schema theory of discrete motor skill learning. *Psychological Review, 82*, 225-260.

Silva, J.M., & Applebaum, M.I. (1989). Association and dissociation patterns of United States Olympic Marathon Trial Contestants. *Cognitive Therapy and Research, 13*, 185-192.

Tarshis, B. (1977). *Tennis and the mind*. New York: Tennis Magazine.

Van Schoyck, S.R., & Grasha, A.F. (1981). Attentional style variations and athletic ability: The advantages of sport-specific test. *Journal of Sport Psychology, 3*, 149-165.

Weinberg, R. (1988). *The mental advantage: Developing your psychological skills in tennis*. Champaign, IL: Human Kinetics.

Enhancing Health and Well-Being

I n the last 20 years we have witnessed an increased interest in
health, exercise, and wellness, including exercise and health
psychology. With greater attention has come more understanding of the role that psychological factors play in health and
exercise. This part focuses on what we have learned in this area.

The part begins with two chapters that specifically address exercise. In chapter 19 we examine the psychological benefits of exercise, such as reduced depression and anxiety, and tell you how
to maximize these benefits. Chapter 20 contains discussion of
exercise motivation and ways to keep people exercising regularly.

Chapters 21, 22, and 23 all deal with more general health-related concerns. Chapter 21 focuses on the psychological antecedents and consequences of athletic- and exercise-induced injuries and the role of psychological factors in injury rehabilitation. In chapter 22, we'll examine two of today's most critical concerns—substance abuse and eating disorders. We'll prepare you to recognize the signs of such problems and help those who are afflicted receive the specialized assistance they require. Finally, chapter 23 examines the potential negative effects of athletic and exercise participation, including close looks at burnout and overtraining.

After reading this part you'll have an excellent understanding of the interrelations of psychological factors and exercise and health, which will help you develop safe, effective programs for the participants you work with. You will also know how to deal with such problems as athletic injuries, overtraining, eating disorders, and substance abuse.

Exercise and Psychological Well-Being

Much of technology was meant to make our lives easier. In fact, the advent of car phones, fax machines, computers, and other communication devices has made our world increasingly complex and pressured. Ever more demands seem to be built into our daily existence, and noise, smog, inflation, unemployment, drug abuse, and random violence add still more stress to our lives. These demands have affected the mental health and psychological well-being of our society.

About 15 million Americans suffer from depression and between 10 and 12 million now suffer from anxiety or stress reactions. Although people typically deal with these mood disturbances through psychological counseling, drug therapy, or both, some are looking to exercise to promote their psychological well-being (see Table 19.1). Which benefits are wishful thinking and which are supported by empirical research? We hope you will find the answers in this chapter.

In this chapter you will learn about

▌ the short- and long-term effects of exercise on anxiety and depression,

▌ runner's high,

▌ positive and negative addiction to exercise,

▌ the relation among exercise, personality changes, and cognitive functioning,

▌ how to explain the effects exercise has on psychological well-being, and

▌ exercise as an adjunct to therapy.

Table 19.1 Psychological Benefits of Exercise in Clinical and Nonclinical Populations	
Increases	**Decreases**
Academic performance	Absenteeism at work
Assertiveness	Alcohol abuse
Confidence	Anger
Emotional stability	Anxiety
Intellectual functioning	Confusion
Internal locus of control	Depression
Memory	Headaches
Perception	Hostility
Positive body image	Phobias
Self-control	Psychotic behavior
Sexual satisfaction	Tension
Well-being	Type A behavior
Work efficiency	Work errors

Adapted from Taylor, Sallis, and Needle (1985).

Exercise in the Reduction of Anxiety and Depression

Mental health problems account for some 30% of the total days of hospitalization in the United States and about 9% of total medical costs, with the Social Security Administration ranking them third as a cause of disability. The psychological variables that have received the most attention are anxiety and depression. Although millions of Americans suffer from anxiety disorders and depression, not all of them have psychopathological states; many simply have subjective distress, a broader description of unpleasant emotions. For these people, regular exercise appears to have therapeutic value in reducing feelings of anxiety and depression.

So far, most studies investigating the relation of exercise and reductions in anxiety and depression have been correlational, which means we cannot conclusively state that exercise caused or produced the change in mood state. Rather, exercise appears to be *associated* with positive changes in mood states.

The vast majority of research investigating the relation between exercise and psychological well-being has used aerobic exercise. It has shown that exercise needs to be of sufficient duration and intensity to produce positive psychological effects. Therefore, the discussion in this chapter is about the relation of *aerobic* activity and psychological well-being.

Acute Effects of Aerobic Exercise

Acute effects refer to immediate and possibly, but not necessarily, transitory effects arising from a single bout of exercise. They are usually measured to assess psychological states directly after exercise. Most research on acute effects of exercise has focused on reducing anxiety. When researchers refer to the tranquilizing effect of exercise on anxiety, they usually mean *somatic* anxiety, not cognitive anxiety (see chapter 6).

Bahrke and Morgan (1978) compared the effects of walking on a treadmill for 20 minutes at 70% of maximal heart rate to meditating or to resting quietly and found these three treatments all lowered state anxiety scores. They concluded that exercise, like rest or meditation, acts as a "time out" or diversion from the usual routine and that the physical aspect of exercise was not the main factor in lowering state anxiety. (An earlier study on an anaerobic activity, bowling, yielded similar results; see Byrd, 1964). We will return later in the chapter to this idea that exercise acts simply as a time out in reducing anxiety.

Exercise intensity, however, appears to be important in determining how well exercise reduces state anxiety. In a series of 7 experiments summarized by Morgan (1987), reductions in state anxiety were found only when exercise was performed at 70% of maximal heart rate. Exercise bouts of low or moderate intensity were not effective in reducing state anxiety.

Some studies have investigated whether exercise can reduce muscular tension. For example, deVries (1981) found that neuromuscular tension levels, as measured electromyographically, were reduced significantly after acute exercise bouts. The magnitude of the reported EMG changes over a 20-year period ranged from 25% to 58%.

How long does the tranquilizing effect of exercise last? Raglin and Morgan (1987) found that state anxiety was reduced for 2 hours after the exercise bout—whereas subjects in a control rest condition returned to baseline levels within 30 minutes. Another study evaluated men and women before and after

Although a cause-effect relation has not been established, regular exercise is associated with reductions in anxiety and depression.

Exercise needs to be of sufficient duration and intensity to produce positive psychological effects.

CAN'T THIS WAIT TILL I'M OLD, CAN I LIVE WHILE I'M YOUNG?
–PHISH

Aerobic and Anaerobic Exercise

Aerobic exercise is physical activity that increases the activity of pulmonary and cardiovascular systems. During aerobic exercise the body uses and transports oxygen to the working muscles to maintain the activity. Aerobic exercise includes such activities as brisk walking, running, swimming, step aerobics, cycling, aerobic dance, cross-country skiing, and rowing. The American College of Sports Medicine has suggested that to receive cardiovascular benefits from exercise, the exercise must be performed at least 20 to 30 minutes (duration) 3 to 5 times a week (frequency) at 60% to 85% of maximal heart rate (intensity). *Anaerobic* exercise, in contrast, is either of short duration or of insufficient intensity to require much transporting of oxygen to the working muscles. Anaerobic activities include weight lifting, golf, bowling, and baseball.

45 minutes of aerobic exercise. Both genders experienced significant decreases in state anxiety levels immediately after the exercise, but levels returned to the preexercise level within 4 to 6 hours (Seeman, 1978). After 24 hours the mean state anxiety levels were identical to the values before the exercise session. These findings suggest that regular exercise on a daily basis might reduce anxiety and prevent the onset of chronic anxiety.

Chronic Effects of Aerobic Exercise

Psychologists also have studied the long-term, or *chronic*, benefits of exercise, investigating in effect the axiom "a sound mind in a sound body." Research on the chronic effects of exercise has focused on changes in both anxiety and depression over time.

Exercise and Depression.   One early attempt to evaluate the influence of exercise on depression (Morgan, Roberts, Brand, & Feinerman, 1970) looked at groups of middle-aged men who participated in various 6-week training programs (e.g., jogging, swimming, circuit training, and cycling), comparing them to controls who remained sedentary for the 6 weeks. The exercise groups became more physically fit, whereas the control group did not, but neither

Acute Effects of Exercise on Anxiety

- Aerobic exercise is associated with more consistent reductions in state anxiety than anaerobic exercise is.

- Reductions in state anxiety after exercise may not be due to the physical activity but to the "time out" from daily stress and hassles.

- Exercise intensity of at least 70% of maximal heart rate appears to be associated with the greatest reductions in postexercise state anxiety.

- Postexercise reductions in state anxiety return to preexercise anxiety levels within 24 hours.

- Exercise is associated with reductions in muscle tension.

group's subjects with no history of clinical depression exhibited changes in depression levels. However, all 11 of the subjects who manifested depression at the outset of the study did experience a decrease in depression after training. These results are consistent with several other research studies that have found that exercise appears most helpful in relieving depression for subjects who are clinically depressed as opposed to "normal" (North, McCullagh, & Tran, 1990).

In another interesting study, depressed subjects (as diagnosed by the National Institute of Mental Health) were randomly divided into (a) running, (b) time-limited psychotherapy, or (c) time-unlimited psychotherapy groups. The runners met individually with a running therapist three times a week for 45 minutes. The psychotherapy subjects also met individually with a therapist, in 10-minute sessions for the time-limited therapy and without a time limit for the time-unlimited therapy. After 10 weeks, the runners showed a significant decrease in depression scores, comparable to the best outcomes obtained by either psychotherapy group (Griest, Klein, Eischens, & Faris, 1978).

Exercise and Anxiety.   Researchers have studied the possible association of long-term exercise and reduced anxiety. Investigations have involved programs that typically last about 2 to 4 months with 2 to 4 exercise sessions per week. Two studies (Long, 1984; Long & Haney, 1988) compared different anxiety-reduction techniques, such as stress inoculation and progressive relaxation, to jogging as stress-management interventions. In both studies, the jogging groups and stress-management groups exhibited significant decreases in state anxiety over the course of the intervention period. But, more important, these reductions in state anxiety were maintained in follow-ups of up to 15 weeks (see Figure 19.1).

In one interesting study, subjects were randomly assigned to either a high-intensity aerobic training regimen, moderate-intensity training regimen, or a strengthening and stretching regimen, which served as a placebo condition (Moses, Steptoe, Mathews, & Edwards, 1989). All three regimens were equated for frequency (four sessions per week) and duration (10 weeks) of sessions. The moderate-intensity aerobic exercise group exhibited a decrease in anxiety, whereas the other two groups showed no changes in anxiety. The high-intensity

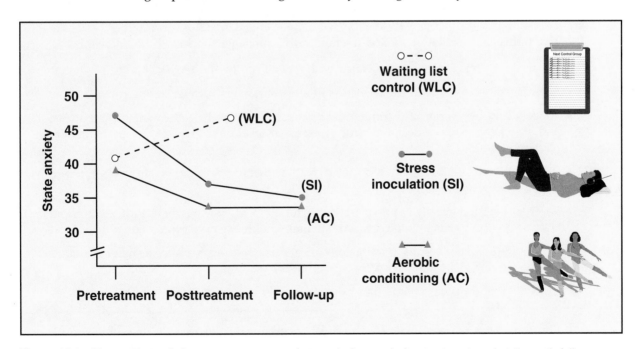

Figure 19.1   Mean ratings of change on measures of stress before and after treatment, and at 3-month follow-up. Adapted from Long (1984).

Exercise and Depression

- Regular exercise has been shown to be related to long-term decreases in depression.

- The greater the total number of exercise sessions, the greater the decrease in depression.

- Exercise intensity is not related to changes in depression.

- The longer the exercise program, the greater the reduction in depression.

- The total exercise time per week is not related to changes in depression.

aerobics group showed the greatest gains in fitness. These results suggest that greater physiological gain does not necessarily lead to greater psychological gain. Other studies also show a relation between exercise and anxiety reduction over time, but definitive conclusions cannot yet be drawn.

The consensus statements in the box below maintain that exercise is associated with but does not *cause* changes in emotional states. Furthermore, we need to understand that the improvement in mental and emotional health associated with regular physical activity does not typically occur among people in the normal range of mental and psychological functioning for anxiety and depression.

Exercise and Mood Changes

Mood is generally defined as a state of emotional or affective arousal of varying but not permanent duration. Feelings of elation or happiness lasting a few

Chronic Exercise and Mental Health

The National Institute of Mental Health convened a panel to discuss the possibilities and limitations of physical activity for coping with stress and depression (Morgan & Goldston, 1987). In terms of chronic exercise and mental health, the panel concluded the following:

- Physical fitness is positively associated with mental health and well-being.

- Exercise is associated with the reduction of stress emotions such as state anxiety.

- Anxiety and depression are common symptoms of failure to cope with mental stress, and exercise has been associated with a decreased level of mild to moderate depression and anxiety.

- Long-term exercise is usually associated with reductions in traits such as neuroticism and anxiety.

- Severe depression usually requires professional treatment, which may include medication, electroconvulsive therapy, and/or psychotherapy, with exercise as an adjunct.

- Appropriate exercise results in reductions in various stress indexes such as neuromuscular tension, resting heart rate, and some stress hormones.

- Current clinical opinion holds that exercise has beneficial emotional effects across ages and genders.

- Physically healthy people who require psychotropic medication may safely exercise under close medical supervision.

hours or even a few days are examples of moods, whereas confidence or self-esteem are more representative of a personality trait. Mood changes have been studied in a variety of settings, but a particular focus has been on runners.

Mood is generally defined as a state of emotional or affective arousal of varying impermanent duration.

The Runner's High

Many regular exercisers report feeling better psychologically, emotionally, and spiritually after exercising. This phenomenon is so pervasive among runners that the feeling has been dubbed the "runner's high." The feeling includes a sense of mental alertness and awareness, liberation, a lift in the legs, suppressed pain or discomfort, ease, perfect rhythm, and exhilaration.

Defining the Runner's High. Sachs found 27 different adjectives or phrases used in the literature to describe the runner's high (1984), including euphoria, spirituality, power, gracefulness, moving without effort, glimpse of perfection, and spinning out. He consolidated these to define the runner's high as a euphoric sensation experienced during running, usually unexpected, in which the runner feels a heightened sense of well-being, enhanced appreciation of nature, and a transcendence of time and space. This definition resembles aspects of peak performance and especially of flow (Csikszentmihalyi, 1975; see chapter 8) in that the runner's high requires rhythmic, long-lasting, and uninterrupted activity.

The runner's high is a euphoric sensation, usually unexpected, of heightened well-being, enhanced appreciation of nature, and transcendence of time and space.

Characteristics of the Runner's High. In a qualitative study, Sachs (1980) interviewed 60 regular runners to discover what conditions (internal to the runner and external in the environment) facilitate the runner's high. They told him that the runner's high cannot be reliably predicted but is facilitated by few distractions and cool, calm weather with low humidity. It requires long distances (6 or more miles) and at least 30 minutes of running at a comfortable

---

The Runner's High

Runners themselves probably best describe the runner's high:

The first half hour is pure agony—exaggerated body pain and philosophical crisis. Thirty minutes out and something lifts. Legs and arms become light and rhythmic. The fatigue goes away and feelings of power begin. "I think I'll run 25 miles today. I'll double the size of the research grant request. I'll have that talk with the dean and tolerate no equivocating. . . ." Then, another switch, from fourth gear into overdrive. . . . Sometime into the second hour comes the spooky time. Colors are bright and beautiful, water sparkles, clouds breathe, and my body, swimming, detaches from the earth. A loving contentment invades the basement of my mind, and thoughts bubble up without trails. I find the place I need to live if I'm going to live. (Black, 1979, p. 79)

My first step I felt lighter and looser than ever before. My shirt clung to me, and I felt like a skeleton flying down a wind tunnel. My times at the mile were so fast that I almost felt like I was cheating. It was like getting a new body that no one else had heard about. My mind was so crystal clear that I could have held a conversation. The only sensation was the rhythm and the beat, all perfectly natural, all and everything part of everything else. . . . Distance, time, motion were all one. There were myself, the cement, a vague feeling of legs, and the coming dusk. I tore on. I could have run and run. Perhaps I had experienced a physiological change, but whatever, it was magic. I came to the side of the road and cried tears of joy and sorrow. Joy for being alive; sorrow for a vague feeling of temporalness, and a knowledge of the impossibility of giving this experience to anyone. (Mike Spino, 1971, p. 222)

pace—although there must be no concern with pace or time. The runners described the mood as a very positive psychological state with feelings of well-being, euphoria, relaxation, and effortlessness.

Individual Differences in the Runner's High.   Not every runner who puts on running shoes experiences a runner's high. But Lilliefors (1978) found that 78% of runners surveyed reported a sense of euphoria during their runs. Forty-nine percent said the euphoria was occasionally spiritual in nature. Along these lines, Sachs (1980) found that 77% of 60 runners he interviewed reported that they had experienced the runner's high at least a few times. Several runners said they experienced the high in nearly 30% of their regular runs. On the other hand, only 10% of another group of runners Sachs (1978) surveyed earlier had experienced the runner's high.

> Runners differ regarding how often they experience the runner's high, and each may require a slightly different set of conditions.

Exercise and Mood Changes—Research Findings

Considerable experiential and anecdotal evidence supports the existence of the runner's high. Other findings have emerged from research about the relation between various forms of exercise and changes in mood states. These include the following:

- Aerobic activities such as running, swimming, and aerobic dance are associated with more positive changes in mood than are anaerobic activities.
- Low-intensity exercise activities (e.g., walking) are associated with more positive changes in mood than are high-intensity activities.
- Exercisers demonstrate more positive mood states than do nonexercisers.
- Massage also is related to increases in positive mood states.

How Exercise Enhances Psychological Well-Being

The evidence we've reviewed thus far suggests a positive relation between exercise and psychological well-being. Several hypotheses, both psychological and physiological, have been proposed to explain how exercise works to enhance well-being. We will focus on two of them: the distraction hypothesis (psychological) and the endorphin hypothesis (physiological).

Distraction Hypothesis

As we touched upon earlier, one psychological explanation is that *distraction* from stressful events rather than the activity itself accounts for the improved feelings associated with exercise. Support for the distraction hypothesis comes from the Bahrke and Morgan experiment (1978) where subjects were randomly assigned to an exercise, meditation, or distraction group and given the various treatments for 20 minutes each. The exercise group ran on a treadmill; the meditation group practiced a relaxation procedure; and the distraction group rested quietly in easy chairs in a sound-filtered room. It turned out that exercise at 70% intensity, meditation, and quiet rest all were equally effective in reducing anxiety immediately after the conclusion of the treatment.

The distraction hypothesis maintains that exercise acts as a "time out" from stressful life events. Exercise does not produce greater reductions in anxiety than control conditions, but the anxiety-reduction effects last longer after exercise.

In another experiment a running group, an exercise class, and a group eating lunch all had significant decreases in state anxiety immediately after completing their activities (Wilson, Berger, & Bird, 1981). Thus, exercise appears to reduce anxiety by providing a "time out" from stress. However, as previously noted, this reduction in anxiety lasts longer after exercise than after simply resting.

Endorphin Hypothesis

The *endorphin hypothesis* is the most popular physiologically based explanation for the benefits derived from exercise. Not all studies support this hypothesis, but from the weight of the evidence it appears tenable. As you may know, the brain, pituitary gland, and other tissues produce various endorphins that can reduce the sensation of pain and produce a state of euphoria. In a typical study, mood state and endorphin levels are measured before and after an exercise bout. Postexercise improvements in mood accompanied by increases in endorphin levels provide support for the endorphin theory. However, more research should test the theory before we draw definitive conclusions. It appears likely that the improvement in well-being following exercise is due to a combination of psychological and physiological mechanisms.

The endorphin hypothesis states that exercise releases endorphins that can give the exerciser a "natural high."

Addiction to Exercise

> I have run since infancy. . . . It's the passion of my life. Running as long as possible—I've made that into a sport. I have no other secrets. Without running I wouldn't be able to live.
>
> *Waldemar Cierpinski, 1980*

Cierpinski, the two-time gold medalist from East Germany, describes the exceptionally strong feelings about running that many runners share. The intense involvement with exercise, particularly running, has been described in such terms as compulsion (Abell, 1975), dependence (Sachs & Pargman, 1984), obsession (Waters, 1981), and addiction (Glasser, 1976). In the exercise psychology literature, most writers use the term *addiction* to refer to an intense involvement in exercise.

What Is Exercise Addiction?

Addiction to exercise is a psychological and/or physiological dependence on a regular regimen of exercise characterized by withdrawal symptoms after 24 to 36 hours without exercise (Sachs, 1981). Note that this definition incorporates both psychological and physiological factors. Some withdrawal symptoms are commonly associated with ceasing exercising, including anxiety, irritability, guilt, muscle twitching, a bloated feeling, and nervousness. But these occur only if an individual is prevented from exercising for some reason (e.g., injury, work, or family commitments) as opposed to purposefully taking a day or two off.

Positive Addiction to Exercise

The concept of positive addiction to exercise, running in particular, was popularized by William Glasser in his book *Positive Addiction*. Glasser argues that positive addictions such as running and meditation promote psychological strength and increase life satisfaction (1976). This is in sharp contrast to negative addictions, such as heroin or cocaine, that inevitably undermine psychological and physiological functioning. Furthermore, Glasser notes that people can use a positive addiction to help themselves become stronger. He sees exercise as a positive addiction that increases an individual's psychological and physical strength, thereby enhancing his or her state of well-being and functioning. Rather than standard quantitative assessments and analyses, Glasser's work includes qualitative data from clinical and psychiatric assessments. For example, reports of the runner's high and the general "feel good phenomenon" after exercise are sources that support Glasser's concept of positive addiction. (Kostrubala's book *The Joy of Running* [1976] also notes the positively addicting aspects of running.)

Exercise as a positive addiction means that a variety of psychological and physiological benefits will typically occur as a person continues to participate in regular physical activity. A positive addiction to exercise means that exercisers view their involvement in regular physical activity as important to their lives and can successfully integrate it with other aspects of their lives such as work, family, and friends.

Positive addiction to exercise implies that a variety of physiological and psychological benefits occur with regular physical activity.

Negative Addiction to Exercise

For most regular exercisers, exercise becomes a habit of daily activity, and this level of involvement represents a "healthy habit." That is, exercise complements other important aspects of life and is effective for managing anxiety and depression.

However, for a small percentage of people, exercise can control their lives (Morgan, 1979). Exercise then becomes a negative addiction that eliminates other choices in life. Lives become structured around exercise to such an extent that home and work responsibilities suffer and relationships take a backseat. This condition apparently reflects personal or social maladjustment and parallels other addictive processes with increasing dose dependence and withdrawal symptoms under deprivation. Table 19.2 provides criteria for classifying an activity as addictive.

Table 19.2 Criteria for Classifying an Activity as Addictive

1. The activity is noncompetitive and of one's own choice. About an hour each day is devoted to the activity.
2. The activity requires little skill or mental effort.
3. The activity is not dependent on others and is usually done alone.
4. The exerciser believes the activity is valuable.
5. The exerciser believes that persistence in the activity will lead to improvement.
6. The activity can be done without self-criticism.

Symptoms of Negative Addiction to Exercise

Several case studies about addicted runners reveal that they are totally consumed by the need to run, this being the driving force in their lives. Exercise addicts who are forced to stop running for a while often become depressed, anxious, and extremely irritable. Interpersonal relations in the home, work, and social settings decay, accompanied by restlessness, insomnia, and general fatigue. Tics, muscle tension and soreness, decreased appetite, and constipation or irregularity often develop. The true exercise addict continues even when the exercise is medically, vocationally, and socially contraindicated (Morgan, 1979). Diagnostic criteria for exercise dependence are:

- Stereotyped pattern of exercise with a regular schedule once or more daily
- Giving increasing priority over other activities to maintain the pattern of exercise
- Increased tolerance to the amount of exercise performed
- Withdrawal symptoms related to mood disorder following cessation of the exercise

- Relief of withdrawal symptoms by further exercise
- Subjective awareness of a compulsion to exercise
- Rapid reinstatement of the previous pattern of exercise and withdrawal symptoms after a period of abstinence

Many addicted exercisers recognize their symptoms of negative addiction themselves. The toll of strenuous training often shows itself in decreased ability to concentrate, listlessness, fatigue, lapses in judgment, and impaired social activity and work productivity. Because exercise addicts tend to be well-educated, many negatively addicted people can acknowledge these symptoms and recognize the effects that exercise is having on their lives (Sachs & Pargman, 1984). Still, accepting help is another matter. Exercise addicts often feel that though exercise may control their life, it enhances their existence. Runner and physician George Sheehan demonstrated this perspective when he wrote:

> The world will wait. Job, family, friends will wait; in fact, they must wait on the outcome. . . . Can anything have a higher priority than running? It defines me, adds to me, makes me whole. I have a job and family and friends that can attest to that. (1979, p. 49)

When an Addicted Exerciser Can't Exercise

What happens when an addicted exerciser is injured and cannot exercise? The exerciser will probably suffer withdrawal symptoms including tension, restlessness, irritability, depression, interpersonal problems, and feelings of guilt. One way to cope with an injury is to try other activities. A runner who injures her lower leg might still swim and possibly ride a bicycle. However, substitution will likely not satisfy the true addict. As one woman said when she pulled an Achilles tendon and had to substitute bicycling for running: "It was like methadone maintenance for a heroin addict." In such cases, other types of psychological therapy might be appropriate.

Negative addiction to exercise is characterized by a dependence on exercise. The addiction can result in problems at home, work, and in relationships. Not being able to exercise can cause severe depression.

Exercise and Changes in Personality and Cognitive Functioning

Our discussion thus far has been on the relation among exercise and anxiety, depression, and mood and on the concepts of positive and negative addiction to exercise. People have also wondered whether exercise has the potential to change personality and mental (cognitive) functioning. We'll briefly review the research in these areas and offer some suggestions to practitioners.

Personality

A classic study originally designed to determine the effects of a fitness program on middle-aged men led to some information on how exercise might change personality (Ismail & Young, 1973). Over the course of the program, the men improved their fitness levels and reported feeling dramatic psychological effects. They reported higher levels of self-confidence, greater feelings of control, improved imagination, and a greater sense of self-sufficiency. Recent research has lent support to these initial findings. However, overall the research is inconclusive and more study is needed in this area.

Exercise and Self-Concept. It is now commonly believed that changes in the body as a result of physical fitness training can alter one's body image and

thus enhance self-concept. Several studies support a positive relation between changes in fitness and increased self-esteem (Sonstroem & Morgan, 1989). Populations as diverse as adult females, college students, obese teenage males, 7th-grade males, elementary school children, and adult male rehabilitation clients have shown improvement in self-esteem after fitness programs. Similar changes in self-concept have been associated with directed play or physical education programs. Physical fitness activities were superior to other components of elementary school physical education programs in developing self-concept.

Regular exercise has been shown to be related to increased self-esteem.

There is a robust relation between fitness and self-concept that professionals in physical education need to be aware of. A strong self-concept is critical to the healthy psychological development and adjustment of children, and exercise can be an important ingredient in helping children and adults feel good about themselves. Exercise can influence self-esteem via agents such as:

- An increase in physical fitness
- Goal achievement
- Feelings of somatic well-being
- A sense of competence, mastery, or control
- Adoption of associated health behaviors
- Social experiences
- Experimental attention
- Reinforcement by significant others (Sonstroem, 1984)

Exercise and Hardiness. Hardiness is a personality style that enables a person to withstand or cope with stressful situations. Stress produces minimal debilitating effects in a hardy personality. You are hardy if you have these three traits:

- a sense of personal control over external events,
- a sense of involvement, commitment, and purpose in daily life, and
- the flexibility to adapt to unexpected changes by perceiving them as challenges or opportunities for further growth (Gentry & Kosaba, 1979).

Exercise can help protect against stress-related illness, especially for hardy people.

Some research has focused on how exercise combined with hardiness can reduce some of the negative effects of stress. One study found that business executives who scored high in both hardiness and exercise remained healthier than those who scored high in only one or the other component. In other words, a hardy personality and exercise in combination are more effective in preserving health than either one alone.

Cognitive Functioning

For a long time we have assumed motor development to be important to the development of intelligence in children (Piaget, 1936). Learning potential presumably will vary with physical fitness level. Since the 1970s researchers have looked for evidence that these two assumptions are valid. So far the search has yielded conflicting findings (Tomporowski & Ellis, 1986). Specifically, some researchers report that exercise facilitates cognitive abilities during and after exercise, whereas others show that exercise either impairs or has no effect on mental functioning. Let's look more closely.

Short-duration, high-intensity exercise enhances mental functioning, whereas strenuous exercise for long durations can inhibit performance unless the athlete is extremely physically fit.

Subjects who perform very brief but intense exercise (e.g., lifting weights) exhibit improved mental processes. This suggests that exercise may initially facilitate attentional processes by directly affecting the central nervous system. However, as the exercise increases in duration, the facilitating effects may be offset by muscular fatigue. Thus, physical fitness level is critical in determining whether exercise will be beneficial or detrimental to mental functioning.

This is an important point. Athletes are asked increasingly to make critical, split-second decisions that involve analyzing a great deal of information quickly and correctly. An athlete who is physically fit might be better able to react mentally and respond effectively as fatigue becomes a factor late in a contest.

Picture a football quarterback at the end of a game. His team is losing by two points and driving for a potentially winning field goal. The quarterback, tired after scrambling throughout the game on a hot and humid afternoon, goes back to throw a pass. He sees all of his receivers are covered and a blitzing linebacker coming right at him. Instead of just taking a sack and a loss of yardage, he decides to throw the ball into a crowd. It is intercepted, and any chance of winning vanishes. The poor decision to throw the ball up for grabs might have been partly due to fatigue clouding his thinking.

Exercise as an Adjunct to Therapy

The mind can have a great impact on the body. Just think how common psychosomatic disorders are, such as migraine headaches, peptic ulcers, hypertension, and sexual impotence. Fortunately, research has found that the body, appropriately used, can affect the mind in constructive ways (Folkins & Sime, 1981).

Literally millions of Americans suffer from some sort of depression or anxiety disorder every year, yet research demonstrates that exercise can help reduce such negative psychological states. It also suggests that aerobic exercise is related to other positive changes, including enhanced self-esteem, improved mood, and higher levels of work productivity. Not surprisingly, the use of physical interventions, including some form of exercise, has received increased attention since the late 1970s (Griest, Klein, Eischens, & Faris, 1978).

Running as an Adjunct to Therapy

Of all the aerobic activities shown to enhance psychological well-being, running has received the most attention in both the professional and popular literature. Running provides a natural, practical, inexpensive, and time-efficient adjunct to traditional psychotherapies. For example, one study on the use of running for treating depression found that running was four times more cost-effective than more traditional verbal-oriented psychotherapies (Griest et al., 1978). These results take on added importance considering the spiraling cost of health care and the present trend toward cost-effective counseling. Running therapies also provide additional health benefits, such as increased respiratory efficiency and cardiovascular endurance, as well as improvement in muscle tone, weight

Running can be an inexpensive, time-efficient adjunct to traditional psychotherapies and offers added health benefits such as increased cardiovascular efficiency and weight control.

Using Exercise as Therapy

Here are a few important points for using exercise as part of therapy:

- A precise diagnosis of the psychological problem and an individually tailored exercise program are optimal for enhancing well-being.

- Exercise should be an adjunct to other forms of therapy. A multimodal therapeutic approach is more effective than the use of a single intervention (Lazarus, 1976).

- Aerobic activities maintained over a period of time appear to produce the most positive psychological effects. A variety of aerobic activities is preferable to just one, as this enhances adherence to the exercise regimen.

- Exercise therapy should be done only by qualified professionals. Although no exact criteria has been established, Buffone (1984) suggests that formal training and practical experience in both the psychological and sport sciences is necessary since exercise therapy takes a multidisciplinary approach to treatment.

control, and blood volume. Finally, the use of running as therapy can encourage a positive approach to health promotion as clients can learn a healthier style of living through exercise.

Although exercise certainly appears to offer some psychological benefits, it certainly should not be used in all cases of depression, stress, or other emotional disorders. For example, Buffone (1984) argues that aerobic exercise therapy should not be prescribed for obese people (40% or more over ideal body weight), those with severe heart disease, or those with high blood pressure that cannot be controlled by medication. Exercise may also be contraindicated for the severely depressed and those with a tenuous contact with reality or suicidal tendencies (Kostrubala, 1976).

Summary

The role of exercise in enhancing well-being is becoming more important as increasing numbers of people face problems with anxiety and depression. Aerobic exercise is associated with reductions in anxiety and depression. Its relation to psychological well-being is correlational rather than causal in nature. Exercise effects tend to be more acute than chronic and people report feeling better immediately following exercise, an effect that tends to last for several hours. Runners especially have reported this "feel-better" phenomenon, often known as the runner's high. This feeling is felt only after running a considerable distance (usually at least 5 miles) at a comfortable pace.

Some runners and exercisers become so engaged in their exercise regimens that they become addicted to exercise. A positive addiction to exercise can be of great benefit psychologically and physiologically. However, when someone becomes controlled by the exercise, a positive addiction can turn into a negative one with adverse effects on personal relationships and the work environment.

Exercise has demonstrated a positive impact on a variety of areas such as building self-esteem, increasing feeling of control, improving self-confidence, and enhancing mental functioning. Both psychological and physiological explanations have been suggested for how exercise enhances psychological well-being, two of the most noted being the distraction and endorphin hypotheses. Because exercise is associated with positive psychological changes, it is commonly used as an adjunct to more traditional psychological therapies.

Review Questions

1. What is the difference between anaerobic and aerobic exercise? Which is more critical for improving psychological well-being?

2. Discuss the research findings on the acute effects of exercise on psychological well-being.

3. Discuss the chronic effects of exercise on psychological well-being as demonstrated by research findings.

4. List five conclusions about exercise and mental health reached by a National Institute of Mental Health panel.

5. Describe the characteristics of the "runner's high."

6. How do the distraction and endorphin hypotheses explain how exercise enhances psychological well-being?

7. Compare and contrast the characteristics of positive and negative addictions.

8. Describe the relation between exercise and changes in personality. What practical implications do these results have?

9. How does exercise affect cognitive functioning?

10. What limitations should you remember in using exercise as an adjunct to other types of therapy?

References

Abell, R. (1975). Confessions of a compulsive. *Runner's World*, **10**, 30-31.

Bahrke, M.S., & Morgan, W.P. (1978). Anxiety reduction following exercise and meditation. *Cognitive Therapy and Research*, **2**, 323-334.

Black, J. (1979). The brain according to Mandell. *Runner*, 1(7):78-80, 82, 84, 87.

Buffone, G. (1984). Exercise as a therapeutic adjunct. In J.M. Silva & R.S. Weinberg (Eds.), *Psychological foundations in sport and exercise* (pp. 445-451). Champaign, IL: Human Kinetics.

Byrd, D.E. (1964). Viewpoints of bowlers in respect to the relief of tension. *Physical Educator*, **21**, 119.

Cierpinski, W. (1980). *Track and Field News*, 27.

Csikszentmihalyi, M. (1975). *Beyond boredom and anxiety*. San Francisco: Jossey-Bass.

deVries, H.A. (1981). Tranquilizer effects of exercise: A critical review. *The Physician and Sportsmedicine*, **9**, 46-55.

Folkins, C.H., & Sime, W.E. (1981). Physical fitness training and mental health. *American Psychologist*, **36**, 373-389.

Gentry, W.D., & Kosaba, S.C. (1979). Social and psychological resources mediating stress illness relationships in humans. In R.B. Haynes, D.W. Taylor, & D. Sackett (Eds.), *Compliance in health care* (pp. 87-116). Baltimore: Johns Hopkins University Press.

Glasser, W. (1976). *Positive addition*. New York: Harper and Row.

Griest, J.H., Klein, M.H., Eischens, R.R., & Faris, J.T. (1978). Running out of depression. *The Physician and Sportsmedicine*, **6**, 49-56.

Ismail, A. II, & Young, R.J. (1973). The effect of chronic exercise on the personality of middle-aged men by univariate and multivariate approaches. *Journal of Human Ergology*, **2**, 47-57.

Kostrubala, T. (1976). *The joy of running*. Philadelphia: J.B. Lippincott.

Lazarus, A.A. (1976). *Multimodal behavior therapy*. New York: Springer.

Lilliefors, J. (1978). *The running mind*. Mountain View, CA: World Publications.

Long, B.C. (1984). Aerobic conditioning and stress inoculations: A comparison of stress management intervention. *Cognitive Therapy and Research*, **8**, 517-542.

Long, B.C., & Haney, C.J. (1988). Coping strategies for working women: Aerobic exercise and relaxation interventions. *Behavior Therapy*, **19**, 75-83.

Morgan, W.P. (1979). Negative addiction in runners. *Physician and Sportsmedicine*, 7(2):56-63, 67-70.

Morgan, W.P. (1987). Reduction of state anxiety following acute physical activity. In W.P. Morgan & S.E. Goldston (Eds.), *Exercise and mental health* (pp. 105-109). Washington, DC: Hemisphere.

Morgan, W.P., & Goldson, S.E. (1987). *Exercise and mental health*. Washington, DC: Hemisphere.

Morgan, W.P., Roberts, J.A., Brand, F.R., & Feinerman, A.D. (1970). Psychological effect of chronic physical activity. *Medicine and Science in Sports*, **2**, 213-217.

Moses, J., Steptoe, A., Mathews, A., & Edwards, S. (1989). The effects of exercise training on mental well-being in the normal population: A controlled trial. *Psychosomatic Research*, **33**, 47-61.

North, T.C., McCullagh, P., & Tran, Z.V. (1990). Effects of exercise on depression. *Exercise and Sport Science Reviews*, **18**, 379-415.

Piaget, J. (1936). *The moral judgment of the child*. New York: Harcourt & Brace.

Raglin, J.S., & Morgan, W.P. (1987). Influence of exercise and "distraction therapy" on state anxiety and blood pressure. *Medicine and Science in Sport and Exercise*, **19**, 456-463.

Sachs, M.L. (1978). *Selected psychological considerations in running*. Invited presentation at a running clinic. Tallahassee, FL.

Sachs, M.L. (1980). *On the trail of the runner's high—a descriptive and experimental investigation of characteristics of an elusive phenomenon*. Unpublished doctoral dissertation, Florida State University.

Sachs, M.L. (1981). Running addiction. In M.H. Sacks & M.L. Sachs (Eds.), *Psychology of running* (pp. 116-121). Champaign, IL: Human Kinetics.

Sachs, M.L. (1984). The runner's high. In M.L. Sachs & G.W. Buffone (Eds.), *Running as therapy: An integrated approach* (pp. 273-287). Lincoln: University of Nebraska Press.

Sachs, M.L., & Pargman, D. (1984). Running addiction. In M.L. Sachs & G.W. Buffone (Eds.), *Running as therapy: An integrated approach* (pp. 231-253). Lincoln: University of Nebraska Press.

Seeman, J.C. (1978). *Changes in state anxiety following vigorous exercise*. Unpublished master's thesis, University of Arizona.

Sheehan, G. (1979). Negative addiction: A runner's perspective. *Physician and Sportsmedicine*, **7**(6), 49.

Sonstroem, R.J. (1984). Exercise and self-esteem. In R.L. Terjung (Ed.), *Exercise and Sport Sciences Reviews* (pp. 123-125). Toronto: Collare.

Sonstroem, R.J., & Morgan, W.P. (1989). Exercise and self-esteem: Rationale and model. *Medicine and Science in Sport and Exercise*, **21**, 329-337.

Spino, M. (1971). Running as a spiritual experience. In J. Scott (Ed.), *The athletic revolution* (p. 222). New York: Free Press.

Tomporowski, P.D., & Ellis, N.R. (1986). Effects of exercise on cognitive process: A review. *Psychological Bulletin*, **99**, 338-346.

Waters, B. (1981). Defining the runner's personality. *Runner's World*, **33**, 48-51.

Wilson, V.E., Berger, B.G., & Bird, E.I. (1981). Effects of running on an exercise class. *Perceptual and Motor Skills*, **53**, 472-474.

CHAPTER 20

Exercise Adherence

From the looks of store windows we seem in the midst of a fitness craze. Athletic footwear appears in every color and for every sport. Athletic sportswear is in vogue not only for sport and physical activity but for leisure and even work apparel. The fitness clubs seem overrun by firm bodies, rippling muscles, and lean muscle mass. It seems that almost everyone wants to get fit. But the fact is that *most Americans do not regularly participate in physical activity* (Rejeski & Kenney, 1988).

Let's look at some statistics to get a better idea of the level of exercise participation in the United States. The Department of Health and Human Services (1986) set national goals for participation in regular and vigorous physical activity at 90% for youth and 60% for adults by 1990. However, we fell far short of these goals (Dishman, 1988). Here's where we currently stand:

- 45% of adults are sedentary.
- 65% of children participate regularly in physical activity.
- 35% of adults participate in exercise about once a week.
- 10% of adults participate in vigorous and frequent activity.
- 10% of sedentary adults are likely to begin a program of regular exercise within a year.
- 50% of people who start an exercise program will drop out within 6 months.

Even with the many demonstrated physiological and psychological benefits of exercise, including reduced tension and depression, increased self-esteem, lowered risk of cardiovascular disease, and better weight control, only half the adults who begin exercise programs continue their participation.

In this chapter you will learn about

■ the reasons people exercise,

■ why people do not exercise,

■ factors associated with exercise adherence, and

■ techniques and strategies for increasing exercise adherence.

Reasons to Exercise

With half of the adult population sedentary, the first problem we face is how to get these people to start exercising. People are motivated for different reasons (see chapter 4), but a good starting place to get people to initiate an exercise program is to emphasize the several diverse benefits of exercise.

1. Weight control. Our society values fitness, good looks, and thinness, so staying in shape and keeping trim concerns many people. However, an estimated 60 to 70 million American adults and 10 to 15 million American teenagers are overweight. For most people, when they face that they are overweight, the first thing they think to do is diet. Although dieting certainly helps to lose weight, exercise plays an important role that is often underrated. People worry that exercise increases appetite, but this isn't true of workouts of moderate and short duration. Some people assume that exercise does not burn enough calories to make a significant difference in weight loss, but this is contrary to fact. For example, running 3 miles five times a week can produce a weight loss of 20 to 25 pounds in a year if caloric intake remains the same.

Weight loss can have important health consequences beyond looking and feeling good. Obesity and physical inactivity are primary risk factors for coronary heart disease. Thus, regular exercise will not only help in weight control and appearance but will also eliminate physical inactivity as a risk factor.

2. Reduced risk of hypertension. Another health-related benefit of regular exercise is the lowering of both systolic and diastolic blood pressure. Like obesity, hypertension is a prime risk factor in coronary heart disease. Statistics indicate that 110 mm Hg systolic and 70 mm Hg diastolic is considered optimal blood pressure for longevity. A rise in systolic blood pressure to 150 mm Hg increases the risk of heart disease by more than two times. Yet research has indicated that blood pressure can be reduced through regular exercise.

3. Reduction in stress and depression. Regular exercise is associated with increased well-being. Our society has seen recently a tremendous increase in the number of people suffering from anxiety disorders and depression. Exercise is one way to cope more effectively with the world around us.

4. Enjoyment. Although many people start exercise programs to improve their health and lose weight, it is rare for people to continue these programs unless they find the experience enjoyable. In general, people continue an exercise program because of the fun, happiness, and satisfaction it brings. The major reason for participation in organized youth sports is to have fun. Yet,

Exercise combined with proper eating habits can help you lose weight. But weight loss should be slow and steady, occurring as you change your exercise and eating patterns.

as people mature, the fun aspect of sport and physical activity seems to be ousted by needs to be productive, hard working, and successful.

5. Building self-esteem. Exercise is associated with increased feelings of self-esteem and self-confidence. Many people get a sense of satisfaction from accomplishing something they couldn't do before. Something as simple as walking around the block or jogging a mile makes them feel good to be moving toward their goals. In addition, people who exercise regularly feel more confident about the way they look. They may get more recognition from a variety of sources.

6. Socializing. Often people start an exercise program for the chance to socialize and be with others. They can meet people, fight loneliness, and shed social isolation. Group experiences often lead to camaraderie and friendship. Aerobics classes, for example, usually meet regularly to exercise and have some fun while doing it. Many people who lead busy lives find the only time they have to spend with friends is exercising together. Regular exercisers often find sharing the experience makes exercise more enjoyable. Almost 90% of exercise program participants prefer to exercise with a partner or group rather than alone. Exercising together gives people a sense of personal commitment to continue the opportunity and to derive social support from each other (Willis & Campbell, 1992).

> Both the physiological and psychological benefits of exercising can be cited to help persuade sedentary people to initiate an exercise program.

Excuses for Not Exercising

Despite the social, health, and personal benefits of exercising, many people still choose not to exercise, usually citing lack of time, lack of knowledge about fitness, inadequate facilities, and fatigue as their reasons for inactivity (Willis & Campbell, 1992). These are reasons both for dropping out of exercise programs and for not getting started in the first place. A clear understanding of why people don't exercise can help the fitness professional develop strategies to counteract these barriers.

1. Lack of time. The most frequent reason given for inactivity is lack of time. However, a close look at schedules usually reveals that this lack of time is more a perception than a reality. The problem is in *priorities*—after all, people seem to find time to watch TV, hang out, or read the newspaper. When fitness professionals make programs enjoyable, satisfying, meaningful, and convenient, exercising can compete well against other leisure activities. But professionals should also clarify the benefits of exercise to help motivate a sedentary person to start an exercise program.

2. Lack of knowledge about fitness. Many people simply don't know how to begin. They wonder how much to exercise, what types of exercise are best, and how intensely to exercise. Some self-proclaimed "experts" armed with books, videos, and TV shows have misinformed the public about proper exercise. To dispel the misinformation, exercise professionals need to share what they know. Expectations of exercise should be kept realistic in terms of the potential benefits (e.g., weight loss, changes in muscular development) so that new exercisers are not disappointed when results are slow.

3. Lack of facilities. Inadequate, inconvenient, or nonexistent facilities are often-cited reasons for not exercising. But you don't need a big weight room, fancy exercise bikes, treadmills, swimming pool, track, and other amenities to benefit from exercise. A pair of shorts and running shoes or a bicycle are sufficient for a good workout. Usually people are really balking at a lack of *convenient* facilities. Certainly, convenient exercise facilities can entice some people to start exercising, especially when they have attractive ambiance, equip-

Exercise professionals should highlight the benefits of exercise and provide a supportive environment to involve sedentary people in physical activity.

ment, and space. But professional, friendly instructors can compensate if these are missing by making people feel unique and comfortable.

4. Fatigue. Many people keep such busy schedules that fatigue becomes an excuse for not exercising. Fatigue typically is more mental than physical and is often stress-related. Fitness professionals should emphasize that a brisk walk, bicycle ride, or tennis game can relieve tension and stress and be energizing. If these activities are structured to be fun, the harried worker will look forward to them after a day filled with hassles.

The Problem of Exercise Adherence

Once sedentary people have overcome inertia and started exercising, the next barrier is to keep on exercising. Evidently many people find it much easier to start an exercise program than to stick with it (see Figure 20.1). In this respect, exercise is like dieting, quitting smoking, or cutting down on drinking alcohol. People intend to change a habit that affects their health and well-being negatively. In fact, fitness clubs traditionally have their highest new enrollments in January and February after sedentary individuals feel charged by New Year's resolutions to turn over a new leaf and get in shape. The marketing of exercise has accelerated in North America in a mass persuasion campaign, with heavy media advertising from sportswear companies. So, when people start an exercise program, why don't they stick with it?

What determines adherence to physical activity and exercise? In a broad sense, the determinants fall into these categories:

- Personal
- Situational
- Behavioral
- Programmatic

We'll examine each of these categories, highlighting the most consistent specific factors related to adherence and dropout rates. Table 20.1 summarizes the positive and negative influences and which variables have no influence on exercise adherence.

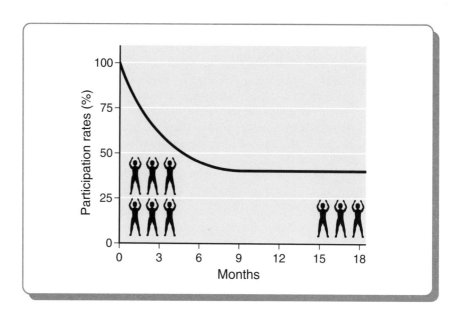

Figure 20.1 Change in rate of exercise program participation over time.

Table 20.1 Factors Associated With Participation in Supervised Exercise Programs

Factor category	Positive	Negative	Neutral
Personal factors			
Past program participation	✓		
Health beliefs/knowledge			✓
Self-motivation	✓		
Age		✓	
Education	✓		
Perceived health/fitness	✓		
Mood disturbance		✓	
Physiological factors			
Body weight		✓	
Cardiovascular disease	✓		
Injuries		✓	
General medical problems		✓	
Situational factors			
Social support	✓		
Convenience to facilities	✓		
Perceived lack of time	✓		
Climate		✓	
Cost			✓
Family/personal problems		✓	
Disruptions in routine		✓	
Behavioral factors			
Smoking		✓	
Blue collar occupation		✓	
Type A behavior		✓	
Programmatic factors			
High exercise intensity		✓	
Group program	✓		
Leader qualities	✓		
Perceived choice of activity	✓		

The Evaporation of an Exercise Program: A Case Study

Maria, a 4-year varsity college basketball player, loved the sport. She was in excellent condition, complementing basketball with weight-lifting workouts and other conditioning drills. After graduation Maria was hired as an accountant but continued working out regularly and playing basketball twice weekly. After a few years, she was promoted to junior partner and began working 50- and 60-hour weeks. She tried to keep up, but her basketball playing dwindled to once a week, with weightlifting maybe once weekly also. Maria got married and had children. Her husband was a lawyer who also worked long hours, so they had to juggle family and professional responsibilities. Even the weekends were hectic, and her basketball playing became sporadic. Maria rarely played basketball or worked out—her lifestyle had changed and physical activity was no longer a top priority.

Personal Factors

Personal characteristics that may influence exercise adherence are previous exercise history, knowledge and attitudes toward exercise, and personality characteristics.

Exercise History.   In supervised programs where activity can be directly observed, past participation in an exercise program is the most reliable predictor of current participation (Dishman, 1987). In other words, someone who has remained active in an organized program for 6 months is likely to remain active a year or two later. As one exerciser put it, "Once I was in a program, I knew what it took to stay active and learned the importance of exercise, so it was just a matter of time before I was going to start another program." This prediction holds for adult men and women in supervised fitness programs and is consistent with observations in treatment programs for patients with coronary heart disease and obesity.

Younger sport and exercise participants have similar adherence patterns. For example, high school and college sport experience predicts a higher level of adult adherence. Similarly, active children who receive parental encouragement for physical activity will be more active as adults than will children who were sedentary and did not receive parental support.

Knowledge of and Beliefs in the Health Benefits of Exercise.   Although knowing and believing in the health benefits of physical activity are motivational, they do not predict adherence to exercise. In one experiment, subjects received written information about why and how to exercise but within 6 months reverted back to the same adherence levels as the control group (Reid & Morgan, 1979).

Early involvement in sport and physical activity should be encouraged because there is a positive relation between childhood exercise and adult physical activity patterns.

Still, a lack of knowledge about appropriate physical activity and negative attitudes about physical activity may impede exercise adherence for some people. Thus, physical educators need to spread information about the benefits of exercise from a psychological as well as a physiological point of view.

Personality.   Self-motivation is consistently related to exercise adherence (Dishman, 1981) and has distinguished adherents from dropouts across many settings, including athletic conditioning, adult fitness, preventive medicine, cardiac rehabilitation, commercial spas, and corporate fitness. Combined with other measures self-motivation can predict adherence. For example, when self-motivation scores were combined with percent body fat, about 80% of subjects were correctly predicted to be either adherents or dropouts.

Another good predictor of adherence to exercise programs is personality trait. Type A individuals are generally more aggressive, achievement oriented, ambitious, and time conscious than Type B individuals. Thus, you might predict that Type A individuals are more likely to adhere to exercise programs. However, these people often feel so stressed for time that they don't make time to stay with an exercise program. Research shows that Type A individuals are more likely to drop out of exercise programs than are Type B people.

Situational Factors

Situational or environmental factors can help or hinder regular participation in physical activity. These factors include the social environment, such as family and peers, as well as the physical environment, such as weather, time pressures, and distance from facilities.

Social Support.   A spouse has great influence on exercise adherence. In fact, a spouse's attitude can exert even more influence than one's own attitude (Dishman, 1988). For example, in the Ontario Exercise-Heart Collaborative Study (Oldridge et al., 1983) the dropout rate among patients whose spouses were indifferent or negative toward the program was three times greater than among patients with spousal support. Spousal support is generally defined as the demonstration of a positive attitude toward an exercise program and the encouragement of involvement in it. Expressing interest in program activities, enthusiasm for the spouse's progress, and a willingness to juggle schedules to facilitate the mate's exercise program are examples of this support.

Exercise professionals can utilize spousal support. They might arrange an orientation session for family members, offer a parallel exercise program for them, or educate spouses on all aspects of the exercise program to foster an understanding of the goals. In Erling and Oldridge's cardiac rehabilitation study the dropout rate, which had been 56% before initiation of the spouse program, reduced to only 10% for patients with a spouse in the support program (1985).

Encouragement for friends, family, and peers who are trying to get back or stay in an exercise program can be as simple as saying, "Way to go" or "I'm proud of you." Such personalized social reinforcement can exert a positive influence on exercise adherence (Wankel, 1984).

Convenience of Exercise Facility.   A convenient location appears necessary for regular participation in community based exercise programs. Both the perceived convenience and actual proximity to home or worksite are consistent factors in whether someone chooses to exercise and adheres to a supervised exercise program (Gettman, Pollock, & Ward, 1983). The closer to home or work the exercise setting is to the individual, the greater the likelihood of his or her beginning and staying with a program.

Exercise professionals should consistently provide sound scientific information about exercise and physical activity to increase the likelihood of adherence to a fitness program.

People with Type B personalities exhibited higher levels of adherence than individuals with Type A personalities.

Spousal support is critical to enhance adherence rates for people in exercise programs. Spouses should be involved in orientation sessions or in parallel exercise programs.

Time.   When time seems short, people typically drop exercise. One of the most common reasons for dropping out of supervised exercise programs is the perceived lack of time (Oldridge, 1982). How many times have you heard someone say "I'd like to exercise but I just don't have the time." For many people, however, this perceived lack of time reflects a lack of interest or commitment. Regular exercisers are at least as likely as the sedentary to view time as a barrier to exercise. For example, working women are more likely than nonworking women to exercise regularly, and single parents are more physically active than families with two parents. So it is not clear that time constraints truly predict or determine exercise participation.

People often cite time constraints for not exercising but such constraints are more perceived than real and often reveal a person's priorities.

Many sedentary people who lack motivation may rationalize that they lack time—it becomes an easy excuse for not exercising. Still, exercise leaders should try to schedule programs at optimal times for busy people. Before and after the work day seem to be more popular than during lunch. Studies have shown that trying to squeeze an exercise class in during the lunch hour causes people to drop out.

Climate or Region.   Weather conditions apparently affect activity patterns except for the most committed and habitual exercisers. For instance, runners commonly interrupt their routines in very poor weather. As for regional tendencies, American adults in the West or Midwest are more apt to be highly active than adults in the East or South (Stephens, Jacobs, & White, 1986). Similarly, the most active Canadians reside in the West (British Columbia) and the least active in the Atlantic provinces and Quebec. These geographic differences may reflect age and socioeconomic differences as much as differences in climate.

Behavioral Factors

Behavioral factors often influence exercise adherence. Some important behavioral factors are not obvious, including smoking and occupational status.

Smoking.   Smokers are likely to drop out of exercise programs. They are also unlikely to use worksite exercise facilities (Conrad, 1987). Smokers especially seem to avoid high-intensity, high-frequency exercise regimens. Sedentary people who smoke are likely to complain of exertional fatigue, regardless of the type of activity. This discomfort further deters participation in exercise. The well-documented negative health effects of smoking are ample reason for exercise leaders to encourage smokers to quit immediately.

Occupation and Income.   People with higher incomes, more education, and higher occupational status are more likely to be physically active. Blue collar workers are more likely than white collar workers to drop out of exercise programs (Cox, 1984), whether they be cardiac rehabilitation exercise or corporate exercise programs. Blue collar workers are also less likely to be active than white collar workers when total leisure is considered. Perhaps blue collar occupations are perceived to have on-job activity adequate for health and fitness, despite low actual exertion. In any case, the high dropout rate of blue collar workers is not inevitable. A study of over 7,000 blue collar employees stressed counseling and tailored programs to individual needs; workers were allowed to choose specific components of their program, such as recreational or competitive activities and group or individual programs. After 2 years the dropout rate was about 25%, half the normal dropout rate (Cox, 1984). This program is a good example of effective, targeted intervention.

Blue collar workers typically have lower exercise adherence rates than white collar workers. However, increased choices can increase their adherence rates.

Programmatic Factors

The success or failure of exercise programs can depend on several structural factors. Some of the more important factors are the intensity of the exercise, group or individual program, and qualities of the exercise leader.

Exercise Intensity.   Discomfort while exercising certainly affects adherence to a program. High-intensity exercise is more stressful on the system than low-intensity exercise, especially for people who have been sedentary. People in walking programs, for example, continue their regimens longer than people in running programs. One study showed a moderate-activity dropout rate (25% to 35%) roughly half that seen for vigorous exercise (50%) (Sallis et al., 1986). By lowering the intensity level and extending the workout's duration, a person can achieve nearly the same benefits as from a high-intensity workout.

Vigorous physical activity carries a greater risk for injury. In starting an exercise program many people try to do too much the first couple of times out and wind up with sore muscles, injuries to sore tissues, or orthopedic problems. Of course such an injury is just the excuse they need to quit exercising. The message is that you are much better off doing some moderate exercise like walking or light aerobics than trying to shape up in a few weeks by doing too much too soon.

Exercise intensities should be kept at moderate levels to enhance the probability of long-term adherence to exercise programs.

Group or Individual Program.   Group exercising leads to better adherence than exercising alone (Massie & Shephard, 1971). Group programs offer enjoyment, social support, an increased sense of personal commitment to continue, and an opportunity to compare progress and fitness levels with others. One reason people exercise is for affiliation. Being part of a group fulfills this need and also provides other psychological and physiological benefits. There tends to be a greater commitment to exercise when others are counting on you. For example, if you and a friend agree to meet at 7 in the morning 4 times a week to run for 30 minutes, you are likely to keep each appointment so you don't disappoint your friend.

Although group programs are generally more effective than individual programs, certain people prefer to exercise alone for convenience. To accommodate these people, a successful unsupervised program should include the following:

- Teach clients how to start a program
- Provide early supervision
- Have clients report progress periodically
- Encourage a home-based program for clients' convenience

Qualities of the Exercise Leader.   Program leadership is the most important factor exercisers identify in programs they like best. Not surprisingly,

Although group exercising generally produces higher levels of adherence than exercising alone, tailoring programs to fit individuals' constraints can help those who exercise alone adhere to the program.

likeable and knowledgeable leaders tend to foster high adherence rates. A good leader can compensate to some extent for other program deficiencies, such as lack of space or equipment. By the same token, weak leadership can result in a breakdown in the program, regardless of how elaborate the facility.

This underscores the importance of evaluating not only a program's activities and facilities but also the expertise and personality of the program leader(s). Most people starting a program need extra motivation, and the leader's encouragement, enthusiasm, and knowledge is critical in this area. Good leaders also show concern for safety and psychological comfort, expertise in answering questions about exercise, and personal qualities that participants can identify with.

An exercise leader may not be equally effective in all situations. Take the examples of Jane Fonda, Richard Simmons, and Arnold Schwarzenegger, all of whom have had a large impact on fitness. They are all successful leaders but they appeal to different types of people. Thus, someone trying to start an exercise program should find a good match in style with a leader who is appealing and motivating.

Exercise leaders influence the success of an exercise program. Leaders should be knowledgeable, give lots of feedback and praise, help set flexible goals, and show concern for safety and psychological comfort.

Strategies to Enhance Adherence to Exercise

Presumably, you now know numerous factors that influence people to stay in or drop out of exercise programs. These reasons and factors are correlational, telling us little about the cause-effect relation between specific strategies and actual behavior. Sport psychologists have recently tested the effectiveness of different strategies and techniques to encourage exercisers to stay with their programs. These different techniques fall into five categories:

- Environmental approaches
- Reinforcement approaches
- Goal setting and cognitive approaches
- Decision-making approaches
- Social support approaches

We'll discuss each of these approaches in some detail.

Environmental Approaches

Usually something in the physical environment acts as a cue for behavior habits. The sight and smell of food is a cue to eat; the sight of a television after work is a cue to sit down and relax. If you want to promote exercise, one technique is to provide cues that will eventually become associated with exercise. Here are some interventions that have attempted to do just that:

1. *Prompts.* A prompt is a cue that initiates a behavior. Prompts can be verbal, physical, or symbolic. For example, cartoon posters (symbolic prompt) can be placed near elevators in a public building to encourage stair climbing (Brownell, Stunkard, & Albaum, 1980). In one study the percentage of people using the stairs rather than the escalators increased from 6% to 14% after posters were put in place. The posters were removed, and after 3 months stair use returned to 6% (see Figure 20.2). Removing a prompt can have an adverse effect on adherence behavior; signs, posters, and other materials should be kept in clear view of exercisers to encourage program adherence. Eventually, prompts can be gradually eliminated through a process called *fading*. Using a prompt less and

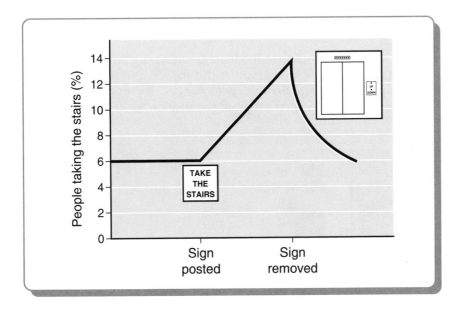

Figure 20.2 Effects of a sign "take the stairs."

less over time allows an individual to gain increasing independence without the sudden withdrawal of support, which occurred in the stair-climbing study.

2. *Sign a statement of intent.* Another way to change exercise behavior is to have subjects sign a statement of intent to comply with the exercise regimen (Oldridge & Jones, 1983). Research has found that people who sign such a statement have significantly better attendance than those who refuse to sign. Thus, people's choosing not to sign a statement of intent to comply can be a signal that they need special measures to enhance their motivation.

3. *Perceived choice.* Having a choice of activities to choose from appears to promote subsequent adherence. Thompson and Wankel (1980) found that people given a choice of activities had higher levels of adherence than those given no choice. This held true even when people only *perceived* that they had a choice (when in reality the experimenter was manipulating their choices of activities).

Reinforcement Approaches

Reinforcement, either positive or negative, is a powerful determinant of future action. To increase exercise adherence, incentives or rewards (e.g., T-shirts) can be given for staying with the program. We'll discuss a few reinforcement interventions in detail.

1. *Rewards for attendance and participation.* One positive reinforcement is rewarding attendance. In one study two rewards were given for attendance during a 5-week jogging program: a $1 weekly deposit return contingent on participation and an attendance lottery (a coupon to win a prize was awarded for each class attended). The two interventions resulted in 64% attendance, whereas subjects in a control group attended only 40% of the classes (Epstein, Wing, Thompson, & Griffiths, 1980). Another study found that contracting for aerobic points to earn back deposited personal items led 7 of 12 subjects to greatly increase aerobic points earned (Wysocki, Hall, Iwata, & Riordan, 1979). In general, results are encouraging for initial attendance or adherence but less so for long-term improvement. Additional incentives or reinforcement must

Manipulating the environment by providing cues to exercise and perceived choices of activities can greatly enhance adherence to exercise programs.

Rewards for attendance and program participation can help improve adherence rates. However, rewards must be provided throughout the length of a program to promote adherence in the long term.

be provided throughout the program to encourage adherence over longer time periods.

2. *Feedback*. Giving feedback to individuals *during* a program session is more effective than praising the whole group at the end (Martin et al., 1984). In a study on giving feedback to runners, this held true both for program attendance and for adherence 3 months after program termination (see Figure 20.3).

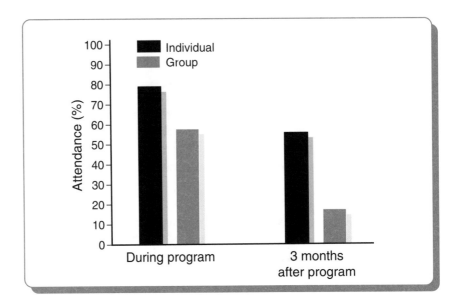

Figure 20.3 Effect of individual and group feedback on adherence.

3. *Self-monitoring/self-reward*. Learning to monitor your own behavior and to reward yourself for positive behaviors enhances your adherence to exercise. For example, one young adult woman used self-monitoring and self-reward to increase exercise participation and fitness over a 5-month period (Turner, Polly, & Sherman, 1976). Keefe and Blumenthal (1980) set up a successful program for three adult men of self-reinforcement combined with self-set, easily attainable goals. All three developed positive exercise habits and after 2 years no longer relied on the self-reinforcement techniques (the activity itself effectively replaced the programmed reinforcements). People can reward themselves for reaching a specific goal or just for hanging in there.

Goal Setting and Cognitive Approaches

Goal setting can be used as a motivational technique (see chapter 17) and as a strategy to improve exercise behavior and adherence. Martin and his colleagues (1984) found that flexible goals that participants set themselves resulted in better attendance and 3-month maintenance of exercise behavior than did fixed, instructor-set goals. Specifically, attendance rates were 83% when subjects set their own goals, compared to 67% when instructors set the goals. Furthermore, 47% of those who set their own goals were still exercising 3 months after the program ended (compared to 28% of the people for whom the instructor set goals).

Time-based goals resulted in better attendance (69%) than did distance-based goals (47%). Longer term, or distal (6-week), goal setting produced better attendance (83% vs. 71%) and better 3-month exercise maintenance (67% vs. 33%) than did proximal (weekly) goal setting (Martin et al., 1984).

Thoughts (*cognition*)—what people focus their attention on—while exercising are also important. When the focus is on internal body feedback (e.g., how their muscles feel or their breathing), it is called *association*; when the focus is on the external environment (e.g., how pretty the scenery is), it is called *dissociation* (a distraction). People who dissociate have significantly better attendance (77%) than those whose thinking is associative (58%). In a study of a 12-week exercise program the dissociative subjects were also superior in long-term maintenance of exercise after 3 months (87% vs. 37%) and 6 months (67% vs. 43%) than associative subjects were (see Figure 20.4; Martin et al., 1984). Focusing on the environment instead of on how you feel is apparently helpful for exercise adherence rates, perhaps because thinking about other things reduces boredom and fatigue.

Dissociative strategies emphasizing external distraction produce significantly higher levels of exercise adherence than associative strategies focusing on internal body feedback.

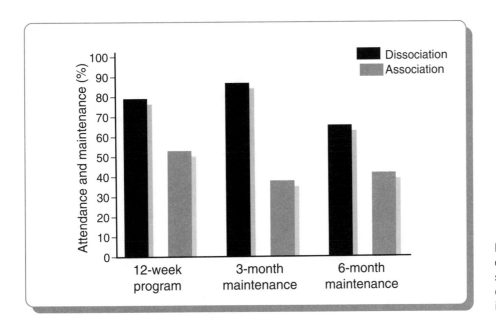

Figure 20.4 Effects of associative and dissociative strategies on exercise program involvement.

Decision-Making Approaches

Involving people in deciding on a program's structure can improve long-term participation. In one study small group discussions about exercise involvement were more effective than a large lecture approach (Heinzelmann & Bagley, 1970). Another study combined small group discussion with an individual fitness test to recruit participants for an employee fitness program; this combination was more effective than was a fitness test alone, a poster-brochure awareness campaign, or an educational seminar approach (Faulkner & Stewart, 1978). Discussing with others their potential involvement in an exercise program apparently helps people act on the decision to join a program.

Another technique to involve participants is using a *decision balance sheet* (Hoyt & Janis, 1975; Wankel, 1984; see Table 20.2) to make them aware of potential benefits and costs of an exercise program. In devising a decision balance sheet, individuals write down the anticipated consequences of exercise participation in terms of

- gains to self,
- losses to self,
- gains to important others,
- losses to important others,
- approval to others,
- disapproval to others,
- self-approval, and
- self-disapproval.

Table 20.2 A Decision Balance Sheet	
Gains to self	**Losses to self**
Better physical condition More energy Loss of weight	Less time with hobbies
To important others	**To important others**
Healthier so I can play baseball with my kids Become more attractive to my spouse	Less time with my family Less time to devote to work
Approval to others	**Disapproval to others**
My children would like to see me more active My spouse would like me to lead a healthier lifestyle	My boss thinks it takes time away from work
Self-approval	**Self-disapproval**
Feel more confident Improved self-concept	I look foolish exercising because I'm out of shape

In one study participants who completed a decision balance sheet attended 84% of the classes over a 7-week period, whereas controls attended only 40% of the classes (Hoyt & Janis, 1975). In a variant of this study, Wankel and Thompson (Wankel, 1984) compared using a full balance sheet (identical to the one in the Hoyt and Janis study) to using a positive-only balance sheet, which deleted reference to any anticipated negative outcomes. Both types of balance sheet produced higher attendance rates than a control condition.

Collectively, the evidence available demonstrates the effectiveness of involving participants in decisions before initiating an exercise program.

Social Support Approaches

Completing a decision balance sheet to increase awareness of the costs and benefits of participating in an exercise program can enhance exercise adherence.

In our context, social support refers to an individual's favorable attitude toward another individual's involvement in an exercise program. Social and family interactions may influence physical activity in many ways. Spouses, family members, and friends can cue exercise through verbal reminders. Significant others who exercise may model and cue physical activity by their behavior and reinforce it by their companionship during exercise. Sometimes family routine is adjusted to allow exercise time. Often people give practical assistance, providing transportation, measuring exercise routes, or lending exercise clothing or equipment.

Wankel (1984) developed a program to enhance social support that included the leader, the class, a buddy (partner), and family members. The leader regularly encouraged the participants to establish and maintain their home and buddy support systems, attempted to develop a positive class atmosphere, and ensured that class attendance and social support charts were systematically marked. Results showed that participants receiving social support had better attendance than members of a control group.

King and Frederiksen (1984) set up 3 or 4 member groups and instructed them to jog with at least one group member throughout the study. In addition, the groups took part in team-building exercises to promote group cohesiveness. These small social support groups increased attendance and improved exercise behavior. Finally, Martin et al. (1984) found that when a leader gives personalized, immediate feedback and praises attendance and maintenance of exercise, adherence improves. These studies all show the important role that social support plays in promoting adherence to exercise programs.

To summarize, here is a list of ways an instructor can get people to adhere to exercise programs:

Using small groups, personalized feedback, and a buddy system to enhance social support has been shown to increase exercise adherence.

- Provide cues for exercise (signs, posters, cartoons).
- Have participants sign a statement of intent to comply with the exercise program.
- Offer a choice of activities to choose from.
- Provide rewards for attendance and participation.
- Give individualized feedback.
- Have participants reward themselves for achieving certain goals.
- Encourage goals to be self-set, flexible, and time based, not distance based.
- Remind participants to focus on environmental cues (not bodily cues) when exercising.
- Use small group discussions.
- Have participants complete a decision balance sheet before starting the exercise program.
- Obtain social support from spouse, family members, and peers.
- Encourage exercising with a friend or a group.

Guidelines for Improving Exercise Adherence

Several elements have emerged in this chapter as keys to enhancing adherence to exercise. We'll consolidate these elements now into guidelines for the aspiring fitness professional.

1. **Make the exercise enjoyable.** It isn't easy for a sedentary person to start exercising regularly, especially if the exercise is not perceived as enjoyable. So you will want to provide a variety of activities for participants to choose from. Running is not ideal for everyone, but cycling, swimming, racquetball, and tennis also make for good aerobic workouts. A variety of activities not only provides cross training and increases fitness but also prevents boredom and reduces the chance of injury from continued stress on the same set of muscles or joints.

2. **Tailor the intensity, duration, and frequency of exercise.** The American College of Sports Medicine has developed guidelines for exercising so as to receive health benefits (3 to 4 days a week, 20 to 30 minutes per exercise bout at 50% to 80% of maximal heart rate, which is 220 minus your age), but some people might have difficulty following them. For example, older adults might wisely start on a walking program before moving into more vigorous activities. Maybe circumstances allow exercising only twice a week. Remember, something is better than nothing, and in time participants can work themselves

into condition to meet the ACSM guidelines. People should train within their comfort zone because exercise loses appeal when it becomes too difficult.

3. **Promote exercising with a group**. Research indicates that exercising with other people enhances adherence to exercise. Two things appear to be operating here. First, commitment is increased because you don't want to let down a friend. Second, many people enjoy social exercise. Part of the success of aerobics classes rests in the fun of exercising in a group.

4. **Suggest keeping daily exercise logs**. Keeping a log is a standard technique for changing a habit. An exercise log details the type, frequency, duration, and intensity of exercise. A log provides information about your exercise patterns and also serves to reinforce your participation.

5. **Reinforce success**. It takes will power and effort to exercise daily, so it is important to reinforce people for sticking to their exercise program. Verbal praise is free and can be extremely helpful in motivating participants. Material rewards also can underscore successful attendance and continued participation. And if you're trying to get started or to stay with an exercise program, don't forget to reward yourself. Going out somewhere or buying yourself something (like a new workout outfit) rewards your consistent participation.

6. **Find a convenient place to exercise**. It's easy to find excuses for not exercising. A favorite excuse is not having time to get to the exercise site. Be sure to identify one or more good places to exercise. The exercise program might be held at a fitness facility, but participants can also exercise at home or walk, jog, or bicycle in their neighborhood. Don't let location be an excuse.

Praise is free, so be free with your praise.

Increasing Exercise Adherence: A Case Study

Jennifer was just hired at a local fitness facility. The club owners told her that her major job would be to increase exercise member participation and adherence—that is, to get and keep people exercising. Jennifer reviewed her college books and notes for programs and techniques to enhance exercise adherence. She then devised a plan to implement after the first of the year, when attendance was typically highest.

First, Jennifer called a meeting of all the fitness instructors at the club. She wanted to get input from the instructors about keeping people exercising and to present her philosophy on exercise adherence so that her staff would know where she was coming from. She detailed the problems in keeping members coming back, made several suggestions for what could and would be done to change things, and emphasized that the instructors would all need to work together and support each other to put the new programs into action.

The first step was for the instructors to set aside time to meet with each member one-on-one for 30 minutes. Jennifer felt individualized meetings were critical for the instructors to find out more about each member. In these meetings members were asked to complete a decision balance sheet noting the potential benefits and costs of participation in the exercise program. They were also asked what barriers might potentially block their way from staying with the program and what the club could do to help them in their quest to stay in shape. Finally, members were asked to set some flexible short- and long-term goals for themselves, which were written down for both the member and exercise leader.

This information helped Jennifer fine tune the program and open up communication lines between the members and exercise leaders. Several themes emerged from these individual meetings, and Jennifer tried to tailor the club's program to meet the needs of the majority of the members. She then summarized and shared this information with her staff.

Jennifer soon scheduled exercise programs and classes at the times members said were convenient (because time and inconvenience was a major factor in whether they exercised or not). The scheduling was flexible and classes were held even if only a few members could attend at a given time. Classes included exercises that met the minimum guidelines developed by the American College of Sports Medicine for intensity and duration to receive health benefits. A variety of exercise classes and activities were planned so that each member could find something she or he enjoyed doing. The variety would also help keep them from getting bored (or injured).

Jennifer implemented a buddy system—each member was paired off with another member identified as having similar interests and a similar time schedule. This system was designed to acquaint members and allow them to set up exercise dates outside of class if they couldn't make a class meeting.

As an extension of the buddy system, Jennifer learned the names of members' spouses or significant others. When possible, these people were telephoned and told how important their support was for keeping the member motivated. Spouses were encouraged to start exercising themselves with the assistance of the trained exercise leaders at the club.

Finally, Jennifer planned contests in different categories including best attendance record for the month, most consecutive days of attendance, and most enthusiasm (as chosen by the exercise leaders). Prizes included T-shirts, free dinners, free massages, and an extra month's membership free.

After 6 months, Jennifer evaluated the program and found that the attendance rate for formal exercise classes was up about 25% and general club attendance had increased by about 20%. In addition, new memberships had increased by 30% over the previous year. Jennifer and the club owners were pleased with this progress. By using the input of the club members and her staff and the latest concepts from the research on exercise adherence, Jennifer made the program a success.

7. **Use music**. Playing music in exercise and fitness programs has become a popular motivational technique. Portable radios and tape players are standard gear for walkers, joggers, and cyclists. In fact, energy expenditure is slightly higher with music, yet participants perceive the exercise to be easier. We noted earlier that the technique of dissociation is associated with higher adherence rates, and music can function in this way, providing a distraction from unpleasant physical sensations to more pleasant auditory ones. This is especially helpful for beginning exercisers, as it makes the entire experience more enjoyable and feel less like work.

Music can serve as a distraction and make exercising more enjoyable.

Many participants prefer to work out to music. The appropriate tempo is important to consider in choosing music for exercise programs. Because tastes vary, some fitness instructors ask participants to bring their own music.

Summary

Although the notion of a fitness boom has been sold to the public, most adults still do not exercise regularly and only a small percentage of those who do exercise work out enough to receive health benefits. The first problem is getting people started in an exercise program. The potential benefits, both psychological and physiological, can help motivate people to start exercising, but of those who do initiate a program about half will drop out within 2 months. This low exercise adherence rate has prompted researchers to study the factors associated with adherence. These factors can be categorized as personal, situational, behavioral, and programmatic. The predictors of persisting with or dropping out of exercise programs are self-motivation (in combination with percent body fat), support from a spouse, location of the exercise facility, group programs, past program participation, exercise intensity, smoking, perceived lack of time, and occupation. Recently, interventions have been developed to enhance adherence to an exercise program. These approaches can be characterized as environmental/reinforcement, decision-making, goal setting, and cognitive and social support. Although initial results are promising, more well-controlled studies are necessary to test how effective these interventions are.

Review Questions

1. Why is it important to understand the reasons people start and adhere to exercise programs? Use data from the Department of Health and Human Services to discuss your answer.

2. Your friend is sedentary and needs to start a regular exercise program but doesn't consider it important. What are three reasons you would cite to convince your friend?

3. Why is exercise adherence a problem?

4. Discuss two personal factors and how they affect and predict adherence rates.

5. What are the relations among body fat, risk of cardiovascular disease, and adherence? What implications do these have for the practitioner?

6. Discuss three situational factors as they relate to exercise adherence and the structuring of exercise programs.

7. Discuss two programmatic factors as they relate to exercise adherence and the structuring of exercise programs.

8. What type of exercise program fosters high adherence rates?

9. Compare and contrast the environmental and reinforcement approaches to exercise adherence. Include different methods for each and describe studies that have found these approaches effective.

10. Based on research about the effects of goal setting on adherence, how would you use goals in setting up an exercise program?

11. How is a decision balance sheet used to help people stick with an exercise program? What research studies demonstrate its effectiveness?

12. Discuss two studies of using social support for enhancing adherence.

13. Using the guidelines for enhancing exercise adherence, design a program that would maximize adherence rates.

References

Brownell, K., Stunkard, A., & Albaum, J. (1980). Evaluation and modification of exercise patterns in the natural environment. *American Journal of Psychiatry*, **137**, 1540-1545.

Conrad, P. (1987). Who comes to work-site wellness programs? A preliminary review. *Journal of Occupational Medicine*, **29**, 317-320.

Cox, M.H. (1984). Fitness and lifestyle programs for business and industry: problems in recruitment and retention. *Journal of Cardiac Rehabilitation*, **4**, 136-142.

Department of Health and Human Services. (1986). *Midcourse review: 1990 physical fitness and exercise objectives*. Washington, DC: U.S. Government Printing Office.

Dishman, R.K. (1981). Biologic influences on exercise adherence. *Res. Q. Exerc. Sport*, **52**, 143-159.

Dishman, R.K. (1987). Exercise adherence. In W.P. Morgan & S.N. Goldston (Eds.), *Exercise and mental health* (pp. 57-83). New York: Hemisphere.

Dishman, R.K. (Ed.) (1988). *Exercise adherence: Its impact on public health*. Champaign, IL: Human Kinetics.

Epstein, L.H., Wing, R.R., Thompson, J.K., & Griffiths, M. (1980). Attendance and fitness in aerobics exercise: The effects of contract and lottery procedures. *Behavior Modification*, **4**, 465-479.

Erling, J., & Oldridge, N.B. (1985). Effect of a spousal support program on compliance with cardiac rehabilitation. *Medicine and Science in Sport and Exercise*, **17**, 284.

Faulkner, R.A., & Stewart, G.W. (1978). Exercise programmes—recruitment/retention of participants. *Recreation Canada*, **36**, 21-27.

Gettman, L.R., Pollock, M.L., & Ward, A. (1983). Adherence to unsupervised exercise. *Physician and Sportsmedicine*, **11**, 56-66.

Heinzelmann, F., & Bagley, R.W. (1970). Response to physical activity programs and their effects on health behavior. *Public Health Reports*, **85**, 905-911.

Hoyt, M.F., & Janis, I.L. (1975). Increasing adherence to a stressful decision via a motivational balance-sheet procedure: A field experiment. *Journal of Personality and Social Psychology*, **35**, 833-839.

Keefe, F.J., & Blumenthal, J.A. (1980). The life fitness program: A behavioral approach to making exercise a habit. *Journal of Behavior Therapy and Experimental Psychiatry*, **11**, 31-34.

King, A.C., & Frederiksen, L.W. (1984). Low-cost strategies for increasing exercise behavior: Relapse preparation training and social support. *Behavior Modification*, **8**, 3-21.

Martin, J., Dubbert, P.M., Katell, A.D., Thompson, J.K., Raczynski, J.R., Lake, M., Smith, P.O., Webster, J.S., Sikora, T., & Cohen, R.E. (1984). The behavioral control of exercise in sedentary adults: Studies 1 through 6. *Journal of Consulting and Clinical Psychology*, **52**, 795-811.

Massie, J.F., & Shephard, R.J. (1971). Physiological and psychological effects of training. *Medicine and Science in Sports*, **3**, 110-117.

Oldridge, N.B. (1982). Compliance and exercise in primary and secondary prevention of coronary heart disease: A review. *Preventive Medicine*, **11**, 56-70.

Oldridge, N.B., Donner, A.P., Buck, C.W., Jones, N.L., Andrew, G.M., Parker, J.O., Cunningham, D.A., Kavanagh, T., Rechnitzer, P.A., & Sutton, J.R. (1983). Predictors of dropouts from cardiac exercise rehabilitation: Ontario exercise-heart collaborative study. *American Journal of Cardiology*, **51**, 70-74.

Oldridge, N.B., & Jones, N.L. (1983). Improving patient compliance in cardiac rehabilitation: Effects of written agreement and self-monitoring. *Journal of Cardiac Rehabilitation*, **3**, 257-262.

Reid, E.L., & Morgan, W.P. (1979). Exercise prescription: A clinical trial. *American Journal of Public Health*, **69**, 591-595.

Rejeski, W.J., & Kenney, E.A. (1988). *Fitness motivation: Preventing participant drop-out*. Champaign, IL: Human Kinetics.

Sallis, J.F., Haskell, W.L., Fortmann, S.P., Vranizan, K.M., Taylor, C.B., & Solomon, D.S. (1986). Predictors of adoption and maintenance of physical activity in a community sample. *Preventive Medicine*, **15**, 331-341.

Stephens, T., Jacobs, D.R., Jr., & White, C.C. (1986). A descriptive epidemiology of leisure-time physical activity. *Public Health Reports*, **100**, 147-158.

Thompson, C.E., & Wankel, L.M. (1980). The effects of perceived choice upon frequency of exercise behavior. *Journal of Applied Social Psychology*, **19**, 436-443.

Turner, R.D., Polly, S., & Sherman, A.R. (1976). A behavioral approach to individualized exercise programming. In J.D. Krumboltz & C.E. Thoreson (Eds.), *Counseling methods*. New York: Holt, Rinehart and Winston.

Wankel, L.M. (1984). Decision-making and social support strategies for increasing exercise adherence. *Journal of Cardiac Rehabilitation*, **4**, 124-135.

Willis, J.D., & Campbell, L.F. (1992). *Exercise psychology*. Champaign, IL: Human Kinetics.

Wysocki, T., Hall, G., Iwata, B., & Riordan, M. (1979). Behavioral management of exercise: Contracting for aerobic points. *Journal of Applied Behavior Analysis*, **12**, 55-64.

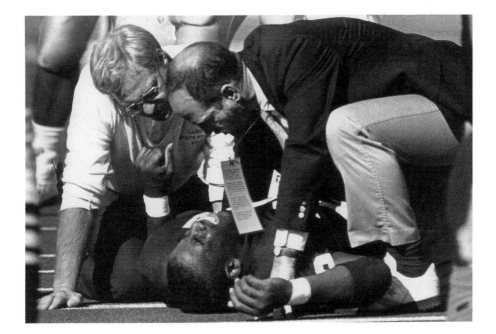

CHAPTER 21

Psychology and Athletic Injuries

At the start of the 1990 football season Minnesota Vikings' defensive tackle Keith Millard was one of the premier players in the NFL. But on September 30, while rushing quarterback Vinny Testaverde of the Tampa Bay Buccaneers, Millard went down with a serious knee injury. Sportswriter Jill Lieber (1991) captured his reaction in an interview:

> "My knee's shot. My knee's shot. There goes my whole career. It's over. I'm through." Agonizing over his misfortune, Millard buried his head in his hands and cried so hard that his 6'5", 265-pound body shook. . . . He was impossible to be around, lashing out at nurses, refusing to eat, slamming his crutches to the floor instead of learning how to use them. . . . Embarrassed by how vulnerable he looked in bed, Millard was so uncomfortable when Viking coaches and players came to visit that he finally phoned Dan Endy of the team's p.r. department and dictated a terse letter specifying no more visitors. . . . When Millard began rehabilitating his knee at the Vikings' practice facility in mid-October, he acted tough and invincible and didn't let on to his teammates that the pain was excruciating. (pp. 37-38)

Millard did recover to play again. But his reactions after the injury clearly showed that he had been hurt psychologically as well as physically. Because of cases like Millard's, the psychology of athletic injuries has become an area of great concern—and involving a much broader population than elite athletes. The area focuses on anyone who has sustained a physical activity–related injury, whether an athlete, exercise enthusiast, or dancer.

In this chapter you will learn about

▌ the role of psychological factors in athletic and exercise injuries,

▌ psychological antecedents that may predispose people to athletic injuries,

▌ explanations for the stress-injury relationship,

▌ typical psychological reactions to injuries,

▌ signs of poor adjustment to injury, and

▌ psychological skills and strategies to speed the rehabilitation process.

The Role of Psychological Factors in Athletic Injuries

It is conservatively estimated that 3 to 5 million adults and children are injured each year in U.S. sport, exercise, and recreational settings (Kraus & Conroy, 1984). Thus, whether your goal is becoming a physical educator, high school coach, personal trainer, strength and conditioning specialist, athletic director, physical therapist, or athletic trainer you will encounter and work with your share of injured participants.

Physical factors are the primary cause of athletic injuries, but psychological factors can also contribute. Thus, fitness professionals need to understand psychological reactions to injuries and how mental strategies can facilitate recovery.

Sport psychologists Mark Anderson and Jean Williams (1988) have helped clarify the role psychological factors play in athletic injuries. Figure 21.1 shows a simplified version of their model. You can see that the relation between athletic injuries and psychological factors is viewed as primarily stress-related. In particular, a potentially stressful athletic situation (e.g., competition, practice, poor performance) can contribute to injury, depending on the athlete and how threatening he or she perceives the situation to be (see chapter 6). A situation perceived as threatening increases state anxiety, which causes a variety of attentional and muscle tension changes (e.g., distraction and tightening up). This in turn leads to an increased chance of being injured.

Stress isn't the only psychological factor to influence athletic injuries, however. As you see in Figure 21.1, personality factors, a history of stressors, and coping resources all influence the stress process and, in turn, the probability of injury. Moreover, after one sustains an injury these same factors influence how much stress the injury causes and subsequent rehabilitation and recovery. Finally, as seen at the bottom of Figure 21.1, people who develop psychological skills (e.g., goal setting, imagery, and relaxation) may deal better with stress, reducing both their chances of being injured and the stress of injury.

Understanding this overview of the roles that psychological factors play in athletic- and exercise-related injuries, we can now examine in more depth the pieces of the model.

It is estimated that 3 to 5 million adults and children are injured each year in sport, exercise, and recreational settings.

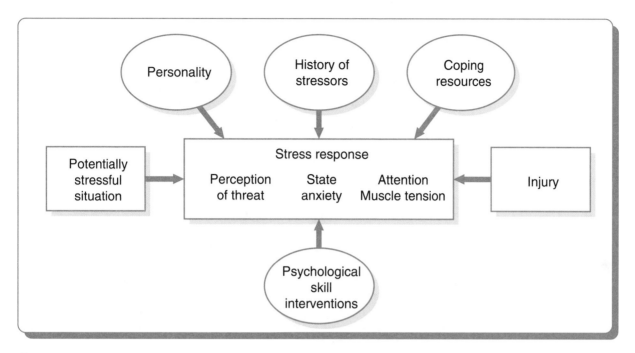

Figure 21.1   A model of stress and athletic injury. Adapted from Anderson and Williams (1988).

How Injuries Happen—Antecedents

Physical factors such as muscle imbalances, high-speed collisions, overtraining, and physical fatigue are the primary causes of exercise and sport injuries. However, psychological factors may also play a role. Personality factors, stress levels, and certain predisposing attitudes have all been identified (Rotella & Heyman, 1986; Wiese & Weiss, 1987) as psychological antecedents to athletic injuries.

Personality Factors

Personality traits were among the first psychological factors associated with athletic injuries. Investigators wanted to understand whether such traits as self-concept, introversion-extroversion, and tough-mindedness were related to injury. For example, would athletes with low self-concept have higher injury rates than their high self-concept counterparts? Unfortunately, most of the research on personality and injury has suffered from inconsistency and the problems that have plagued sport personality research in general (Feltz, 1984; see chapter 3). Of course, this does not mean that personality is not related to injury rates—it means only that to date we have not successfully identified and measured the particular personality characteristics associated with athletic injuries.

Stress Levels

Stress level, on the other hand, has been identified as an important antecedent of athletic injuries. Research has examined the relation between life stress and injury rates (Anderson & Williams, 1988). Measures of these stresses focus on major life changes, such as losing a loved one, moving to a different town, getting married, or experiencing a change in economic status. Minor stressors and daily hassles such as driving in traffic have also been studied. Overall, the research suggests that athletes with higher levels of life stress experience more injuries. Thus, fitness and sport professionals should ask about major changes and stressors in athletes' lives and, when such changes occur, carefully monitor and adjust training regimens and provide psychological support.

The relation between stress and injuries is complex. A study of 452 male and female high school athletes (in basketball, wrestling, and gymnastics) examined the relation between stressful life events; social and emotional support from family, friends, and coaches; coping skills; and the number of days of non-participation in athletics due to injury (Smith, Smoll, & Ptacek, 1990). No relation was found among these factors across a school season. However, life stress was associated with athletic injuries in the specific subgroup of athletes who had both low levels of social support and low coping skills. These results suggest that when an athlete possessing few coping skills and little social support experiences major life changes, he or she is at a greater risk of athletic injury. Athletic trainers and coaches need to be on the lookout for these at-risk individuals. This finding supports the Anderson and Williams model, emphasizing the importance of looking at the multiple psychological factors in the stress-injury relationship.

Explaining the Stress-Injury Relationship

Understanding why athletes who experience high life stress are more prone to injury is important because such understanding could facilitate designing preventive sports medicine programs. To date, two major theories have been advanced to explain the stress-injury relationship.

Attentional Disruption

One promising view is that stress disrupts an athlete's attention by reducing peripheral attention (Williams, Tonyman, & Anderson, 1991). Thus, a football quarterback under great stress might be prone to injury because he does not see a charging defender rushing in from his off side. Under lower stress levels, the quarterback would have a wider field of peripheral vision and thus see the defender in time to avoid a sack and subsequent injury.

It has also been suggested that increased state anxiety causes distraction and irrelevant thoughts. For instance, an executive who jogs at lunch after an argument with a colleague might be inattentive to the running path and step into a hole, twisting her ankle.

Increased Muscle Tension

High stress might be accompanied by considerable muscle tension that interferes with normal coordination and increases the chance of injury (Nideffer, 1983). For example, a highly stressed gymnast might experience more muscle tension than is desirable and fall from the balance beam, injuring herself.

Teachers and coaches who work with an athlete experiencing major life changes (e.g., a high school student whose parents are in the midst of a divorce) should watch the athlete's behavior closely. If he shows signs of increased muscle tension or abnormal attentional difficulties when performing, it would be wise to ease training and initiate stress-management strategies (see chapter 14).

Other Stress-Injury Relationship Explanations

Sport psychologists working with injured athletes have identified attitudes that appear to predispose players to injury. Rotella and Heyman (1986) observed that the "Act tough and always give 110%" and "If you're injured, you're worthless" attitudes held by some coaches increase the probability of athlete injury.

Act Tough and Give 110%.   Slogans such as "Go hard or go home," "No pain, no gain," and "Go for the burn" typify the 110% effort orientation many coaches promote. Coaches who reward such effort without also emphasizing the need to recognize and accept injuries encourage athletes to play hurt or take undue risks (Rotella & Heyman, 1986). A college football player, for instance, may be repeatedly rewarded for sacrificing his body on specialty teams. He becomes ever more daring, running down to cover kickoffs, until one day he throws his body into another player and sustains a serious injury.

This is not to say that athletes should not play assertively and hit hard in football, wrestling, and rugby. But giving 110% should not be emphasized so much that athletes take undue risks—such as spearing or tackling with the head down in football—and increase their chances of severe injuries.

The act tough orientation is not limited to contact sports. Many athletes and exercisers are socialized into believing that they must "train through pain" and that "more is always better." They consequently overtrain and are stricken by tennis elbow, shin splints, swimmer's shoulder, and other injuries. Hard physical training does involve discomfort, but athletes and exercisers must be taught to distinguish between the normal discomfort that accompanies overloading and increased training volumes and the pain that accompanies the onset of injuries.

Teach athletes and exercisers to distinguish the normal discomfort accompanying overload and increased training volumes from the pain accompanying the onset of injuries.

Worthlessness Attitude.   Some people learn to feel worthless if they are hurt, an attitude that develops in several ways. Coaches may convey, consciously or otherwise, that winning is more important than the athletes' well-being. When a player is hurt, that player no longer contributes toward winning.

Thus, the coach has no use for the player—and the players quickly pick up on this. They want to feel worthy (like winners) so they play while hurt and sustain even worse injuries. A less direct way of conveying this attitude is to say the correct things (e.g., "Tell me when you're hurting; your health is more important than winning") but then act very differently when a player is hurt. The player is ignored, which tells her that to be hurt is to be less worthy. Athletes quickly adopt the attitude to play even when hurt.

The following case study shows how athletes should be encouraged to train hard without risking injury.

Psychological Reactions to Athletic Injuries

Despite taking physical and psychological precautions, many people engaged in vigorous physical activity will sustain injuries. Even in the best staffed, equipped, and supervised programs injury is an inherent risk. So it is important to understand psychological reactions to activity injuries.

Sport psychology specialists and athletic trainers have identified typical psychological reactions to injuries. Some people view an injury as a disaster, as did football player Keith Millard. Others may view their injury as a relief—a way to get a break from tedious practices, save face if they are not playing well, or even as an acceptable excuse for quitting. Sport and fitness professionals need to observe how different individuals handle injuries.

The Grief Reaction

The most widely accepted framework for how people react to exercise and athletic injury is Kubler-Ross's (1969) *grief reaction response*. That is, exercisers

---

Injury Pain and Training Discomfort

Sharon Taylor coaches a swimming team that over the years has been plagued by overuse injuries. Yet her team is proud of its hard work ethic. Incorporating swimming psychologist Keith Bell's guidelines (1980), Sharon has taught the team to view the normal discomfort of training (pain) as a sign of growth and progress, as opposed to something awful or intolerable. For her team, normal training discomfort is not a signal to stop but a challenge to do more.

Because Sharon's swimmers have taken their training philosophy too far and misinterpreted Bell's point, Sharon set a goal of having her swimmers distinguish between the discomfort of training and injury pain. At the start of the season she discussed her concerns and asked swimmers who had received overuse injuries the season before to talk about the differences between pushing through workouts (overcoming discomfort) and injury pain (e.g., not stopping or telling the coach when a shoulder ached). She changed the team slogan from "No pain, no gain" to "Train hard and smart." She also revamped the training cycling scheme to include more off days and initiated a team rule that no one could swim or lift weights on the off days. She discussed injury versus discomfort with her swimmers periodically during the season and reinforced correct behavior with praise and occasional rewards. Sharon also informed parents of the need to monitor their children's chronic pains.

As the season progressed, the swimmers began to understand the difference between injury pain and the normal discomfort of hard training. By the end of the season, most of her swimmers remained healthy and excited about the State meet.

and athletes who become injured often follow a five-stage process following an injury (Hardy & Crace, 1990). These stages include

1. denial,
2. anger,
3. bargaining,
4. depression, and
5. acceptance and reorganization.

After an injury most people first enter a denial stage. In shock, they can't believe the injury has happened to them and tend to play down the injury and its significance. After the reality of the injury sets in, anger often follows. Athletes may lash out at themselves and those around them. Then comes bargaining: The injured athlete tries rationalizing to avoid the reality of the situation. For instance, an injured runner may promise herself to train extra hard or to always be nice to those around her if she is allowed to recover quickly. In the fourth stage recognition of the injury and its consequences fully sets in. Realizing that he or she may not be able to continue full participation, the athlete experiences depression and uncertainty about future activity. The final stage is acceptance, when the athlete has worked through depression and is ready to focus on rehabilitation and return to activity.

Most athletes will move through these stages in reaction to injury, but the speed and ease with which they progress varies widely. One person may move through the process in a day or two; others may take weeks or even months.

All five stages may not hold equal significance to the athlete or exerciser. A survey of athletic trainers, for example, found that athletes experienced all the stages, but that denial and bargaining stages were observed more frequently than the depression and anger stages (Gordon, Milios, & Grove, 1991).

> Most people experience a typical reaction to injury, but the speed and ease with which they progress through the stages can vary widely.

Other Reactions to Being Injured

Additional psychological reactions to injury athletes and exercisers experience are listed in Table 21.1 (Petitpas & Danish, 1995). The loss of personal identity is especially significant to athletes who define themselves solely through sport. Individuals who suffer a career or activity-ending injury may require special, often long-term, psychological care.

> **Table 21.1   Psychological Reactions Associated With Athletic Injuries**
>
> **Identity loss**
>
> When athletes can no longer participate because of an injury they may experience a loss of personal identity. That is, an important part of themselves is lost, seriously affecting self-concept.
>
> **Fear and anxiety**
>
> When injured, athletes can experience high levels of fear and anxiety. They worry whether they will recover, if reinjury will occur, and whether someone will replace them permanently in the lineup. Because the athlete cannot practice and compete there's plenty of time for worry.
>
> **Lack of confidence**
>
> Given their inability to practice and compete and their deteriorated physical status, athletes can lose confidence after an injury. Lowered confidence can result in decreased motivation, inferior performance, or additional injury because the athlete overcompensates.
>
> **Performance decrements**
>
> Because of the lowered confidence and missed practice time, athletes may suffer postinjury performance declines. Many athletes have difficulty lowering expectations after an injury and expect to return to a preinjury level of performance.

Based on Petitpas and Danish (1995).

Signs of Poor Adjustment to Injury

Most people work through the grief process stages (or other responses to injury) showing some negative emotions, but without great difficulty. How can we tell whether an athlete or exerciser exhibits a "normal" injury response or is having serious difficulties and needs special attention?

Table 21.2 lists symptoms that are warning signs of poor adjustment to athletic injuries (Petitpas & Danish, 1995). If a fitness instructor or coach observes someone with these symptoms, he or she should discuss the situation with a sports medicine specialist and suggest the specialized help of a sport psychologist or counselor.

The Role of Sport Psychology in Injury Rehabilitation

A holistic approach emphasizes healing both mind and body.

Tremendous gains have been made in recent years in the rehabilitation of athletic and exercise-related injuries. Active recovery, less invasive surgical techniques, and weight training are among these advances. New psychological techniques also facilitate the injury recovery process, including an increased holistic approach to healing both the mind and body.

Psychology of Recovery

In a study of how psychological strategies help injury rehabilitation, investigators tried to determine if athletes with fast-healing (less than 5 weeks) Grade II knee and ankle injuries demonstrated greater use of psychological strategies

Table 21.2   Signs of Potential Problematic Adjustment to Athletic Injuries
Feelings of anger and confusion
Obsession with the question of when one can return to play
Denial (e.g., "The injury is no big deal.")
Repeatedly coming back too soon and experiencing reinjury
Exaggerated braggings about accomplishments
Dwelling on minor physical complaints
Guilt about letting the team down
Withdrawal from significant others
Rapid mood swings
Statements indicating that no matter what is done, recovery will not occur

Adapted from Petitpas and Danish (1995).

and skills than those with slow-healing injuries (over 16 weeks) (Ievleva & Orlick, 1991). The researchers conducted interviews, assessing attitude and outlook, stress and stress control, social support, positive self-talk, healing imagery, goal setting, and beliefs, and found that faster healers used more goal setting, positive self-talk strategies, and, to a lesser degree, healing imagery than did slow-healing athletes. This suggests that psychological factors play an important role in injury recovery.

Surveys of athletic trainers support this conclusion. Wiese, Weiss, and Yukelson (1991) asked 115 athletic trainers to identify the primary characteristics of athletes who coped most and least successfully with their injuries. The trainers observed that willingness to listen to the trainer, maintaining a positive attitude about the injury and the rehabilitation process, and intrinsic motivation (i.e., self-generated motivation to recover) best distinguished successful from less successful injured athletes.

Conversely, another study found that failure to take responsibility for one's own rehabilitation, nonacceptance of injury, and noncompliance with rehabilitation regimens were signs of a poor response to injury (Gordon, Milios, & Grove, 1991). The trainers in this study cited asking questions of the trainer, listening to medical advice, cooperating with the trainer, and accepting physical restrictions as positive psychological responses to injury.

Implications for Injury Treatment and Recovery

Descriptive studies clearly show that the time has come for a more holistic approach that supplements physical therapy with psychological strategies for facilitating recovery from injuries. The psychological aspects of injury rehabilitation are derived from understanding responses to injury. However, just understanding the process of injury response is not enough. Several sport psychological procedures and techniques facilitate the rehabilitation process, including

For complete recovery, both physical and psychological aspects of injury rehabilitation must be considered.

1. building rapport with the injured person,
2. educating her or him about the injury and recovery process,
3. teaching specific psychological coping skills,
4. preparing her or him to cope with setbacks, and
5. fostering social support.

It is the sport psychologist's or trainer's responsibility to learn and administer these procedures as appropriate.

Build Rapport With the Injured Party.   When athletes and exercisers become injured, they often experience disbelief, frustration, anger, confusion, and vulnerability. Blocked out by all these emotions, it can be difficult for anyone to establish rapport with the injured person. It helps to show empathy—that is, trying to understand how the injured person feels. Also, strive to show emotional support and to be there for the injured party. Visit, phone, and show interest. This is especially important after the novelty of the injury has worn off and athletes feel forgotten. In building rapport, be careful not to be overly optimistic about a quick recovery. Instead, be positive and stress a team approach to recovery. ("This is a tough break, Mary, and you'll have to work hard to get through this injury. But I'm in this with you and together we'll get you back.")

Educate the Injured Person About the Injury and Recovery Process. Especially when working with someone through a first injury, it is important to tell him what to expect during the recovery process. Help him understand the injury in practical terms. For example, if a high school wrestler suffers a clavicular fracture (broken collar bone), you might bring in a green stick and show him what his partial "green stick" break looks like. Explain that he will be out of competition for about 3 months. Equally important, you should tell him that in 1 month his shoulder will feel much better. Tell him he will likely be tempted to try to resume some normal activities too soon, which might cause a setback.

Outlining the *specific* recovery process is important. For instance, the athletic trainer may indicate that a wrestler can ride an exercise cycle in 2 to 3 weeks, begin range-of-movement exercises in 2 months, and follow this with a weight program until his preinjury strength levels in the affected area have been

Build rapport with the injured party by

- taking her perspective (think how she must feel),
- providing emotional support, and
- being realistic but positive and optimistic.

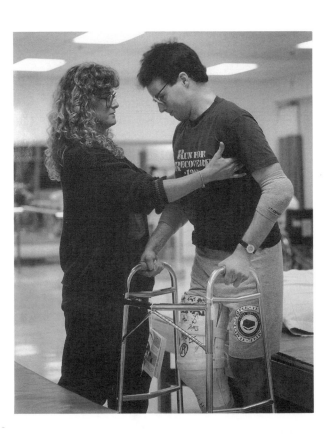

regained. Then and only then can he return to wrestling, first in drill situations and slowly progressing back to full contact. (For a comprehensive discussion of the progressive rehabilitation process, see Tippett's *Functional Progressions for Sport Rehabilitation*, 1994.)

Teach Specific Psychological Coping Skills.   The most important psychological skills to learn for rehabilitation are

- goal setting,
- positive self-talk,
- imagery visualization, and
- relaxation training (Hardy & Crace, 1990; Petitpas & Danish, 1995; Wiese & Weiss, 1987).

Goal-setting strategies can include a date to return to competition, the number of times per week to come to the training room for therapy, and the number of range-of-motion, strength, and endurance exercises to do during recovery sessions. Highly motivated athletes tend to do more than required during therapy, and they may reinjure themselves by overdoing it. Thus, it is important to emphasize the need to stick to goal plans and not do more because they feel better on a given day.

Self-talk strategies are important for counteracting the lowered confidence that can follow injury. Athletes should learn to stop negative thoughts ("I am never going to get better") and replace them with realistic, positive ones ("I'm feeling down today but I'm still on target with my rehabilitation plan—just be patient and I'll make it back").

Visualization is useful in several ways during rehabilitation. An injured player can visualize herself in game conditions to maintain her playing skills and facilitate her return to competition. Or someone might use imagery to visualize the removal of injured tissue and the growth of new healthy tissue and muscle and thereby quicken recovery (Figure 21.2). This may sound far

> Highly motivated people tend to over-do. A recovering athlete should not exceed the program because she feels better on a given day.

Figure 21.2 Visualization using healing imagery.

fetched to some, but Ievleva and Orlick (1991) found healing imagery characterized fast-healing knee injury patients. (Healing imagery originated from advances in nontraditional cancer treatments.)

Relaxation training can be useful to relieve pain and stress, which usually
accompany severe injury and injury recovery. Athletes can also employ relaxation techniques to facilitate sleep and reduce general levels of tension.

Teach How to Cope With Setbacks.   Injury rehabilitation is not a precise
science. People recover at different rates, and setbacks are not uncommon.
Thus, it is extremely important to prepare an injured person to cope with
setbacks. Inform him or her during the rapport stage that setbacks will likely
occur. At the same time, encourage the athlete to keep a positive attitude
toward recovery. Setbacks are normal and not a cause for panic, so there's no
reason to be discouraged.

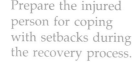

Prepare the injured
person for coping
with setbacks during
the recovery process.

Similarly, rehabilitation goals will need evaluation and periodic redefining
from the start. To help teach people coping skills, encourage them to inform
significant others when they experience setbacks. By discussing their feelings,
they can receive the necessary social support.

Foster Social Support.   Social support can take many forms but is best
defined as "an exchange of resources between at least two people, with a
beneficial outcome for the recipient" (Hardy & Crace, 1991, p. 1). This may be
emotional support from friends and loved ones, informational support from
a coach (e.g., "you're on the right track"), or tangible support (e.g., money
from parents).

Injured athletes need social support. They need to know that their coaches
and teammates care, that people will listen to their concerns without judging
them, and how others have recovered from similar injuries. It is a mistake to
assume that adequate social support occurs automatically. As previously noted,

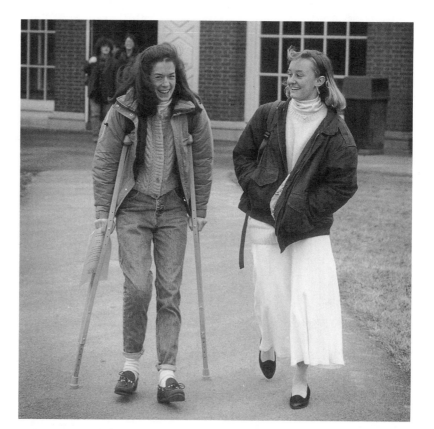

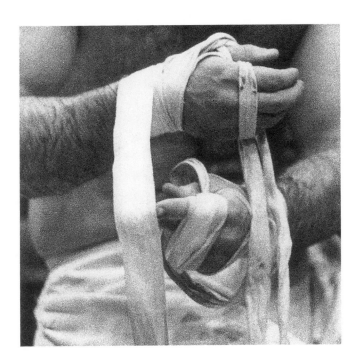

social support tends to be more available immediately after an injury and become less frequent during the later stages of recovery. Remember that adequate social support is needed throughout the recovery process.

Summary

Psychological factors influence the incidence of injury, responses to injury, and injury recovery. Psychological factors such as stress and attitudes can predispose athletes and exercisers to injuries. Professionals in our field must recognize antecedent conditions, especially major life stressors, in individuals with poor coping skills and little social support. When high levels of stress are identified, stress-management procedures should be implemented and training regimens adjusted. Athletes must learn to distinguish between the normal discomfort of training and the pain of injury. They should understand that a "no pain, no gain" attitude can predispose them to injury.

Injured athletes and exercisers exhibit various psychological reactions, typically including a grief response, which is a five-stage process of denial, anger, bargaining, depression and loss of personal identity, and acceptance-reorganization. Increased fear and anxiety, lower confidence, and performance decrements also often occur in injured athletes. If you work with an injured athlete or exerciser, be vigilant in monitoring warning signs of poor injury adjustment.

Psychological foundations of injury rehabilitation include building rapport with the injured individual; educating him or her about the nature of the injury and injury recovery process; teaching specific psychological coping skills, such as goal setting, relaxation techniques, and imagery; preparing him or her to cope with rehabilitation setbacks; and fostering social support.

Professionals in our field must be prepared to initiate teaching and coaching practices that help prevent the onset of injuries, assist in the injury coping process when injuries are sustained, and provide supportive psychological environments to facilitate injury recovery.

Review Questions

1. What is the Anderson and Williams (1988) stress-injury relationship model? Why is it important?

2. What three categories of psychological factors are related to the occurrence of athletic and exercise injuries?

3. Identify two explanations for the stress-injury relationship.

4. Describe the five-stage grief reaction response to athletic injuries.

5. What are common symptoms of poor adjustment to athletic and exercise injuries?

6. What strategies did Ievleva and Orlick (1991) find associated with enhanced healing in knee-injured athletes? Why are these findings important?

7. Give five implications for athletic injury treatment and recovery, briefly identifying and describing each.

References

Anderson, M.B., & Williams, J.M. (1988). A model of stress and athletic injury: Prediction and prevention. *Journal of Sport and Exercise Psychology*, **10**, 294-306.

Bell, K. (1980). *The nuts and bolts of psychology for swimmers*. Austin, TX: Author.

Danish, S. (1992, February 28). *Teaching life skills through sport*. Presentation made to the Exercise and Sport Psychology Seminar, University of North Carolina at Greensboro, Greensboro, North Carolina.

Feltz, D.L. (1984). The psychology of sport injuries. In P.E. Vinger & E.F. Hoerner (Eds.), *Sport injuries: The unthwarted epidemic* (2nd ed.) (pp. 336-344). Boston: John Wright, PSG.

Gordon, S., Milios, D., & Grove, R.J. (1991). Psychological aspects of recovery process from sport injury: The perspective of sport physiotherapists. *The Australian Journal of Science and Medicine in Sport*, **23**(2), 53-60.

Hardy, C.J., & Crace, R.K. (1990). Dealing with injury. *Sport Psychology Training Bulletin*, **1**(6), 1-8.

Hardy, C.J., & Crace, R.K. (1991). Social support within sport. *Sport Psychology Training Bulletin*, **3**(1), 1-8.

Ievleva, L., & Orlick, T. (1991). Mental links to enhanced healing. *The Sport Psychologist*, **5**(1), 25-40.

Kraus, J.F., & Conroy, C. (1984). Mortality and morbidity from injuries in sports and recreation. *Annual Review of Public Health*, **5**, 163-192.

Kubler-Ross, E. (1969). *On death and dying*. London, England: Macmillan.

Lieber, J. (1991). Deep scars. *Sports Illustrated*, **75**(5), 36-44.

Nideffer, R.M. (1983). The injured athlete: Psychological factors in treatment. *Orthopedic Clinics of North America*, **14**, 373-385.

Petitpas, A., & Danish, S. (1995). Caring for injured athletes. In S. Murphy (Ed.), *Sport psychology interventions* (pp. 255-281). Champaign, IL: Human Kinetics.

Rotella, R.J., & Heyman, S.R. (1986). Stress, injury and the psychological rehabilitation of athletes. In J.M. Williams (Ed.), *Applied sport psychology: Personal growth to peak performance* (pp. 343-364). Palo Alto, CA: Mayfield.

Smith, R.E., Smoll, F.L., & Ptacek, J.T. (1990). Conjunctive moderator variables in vulnerability and resiliency research: Life stress, social support and coping skills and adolescent sport injuries. *Journal of Personality and Social Psychology*, **58**(2), 360-369.

Tippett, S.R., & Voight, M.L. (1994). *Functional progressions for sport rehabilitation*. Champaign, IL: Human Kinetics.

Wiese, D.M., & Weiss, M.R. (1987). Psychological rehabilitation and physical injury: Implications for the sportsmedicine team. *The Sport Psychologist*, 1(4), 318-330.

Wiese, D.M., Weiss, M.R., & Yukelson, D.P. (1991). Sport psychology in the training room: A survey of athletic trainers. *The Sport Psychologist*, **5**(1), 15-24.

Williams, J.M., Tonyman, P., & Anderson, M.B. (1991). The effects of stressors and coping resources on anxiety and peripheral narrowing. *Journal of Applied Sport Psychology*, **3**, 126-141.

Substance Abuse
and Eating Disorders

In 1988 Canadian sprinter Ben Johnson set a world and Olympic record in the 100-meter dash but was later disqualified when he tested positive for steroid use. Johnson left the Olympic games in shame. Former NFL great Lyle Alzado was never caught taking steroids, but after retirement he admitted using massive amounts of steroids throughout his career and attributed health problems (cancer) that ended his life prematurely to substance abuse. University of Maryland basketball star Len Bias did not use steroids. He tried cocaine only once—and died of cocaine-induced heart failure just before embarking on his NBA career. He died not because he was a drug addict but because he decided to celebrate with a recreational drug. Tennis star Zina Garrison never abused drugs, but she too had a substance abuse problem—in her case, food. In response to stress and other psychological problems, she suffered from bulimia, an eating disorder that involves food binges and self-induced vomiting. Substance abuse is not limited to elite athletes. Drugs, steroids, alcohol, and smokeless tobacco are used even by high school and youth sport participants. Like it or not, physical education, sport, or exercise science professionals must be prepared to deal with these issues.

Eating disorders are prevalent in athletic populations, especially among females. Many people become heavily involved in exercise as a means to control their weight. They also resort to extreme, even dangerous, diets to lose weight fast. Unchecked, these behavior patterns can lead to life-threatening conditions such as anorexia nervosa.

Substance abuse and eating disorders are clinical issues requiring treatment by specialists. Still, nonspecialists must learn to detect signs of these conditions and refer afflicted exercisers, students, and athletes to specialists for the treatment they need.

In this chapter you will learn about

▮ eating disorders and substance abuse,

▮ how to detect these disorders,

▮ how teaching and coaching practices unwittingly may foster these conditions, and

▮ how you might help prevent them.

Eating Disorders

Anorexia nervosa is a psychobiological disease characterized by an intense fear of becoming obese, a disturbed body image, a significant weight loss, the refusal to maintain normal body weight, and amenorrhea.

Bulimia is an episodic eating pattern of uncontrollable food bingeing followed by purging and characterized by an awareness that the pattern is abnormal, fear of being unable to stop eating voluntarily, depressed mood, and self-deprecation.

Anorexia nervosa and bulimia are the two most common eating disorders. *Anorexia nervosa* is a psychobiological disease ". . . characterized by intense fear of becoming obese, disturbance of body image, significant weight loss, refusal to maintain normal body weight, and amenorrhea" (Thompson, 1987, p. 115). It can lead to starvation, other medical complications such as heart disease, and death. Anorexia is a severe condition made worse because the affected individual often doesn't see himself or herself as abnormal.

Bulimia has been defined as ". . . an episodic eating pattern characterized by an awareness that the pattern is abnormal, fear of being unable to stop eating voluntarily, and depressed mood and self-deprecating thoughts following binges" (Thompson, 1987, p. 115). A bulimic person often becomes depressed because of low self-esteem, eats excessively in an effort to feel better (bingeing), then feels guilty about eating and induces vomiting or takes laxatives to purge the food. Although a severe problem, bulimia is usually less severe than anorexia. The person with bulimia is aware he or she has a problem whereas the anorexic is not. Bulimia can lead to anorexia, and some individuals are characterized as bulimarexic. Within each disorder are progressive stages of involvement.

Although eating disorders are physical, they are driven by psychological factors. In particular, they appear together with certain personality characteristics (often low self-esteem), and in people who experience high levels of stress relative to achieving and pleasing others, especially their families (Thompson, 1987). In anorexics, self-esteem is so low it affects perception of the physical self. When an anorexic looks in a mirror she sees an obese person when actually she is excessively underweight.

Maggie's Weight Loss Tragedy

Maggie is 26 years old and weighs 73 pounds. She was once a sleek and powerful all-conference athlete in soccer and an Academic All-American. Before that she was a high school homecoming queen voted most likely to succeed. Now Maggie is in intensive care at Tacoma University Hospital. Her doctors give her only a few weeks to live as heart complications resulting from her 15-year battle with anorexia and bulimia have gone well beyond the treatment phase. Ironically, even now Maggie sees herself not as emaciated and malnourished but as bloated and obese.

Maggie came from an upper middle-class home and had two loving parents and a wonderful older sister. Yet ever since her early teenage years she felt pressure to live up to her parents' high expectations—socially, academically, and athletically. Moreover, following in the footsteps of a highly successful sister was no easy task.

No one ever chastised Maggie for failing or even voiced specific expectations. However, her parents and friends always seemed so pleased when she did well in school or on the athletic field and constantly talked about the contributions she would make to her community. And Maggie always remembered how much her mom and dad bragged to the relatives about her achievements.

Inside, however, Maggie was not doing well. She was not confident, despite her many accomplishments and immense talent. In fact, she began to dread succeeding because with each new accomplishment came higher expectations from her parents, coaches, teachers, and even peers. By the time Maggie entered college, she felt she had to be perfect.

Maggie also wanted to look like the swimsuit models who saturated popular magazines and was very conscious of her weight. However, she was a short, mesomorphic woman who added muscle mass to her frame easily, especially when she lifted weights. She can still remember how hurt she was when she overheard one of her teammates refer to her as "thunderthighs." She dreaded every Monday when she had to be weighed in front of her soccer teammates. Finally, Coach Peterson challenged the team to develop speed by everyone shedding a few pounds.

The more Maggie's coaches talked about weight, the more self-conscious she became about her appearance and eating. She tried the water diet, the grapefruit diet, and the protein diet, but she felt so hungry after practice and with the academic, social, and athletic stresses that she ate more. Although she was never overweight, her weight bounced around like a yo-yo.

Then one day Maggie finally found the solution: She would eat whatever she pleased whenever she wanted and then later, in private, either make herself throw up or take an abundance of laxatives. This made her feel like she had some control over her weight, although her energy level was down and she often felt guilty about her uncontrolled eating. She also started exercising more, getting up and running 4 miles in the morning, going to practice in the afternoon, and then running again and working on the StairMaster in the evening.

Maggie hid her eating habits throughout her college days, but after college she slipped slowly into a pattern of eating less and less. Her weight dropped and she began to exercise more, despite developing a stress fracture from running. At first she felt good about her weight loss and her friends' comments about it. Later, when her weight dropped well below her optimal level, she did not believe her friends' and parents' concerns about her "low" body weight. If they asked about her eating habits and low weight, she would change the subject and deny the problem. In fact, convinced she was still overweight, she wore baggy clothes to cover up the layers of fat she perceived. She dreaded looking in the mirror because she hated the obese person she saw.

One day Maggie fainted while visiting her parents, and when her dad picked her up to put her on the couch, he realized she was just skin and bones under all those sweatshirts. Her parents insisted that she see the family doctor, who immediately recommended an institution, where Maggie was force fed. Behavior therapy helped some, but suffering from her severe eating disorder for over a decade caused permanent damage to Maggie's internal organs and the prognosis remains bleak.

Anorexia and bulimia are a special concern in sports emphasizing form (e.g., gymnastics, diving, and figure skating) or weight (e.g., wrestling), but athletes with eating disorders are probably found in all sports. Here a national champion figure skater describes how sport experience can influence the development and consequences of eating disorders.

> Figure skating is such an appearance sport. You have to go up there with barely anything on. . . . I'm definitely aware of [my weight]. I mean I have dreams about it sometimes. So it's hard having people look at my thigh and saying "oops, she's an eighth of an inch bigger" or something. It's hard. . . . Weight is continually on my mind. I am never, never allowed to be on vacation. (Gould, Jackson, & Finch, 1992, p. 22)

And here a bulimic athlete describes the turmoil of her disorder.

> I would get so hungry—sometimes I'd give in and eat with the others and then I felt so guilty. Once I started eating I had to get away from the others so I could go finish the binge and get rid of it. I was afraid someone would find me. (ACEP, 1992, p. 4)

Fitness professionals need to recognize the physical and psychological signs of eating disorders.

Physical educators, exercise leaders, and coaches are in an excellent position to spot individuals with eating disorders. Thus, they must be able to recognize the physical and psychological signs and symptoms of these conditions (see Table 22.1).

Often, unusual eating patterns are among the best indicators of problems. Anorexics often pick at their food, push it around their plates, eat predominantly low-calorie foods, and then lie about their eating. Bulimics often hide food and

Table 22.1 Physical and Psychological-Behavioral Signs of Eating Disorders

Physical signs	Psychological-behavioral signs
Weight too low	Excessive dieting
Considerable weight loss	Excessive eating without weight gain
Extreme weight fluctuations	Excessive exercise that is not part of normal training program
Bloating	
Swollen salivary glands	Guilt about eating
Amenorrhea	Claims of feeling fat at normal weight despite reassurance from others
Carotinemia—yellowish palms or soles of feet	Preoccupation with food
Sores or callouses on knuckles or back of hand from inducing vomiting	Avoidance of eating in public and denial of hunger
Hypoglycemia—low blood sugar	Hoarding food
Muscle cramps	Disappearing after meals
Stomach complaints	Frequent weighing
Headaches, dizziness, or weakness from electrolyte disturbances	Binge eating
	Evidence of self-induced vomiting
Numbness and tingling in limbs due to electrolyte disturbances	Use of drugs such as diet pills, laxatives, or diuretics to control weight
Stress fractures	

Adapted from Garner and Rosen (1991).

disappear after eating (so they can purge the food just eaten). Whenever possible, fitness educators should observe the eating patterns of students and athletes, looking for abnormalities.

If as a coach or exercise leader you identify someone who demonstrates symptoms, you'll need to solicit help from a specialist familiar with eating disorders. Some people exhibit some of these signs without having a disorder. Others are afflicted, and it would be a serious mistake to think the problem will correct itself.

If you or a colleague suspects an eating disorder, the person who has the best rapport with the individual should schedule a private meeting to discuss his or her concerns (Garner & Rosen, 1991). Be supportive but direct in such instances and keep all information confidential. Equally important are several dos and don'ts regarding eating disorders (see the guidelines in Table 22.2).

Table 22.2 Dealing With Eating Disorders: Dos and Don'ts

Dos	Don'ts
Get help and advice from a specialist	Ask the athlete to leave team or curtail participation, unless instructed to by a specialist
Be supportive and empathetic	
Express concern about general feelings, not weight specifically	Recommend weight loss or gain
Make referrals to a specific person and, when possible, make appointments for them	Hold team weigh-ins
	Single the individual out or treat unlike other participants
Emphasize the importance of long-term good nutrition	Talk about the problem with nonprofessionals who are not directly involved
Provide information about eating disorders	Demand the problem be stopped immediately
	Make insensitive remarks or tease individuals regarding their weight

Adapted from American Coaching Effectiveness Program (1992), Thompson (1987), and Garner and Rosen (1991).

Practice good preventive medicine by being careful about how you comment about weight gain or weight loss to students, athletes, and clients with whom you work. You never know when an off-hand comment meant in jest could be taken the wrong way and contribute to an eating disorder. (For comprehensive treatment of the many issues and variables of this complex subject, see Thompson and Sherman's *Helping Athletes With Eating Disorders* [1993].)

Substance Abuse

Not all drugs are bad or even out of place in sport or physical activity settings. Drugs are useful tools in sports medicine. Imagine undergoing surgery without pain-killing drugs or treating a serious infection without antibiotics. Some drugs can offset intense pain and enhance healing.

So, drugs per se are not the problem—it's the *misuse* of drugs. Thus, substance *abuse*, not use, is the issue. And abuse occurs both with performance-enhancing drugs and so-called recreational or social drugs. People abuse drugs for different reasons but with the same negative consequences. Drug abuse can lead to long-term, sometimes fatal, health and psychological problems, including addiction.

Drug addiction or psychological dependence on drugs is defined as "the state where discontinued use of a drug or continuous use of a drug creates an overwhelming desire, need, and craving for more of the drug" (Asken, 1988, p. 80). This is one of the most devastating side-effects of drug use: It is extremely difficult for an abuser to kick the habit. Instead, the habit becomes self-fueling, often leading to increasing destruction. Dexter Manley of the Washington Redskins and Roy Tarpley of the Dallas Mavericks are two examples of athletes who tried repeatedly to overcome substance abuse problems and had their careers ended prematurely by league sanctions. Abusers *can* kick their habits, but they need specialized assistance. Clearly, drug education and prevention efforts are important—it is much easier not to become a substance abuser than to overcome a substance abuse problem.

Drug abuse now affects all elements of our society, including sport at virtually every level. Up to 20% of college athletes have used drugs (McGuire, 1990). Buckley and his colleagues (1988) found that almost 7% of high school males had taken steroids by their senior year—an especially startling statistic because many of these boys were nonathletes who took steroids to become more muscular and thus increase self-esteem and peer approval.

Still, the use of illegal drugs is minimal compared to the wide-spread use of legal drugs such as alcohol and tobacco, the two most abused drugs in America. Sustained use of these substances has been linked to a host of negative health effects (see Table 22.3).

> Drug addiction is a state where both discontinuing or continuous use of a drug creates an overwhelming desire, need, and craving for more of the substance.

Table 22.3 Negative Health Effects Associated With Prolonged Use of Alcohol and Tobacco

Substance	Negative health effect
Alcohol	Gastrointestinal diseases (e.g., ulcers) Liver damage Cardiovascular disease Cancers Brain damage Accidents, murders, and suicides
Nicotine	Lung, mouth, larynx, and esophagus cancers Emphysema Heart disease and irregularities
Smokeless tobacco (snuff)	Mouth cancer Gum damage

An in-depth examination of athletes and substance abuse is beyond our scope here. For more detailed information, we recommend several excellent books on the subject (Asken, 1988; Tricker & Cook, 1990; Voy & Deeter, 1991). For our purposes here we'll concentrate on three issues:

1. Why athletes and exercisers take drugs
2. Major drug categories and their effects
3. The fitness professional's role in preventing and detecting substance abuse

Why Athletes and Exercisers Take Drugs

Athletes and exercisers do not start out abusing drugs. Rather, they take them for what they perceive to be good reasons. Usually these reasons fall into four general categories (Bump, 1988; Danish, 1992):

- Peer pressure
- Thrill-seeking and curiosity
- The need to achieve success
- Issues related to self-esteem

The first category, peer pressure, is especially apparent among adolescents who want to fit in. They may drink, smoke, or take performance-enhancing drugs not so much because they want to, but to be accepted by their peers. Sometimes they become addicted before they recognize that real friends like people for who they are, not for going along with the crowd. Thus, it is important for teachers and coaches to repeatedly communicate the importance of being oneself and not giving in to pressure from so-called friends.

Thrill seekers like to test themselves and experiment with new things. Such people may try drugs out of curiosity. But thrill seekers, despite what they think, are not immune to the dangers of addiction. Plus, their personalities and drug use are a particularly bad mix. The drug leads them to recklessness, and they often hurt themselves in accidents. Thrill seekers are much better off physically challenging themselves through sport and physical activities that allow them control of their destinies.

Reasons athletes and exercisers take drugs include

- peer pressure,
- thrill-seeking and curiosity,
- the need to achieve success, and
- to increase self-esteem.

The third category of reasons for drug use concerns the needs of athletes to achieve success. Athletes take steroids to develop size and strength, painkillers to help them endure, beta blockers to calm nerves, and diuretics to lose weight. In some cases, drugs can facilitate sport performance. However, performance-enhancing drugs have clearly documented health risks. In addition, taking drugs to enhance performance is clearly cheating. Those who take drugs and win must realize that winning is not a sole result of their action but is in part a result of cheating. If caught, they will be subjected to considerable public scorn. Even if they are not caught, they'll always know the victory was not their own.

Finally, people take drugs because of low self-esteem and feelings of helplessness (Danish, 1992). Some people feel that no matter what they do they will remain impoverished, fail in school, or not be liked. Thus, one of the most important roles of fitness and sport professionals is to enhance participants' self-esteem. By doing so, they can provide an important barrier to substance abuse. Fortunately, sport and physical activity themselves are excellent vehicles for improving self-esteem.

Major Drug Categories and Their Effects

In the sport and exercise realm drugs are classified by their purpose: (a) performance-enhancing drugs and (b) recreational, social, or street drugs. Performance-enhancing drugs include anabolic steroids, beta blockers, and stimulants used by athletes or exercisers to increase strength, calm nerves, or block pain. Table 22.4 lists six general categories of performance-enhancing drugs, their potential performance-enhancing effects, and psychological and medical side-effects associated with their use.

Recreational or street drugs are substances that people seek out and use for personal pleasure. They may be trying to escape pressures, to fit in with friends who use drugs, or to look for thrills and excitement that seem to escape them in everyday life. Table 22.5 lists three common recreational drugs—alcohol, cocaine, and marijuana—and their side-effects. Tobacco is another widely used recreational drug associated with negative health effects. Most people know

Snuff and chewing tobacco are associated with lip, gum, and other oral cancers, but the use of smokeless tobacco is on the rise among some populations.

Table 22.4   Major Categories of Performance-Enhancing Drugs in Sport

Drug category	Definition/use	Performance-enhancing effect	Side-effects
Stimulants	Various types of drugs that increase alertness, reduce fatigue, and may increase competitiveness and hostility	Reduced fatigue, increased alertness, endurance, and aggression	Anxiety, insomnia, increased heart rate and blood pressure, dehydration, stroke, heart irregularities, psychological problems, death
Narcotic analgesics	Various types of drugs that kill pain through psychological stimulation	Reduced pain	Constricted pupil size, dry mouth, heaviness of limbs, skin itchiness, suppression of hunger, constipation, inability to concentrate, drowsiness, fear and anxiety, physical and psychological dependence
Anabolic steroids	Derivatives of the male hormone testosterone	Increased strength and endurance, improved mental attitude, faster training and recovery rates	Increased risk of liver disease and premature heart disease, increased aggression, loss of coordination, a variety of gender-related effects (e.g., infertility in males and development of male sex characteristics in females)
Beta blockers	Drugs used to lower blood pressure, decrease heart rate, and block stimulatory responses	Steadied nerves in sports such as shooting	Excessively slowed heart rate, heart failure, low blood pressure, light-headedness, depression, insomnia, weakness, nausea, vomiting, cramps, diarrhea, bronchial spasm, tingling, numbness
Diuretics	Used to help eliminate fluids from the tissue (increase secretion of urine)	Temporary weight loss	Increased cholesterol levels, stomach distress, dizziness, blood disorders, muscle spasms, weakness, impaired cardiovascular functioning, decreased aerobic endurance
Peptide hormones and analogues (e.g., human growth hormone)	Chemically produced drugs designed to be chemically similar or to have similar effects to already existing drugs	Increased strength and endurance and muscle growth	Increased growth of organs, heart disease thyroid disease, menstrual disorders, decreased sexual drive, shortened life span

Adapted from Bump (1988) and Newsom (1989).

the negative effects of cigarettes and cigars, but smokeless tobacco should not be forgotten, as its use has recently increased in teenage athletic populations. Snuff and chewing tobacco are associated with lip, gum, and other oral cancers.

Table 22.5 **Common Recreational Drugs and Their Side-Effects**

Drug	Side-effects	
Alcohol	Mood swings	Emotional outbursts
	Euphoria	Lost inhibitions
	False confidence	Muscular weakness
	Slowed reaction time	Decreased reaction time
	Distorted depth perception	Dizziness
	Difficulty staying alert	Liver damage
	Reduced strength	Reduced power
	Reduced speed	Reduced endurance
Marijuana	Drowsiness	Decreased alertness
	Decreased hand-eye coordination	Increased heart rate
		Memory loss
	Increased blood pressure	Slowed reaction time
	Distorted vision	Decreased mental performance
	Decreased physical performance	
Cocaine	Physical and psychological addiction	Death from circulatory problems
	Increased strength	Violent mood swings
	Dizziness	Decreased reaction time
	Rapid blood pressure fluctuations	Vomiting
		Distorted depth perception
	Anxiety	Hallucination

Adapted from Bump (1988).

Preventing and Detecting Substance Abuse

Because drug abuse is a clinical matter, without additional training sport and fitness personnel are unlikely to be involved in drug treatment programs. However, we can play major roles in drug prevention and detection.

Linda Bump (1988) has indicated several steps coaches and exercise leaders can implement to help prevent drug use.

1. Provide a supportive environment that addresses the reasons individuals take drugs. Coaches can initiate programs allowing people to physically challenge themselves and get high on physical activity, not drugs. They can consistently work toward empowering participants through increased self-esteem, because people who feel good about themselves are less likely to take drugs. Finally, in competitive athletics, coaches should avoid emphasizing winning at all costs.

Bystander apathy to drugs in sport, whether from administrators or coaches, is not acceptable. That is, telling athletes not to take drugs but then ignoring substance abuse symptoms is inappropriate and unethical. Drug use and abuse is growing in sport, and fitness professionals must become involved in drug prevention and education efforts.

2. Educate participants about the effects of drug use. Although it is imperative to emphasize the greater negative side-effects of drug use, coaches should be sure to indicate that performance-enhancing drugs can facilitate strength and performance. For years the sports medicine community told athletes that steroids do not enhance performance (when actually they do), which resulted in a loss of credibility: Athletes discounted negative information on side-effects because of earlier false information.

3. Inform participants of legal sanctions against drug use. Coaches can discuss such examples as former Miami Dolphin football star Mercury Morris imprisoned for involvement with drugs, basketball player Roy Tarpley suspended from professional basketball because of repeated drug use, and Canadian sprint star Ben Johnson suspended for 2 years and having his Olympic gold medal revoked for using performance-enhancing drugs.

4. Solicit information on their organization's drug use policy or initiate a policy if one does not exist. Coaches should convey these policies to both students and parents involved in the program.

5. Set a good example. Actions speak louder than words, so coaches and exercise leaders should monitor their own actions and not smoke, chew tobacco, or drink excessively. This sends a powerful message against the use of drugs. Professionals are not themselves immune to drug abuse. If a coach has personal concerns, he or she should get help.

Fitness professionals are not the police, charged with fighting the war on drugs. However, without our help, the war on drugs could well be lost. As members of a helping profession, we must be alert to substance abuse and do what we can to deter it.

Drug use and abuse is detected by both formal procedures, such as drug testing, and informal procedures, such as observation and listening. Properly conducted drug testing is very expensive. Here we'll focus on less formal but still very effective methods of observing and listening.

Table 22.6 depicts many of the signs and symptoms that characterize people who use drugs. Observing these symptoms in athletes and exercisers does not necessarily mean they are drug users or abusers, as these symptoms could also reflect other emotional problems. Thus, a fitness professional who observes these symptoms should first talk to the concerned party to validate his or her suspicions. Hard core substance abusers are notorious for lying and denying the problem, however. So, if doubts remain after the initial talk with the individual, confidential advice should be solicited from a substance abuse specialist.

> Hard core substance abusers are notorious for lying and denying their substance abuse problem.

Table 22.6 Signs of Drug Use in Athletes and Exercisers
Change in behavior (lack of motivation, tardiness, absenteeism)
Change in peer group
Major change in personality
Major change in performance (academic or athletic)
Apathetic or listless behavior
Impaired judgment
Poor coordination
Poor hygiene and grooming
Profuse sweating
Muscular twitches or tremors

Listening is a simple but excellent way to obtain information about drug use. We are not suggesting that sport and fitness professionals eavesdrop on students, athletes, or clients. But if you hear drug use being discussed, you should address the issue in a nonaccusatory manner (e.g., "I didn't recognize the voices, but I heard someone talking about steroids in the locker room the other day. Let me tell you a few things about performance-enhancing drugs in case anyone has gotten misinformation about them and their effects . . .''). If individuals tell you that they are using drugs, respect their confidentiality but solicit professional help.

Summary

Anorexia and bulimia are potentially life-threatening psychologically based disorders. Although they have grown more prevalent in recent years, you will not frequently encounter anorexic or bulimic athletes, exercisers, and students. However, we must be prepared to recognize those who suffer from these conditions and assist them in getting appropriate specialized assistance. Watch for signs and symptoms of bulimia and anorexia nervosa and be sensitive to the psychological underpinnings of these disorders.

Substance abuse is one of the most severe problems facing our society today. Athletes and exercisers take both performance-enhancing drugs and recreational drugs, and both have dangerous side-effects. We must understand why people take drugs, gain knowledge about the major drugs used and their effects on health and performance, and initiate strategies to prevent and detect drug use among those we serve.

Because eating disorders and substance abuse have increased markedly in exercisers and athletes in recent years, professionals in our field should be prepared to initiate teaching and coaching practices to help prevent the onset of these conditions.

Review Questions

1. Define, compare, and contrast anorexia nervosa and bulimia.

2. How do you recognize individuals with eating disorders? (Describe signs and symptoms.)

3. How are eating disorders related to psychological factors?

4. If you suspect someone has an eating disorder, how would you approach him or her with your concern? What should and should not be done?

5. Why do athletes and exercisers take drugs?

6. What are the two major drug categories?

7. Identify the major categories of performance-enhancing drugs and their reported benefits.

8. What are five strategies to prevent and detect substance abuse?

9. Identify the relation between substance abuse and feelings of self-worth and competence.

10. What signs and symptoms help identify drug abusers?

11. What is the role of the fitness professional in the war on drugs?

References

American Coaching Effectiveness Program (ACEP). (1992). Detecting and helping bulimic athletes. *The Coaches' Coach*, **5**(5), 4-5.

Asken, M.J. (1988). *Dying to win: The athletes' guide to safe and unsafe drugs in sports.* Washington, DC: Acropolis Books Ltd.

Buckley, W.E., Yesalis, C.E., Friedl, K.E., Anderson, W.A., Streit, A.L., & Wright, J.E. (1988). Estimated prevalence of anabolic steroid use among male high school seniors. *Journal of the American Medical Association,* **260,** 3441-3445.

Bump, L.A. (1988). Drugs and sport performance. In R. Martens (Ed.), *Successful coaching* (pp. 135-147). Champaign, IL: Human Kinetics.

Danish, S. (1992, February). *Teaching life skills through sport.* Presentation made to the Exercise and Sport Psychology Seminar, University of North Carolina at Greensboro, Greensboro, North Carolina.

Garner, D.M., & Rosen, L.W. (1991). Eating disorders among athletes: Research and recommendations. *Journal of Applied Sport Science Research,* **5**(2), 100-107.

Gould, D., Jackson, S., & Finch, L. (1992). *Sources of stress experienced by national champion figure skaters.* Final Sport Science grant report submitted to the U.S. Olympic Committee, Colorado Springs, Colorado.

McGuire, R. (1990). Athletes at risk. In R. Tricker & D.L. Cook (Eds.), *Athletes at risk: Drugs and sport* (pp. 1-14). Dubuque, IA: William C. Brown.

Newsom, M.M. (1989). (Ed.). *Drug free: The goals of the U.S. Olympic Committee.* Colorado Springs: United States Olympic Committee.

Thompson, R.A. (1987). Management of the athlete with an eating disorder: Implications for the sport management team. *The Sport Psychologist,* **1,** 114-126.

Thompson, R.A., & Sherman, R. (1993). *Helping athletes with eating disorders.* Champaign, IL: Human Kinetics.

Tricker, R., & Cook, D.L. (1990). (Eds.). *Athletes at risk: Drugs and sport.* Dubuque, IA: William C. Brown.

Voy, R., & Deeter, K.D. (1991). *Drugs, sport and politics.* Champaign, IL: Human Kinetics.

CHAPTER

23

Burnout and Overtraining

Often in the middle of a game I'd think to myself, *What am I doing here*? These guys are going to eat me alive. The frustrations, abuse, and hassles sort of wear on you.

High school basketball and football official

I was very paranoid about being a high school burnout. All I'd hear after a good race was "it's about time." I ran all winter and spring on an injured Achilles tendon. I'd spend each week just trying to recover from the last race so I could run the next one. A lot of times I blamed myself for not running well; I thought it was a lack of character or mental toughness.

Nationally ranked high school miler

It's a long, long grind. It's either preseason practice, the season itself, postseason weight training, or recruiting. The demands to win can also be very stressful. When we were successful, there was pressure and high expectations to stay successful. When we were losing, there was pressure to start winning real soon. This schedule and pressure can wear you down and make you just want to leave everything behind for awhile.

College football coach

Officials, athletes, and coaches—they all face the risk of burnout or overtraining. Competition and athletic accomplishment have increased dramatically since the 1970s, and financial rewards, publicity, status, and the intrinsic satisfaction associated with athletic success all add motivation to train with vigor and intensity. Accordingly, the time commitment involved to compete successfully at all levels of sport is enormous.

In this chapter you will learn about

▪ what burnout, overtraining, and staleness are,

▪ what causes overtraining and burnout,

▪ symptoms of overtraining and burnout

▪ how overtraining affects sport performance,

▪ a model of burnout,

▪ measuring burnout,

▪ research evidence of burnout in sport, and

▪ the treatment and prevention of overtraining and burnout.

Defining Overtraining, Staleness, and Burnout

Some confusion still exists among common definitions for the related terms overtraining, burnout, and staleness. We'll present a set of definitions that represent our viewpoint, although we recognize that not all sport and exercise psychologists would define these terms exactly the same way.

Overtraining

To put it simply, *overtraining* refers to training loads that are too intense and prolonged for individuals to adapt to, which results in a subsequent decrease in performance (Murphy, Fleck, Dudley, & Callister, 1990). In essence, overtraining is an abnormal extension of the training process culminating in a state of staleness (Morgan et al., 1987a). Unlike overtraining, which results in a decrease in performance, the deliberate strategy of exposing athletes to high-volume/high-intensity training loads (what we call *periodized training*) promotes performance enhancement. The goal in periodized training is to condition athletes so that performance peaks at a later date.

The difference between overtraining and periodized training depends largely on individual differences and capabilities. That is, what is seen as overtraining (detrimental) for one athlete can be seen as positive for another. For example, Mark Spitz, who broke seven world records in swimming and won seven gold medals at the 1972 Olympics, never trained more than 10,000 yards per day. On the other hand, Vladimir Salnikov, a Soviet Olympic swimming champion, trains at 2-week schedules called "attack mesocycles," which involve swimming up to 20,000 meters (21,880 yards) a day. His distances would be excessive for many elite swimmers, but they apparently facilitate Salnikov's performance (Raglin, 1993).

This substantial variability in prescribing exercise to athletes must be considered, and it should be recognized that the most talented performers are not

Overtraining is an abnormal extension of the training process culminating in staleness.

necessarily the ones with the greatest capacity to endure periods of overtraining. Furthermore, it has been demonstrated that athletes of similar capacity respond differently to standard training regimens: Some resist the negative effects of intensive training, whereas others are quite vulnerable. Thus, a particular training schedule may improve the performance of one athlete, be insufficient for another, and be downright damaging for a third.

One athlete's overtraining might be another athlete's optimal training regimen.

Staleness

Staleness is commonly defined as the end result or outcome of overtraining. It is a state in which the athlete has difficulty maintaining standard training regimens and can no longer achieve previous performance results. Overtraining can be viewed as a stimulus, and staleness as a response (Morgan, Brown, Raglin, O'Connor, & Ellickson, 1987a; see Figure 23.1). Although staleness is associated with an array of behavioral symptoms and disturbances, the primary psychological feature of staleness is depression.

A stale athlete has difficulty maintaining standard training regimens and can no longer achieve previous performance results.

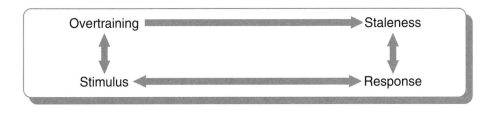

Figure 23.1 Relationship of overtraining and staleness.

Burnout

Burnout has received more attention than overtraining or staleness (e.g., Duda, 1990; Smith, 1986). A complex concept, *burnout* is an exhaustive psychophysiological response exhibited as a result of frequent, sometimes extreme but generally ineffective efforts to meet excessive training and competitive demands. Burnout involves a psychological, emotional, and sometimes physical withdrawal from an activity in response to excessive stress or dissatisfaction (Smith, 1986).

Unlike other phases of the training stress syndrome, once a person experiences burnout, withdrawal from the stress environment is often inevitable. In sport, burnout differs from simply dropping out. It involves psychological and emotional exhaustion. There are many reasons why athletes drop out of sport participation, and burnout is just one of them.

Characteristics of Burnout

- Exhaustion, both physical and emotional, in the form of lost concern, energy, interest, and trust.

- Exhaustion causes a more negative response to others, seen as being impersonal and unfeeling.

- Feelings of low personal accomplishment, low self-esteem, failure, and depression. This is often visible in low job productivity or a decreased performance level.

- Reaction to chronic, everyday stress that occurs over time.

Frequency and Causes of Overtraining and Burnout

A survey of college varsity athletes from the Atlantic Coast Conference regarding their experiences dealing with training stress revealed that 66% of them felt they had experienced overtraining, with almost 50% indicating that it was a bad experience (Silva, 1990). Other research found that 60% of females and 64% of males have had at least one episode of staleness in their running careers (Morgan, O'Connor, Sparling, & Pate, 1987b; Morgan, O'Connor, Ellickson, & Bradley, 1988). And this staleness is not confined to elite athletes, as is commonly assumed.

On the average, the college athletes in Silva's study reported that they experienced overtraining about twice during college. Some interesting research by Raglin and Morgan (1989) found that of swimmers who developed staleness during their freshman year, 91% became stale in one or more subsequent seasons. Yet only 30% of the swimmers who did not become stale as freshmen later developed the disorder in a subsequent season. Apparently, once staleness is experienced, subsequent bouts become more probable.

Year-Round Training

Training in most sports now requires year-round workouts, with off seasons becoming ever shorter. In fact, in sports such as tennis, gymnastics, and swimming there really is no "off season." In addition, the increase in volume and intensity of the training loads carried out by some athletes is so demanding that it limits the athlete's ability to adapt, which results in performance deterioration instead of improvement. Basketball, football, baseball, and soccer seasons are now so long that there is little break between the end of one season and training for the next. With these intense and prolonged training requirements, it is almost impossible to compete with success in more than one sport (Bo Jackson and Deion Sanders provided noteworthy exceptions).

Training From an Early Age

Athletes now start training at a young age, some as early as 5 years old. And some, like young tennis player Venus Williams, are being pressured to turn pro at the ripe old age of 12 years. Another teenage tennis phenomenon, Jennifer Capriati, turned pro at age 13 and was a millionaire before she ever hit a ball as a professional, due to a clothing contract. Her early fame and fortune might be partly to blame for her dropping out of tennis and experimenting with drugs. The names of Vince Cartier, Curtis Beck, and Eric Hulst (all elite junior runners) are probably less familiar, but what these athletes have in common is that they were national champions as teenagers, only to discontinue their participation in competitive sport just a few years after either setting national records or winning junior division titles. Specialized training camps or academies in ice skating, tennis, golf, and gymnastics are residences where young athletes live (generally without parents), attend school, and train, aspiring for an Olympic medal, professional career, or athletic scholarship. In these environments, young athletes practice 25 to 30 hours a week with little time off for vacation.

Sometimes this same intensity, duration of training, and associated pressure are undertaken while the athlete tries to maintain a normal home and family life. And of course many of these young athletes have their self-esteem or self-worth tied closely to their performances on the athletic field, which creates additional pressures to succeed. Many young athletes fail to develop the coping skills they'll need when they are no longer able to continue participation in their chosen sport. Whether such retrenchment is self-imposed (i.e., burnout) or other-imposed (i.e., not being good enough), it can lead to a difficult adjustment period.

Causes of Overtraining and Burnout

The causes of overtraining most often cited by athletes include the following, in ranked order (Raglin & Morgan, 1989):

1. Too much stress and pressure
2. Too much practice and physical training
3. Physical exhaustion and all-over soreness
4. Boredom because of too much repetition
5. Poor rest or lack of proper sleep

Burnout was experienced by 47% of the athletes, with 81% indicating that burnout was the worst response to training stress an athlete can experience. On the average, athletes also reported being burned out once or twice during their college career. The causes of burnout they cited most often included the following, in ranked order:

1. Severe practice conditions
2. Extreme physical fatigue
3. Not enough time to recover from competitive stress
4. Boredom
5. Emotional and physical exhaustion

> Training in many sports is virtually year-round and the intensity of training loads makes it almost impossible to compete successfully in more than one sport.

> Athletes are starting to train at younger ages, which can have negative effects on their home and family life.

Thus, most college athletes in Raglin and Morgan's sample reported that they experienced overtraining and burnout at least once during their collegiate career, with overtraining being more prevalent than burnout. The causes of overtraining and burnout often overlapped, each including too much practice, stress, fatigue, and boredom. Increased training volume, competition, physical training demands on the body and mind, job pressures, and criticism without corresponding praise all replace the game's fun with undue pressures that lead to burnout.

Characteristics and Symptoms of Overtraining and Burnout

Overtraining and burnout are both physical and psychological in nature. Some common symptoms of overtraining include physical fatigue, mental exhaustion, grouchiness, depression, apathy, and sleep disturbances. Symptoms of burnout include a loss of interest, no desire to play, physical and mental exhaustion, lack of caring, depression, and increased anxiety. Research summarizing the characteristics of overtraining and burnout (Hackney, Perlman & Nowacki, 1990) is presented in Table 23.1.

Table 23.1 Signs and Symptoms of Overtraining and Burnout	
Overtraining	**Burnout**
Apathy	Loss of desire to play
Lethargy	Lack of caring
Sleep disturbance	Sleep disturbance
Weight loss	Physical and mental exhaustion
Elevated resting heart rate	Lowered self-esteem
Muscle pain or soreness	Headaches
Mood changes	Mood changes
Elevated resting blood pressure	Substance abuse
Gastrointestinal disturbances	Change in values and beliefs
Retarded recovery from exertion	Emotional isolation
Appetite loss	Increased anxiety

Adapted from Hackney, Perlman, and Nowacki (1990).

Overtraining and Mood States

Overtraining is assumed to affect athletic performance and mental health; a few researchers have asked how. For example, Morgan and his colleagues at the University of Wisconsin have investigated the relation between overtraining and psychological mood states. To measure mood, they administered the Profile of Mood States (POMS; McNair, Lorr, & Droppleman, 1971) to 400 competitive swimmers during different parts of the training and competitive season. The POMS measures six transitory emotional states (tension, depression, anger, vigor, fatigue, and confusion). After analyzing the data from studies done over a 10-year period, Morgan et al. (1987a) concluded that mood state disturbances increase as the training stimulus increases (in a dose-response manner). The heavier the training (in this case the distance swam each week), the greater the mood disturbance. This mood disturbance included increases in depression, anger, and fatigue and decreased vigor.

Athletes experience increased mood disturbance under especially heavy training workloads, especially over time. The heavier the workload, the greater the mood disturbance.

The psychological mood profile of successful athletes differed from that of unsuccessful athletes. Specifically, top-level athletic performers had what Morgan has called an iceberg profile (see chapter 3). As seen in Figure 23.2, the iceberg profile shows that more successful athletes tend to score higher on vigor and lower on anxiety, depression, fatigue, and confusion than the population average. Interestingly enough, when athletes are *over*trained and become stale due to increased training demands, they display an inverted iceberg profile. That is, all the negative states of depression, anxiety, fatigue, confusion, and tension become elevated while vigor is decreased. There was a stepwise increase in the swimmer's mood disturbance that coincided directly with increases in swimming training. And subsequent decreases in the training regimen (i.e., tapering off) were associated with improvements in mood state.

> Successful athletes exhibit high levels of vigor and low levels of negative mood states, an optimal combination. Overtrained athletes show an inverted iceberg profile, with negative states pronounced.

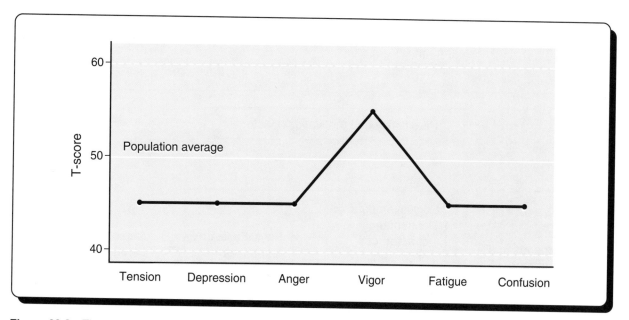

Figure 23.2   The "Iceberg" Profile.

Overtraining and Performance

One well-controlled study investigated the effects of increased training loads on mood states and performance for Olympic judoists (Murphy et al., 1990). For 4 weeks the conditioning training volume was increased, and then for 2 weeks sport-specific training volume was increased. The increased conditioning training volume did not result in negative mood state increases, whereas the increased sport-specific training volume did increase anger and anxiety levels (although there were no signs of clinical distress, such as depression or irrational thinking). However, both the conditioning and sport-specific training

Mood States and Training Stress

- High training demands are associated with negative mood states.
- Lower training demands are associated with positive mood states.
- Positive mental health is associated with higher performance levels.
- Mood disturbance is associated with lower performance levels.

sessions showed *decreases* in physical performance measures of strength and anaerobic endurance.

Overtrained and stale athletes are at risk of developing mood disturbances, which can result in decreased performance levels and dropout. Thus sport and exercise professionals should carefully monitor how much training they require: The old strategy "more is better" may backfire in the long run.

A Model of Burnout in Sport and Exercise

R.E. Smith (1986) developed a model of burnout in sport that can help you understand the burnout syndrome. The model, depicted in Figure 23.3., shows how factors in the situation, appraisal of the situation, physiological responses, and behavioral responses are related. Each of these components is influenced by level of motivation and personality. Let's examine the major components of Smith's model.

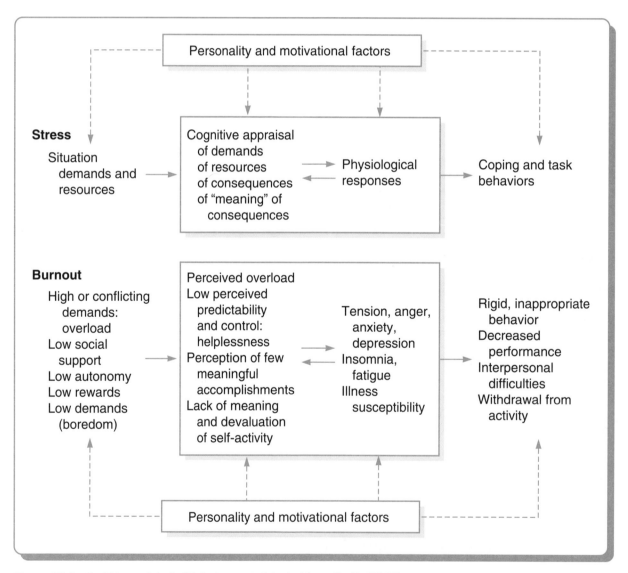

Figure 23.3   Smith's model of athletic burnout. Adapted from Smith (1986).

The Situation

The situation involves how demands and resources interact. Typically, when the demands of a situation outweigh potential resources, stress occurs, which over time can lead to burnout. For example, with young athletes, such factors as time and energy demands, boredom, insufficient skills, difficulty with coaches, and high competitive demands can all be sources of stress.

Cognitive Appraisal

The second component of the model, which Smith labels *cognitive appraisal*, is how someone interprets the situation. Imbalance between demands and resources over time can feel like overload. For example, if Jeff perceives low accomplishment long enough, he will eventually perceive little control over the situation—he'll feel helpless to change his environment.

As we discussed earlier in chapter 5, although people often assume situations are to blame for their emotional and physical reactions, it is usually the *perception* (i.e., cognitive appraisal) of the situation that matters (Lazarus, 1982). For example, one football coach whose team loses three games in a row might get uptight and fear that he will lose his job, whereas another coach in the same situation might see the losing streak as a challenge and an opportunity to show that the team can come back from adversity. Thus, it is often not the event that causes one's reaction but how that event is viewed and interpreted. Many

Cognitive appraisal: Nothing is either good nor bad, but thinking makes it so.
Hamlet

people are victimized by their irrational beliefs about the importance of success and social approval, and their beliefs then predispose them to inappropriate stress reactions (Ellis, 1962).

Physiological Responses

If you appraise a situation as harmful or threatening, then over time, as your perception becomes chronic, stress can produce physiological changes such as increases in tension, irritability, and fatigue. Typically, victims of athletic burnout feel emotionally depleted and have little positive emotion. They may develop sleep-related disorders, susceptibility to illness, and lethargy. The sport that once produced fun and enjoyment now brings only tension and anger.

Coping and Task Behaviors

People differ in how they respond to prolonged stress in sport and exercise settings.

The model's final component is the behavioral consequences of burnout, including decreased performance, interpersonal difficulties, rigid behavior, and finally withdrawal from the activity. Smith argues that reaction to stress in sport is moderated by personality and motivation. One person will burn out while another copes and remains in sport. For example, one study found that coaches who had a relationship-oriented style of leadership showed greater degrees of burnout than coaches who had a task-oriented style of leadership (Dale & Weinberg, 1990). A person's personality and motivation often determine whether she will burn out or cope.

Stages of Burnout

Burnout takes time to develop; it doesn't happen overnight. Typically, a person passes through a series of stages leading to burnout (see box), although these stages differ depending on the person's strengths and weaknesses and the particular environmental demands that he or she might encounter (see Smith's model).

Measuring Burnout

Probably the best way to study burnout would be to find people who have left sport because they felt burned out and compare them to those who are

Stages of Burnout

1. *Depersonalization*—You dissociate yourself from others as you become emotionally removed, distant, and unconcerned.

2. *Decreased feelings of personal accomplishment*—You feel you're no longer making a contribution, that you're not accomplishing what you set out to do. You no longer gain satisfaction from your sport or activity.

3. *Isolation*—You insulate yourself from teammates or partners and look for excuses not to compete or exercise.

4. *Emotional and physical exhaustion*—You break down emotionally and/or physically. The slow burnout process is complete as you have no desire to compete or exercise nor the energy to do so.

currently participating in sport and exercise. However, besides the difficulty of locating these people, many burned out players remain in sport for reasons such as money, prestige, or pressure from a coach or parent. So researchers have instead developed a paper and pencil method to measure burnout.

The most widely used and accepted instrument is the Maslach Burnout Inventory (Maslach & Jackson, 1981), which measures both the frequency and intensity of the feelings of burnout. From their research, Maslach and Jackson identified three components of burnout:

- Emotional exhaustion—assesses feelings of emotional overextension and exhaustion.
- Depersonalization—measures an unfeeling and impersonal response to other people in one's environment. There are detached feelings toward people and a sense of just going through the motions.
- Personal accomplishment—measures the feeling of competence and successful achievement in one's work with people. Low feelings of achievement often result in perceived lack of ability to control situations.

Maslach's Burnout Inventory has been used with professionals in a variety of potentially stressful occupations including nurses, lawyers, social workers, physicians, psychologists, police officers, counselors, and probation officers. It has been especially useful in studying teachers, whose work environment typically includes long hours, excessive expenditure of mental and emotional energy, and high expectations from principals and parents. Coaches and athletes face similar stressors in competitive sport: long hours of practice, great physical and mental energy expenditure, and performance pressures on game days. However, only recently has empirical research focused on burnout in competitive sport, spurred by Smith's model of athletic burnout. Some of this research has adapted Maslach's Burnout Inventory to sport (Weinberg & Richardson, 1990; see Table 23.2). We'll now review some of the major findings regarding burnout in competitive sports.

> The Maslach Burnout Inventory is a reliable instrument to measure burnout and has been adapted and modified for use in sport and exercise settings.

Burnout in Sport

Not much research has been conducted on burnout in sport. In the few existing studies, coaches, athletic trainers, and officials have received the most scrutiny. We'll examine this literature first before moving on to discuss athletes and burnout (also see chapter 24 on burnout with youngsters in sport).

Burnout and Athletic Trainers

Few people are aware of the long hours trainers put in before and after games and during practice. Trainers at the high school or college level are often responsible for several teams, working in the training room or on the field most of the day. Coaches pressure them to prepare athletes for game day, which adds stress. Gieck, Brown, and Shank (1982) were the first to study how burnout affects athletic trainers, and they demonstrated that trainers experience great job stress. Many trainers reported that being at the beck and call of several teams made it difficult to devote enough quality time to individuals. Trainers with Type A personalities (i.e., excessive anxiety about time urgency) were especially prone to burnout.

> Trainers with Type A personalities are more likely to burn out than their Type B counterparts.

Some trainers feel when their several roles become blurred (role ambiguity) they are more likely to feel burned out (Capel, 1986). Conversely, athletic trainers who feel more in control of their situations (i.e., internal locus of

Table 23.2 Officiating Burnout

Please read each statement carefully and decide if you ever feel this way about officiating. Indicate how often by writing in the blank a number from 1 to 7. Then describe how strong the feeling is when you experience it by again writing in a number from 1 to 7.

How often	1	2	3	4	5	6	7
	Not often at all						Extremely often

How strong	1	2	3	4	5	6	7
	Not often at all						Extremely often

How often 1-7	How strong 1-7	
1. _____	_____	I feel used up at the end of officiating an event.
2. _____	_____	I feel fatigued when I get up in the morning and have to face another officiating assignment.
3. _____	_____	I feel I treat players and coaches as if they were impersonal objects.
4. _____	_____	Working with players and coaches is really a strain for me.
5. _____	_____	I feel I'm positively influencing other people's lives through my officiating.
6. _____	_____	I worry that officiating is hardening me emotionally.
7. _____	_____	I feel very energetic.
8. _____	_____	I feel frustrated by officiating.
9. _____	_____	I feel I'm working too hard at officiating.
10. _____	_____	I feel like I'm at the end of my rope.
11. _____	_____	I feel coaches and athletes blame me for some of their problems.

Adapted from Weinberg and Richardson (1990).

control) experience less burnout than colleagues with little sense of control (i.e., external locus of control). For example, trainers often play the role of counselor and friend, which can conflict with their official role.

Burnout and Officials

Officials also face great stress—and few compensations for it other than the satisfaction of a job well done. This leads to high turnover rates and a shortage of officials. Evidently the fear of failure is the strongest predictor of burnout with sport officials (Taylor, Daniel, Leith, & Burke, 1990). Officials report that making bad calls is a major stressor related to perceived burnout and that players, coaches, and spectators are more likely to evaluate them negatively than positively. Like athletic trainers, officials who feel role conflicts have higher levels of perceived burnout.

Role conflict and role ambiguity are related to burnout in both trainers and sport officials.

Burnout and Coaches

Coaches are prime candidates for burnout (Kroll & Gunderscheim, 1982). They are subject to

- pressure to win,
- administrative and parental interference and indifference,
- disciplinary problems,
- multiple roles to fulfill,
- extensive travel commitments, and
- intense personal involvement.

Professional football coach Dick Vermeil stepped down as coach of the Philadelphia Eagles saying that the long grind of 14-hour days and the great pressure to win had simply burned him out. Many coaches share his feelings.

Gender Differences. More and more female coaches are feeling the pressure that their male counterparts have felt for years. Some studies (Caccese & Mayerberg, 1984; Haggerty, 1982) have found that females have higher levels of perceived burnout than males, whereas others have found no differences (Wilson, Haggerty, & Bird, 1986). Some studies report higher levels of burnout in males (Dale & Weinberg, 1989). Likely the inconsistency of the findings simply reflects the great variety of samples in the research.

Age Differences. Studies have found that younger coaches have higher levels of perceived burnout than older coaches (Dale & Weinberg, 1989; Taylor et al., 1990). Of course coaches who felt extremely high levels of stress and burnout have probably quit coaching already. Thus, the older coaches who remain probably have good coping skills for stressors in their environment. Researchers thus face the problem that those coaches who have truly burned out (i.e., out of the profession) are unavailable for study.

Coaching Style. Dale and Weinberg (1989) investigated high school and college coaches and found that those with a consideration style of leadership (caring and people oriented) had higher levels of perceived burnout than coaches who were more goal oriented and authoritarian (initiating structure style of leadership). It may well be that coaches who develop closer personal ties with their athletes suffer greater burnout because they care more. Which is not to say that coaches should care less—rather, they should be aware that this style generally requires a lot of energy, emotion, and time and can take its toll long-term.

Burnout and Athletes

On the subject of burnout in sport, athletes have received the most attention, at least anecdotally. Flippen (1981) states that "burning out applies generally to an athlete who quits, breaks down, or loses competitive drive before he or she has reached full athletic development" (p. 78). Athletes personally describe themselves as leaving their sport because of too much pressure or because they don't have fun anymore. Their situations place high expectations on them, and they may react to the pressure by developing a fear of failure, anxiety, frustration with coaches, feelings of overwork (i.e., overtraining), or depression.

Anecdotal reports of burned-out athletes share common themes: Athletes feel pressure from coaches and parents to perform at high levels and have trained extremely hard for too long at the expense of other pleasures in life. Despite the inherent interest in burnout among athletes, only a few systematic, empirical studies have been conducted (e.g., Feigley, 1984; Fender, 1989;

It has yet to be established whether male coaches or female coaches experience higher levels of burnout.

Young coaches appear to have higher levels of perceived burnout than older coaches, partly because some older coaches have burned out of the profession.

Coaches who are more caring and people oriented appear more vulnerable to perceived burnout than goal-oriented, authoritarian coaches.

Greenspan, 1983). However, a noteworthy study by Silva (1990) found that collegiate athletes experienced burnout about once or twice during their college career, usually at the end of a season. These athletes indicated causes of their burnout were severe practice conditions, extreme physical fatigue, insufficient time to recover from competitive stress, inability to cope, and frustration with trying to satisfy everyone.

Here is a typical scenario that could lead to athlete burnout. First, the athlete gets into a slump (i.e., an extended period of low personal performance). Although execution problems are not detected, his performance outcome isn't up to his usual personal standards. He reacts by overcompensating with extra training. This begins a vicious cycle, with overtraining leading to staleness. If the problem becomes severe, burnout results.

Anecdotal evidence suggests that athlete burnout follows high training loads, pressure from coaches and parents, and competition over a long time period. Systematic research is needed.

Treatment and Prevention of Burnout

The goal in studying overtraining, staleness, and burnout is to learn how to develop programs and strategies that help sport personnel either prevent these conditions or at least treat them effectively. We offer these suggestions:

1. *Set short-term goals for competition and practice.* Setting short-term goals with incentives for reaching them not only provides feedback that the athlete is on the right course but also enhances long-term motivation. Meeting short-term goals is a success, which can enhance self-concept. Toward the end of the season it is particularly important to include fun goals. Most of an athlete's time is taken up in practice, rather than competition, so incorporate fun goals there. For example, if a team has been working really hard, its coach could say the practice goal is to simply have fun. She might let a soccer team play basketball or relax the game so that "everything goes" (no rules). These activities provide a break and reduce monotony.

Burnout in Young Tennis Players

Recently, teenagers and players in their early 20s have dominated the tennis scene. Steffi Graf and Monica Seles dominate on the women's professional tour while Jim Courier, Pete Sampras, Todd Martin, and Michael Chang are among the top men touring the tennis world. These young players are all excelling, but many more young players who were catapulted into professional tennis before they were emotionally and physically prepared to deal with its lifestyle have subsequently burned out.

The tennis establishment has been considering how to keep talented players in the game for 10 to 12 years instead of having them drop out after 3- or 4-year careers. The following suggestions have surfaced for reducing burnout in young tennis players:

- Hire staff psychologists to help young players handle the emotional stress of professional tennis.

- Decrease the number of tournaments players under the age of 16 can play.

- Set a "futures tour" for players 14 to 18 years of age. This would be a team concept with play limited to the summer to avoid interfering with school.

- Require a high school diploma of any player 18 years or older to compete on the professional tour.

- Hire multilingual teachers to tutor young players on tour.

2. *Communicate*. When professionals constructively analyze and communicate their feelings to others, burnout is less likely and less severe (Maslach, 1976). Following this concept, coaches, athletes, officials, trainers, and physical education teachers can be encouraged to express their feelings of frustration, anxiety, and disappointment and seek out social support from colleagues. Self-awareness early on might prevent burnout later. By sharing negative feelings, colleagues can often discover a humorous twist and necessary detachment from a particular situation.

3. *Take relaxation (time-out) breaks*. It is essential for mental and physical well-being to take some time out from our jobs and other stresses. The business world has vacations, holidays, and weekends away from work. But in competitive sport many people work almost year-round under continuous pressure.

Time-Out

An Olympic athlete used to live and train in southern California, where the weather is typically good year-round. In that sunny, warm environment she said she always felt guilty for missing a practice or taking a day off, but with her year-round training regimen she found herself getting injured often and feeling stressed and somewhat burned out. She moved to the middle of the country, where the weather was more variable—often extremely hot in the summer and extremely cold in the winter. When the weather was very bad she either took the day off or shortened her workout. To her surprise, the days off did not hurt her performance; instead her performance actually improved because she avoided injury and started to regain her enthusiasm. This led her to schedule relaxation or "off" days into her training.

The myth that more is better is still floating around when it comes to practice and workouts. Time off is seen as falling behind your opposition. Yet the weekly grind of practice and competitions produces mental and physical fatigue. In truth, cutting back on training loads and intensities as a burnout treatment or prevention is associated with increases in positive mental health. More is not necessarily better—in fact, more can sometimes be worse.

4. *Learn self-regulation skills.* Developing psychological skills such as relaxation, imagery, goal setting, and positive self-talk can ward off much of the stress that leads to burnout. For example, setting realistic goals can help manage time for balancing professional and personal lives. People who overtrain in sport usually do so at the expense of their family and personal lives. By setting realistic goals, you have time for both your sport and other responsibilities, helping you avoid the burnout syndrome.

5. *Keep a positive outlook.* It is easy for officials, for example, to let news commentary and criticism from coaches, spectators, and players get them down. Even when they officiate a great game, the losing coach may be upset and blame them. The antidote is to focus on what they do well. Seek people who provide social support (in this example, maybe other officials) to help you keep a positive outlook.

6. *Manage postcompetition emotions.* Although many coaches and athletes know to control pregame anxiety and tension, few consider what happens after competition. The final buzzer does not necessarily stop the intense psychological feelings aroused by the competition. Emotions often intensify and erupt into postgame quarrels, fights, drinking binges, and other destructive behaviors. On the other hand, some athletes become depressed, despondent, and withdrawn after losing or performing poorly. Henschen (1992) suggests some ways for coaches to handle postcompetition stress in athletes (see Table 23.3).

Table 23.3 Ways Coaches Can Reduce Postcompetition Stress in Athletes

1. Provide a supportive atmosphere immediately following a contest.
2. Concentrate on your players' emotions, not your own.
3. Try to be with your team after a contest (not on the radio or TV).
4. Provide an unemotional, realistic assessment of each athlete's performance.
5. Talk to all team members, even those who did not play.
6. Once athletes have dressed, have a team group activity (e.g., postgame meal, swimming, bowling, movie).
7. Keep athletes away from well-meaning but demanding peers and parents.
8. Do not allow team members to gloat over success or be depressed over a loss.
9. Begin preparation for the next opponent at the very next practice.

Adapted from Henschen (1992).

7. *Stay in good physical condition.* Your body and mind have a reciprocal relationship: Each affects the other. Chronic stress usually takes a toll on your body—so it's critical that you take good care of yourself through diet and exercise. Eating improperly, gaining weight, or losing too much weight only contribute to low self-esteem and self-worth, feeding into the burnout syndrome. When you feel particular stress, make a special attempt to stay in good physical condition to help your mental state stay strong.

Summary

With mounting pressures to win and year-round competition and practice in sport, overtraining and burnout have become more common. Only recently have researchers begun to systematically study these states. Overtraining is the abnormal extension of the training process with loads too intense for athletes to adapt to. Staleness is the end result of overtraining, a state in which athletes have difficulty maintaining standard training regimens and performance results. Burnout is another, more exhaustive psychophysiological response of withdrawal from excessive training and competitive demands. Excessive pressure and physical demands, boredom, and physical exhaustion are common causes of burnout, which is signaled by a variety of signs and symptoms, both physical and emotional.

Overtraining is generally associated with impaired performance and psychological distress. Smith's model of burnout shows a process of several stages involving a complex interaction of personal factors and environmental demands. Initial research into burnout with athletes, coaches, officials, and athletic trainers yields interesting observations, but more studies are needed to reach definitive conclusions. The chapter concluded with seven suggestions for preventing and managing overtraining and burnout in sport.

Review Questions

1. What are some causes of overtraining and burnout in athletes? In coaches?

2. Define the terms *overtraining*, *burnout*, and *staleness*, pointing out similarities and differences.

3. Use Morgan's "iceberg profile" to discuss the relation between psychological mood and performance.

4. Summarize the four major components of Smith's model of burnout.

5. Discuss two of the components of Smith's model of burnout in depth.

6. What are the four stages of burnout? Describe each in detail.

7. Discuss the findings of research on burnout among trainers and officials.

8. Discuss the inconsistency of findings on the relations of gender and age of coaches to burnout.

9. Describe three different antidotes, or treatments, for burnout and overtraining in sport.

References

Caccese, T.M., & Mayerberg, C.K. (1984). Gender differences in perceived burnout of college coaches. *Journal of Sport Psychology*, **6**, 279-288.

Capel, S.A. (1986). Psychological and organizational factors related to burnout in athletic trainers. *Research Quarterly for Exercise & Sport*, **57**, 321-328.

Dale, J., & Weinberg, R.S. (1990). Burnout in sport: A review and critique. *Journal of Applied Sport Psychology*, **2**, 67-83.

Duda, J.L. (Ed.). (1990). [Special issue]. *Journal of Applied Sport Psychology*, **2**(1).

Ellis, A. (1962). *Reason and emotion in psychotherapy*. Secaucus, NJ: Lyle Stuart.

Feigley, D.A. (1984). Psychological burnout in high-level athletes. *The Physician & Sportsmedicine*, **12**, 109-119.

Fender, L.K. (1989). Athlete burnout: Potential for research and intervention strategies. *The Sport Psychologist*, **3**, 63-71.

Flippin, R. (1981, July). Burnout out. *The Runner*, 77-83.

Gieck, J., Brown, R.S., & Shank, R.H. (1982, August). The burnout syndrome among athletic trainers. *Athletic Training*, 36-41.

Greenspan, E. (1983). Some athletes feel a burning desire to reach the top. Others feel burnout. *Women's Sport*, **5**, 50-53, 74.

Hackney, A.C., Perlman, S.N., & Nowacki, J.M. (1990). Psychological profiles of overtrained and stale athletes: A review. *Journal of Applied Sport Psychology*, **2**, 21-33.

Haggerty, T. (1982). An assessment of the degree of burnout on Canadian University coaches: A national survey. Unpublished master's thesis, York University.

Henschen, K. (1992). Athletic staleness and burnout: Diagnosis, prevention and treatment. In J. Williams (Ed.), *Sport psychology: Personal growth to peak performance* (pp. 328-337). Palo Alto: Mayfield.

Kroll, W., & Gunderscheim, J. (1982). Stress factors in coaching. *Coaching Science Update*, 47-49.

Lazarus, R.S. (1982). Thoughts on the relation between emotion and cognition. *American Psychologist*, **37**, 1019-1024.

Maslach, C. (1976). Burned-out. *Human Behavior*, **5**, 16-22.

Maslach, C., & Jackson, S.E. (1981). The measurement of experienced burnout. *Journal of Occupational Behavior*, **2**, 99-113.

McNair, D., Lorr, M., & Droppleman, L. (1971). *Profile of mood states manual.* San Diego: Educational and Testing Service.

Morgan, W.P., Brown, D.R., Raglin, J.S., O'Connor, P.J., & Ellickson, K.A. (1987a). Psychological monitoring of overtraining and staleness. *British Journal of Sport Medicine*, **21**(3), 107-114.

Morgan, W.P., O'Connor, P.J., Ellickson, K.A, & Bradley, P.W. (1988). Personality structure, mood states, and performance in elite distance runners. *International Journal of Sport Psychology*, **19**, 247-269.

Morgan, W.P., O'Connor, P.J., Sparling, P.B., & Pate, R.R. (1987b). Psychologic characterization of the elite female distance runner. *International Journal of Sports Medicine*, **8**, 124-131.

Murphy, S.M., Fleck, S.J., Dudley, G., & Callister, R. (1990). Psychological and performance concomitants of increased volume training in athletes. *Journal of Applied Sport Psychology*, **2**, 34-50.

Raglin, J.S. (1993). Overtraining and staleness: Psychometric monitoring of endurance athletes. In R. Singer, M. Murphey, & K. Tennent (Eds.), *Handbook of research on sport psychology* (pp. 840-850). New York: Macmillan.

Raglin, J.S., & Morgan, W.P. (1989). Development of a scale to measure training induced distress. *Medicine and Science in Sport and Exercise*, **21** (suppl.) 60.

Silva, J.M. (1990). An analysis of the training stress syndrome in competitive athletics. *Journal of Applied Sport Psychology*, **2**, 5-20.

Smith, R.E. (1986). Toward a cognitive-affective model of athletic burnout. *Journal of Sport Psychology*, **8**, 36-50.

Taylor, A.H., Daniel, J.V., Leith, L., & Burke, R.J. (1990). Perceived stress, psychological burnout and paths to turnover intentions among sport officials. *Journal of Applied Sport Psychology*, **2**, 84-97.

Weinberg, R.S., & Richardson, P.A. (1990). *Psychology of officiating.* Champaign, IL: Human Kinetics.

Wilson, V.E., Haggerty, T., & Bird, E. (1986, September). *Burnout in coaching sports.* Ottawa: The Coaching Association of Canada.

Facilitating Psychological Growth and Development

As we have learned, sport and exercise psychology focuses on helping people enhance performance through the use of mental skills. But this represents only part of the field. Sport psychology also deals with how psychological development and well-being occur as consequences of participation in sport and physical activity. The four chapters in this part concern four topics of psychological development and well-being important to both society and sport and exercise psychology.

Chapter 24 examines children's psychological development through sport participation, looking at such important issues as levels of stress experienced, self-esteem development, and effective coaching practices. Controlling aggression in sport and physical activity settings is the focus of chapter 25, whereas chapter 26 examines the related topic of moral development and sportsmanship. In these chapters you'll learn how to eliminate unwanted aggression and maximize character development through participation in sport and physical education. Last, chapter 27 looks at ways gender influences participation and motivation in sport.

Study of these chapters will help prepare you to assist your future students, athletes, and exercise clients in developing both strong bodies and strong minds. Given the prevalence of violence and other immoral behavior in today's society, promoting psychological development through sport and exercise will be among your top priorities.

CHAPTER 24

Children's Psychological Development Through Sport

Twenty-five million children participate in sport. What motivates them? Is competitive sport too stressful for them? Why do so many youngsters drop out of sport after the age of 12? Is there something wrong with how they're being coached? These are among the important questions we'll try to answer in this chapter.

It is ironic that most people think of sport psychology as applied to elite athletes. In fact, youngsters comprise the greatest population of sport participants, and since the mid-1970s a small but highly committed number of sport psychologists have devoted their careers to examining the important psychological issues in children's sport participation. Their work has major implications for creating safe and psychologically healthy sport programs for children.

In this chapter you will learn about

▌ the importance of studying the psychology of the young athlete,

▌ reasons children participate in sport,

■ reasons children drop out of sport,

■ stress and burnout effects in young athletes, and

■ effective coaching practices to use with youngsters.

Why a Psychology of the Young Athlete?

Some of the most important implications of sport psychology are in the children's sports arena.

In the United States alone, an estimated 25 million children under the age of 18 years are involved in school and extracurricular physical activity programs, ranging from youth basketball and baseball to cross-country skiing and rodeo (Martens, 1986). Some of sport psychology's most important contributions, therefore, are to children's sport.

Many children are intensely involved in organized sports. On average, they participate in their specific sport 11 hours weekly for an 18-week season (Gould & Martens, 1979). Sport is one of the few areas in children's lives in which they can intensively participate in activity that has meaningful consequences for themselves, peers, family, and community alike (Coleman, 1974).

For most children, sport participation peaks around the age of 12 years.

For most children sport participation peaks around the age of 12 years (State of Michigan, 1976). And we know from the developmental psychology literature that this age and the time leading up to it are critical times for children, having important consequences on self-esteem and social development. Thus, the youth sport experience can have important life-long effects on the personality and psychological development of children.

Finally, contrary to popular belief, participation in organized sport is not automatically beneficial for the child (Martens, 1978). Character development, leadership, sportsmanship, and achievement orientations do not magically occur through mere participation. These benefits usually follow competent, adult supervision from leaders who understand children and know how to structure programs that provide positive learning experiences. An important first step to becoming a qualified youth sport leader is understanding the psychology of young athletes.

Why Children Participate in Youth Sport

Some 8,000 youths (49% male, 51% female) involved in sponsored sports throughout the United States both in school and after school were asked to rank in importance a number of possible reasons for their participating (Ewing & Seefeldt, 1989). Both boys and girls in both school and nonschool athletic programs had similar responses (see Table 24.1) that were consistent

Why Sport Psychology for Young Athletes?

1. 25 million children participate in sport.

2. Children are intensely involved in sport.

3. Sport participation peaks at a critical time in children's lives.

4. Benefits of sport participation come only with qualified adult leadership.

Table 24.1   Motives for Participation in Youth Sports

Reasons for participating (nonschool sports)

Boys	Girls
1. To have fun	1. To have fun
2. To do something I'm good at	2. To stay in shape
3. To improve my skills	3. To get exercise
4. For the excitement of competition	4. To improve my skills
5. To stay in shape	5. To do something I'm good at
6. For the challenge of competition	6. To learn new skills
7. To get exercise	7. For the excitement of competition
8. To learn new skills	8. To play as part of a team
9. To play as part of a team	9. To make new friends
10. To go to a higher level of competition	10. For the challenge of competition

Reasons for participating (school sports)

Boys	Girls
1. To have fun	1. To have fun
2. To improve my skills	2. To stay in shape
3. For the excitement of competition	3. To get exercise
4. To do something I'm good at	4. To improve my skills
5. To stay in shape	5. To do something I'm good at
6. For the challenge of competition	6. To be part of a team
7. To be part of a team	7. For the excitement of competition
8. To win	8. To learn new skills
9. To go to a higher level of competition	9. For team spirit
10. To get exercise	10. For the challenge of competition

Adapted from Ewing and Seefeldt (1989).

with previous participation motivation research (Gould & Horn, 1984). Most children participate in sport to have fun, do something they are good at, improve their skills, get exercise and become fit, be with their friends and make new friends, and compete.

Why Children Discontinue Participation

Children's sport participation peaks between the ages of 10 and 13 years and then consistently declines to the age of 18, when a relatively small percentage of youths remain involved in organized sport (Ewing & Seefeldt, 1989; State of Michigan, 1976). Moreover, dropout rates for organized youth sport programs average 35% in any given year (Gould & Petlichkoff, 1988). So, of every 10 children who begin a sport season, 3 to 4 of them will drop out.

In an in-depth study of 50 swimming dropouts ranging in age from 10 to 18 years, "other things to do" and "a change in interest" were the major reasons children gave for discontinued involvement (Gould, Feltz, Horn, & Weiss, 1982). Other reasons 40% of the sample rated as important included

For every 10 children who begin a sports season, 3 to 4 quit before the season ends.

- not as good as I wanted to be,
- not enough fun,
- wanted to play another sport,

- didn't like the pressure,
- boredom,
- didn't like the coach,
- training was too hard, and
- not exciting enough.

So most young swimmers who quit did so not because of excessive pressure, dislike of the coach, failure, a lack of fun, or an overemphasis on winning. Rather, they discontinued because of interest in other activities. However, as many as 28% of the swimmers cited negative factors as major influences on their decision to withdraw.

The Importance of Perceived Competence

Of course the reasons youths give for participation and dropping out are their surface-level reasons, not the deeper, underlying motives some sport psychologists have sought (see Figure 24.1).

Figure 24.1 A motivation model of youth sport participation and withdrawal. Adapted from Gould and Petlichkoff (1988).

Motivation for Youth Sport Participation and Withdrawal

Why youngsters participate	*Why youngsters withdraw*
* Learn new skills	* Failure to learn new skills
* Fun	* Lack of fun
* Affiliation	* Lack of affiliation
* Thrills and excitement	* Lack of thrills and excitement
* Exercise and fitness	* Lack of exercise and fitness
* Competitive challenge/winning	* No challenge/failure

Underlying psychological motives for participation and withdrawal

- Perceived competence   • Goal orientations   • Stress response

Children with low perceptions of their athletic abilities drop out of or do not participate in sport, whereas children with high perceptions of their competence participate and persist.

Maureen Weiss, a leading researcher in this area, concluded that youth sport participants differ from nonparticipants and those who drop out in their level of perceived competence (Weiss & Chaumeton, 1992). That is, children with low perceptions of their abilities to learn and perform sport skills do not participate (or they drop out), whereas children who persist have higher levels of perceived competence.

From this information, you can infer that one very important task of youth sport leaders and coaches is to discover ways to enhance children's self-perceived ability. One way to do this is to teach children to evaluate their performances by their own standards of improvement rather than on competitive outcomes (winning or losing).

Sport-Specific and Sport-General Dropouts

Learn whether children are withdrawing from a particular sport or program or from sport participation altogether.

Youth sport leaders would want to know if children are withdrawing from their programs and entering other sports or withdrawing from sport participation altogether. For example, in the swimming study cited earlier, 68% of the youngsters who discontinued competitive swimming were active in other sports (Gould et al., 1982). Similarly, in a study of former competitive gymnasts, 95% were participating in another sport or were still in gymnastics, but at a less intense level (Klint & Weiss, 1986). Thus, we need to distinguish between sport-specific dropouts and sport transfers and those children who discontinue involvement in *all* of sport (Gould & Petlichkoff, 1988).

Implications for Practice

The research on why children participate or withdraw from sports leads to a number of general conclusions:

1. Most of the motivations children have for participating in sport (i.e., having fun, learning new skills, doing something one is good at, being with friends, making new friends, fitness, exercise, and to experience success) are intrinsic in nature. Winning clearly is neither the only nor the most common reason for participation.

2. Most young athletes have multiple reasons for participation, not a single motive.

3. Although most children withdraw because of interest in other activities, a significant minority discontinue for negative reasons such as a lack of fun, too much pressure, and disliking the coach.

4. Underlying the descriptive reasons for sport withdrawal (e.g., no fun) is the child's need to feel worthy and competent. When young athletes feel worthy and competent about the activity, they tend to participate. If they don't feel confident about performing the skills, they tend to withdraw.

Think about the interactional model of motivation—how a person interacts with a situation (see chapter 4). If you understand the reasons children participate in sport, you can enhance their motivation by structuring environments that better meet their needs. Study Table 24.2, which shows strategies a coach can use to structure the environment for skill development, fun, affiliation, excitement, success, and fitness.

Table 24.2 Structuring Sport Situations to Meet the Most Prevalent Needs of Young Athletes

Need	Coaching strategy
Learn and improve new skills	Implement effective instructional practices (e.g., effective demonstrations; contingent feedback) Foster a positive approach to instruction, emphasizing what the child does correctly Know the technical and strategic aspects of the sport
To have fun	Form realistic expectations to avoid negative coaching results and frustration Keep practices active—avoid lines and standing around Joke and kid around freely with the children
Affiliation	Provide time for children to make friends Schedule social events (e.g., pizza party) outside practice Incorporate periods of free time before and during practices
Excitement	Do not overemphasize time spent on drills; incorporate variety into practices Incorporate change-of-pace activities (e.g., water polo for swimmers) into practices Focus on short, crisp practices
Exercise and fitness	Teach young athletes how to monitor their own fitness Organize planned, purposeful practices specifically designed to enhance fitness
Competitive challenge and winning	Allow children to compete Help children define winning as not only beating others but as achieving one's own goals and standards

Teach young athletes to view success as exceeding their own goals, not merely as winning contests.

Rigorously analyze why young athletes withdraw from sport.

By emphasizing individual goal setting where children compare their athletic performances to their own standards (self-referenced standards), you will help them not focus sole attention on the outcomes of competitions (Martens, Christina, Harvey, & Sharkey, 1981) and they will more likely feel competent. When self-evaluation depends on winning and losing, 50% of young athletes can lose and develop low self-worth, making them less likely to continue sport participation.

Youth sport leaders can keep—and analyze—participation statistics and conduct exit interviews with children who drop out. In this way they can track how many children begin, continue, and complete seasons and, if they discontinue, whether they chose to participate in another sport or to discontinue involvement in sport altogether. They can ask whether young athletes discontinue because of conflicts with other interests (something adult leaders may not have control over) or because of poor coaching, competitive pressure, or lack of fun (which adult leaders can better control).

For example, a high school football coach was concerned by the low number of players coming out for his squad. He examined previous participation records at all levels of play and saw that many youngsters had participated in elementary school and summer programs but few had participated through the ninth grade. The coach spoke with some of the players who had discontinued during middle school and discovered that some very negative coaching had occurred at the seventh- and eighth-grade levels. He discussed with these coaches the advantages of a positive approach to coaching (explained later in this chapter) and found in subsequent years that more players were coming out for his high school team.

Stress and Burnout Effects

Stress and burnout are among the most controversial concerns in children's competitive sport. Critics argue that competitive sport places excessive levels of stress on youngsters, who often burn out from it. Proponents contend that young athletes do not experience excessive competition and that competition teaches children coping strategies, which transfer to other aspects of their lives.

Are Young Athletes Under Too Much Stress?

Levels of stress in young athletes have been assessed by using state anxiety measures administered in competitive game situations (where stress is predicted to be maximal). Most young athletes do *not* experience excessive levels of state anxiety in competition. For example, 13- and 14-year-old wrestlers took the Competitive State Anxiety Inventory for Children just before competition (see Figure 24.2, showing the distribution of anxiety scores of the 112 wrestlers). Their prematch state anxiety level averaged 18.9 out of a possible 30. Only 9% of the wrestlers had scores in the upper 25% of the scale, which could be considered extremely high. Thus, 91% of the wrestlers did not experience excessive stress (Gould et al., 1991).

Simon and Martens (1979) measured state anxiety levels of boys, ages 9 to 14, in both practice and socially evaluative settings. Of prime interest in this study is that state anxiety levels were compared among participants in band music solos, band group competitions, academic tests, competitive PE classes and in competitive baseball, basketball, tackle football, gymnastics, ice hockey, swimming, and wrestling. State anxiety was elevated more in competition than in practices, but this change was not dramatic. Also, levels exhibited in sport competition were not significantly greater than that in the other activities tested. In fact, band soloists reported the greatest state anxiety levels (M = 21.5 out of 30).

> State anxiety levels in children during sport competitions were not significantly higher than those during other childhood evaluative activities.

After these studies the question still remained whether there might be long-term stress effects apparent in the children's trait anxiety levels. Investigators examined sport participation's influence on children's trait anxiety (i.e., their predisposition to perceive competition as threatening and respond with heightened nervousness). From this research, it appears that young athletes have at most only slightly elevated trait anxiety levels. Moreover, in half the studies no differences were found (see Gould, 1993, for a detailed review).

> Excessive trait anxiety does not appear to be associated with youth sport participation.

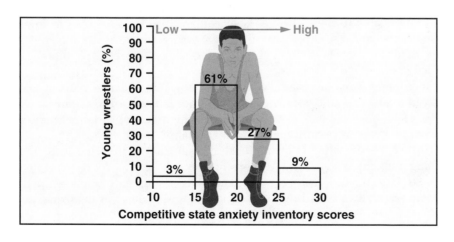

Figure 24.2 Prematch state anxiety levels in youth wrestlers.

Heightened State Anxiety in Young Athletes

Although most children who participate in sport do not experience excessive state or trait anxiety levels, stress can be a problem for certain children in specific situations. And while this may be true of only 1 of 10 children who participate, with 25 million young participants, that is 2.5 million children with heightened stress. For this reason, sport psychologists are examining what personal and situational factors are associated with heightened state anxiety by administering various background and personality measures away from the competitive setting (e.g., trait anxiety, self-esteem, team and individual performance expectancies, ratings of parental pressure to participate), as well as state anxiety assessments in practice, just before competition, and immediately after it. Links are then made between heightened levels of state anxiety and factors related to these changes (see Scanlan, 1986 for a detailed review).

Researchers have developed a profile of the young athlete at risk for experiencing unhealthy levels of competitive state anxiety (see box). A thorough knowledge of these characteristics will help you detect a child at risk.

Most of the research has examined at risk youngsters under 14 years of age, usually in local competitions. However, some studies have looked at elite junior athletes of high school age. For instance, elite high school distance runners experienced stress in performing up to their ability, improving on their last performance, participating in championship meets, not performing well, and not being mentally ready (Feltz & Albrecht, 1986). Elite junior wrestlers cited similar stressors (Gould, Horn, & Spreemann, 1983). Thus, elite junior competitors seem primarily stressed by a fear of failure and feelings of inadequacy.

High stress levels are relatively rare but can still affect over 2.5 million children in specific situations.

Stress in elite junior competitors is caused by a fear of failure and feelings of inadequacy.

Personal Characteristics of Children at Risk for Heightened Competitive State Anxiety

- High trait anxiety disposition
- Low self-esteem
- Low performance expectancies relative to his or her team
- Low self-performance expectancies
- Frequent worries about failure
- Frequent worries about adult expectations and social evaluation by others
- Less perceived fun
- Less satisfaction with his or her performance, regardless of winning or losing
- Perceived importance to parents that he or she participate in sport

Situational Sources of Stress

Situations too cause increased stress, particularly the following:

- Defeat or victory—children experience more state anxiety after losing than winning.
- Event importance—the more importance placed on a contest, the more state anxiety experienced by the participants.
- Sport type—children in individual sports experience more state anxiety than children in team sports.

Consequently, youth sport leaders must understand both the personalities of children at risk for high levels of competitive stress and the situations most likely to produce heightened state anxiety. We cannot help children deal with excessive stress until we identify the particular stresses specific situations elicit for each of them.

Stress-Induced Burnout

We discussed burnout at length in the previous chapter, including its implications for children. Here we'll only elaborate on earlier points, focusing on burnout as a stress-induced phenomenon in young athletes. See chapter 23 for greater development of some of the points touched on here.

Burnout is a growing concern in children's competitive sport and is thought to occur when children lose interest as a result of specializing in a specific sport at a very early age, for long hours, under intense pressure, and over several years. Children as young as age 4 begin participating in sports like gymnastics, swimming, and tennis and sometimes attain world-class levels by their early teens. When careers end early, or performance declines prematurely, burnout is suspected.

Recent studies have contributed to our understanding of burnout as a special case of sport withdrawal where a young athlete discontinues or curtails sport involvement in response to chronic or long-term stress (Smith, 1986). A previously enjoyable activity is no longer pleasurable because of the stress it causes. Children withdraw from sport, however, for reasons other than burnout.

Burnout is a special case of sport withdrawal in which a young athlete discontinues sport involvement in response to chronic stress.

Coakley (1992) found that adolescents who burned out of sport typically had one-dimensional self-definitions, seeing themselves only as athletes and not in other possible roles such as students, musicians, or school activity leaders. Also, young athletes who burned out had seriously restricted control of their own destinies, both in and out of sport. Their parents and coaches made the important decisions regarding their lives, with little or no input from them. As you learned in the section on feedback and reinforcement, someone else controlling your destiny almost always results in decreased intrinsic motivation.

Some prominent factors associated with burnout have been reported (see following box; Gould, 1993), with the end result being increased state anxiety. Unlike the usual state anxiety we experience before a contest, however, for a child en route to burnout, the stress does not abate but constantly builds. Thus, burnout is best viewed as the end result of long-term stress.

Practical Implications for Dealing With Stressed Children

Once you have identified children with stress or at high risk of experiencing stress, you must help these young athletes learn to cope.

Adult leaders should make concerted efforts to help children develop confidence by creating a positive environment and a positive, constructive attitude toward mistakes. Stress can be alleviated by reducing social evaluation and the importance of winning (e.g., no more "win one for the gipper" pep talks). Adult anxiety reduction techniques (progressive muscle relaxation, breath control, mental training, autogenic training, systematic desensitization, biofeedback, and cognitive-affective stress-management strategies) can be adapted for use with children. For instance, Terry Orlick (1992) has adapted progressive muscle relaxation for children by creating a "spaghetti toes" exercise (see box on page 459). Orlick and McCaffrey (1991) also have these suggestions for modifying arousal regulation and stress-management strategies for children:

- Use concrete and physical strategies (e.g., a little "stress bag" for children to put their worries in).
- Use fun strategies (e.g., have children release muscle tension by making their bellies turn to jello).

Factors Associated With Burnout in Young Athletes

- Overtraining
- Very high self- and other-imposed expectations
- Win-at-all-costs attitude
- Parental pressure
- Long repetitive practices with little variety
- Inconsistent coaching practices
- Overuse injuries from excessive practice
- Excessive time demands
- High travel demands
- Love from others distributed on the basis of winning and losing
- Perfectionism

- Use simple strategies (e.g., imagine changing TV channels to change one's mind focus).
- Vary approaches to the same exercise.
- Individualize approaches to the children's interests.
- Remain positive and optimistic.
- Use role models (e.g., tell them Michael Jordan uses positive self-talk).

General directions like "just relax" or "you can do it" are not enough to help children manage stress. You'll need to develop strategies to make the directions fun and seem relevant to the children.

Orlick's Spaghetti Toes Relaxation Exercise

There are lots of games you can play with your body. We'll start with one called Spaghetti Toes. I wonder how good you are at talking to your toes. I'll bet you're pretty good. Let's find out.

Tell the toes on one of your feet to wiggle. Are they wiggling? On just one foot? Good! Now tell these toes to stop wiggling. Tell the toes on your other foot to wiggle. Tell them to wiggle real slow . . . and faster . . . and real slow again . . . slower . . . stop. Did your toes listen to you? Good.

If you talk to different parts of your body, like you just did with your toes, your body will listen to you . . . especially if you talk to it a lot. I'm going to show you how you can be the boss of your body by talking to it.

First, I want to tell you something about spaghetti. I like spaghetti. I bet you do, too. But did you ever see spaghetti before it's cooked? It's kind of cold and hard and stiff and it's easy to break. When it's cooked, it's warm and soft and kinda lies down and curls up on your plate.

I want to see if you can talk to your toes to get them to go soft and warm and sleepy like cooked spaghetti lying on your plate. You might have to talk to them quite a bit to make them know what you want them to do, but I know they can do it.

Wiggle your toes on one foot. Now tell these toes to stop wiggling. Tell them to go soft and sleepy like warm spaghetti lying on your plate. Now wiggle the toes on your other foot. Stop wiggling. Turn those toes into soft spaghetti. Good.

Now wiggle one leg. Stop wiggling. Tell the leg to go soft and sleepy like warm spaghetti. Now wiggle the other leg. Stop. Tell it to go soft and sleepy. Wiggle your behind. Let it go soft and sleepy.

Wiggle your fingers on one hand. Tell your fingers to stop wiggling. See if you can make those fingers feel warm and soft and sleepy like spaghetti lying on your plate. Now wiggle your fingers on your other hand. Slowly. Stop. Make those fingers feel warm. Tell them to go soft and sleepy.

Now wiggle one arm. Stop. Tell your arm to go soft and sleepy. Now wiggle the other arm and tell it to go soft and sleepy. Good.

Try to let your whole you go soft and warm and sleepy like soft spaghetti lying on your plate. [Pause] That's really good. Your body is listening well. Let your body stay like spaghetti and just listen to me. I want to tell you about when spaghetti toes can help you.

When you are worried or scared of something, or when something hurts, your toes and your hands and muscles get kinda hard and stiff—like hard spaghetti before it's cooked. If you are worried, scared, or something hurts you, you feel a lot better and it doesn't hurt so much if your hands and toes and muscles are like warm, soft spaghetti lying on a plate. If you practice doing your spaghetti toes you'll get real good at it. Then you can tell your hands and toes and muscles to help you by going warm and soft and sleepy, even if you are scared or something hurts.

Before you go, let's try talking to your mouth. Wiggle your mouth. Let it go soft and sleepy. Wiggle your tongue. Let it go soft and sleepy. Wiggle your eyebrows. Let them go soft and sleepy. Let your whole you go warm and soft and sleepy. Let your whole you feel good.
(Orlick, 1992a, p. 325)

Effective Coaching Practices

You may have heard about or seen Little League coaches who emulate big-time college or professional coaches to try to achieve success and impress people. For example, former Vice President Dan Quayle once boasted that he modeled his coaching of his 12-year-old son's basketball team after Indiana University basketball coach Bobby Knight. But is Knight's style (especially his use of punishment, severe criticism, and emotional outbursts) appropriate to use with 12-year-olds? Probably not. Coaching practices designed for adult elite athletes are often inappropriate for developing young athletes. Sport psychologists have found many coaching practices that are effective with youngsters.

What the Research Says About Coaching Children

The classic research about coaching children was conducted at the University of Washington by Ron Smith, Frank Smoll, and their colleagues. They examined the relation between coaching behaviors (e.g., reinforcement, mistake-contingent technical instruction) and self-esteem in young baseball players and whether coaches could learn effective coaching practices (Smith, Smoll, & Curtis, 1979). Their study had two phases. In the first phase, 52 male youth baseball coaches were observed while coaching and assessed using a specially developed instrument, the Coaching Behavior Assessment System (CBAS). The researchers also interviewed 542 players about their Little League baseball experiences and found that coaches who gave technical instruction were rated more positively than those who gave general communication and encouragement. The coaches who used more reinforcement and mistake-contingent technical instruction (gave instruction after errors) were also highly rated—and these results held even when team win-loss records were considered. Positive reinforcement and mistake-contingent encouragement (encouraging a player after a mistake) positively affected postseason self-esteem measures, liking of teammates, and liking of baseball.

Unfortunately, the first phase did not show that the coaching behaviors actually *caused* changes in the athletes' perceptions, only that these factors were correlated. In a second phase investigators assigned 32 baseball coaches to either a control condition—where they coached as they had always done—or to an experimental coaching education program where they received training based on the first phase results. The experimental group received guidelines on desirable coaching behaviors, saw these behaviors modeled, and were monitored until they increased the frequency of their encouraging remarks by 25%. The control group did not receive any special training (their coaching, however, was not excessively negative).

As you might expect, the experimental group coached different from the control group: They were more encouraging, gave more reinforcement, and were less punitive. The players in the experimental group rated their coaches as better teachers, liked their teammates more, liked their coaches more, and showed greater positive changes in self-esteem than the control group players.

These findings clearly identify coaching behaviors associated with positive psychological development in children. Moreover, the research shows that coaches can learn these positive behaviors.

Other studies have found that remarks from coaches must be not only positive but also sincere to be effective (Horn, 1985); giving information frequently after good performances and encouragement combined with information after poorer performances is associated with effectiveness, competence, and enjoyment (Black & Weiss, 1992); and learning a positive approach to coaching results in lower player dropout rates (5%, compared to 26% with untrained coaches) (Barnett, Smoll, & Smith, 1992).

A coach's technical instruction, reinforcement, and mistake-contingent encouragement correlate with a player's self-esteem, motivation, and positive attitudes.

Implications for Practice

Some ready observations for practical work follow from these studies. The following 11 coaching guidelines are drawn from Smoll and Smith (1980) and Weiss (1991).

1. Catch kids doing things right and give them plenty of praise and encouragement. Praise young children frequently. Add such rewards as a pat on the back and a friendly smile. The best way to give encouragement is to focus on what youngsters do correctly rather than on the errors they make.

2. Give praise sincerely. Praise and encouragement are ineffective unless they are sincere. Telling a young athlete she did a good job when she knows she did not conveys that you are trying only to make her feel better. Insincerity destroys your credibility as a leader or coach. Recognize poor performance in a nonpunitive specific way (put your arm around the child and say, "It can be really tough out there"), but also offer some encouragement ("stick with it, it will come").

3. Develop realistic expectations. Realistic expectations appropriate to the child's age and ability level make it much easier for a coach to offer sincere praise. You can't expect of an 11-year-old what you might of a 16-year-old.

4. Reward effort as much as outcome. It's easy to be positive when everything is going well. Unfortunately, things don't always go well—teams lose and sometimes perform poorly. However, if a youngster gives 100% effort, what more can you ask? Reward efforts of young athletes as much as—or even more than—game outcomes.

5. Focus on teaching and practicing skills. All the positive coaching techniques in the world will do little good unless youngsters see improvement in their physical skills. Design practices that maximize participation and include plenty of activity and drill variety. Keep instructions short and simple. Give plenty of demonstrations from multiple angles. Maximize equipment and facility use.

6. Modify skills and activities. One of our goals is for children to experience performance successes. Modifying activities so they are developmentally appropriate is an excellent way to ensure success. For example, make sure baskets are lowered, batting tees used, and field distances modified. "Match the activity to the child, not the child to the activity" (Weiss, 1991, p. 347). Use appropriate skill progressions.

7. Modify rules to maximize action and participation. Rules can be modified to ensure success and enhance motivation. You might modify the traditional baseball or softball rules so that coaches pitch to their own teams, which greatly increases the probability of hits. In basketball, instruct referees to call only the most obvious fouls until the child becomes more skilled. Children can rotate positions to give everyone a chance to be in the action. Modify rules to increase scoring and action. This will keep scores close and games exciting.

8. Reward correct technique, not just outcome. A common mistake in coaching youngsters is to reward the *outcome* of a skill (e.g., getting a base hit in baseball or softball), even when the *process* of skill execution is done incorrectly (poor swing). In the long run, this isn't helpful: Proper form is usually needed to achieve desirable outcomes consistently. Encourage and reward correct technique regardless of outcome.

9. Use a positive "sandwich" approach when you correct errors. How can you give frequent praise when young athletes are learning and making many mistakes? One way is to use the positive sandwich approach, as discussed in chapter 12. When a child makes a mistake, first mention something she did

correctly ("Good try, you didn't give up on the dive"). This will help reduce her frustration in making the error. Second, provide information to correct the error made (e.g., "Tuck earlier and tighter on the dive"). Then end positively with an encouraging remark ("Stick with it—it's a tough dive, but you'll get it"). Thus, you will have created a psychological sandwich, as illustrated in Figure 24.3.

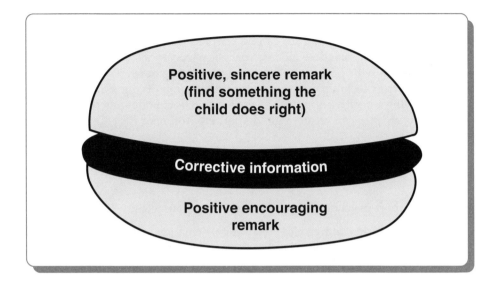

Figure 24.3 A positive psychological sandwich approach to error correction.

10. Create an environment that reduces fear of trying new skills. Mistakes are a natural part of the learning process, what UCLA basketball coach John Wooden called the building blocks of success. Provide an encouraging atmosphere where ridicule is not tolerated.

11. Be enthusiastic! Children respond well to positive, stimulating environments. Breed enthusiasm in the pool, gym, or on the playing field. As leading youth sport expert Maureen Weiss says, enthusiasm is contagious! Smile, interact, and listen.

Summary

Applying strategies from sport psychology is vital in youth sport settings because children are at such critical points in their developmental cycles. Qualified adult leadership is crucial to assure a beneficial experience. Children cite many reasons for sport participation, including having fun, skill improvement, and being with friends. They also have various reasons for dropping out of sport, including changing interests and interest in other activities. Underlying these motives is the young athlete's need to feel worthy and competent. Children who perceive themselves as competent seek out participation and stay involved in sport, whereas children who see themselves as failing often drop out.

Adult leaders can facilitate children's participation and deter withdrawal by structuring the athletic environment to meet young athletes' motives for involvement, enhancing self-worth by focusing on individual performance goals and downplaying socially compared outcome goals, tracking participation and dropout statistics, and conducting exit interviews to determine why youngsters discontinue program involvement.

Most young athletes do not experience excessive levels of competitive stress in sport, but a significant number do. High trait anxiety, low self-esteem, low self-performance expectations, frequent worry about evaluation, less fun and satisfaction, and parental pressure combine to put children at risk for excessive state anxiety. Losing, attaching great importance to an event, and individual competition are situational factors that add to stress.

Stress-induced burnout is a specialized withdrawal where a young athlete discontinues or curtails involvement in response to long-term stress. Knowing potential causes of burnout helps adults teach children to cope with stress. Arousal-management techniques can be adapted for use with children.

Effective coaching practices include realistic expectations; techniques to provide youngsters with positive, encouraging, and sincere feedback; rewarding effort and correct technique as much as outcome; modifying skills and rules; and employing a positive approach to error correction. Following the 11 guidelines in this chapter can create a good sport environment for children.

Review Questions

1. Why is sport psychology important for young athletes?

2. What reasons do children cite for sport participation and withdrawal? How does a child's level of perceived athletic competence relate to participation and withdrawal?

3. Distinguish between sport-specific and sport-general withdrawal. Why is this distinction important?

4. How can we make young athletes feel worthy?

5. Are young athletes placed under too much stress in sport? What children in what situations are at risk of experiencing the highest levels of stress?

6. What is burnout? What causes young athletes to burn out of sport?

7. What can be done to help young athletes cope with stress? What strategies can be employed?

8. What were the major findings of Smith, Smoll, and their colleagues' research?

9. Identify and describe 11 practical coaching guidelines from the youth sport coaching effectiveness research.

References

Barnett, N.P., Smoll, F.L., & Smith, R.E. (1992). Effects of enhancing coach-athlete relationships on youth sport attrition. *The Sport Psychologist*, **6**, 111-127.

Black, S.J., & Weiss, M.R. (1992). The relationship among perceived coaching behaviors, perceptions of ability, and motivation in competitive age-group swimmers. *Journal of Sport and Exercise Psychology*, **14**, 309-325.

Coakley, J. (1992). Burnout among adolescent athletes: A personal failure or social problem? *Sociology of Sport Journal*, **9**, 271-285.

Coleman, J.S. (1974). *Youth: Transition to adulthood*. Chicago, IL: University of Chicago Press.

Ewing, M.E., & Seefeldt, V. (1989). *Participation and attrition patterns in American agency-sponsored and interscholastic sports: An executive summary.* Final Report. Sporting Goods Manufacturer's Association, North Palm Beach, FL.

Feltz, D.L., & Albrecht, R.R. (1986). Psychological implications of competitive running. In M.R. Weiss & D. Gould (Eds.), *Sports for children and youth* (pp. 225-230). Champaign, IL: Human Kinetics.

Gould, D. (1993). Intensive sport participation and the prepubescent athlete: Competitive stress and burnout. In B.R. Cahill & A.J. Pearl (Eds.), *Intensive participation in children's sports* (pp. 19-38). Champaign, IL: Human Kinetics.

Gould, D., Eklund, R., Petlichkoff, L., Peterson, K., & Bump, L. (1991). Psychological predictors of state anxiety and performance in age-group wrestlers. *Pediatric Exercise Science, 3,* 198-208.

Gould, D., Feltz, D., Horn, T., & Weiss, M. (1982). Reasons for attrition in competitive youth swimming. *Journal of Sport Behavior, 5,* 155-165.

Gould, D., & Horn, T. (1984). Participation motivation in young athletes. In J.M. Silva & R.S. Weinberg (Eds.), *Psychological foundations of sport* (pp. 359-370). Champaign, IL: Human Kinetics.

Gould, D., Horn, T., & Spreemann, J. (1983). Sources of stress in junior elite wrestlers. *Journal of Sport Psychology, 5,* 159-171.

Gould, D., & Martens, R. (1979). Attitudes of volunteer coaches toward significant youth sport issues. *Research Quarterly, 50*(3), 369-380.

Gould, D., & Petlichkoff, L. (1988). Participation motivation and attrition in young athletes. In F. Smoll, R. Magill, & M. Ash (Eds.), *Children in sport* (3rd ed., pp. 161-178). Champaign, IL: Human Kinetics.

Horn, T.S. (1985). Coaches' feedback and children's perception of their physical competence. *Journal of Educational Psychology, 77,* 174-186.

Klint, K.A., & Weiss, M.R. (1986). Dropping in and dropping out: Participation motives of current and former youth gymnasts. *Canadian Journal of Applied Sport Sciences, 11,* 106-114.

Martens, R. (1978). *Joy and sadness in children's sports.* Champaign, IL: Human Kinetics.

Martens, R. (1986). Youth sports in the USA. In M.R. Weiss & D. Gould (Eds.), *Sport for children and youths* (pp. 27-33). Champaign, IL: Human Kinetics.

Martens, R., Christina, R.W., Harvey, J.S., & Sharkey, B.J. (1981). *Coaching young athletes.* Champaign, IL: Human Kinetics.

Orlick, T. (1992). *Freeing children from stress: Focusing and stress control activities for children.* ITA Publications, PO Box 1599, Willits, CA.

Orlick, T., & McCaffrey, N. (1991). Mental training with children for sport and life. *The Sport Psychologist, 5,* 322-334.

Scanlan, T.K. (1986). Competitive stress in children. In M.R. Weiss & D. Gould (Eds.), *Sport for children and youth* (pp. 113-118). Champaign, IL: Human Kinetics.

Seefeldt, V., Ewing, M., & Walk, S. (1993). *Overview of youth sports programs in the United States.* Unpublished manuscript commissioned by the Carnegie Council on Adolescent Development.

Simon, J., & Martens, R. (1979). Children's anxiety and sport and nonsport evaluative activities. *Journal of Sport Psychology, 1*(1), 160-169.

Smith, R.E. (1986). Toward a cognitive-affective model of athletic burnout. *Journal of Sport Psychology, 8,* 36-50.

Smith, R.E., Smoll, F.L., & Curtis, B. (1979). Coach effectiveness training: A cognitive-behavioral approach to enhancing relationship skills in youth sport coaches. *Journal of Sport Psychology, 1,* 59-75.

Smoll, F.L., & Smith, R.E. (1980). Psychologically oriented coach training programs: Design, implementation, and assessment. In C.H. Nadeau, W.R. Halliwell, K.M. Newell, & G.C. Roberts (Eds.), *Psychology of motor behavior and sport—1979*. Champaign, IL: Human Kinetics.

State of Michigan (1976). *Joint legislative study on youth sports programs. Phase 2.* East Lansing, MI: Author.

Weiss, M.R. (1991). Psychological skill development in children and adolescents. *The Sport Psychologist*, **5**, 335-354.

Weiss, M.R., & Chaumeton, N. (1992). Motivational orientations in sport. In T.S. Horn (Ed.), *Advances in sport psychology* (pp. 61-99). Champaign, IL: Human Kinetics.

Aggression in Sport

Aggression in sport has become all too common. We see it in the bleachers, on the benches, and most commonly on the fields or courts of sport arenas: bench-clearing brawls, brushback pitches and retaliatory beanings, ice hockey fights, moats and electric fences surrounding soccer fields, city-wide riots during postcontest celebrations, stalkers preying on star athletes, weapon searches at high school football games, an Australian sport psychologist held hostage at gunpoint by a disgruntled athlete, and a frenzied fan attacking a popular tennis star during a break between games. Even Little League sport coaches settle altercations with their fists, and one father murdered a coach in a dispute over his son's playing time.

In the last 20 years society has become more violent in general, and sport reflects this. Yet sport can also be a vehicle to control or curb violence. Midnight inner-city basketball games have become popular because they are thought to keep gang members off the street, and boxing, wrestling, and, to a lesser extent, football are seen by many as socially acceptable channels for aggression.

In this chapter you will learn about

▌ what is meant by aggression,

▌ the causes of aggression,

▌ some common myths about aggression,

▌ spectator aggression,

▌ the aggression-performance relation, and

▌ implications for practice.

What Is Aggression?

The term *aggression* is used in several ways. We speak of "good" aggression (e.g., going after a loose ball in volleyball or lowering your shoulder in a drive toward the basket) and "bad" aggression (e.g., taking a cheap shot in soccer or committing a flagrant foul in basketball). The term seems to draw automatic associations and produce positive or negative value judgments and emotional responses (Gill, 1986). However, most aggressive behavior in sport and physical activity settings appears not to be inherently desirable or undesirable but to depend on interpretation. Two people watching a particular hard but clean check in ice hockey might disagree whether the hit was good or bad aggression. Aggression is easier to talk about if you avoid the good/bad dichotomy and view it neutrally as a behavior you want to understand (Gill, 1986).

Criteria for Aggression

Psychologists define aggression as "any form of behavior directed toward the goal of harming or injuring another living being who is motivated to avoid such treatment" (Baron, 1977, p. 7).

In examining this and similar definitions, four criteria of aggression emerge (Gill, 1986):

> 1. Aggression is a behavior.
> 2. It involves harm or injury.
> 3. It is directed toward a living organism.
> 4. It involves intent.

Aggression is physical or verbal behavior: It is *not* an attitude or emotion. Aggression involves harm or injury, which may be either physical or psychological (e.g., we would all agree that hitting someone with a baseball bat is an aggressive act, but so too is purposely embarrassing someone or saying something hurtful). Aggression is directed toward another living thing. Punching someone is certainly aggressive, as is slapping a cat who scratches your new chair. But throwing your helmet in disgust after striking out in softball while in bad taste is not aggressive. Finally, aggression is intentional. Accidental harm, even unintentionally shooting someone, is not aggressive because you did not intend to do harm.

So, when sport psychologists are discussing aggression in general they are referring to what many people would call bad aggression. By the same token, not all "bad" aggression would be aggressive according to the sport psychology definition.

What many people call examples of good aggression in sport (e.g., charging the net in tennis) are labelled *assertive* behaviors in sport psychology (Husman &

Aggression is defined as any behavior directed toward intentionally harming or injuring another living being.

Silva, 1984)—that is, playing within the rules with high intensity and emotion but without intention to do harm.

Now that you're getting comfortable with this new way of thinking about aggression, try the test in the following box to check your understanding of the criteria marking aggression.

Defining Aggression

Using Gill's four criteria, circle A or N to indicate whether you consider the behavior in each of these situations to be aggressive (A) or nonaggressive (N).

A   N   1. A football safety delivers an extremely vicious but legal hit to a wide receiver and later indicates he wanted to punish the receiver and make him think twice about coming across the middle again.

A   N   2. A football safety delivers an extremely vicious and illegal hit to a wide receiver and later indicates he wanted to punish the receiver and make him think twice about coming across the middle again.

A   N   3. A basketball coach breaks a chair in protesting a disputed call.

A   N   4. Marcia, a field hockey midfielder, uses her stick to purposely hit her opponent in the shin in retaliation for her opponent's doing the same thing to her.

A   N   5. A race car driver kills a fellow competitor by running into the competitor's stalled car coming out of a turn.

A   N   6. Trying to make an opposing field goal kicker worry and think about the negative ramifications of a game-winning field goal, Coach Sullivan calls a time out.

A   N   7. Barry knows that John is very sensitive and self-conscious about his ability to putt under pressure, so he tells John that Coach Hall said if he does not putt better he will be replaced in the line-up. Coach Hall never said this.

A   N   8. Jane beans Fran with a fastball that got away from her.

Defining Aggression—Test Key

Question 1—Aggressive (Although the hit was legal, the intent was to inflict harm.)

Question 2—Aggressive (The intent was to inflict harm.)

Question 3—Nonaggressive (The action was not directed at another living being.)

Question 4—Aggressive (Although the athlete felt she was hit first, her intent was to inflict harm.)

Question 5—Nonaggressive (Although the other driver was killed, there was no intent to do harm.)

Question 6—Aggressive (Although many would consider this a tactically smart move, the intent was to inflict psychological harm in the form of fear and anxiety to another.)

Question 7—Aggressive (As in Question 6, the intent was to inflict psychological harm.)

Question 8—Nonaggressive (Although harm resulted, there was no intent to harm.)

Hostile and Instrumental Aggression

In hostile aggression the primary goal is to inflict injury or psychological harm on another, whereas instrumental aggression occurs in the quest of some non-aggressive goal.

Psychologists distinguish two types of aggression (Husman & Silva, 1984): reactive, or hostile, and instrumental. With *hostile* aggression the primary goal is to inflict injury or psychological harm on someone else. *Instrumental* aggression, on the other hand, occurs in the quest of some nonaggressive goal. For instance, when a boxer lands a solid blow to an opponent's head, injury or harm is usually inflicted. However, usually such an action is an example of instrumental aggression—the boxer's primary goal is to win the bout and by inflicting harm to his opponent (scoring points or by knocking him out) he can do that. If a boxer pinned his opponent to the ropes and purposely tried to punish him with blows to the head and body while consciously trying *not* to end the match, this would qualify as hostile (reactive) aggression.

Most aggression in sport is instrumental, such as

- a wrestler squeezing an opponent's ribs to create discomfort and turn him over,
- a cornerback delivering a particularly hard hit to a receiver to deter him from running a pass route across the middle of the field, or
- a basketball coach calling a time-out when an opposing player is on the foul line, trying to cause psychological discomfort (heightened state anxiety) and poor performance.

Professionals in sport and exercise science must have well-thought-out philosophies distinguishing acceptable and unacceptable instrumental aggressive behaviors.

Of course, hostile and instrumental aggression both involve the intent to injure and harm. Although most sporting aggression is instrumental, that does not make it acceptable. Professionals in sport and exercise science must have a well-thought-out philosophy as to what is acceptable and unacceptable instrumental aggressive behavior.

Causes of Aggression

Why are some children more aggressive than others? What causes some athletes to lose control? Are aggressive individuals born or are they a product of their environment? Psychologists have advanced four important theories regarding causes of aggression:

1. Instinct theory
2. Frustration-aggression theory
3. Social learning theory
4. Revised frustration-aggression theory

We'll discuss each of these theories below.

Instinct Theory

According to the *instinct theory* (Gill, 1986), people have an innate instinct to be aggressive that builds up until it must inevitably be expressed. This instinct can either be expressed directly by attacking another living being or displaced through *catharsis*, where aggression is released or "blown off" through socially desirable means such as sport. Thus, for an instinct theorist, sport and exercise play an extremely important function in society in that they allow people to channel their aggressive instincts in socially acceptable ways.

Unfortunately, no biologically innate aggressive instinct has ever been identified and no support has been found for the notion of catharsis. So we cannot cite the instinct theory in claiming that physical education and sport programs provide a socially acceptable means of channeling natural aggressive urges.

There is little support for the instinct theory of aggression or its tangent notion of catharsis.

Frustration-Aggression Theory

The *frustration-aggression theory*, sometimes called the *drive theory*, states simply that aggression is the direct result of a frustration that occurs because of goal blockage or failure (Dollard, Doob, Miller, Mowrer, & Sears, 1939). The hypothesis at first made intuitive sense to psychologists because most aggressive acts are committed when people are frustrated. For example, when a soccer player feels she has been illegally held by her opponent, she becomes frustrated and takes a swing at the defender. However, this view has little support today because of its insistence that frustration must *always* cause aggression. Research and experience repeatedly show that people often cope with their frustration or express it in nonaggressive ways.

Frustration-aggression theorists counter that aggressive responses that occur are not always obvious: They may get channeled through socially acceptable outlets like competitive contact sports. Thus, like instinct theorists, frustration-aggression proponents view catharsis as playing a major role. As we've mentioned, little evidence exists of catharsis in sport. Consequently, there's also little evidence that frustrated, aggressive participants in contact sports lower their aggression levels through participation (Gill, 1986). In fact, in some instances they may become more aggressive (Arms, Russell, & Sandilands, 1979).

Despite its shortcomings, the frustration-aggression hypothesis has contributed a valuable awareness of frustration's role in the aggression process.

Social Learning Theory

Social learning theory explains aggression as behavior learned through observing others model behaviors then getting reinforcement for exhibiting similar actions. Psychologist Albert Bandura (1973) found that children who watched adult models commit violent acts (beat up bobo dolls) repeated those acts more than children unexposed to such aggressive models. These effects were especially powerful when the children were reinforced for copying the actions of the adult models.

Sport psychologists and sociologists have studied ice hockey because of the pervasiveness of illegal aggressive actions, like fighting, in the sport. Smith (1988) found that the violence prevalent in the professional game is modeled by young amateur players. In fact, in ice hockey aggression is valued and players quickly learn that being aggressive is a way to gain personal recognition. Many coaches, parents, and teammates accept and reinforce these aggressive acts (Smith, 1988). Young hockey players watch their heroes on television model aggressive behavior and receive reinforcement for exhibiting similar behavior.

Social-learning research in sport shows that most athletes are not taught to be blatantly violent. However, aggression can and does occur in every sport. A figure skater, for example, may attempt to psych out an opponent and make upsetting remarks, such as "I heard that the judges said a costume like that is illegal this year." And this is more subtle aggression: The intent still is to harm another. Most parents and coaches do not condone unprovoked attacks on others, yet aggression is often sanctioned in response to another's aggressive act. For example, a young basketball player is instructed not to violate rules and hit others, but in a particularly rough game with shoving and elbowing under the boards, he or she is taught to retaliate in kind.

Social learning theory has considerable scientific support. It emphasizes the important role that significant others have on the development or control of aggression.

The frustration-aggression hypothesis, which maintains that frustration *always* causes aggression, is generally dismissed today.

There's little or no evidence to indicate that frustrated athletes lower their aggression levels through participation in contact sports.

The social learning theory, which explains aggression as behavior learned through observing others and then having similar behavior reinforced, has considerable scientific support.

The Case of Bad Billy

Seven-year-old Billy, a goalie with the midget hockey league's Buffalo Bombers, gets entangled with teammates and opponents in a skirmish around his net. Billy is hit and dazed but is uncertain by whom or what. Angry, he retaliates by punching the nearest opponent in the nose. The referee throws Billy out of the game. Billy's coach tells him he shouldn't throw a punch because the team needs him and he is no help sitting on the bench. However, Billy later overhears his coach boast to an assistant, "What a scrapper and competitor that Billy is," which made Billy feel good.

At home, Billy's dad seems proud of Billy's performance. He tells Billy never to start a fight and just hit anybody out there on the ice, but he's got to be a man and defend himself: "Hockey is a dog-eat-dog game, and you can't let anybody push you around out there—after all, you don't see the NHL goalies take any guff."

Lately, Billy has become a goalie his opponents fear—anybody in the crease is liable to get extra rough treatment from him. Billy now watches the pros to learn how to be rough and tough without getting kicked out of the game! (Adapted from Martens, 1982)

Revised Frustration-Aggression Theory

A revised frustration-aggression theory combines elements of the original frustration-aggression hypothesis with social learning theory. This widely held view holds that although frustration does not always lead to aggression, it increases the likelihood of aggression by increasing arousal and anger (Leonard Berkowitz, 1965, 1969). However, increased arousal and anger only result in aggression when socially learned cues signal the appropriateness of aggression in the particular situation. If the socially learned cues signal that aggression is inappropriate, it will not result.

Figure 25.1 depicts the aggression process, based on Berkowitz's model. First, the individual becomes frustrated in some way, perhaps by losing the game or playing poorly. Then increased arousal, usually in the form of anger or pain, results from the frustration. Aggression will not automatically result, and increased arousal and anger lead to aggression only if the individual has learned that it is appropriate to be aggressive in such a situation. Thus, a football safety who is frustrated after being badly beaten on a deep pass pattern for a touchdown may lash out at his opponent if his coaches have previously tolerated this behavior.

The strengths of the revised frustration-aggression theory are that it combines the best elements of the original frustration-aggression and social learning theories and uses an interactional model (the individual's level of arousal-anger within the context of socially learned environmental cues) to explain behavior.

The revised frustration-aggression theory is currently one of the most popular theories on aggression.

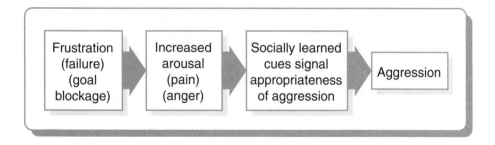

Figure 25.1 Revised frustration-aggression theory.

Aggression in Sport: Special Considerations

Competitive sport differs from many activities in that it is usually conducted in the presence of fans and spectators. Fans are not passive observers—they actively identify with their teams. Their involvement is usually well-mannered and supportive, but instances of fan violence appear to be on the rise. In response to concerns about fan violence, sport psychologists have studied spectator aggression.

Spectators and Aggression

Psychologists first tested the catharsis theory to determine whether fans become more or less aggressive after watching sport events. In general, they found that observing a sporting event does not lower the level of the spectator's aggression. Moreover, watching some violent contact sports actually increases a spectator's readiness to be aggressive (Isoahola & Hatfield, 1986). However, aggression usually does not occur without other environmental or game-related factors. For instance, a study of 1,500 hockey spectators found that fan aggression is more likely with younger spectators in crowded conditions and under the influence of alcohol (Cavanaugh & Silva, 1980). Rivalries are also associated with fan violence. Smith (1983) found these additional factors are triggers for or associated with spectator aggression:

- Small-scale aggressive acts on the field (e.g., a brief shoving match between players or a heated argument over a call)
- Male gender
- Working-class economic status

Those in sport management and administration should note these findings to help decrease the probability of violence (e.g., by eliminating sales of alcohol and enforcing strict seating capacities to minimize crowd density). Obviously, coaches and players should maintain emotional control on the field to ensure they are not triggers for fan aggression.

Game Reasoning and Aggression

An alarming research finding is that many athletes view some aggressive acts as inappropriate in general but appropriate in the sport environment (Bredemeier & Shields, 1986). For example, in certain sport situations fighting is deemed appropriate (e.g., if a pitcher intentionally beans you), whereas no form of fighting would be tolerated in the school band. This double standard is called *game reasoning* or *bracketed morality*.

Unfortunately, people are learning and believing it is okay to be more aggressive in sport than in other life contexts. This presents a problem. First, aggression carries the risk of injury and harm. Also, sport can and should serve to teach children how to behave appropriately inside and outside of sport. Allowing (or applauding) aggressive behavior in sport sends the wrong message to children. Sport professionals must specifically define appropriate behavior and make clear that any form of aggression not sanctioned in society is also inappropriate in sport.

Athletic Performance and Aggression

Some coaches and athletes feel that aggressiveness enhances athletic performance, either at the team or individual level. For instance, basketball player Kermit Washington said that being mean helped keep him from being pushed around on the court. Football safety Jack Tatum said his team had a greater likelihood of succeeding if he punished his opponent on every play (Papanek, 1977). Certainly, the relation between aggression and performance is complex, and there have been many cases where aggressive acts have "paid off" regarding outcome. Consider, for example, the strategy of having a lower-skilled player commit aggressive acts against a higher-skilled opponent to distract the superior player or draw him into a fight.

Some sport psychologists agree that aggression facilitates performance outcome (Widmeyer, 1984), whereas others feel it does not (Gill, 1986). The research is difficult to interpret because clear distinctions have not been drawn between aggression and assertive behavior. Silva (1980) argues that aggression would not facilitate performance because it elevates a person's arousal level and shifts attention to nonperformance issues (e.g., hurting the opponent).

In the end, the relation of aggression to performance may be of secondary importance. More central issues are whether you value performance at any cost, your concern about sport participants, and ensuring that aggression does not pay—but that those acting aggressively do (Widmeyer, 1984).

> Sport and exercise science professionals must decide if they value enhanced performance at the cost of increased aggression or if they are more concerned about how sport affects its participants.

Implications for Guiding Practice

Let's now consolidate what we know of aggression and discuss how we might develop strategies to control aggression in sport and physical activity settings. First, we'll examine situations where aggression is most likely to occur. Next, we'll discuss strategies for teaching appropriate behavior and modifying aggressive actions.

When Aggression Is Most Likely to Occur

Expect certain situations to provoke aggressive behavior. Aggression is likely when athletes are frustrated and thus aroused. Participants typically feel frustrated when they

- are losing,
- perceive unfair officiating,
- are embarrassed,
- are physically in pain, or
- are playing below their capabilities.

Controlling Aggression

Stress-management training can help students or athletes deal with frustrating situations.

Sport and exercise professionals have a moral responsibility to clearly distinguish between assertive behavior and aggression with the intent to harm.

Unfortunately, we cannot always control these situations. But we can observe participants more closely and remove them from the situation at the first signs of aggression. Or, better yet, we can teach athletes skills to control their emotions and their reactions to frustration. For example, stress-management skills (see chapter 14) were successfully taught to an ice hockey player who often became frustrated during games, responded aggressively, and spent increasingly more time in the penalty box (Silva, 1982). Through training, the player reduced his aggressive responses and remained in the game instead of in the box.

An overemphasis on winning is the root of much frustration. Trying to win isn't wrong, but winning should not be emphasized to the point that aggression results after a loss. Such frustration is a sign that winning needs to be put into perspective.

Sport and exercise science professionals have a moral responsibility to distinguish between aggression with the intent to harm and assertive behavior. We must delineate aggression from intensity and assertiveness (good aggression) and instruct participants accordingly.

Good Versus Bad Aggression

Tom Martinez is the new head football coach at Aurora High School. He takes over a program with a losing tradition and a reputation for overaggressive players who commit flagrant fouls and take cheap shots. A former major college player himself, Tom knows it takes intensity to be successful, but he is committed to his philosophy that cheap shots and playing to physically hurt opponents are inappropriate. He feels the first step toward remedying the situation at Aurora is to differentiate for the players appropriate and inappropriate aggression. He remembers how confusing and frustrating it was for him when one coach rewarded him for aggressive play and others reprimanded him for the same actions.

Tom meets with his coaching staff and they all agree to be consistent in distinguishing between assertive play and aggression. They adopt guidelines, explain them to the team, and consistently reward the demonstration of good, clean intense play while immediately punishing aggression.

Aurora High School Guidelines

Appropriate actions are

Hard hits within the rules and within the field of play

Helping opponents off the turf after hard hits

Acknowledging good plays by the opponents

Inappropriate aggressive actions are

Out-of-bounds tackles and hits

Legal acts aimed at physically punishing opponents (e.g., forearm shivers to the head of receivers)

Head hunting (tackles aimed at the head) or blind-side blocks aimed at the knees

Pushing and shoving opponents after the whistle has blown

Intimidating remarks (e.g., "if you think that was a hard shot, wait for the next one")

Off-the-field trash talk about hurting or getting opponents

Teaching Appropriate Behavior

Once it has been determined what constitutes aggression and what is appropriate, intense, or assertive play, social-learning strategies (modeling and reinforcement; see chapter 8) can be used to teach participants these behaviors. Explain why behaviors are appropriate and inappropriate. (See chapter 26 on sportsmanship and moral development.)

Not only can we work with athletes to control aggression, strategies can also be used with spectators. Here are some general strategies for controlling spectator aggression:

1. Develop strict alcohol control policies or ban alcohol for spectators at athletic competitions.
2. Penalize spectators (e.g., kick them out) immediately for aggressive acts. Stop aggression as soon as it starts and inform other spectators it will not be tolerated.
3. Request officials who you know won't tolerate aggression on the field.
4. Inform coaches that aggressive displays on their part will not be tolerated.
5. Work with the media to convey the importance of not glorifying aggressive acts in sports coverage.

Summary

Aggression is behavior directed toward the goal of harming or injuring another living being. Aggression is distinct from assertive behavior in sport. Four hypotheses explaining why aggression occurs include the instinct, frustration-aggression, social learning, and revised frustration-aggression theories. Little support has been found for the instinct theory or the original frustration-aggression hypothesis; nor is there support for the notion that catharsis (releasing pent-up aggression through socially acceptable sport and physical activity) abates aggression. Strong support has been found for the revised frustration-aggression and social learning theories.

Frustration predisposes individuals to aggressiveness, and aggression occurs if it has been learned to be an appropriate reaction to frustration. Modeling and reinforcement can be powerful determinants of aggressive behavior. Spectators also use aggression and they as well as sport participants sometimes condone behaviors that would not be considered appropriate in society (game reasoning).

Some research findings have important implications for guiding practice. These include recognizing when aggression is most likely to occur, teaching athletes how to handle these situations, teaching appropriate behavior, and modifying inappropriate aggressive actions.

Review Questions

1. What is aggression? How does it differ from assertive behavior?

2. Describe the four criteria for aggression.

3. What are four theories of aggression? Describe the major contentions of each. Which have the strongest support and why?

4. What is catharsis? What implications does it have for guiding practice?

5. What factors are associated with spectator aggression?

6. What is sport-specific game reasoning, or bracketed morality? What are its implications for professionals?

7. Explain the relation between athlete aggression and performance.

8. In what situations is aggression most likely to occur?

9. How might you curb spectator aggression in sport?

References

Arms, R.L., Russell, G.W., & Sandilands, M.L. (1979). Effects of viewing aggressive sports on the hostility of spectators. *Social Psychology Quarterly*, **42**, 275-279.

Bandura, A. (1973). *Aggression: A social learning analysis.* Englewood Cliffs, NJ: Prentice-Hall.

Baron, R.A. (1977). *Human aggression*. New York: Plenum.

Berkowitz, L. (1965). The concept of aggressive drive: Some additional considerations. In L. Berkowitz (Ed.), *Advances in experimental social psychology* (Vol. 2, 301-329). New York: Academic Press.

Berkowitz, L. (1969). *Roots of aggression*. New York: Atherton Press.

Bredemeier, B., & Shields, D. (1986). Athletic aggression: An issue of contextual morality. *Sociology of Sport Journal*, **3**, 15-28.

Cavanaugh, B.M., & Silva, J.M. (1980). Spectator perceptions of fan misbehavior: An additudinal inquiry. In C.H. Nadeau, W.R. Halliwell, K.M. Newell, & G.C. Roberts (Eds.), *Psychology of motor behavior and sport*. Champaign, IL: Human Kinetics.

Dollard, J., Doob, J., Miller, N., Mowrer, O., & Sears, R. (1939). *Frustration and aggression*. New Haven, CT: Yale University Press.

Gill, D.L. (1986). *Psychological dynamics of sport*. Champaign, IL: Human Kinetics.

Husman, B.F., & Silva, J.M. (1984). Aggression in sport: Definitional and theoretical considerations. In J.M. Silva & R.S. Weinberg (Eds.), *Psychological foundations of sport* (pp. 246-260). Champaign, IL: Human Kinetics.

Isoahola, S.E., & Hatfield, B. (1986). *Psychology of sports: A social psychological approach*. Dubuque, IA: William C. Brown.

Martens, R. (1982). Kids sports: A den of iniquity or land of promise. In R.A. Magill, M.J. Ash, & F.L. Smoll (Eds.), *Children in sport* (2nd ed., pp. 204-218). Champaign, IL: Human Kinetics.

Papanek, J. (1977, October 31). The enforcers. *Sports Illustrated*, pp. 43-49.

Silva, J.M. (1980). Understanding aggressive behavior and its effects upon athletic performance. In W.F. Straub (Ed.), *Sport psychology: An analysis of athlete behavior in sport* (2nd ed.). Ithaca, NY: Mouvement.

Silva, J.M. (1982). Competitive sport environments: Performance enhancement through cognitive intervention. *Behavior Modification*, **6**, 443-463.

Silva, J.M. (1984). Factors related to the acquisition and exhibition of aggressive sport behavior. In J.M. Silva & R.S. Weinberg (Eds.), *Psychological foundations of sport* (pp. 261-273). Champaign, IL: Human Kinetics.

Smith, M.D. (1983). *Violence and sport*. Toronto: Butterworths.

Smith, M.D. (1988). Interpersonal sources of violence in hockey: The influence of parents, coaches, and teammates. In F.L. Smoll, R.A. Magill, & M.J. Ash (Eds.), *Children in sport* (3rd ed., pp. 301-313). Champaign, IL: Human Kinetics.

Widmeyer, W.N. (1984). Aggression-performance relationships in sport. In J.M. Silva & R.S. Weinberg (Eds.), *Psychological foundations of sport* (pp. 274-286). Champaign, IL: Human Kinetics.

CHAPTER 26

Character Development and Sportsmanship

As an undergraduate, Wake Forest football player Chip Reeves began a Santa's helper program to provide gifts to the needy at Christmas. Professional golfer Patty Sheenan sponsors a home for troubled teens. Olympic marathon champion Kip Keino has adopted and raised over 100 orphan children in his native Kenya (Deford, 1987). For years we have been taught that sport and physical activity participation builds character and develops moral values.

Yet some of the most popular role models in recent years have been the "bad boys" of sports—John McEnroe in tennis, Jack Tatum (nicknamed the assassin) in football, and Charles Barkley in basketball, whose antics include spitting on fans he doesn't like. And the coverage of the 1994 Winter Olympics was swamped with news that associates of figure skater Tonya Harding had attacked her rival, Nancy Kerrigan. In the face of what we see, can we really say that sport participation builds character? If so, do sport and exercise science professionals play a role in character development?

In this chapter you will learn about

▌ what character development and sportsmanship are,

▌ how moral reasoning and behavior develops,

▌ the important link between moral reasoning and moral behavior,

▌ how moral reasoning and behavior can be influenced, and

▌ the effects of winning on moral development and sportsmanship.

Defining Character Development and Sportsmanship

Defining character development and sportsmanship is difficult. We all generally know what they mean, but we seldom precisely define them (Martens, 1982) or agree exactly on that meaning. For example, tennis great Chris Evert said that sportsmanship is acting in a classy, dignified way (Ross, 1992). Basketball great David Robinson defined it as playing with all your heart and intensity yet still showing respect for your opponents (Ross, 1992). Two very different definitions. And what exactly *is* acting respectfully or in a classy and dignified manner? A golfer might say it means you don't talk to your opponent during play, but a baseball player might think it's fine to talk to the opposing pitcher. Similarly, in college baseball sliding hard into second base to break up a double play is expected and not inappropriate, yet most of us would discourage it in T-ball with 6- and 7-year-olds.

> There is no one universally accepted definition of sportsmanship.

Thus, Martens (1982) concluded that there is no one universally accepted definition of sportsmanship. Rather, sportsmanlike behaviors must be specifically identified, and they are tied to the type of sport, level of play, and age of the participant. Some people prefer the term *sportspersonship* in recognition that girls and women derive the same benefits from sport participation as do boys and men—a belief we hold even while using the dictionary term of sportsmanship, which makes no reference to gender.

Although there is no one definition of the term, it is important that we each develop situation-specific definitions of sportsmanship to work professionally in sport, physical education, and exercise settings. Sport psychologists *have* derived definitions of character development, moral reasoning, and moral behavior. We use *character development* as the general term, which is basically the same as *moral development* but lacking the implication of a religious context. And when we use the term *moral*, we do not mean to imply religious values.

- Moral reasoning is the decision process where the rightness or wrongness of a course of action is determined.
- Moral development is the process of experience and growth through which a person develops the capacity to morally reason.
- Moral behavior is the execution of an act that is deemed right or wrong.

In particular, *moral reasoning* is defined as the decision process in which the rightness or wrongness of a course of action is determined. Thus, moral reasoning focuses on how one decides if some course of action (e.g., a coach violating NCAA rules by paying to fly a player home to see her dying mother) is right or wrong. In contrast, *moral*, or *character*, *development* is the process of experience and growth through which a person develops the capacity to reason morally. For example, in planning a system-wide PE curriculum, a district PE coordinator would want to understand what experiences and cognitive developmental changes are most likely to enhance children's abilities to decide the rightness or wrongness of an action. Lastly, *moral behavior* is actually carrying out an act that is deemed right or wrong.

So, moral reasoning results from individual experiences, as well as the psychological growth and development of the child, and is thought to guide moral behavior. Moreover, moral reasoning is seen as a series of general ethical principles that underlie situationally specific acts of sportsmanship.

Developing Sportsmanlike Attitudes, Behaviors, and Moral Reasoning

Although views differ about how sportsmanlike attitudes and behaviors—and in a larger sense, moral reasoning—develop, two particular views are most accepted today (Weiss & Bredemeier, 1991): the *social-learning* approach and the *structural-developmental* approach.

The Social-Learning Approach

Aggression and character development are linked in many ways, and similar theories explain both. The social-learning approach to character development, best summarized in the work of Albert Bandura (1977), views specific sportsmanlike attitudes and behaviors as learned by modeling or observational learning, reinforcement, and social comparison (see Figure 26.1).

For example, by observing other children being praised for reporting false sit-up scores to the instructor, Zoe learns in PE that it is acceptable to cheat on a fitness test. Wanting praise and attention from the teacher, she copies or models the behavior of the other students that she compares herself to and begins to report more sit-ups than she really did. The physical educator notes the reported improvement in the number of sit-ups executed and praises her.

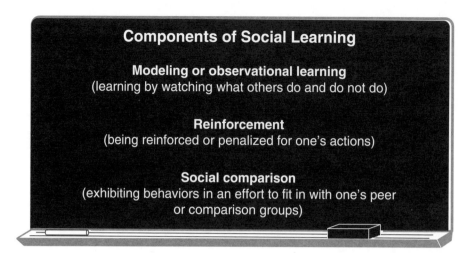

Figure 26.1 Social learning components.

Thus, Zoe learns from observing the other children and through her own experience that if she lies about the number of sit-ups, she receives reinforcement.

Conversely, a selfish child may learn to share and be more caring by observing classmates receive attention and praise for helping. And, over time, when the child models these helping actions and is praised, the prosocial behavior is reinforced. Thus, both sportsmanlike and unsportsmanlike attitudes and behavior are affected by the social-learning process.

In one study of social learning theory, fifth-grade boys who acted unsportsmanlike (e.g., swore) received instruction about their inappropriate behaviors, saw the appropriate behaviors modeled, and took part in a reinforcement system (points leading to desired prizes could be earned for exhibiting sportsmanlike behaviors). Over time, the reinforcement system was effective, although more in eliminating undesirable behaviors than in getting the boys to exhibit sportsmanlike or desirable behaviors (Geibenk & McKenzie, 1985).

Former tennis great Bjorn Borg was known for his excellent sportsmanlike behavior, but he hadn't always behaved that way. When he was 12, Borg threw his racquet in disgust, exhibiting a temper tantrum on the court. Such actions were quickly curtailed because his mother would not tolerate them. Borg had his racquet taken away for 6 months and was not allowed to play.

Sportsmanlike attitudes and behavior are learned through modeling, reinforcement, and social comparison.

The Structural-Developmental Approach

Instead of focusing on modeling, reinforcement, and social comparison, the structural-developmental approach focuses on how psychological growth and developmental changes in a child interact with environmental experiences to shape moral reasoning (Weiss & Bredemeier, 1991). The ability to reason morally is thought to depend on a person's level of cognitive or mental development (e.g., a child's ability to think in concrete versus abstract terms). Thus, if a 4-year-old boy, able to think in only very concrete terms, is inadvertently pushed in line at preschool, he responds by hitting the child who was pushed into him. This child is not able to judge intent and knows only that the other child hit him. However, given the process of normal growth and cognitive development, an 11-year-old child who is inadvertently pushed in line will not necessarily push back because he can already judge intent and realizes the other child didn't bump him on purpose. Thus, structural developmentalists view moral reasoning and behavior as dependent, in large part, on cognitive development.

Moral reasoning and behavior depend on the level of cognitive development of the individual.

Developmental psychologists have identified sequential stages of character development in children. Figure 26.2 depicts the five stages, or levels, of moral development first identified by Norma Haan (Haan, Aeerts, & Cooper, 1985) and later explained in more practical sport psychological terms by Maureen Weiss (1987; Weiss & Bredemeier, 1991). As a child matures, she progresses in moral reasoning from Level 1 to Level 5. Not everyone reaches Level 5, however, and we don't always use the highest level of moral thinking that we're capable of. In fact, we may use several different levels at once.

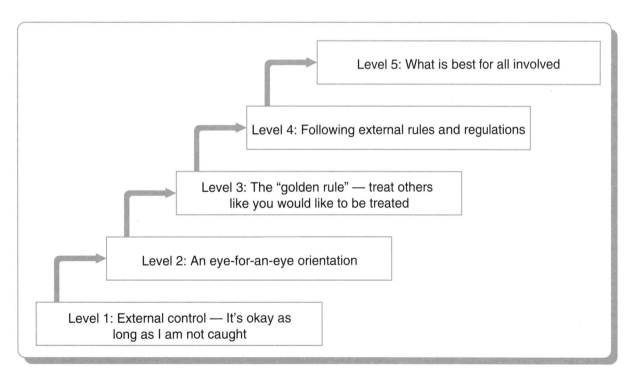

Figure 26.2 Levels of moral reasoning. Adapted from Weiss (1987).

Level 1 reasoning is at the external control stage: the "It's okay as long as I don't get caught" stage. At this level a child's determination of what is right or wrong is based on self-interest and, in particular, the outcome of her actions. Thus, Kim would decide whether kicking an opponent in soccer (illegally playing the person, not the ball) is right or wrong depending on whether she got away with it. If she did get away with it, she would think it was an acceptable course of action. But if she were penalized for it, she would view playing the person as inappropriate behavior.

Level 2 still focuses on maximizing self-interests, but the child now doesn't see only the action's outcome. Instead, this is an "eye-for-an-eye" stage, where the individual can compromise and make tradeoffs to maximize self-interest. For instance, Kim decides that it is acceptable to illegally kick another player because Lee has been doing just that to her for most of the first half. Or an elite track-and-field athlete takes illegal performance-enhancing drugs, defending the action on the premise that "everybody does it."

Level 3 is to treat others as you would like to be treated. Unlike the first two levels, self-interest is not the sole focus here. The person adopts a helping or altruistic view. Kim now would view illegally kicking another player as inappropriate because she would not want to be treated that way.

Level 4 of moral reasoning focuses on following external rules. The person has learned that not all people can be trusted to do the right thing and recognizes that official rules were developed for the common good. At this stage, for instance, Kim views illegally kicking an opponent as inappropriate because it is against the rules, and one must play by the rules because they are designed to promote everyone's self-interest.

Moral reasoning at Level 5 focuses on what is best for everyone involved, whether or not it is in accordance with official rules and regulations. This reasoning is considered the most mature because the individual seeks to maximize the interests of the group through mutual agreements or "moral balances." Thus, Kim reasons that it is inappropriate to kick another player not only because it is against the rules but also because it violates the fundamental rights of both parties—the right to play in a safe and healthy environment.

In summary, with character development, reasoning progresses from decisions based on self-centered interests to a concern with mutual interests of all the people involved. This development depends on the person's ability to think abstractly.

Moral Reasoning and Moral Behavior

A consistent relation exists between aggression and people with less mature moral reasoning (Bredemeier & Shields, 1987). Not surprisingly, the link between moral reasoning and behavior is not perfect. Nor would you expect it to be—all of us at one time or another have known that something was wrong but went ahead and did it anyway.

Enhancing Character Development and Sportsmanship

Cultural attitudes, values, norms of the particular individuals and groups, and the stage of moral reasoning must all be considered to understand how to enhance character development and sportsmanship. Consequently, it is best to take advantage of what has been learned through both the social-learning and structural-developmental approaches.

Character development progresses from basing decisions about the rightness or wrongness of actions on self-centered interests to a concern with the mutual interests of all involved.

Although aggression is linked with immature moral reasoning, the connection between reasoning and behavior is not perfectly understood.

Does Physical Education Enhance Character Development?

Most of us like to believe that participation in physical activity programs automatically builds character, enhances moral reasoning, and teaches sportsmanship, but little evidence supports this fallacy (Hodge, 1989). Participation in sport and physical education settings does not automatically produce better or worse people. Character is not caught, but *taught* in sport and physical activity settings. And teaching moral reasoning and sportsmanship involves the systematic use of certain strategies.

For example, in one field study fifth-grade physical education students were divided into experimental and control groups (Romance, Weiss, & Bockoven, 1986). All children participated in an 8-week program, playing the same activity games for identical lengths of time. However, the experimental group was also exposed to specific game-related moral reasoning strategies. For instance, teams of two students were asked to compete in basketball, with the first team to reach 10 points winning. After the activity, a discussion was held during which each student explained how it was determined who would shoot and if that was fair. The control group children did not participate in such activities.

The children in the experimental group demonstrated significantly greater moral reasoning gains, both in sport and in everyday life situations. Evidently, when well-designed strategies are used, moral reasoning can be taught through physical education participation. That changes did not occur in the control group of children suggests that participation in physical education alone does not enhance moral reasoning.

Character is not caught but taught in sport, exercise, and physical activity settings.

Strategies for Enhancing Character Development

Both the social-learning and structural-developmental approaches have facilitated our understanding of sportsmanship and enhanced character development. Figure 26.3 lists six strategies derived from these approaches. We'll discuss each of these strategies to learn how it can enhance character development.

Strategy 1:	Define sportsmanship in your particular context
Strategy 2:	Reinforce and encourage sportsmanlike behaviors and penalize and discourage unsportsmanlike behaviors
Strategy 3:	Model appropriate behaviors
Strategy 4:	Convey rationales • Emphasize "why" • Emphasize the "intent" of actions • Emphasize "role taking" • Encourage empathy
Strategy 5:	Discuss moral dilemmas
Strategy 6:	Build moral dilemmas and choices into practices and classes

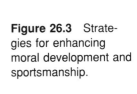

Figure 26.3 Strategies for enhancing moral development and sportsmanship.

If sportsmanship is
not specifically de-
fined, people do not
know what consti-
tutes acceptable and
unacceptable be-
havior.

1. Define Sportsmanship in Your Particular Context or Program. As
you learned, there is no one universal definition of sportsmanship. And without
a specific definition, people in your program will not know what you mean
by appropriate and acceptable behavior or inappropriate and unacceptable
behavior. You can develop a personal definition of the term, however. Table
26.1 contains an example of such a written code for a children's sports program,
specifically identifying sportsmanlike and unsportsmanlike behaviors.

Table 26.1 A Written Code of Sportsmanship for a Youth Sport Program		
Areas of concern	**Sportsmanlike behaviors**	**Unsportsmanlike behaviors**
Behavior toward officials	• Questioning officials in the appropriate manner (e.g., lodging an official protest, having only designated individuals, such as a captain, address officials)	• Arguing with officials • Swearing at officials
Behavior toward opponents	• Treating all opponents with respect and dignity at all times	• Arguing with opponents • Making sarcastic remarks about opponents • Making aggressive actions toward opponents
Behavior toward teammates	• Giving only constructive criticism and positive encouragement	• Making negative comments or sarcastic remarks • Swearing at or arguing with teammates
Behavior toward spectators	• Making only positive comments to spectators	• Arguing with spectators • Making negative remarks and swearing at spectators
Rule acceptance and infractions	• Obeying all league rules	• Taking advantage of loopholes in rules (e.g., every child must play, so coach tells unskilled players to be sick on day of important game)

Adapted from Gould (1981).

2. Reinforce and Encourage Sportsmanlike Behaviors. Conversely,
penalize and discourage inappropriate behaviors. Consistency in reinforcing
and penalizing these behaviors and actions is essential. Follow the behavior
modification guidelines in chapter 8.

Fitness and sport
professionals must
be models of sports-
manship.

3. Model Appropriate Behaviors. Many people look up to professionals
in our field, identifying with them and modeling their actions. Because actions
speak louder than words, it is important that exercise and sport professionals
provide a good model of sportsmanship. Easier said than done, you say?

Indeed, professionals may make mistakes (e.g., lose control and be charged with a technical foul for arguing with the officials). When they lose control, they should admit their error and apologize to the players or students.

Some coaches with strict sportsmanlike guidelines for their players believe it is their job to argue with officials and stick up for their team. Their efforts may be well-intended, but coaches should realize that by demonstrating poor sportsmanship they send mixed messages that undermine their efforts to enhance sportsmanship.

4. Explain Your Thinking About Appropriate Behaviors.

Only when people have internalized a guiding moral principle for determining right or wrong can we expect them to consistently behave well in different situations. Thus, it is important to include an accompanying rationale for the various components of your sportsmanship code. Rationales provide explanations based on the key elements underlying the levels of moral reasoning: That is, altruism, self-interest, impartial rules, and moral balances based on mutually determined agreements (Weiss, 1987). Most important, rationales should be regularly conveyed to participants. For example, if several youngsters are excluding a less-skilled classmate in a physical education game, you need to ensure that the less-skilled child is included and also to emphasize the reason behind the decision (e.g., "It is important to treat others as you want them to treat you instead of just doing what you want").

It should also be emphasized how important intention is in actions. The ability to judge intent starts developing around the age of seven or eight (Martens, 1982). With children about 10 years old, you can already emphasize role taking (i.e., seeing oneself in someone else's role). Then you can add higher levels of *empathy*, the ability of two people to take each other's perspectives into account when deciding how to act (Newman & Newman, 1991). Many coaches like to have players officiate practice scrimmages of their teammates. The players can then better understand the rules of the game and see things from an official's perspective. By adding a brief postscrimmage discussion, this role taking can serve as a valuable tool for helping players learn to empathize.

Explain rationales for the rightness or wrongness of actions regularly.

5. Discuss Moral Dilemmas and Choices.

For effective moral education participants should engage in self-dialogue and group discussions about choices and moral dilemmas. A moral dilemma requires participants to decide what is morally correct or incorrect. (Read the script for discussion in the box about wrestling.) Rule violations, when and why injured participants should play, and who should play are other excellent topics for discussion (Bredemeier & Shields, 1987). Discuss those gray areas of right and wrong that may or may not be against the rules (e.g., is it okay to intentionally say something upsetting to an opponent at the start of a contest? [Weiss, 1987)]).

6. Build Moral Dilemmas and Choices Into Practices.   Some dilemmas you might pose to young athletes during practice include the following (Weiss, 1987, p. 148):

- Not putting out enough of the "best" equipment for all athletes.
- Devising a drill with unequal opportunities for practice; for example, one person is always on defense.

When to Shoot Toward an Opponent's Injured Leg

Rodd and Kevin are two evenly matched 150-pound wrestlers involved in a close match. Rodd injures his left knee, takes an injury time-out for treatment, and then returns to the mat. He is in obvious pain with greatly constrained movement and cannot place weight on his injured leg. Imagine that you are Kevin and respond to the following questions.

Should you execute moves to the side of the injured leg because it will be easier to score points?

Once you are in contact with your injured opponent, should you put extra pressure on his injured leg to cause him pain and allow you to turn him to his back and pin him?

Should you avoid executing moves toward his injured leg unless the match is close in score?

Should you avoid executing moves toward his injured leg entirely and try to beat him at his best?

- Devising a drill where players might be tempted to hurt with words (laughing, yelling), such as having someone demonstrate weak skills or having unfair relay teams.
- Devising a drill that provides possible opportunities for rough play—for example, the hamburger rebound drill, in which two individuals block out one person simultaneously and go for the ball.

After the players try to solve the dilemmas, follow up with discussion about the underlying moral reasoning.

These strategies for enhancing character development and sportsmanship require time, planning, and effort. For optimal effect, they should be repeated consistently across time, not just once or twice at the start of the season or when a child is causing a problem.

Critical Considerations in Character Development

To guide practice, several philosophically oriented issues should be considered. They cover a broad range and include the physical educator's and coach's role in moral development; the role of winning; how to make teaching moral behavior transfer beyond the playing field; and recognizing the imperfect nature of character development.

The Educator's Role in Character Development

Some people believe teachers and coaches have no business teaching morals and values to youth. Character and morals are the domain of parents and the church, they argue, not the school, especially public schools. We certainly agree that it is not sound practice to mix religious values into the public school curriculum. However, avoiding character education in basic values like honesty, empathy, and methods of solving disputes is a grave mistake. And we contend that physical educators, coaches, and exercise leaders influence many values, intentionally or not. For example, coaches decide whether to argue with officials, physical educators take positions on teaching competitive or cooperative games, athletic trainers decide when to play an injured athlete. Such decisions often affect the development of participants, and so it is important to have developed a philosophical stance on these issues. It is much better to recognize the moral values you're fostering and discouraging than to affect someone else's values haphazardly.

Physical educators, coaches, and exercise leaders are in positions to positively influence character behavior and development.

The Double-Sided Role of Winning

Winning plays a dual role in character development (Martens, 1982). On one hand, an emphasis on winning pressures some individuals to cheat, break rules, and behave in ways they would consider inappropriate off the field. On the other hand, when a player resists the temptations to cheat or commit other immoral acts, despite a high value placed on winning, moral lessons may be much more meaningful. Winning itself is neutral to moral development. The key is to consider the right emphasis to place on winning.

Teaching for Transfer

It is a myth that the lessons and values learned in the gym or pool or on the athletic field transfer automatically to other environments. For such a transfer to occur, the lesson must be drawn out, extended (Danish, Petitpas, & Hale,

1992). If you want to teach values through sport and physical activity, you must discuss how the values transfer to the nonsport environment. For instance, a coach who wants to teach young athletes an attitude of cooperation to carry over to nonsport situations should discuss how and when teamwork can be used in other contexts (e.g., working on a school project). In fact, this is one advantage of a structural-developmental approach. Social-learning principles, which enhance specific sportsmanlike attitudes and behaviors, tend to be highly situation-specific. That is, teaching a child to be honest in gym class will not transfer to math class. However, if someone's underlying moral reasoning level can be raised, his or her behavior tends to be affected across a variety of situations.

Realistic Expectations

Unfortunately, sportsmanship enhancement and character development through sport and physical activity involvement is an imperfect process (Martens, 1982). We cannot reach all individuals at all times. More likely we'll experience tremendous successes along with dismal failures. Recognizing the imperfect nature of character development and being realistic in our expectations enables us to remain optimistic despite our setbacks.

Summary

There is no one definition of sportsmanship. Moral reasoning, closely linked to sportsmanship, is related to a person's level of cognitive development. The analysis of five levels in moral reasoning (Haan, Aeerts, & Cooper, 1985) reflects a progression from judging an action's rightness or wrongness on self-centered interests to a concern with the mutual interests of all involved. Six strategies of moral development were delineated, based on the social-learning and structural-developmental approaches. These included the need to (1) define what you consider sportsmanship in precise terms; (2) reinforce and encourage sportsmanlike behaviors and penalize and discourage unsportsmanlike behaviors; (3) model appropriate behaviors; (4) convey rationales, emphasizing why actions are appropriate or inappropriate, emphasizing the intent of actions, role taking, and the need to empathize; (5) discuss moral dilemmas; and (6) build moral dilemmas and choices into practice and class contexts.

Some philosophically oriented issues to consider in facilitating character development are the professional's role in character development, the two-sided role of winning, teaching for transfer, and maintaining realistic expectations of the character-development process.

Review Questions

1. Define moral reasoning, character development, and moral behavior.
2. What is the social-learning approach to sportsmanship and character development? Name the three major means through which social learning takes place.
3. Describe the structural-developmental approach to moral reasoning and development.
4. What are Haan's five stages of moral reasoning? Why are these important?

5. Describe the relation between moral reasoning and moral behavior. What implication does this have for guiding practice?

6. Explain each of the following strategies for enhancing character development and sportsmanship:

   - Define sportsmanship in your particular context.
   - Reinforce and encourage sportsmanlike behaviors and penalize and discourage nonsportsmanlike behaviors.
   - Explain your thinking about appropriate behaviors.
   - Discuss moral dilemmas.
   - Build moral dilemmas and choices into practices and classes.

7. What should the role of the physical educator be in enhancing character development and teaching sportsmanship?

8. How can winning both enhance and deter the development of sportsmanship and moral reasoning?

9. Why is it important to teach character development for transfer?

References

Bandura, A. (1977). *Social learning theory.* Englewood Cliffs, NJ: Prentice Hall.

Bredemeier, B.J., & Shields, D. (1984). Divergence in moral reasoning about sport and everyday life. *Sociology of Sport Journal*, **1**, 234-257.

Bredemeier, B.J., & Shields, D. (1987). Moral growth through physical activity: A structural developmental approach. In D. Gould & M.R. Weiss (Eds.), *Advances in pediatric sport sciences: Behavioral issues.* (Vol. 2, pp. 143-165). Champaign, IL: Human Kinetics.

Danish, S.J., Petitpas, A.S., & Hale, B.D. (1992). A developmental-educational intervention model of sport psychology. *The Sport Psychologist*, **6**, 403-415.

Deford, P. (1987). A little lower than angels. *Sports Illustrated*, **71**(12), 12-31.

Geibink, M.P., & McKenzie, T.C. (1985). Teaching sportsmanship in physical education and recreation: An analysis of intervention and generalization efforts. *Journal of Teaching Physical Education*, **4**, 167-177.

Haan, N., Aeerts, E., & Cooper, B. (1985). *On moral grounds.* New York: University Press.

Hodge, K.P. (1989). Character-building in sport: Fact or fiction? *New Zealand Journal of Sports Medicine*, **17**(2), 23-25.

Martens, R. (1982). Kids sports: A den of iniquity or land of promise. In R.A. Magill, M.J. Ash, & F.L. Smoll (Eds.), *Children in sport* (2nd ed., pp. 204-218). Champaign, IL: Human Kinetics.

Newman, B.M., & Newman, P.R. (1991). *Development through life: A psychological approach.* Pacific Grove, CA: Brooks/Cole.

Romance, T.J., Weiss, M.R., & Bockoven, J. (1986). A program to promote moral development through elementary school physical education. *Journal of Teaching Physical Education*, **5**, 126-136.

Ross, M.S. (1992). Good sports report. *Fantastic Flyer*, Summer, 16-17.

Weiss, M.R. (1987). Teaching sportsmanship and values. In V. Seefeldt (Ed.), *Handbook for youth sports coaches* (pp. 137-151). Reston, VA: AAHPERD.

Weiss, M.R., & Bredemeier, B.J. (1991). Moral development in sport. In K.B. Pandolf & J.O. Holloszy (Eds.), *Exercise and Sport Science Reviews*, **18**, 331-378.

CHAPTER 27

Gender Issues in Sport and Exercise

When I first started running, I was so embarrassed I'd walk when cars passed me. I'd pretend I was looking at the flowers.

Joan Benoit, 1984 Olympic marathon gold medalist

Many colleges resisted Title IX at first, and even now, discrimination is rampant. Men have their uniforms washed for them; women do their own. Men get better practice times and facilities. Men take airplanes while women's teams drive their own cars. Men eat steak; women hamburger.

Sally Goldfarb, National Women's Law Center

This is the message you get from male judges: If you're going to have muscles, you damn well better be feminine. I didn't want to be a man. . . . I kind of felt . . . caught in the twilight zone.

Woman body builder

Despite changes in the past 20 years, females still experience special problems in exercise and sport settings. Differences between the male and female sport experience persist in opportunity, psychosocial orientations, and reactions to sport participation.

In this chapter you will learn about

▌ whether evidence supports stereotypical views of males and females in sport,

▌ socialization differences between males and females,

▌ gender inequities in sport,

▌ gender role orientation,

▌ how gender affects achievement orientations and expectations,

▌ role conflict and female athletes, and

▌ female perspectives on sport and exercise concerns.

Sex Differences—Fact and Myth

Sex differences refer to biologically based differences between males and females, whereas *gender differences* refer to social and psychological characteristics and behaviors associated with males and females (Gill, 1992). The phrase *gender role*, on the other hand, refers to the pattern of beliefs, attitudes, behaviors, skills, and interests that a culture identifies as reflecting femininity or masculinity. Most of the early work investigating disparity between males and females in sport and exercise took a sex difference approach, focusing on biological differences.

In 1974 Maccoby and Jacklin reviewed over 2,000 books and articles to determine which beliefs about biological sex differences in social behavior, intellectual ability, and motivation were supported by evidence. Before we present their conclusions, first see if you consider the following statements true or false.

1. Females are more social than males.
2. Females have lower self-esteem than males.
3. Females have greater verbal ability than males.
4. Males are more aggressive than females.
5. Males are more analytical than females.
6. Males excel in visual-spatial ability.
7. Males excel in mathematical ability.
8. Females lack motivation to achieve.

Recent research finds more overlap and similarity than difference between males' and females' abilities—and the differences are culturally, not biologically, based.

Maccoby and Jacklin (1974) found only four areas where sex differences had a notable effect: mathematical ability, visual-spatial ability, verbal ability, and aggressive ability. Since then, a more recent review (Jacklin, 1989) of research findings suggested that sex differences in these areas are minimal. The differences in these abilities are not biologically based, and overlap and similarities far outweigh differences. Where apparent distinctions exist in the perceptions and behaviors of males and females, situational factors play a critical role. In other words, differences arise when males and females adopt distinct roles in diverse settings. A biological approach to studying male-female differences ignores the complexity and variations in gender-related behavior. Thus, psychologists now tend to study psychosocially based gender differences.

Socialization Patterns of Girls and Boys

Virtually from birth, girls and boys are treated differently by adults and society. Little boys are allowed to explore more of their physical environment before being picked up by their parents than little girls are. In most North American families even when young girls are not actually discouraged from participating in sports, they are less likely to learn that physical activity and sport achievement can be rewarding aspects of their lives. Girls are often restricted more in their time away from home than boys are, and this hampers girls' freedom to participate in competitive sports and games. Typically, young girls hear these kinds of warnings:

- Don't play rough or get hurt
- Keep your clothes clean
- Don't go too far from the house

Daughters are Daddy's little girls and Mother's little helpers, protected and encouraged to be caretaking, nurturing homebodies (Coakley, 1990). These roles can discourage girls from developing social independence and competence in sport.

Virtually from walking age, boys are encouraged to explore the environment and be active in physical activity, whereas girls are more restricted and protected from the environment.

Patterns of Sport Participation

As girls move toward adolescence they typically learn that engaging in contact sports that involve great strength and power can jeopardize their popularity,

The Socialization of Cheerleaders

All-female cheerleader squads stand out as symbols of the past. In many high schools and colleges their main purpose is to provide support for the men on the athletic field. Although cheerleaders are selected on the basis of many attributes, including spirit, popularity, gymnastic ability, and grades, physical attractiveness is usually the key criterion. Certainly coaches would be fired or laughed out of school if they used attractiveness as a criterion for making the team or starting lineup.

Still, being a cheerleader often carries greater status among high school girls than being an athlete. Traditional definitions of femininity are nourished by television coverage, for example, that showcases cheerleaders who are alluring and sensuous.

Girls prefer different sports than boys do and participate in far fewer numbers, even in their favorite sports.

and they soon give low priority to these (Coakley, 1990). A survey of 712 midwestern high schools (State Association Summary, 1989) showed that boys were most likely to play football (42,299), basketball (26,662), and baseball (19,368), whereas girls were most likely to play basketball (17,011), volleyball (16,306), and track and field (13,478). Girls and boys preferred different sports, and far fewer of the girls participated in even their most preferred sport. When girls do choose to participate in sport, they often experience discrimination.

Gender Inequity in Sport

For many years, men's sport programs received substantially more money than women's to run their athletic departments. In fact, in many schools women's athletic programs in the 1960s and early 1970s received less than 1% of the funding men's programs received (Gilbert & Williamson, 1973). In 1974, the estimated budgets for boys' sport activities in U.S. high schools were on the average five times larger than those for girls' sport activities. That year, men's intercollegiate programs received an average of 30 times more than women's programs, and in some universities it was 100 times more.

Such inequity prompted passage of Title IX in 1972. Basically, Title IX states that no persons in the United States shall, on the basis of sex, be excluded from participation in, be denied the benefits of, or be subjected to discrimination under any education program or activity receiving Federal financial assistance. However, implementing Title IX has been difficult and politically controversial, and although changes have occurred, many of the gender inequities listed in the following box persist.

Participation Rates

Participation rates in women's athletics increased significantly in the first 10 years after the passage of Title IX, but there has been little change since.

In 1971, before passage of Title IX, 300,000 girls participated in high school sports; by 1991, participation had increased to 1.9 million girls—36% of all high school athletes (compared to 7.5% in 1971). Although boys still outnumber girls nearly 2 to 1 in interscholastic athletics, this increase reflects tremendous progress. Most of this progress, however, occurred in the first 10 years after Title IX was implemented and has not changed much since. Girls continue to lag far behind boys in their levels of participation. The goal should be a mix of male and female athletes that mirrors the school's overall enrollment.

Gender Inequity in College Sports

- Males dominated the use of facilities.
- Male coaches were paid higher salaries.
- Scholarship opportunities for female athletes were severely limited.
- Males received better publicity and press coverage.
- Males were provided with more, better, and newer equipment.
- Few females were in positions of administrative authority.
- Significantly less overall funding was provided for women's programs. (Poindexter, 1974)

Maintaining Inequity Through Myths

Many myths about the consequences of sport participation and the physical and psychological abilities of girls and women have been used to rationalize unequal opportunities. These are myths that medical and sport science research have proven incorrect or unsubstantiated:

- Strenuous participation in sport may lead to problems in childbearing.

- The activity in many sports damages a woman's reproductive organs or breasts.

- Women have a more fragile bone structure than men, making injuries more likely.

- Intense involvement in sport causes menstrual problems.

- Sport involvement leads to the development of unattractive, bulging muscles.

- Participation in aggressive, body contact sports diminishes femininity.

Other Inequities Affecting Female Athletes

Many inequities between male and female sports are more subtle (Peggy Kellers, Director of the National Association for Girls and Women in Sports, 1992). Consider these persisting inequities in men's and women's intercollegiate athletic programs:

- Travel and per diem expenses
- Provision of medical and training services and facilities
- Provision of locker rooms, practice, and competitive facilities
- Coaching and academic tutoring opportunities
- Provision and maintenance of equipment and supplies
- Scheduling of games and practice times
- Provision of housing and dining services and facilities
- Media and press coverage

For example, in reviewing the four major Canadian newspapers, Theberge (1991) found the percentage of articles on female sports alone ranged from 2% to 14%, whereas articles on male sports ranged from 25% to 56%. In addition, the coverage of women's physical activities tended to be stereotypical, focusing on aerobics or aquatics, whereas the men's coverage ranged across many sports and activities.

Inequities Concerning Women Coaches

Perhaps the greatest irony of Title IX is the devastating effect it has had on women coaches. For reasons not understood or agreed upon (see following box), women actually *lost* 294 head coach positions in 335 women's inter-collegiate sport programs between 1974 and 1979, whereas men gained 437 coaching positions on women's teams (Holmen & Parkhouse, 1981). Grouping together head and assistant coaches, men gained 724 new positions (an 184% increase over the 5-year period), while women gained only 44 new positions (a 3% increase over the 5-year period). Between 1977 and 1984 the pattern continued, with women coaching positions actually declining in number (Acosta & Carpenter, 1987; see Table 27.1).

Explaining the Decline of Female Coaches and Administrators

Men say it is because of the

- lack of qualified women in coaching and administration,

- unwillingness of women to travel to recruit athletes,

- lack of women applicants for job openings, and

- family-related time constraints women have in American society.

Women say it is because of the

- success of the "good old boys network" in the hiring process (i.e., men tending to hire men),

- weakness of the "good old girls club" in the hiring process,

- unconscious sex discrimination in the process of selecting coaches and administrators, and

- lack of qualified women in coaching and administration.

Table 27.1   Percentage of Women Coaches for the 10 Most Popular Women's Intercollegiate Sports From 1977 and 1984

Sport	1977	1984	% change
Basketball	79.4%	64.9%	−14.5
Volleyball	86.67	75.5	−11.1
Tennis	72.9	59.7	−13.2
Softball	83.5	68.6	−14.9
Cross country	35.2	19.7	−15.5
Track	52.3	26.6	−25.5
Swimming/diving	53.6	33.2	−20.4
Field hockey	99.1	98.2	−.9
Golf	54.6	39.7	−14.9
Soccer	29.4	26.8	−2.6

Coaching and administrative positions for women have dropped significantly since the inception of Title IX, whereas the percentage of men coaching women's teams has risen dramatically.

Between 1972 and 1992, the percentage of women coaching women's teams plummeted from more than 90% to about 48% (Acosta & Carpenter, 1994; see Figure 27.1). Women held only 181 more coaching jobs in 1992 than they did in 1982, while men held 631 more coaching positions of women's teams. Yet only 2% of men's teams were coached by women. The merging of men's and women's programs accounts for some of this drop. Unfortunately, the result is that fewer female coaches and administrators can serve as valuable role models. The small rise in the 1994 figure (only about 1%) hopefully represents an upward trend in women's coaching.

Gender Role Orientation

The assumption that males should have masculine characteristics and females feminine characteristics has attracted scrutiny and debate both inside and out-

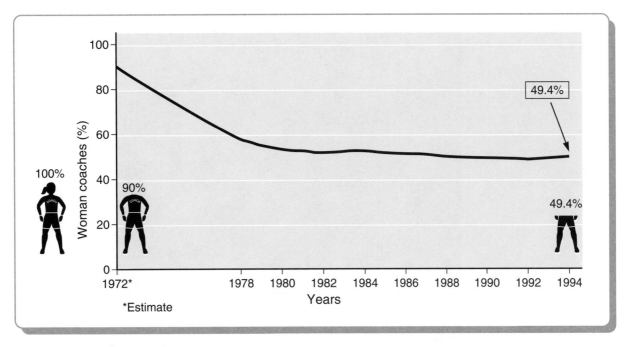

Figure 27.1 Percentage of women coaching women's teams in all four-year NCAA colleges and universities with intercollegiate programs for women. Adapted from Acosta and Carpenter (1994).

Women in Coaching: Some Recommendations

1. All coaching associations should host consciousness-raising sessions on subtle discrimination and other behaviors that exclude women (and minorities) from coaching.

2. As parents and professionals we must vigilantly counter any effort to reduce participation opportunities for women, even in bad economic times.

3. Women's sports should be developed to be greater revenue-producers. Both men's and women's sports programs should try to produce revenues to defray program expenses.

4. We must insist on open and fair employment practices and act affirmatively to redistribute coaching opportunities fairly among women and minorities.

5. School districts, universities, and national governing bodies must maintain, publish, and review data on gender, salaries, and positions of sport coaches and administrators.

6. We must all be advocates and watchdogs within the athletic establishment. Laws don't prevent discrimination in employment or opportunity to participate—people do. When we recognize unfairness, we must speak up.

7. To help prevent employment discrimination, we must advocate certification that mandates objective criteria to weigh the qualifications of athletes.

8. We must sell coaching as both a profession and a volunteer activity.

9. We need to establish more widely inclusive networks for recruiting female professionals.

10. Publications on sport and physical activity should include women in coaching, leadership, and athletic roles.

11. Every new woman or minority employee should have an assigned mentor. (adapted from Donna Lopiano, 1992)

side the world of sport. Sport was long considered a masculine (male-appropriate) activity. Males uninterested and females interested in sport are viewed as unusual, and their behavior is often labeled inappropriate.

The Bem Sex-Role Inventory

In the 1970s, some psychologists began investigating the rigid interpretation of masculinity and femininity, sex-appropriate behavior, and gender role orientation (Bem, 1974, 1978; Spence & Helmreich, 1978). Through the development of the Bem Sex-Role Inventory (BSRI) and the Personal Attributes Questionnaire (PAQ) these researchers provided the means for studying gender roles. Bem argued that masculinity and femininity are not opposite ends of the same personality dimension, as had previously been advanced in the literature. Rather, although masculine characteristics are typically more desirable for men than women, and feminine characteristics more desirable for women than men, there is no reason why males should possess only masculine characteristics and females only feminine characteristics.

Research using the BSRI and the PAQ has typically classified subjects based on their scores on the masculinity and femininity subscales. Those scoring high on femininity and low on masculinity were classified as feminine; those scoring high on masculinity and low on femininity were classified as masculine; those high on both masculinity and femininity were classified as androgynous; and those scoring low on both scales were classified as undifferentiated (see Table 27.2).

The BSRI and PAQ have been used to study participants in many sports, and female athletes were generally classified as either androgynous—having both desirable masculine and feminine characteristics—or masculine (Gill, 1992). Wrisberg, Draper, and Everett (1988) found some differences depended on whether athletes participated in individual or team sports. For example, with team sports, both male and female athletes were classified most often as either masculine or androgynous, but with individual sports the males were equally distributed across the classifications, whereas the females were mostly feminine.

> Males and females can (and probably should) possess both masculine and feminine characteristics.

Table 27.2 Classification According to Scores on Femininity and Masculinity		
	Masculinity	
	Low	**High**
Low	Undifferentiated	Masculine
Femininity		
High	Feminine	Androgynous

Gender-Related Behavior

The findings just discussed tell us little about gender-related behavior in sport and exercise and do not explain male and female behavior in these settings (Gill, 1992). For example, competitive sport requires that individuals exhibit assertive, competitive behavior. The higher masculine scores of female athletes probably reflect an overlap with competitiveness or achievement orientation (Gill & Deeter, 1988). Indeed, another study found that both male and female athletes were more competitive than male and female nonathletes (Gill & Dzewaltowski, 1988): That is, athletes have higher levels of competitiveness unrelated to gender.

Two studies indicate that gender roles, more than gender alone, influence how males and females react to sport and exercise environments. In one study, male and female nonvarsity athletes in university physical activity classes completed the Bem Sex-Role Inventory and the Sport Competition Anxiety Test, a measure of competitive trait anxiety (see chapter 6). The feminine females had the highest competitive trait anxiety, whereas masculine males had the lowest levels (see Figure 27.2; Anderson & Williams, 1987). The men and women showing androgynous gender roles had moderate levels of competitive trait anxiety. The second study investigated how men perceived effort and pain while performing strenuous physical exercise on a bicycle ergometer. The masculine and androgynous males reported lower levels of effort and physical strain than the feminine males did (Rejeski, Best, Griffith, & Kenney, 1987). Looking only at the simple male/female or masculine/feminine dichotomy, then, isn't really helpful in understanding gender-related behaviors in sport and exercise settings.

To better understand gender-related behavior in sport and exercise environments, we need to relate traditional male/female differences to the larger context of culture and societal expectations.

Gender and Achievement-Related Motives

Many people have wondered if males and females approach achievement-related situations differently, particularly if they have different motivations. Early research on the motive to achieve success and the motive to avoid failure (the two major constructs in achievement motivation theory) found that women's achievement motives did not predict their achievement behavior, whereas men's did (McClelland, Atkinson, Clark, & Lowell, 1953). Consequently, women were eliminated as subjects in most later studies on achievement motivation theory.

Most early studies investigating achievement-related behaviors used only male subjects. Their findings cannot be generalized to females.

Gender Differences in Achievement Settings

Other early research focused on gender differences in the motive to avoid success, or what was called the *fear of success*. Matina Horner (1972) argued that the fear of success affects achievement behavior. She hypothesized that

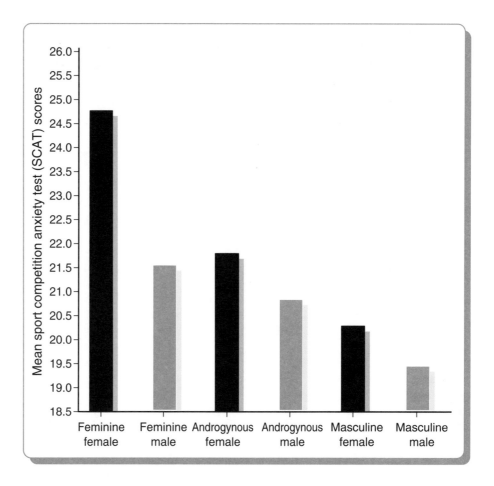

Figure 27.2 Mean sport competitive anxiety scores by gender role classification and sex. Adapted from Anderson and Williams (1987).

Research suggests that women's low-achievement responses are due to fear of sex-role inappropriate behavior, not to fear of success.

women would have higher fear of success than men because success has negative consequences for women, especially in achievement-oriented situations. The competitive achievement behaviors, which success requires, could be in conflict with the more traditional feminine roles expected of females.

To investigate this hypothesis, Horner (1972) gave college students a cue and asked them to complete short stories about the key character. A sample sentence cue might be, "After midterm exams, Mary (or Tom) found that she was at the top of her medical school class." If the stories contained negative consequences as a result of this success, the subject was classified as having fear of success. Results revealed that 10% of the men wrote negative stories about the successful male, whereas 62% of the women wrote negative stories about the successful female. On the basis of this data, as well as findings that females high in fear of success performed poorer than females low in fear of success in a competitive achievement situation, Horner concluded that females are higher in fear of success than males and that this motive undermines performance in achievement situations.

However, later research called Horner's conclusions into question. For example, men as well as women wrote more negative stories in response to the female cue. Thus, researchers have concluded that females do not have a higher fear of success than males; rather the responses were influenced by a "fear of sex-role inappropriate behavior" (i.e., a woman should not be successful, especially in a "male-oriented" occupation such as medicine).

Gender Differences in Competitive Sport

More recently, Gill and Deeter (1988) devised the Sport Orientation Questionnaire (SOQ), which measures three different motivations in competitive sport:

- Competitiveness—an achievement orientation to enter and strive for success
- Win orientation—a desire to win and avoid losing
- Goal orientation—an emphasis on achieving personal goals

Using the SOQ, researchers have found these differences between males and females:

- Males score higher on competitiveness and win orientation than females, whereas females score higher than men on goal orientation.
- Males report more competitive sport activity and experience than females.
- Females are just as likely as males to participate in noncompetitive sport and to report nonsport achievement activities and interests.

From these studies we can infer that males are more sensitive to social comparison and oriented toward winning, whereas females tend to be more interested in personal improvement. These differences refer to sport, however, and do not extend to general achievement activities. Apparently, the competitive nature of sport brings out the different achievement orientations of males and females.

> Males in sport are generally more oriented toward winning, whereas females are more oriented toward personal improvement.

Gender and Expectations

Expectations are good predictors of achievement behavior and performance (e.g., Eccles & Harold, 1991; Feltz, 1988), and there is good indication that males and females differ in their expectations. Early studies found that females typically report lower expectations and take less responsibility for success than males.

Task and Situational Considerations

Gender differences in confidence generally occur in achievement situations that

- emphasize social comparison and evaluation (i.e., competition),
- provide feedback that is ambiguous, and
- involve tasks perceived as male-oriented (Lenney, 1977).

Gender Differences and Confidence: An Update

- The more masculine a task is considered, the greater the confidence for males as compared to females. This is the most important variable affecting confidence and gender.

- In general, males appear more confident than females in performing motor tasks, although the differences are only about one-half of one standard deviation.

- Males perform slightly better than females regardless of whether tasks are performed competitively or alone.

- Differences in confidence levels appear to be widening between males and females in recent years. (from a review of research from 1977-1991; Lirgg, 1991)

In particular, females tend to have lower expectations when they view the task as masculine, when feedback is ambiguous, and when social comparison is high. When tasks are gender-neutral (i.e., seen as appropriate for either men or women) and social comparison was kept to a minimum, females did not show lower levels of self-confidence (Corbin & Nix, 1979; Petruzzello & Corbin, 1988; Stewart & Corbin, 1988). Specific performance feedback can also improve women's self-confidence.

Eccles' Expectancy Model of Activity Choice

Expectations (as well as the social environment, gender roles, and individual differences) are key determinants of achievement choices and behavior.

Eccles argues that gender differences in expectations and values do not suddenly appear in a particular setting. Rather, they develop over time and are influenced by gender role, sociocultural norms, socialization, and an individual's characteristics and experiences (Eccles, 1985, 1987; Eccles & Harold, 1991). We noted earlier how important the socialization process can be in determining how boys and girls develop sex-role appropriate behavior, and Eccles' model considers these factors. Her model also recognizes that expectations are key determinants of achievement choices and behavior (see Figure 27.3).

Eccles first provided evidence supporting her model for a variety of academic activities (Eccles et al., 1983), but more recently she has studied activity choice in sport settings, focusing on gender differences resulting from socialization differences of young boys and girls. She surveyed 3,000 adolescents about

Gender Differences in Sport and Physical Activity: An Application of Eccles' Model

- Parents rate a daughter's talent for sport substantially lower than a son's, even when the children are in kindergarten.

- Parents provide sons with more opportunities to participate in sport activities than they provide daughters.

- Teachers rate boys higher in sport ability than girls, although they do not rate the genders differently for math and reading abilities.

- Boys perceive a greater importance to their parents that they do well in sports than girls perceive.

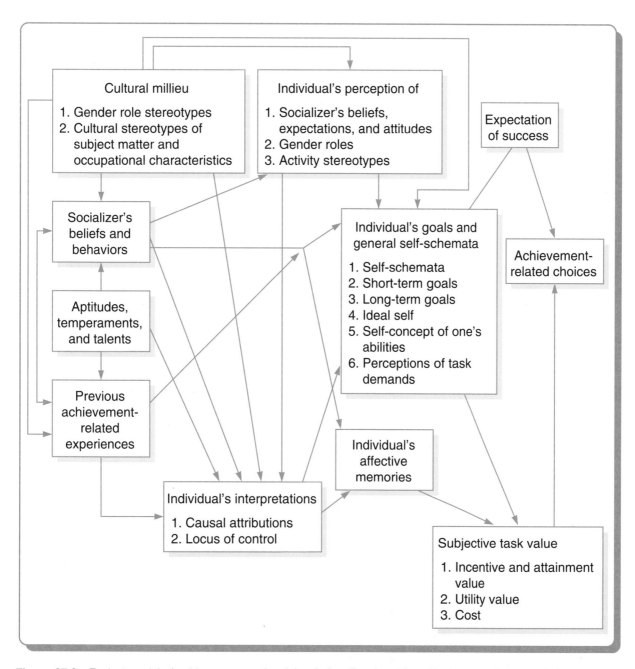

Figure 27.3 Eccles' model of achievement and activity choice. Reprinted from Eccles and Harold (1991).

activity choice and followed about 1,000 of them for 3 years to determine changes in choice over time. She found that gender differences in children's attitudes toward sports are quite strong and emerge at a very young age. These differences affect how teenagers estimate their ability and what value they attach to sport. Gender differences seem to emerge more from socialization of gender roles than from innate differences in aptitude. By the first grade, girls assess their general athletic ability more negatively than boys do and attach less importance to the sport domain. They see themselves as less able in sport than in academic areas and see sports as less important than other areas. Boys, however, see sport as equally or more important than other areas and feel more confident of their abilities in sport than in other domains.

Eccles' model provides a theoretical framework to investigate gender differences in sport achievement and participation, and gender differences do indeed exist in these areas. They are a result of how parental influences, school influences, and sex-role stereotyping affect values and expectations. Although we still cannot specify which sociocultural factors are most important in predicting gender differences in sport and exercise settings, we do know the socialization process is central to understanding gender and sport achievement.

Role Conflict and the Female Athlete

Many researchers have suspected that females feel conflict about how participation in competitive sport and exercise affects their femininity. Society's images, definitions, and expectations of athletes would seem to collide with its concepts of remaining feminine. Allison (1991) notes that the Victorian ideals of femininity—submissiveness, grace, beauty, and passivity—have been said to conflict with the ideal images of competitive sport—aggressiveness, strength, toughness, and achievement. Indeed, society's view of the least acceptable sports for women, such as boxing, football, powerlifting, or hockey, are attempts "to physically subdue the opponent by bodily contact" (Metheny, 1965, p. 282). Thus, female athletes seem placed in a double bind: If they succeed in competitive sport and portray behavior typical of male athletes, they compromise their sense of femininity, risking psychological anxiety over trying to reconcile these conflicting expectations.

Women may find themselves in a double bind if success in competitive sport is equated with a lack of femininity.

The Double Bind

Researchers have accumulated data supporting the notion that participating in sport competition and ideas about femininity are not compatible. For example, negative stereotypes still exist about how gender-appropriate various activities

are. Kane (1988) found that being an athlete was the greatest source of status for high school males but the least-valued role for high school females. Female athletes who participated in team sports especially had significantly less status with their peers (both male and female) than those in individual sports, such as tennis and golf, which were deemed more appropriate.

Frequency of Role Conflict

Most research on the role conflict of female athletes studied the appropriateness of females participating in a variety of sport and physical activities. However, Sage and Loudermilk (1979) assessed role conflict as actually experienced by female athletes. Only 20% of sampled athletes perceived role conflict, and only 20% experienced role conflict to a great or very great extent. Perhaps college-age females had enough maturity to feel competent in their roles as athletes. To test this explanation, Anthrop and Allison (1983) assessed female high school athletes—and found similar results. Only 11% felt that role conflict was a great problem. Findings of other studies were the same (e.g., Allison & Butler, 1984; Deseretrain & Weiss, 1988). Still, despite the lack of empirical support, researchers continued to pursue the topic (Allison, 1991). Their preoccupation with role conflict reflects a lack of willingness to give up the traditional images of the female athletes. As Boutilier and SanGiovanni (1983) state, "To ask if a woman can remain a woman and still play sports means that one has in mind a view of women and of sport that accepts the socially constructed definitions of these two realities as contradictory and conflicting" (p. 117).

It is inappropriate to assume that role conflict is the root of performance problems for female athletes; rather, the problems are probably within the

> Despite an apparent reluctance of researchers to admit it, role conflict does not appear to be a significant problem for women athletes.

Coaching Female Athletes

Practice and research have identified some consistent themes and concerns that motivate females competing in sport. Coaches should understand these characteristics and concerns as they consider how to make the environment optimal for females to achieve excellence both on and off the playing field.

Female athletes . . .

- value friendship and camaraderie,

- cooperate with and support each other, focusing on team unity,

- value personal improvement over winning,

- have realistic views of their capabilities,

- tend to be sensitive to teammates' feelings and willing to share feelings,

- respond best to a democratic coach,

- work hard to achieve personal and team goals,

- need to have their self-confidence nurtured, not attacked,

- like to establish personal relationships with coaches,

- prefer coaches who are empathetic and communicate openly, and

- respond better to positive feedback rather than criticism.

The Athletic Experience: A Female Perspective

A few generalizations . . .

- Female athletes generally view their coach's power as more absolute than the power held by other authorities and describe coaches as more "connected" authorities with whom they can discuss either personal or athletic matters.

- Female athletes tend to avoid competition in daily life and physical activity settings, feeling most comfortable in relationships where power is shared equally by all.

- Female participants prefer and value cooperation.

- Female participants tend to favor disclosing feelings to other females rather than to males and have a strong need for a female coach to relate to.

. . . and a sampling of women's comments on various aspects in sport and physical activity:

- "I give a lot of credit to getting into weight training and how that's changed my life. . . . My sense of myself is completely different. There's nothing as empowering as to go out, set a goal, and succeed at it."

- "It's the desire to win, but also it's the desire to play well and the desire to coordinate with others."

- "Women are very sensitive. They react strongly to minor comments from the coach. It seems we need more positive strokes than the guys."

- "When I have less self-confidence, the coach's negative comments are more difficult to deal with. It's like kicking me when I'm down."

- "Men shouldn't think that a woman athlete's tears are a sign of weakness. Tears help me express how I feel. It's okay to feel and appear upset. Tears are my way of dealing with feeling down, but they don't say I'm out."

- "I love being an athlete. My teammates are great friends, and even the guys seem to respect me for my skills."

- "Women athletes are not too receptive to aggressive commands from coaches. My coach demands that I charge the net, when I'm more comfortable playing the baseline. His assertiveness reduces my concentration and self-confidence."

- "If my opponent is too easy, I don't feel very satisfied after winning."

- "Female coaches seem to have greater insight into the feelings of players than male coaches. I think the word is *empathy*."

- "To be emotionally up for the game, I need a low-key pregame approach, which I get. I'm glad my coach doesn't rant or rave before the game; it would destroy my concentration." (from Bredemeier et al., 1991 and Anshel, 1990)

athlete and not a result of societal stereotypes. In addition, continuing to reinforce the notion of role conflicts for female athletes may only create a self-fulfilling prophesy. Therefore, we should focus on the positive aspects of female participation in sport and physical activity instead of reinforcing a concept that does not exist in the minds of most female athletes.

Women's Experiences in Sport

Women scholars in a variety of scientific contexts have called for more women-centered research as a response to the historic problem of assuming males to be the standard for the entire population. And women-centered research begins with women's experience, as described by women (Messmer, 1988).

In many ways, the thoughts and feelings of female athletes are similar to those of males. However, women show strong affiliation needs and a cooperation orientation. If future research continues to elicit the female sport perspective, we will eventually have a more well-rounded and accurate view of male and female experiences in sport and physical activity settings.

Summary

Research has found that from early in life, boys and girls are socialized into different role expectations. Many differences in their behavior in sport and other situations stem more from gender role orientation than from biological sex. These differences, however, have contributed to inequities in relation to opportunities and funding for women's sports. Despite the passage of Title IX in 1972, many inequities still exist between men's and women's intercollegiate athletics.

Differences in expectations and confidence emerge between males and females who participate in sport, especially when females feel they are in a masculine-oriented activity. Eccles' model of activity choice provides a good theoretical framework for investigating potential differences in sport participation between males and females. Although much as been written about the supposed role conflict of female athletes, recent interviews of female athletes reveal little actual role conflict. Some recent research has been women-focused in an attempt to provide women athletes and participants a forum to describe their experiences in sport, as most previous research has focused on men.

Review Questions

1. What are three ways in which boys and girls are socialized differently in terms of sport participation? Discuss each briefly.

2. Discuss the intent and success of Title IX in changing participation rates of females in sports and coaching.

3. Describe Bem's Sex-Role Orientation Inventory, including the classification scheme for studying gender role orientation.

4. Describe Horner's research concerning the concept of fear of success. What were her conclusions and how has later research refined her findings?

5. What different motives are measured by the Sport Orientation Questionnaire?

6. In what situations do females have lower self-confidence than males?

7. Briefly describe Eccles' model of achievement, focusing on choice of activity and expectations, gender differences, and explanations for these gender differences.

8. React to the statement, "Females experience a role conflict when competing in sports." Does research support this statement?

9. Recent research has focused on asking women to describe their experiences participating in sport and exercise settings. List three themes that emerge in this type of research and their implications for practitioners.

10. Describe some attributes and characteristics of women athletes and the implications they have for coaching.

References

Acosta, R.V., & Carpenter, L.J. (1987, April). *Women in intercollegiate sport. A longitudinal study—nine year update 1977-1986.* Paper presented at the American Alliance for Health, Physical Education, Recreation, and Dance Convention, Las Vegas, NV.

Acosta, R.V., & Carpenter, L.J. (1994). *Women in intercollegiate sport. A longitudinal study—seventeen year update 1977-1994.* Unpublished manuscript, Brooklyn College, Brooklyn, NY.

Allison, M.T. (1991). Role conflict and the female athlete: Preoccupations with little grounding. *Journal of Applied Sport Psychology,* **3**, 49-60.

Allison, M., & Butler, B. (1984). Role conflict and the elite female athlete: Empirical findings and conceptual dilemmas. *International Review for Sociology of Sport,* **19**, 157-167.

Anderson, M.B., & Williams, J. (1987). Gender role and sport competition anxiety: A re-examination. *Research Quarterly for Exercise and Sport,* **58**, 52-56.

Anshel, M. (1990). *Sport psychology: From theory to practice.* Scottsdale, AZ: Gossuch Scarisbrick.

Anthrop, J., & Allison, M. (1983). Role conflict and the high school female athlete. *Research Quarterly,* **54**, 104-111.

Bem, S.L. (1974). The measurement of psychological androgyny. *Journal of Consulting and Clinical Psychology,* **42**, 155-162.

Bem, S.L. (1978). Beyond androgyny: Some presumptuous prescriptions for a liberated sexual identity. In J. Sherman & F. Denmark (Eds.), *Psychology of women: Future directions for research* (pp. 1-23). New York: Psychological Dimensions.

Boutilier, M., & SanGiovanni, L. (1983). *The sporting woman.* Champaign, IL: Human Kinetics.

Bredemeier, B.J.L., Deseretrain, G.S., Fisher, L.A., Getty, D., Slocum, N.E., Stephens, D.W., & Warren, J.E. (1991). Epistemological perspectives among women who participate in physical activity. *Journal of Applied Sport Psychology,* **3**, 87.

Coakley, J. (1990). *Sport and society: Issues and controversies* (4th ed.). St. Louis: Mosby.

Corbin, C.B., & Nix, C. (1979). Sex-typing of physical activities and success predictions of children before and after cross-sex competition. *Journal of Sport Psychology,* **1**, 43-52.

Deseretrain, G., & Weiss, M. (1988). Being female and athletic: A cause for conflict? *Sex Roles,* **18**, 567-582.

Eccles, J.S. (1985). Sex differences in achievement patterns. In T. Sonderegger (Ed.), Nebraska symposium on motivation, 1984: *Psychology and gender* (pp. 97-132). Lincoln: University of Nebraska Press.

Eccles, J.S. (1987). Gender roles and women's achievement related decisions. *Psychology of Women Quarterly,* **11**, 135-172.

Eccles, J.S., Adler, T.F., Futterman, R., Goff, S.B., Kaczala, C.M., Meece, J.L., & Midgley, C. (1983). Expectations, values, and academic behaviors. In J. Spence (Ed.), *Achievement and achievement motive* (pp. 75-146). San Francisco: Freeman.

Eccles, J.S., & Harold, R.D. (1991). Gender differences in sport involvement: Applying the Eccles' expectancy-value model. *Journal of Applied Sport Psychology,* **3**, 7-35.

Feltz, D.L. (1988). Self-confidence and sports performance. In K. Pandolf (Ed.), *Exercise and sport sciences reviews* (Vol. 16, pp. 423-457). New York: Macmillan.

Gilbert, B., & Williamson, N. (1973). Women in sport (3 part series). *Sports Illustrated*, May 28, June 4, June 11.

Gill, D. (1992). Gender and sport behavior. In T. Horn (Ed.), *Advances in sport psychology* (pp. 143-160). Champaign, IL: Human Kinetics.

Gill, D.L., & Deeter, T.E. (1988). Development of the Sport Orientation Questionnaire. *Research Quarterly for Exercise and Sport*, **59**, 191-202.

Gill, D.L., & Dzewaltowski, D.A. (1988). Competitive orientations among intercollegiate athletes: Is winning the only thing? *The Sport Psychologist*, **2**, 212-221.

Holmen, M.G., & Parkhouse, B.L. (1981). Trends in the selection of coaches for female athletes: A demographic inquiry. *Research Quarterly for Exercise and Sport*, **52**, 9-18.

Horner, M.S. (1972). Toward an understanding of achievement-related conflicts in women. *Journal of Social Issues*, **28**, 157-176.

Jacklin, C.N. (1989). Female and male: Issues of gender. *American Psychologist*, **44**, 128-133.

Kane, M. (1988). The female athletic role as a status determinant within the social systems of high school adolescents. *Adolescence*, **23**, 252-264.

Kellers, P. (1992). *USA Today*, p. 9.

Lenney, E. (1977). Women's self-confidence in achievement settings. *Psychological Bulletin*, **84**, 1-13.

Lirgg, C.D. (1991). Gender differences in self-confidence in physical activity: A meta-analysis of recent studies. *Journal of Sport and Exercise Psychology*, **8**, 294-310.

Lopiano, D. (1992). Women in coaching: Some recommendations. *Olympic Coach*, **2**, 6-7.

Maccoby, E., & Jacklin, C. (1974). *The psychology of sex differences*. Stanford, CA: Stanford University Press.

McClelland, D.C., Atkinson, J.W., Clark, R.A., & Lowell, E.C. (1953). *The achievement motive*. New York: Appleton-Century-Crofts.

Messmer, M.A. (1988). Sports and male domination. *Sociology of Sport Journal*, **5**, 197-211.

Metheny, E. (1965). *Connotations of movement in sport and dance*. Dubuque, IA: William C. Brown.

Petruzzello, S.J., & Corbin, C.B. (1988). The effects of performance feedback on female self-confidence. *Journal of Sport and Exercise Psychology*, **10**, 174-183.

Poindexter, H.W. (1974). *Women's athletics: Issues and directions*. Proceedings NCPEAM, 58-63.

Rejeski, W.J., Best, D., Griffith, P., & Kenney, E. (1987). Sex-role orientation and the responses of men to exercise stress. *Research Quarterly for Exercise and Sport*, **58**, 260-264.

Sage, G., & Loudermilk, S. (1979). The female athlete and role conflict. *Research Quarterly*, **50**, 88-96.

Spence, J.T., & Helmreich, R.L. (1978). *Masculinity and femininity*. Austin: University of Texas Press.

State Association Summary. (1989). *1988-89 sports participation survey*. Michigan High School Athletics Association.

Stewart, M.J., & Corbin, C.B. (1988). Feedback dependence among low confidence preadolescent boys and girls. *Research Quarterly for Exercise and Sport*, **59**, 160-164.

Theberge, N. (1991). A content analysis of print media coverage of gender, women and physical activity. *Journal of Applied Sport Psychology*, **3**, 36-48.

Wrisberg, C.A., Draper, M.V., & Everett, J.J. (1988). Sex role orientations of male and female collegiate athletes from selected individual and team sports. *Sex Roles*, **19**, 81-90.

Finish

Y ou should now have a good grasp of strategies that can be used to foster psychological change and development. This knowledge will help you to choose the most appropriate ways to achieve the objectives of your psychological skills program. However, unless this knowledge is put into practice, it will be of little use.

As a professional in sport and exercise science you will be responsible for implementing what you have learned. You now know that a knowledge of sport and exercise psychology can have tremendous payoffs when applied in professional practice settings. So adopt the active approach to professional practice that we discussed in the beginning of this text; implement the ideas conveyed here and consistently evaluate your strategies in light of your professional experience. Be aware of current research and use the gym, pool, and athletic field as your professional laboratory for continued growth and development. Don't make the mistake of simply taking your final exam and finishing this course, and then never thinking about the material again. Refer to the text when you are faced with practical problems. Use what you have learned and apply and try to improve upon it. Take it from us, seeing someone achieve his or her goals through psychological skills development is one of the most rewarding professional experiences you will have.

Credits

Tables 2.2, 12.1, and 12.2 and Figures 11.2 and 12.1: From *Coaches Guide to Sport Psychology* (Table 12.1, pp. 51-53; Table 12.2, p. 56; Figure 11.2, p. 35; Figure 12.1, p. 48), by R. Martens, 1987, Champaign, IL: Human Kinetics. Copyright 1987 by Rainer Martens. Adapted by permission.

Figures 3.1 and 7.1: From *Social Psychology and Physical Activity* (pp. 146 and 69), by R. Martens, 1975, New York: Harper and Row. Copyright 1975 by Rainer Martens. Adapted by permission of the author.

Tables 3.1 and 3.2: From "Sport Confidence and Competitive Orientation: Preliminary Investigation and Instrument Development" by R.S. Vealey, 1986, *Journal of Sport Psychology*, **8**, pp. 221-246. Copyright 1986 by Human Kinetics. Adapted by permission.

Figures 3.2 and 3.3: From "Prediction of Performance in Athletics" by W.P. Morgan. In *Coach, Athlete and the Sport Psychologist* (pp. 185 and 183), by P. Klavora and J.V. Daniel (Eds.), 1979, Toronto: University of Toronto School of Physical and Health Education. Copyright 1979 by Publishing Division, School of Physical and Health Education, University of Toronto. Adapted by permission.

Table 3.3: From "Test of Attentional and Interpersonal Style" by R. Nideffer, 1976, *Journal of Personality and Social Psychology*, **34**, pp. 394-403. Copyright 1976 by the American Psychological Association. Adapted by permission.

Table 3.5: From "Attentional Style Variations and Athletic Ability" by S.R. van Schoyck and A.F. Grasha, 1981, *Journal of Sport Psychology*, **3**, pp. 149-165. Copyright 1981 by Human Kinetics. Adapted by permission.

Tables 3.6 and 17.1: From *Psyching for Sport: Mental Training for Athletes* (Table 3.6 pp. 68-69; Table 17.1, 15-16), by T. Orlick, 1986, Champaign, IL: Human Kinetics. Copyright 1986 by T. Orlick. Adapted by permission.

Table 4.1 and Figure 24.1: From "Participation Motivation and Attrition in Young Athletes" by D. Gould and L. Petlichkoff. In *Children in Sport* (3rd ed.) (pp. 161-178) by F.L. Smoll, R.A. Magill, and M.J. Ash (Eds.), 1988, Champaign, IL: Human Kinetics. Copyright 1988 by F.L. Smoll, R.A. Magill, and M.J. Ash. Adapted by permission.

Table 4.3: From *Mental Training for Peak Performance*, by E.F. Gauron, 1984, Lansing, NY: Sport Science Associates. Adapted by permission of Sport Science Associates.

Tables 6.1 and 6.2: From *Competitive Anxiety in Sport*, by R. Martens, R.S. Vealey, and D. Burton (Eds.), 1990, Champaign, IL: Human Kinetics. Copyright 1990 by Human Kinetics. Adapted by permission.

Table 7.1: From "Development of the Sport Orientation Questionnaire" by D.L. Gill and T.E. Deeter, 1988, *Research Quarterly for Exercise and Sport*, **59**, pp. 191-202. Adapted with permission from the American Alliance for Health, Physical Education, Recreation and Dance, Reston, VA.

Figure 8.1: From "Examining Flow Experiences in Sport Contexts: Conceptual Issues and Methodological Concerns" by J. Kimiecik and G. Stein, 1992, *Journal of Applied Sport Psychology*, **4**(2), p. 147. Adapted by permission of the Association for the Advancement of Applied Sport Psychology.

Table 8.1: From *Coaching: An Effective Behavioral Approach*, by F. Martin and J. Lumsden, 1987, St. Louis: Mosby-Year Book, Inc. Adapted by permission of Mosby-Year Book, Inc.

Table 9.1: Adapted from M. Anshel, *Sport Psychology: From Theory to Practice*, 2nd edition. Copyright 1994 by Gorsuch Scarisbrick, Publishers (Scottsdale, AZ). Used with permission.

Figure 10.1: From "Cohesiveness in Sport Groups: Interpretations and Considerations" by A.V. Carron, 1982, *Journal of Sport Psychology*, **4**, p. 131. Copyright 1982 by Human Kinetics. Adapted by permission.

Table 10.1: From Carron, A.V., Brawley, L.R., and Widmeyer, W.N. (1985). Used with permission.

Figure 10.2: From "The Development of an Instrument to Assess Cohesion in Sport Teams: The Group Environment Questionnaire" by A.V. Carron, W. Widmeyer, and L. Brawley, 1985, *Journal of Sport Psychology*, **7**, p. 248. Copyright 1985 by Human Kinetics. Adapted by permission.

Table 10.2: From "Team Building in an Exercise Setting" by A.V. Carron and H.S. Spink, 1993, *The Sport Psychologist*, **7**, pp. 8-180. Copyright 1993 by Human Kinetics. Adapted by permission.

Index